VITICULTURE

VOLUME 1 — RESOURCES

2ND EDITION

VITICULTURE

VOLUME 1 — RESOURCES

2ND EDITION

EDITED BY P.R. DRY AND B.G. COOMBE

CONTRIBUTING AUTHORS

C.J. Anderson, S-J. Bell, J.S. Gladstones, W.S. Goodchild
P.G. Iland, D.J. Maschmedt, P.R. Nicholas, I. Pearce
E. Riley, R.E. Smart, M.R. Thomas, R. van Heeswijck, J.R.Whiting

[W] winetitles

Published by Winetitles Pty Ltd
67 Anzac Highway, Ashford
South Australia 5035
www.winebiz.com.au

First edition published in 1988
Reprinted with alterations in 1990, 1992
Reprinted in 1995, 1997, 1998, 2000, 2003
Second edition published in 2004
Reprinted with alterations in 2005

National Library of Australia
Cataloguing in Publication data

    Viticulture. Volume 1, Resources.

    2nd ed.
    Bibliography.
    Includes index.
    For tertiary students.
    ISBN 0 9756850 2 3 (set).

    ISBN 0 9756850 0 7 (v. 1).

    1. Viticulture – Australia. 2. Grapes – Australia. I. Dry,
    P. R. II. Coombe, B. G. (Bryan George).

    634.80994

Viticulture. Volume 2, Practices
ISBN 0 9756850 1 5

Wholly produced in Adelaide, South Australia.
Designed and produced by Chris Potter and Larry Ellenwood.
Printed by Hyde Park Press.

CONTENTS

ACKNOWLEDGEMENTS

Many people have made important contributions to the writing of this book. In particular, the editors, authors and publishers acknowledge the contribution of the authors of the equivalent chapters in the previous version of Viticulture Volume 1 (Coombe and Dry 1988) who did not participate directly in the production of this text: G.R. Gregory (deceased), K.H. Northcote (deceased), D.I Jackson, M.B. Spurling, A.J. Antcliff (deceased), W.J. Hardie, R.M. Cirami and M.G. McCarthy.

We gratefully acknowledge those who have helped in the writing, reading and advising on the early drafts of chapters: their advice has helped to make this text more accurate and relevant: Bob Barrett, Melanie Coombe, Jim Hardie, Steve Martin, Peter May, Julie-Ann Payne, Ernie Sullivan. We also thank those authors who acted as referees for other chapters.

Many people have contributed to individual chapters and the authors of these chapters gratefully acknowledge these specific contributions:

Chapter 2: Information on soils of respective states was provided by Mark Imhof and Siggy Engleitner (Vic.), Peter Tille (WA), Richard Doyle (Tas.) and Bernie Powell (Qld).

The following persons provided information on individual regions in response to a survey:

Brian Addison (Mt Benson)
Leon Andretzke (Barossa Valley)
Ian Bell (Margaret River)
John Beresford (Goulburn Valley)
Peter and Sarah Bird (Wrattonbully)
Nigel Blieschke (Sth. Flinders)
Jim Campbell-Clause (Margaret River)
Joe Ceravolo (Adelaide Plains)
Neville Coats (Riverland),
Alan Cooper (Macedon Ranges)
Patrick Coutts (Pemberton)
Sean Cox (South Burnett)
Michael Dalbosco (Alpine Valleys)
David Dean (McLaren Vale)
Louise Eather (Cowra)
Duncan Farquhar (Tasmania)
Ralph Fowler (Mt Benson)
Brian Freeman (Hilltops)
Brett Grocke (Sth. Flinders)
Bruce Guthrie (Tumbarumba)
Geoff Hardy (McLaren Vale)
Lee Haselgrove (Coonawarra)
Peter Hedberg (Orange)
Stephen Henschke (Eden Valley)

Prue Henschke (Eden Valley)
Samantha Hilliard (Murray Darling)
Adam Jacobs (McLaren Vale)
Emma Jamieson (Riverina)
Greg Johnstone (Hilltops)
Anthony Koerner (Clare)
Murray Leake (Adelaide Hills)
Mardi Longbottom (Padthaway)
Adam Loveys (Kangaroo Is.)
Michael Lowe (Geographe)
Trevor March (Eden Valley)
Jason Omedei (Pemberton)
Malcolm Orrock (Sth. Flinders)
Malcolm Parish (Clare)
Steve Partridge (Great Southern)
John Petch (Riverland)
Peter Read (King Valley)
Rhys Robinson (Robe)
Craig Rutledge (Qld)
Tracy Sandow (Clare)
Tony Smith (Mt Barker)
Peter Watters (Granite Belt)
Peter Wehl (Mt Benson)
Fiona Wood (Langhorne Creek)

The editors and publishers gratefully acknowledge the financial support provided by the Australian Society of Viticulture and Oenology. This project was supported by Australia's grapegrowers and winemakers through their investment body, the Grape and Wine Research and Development Corporation, with matching funds from the Australian Government.

BIOGRAPHICAL DETAILS

Editors

PETER DRY (BAgSc, MAgSc, PhD) is an Associate Professor in the School of Agriculture and Wine, Faculty of Sciences, University of Adelaide. From 1970 to 1975 he was a Research Officer in the SA Department of Agriculture based at Loxton. Since 1975 he has taught viticulture at both Roseworthy Agricultural College and University of Adelaide, and conducted research on many aspects of viticulture and plant physiology. His research interests since the early 1990s have included: manipulation of grapevine yield and wine quality by canopy management, irrigation and rootstock; effect of canopy microclimate on fruit composition; irrigation strategies for improvement of water-use efficiency of grapevines; and regulation of flowering and fruitset of grapevines. He is co-inventor (with Dr Brian Loveys) of the 'partial rootzone drying' (PRD) irrigation strategy: in 2001, PRD was named as one of the 100 most important technological innovations of the 20th century in Australia by the Australian Academy of Technological Sciences and Engineering.

BRYAN COOMBE (AM, MAgSc, PhD) built his career, since graduation in 1948, around various aspects of grapevine research. The first decade was as Viticultural Research Officer in the South Australian Department of Agriculture (the first such position in Australia), then followed appointments lecturing in Horticultural Science at the University of Adelaide. His research, done in conjunction with a large number of colleagues and graduate students, has emphasised the growth and development of the grapevine, especially the grape berry, and has led to152 publications of which 106 are in refereed journals. The American Society of Enology and Viticulture honoured Dr. Coombe with Best Paper awards (in Viticulture, 1987 and in Enology, 1991) and Honorary Research Lecturer in 1991. Upon retirement at the end of 1992, Dr. Coombe was created an Honorary Visiting Research Fellow of the University of Adelaide, a position he still holds.

BIOGRAPHICAL DETAILS

Senior authors

JOHN GLADSTONES (BScAgric, PhD, HonDScAgric) was formerly Senior Lecturer in Agronomy, University of Western Australia, and later Principal Plant Breeder, Western Australian Department of Agriculture, his major research fields being the botany, agronomy and breeding of crop lupins, subterranean clover and serradella. In 'retirement', he pursues a lifelong interest in the climate ecology of grapevines.

PATRICK ILAND (BAppSc, MAgSc, PhD) was a lecturer in wine chemistry at Roseworthy Agricultural College and a Senior Lecturer in viticulture at the University of Adelaide. His research interests were in grape and wine chemistry. He now writes and publishes educational wine books while maintaining an active interest in research, particularly in grape and wine tannins.

DAVID MASCHMEDT (BAgSc) is a soil scientist with the Department of Water, Land and Biodiversity Conservation. He has had 25 years experience in soil survey and land evaluation, including the implementation and management of a program to describe and map the soils and landscapes of the agricultural zone of South Australia. This work included extensive characterization of soils in vineyards from most of the State's viticultural regions.

PHIL NICHOLAS (BAgSc) is a Senior Research Scientist with the South Australian Research and Development Institute at Loxton. He has had 28 years experience in vine improvement programs involving selection of winegrape clones and rootstocks, virus-testing and maintenance of germplasm collections. Other research interests have included grapevine nutrition and regulating irrigation to improve grape quality. He is compiler and editor of the 'Grape Production Series' of books.

INCA PEARCE (BSc, MVit) is Project Viticulturist for Orlando Wyndham Group. After completing her Masters in Viticulture at the University of Adelaide, Inca joined Orlando Wyndham Group; from 1997 to 1999 as Viticulturist for the South East of South Australia and from 2000 in her current role as Project Viticulturist. In this role Inca is responsible for managing grape and wine research and development projects, with particular focus on the characterisation of grapes, juice and wine.

RICHARD SMART (BAgSc, MScHons, PhD, DScAgr) has been involved in the science of viticulture since 1965. He studied for his PhD at Cornell University under Professor Nelson Shaulis. From 1975 to 1981 he taught at Roseworthy Agricultural College and from 1982 to 1989 he was responsible for the Government viticultural research program of New Zealand. His primary research interests have been in grapevine physiology and canopy management effects on yield and fruit quality. He has been a consultant since 1990.

MARK R. THOMAS (BScHons, PhD) is a Project Coordinator at the Horticulture Unit of CSIRO Plant Industry. Since 1990 his research interests have been grapevine improvement, grapevine diversity and the biology and genetics of grape development.

JOHN WHITING (DipAgSc, BSc) is a Senior Viticulturist with the Department of Primary Industries, Bendigo, Victoria. From 1972 to 1989 he worked as a Research Officer in DPI based at Irymple, covering a broad range of topics including field rootstock research across Victoria. Since 1989 he has worked at DPI Bendigo and Tatura with a major role in viticulture extension, but also a continued involvement in numerous research projects.

FOREWORD

Foreword to the second edition

This publication is a second edition of *Viticulture Volume I Resources*, which was published in 1988. The companion book, *Volume II Practices*, appeared in 1992. We attribute their wide popularity to the policy of emphasising basic principles supported by scientific research.

This edition of *Volume I* is about 50 per cent longer than the first. The authors have searched the literature widely, covering earlier classical works and modern scientific publications; hence, the reference lists are lengthy. Much of the increase, however, is new material within those chapters that were also in the first edition-especially in the sections on regions, soils and climate. In addition, there is an entirely new chapter on berry development and grape quality. The increases in the number of researchers and in research funds and facilities have fuelled the changes.

A wide array of basic science is used in scientific studies concerning viticultural problems. Two in particular are prominent: a) Plant Physiology, now augmented by molecular methods, has helped explain problems of the plant itself; and b) Organic Chemistry has been an important tool for physiologists and for research on the transformation of the grape crop into its marketed products. A recent account of Faraday's early work to purify by distillation the exceptionally stable benzene molecule illustrates how a whole new discipline crucial to the study of all branches of biology—Organic Chemistry—can emerge as a result of a specific endeavour.* This new edition of *Volume I* documents the evolution of viticultural science since the publication of the first edition through the specific endeavours of a burgeoning range of researchers. It also demonstrates the wide-reaching potential for viticultural science to influence, and be influenced by, developments in other areas of science, including new fields.

Bryan Coombe and Peter Dry

* Buckingham, J. (2004) *Chasing the Molecule* (Sutton Publishing: Thrupp-Stroud, UK).

Foreword[#] to the first edition

This book had its genesis in the mid-1970s with a proposal to the Australian Wine Board by Mr Colin Gramp. A publication committee was appointed and editors and authors were selected to write a comprehensive reference book on Australian viticulture. However, the project as originally envisaged proved to be too large and unwieldy, and eventually came to a halt. The project was renewed by the newly-formed Australian Society of Viticulture and Oenology, leading to a grant to T.H. Lee and B.G. Coombe from the Australian Grape and Wine Research Council made in June 1987 to see that the book was published. A new format was developed and the material was divided into two volumes, the first on Resources dealing with those matters that concern pre-planting decisions, and the second on Practices, concerning all aspects of establishing and operating a vineyard. The two volumes are intended to help those who are seeking information on the 'how' and the 'why' as well as the 'what'. Viticulture in Australia is innovative and largely unconstrained by legislative controls. Many new methods have been developed and adopted, most of them motivated towards the lowering of the cost of production to cope with low grape prices, by the reduction of the costs of specific operations and by the cost-benefit effects of increased yield; this latter trend has focussed attention on the vexed question of balance between yield and grape quality. Another significant recent change is the large planting of winegrapes in the cooler areas of Australia. These changes are bringing with them many new problems that require solutions based on principles. It is our hope that these volumes will help people to find answers.

[#]An abbreviated version

THIS BOOK IS DEDICATED TO THE MEMORY OF

ROBYN VAN HEESWIJCK

FRIEND, COLLEAGUE AND OUTSTANDING SCIENTIST.

CHAPTER ONE

Development and Status of Australian Viticulture

P. G. ILAND

1.1 The Australian viticultural industry

Australia's viticultural industry is spread over the southern half of the continent and comprises three enterprises — wine, drying and tablegrape production. Recently, areas involved in winegrape production have been assigned a 'Geographical Indication' designating their location within Australia (**FIGURE 1.1**). Although the 'Geographical Indication' map specifically relates to wine-producing zones, regions and subregions, it provides a reference to locations associated with grape production for all three enterprises.

Initially the wine, table and drying grape industries developed together; however comparison of growth of the different enterprises in the 1800s and early and mid-1900s is difficult as records are scarce. Figures since 1976 clearly show that, in recent times, winegrape production is by far the largest enterprise (**FIGURE 1.2**). From the year 1976 to 2002 the production of winegrapes increased by 3.6 times, with most of the change occurring in the last decade. Tablegrape production increased by about 7.3 times, but drying grape production declined by almost half, again with most change occurring in the last decade. The fluctuations throughout the 1980s and 1990s in drying and tablegrape production in part reflect the degree of diversion of multipurpose varieties such as Sultana and Muscat Gordo Blanco to wine production. The decline in the production of grapes for drying purposes occurred largely because the costs and risks were greater than for the other two enterprises. In 2001–02 the proportions of total tonnes produced were 86% (1.5 million tonnes) for wine, 9% (0.15 million tonnes) for drying and 5% (0.09 million tonnes) for tablegrapes.

Winegrapes are grown in all States and Territories, with the major production occurring in South Australia, New South Wales and Victoria. Drying and tablegrape production is concentrated in Victoria and to a lesser extent in New South Wales. The planted area and production figures for each enterprise in 2001–002 in different zones are provided in **TABLE 1.1**. In 2001–02 the proportions of total planted area (ha) for all enterprises were 43% in South Australia, 24% in Victoria, 24% in New South Wales, 7% in Western Australia, 1% in Queensland and less than 1% in Tasmania, Northern Territory and The Australian Capital Territory. The proportions of the total production (tonnes) were 40% in South Australia, 29% in Victoria, 26% in New South Wales, 4% in Western Australia, and less than 1% in Queensland, Tasmania, Northern Territory and The Australian Capital Territory (**TABLE 1.1**).

1.1.1 THE FIRST VINES
Vines were part of the cargo when the First Fleet arrived in Australia in 1788. Grape cuttings and seeds were collected enroute at Rio de Janiero and the Cape of Good Hope and brought to the new settlement of Sydney.

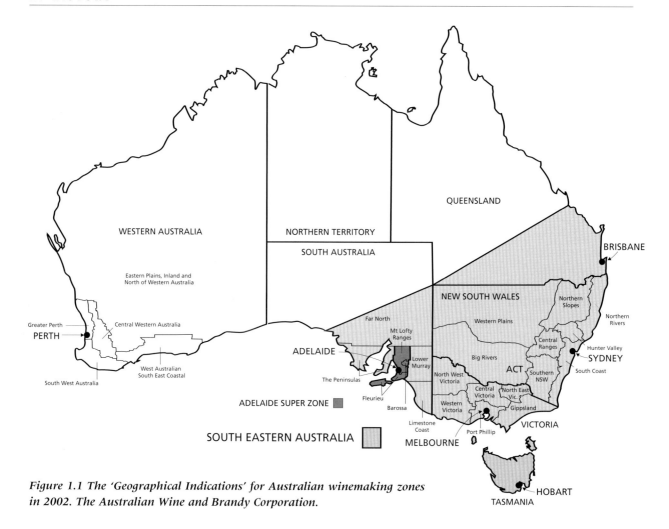

Figure 1.1 The 'Geographical Indications' for Australian winemaking zones in 2002. The Australian Wine and Brandy Corporation.

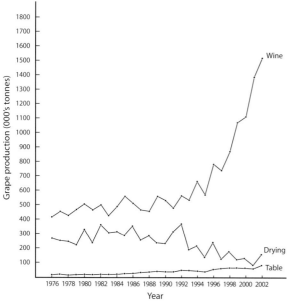

Figure 1.2 Change in wine, drying and table grape production ('000 tonnes) during the period 1976 to 2002. Source: ABS Catalogue No 1329.0, ABS Vineyard Survey 2002 and previous years ABS Catalogues. Drying grape data are as fresh weight.

Governor Phillip commissioned the planting of these vines at Farm Cove, the site of the present Sydney Royal Botanic Gardens. By 1791 vines had also been established at sites to the west of Sydney on the Parramatta River. Australia's first commercial viticultural endeavours were at these sites and produced tablegrapes for the growing population of the new colony. One of the first references to grapes in the official records came from Elizabeth Macarthur, wife of John Macarthur (the founder of the Australian wool industry), when on the 18th March 1791 she wrote from Sydney:

'The grape thrives remarkably well. The Governor sent me some bunches this season, as fine as any I ever tasted, and there is little doubt in a very few years there will be plenty' (Maiden 1917).

Further development of the Australian grape industry is considered in the next section and also in later sections: tablegrapes (1.2), drying grapes (1.3) and wine (1.4).

1.1.2 EXPANSION OF VITICULTURE IN AUSTRALIA
Initially, expansion was slow but by the early 1800s vineyards were established in every Australian State. Changes in vineyard area from 1840 to 2002 are shown in **FIGURE 1.3**. The principal events associated with significant periods

of expansion (A, B, C and D in this figure) were as follows:

A. Initial expansion occurred as a result of natural growth in South Australia, Victoria and New South Wales. The Mediterranean climate in South Australia provided favourable conditions for the culture of the grapevine and much of the early development took place close to the capital, Adelaide. Expansion in Victoria was boosted by a Government bonus of £2 for every acre of vines planted and, by the mid-1870s, Victoria challenged South Australia's position as the State with the largest area planted to vines. By the time of Federation in 1901 Victoria had a total of 12,397 hectares. However, the outbreak of phylloxera and the severe economic depression at that time hindered the development of viticulture in that State.

B. Government-sponsored soldier settlement schemes after the First and Second World Wars resulted in increased plantings along the River Murray Valley in irrigated regions in South Australia and Victoria and in the Murrumbidgee Irrigation Area of New South Wales.

Many of these were mixed horticulture enterprises growing grapes for wine, drying and fresh consumption. Construction of river control systems assured water supply for irrigation.

C. Up to the 1960s winegrape production was dominated by its use for fortified wine production, 80% of production being sherry, port and flavoured dessert wine. However, in the early 1960s there was a shift in consumer preference from fortified wines to table wines, first to red then to white wine. Immigration of Europeans after the Second World War influenced the attitude and approach to food and wine; wine became an acceptable beverage particularly as an accompaniment to food. During the decade 1960–61 to 1970–71 sales of red wines rose from 6.5 million litres to 25.0 million litres. However, during the 1970s there was a swing in consumer preference to white wine. Much of the increase in white wine sales was associated with the introduction of the wine cask. A broader consumer base was created as first-time wine drinkers were introduced

Table 1.1 Planted area (ha) and production ('000 tonnes) of vineyard by state, territory/zone[1], 2001–02 (Winemakers Federation of Australia, 2003). Data were compiled from ABS Vineyard Survey.

STATE/Zone	Bearing ha	Non-bearing ha	% non bearing	Total ha	% of Aust total	Wine '000 t	Drying '000 t	Table '000 t	Total '000 t	% of Aust (wine grapes)	% of Aust (all end uses)
AUSTRALIA	143 373	15 221	10	158 594	100	1 515	152	87	1 754	100	100
SA	60 526	6 513	10	67 039	43	689.6	5.4	2.7	697.8	46	40
Lower Murray	20 626	1 709	8	22 335	14	419.7	4.5	2.4	426.6	28	24
Limestone Coast	12 232	1 234	9	13 466	8	59.7	<0.1	<0.1	59.8	4	3
Fleurieu	11 366	1 303	10	12 669	8	95.6	0.2	<0.1	95.8	6	5
Barossa	9 641	1 137	11	10 778	7	74.5	0.3	<0.1	74.8	5	4
Mt Lofty Ranges	6 493	1 074	14	7 567	5	39.1	0.4	0.2	39.7	3	2
Other	168	56	25	224	<1	1	<0.1	0.1	1.1	<1	<1
Vic.	35 035	3 618	9	38 653	24	338.5	119.2	56.4	514.1	22	29
North West Vic.	23 616	19.8	7	25 524	16	282.7	118.8	56.2	457.8	19	26
Pt Phillip	3 478	558	14	4 036	3	12.2	0.3	<0.1	12.5	<1	20
North East Vic.	3 211	222	6	3 433	2	24.6	<0.1	<0.1	24.6	2	2
Central Vic.	3 331	477	13	3 808	2	15.7	<0.1	0.2	15.9	1	2
Western Vic.	1 237	432	26	1 669	1	3.2	<0.1	<0.1	3.2	<1	1
Other	162	21	11	183	<1	0.1	0.1	<0.1	0.1	<1	<1
NSW	34 005	3 376	9	37 381	24	415	26.2	11.1	452.3	27	26
Big Rivers	20 887	2 069	9	22 956	14	321.8	26	10.1	357.9	21	20
Central Ranges	5 944	471	7	6 415	4	40.8	<0.1	0.1	40.9	3	2
Hunter Valley	4 137	310	7	4 447	3	29.8	<0.1	<0.1	29.8	2	2
Southern NSW	2 167	304	12	2 471	2	17.2	<0.1	0.2	17.4	1	1
Other	870	222	20	1 092	<1	5.4	0.2	0.7	6.3	<1	<1
WA	10 260	1 121	10	11 381	7	63.6	1.8	4.6	70	4	4
South West Aust.	8 405	803	9	9 208	6	54.8	0.2	1	56	4	3
Greater Perth	1 593	262	14	1 855	1	8	1.5	2.5	12	<1	<1
Other	262	56	18	318	<1	0.8	0.1	1.1	2	<1	<1
QLD	2 092	220	10	2 312	1	4.4	0.1	7.9	12.4	<1	<1
Tas.	909	258	22	1 167	<1	3.1	<0.1	<0.1	3.1	<1	<1
NT	455	24	5	479	<1	<0.1	0.1	3.9	4.0	<1	<1
ACT (2003)	90	92	50	182	<1	0.2	<0.1	<0.1	0.2	<1	<1

[1]See Chapter 2 for description of regions within each zone

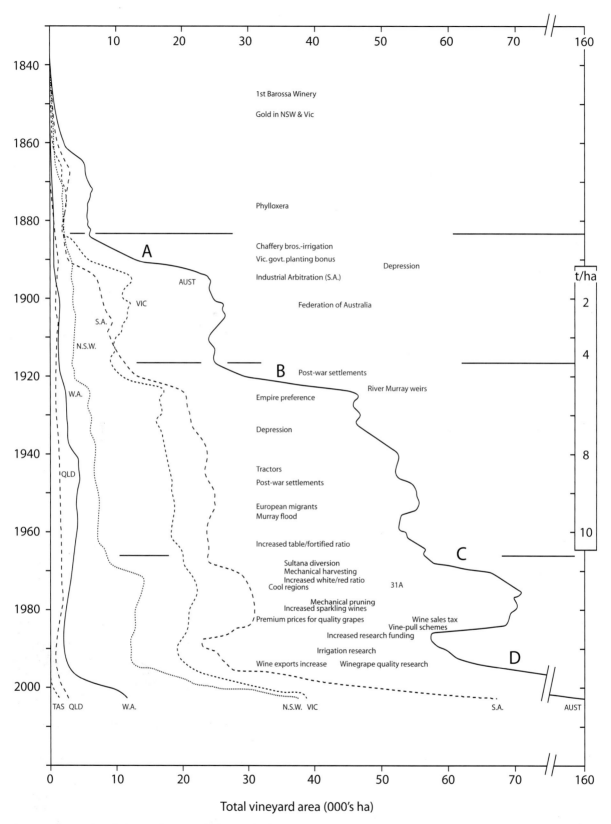

Figure 1.3 Graphs of the total areas of vineyards in all states and in the whole of Australia from 1840 to 2002. The values are the total of vineyards (bearing and non-bearing) supplying grapes used for wine, dried fruit, table purposes, canning, juice and freezing. The average yield in t/ha is shown on the right hand side. Significant events in Australia's viticultural history are shown. The area in 1830 was less than 160 hectares, all in NSW, while that in 2002 had reached 160,000 hectares producing 1.5 million tonnes of winegrapes. Adapted from Coombe (1987).

to sweet white wine styles (formerly called 'moselle') made mainly from the multi-purpose varieties Muscat Gordo Blanco and Sultana (Halliday 1994).

Rationalisation associated with low grape prices and the change in popularity from red to white wine consumption was fostered by the introduction in 1985 of a 'vine pull' scheme, under which subsidies were paid to encourage growers to remove uneconomical plantings and unwanted varieties, such as Grenache, Palomino and Doradillo. The scheme was financed on a basis of $2 from the Commonwealth matched by $1 from the participating States, which included all the mainland, other than New South Wales. The scheme, which operated until 1987, was largely a social rescue programme and resulted in the removal of 2,694 hectares of wine grape varieties and 527 hectares of multi-purpose grapes at a cost to Governments of $6.9 million and $1.9 million respectively. Some old Shiraz, Mataro and Grenache vines were also removed—a somewhat regrettable decision in hindsight, as the remaining old vines are now being used to produce wines for 'niche' markets based on interest and rarity of wines produced from 50 to > 100-year-old vines. These remaining vines represent some of the oldest viticulture plantings in the world, hence the uniqueness and high value of their wines.

D. Wine consumption rate in Australia increased from 18.5 litres per head of population in 1990 to 20.0 litres in 2001, the increase being largely in the consumption of table wines. The rise in vineyard area during this period was due mainly to increased plantings of premium grape varieties, particularly in cool and warm climatic regions, reflecting stronger demand for premium wine. The increase in vineyard plantings was also driven by the expanding export market for Australian wine. During the second half of the 1980s exports of Australian wine quadrupled; the boom continued into the 1990s with exports trebling from 1990 to 1993 (Halliday 1994). In the early 1990s it became obvious that a plan for the future expansion of the Australian wine industry was required and in 1996 the Australian wine industry developed 'Strategy 2025', a pro-active approach detailing the strengths and weaknesses of the industry and suggested action for its continued growth domestically and internationally. This plan predicted that an additional 40,000 hectares of vineyard plantings would be required by the year 2025 to service the anticipated increase in sales of wine. Massive expansion in vineyard development occurred in most States and by the year 2000 the predicted area of plantings had already been achieved. The huge scale of this expansion is illustrated by the steep rise in each of the lines of **FIGURE 1.3** after the mid-1990s; the total vineyard area in Australia doubled within a period of about 7 years (1993 to 2000). During the last decade the volume of wine approved for export increased 5-fold (from about 100,000 kL in 1993 to 507,984 kL in 2003), highlighting the impact of the booming export market on the development of the Australian wine industry. In 2001/2002 Australia's total vineyard area was 158,594 hectares with a total production of 1.7 million tonnes of grapes.

1.1.3 IRRIGATED VITICULTURE

Until the 1880s commercial viticulture was confined to areas where natural rainfall was sufficient for the production of profitable crops. In 1884 a Victorian Royal Commission was set up to investigate irrigation techniques. As a result, the Premier of Victoria, Alfred Deakin, (who subsequently became Prime Minister of Australia in 1901), persuaded the Canadian-born George and William Chaffey to come to Australia to establish irrigation schemes. George, the engineer and William, the horticulturist, brought with them a combination of skills and experience that they had acquired in founding successful irrigation projects in California. They arrived in 1886 and commenced a survey along the River Murray Valley. Land was selected around Mildura, and an agreement was negotiated under which the Victorian Government would set aside 250,000 acres (100,000 ha) at Mildura for occupation under licence for 20 years by the Chaffey Brothers to have the right to construct works on any part of the area for conserving and distributing water. As money was spent, the Chaffeys were to receive titles to the land (Fogarty 1967). This caused a political controversy in Victoria and the enabling Bill was amended requiring the concession to be offered for public tender for two months. The South Australian Government was less apprehensive and, in February 1887, legislation was enacted which secured to the Chaffeys 250,000 acres just west of the Victorian border; this became the Renmark Irrigation Settlement. They received an acre of freehold land for every £4 spent by them or property owners on development. By the end of the year Chaffey pumps were operating at Renmark (**FIGURE 1.4**) and blocks

Figure 1.4 A Chaffey Pumping Engine driving Tangye pumps to lift irrigation water from the Murray River; installed at the end of the 19th century.

were being sold at £20 per acre with 10 years to pay. This prompted Victoria to review its stance and a few months later the original proposals for that state were put into effect under an agreement signed in May 1887. By the end of the year subdivision of the first 25,000 acres had been planned and pumping machinery to lift water 30 metres from the River Murray had been designed (**FIGURE 1.4**). The predominance of furrow irrigation of vineyards (**FIGURE 1.5.a**) meant that establishment was directed by the effect of contours on irrigation runs (**FIGURE 1.5b**). The first settlers began to arrive in 1888 (Fogarty 1967).

Following these settlements along the Murray Valley, completion of the Burrinjuck Dam and Berembed Weir on the Murrumbidgee River in New South Wales enabled development of the Murrumbidgee irrigation areas where the first farms were made available in 1912 and water supplied for irrigation in July of that year. Expansion of irrigated grape plantings was fostered by Government-sponsored soldier settlement schemes following both World Wars, firstly in Renmark, Berri and Waikerie and secondly, after World War 2, at Loxton in South Australia and Robinvale in Victoria. Thus growing of vines in arid and semi-arid regions of Australia began, marking a major turning point in the course of viticultural development.

Since the early 1970s there has been a significant change in the methods of irrigating vineyards. In many areas overhead, micro-jet and drip irrigation systems (**FIGURE 1.6**) have replaced furrow irrigation. These methods have significantly lowered establishment costs, improved irrigation efficiency and permitted extensive plantings such as Angove's Nanya vineyard shown in aerial view in **FIGURE 1.7**. The result is that, at the beginning of the 21st century, vineyards in dry inland districts comprise about half of the total area of Australia's plantings and are responsible for around 70% of Australia's grape production for all purposes.

The introduction of schemes whereby companies and individuals could purchase licences to pump water from the River Murray led to the establishment of large irrigated vineyard holdings; Angoves Nanya vineyard is an example (**FIGURE 1.7**). More recently pipelines have been established where water is pumped from lakes or rivers to vineyard sites, in some cases a considerable number of kilometers from the water source. Many vineyards in the Langhorne Creek region of South Australia have been developed as a result of the availability of water piped from Lake Alexandrina. Similar schemes are in place in other parts of Australia allowing expansion of viticulture, particularly for winegrape production in both established and new regions. Vineyards in the McLaren Vale region started to use treated waste water in the late 1990s. Trading of water has become part of vineyard management schemes. This approach provides the opportunity for vineyard managers to buy water from brokers, who have previously bought licences and allocations. In many Australian viticultural regions water is a limiting resource and proper management of water and water sources is a critical factor in the sustainability of the wine, table and dried fruit industries.

Salinity is also a major concern in many viticultural regions. Major salt interception schemes, where drainage water is pumped away from the river, constructed in the Murray-Darling Basin since 1980 have been successful in reducing average river salinity. More recently, changes in irrigation methods, capping of water licences and greater cooperation between State Governments in controlling the use of water from the River Murray are contributing to improved flow of this important river system and in reducing river salinity. In South Australia the 'Water Allocation Plan for the River Murray Prescribed Watercourse' came into force on July 1, 2002. This plan details criteria for issues such as water allocation, licences, permits and transfers.

Figure 1.5a Furrow irrigation of a newly planted vineyard at Mildura, December 1890.

Figure 1.5b Aerial view of Murray River vineyards showing the mosaic effect imposed by furrow irrigation.

Figure 1.6 A modern vineyard with a drip irrigation system.

Figure 1.7 Angoves Nanya vineyard in the Riverland Region of South Australia of about 500 ha.

The introduction of two new irrigation management techniques—regulated deficit irrigation (RDI) (where water is withheld during specified vine growth stages) (McCarthy 1998) and partial rootzone drying (PRD) (where half the normal levels of irrigation are applied; Dry et al. 2002)—have led to greater efficiencies in water-use as well as improved fruit quality (see Volume II, Chapter 6). Scheduling of irrigation based on grape variety and soil type is also practised in many modern vineyards; vineyard blocks are divided into irrigation units based on these criteria.

1.1.4 MECHANISATION AND TECHNOLOGICAL INNOVATIONS

Important technological achievements based on mechanisation and involving almost all aspects of grapegrowing have accompanied growth in the industry over the last three decades. Mechanical pruning techniques (**FIGURE 1.8**) were developed in the 1970s, but could not be introduced on a large scale until the development and adoption of mechanical harvesting. The first mechanical harvesters (prototypes of the Up-Right vertical impactor and the Chisholm Ryder O-W) were introduced into Australia and tested by Dr Peter May of CSIRO in 1969. Mechanical pruning techniques and mechanical harvesting are now widely used in winegrape vineyards in all viticultural regions. Modern machine harvesters are mostly of the 'slapper' type: curved fibre rods are used to detach the berries from the vine (**FIGURE 1.9**). With modern trellis systems there

may be minimal damage to the vine and the fruit. About 80% of the annual harvest of winegrapes is mechanically harvested. Machine harvesters can now also be used to harvest trellis-dried grapes (**FIGURE 1.10**). The introduction of mechanised pruning and harvesting operations has not only provided economic advantages in managing vineyards but has also allowed expansion of vineyard development into areas where availability of local labour would have been a constraint. An added advantage of mechanical harvesting is that large areas of vineyards can be harvested during the night when fruit temperature is relatively low and potential oxidation is minimised.

As well as pruning and harvesting, other operations have been mechanised, such as foliage-wire lifting, leaf and sucker removal and spray application. Innovative technologies, often as a result of adoption of outcomes of research programs, have been introduced, e.g. yield monitors on mechanical harvesters are currently being assessed as a tool to selectively harvest sections of the vineyard to decrease variability in fruit composition within loads of fruit. 'Precision viticulture', where viticultural management practices are fine-tuned to specific sections within a vineyard, are being introduced into irrigation scheduling, soil management and harvesting operations; this approach often involving advanced technologies such as global positioning systems (GPS), grape yield monitors and geographical information systems software (GIS) (Bramley et al. 2003).

Figure 1.8 A mechanical pruner.

Figure 1.9 A mechanical harvester (slapper type) in operation.

Figure 1.10 A Shaw harvester harvesting trellis dried grapes.

1.1.5 VINEYARD PRODUCTIVITY

As the industry developed during the 1900s vineyard establishment moved from widely spaced non-trellised 'bush' vines (**FIGURE 1.11**) to closer planted trellised systems, thereby creating greater opportunity for mechanisation of operations. Higher yields per hectare have been achieved as a result of changes in vineyard management practices including trellising, irrigation, pruning, use of rootstocks and improved nutrition and disease and pest control. From about 1930 until the late 1980s, before the boom period of vineyard plantings in the 1990s, vineyard area increased from 46,000 to 60,000 hectares (a 30% increase), while wine production increased from 13 to 300 kL (a 20-fold increase). A study by Clingeleffer et al. (1997) detailed the increase in productivity for three winegrape varieties in two regions during the period 1968 to 1998 — highly significant time trends showed increased yield per hectare for all varieties in both regions (**FIGURE 1.12**). Data from 1998 to 2002 indicate that yields per hectare have levelled.

Generally, in the hot, intensively-irrigated regions, where yields of 30 t/ha or more are attainable, there has been a tendency to produce lower yields than in the past. In the main, this has been a consequence of the adoption of deficit irrigation strategies. These regions produce a large proportion of Australia's branded, non-regional, commodity wine on which recent success in the international wine markets has been largely based (Croser 2004). The majority of Australia's regionally-differentiated, quality wines are derived from vineyards across a wide range of climatic regions, usually yielding less than 15 t/ha, and often less than 10 t/ha.

1.1.6 RESEARCH AND DEVELOPMENT

Prior to the late 1980s viticultural research was carried out at the then State Departments of Agriculture, CSIRO, and the teaching Institutions, e.g. the University of Adelaide and Roseworthy Agricultural College. Research topics included mechanical harvesting and pruning, use of rootstocks, irrigation strategies, canopy management and berry development. Significant studies included those of Dr Chris Somers of the Australian Wine Research Institute, which highlighted the importance of grape juice pH measures and the effects of adjustment of must and wine pH and sulfur dioxide concentration on red wine colour (Somers 1998) and the studies of Dr Richard Smart (firstly at Roseworthy Agricultural College, Australia and later at MAF Tech, Ruakura Agriculture Centre, New Zealand) on canopy management of grapevines (Smart and Robinson 1991). However, a problem facing the grape and wine industries prior to the 1980s was lack of long-term research funding. This problem was reduced by the establishment of the Grape and Wine Research Council in 1986, which led to the formation of the Grape and Wine Research and Development Corporation (GWRDC) and The Dried

Fruits Research and Development Council in the early 1990s. These bodies are funded by an industry levy and matching Government funds. They provide support for research and development to their particular enterprises in projects in accordance with industry priorities.

A major development occurred during the 1990s when the Federal Government established Cooperative Research Centres in a number of key industries. The Cooperative Research Centre for Viticulture (CRCV) was established in 1993 and provided a grant of $14 million over a 7-year period to establish collaborative programmes between research institutions. The aims of the various programmes were to investigate methods for the efficient production of grape products, such as wine, dried grapes and tablegrapes that met consumer expectations in terms of quality, low chemical input and production processes. The research programmes included irrigation strategies, canopy management, pest and disease management, product composition, quality indicators and gene technology. As well there was an education and extension programme to relate outcomes of the scientific research to the industry. The Industry was successful in obtaining funding for a second 7-year CRCV programme. The vision and mission statements of the CRCV are —

Vision: The Cooperative Research Centre for Viticulture will be recognised as a leading provider of technologies to enable the viticultural industry in Australia to supply the world with competitively priced, high-value table grapes, dried fruit and wine.

Mission: To provide Australian grapegrowers and processors with readily adoptable, improved technologies based upon cooperative multi-disciplinary research and development, and to effectively promote those technologies.

The Australian Society of Viticulture and Oenology (ASVO), the professional body of personnel involved in the grapegrowing and winemaking industries was founded in 1981: its aim is to improve communication within the different industry sectors and to provide a means for dissemination of research and technical information. The first seminar organised by the ASVO was in 1981 on the topic of 'Grape Quality', an area which is still of great importance (see Chapter 11). The Society was instrumental in the establishment of the Australian Journal of Grape and Wine Research in 1995. Together with the AWRI the ASVO is responsible for organising The Australian Wine Industry Technical Conference, a major industry event comprising lectures, workshops and a trade exhibition held every three years.

Developments up to 1995 in viticulture and especially in winemaking are described by Rankine (1996). Research relating to the chemistry and microbiology of grapes and wines and an understanding of the processes controlling oxidation and preservation of fruit flavours have been, and continue to be, key programmes of

Figure 1.11 Bush vines in the Barossa, South Australia.

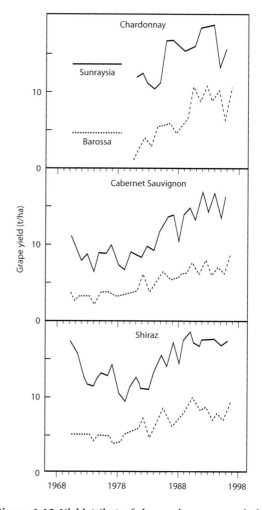

Figure 1.12 Yield (t/ha) of three winegrape varieties in Sunraysia and the Barossa Valley over 27 consecutive years (1970-1996). Redrawn from Clingeleffer et al. (1997).

AWRI, CSIRO, and the two major universities involved in teaching grape and wine studies, The University of Adelaide and Charles Sturt University. Recent research has focussed on grape and wine aroma and flavour compounds and on studies for the development of rapid methods for the measurement of grape and wine composition, e.g. Near Infrared (NIR) technologies. In 1995 the University of Adelaide appointed Dr Peter Høj as Australia's first university Professor of Viticulture. Dr Høj later became Director of the AWRI, the current Professor of Viticulture being Dr Steve Tyerman.

A feature of Australian viticulture has been a readiness by growers to trial and embrace new technology emerging from research programs, examples being mechanical pruning, new trellis systems for tablegrapes, trellis-drying of dried grapes and innovative irrigation techniques, such as RDI and PRD and, more recently, precision viticulture.

1.2 Tablegrapes

1.2.1 EXPANSION IN AUSTRALIA

Grape production for fresh consumption commenced soon after settlement and was, as mentioned previously, Australia's first commercial viticultural enterprise. Compared to wine and drying grapes, production of grapes for fresh consumption has always been minor in Australia. Recorded information is scarce, reflecting its past minor significance in most districts. During the first half of the 1900s vineyards for tablegrape production were established in most Australian states, often as sidelines to other horticultural pursuits. Specialist tablegrape production on a relatively small scale was also established near cities to meet the requirements of the local market. Those who catered for the early market included growers at Stanthorpe in the Queensland Granite Belt and the Pinkenba and Nudgee districts on the outskirts of Brisbane, the Orchard Hills, Liverpool and Camden areas close to Sydney and the Hunter Valley near Newcastle. More remote, cooler growing regions such as Mudgee and Orange in the Central Tablelands of New South Wales also had a significant role in supplying the late markets. Many of the plantings in the above districts were eventually lost to urban development. Specialist tablegrape production has been a long established enterprise in the Swan Valley of Western Australia. Apart from supplying the Perth market, growers in this district developed a steady export trade to south east Asia. In South Australia tablegrape production was concentrated around Adelaide and came mainly from the Marion district on the Sturt River and Payneham on the Torrens River. Since the loss of these areas to residential subdivision in the 1950s specialist tablegrape production has relocated to the South Australian Riverland. The shift of production to inland irrigation districts was aided by the introduction of fast, refrigerated transport.

During the second half of the 1900s there was widespread interest in the use of plant growth regulators, such as gibberellic acid (GA) and ethephon for viticulture. GA is widely used, mainly for increasing berry size of Sultana. In some areas, for example Murray Bridge in South Australia, glasshouses, formerly used for tomato production, have been utilised for producing pre-Christmas tablegrapes. This practice also extended into the Murray-Darling region of Victoria and New South Wales. Purpose-built glasshouses for tablegrape production are used in the Swan Valley and elsewhere. A major shift in the tablegrape industry in recent times has been to extend the marketing season at the 'front end', not only through the planting of early maturing varieties, but also by planting new vineyards in Northern Australia to take advantage of the warmer climate. Substantial plantings have been made in northwest Western Australia, the Northern Territory and Queensland to produce grapes for the pre-Christmas market in the southern States.

1.2.2 VARIETAL PROFILE AND USAGE

In the early years of the industry Muscat Hamburg (syn. Black Muscat) was by far the most important and profitable variety in most districts, while Cannon Hall Muscat and the late maturing Ohanez were major varieties in the Swan Valley of Western Australia. In the 1960s Sultana gained wide acceptance. Today about 30 varieties are used. Red Globe is the major variety, making up more than 80% of sales of tablegrapes. Other varieties include Crimson Seedless, Thompson Seedless (Sultana), Menindee Seedless and Flame Seedless. In 1999 CSIRO established a national breeding program to breed grapes specifically for Australian growing conditions.

1.2.3 GROWTH AND STATUS

Australian production of tablegrapes in 1901–02 was 13,400 tonnes (The Commonwealth Yearbook 1902). According to figures from this source there was little overall growth in production for about 40 years, with 16,002 tonnes being recorded in 1940–41. Production increased to 19,600 tonnes in 1960–61 and 25,300 tonnes in 1970–71 and to 43,400 tonnes in 1986–87. Up to 1987 statistics on fresh grape utilisation in Australia listed three categories; wine, drying and other purposes. For all intents and purposes, prior to 1988, 'other purposes' can be regarded as 'tablegrapes'. In 1988, there was a significant quantity of grapes processed for sale as juice and other fermented grape products. Accordingly, the 'other purpose' statistic subsequent to 1986–87 is no longer a reliable guide to tablegrape production. Expansion which took place in the early 1960s was partly associated with the wide acceptance by consumers of the seedless Sultana. In the early 1980s the potential for expansion of exports of tablegrapes was recognised, prompting a number of growers, mostly located in the Murray-Darling and Swan Hill regions of Victoria and New South Wales, to establish specialist enterprises, utilising modern technology and new varieties, aimed at capturing a greater share of these markets. During the second half of the 1980s exports increased four times and steady increase continued throughout the 1990s. Exports in the 1970s were mostly confined to south east Asia, with limited quantities to the United Kingdom. While these areas remain strong markets, new markets have emerged in Europe, New Zealand and the Middle East. The development of new regions, improved storage technology and refrigerated containers have extended the availability of fresh grapes and have improved fruit quality. This has contributed to the expansion of markets, both nationally and internationally.

The tablegrape industry now comprises hundreds of grape producers and processors with enterprises in each mainland state, with the North West Victorian Zone and the Big Rivers Zone in NSW producing approximately 65% and 13% respectively of total Australian production (**TABLE 1.1**). In the season 2001–02, Table and Other Grape Production was 86,524 tonnes, up from 64,686 tonnes in 2000–01. The Australian industry represents less than 1% of world production. The industry is strongly export-driven with about 45% of total production being exported. Most tablegrapes are now produced to particular market specifications (see Volume II Chapter 15).

1.3 Drying grapes

1.3.1 EXPANSION IN AUSTRALIA

The dried fruits industry developed following the establishment of the Mildura and Renmark irrigation settlements in 1887 under the guidance of the Chaffey brothers (see 1.1.3). In the late 1880s and early 1990s there was emphasis on the production of dried fruits rather than tablegrapes because of the problems associated with transport of fresh fruit. At the peak of summer, just when the fruit was ripe, low water levels (prior to the construction of locks) often prevented the paddle wheelers getting through to the ports along the River Murray. Politicians promised a railway system but this did not eventuate. Because there was no means of quick transport for fresh fruit to the capital cities, interest in the development of vineyards for tablegrapes lessened and the drying grape industry emerged as a viable alternative. The Chaffey brothers brought in experts to help the settlers develop drying techniques and the industry strengthened. The first five tonnes of dried vine fruits was sent to market in 1891.

However, lack of efficient transport systems meant that growers had to hold fruit for long periods and, being without an industry organization, growers were often

forced to sell at low prices. An attempt to introduce better-organised selling arrangements in 1894 was unsuccessful and Mildura's population began to decline as settlers walked off their properties. By 1895, the fortunes of the industry reached their lowest ebb. That year saw the formation of the Mildura and Renmark Raisin Trusts which jointly set a minimum price of 4.5 pence per pound, but few growers, if any, realised this price at the time. Nonetheless, by 1896, Renmark and Mildura were able to achieve some success in a scheme of orderly marketing and the fledging industry weathered the severe economic problems of the 1890s. With the turn of the century, conditions began to improve. Federation of the independent States in 1901, saw the removal of State customs barriers, thereby opening up new markets through interstate trade. Soon after, Mildura received its promised railway—the connection from Melbourne to Mildura was completed in 1903 and the transport problem was solved.

In 1904 the Renmark Raisin Trust and Mildura Dried Fruits' Association (formerly the Mildura Raisin Trust) held their first federal meeting; by 1907 the two organizations had combined to form the Australian Dried Fruits Association (ADFA) which has remained a dominant force in the industry. W.B. Chaffey was the first Chairman of the Association. Expansion was modest up until the First World War. In the following years extensive planting resulted from Government-sponsored soldier settlement schemes. Problems of disposal began to appear, but generally the ADFA was able to maintain stable prices despite the fact that some growers and packers abandoned the scheme of orderly marketing to sell more of their allocation of production on the higher-priced domestic market. Fortunately, the years from 1920 to 1922 were boom years, but in 1923 export prices collapsed, giving producers operating independently of the ADFA a very distinct advantage. The marketing problem eased with the introduction of the Empire preference by the UK in 1925 and by Canada in the following year. This was timely as production had increased to 37,594 tonnes by 1926. The difficulties of the mid-twenties forced a reorganisation of the ADFA, and in 1923 packing companies and selling agents were formally incorporated into the Association as affiliates. This was soon followed by the formation of the Australian Dried Fruits Control Board and the Dried Fruits Boards in producing States, thereby providing statutory powers to control export and domestic marketing.

Further growth was fostered by another Government sponsored soldier settlement scheme after the Second World War. From the 1950s onwards, however there has been no substantive change in the planted areas of drying varieties and the industry remains centred in the areas extending east along the River Murray from Cadell in South Australia to Woorinen near Swan Hill in

Victoria. Developments in drying techniques, involving the use of oil emulsion treatments and more recently trellis-drying practices have helped to advance the industry. Only small quantities of grapes are dried in areas dependent on natural rainfall, namely the Swan Valley and Bindoon in Western Australia where summer rainfall is sufficiently low to permit sun drying of currants.

1.3.2 VARIETAL PROFILE AND USAGE

In Australia 'currants' are dried grapes of the varieties Zante Currant and Carina, 'sultanas' are dried grapes from the variety Sultana and 'raisins' are dried grapes from the varieties Muscat Gordo Blanco and Waltham Cross. Initial plantings for dried grapes comprised Zante Currant, Muscat Gordo Blanco and Waltham Cross. Commercial Sultana vines, synonymous with the American Thompson Seedless, were first planted in 1895 and soon became Australia's principal drying grape. In most seasons, more than 90% of the Australian dried grape production have been sultanas.

1.3.3 GROWTH AND STATUS

Through the late 1880s and until about 1950 growth of vineyards for dried fruit production increased steadily. Since then the planted areas of drying varieties and production has only varied with seasonal conditions, the extent to which the multipurpose varieties Sultana and Muscat Gordo Blanco have been diverted away from drying to winemaking. There was significant production of currants from dryland vineyards in the Barossa, Clare and McLaren Vale Regions up until the 1960s. During the 1990s production of grapes for drying has decreased significantly (**FIGURE 1.2**). This decline has in part been due to the use of multipurpose varieties for wine production but also because costs and risks are higher for drying operations and thus growers have opted for the more reliable enterprises of wine and table grape production.

Production of grapes for drying purposes in 2001–02 was estimated at 152,863 tonnes (fresh weight) which amounts to about 33,500 tonnes of dried products. Victoria is the largest producer with 78% of production followed by New South Wales with 17% (**TABLE 1.1**). About 45% of production is exported to key markets in the UK, Germany, Canada, New Zealand and Japan.

1.4 Winegrapes

1.4.1 EXPANSION IN AUSTRALIA

Although the new colonial administration encouraged and supported development of vineyards for wine production, there was little growth up until the early 1800s. In an attempt to foster the fledgling wine industry, the Duke of Norfolk sent two Frenchmen to Sydney in 1801 to assist with the establishment of vineyards. Although knowledgeable in the cultivation of the vine and of winemaking, their attempts were not very successful, mainly due to the prevalence of vine diseases. Others took up the challenge, including two famous Australian pioneers, John Macarthur, the recognised founder of the Australian wool industry and Gregory Blaxland, who with Wentworth and Lawson were the first to cross the Blue Mountains. It appears that John Macarthur planted vines when he first arrived in 1790 (Maiden 1917), however, his first commercial vineyard was not planted until 1820 at a site near Camden (NSW) after he and his sons had travelled to the wine regions of Europe in 1815–16. During this period, Blaxland was also producing wine at his property in the Parramatta Valley. In 1822, he made history by shipping a fortified red wine to London, for which he gained a Silver Medal from the Society for the Encouragement of the Arts, Manufacturing and Commerce.

During the first half of the 1800s interest in grape production and winemaking gathered momentum. Amongst those who became interested in the culture of the vine was James Busby who, soon after his arrival from Scotland in 1824, was employed by the New South Wales Government to teach viticulture at a male orphanage at Cabramatta. During this period he wrote a number of articles and books on viticulture. In 1830 he published his second book and in this detailed his understanding of the culture of the vine in Australia. This book, 'A Manual of Plain Directions for Planting and Cultivating Vineyards, and for Making Wine in New South Wales', provided a practical guide for viticulturists and winemakers. In 1831 Busby travelled to Spain and France to study viticulture and collect grape cuttings. In a letter sent during this trip Busby wrote —

'I have been careful to collect cuttings of every variety which I found cultivated, and have got to the number of from sixty to seventy. But independently of these I have also made what I call a nursery collection, viz.: two cuttings each of 550 varieties (437 of them are the gift of Mr Delile of Montpellier, the remainder I purchased from the Royal Nursery of the Luxemburg at Paris). I have tendered this collection to the Secretary of State, for the purpose of founding an experimental garden under your direction. The offer has been accepted, and I believe the Governor will receive a dispatch upon the subject by the same ship which conveys this letter.' (Maiden 1917).

The majority of the cuttings collected by Busby were shipped to Sydney in early 1832. The cuttings were packed in closed cases of damp moss, lined around the sides with damp-proof paper. Some of the Spanish varieties, together with duplicates from the French collections, did not reach London for the first shipment and they were shipped later. Official records state that, of the 650 varieties received, 362 varieties were alive and for the most part healthy as at January 1833. They were planted at the Sydney Botanic Gardens. Cuttings from these vines were eventually distributed to sites around

Australia. An important planting was in the Adelaide Botanic Gardens where a representative collection was established from which thousands of cuttings were spread throughout South Australia. Over a period of about 200 years viticulture became established in many regions of Australia, the sequence of which is detailed in **TABLE 1.2.**

The first commercial vineyards in the Hunter Valley were established in 1830 with vines planted in that year by George Wyndham at 'Dalwood' near Branxton: and in the same year at 'Kirkton' near Belford, between Branxton and Singleton by William Helman, Busby's brother-in-law, at that time manager of the property.

In Victoria, Edward Henty took cuttings to Portland in 1834 (the year that State became a separate entity), but there is no further record of Henty or the fate of the cuttings. The initial planting in the Yarra Valley was made in 1838 by William Ryrie at Yering (**FIGURE 1.13**), and by 1848 the area of grapes in the district had increased to 40 hectares (Laffer 1949). Expansion of vineyards was rapid and by the 1880s the vineyard area of Victoria was the largest of all the colonies. However, as previously

Table 1.2 Decade of first 'commercial' plantings in Australian wine regions. Adapted from Dry and Smart (1988); see Chapter 2 for further details.

Decade	SA	NSW	Vic.	Tas.	WA	QLD
			Wine Regions			
1820s		Hunter		Nth Tasmania[a]		Granite Belt
1830s	McLaren Vale Adelaide Plains		Yarra Valley		Swan District	
1840s	Barossa Valley Clare Valley Eden Valley Adelaide Hills		Geelong			
1850s	Langhorne Creek	Mudgee	Rutherglen Sunbury			
1860s			Grampians Bendigo Goulburn Valley Beechworth	Sth Tasmania[a]		Roma[a]
1870s		Cowra				
1880s	Riverland	Murray Darling	King Valley Murray Darling			
1890s	Coonawarra					
1900s		Riverina Hilltops Swan Hill	Pyrenees Swan Hill			
1930s					Geographe	
1950s			Heathcote			
1960s	Currency Creek Padthaway Wrattonbully		*Macedon Ranges Henty Alpine Valleys		Great Southern (Mt Barker, Frankland River) Margaret River	
1970s	Kangaroo Is Mt Benson	Perricoota	Mornington Peninsula *Strathbogie *Gippsland[b]		Blackwood Valley Peel Great Southern (Porongorups, Denmark Albany)	
1980s		*Hastings River Orange *Tumbarumba			Manjimup Pemberton	
1990s	Sth Flinders Ranges	Sth Highlands				Sth Burnett

* Indicates those regions where viticulture may have commenced earlier than indicated; however, in these cases, it may not have been at a commercial scale.
[a] Locations, not regions. [b] Zones.

Figure 1.13a (Left) Grape harvest at Yering in the Yarra Valley circa 1866 (La Trobe Picture Collection, Victorian State Library). Figure 1.13b (Right) Present day vineyards at Yering Station Vineyard, site of the first grape plantings in Victoria (photograph courtesy of Yering Station Vineyard).

mentioned, development of viticulture in this state slowed due to a combination of the outbreak of phylloxera and severe economic depression.

Phylloxera was first recorded in Australia in 1875 at Fyansford, near Geelong. Soon it infested vineyards throughout large areas of Victoria, spreading to Bendigo and up the Goulburn River to Rutherglen. Outbreaks also occurred in table and wine grape holdings near Sydney where it was first detected at Camden in 1884. In Queensland the pest first appeared in vineyards at Enoggera, a suburb of Brisbane in 1910. The parliament of South Australia passed legislation in 1894 imposing rigid quarantine restrictions — which are still largely in force — in a successful campaign to keep phylloxera out of the State. These restrictions involved a total prohibition on the introduction of grape cuttings or any part of the grapevine; they were relaxed only in 1964 to permit the introduction, under close Government quarantine supervision, of new varieties and selected clones. Control of the spread of phylloxera remains an important issue and forms part of the current CRCV programmes. Studies include those aimed at understanding changes in the expression of gene activity of vines when attacked by phylloxera.

In South Australia, grapes were planted soon after settlement of the colony in 1836, much of the early development taking place close to the centre of Adelaide, at Reynella and in the McLaren Vale district. The first vines were planted by John Barton Hack in North Adelaide in 1837 with material obtained from Launceston. However, credit for the first to make wine in South Australia remains disputed, the claimants being John Reynell, Richard Hamilton and Walter Duffield. The latter shipped a case of 1844 vintage white wine made in the Mount Lofty Ranges to Queen Victoria in 1845 (Ilbery 1984). At Watervale (near Clare) the Sevenhills vineyard was planted by Austrian Jesuit fathers in 1848 (Ilbery 1984). Although the Barossa Valley was explored in 1837 by Colonel William Light, and German immigrants began to settle there in 1842, it took until 1847 for the first vines to be planted in the district by Johann Gramp at Jacobs Creek, two km from the present Orlando winery. Although the Barossa Valley has a strong German heritage it is interesting to recall that the German connection with Australian viticulture was first established by William Macarthur, who brought out several German vignerons as colonists in 1839, and there is evidence of several German 'vinedressers' at Camden Park as early as 1832.

In Western Australia it seems that credit for the first vine plantings there should go to Thomas Waters of 'Olive Farm' who arrived in September 1829, soon after the colony came into being on 18 June of that year. Waters was a botanist who brought with him a collection of plants and seeds from South Africa, together with a knowledge of winemaking that he had acquired from

the Boers. He was granted a property on the Swan River soon after arrival. Records indicate that by 1834 he had one-fifth of a hectare of vines planted and in a letter of 1842 he noted that he used wine made at 'Olive Farm' to barter for other goods. Captain John S. Roe came to Western Australia in June 1829 and became the colony's first Surveyor General. He was granted the 'Sandalford' property in 1840, also in the Swan Valley, where he planted tablegrapes and currants (Ilbery 1984). Significant contributions to the development of the wine industry in Western Australia were made by Professor Harold Olmo and Dr John Gladstones (Beeston 2002). In 1955 the Western Australian Government commissioned Professor Olmo of the University of California, Davis, to evaluate the wine industry and advise on its future. This report highlighted the potential of the south-west of Western Australia, particularly the region now known as the Great Southern, for suitability for the production of grapes for table wines. Follow-up studies by Dr John Gladstones supported this conclusion, but also suggested a particular suitability of Margaret River-Busselton for winegrapes. His report stimulated a number of people to establish vineyards and thus began the development of viticulture in the Margaret River region.

Although attempts to establish a viticultural industry in Tasmania were thwarted by both cool climate and disease, it is interesting to note that grapes for wine were grown successfully by Bartholomew Broughton at his 'Prospect Farm' as early as the 1820s. Also in the 1840s Dr Matthias Gaunt of Windermere, East Tamar, was making wine from grapes on his property (Ilbery 1984). In Queensland there has been a small viticultural industry since the state's separation from New South Wales in the 1850s. The first vines in the Stanthorpe area were recorded near Ballandean in 1859. Further to the north at Roma, grapes were planted by Samuel S. Bassett, in 1863. The vineyard is still in existence and remained in the ownership of the Bassett family until the 1970s.

1.4.2 VARIETAL PROFILE AND USAGE

Over the years the varietal composition of vineyard planting has altered to reflect changes in consumer preference for different wine styles. The early vineyard plantings were established with the European varieties, Shiraz, Semillon and Riesling (for table wine) and Palomino and Pedro Ximenez (for fortified wine). Prior to 1960 the major winegrape varieties were those used for fortified production. After this time there was a shift towards varieties more suitable for table wine production, and particularly varietal table wines. Because of this shift in consumer preference towards table wines, plantings of Cabernet Sauvignon and Chardonnay increased dramatically (see Chapter 6). The first statistical record of Cabernet Sauvignon was in 1959 with 68 tonnes crushed, and the first record of Chardonnay in 1974 with 90 tonnes crushed (Halliday 1994).

At times, particularly when yields of winegrapes have been low, the multipurpose varieties, especially Sultana, have been diverted to wine production. This practice caused fluctuations in the supply of dried grapes. Recently, as new winegrape vineyards have come into production, the contribution of multipurpose varieties such as Sultana and Muscat Gordo Blanco has decreased significantly and wine production is now largely based on premium winegrape varieties (see Chapter 6). The change in the varietal mix from 1998 to 2002 is detailed in **TABLE 1.3**, e.g. Shiraz replaced Chardonnay as the variety with the highest production. About 80% of Australian winegrape production in 2001–02 comprised premium winegrape varieties. As new plantings come into production the proportion of the total crush as premium varieties could well rise to near 90%. In 1996 and 1997 black grape varieties dominated new plantings. The significant plantings of black grape varieties has placed the Australian wine industry in a position to capitalise on the worldwide interest in the health benefits of drinking red wine in moderation.

Table 1.3 The top 15 contributors to winegrape production by variety in 1997–98 and 2001–02. From Hoffmann 2003.

1997-98			2001-02		
Variety	(tonnes)	share	Variety	(tonnes)	share
Chardonnay	152,979	17.6%	Shiraz	326,564	21.6%
Shiraz	135,325	15.5%	Cabernet Sauvignon	257,223	17.0%
Sultana	109,306	12.6%	Chardonnay	256,328	16.9%
Cabernet Sauvignon	94,085	10.8%	Merlot	104,423	6.9%
Muscat Gordo Blanco	58,894	6.8%	Semillon	100,785	6.7%
Semillon	57,682	6.6%	Sultana	65,358	4.3%
Riesling	34,028	3.9%	Colombard	60,419	4.0%
Colombard	30,095	3.5%	Muscat Gordo Blanco	51,064	3.4%
Grenache	24,025	2.8%	Sauvignon Blanc	28,567	1.9%
Pinot Noir	19,716	2.3%	Riesling	27,838	1.8%
Sauvignon Blanc	19,608	2.3%	Grenache	26,260	1.7%
Chenin Blanc	16,439	1.9%	Pinot Noir	21,341	1.4%
Merlot	14,468	1.7%	Verdelho	16,121	1.1%
Trebbiano	10,990	1.3%	Chenin Blanc	14,567	1.0%
Doradillo	9,409	1.1%	Mataro	12,452	0.8%
Other	83,578	9.6%	Other	145,193	9.6%
Total winegrapes	870,627	100%	Total winegrapes	1,514,501	100%

Source: All tables are based on Australian Bureau of Statistics, Vineyard Survey data, 1997-98 and 2001-02.

1.4.3 REGULATIONS AND PHILOSOPHIES

The laws which regulate winegrape production in Australia allow viticulturists many options in managing their vineyards; unlike some parts of Europe there are neither yield limitations nor restrictions on use of irrigation. Furthermore, the flexibility of the laws relating to winemaking and labelling of wines gives winemakers the choice to make a wine from either a single variety from one vineyard or from different varieties from different regions to produce a blended wine. Many Australian wines are multi-variety and/or multi-regional blends. The opportunity to blend wines of different varieties from a range of regions provides consistency of wine style, a feature which has been of great benefit in building the reputation of Australian wines both domestically and internationally. As new regions have developed, the suitability of these for different varieties and wine styles has been tested. In the future, alongside multi-regional blends, regional wine styles (e.g. Barossa Valley Shiraz) are likely to play a greater role in the promotion and image of Australian wine. The concept of regionality is being embraced in a number of regions. An example of this is that of Jeffrey Grosset of Grosset Wines in the Clare Valley Region who, recognising that certain tastes in his Riesling wines are closely linked to specific vineyards or sections of vineyards, has suggested the use of the Aboriginal word *pangkarra* to capture this connection between vines and their wine. *Pangkarra* is a word with no direct English translation, but which encompasses the notion of 'a sense of place'. It is a concept similar in many ways to that embraced by the French word *terroir*. Matching of regions and sites to the expression of the character of a wine is also likely to lead to a greater interest in single vineyard wines. Henschke's Hill of Grace, a Shiraz wine made from old vines, some over a hundred years old grown in the Eden Valley region, is Australia's most notable single vineyard wine. However, recognition of other sites is increasing.

Travel by viticulturists and winemakers to overseas wine regions has played a significant part in the development of the Australian wine industry. Notable examples are the visits by James Busby (see 1.4.1) and Max Schubert. The study trip of Max Schubert, the chief winemaker for Penfolds, to Spain and France in 1950 resulted in a new approach to Australian winemaking. He returned determined to produce an Australian red wine that would last at least 20 years and be comparable to those produced in Bordeaux. He chose to make a wine from a blend of Shiraz wines produced from a number of vineyards (not necessarily from the same viticultural region) and he used American rather than French oak for storage. This innovative approach led to the creation of Grange (formally Grange Hermitage), a full-bodied red wine that has become an Australian icon and is recognised as equivalent in status to the First Growths of Bordeaux. This spirit of innovation has continued to drive the Australian viticultural and winemaking industries.

1.4.4 GROWTH AND STATUS

A number of events have shaped the growth of the Australian winegrape industry since it started 200 years ago. These were summarised in sections 1.1.2 and 1.4.1 and illustrated in **FIGURE 1.3**. By far the most dramatic event was the doubling of the area planted to winegrapes during the short period of only seven years beginning in 1993. This achievement is astonishing given that Australia has only 20 million people with just a small proportion living away from cities, and considering the large capital investment required for establishment and management of this type of horticultural enterprise. Many factors contributed to the success of this phenomenal growth: —

a) the increasing appreciation by the international wine community of the value and quality of Australian wines.

b) the availability of suitable land in a range of climatic regions.

c) the wide array of modern technologies that has been developed, many adopted with a high degree of mechanisation.

d) the network of research facilities and supporting organisations that provide direction and funding.

In 2001–02 Australia's total vineyard area was 158,594 hectares with a total production of 1.5 million tonnes of grapes for wine production, being about 1,216 millions of litres of wine. South Australia, New South Wales and Victoria are the main winegrape producing states, with South Australia being the state with the largest area planted with vines and the largest wine producer. About 40% of Australian wine is exported, with the United Kingdom, the United States, New Zealand, Canada and Germany being the key export destinations. In 2001 production of wine in Australia represented about 4% of total world production of 27,544 millions of litres of wine.

1.5 Concluding Remarks

The viticultural industry comprises thousands of private and company-owned vineyards spread across all states and territories. Growing grapes for table, drying and winemaking purposes should continue to provide significant economic benefit to rural Australia, enhancing employment and the development of associated industries. Winegrape production will undoubtedly predominate, however it is unlikely that growth will continue at the pace of the late 1990s. It is likely that there will be a period of some rationalisation as issues of grape quality and potential oversupply of some varieties are resolved. Emphasis on new vineyard establishment will most likely be towards areas targeted for their suitability to produce particular wine styles for domestic and overseas markets. Growth in the table and drying grape industries will probably be minimal. In future all three viticultural enterprises are likely to become more quality-conscious and -focused. A greater proportion of grapes, be they for table, drying or wine purposes will be produced to particular specifications and for defined markets. Environmental issues such as water-use efficiency, water quality, land management

and use of chemicals to control pests and diseases will be important considerations in developing and managing vineyards. The adoption of molecular biology techniques is likely to play a greater role in the viticulture industry in the future; genetic modification of grapevines will continue to be investigated and debated by the scientific and general community. Building of the export sector will be critical for the stability and growth of all three enterprises and the next decade will see a greater focus on market-orientated activities to capitalise on the advances previously made in production.

REFERENCES

Statistical data are sourced from the yearly Australian Bureau of Statistics Vineyard Survey Report. Recent years data of the Australian Bureau of Statistics Vineyard Survey Report are summarised in Vintage – the Australian Wine Industry Statistical Yearbook, a yearly official wine industry annual published by Winetitles in conjunction with the Winemakers' Federation of Australia.

Beeston, J. (2002) The Wine Regions of Australia (Allen & Unwin: Crows Nest).

Bramley, R., Pearse, B. et al. (2003) Being profitable precisely - a case study of precision viticulture from Margaret River. Aust. NZ Grapegrower & Winemaker No. 473a, 84-87.

Clingeleffer, R.R., Sommer, K.J. et al. (1997) Winegrape crop prediction and management. Aust. NZ Wine Industry J. 12, 354-359.

Coombe, B.G. (1987) Viticultural research and technical development in Australia. In: Proc. 6th Aust. Wine Industry Tech. Conf., Adelaide 1986. Ed T.H. Lee (Aust. Industrial Publ.: Adelaide), pp. 20-24.

Croser, B.J. (2004) Brand or authenticity? Aust. NZ Wine Industry J. 19 (2), 12-21.

Dry, P.R., Loveys, B.R. et al. (2000) Partial rootzone drying - an update. Aust. Grapegrower & Winemaker No. 438a, 35-39.

Dry, P.R. and Smart, R.E. (1998) The Grapegrowing Regions of Australia. In: Viticulture Vol. 1, Edition 1. Eds B.G. Coombe and P.R. Dry (Australian Industrial Publishers: Adelaide), pp. 37-60.

Fogarty, J.P. (1967) Great Australians, George Chaffey (Oxford University Press: Oxford).

Gregory, G.R. (1988) Development and Status of Australian Viticulture. In: Viticulture Vol. 1, Edition 1. Eds B.G. Coombe and P.R. Dry (Australian Industrial Publishers: Adelaide), pp. 1-36.

Halliday, J. (1994) A History of the Australian Wine Industry 1949-1994 (Winetitles: Adelaide).

Hoffman D. (2003) The changing face of viticulture. Aust. NZ Wine Industry J. 18 (4), 40-45.

Ilbery, J. (1984) Vineyards and Vignerons of Australia. In: Len Evans Complete Book of Australian Wine (Summit Books: Sydney), pp. 39-180.

Laffer, H.E. (1949) The Wine Industry of Australia (Australian Wine Board: Adelaide).

Maiden, J.H. (1917) The Grapevine. Notes on its introduction into New South Wales. Agric. Gazette of NSW 28, 427-433.

McCarthy, M.G. (1998) Irrigation management to improve winegrape quality - nearly 10 years on. Aust. Grapegrower & Winemaker No. 414, 65-71.

Rankine, B.C. (1996) Evolution of the Modern Australian Wine Industry: A Personal Appraisal (Ryan Publications: Adelaide).

Smart, R.D. and Robinson, M.D. (1991) Sunlight into Wine: a handbook for winegrape canopy management (Winetitles: Adelaide).

Somers, T.C. (1998) The Wine Spectrum (Winetitles: Adelaide).

CHAPTER TWO

The Grapegrowing Regions of Australia

P. R. DRY, D. J. MASCHMEDT, C. J. ANDERSON, E. RILEY, S-J. BELL AND W. S. GOODCHILD

Since their introduction to Australia in 1788, grapevines have been cultivated in many parts of its southern regions. The viticultural significance of these regions has changed with time for a variety of reasons: for instance, the large impact of phylloxera in Victoria last century and more recently, the effect of urban sprawl around Adelaide and Perth, and the renewed interest in table wines from cooler regions. Prior to the 1980s, commercial viticulture in Australia was restricted to a relatively small number of regions (fewer than 30) and, even with the vineyard expansion of the late 1960s associated with increases in wine consumption, most plantings were in 'traditional' areas. However, the planting boom of the 1990s not only increased the total area by 2.5 times, it also resulted in a significant number of new regions and subregions which have now been geographically registered under the aegis of the Geographical Indications (GI) scheme (a full list is available online—Australian Wine and Brandy Corporation 2003). For example, 57 regions and 11 subregions are described in this chapter. Despite this growth in number of regions, plantings irrigated from the Murray and Murrumbidgee Rivers still dominate the grape industry and collectively account for 66% of Australia's winegrape production.

2.1 Classification of grapegrowing regions on the basis of climate

The role of climate in determining both quantity and quality of grape production is regarded as paramount. A classification was developed by Smart and Dry (1980) encompassing the major climate variables of significance to grape production in Australia: temperature, the rainfall-evaporation difference (aridity), humidity and solar radiation. Each of these variables exhibits diurnal and seasonal variation, and the justification for characterising the fluctuations may be found in Smart and Dry (1980) and Chapter 4. The indices are designed to be representative of a standard growing season in the southern hemisphere (October to March inclusively) though it is recognised that the length of actual growing season depends on region, variety and each year's climate. Other climatic indices utilise the October to April period (see Chapter 4). As simplistic as the indices are, they do provide an explanation for differences in yield, quality, disease incidence, irrigation requirements and variety suitability between regions. More precise methods of climatic comparison are available for the purpose of vineyard site selection (see Chapter 10).

2.1.1 THE VARIABLES USED

The climatic variables used are based on readily available, long-term climatic averages (available online: Australian Bureau of Meteorology [2003]) and are as follows:

Temperature

The annual curve of mean temperature is approximately sinusoidal and hence may be essentially described by two values: Smart and Dry (1980) chose the approximate peak of the curve—the mean January temperature (MJT)—and the mean annual range or continentality (CTL) which is the difference between January and July mean temperatures. The implication of a high CTL value for the same MJT is that spring and autumn temperatures will be lower, and so vine development proceeds more slowly in spring and ripening takes place under lower temperatures in autumn. Because of the nature of the temperature-time curve, MJT is well correlated with degree days (Smart and Dry 1980) and is essentially the same as the mean temperature of the warmest month, first brought to notice as a useful index by Prescott (see Chapter 4).

Aridity

Evaporation is measured in Australia with a Class A pan evaporimeter (GSE in **TABLE 2.1**). Mature, well-watered and vigorous vineyards evapotranspire about half of the evaporation rate as measured by a guarded Class A pan evaporimeter (Smart and Coombe 1983). A simple index of irrigation water requirement of vineyards ('aridity') is therefore calculated from monthly totals by subtracting rainfall (mm) from 0.5 of Class A Pan evaporation (mm). However, this is an over-estimate if a deficit irrigation strategy is planned (see Volume II, Chapter 6). The data are summed for the standard growing season (October to March; ARID in **TABLE 2.1**).

Relative humidity

The 9 am per cent relative humidity for January is taken as an index of relative humidity over the growing season. The 9 am value approximates the daily mean figure (RH in **TABLE 2.1**). The 3 pm value has also been used as a climatic index (see Chapter 4).

Sunshine hours

The average daily bright sunshine hours in the standard growing season (October to March) is used as an index of solar radiation (SSH in **TABLE 2.1**).

2.1.2 COMPARISON OF REGIONS: CLIMATE

TABLE 2.1 (a-d) gives details of climatic averages for 61 locations in Australian viticultural regions. As well as the indices listed above, data are presented for annual and growing season (October to March) rainfall (ARF and GSRF respectively in **TABLE 2.1**) and growing season

(October to March) raindays (GSRD in **TABLE 2.1**). Problems associated with the use of climatic data from particular station(s) for a given region have been discussed in Smart and Dry (1979, 1980); also see footnotes of **TABLE 2.1**. The order of the regions listed below is based on temperature and geography. Regions (GI) are grouped into classes on the basis of MJT as follows: MJT > 25°C; MJT from 23.0 to 24.9°C; 21.0 to 22.9°C; 19.0 to 20.9°C; and less than 19°C. Within each MJT class, regions are arranged by state and order is from west to east. Within each state, the regions are ordered on the basis of MJT with the exception that regions are grouped on the basis of zones: this allows regions in close proximity to be considered together. **FIGURE 2.1** shows isotherms of MJT.

2.2 Regional descriptions: background

The history of the development of the GI system is described in detail in Beeston (2002). The whole of Australia is divided into 'wine zones' as follows:

1. *Western Australia:* Eastern Plains, Inland and North of Western Australia, West Australian South East Coastal, South West Australia, Central Western Australia, Greater Perth
2. *South Australia:* Mount Lofty Ranges, Barossa, Fleurieu, Limestone Coast, Lower Murray, Far North, The Peninsulas
3. *Northern Territory* (whole of territory)
4. *Victoria:* Gippsland, Central Victoria, North East Victoria, North West Victoria, Port Phillip and Western Victoria
5. *Tasmania* (whole of state)
6. *New South Wales:* Big Rivers, Western Plains, Northern Slopes, Northern Rivers, Hunter Valley, South Coast, Central Ranges, Southern New South Wales
7. *Queensland* (whole of state)
8. *Australian Capital Territory*

While the zones are not likely to change in the near future, new regions and subregions will continue to be added. **FIGURES 1.1** and **2.2** show the locations of zones and regions respectively. The Chapter is a description of viticultural regions in Australia. Information on the average dates of budburst, flowering and harvest of many regions can be found in **TABLES 7.3, 7.5** and **7.6**. The planting and production statistics (2000–01) were sourced from the Winemakers Federation of Australia (2002), J. Whiting (pers. comm.) and regional associations (the latter were estimates in most cases). Where the main varieties are listed, these data are based on actual statistics of total planted area. Otherwise, the 'principal' varieties have been estimated from both local knowledge and production statistics. The planting and production statistics by state/zone are summarised in **TABLE 1.1**. The decade of first

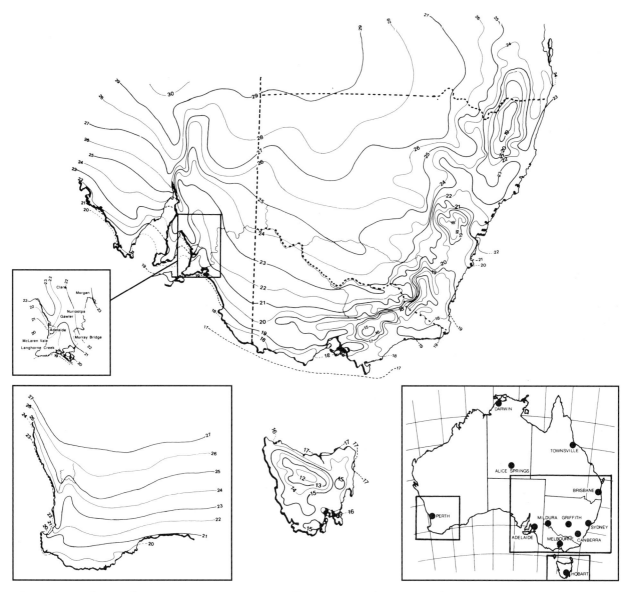

Figure 2.1 Isotherms of Mean January Temperature (Source: Dry and Smart 1988)

commercial planting in a region is listed in **TABLE 1.2.** The landscapes and key soils are summarised for each region. For most regions, soils are assigned a code (bold and in parentheses—e.g. **Class 9.1**) which corresponds exactly to a sub-category according to the scheme described in Chapter 3 and in Maschmedt et al. (2002).

2.3 Regions with MJT > 25°C

2.3.1 QUEENSLAND
The grape industry in Queensland is relatively small (2,335 ha). Grapes destined for the table make up 65% of total production and the remainder is used for wine. The drying grape industry is insignificant. The main winegrape varieties are Shiraz, Cabernet Sauvignon, Chardonnay, Red and Black Frontignac, Sultana and Merlot. Roma, 500 km west of Brisbane (26.58°S,

148.78°E) at an elevation of 300 m, was the traditional centre of winemaking in the state. The first vines were planted here in 1863. There are now just a few hectares of winegrapes remaining in the area. Some of the hottest commercial wine-producing areas in Australia are found in Queensland, e.g. Roma (MJT = 27.3°C); Gayndah [North Burnett] (MJT = 26.3°C); Dalby [Darling Downs] (MJT = 25.2°C). Rainfall is very summer-dominant. Harvest is very early.

2.3.2 OTHER REGIONS
There are small plantings of winegrapes at Alice Springs, NT (MJT = 29.4°C), and tablegrapes at Menindee, NSW near Broken Hill (**TABLE 2.1a**), Townsville, Qld and at other places in Queensland, the Northern Territory and northern Western Australia. The harvest period varies from October to early January.

Table of codes

State	ZONE, Region or *subregion*	Code
WA	Blackwood Valley	BD
	Geographe	GE
	Great Southern	GS
	Albany	AL
	Denmark	DE
	Frankland River	FR
	Mt Barker	MB
	Porongorup	PO
	Manjimup	MA
	Margaret River	MR
	Peel	PE
	Pemberton	PB
	Perth Hills	PH
	Swan District	SW
SA	Adelaide Hills	AH
	Adelaide Plains	AP
	Barossa Valley	BV
	Clare Valley	CL
	Coonawarra	CO
	Currency Creek	CC
	Eden Valley	EV
	Kangaroo Island	KI
	Langhorne Creek	LC
	McLaren Vale	MV
	Mount Benson	ME
	Padthaway	PA
	Penola	PN
	Riverland	RL
	Southern Fleurieu	SF
	Southern Flinders Ranges	FL
	Wrattonbully	WR
Vic	Alpine Valleys	AV
	Bendigo	BE
	Beechworth	BW
	Geelong	GL
	GIPPSLAND	GI
	Glenrowan	GN
	Goulburn Valley	GV
	Grampians	GR
	Heathcote	HE
	Henty	HN
	King Valley	KV
	Macedon Ranges	MC
	Mornington Peninsula	MO
	Murray Darling	MD
	Pyrenees	PY
	Rutherglen	RU
	Strathbogie Ranges	SR
	Sunbury	SU
	Swan Hill	SH
	Upper Goulburn	UG
	Yarra Valley	YV
NSW	Canberra District	CB
	Cowra	CW
	Gundagai	GU
	Hastings River	HR
	Hilltops	HT
	Hunter	HU
	Mudgee	MU
	NORTHERN SLOPES	NS
	Orange	OR
	Perricoota	PR
	Riverina	RI
	Shoalhaven Coast	SO
	Southern Highlands	SI
	Tumbarumba	TU
QLD	Granite Belt	GB
	South Burnett	SB
TAS	TASMANIA	TA

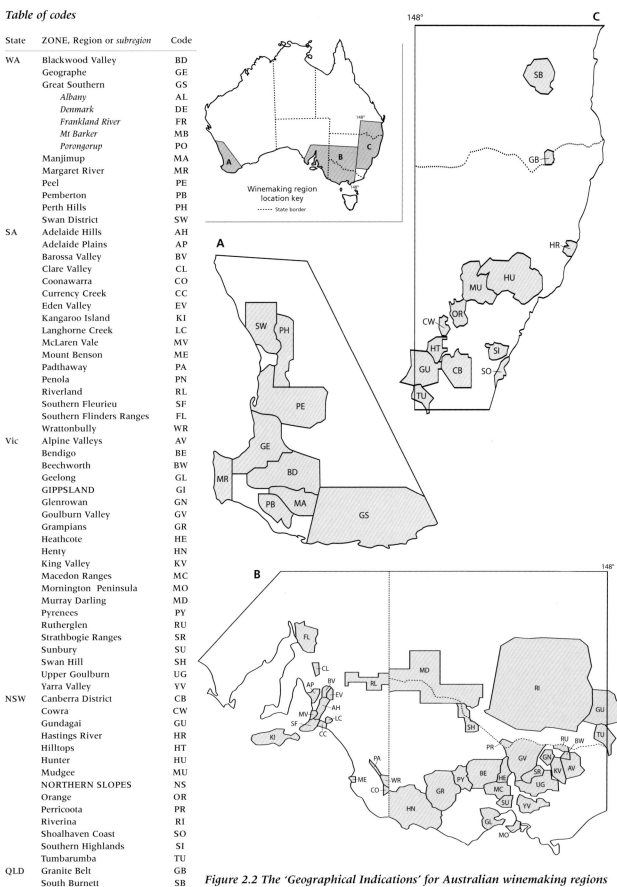

Figure 2.2 The 'Geographical Indications' for Australian winemaking regions in 2004. Redrawn from an Australian Wine and Brandy Corporation map.

20

Table 2.1. Climatic data for viticultural regions in Australia.
Table 2.1a. Regions with mean January temperature (MJT) greater than 23°C.

Region	State	Station	Elevation (m)	MJT[y] °C	CTL °C	ARF mm	GSRF mm	GSRD	GSE mm	ARID mm	RH %	SSH
-	NSW	47019 Menindee	61	26.2	15.7	244	128	17	1587	666	45	(10.0)
Swan District	WA	9021 Perth Airport	15	24.5[x]	11.3	792	123	30	1506	630	51	10.7
Riverina	NSW	75028 Griffith CSIRO	126	23.9	15.3	406	192	29	1347	481	49	9.3
Peel	WA	9572 Mandurah	15	23.7[x]	10.2	877	129	29	1228[c]	485	53	9.3[a]
Hunter	NSW	61009 Cessnock PO	80	23.7	12.8	748	436	45	916[d]	22	59	8.5[a]
Gundagai	NSW	73009 Cootamundra	318	23.6	16.3	626	298	36	(1060)	(232)	57	(9.9)
Murray Darling	NSW, Vic.	76026 Merbein	56	23.6	13.9	285	133	26	1357	546	49	10.1[a]
Cowra	NSW	65091 Cowra Airport	300	23.5	15.7	621	317	40	1030[e]	198	59	9.8[a]
South Burnett	Qld	40112 Kingaroy	442	23.5	12.3	780	542	51	1074	-5	72	(8.5)
Swan Hill	NSW, Vic.	77042 Swan Hill	70	23.4	14.2	349	153	25	1300[b]	497	53	10.0[a]
Hastings River	NSW	59017 Kempsey	10	23.4	10.7	1220	721	64	949[f]	-246	78	(7.5)
Mudgee	NSW	62021 Mudgee	454	23.3	15.4	676	365	38	(1200)	235	63	9.4[a]
Rutherglen	Vic.	Composite[g]	148	23.3	15.6	615	262	36	1205[a]	340	55	9.3[h]
Riverland	SA	24002 Berri	66	23.2	12.8	275	113	23	1363[i]	569	44	9.4
Southern Flinders	SA	21020 Georgetown	273	23.1	13.8	473	160	27	1300[j]	490	42	(9.5)

[a] Gladstones (1992)

[b] Dry and Smart (1988)

[c] 9812 Harvey

[d] 61242 Cessnock (Nulkaba)

[e] 63023 Cowra Research

[f] 0090 Taree

( ) Denotes estimate

[g] Average of 082138 Wangaratta Airport and 074034 Corowa Airport

[h] 082039 Rutherglen Research

[i] 024024 Loxton Research

[j] Estimated from stations 19102, 21114 and 21008

[x] J. Gladstones (pers.comm.)

[y] See 2.1.1 and 2.1.2 in text for explanation of codes

2.4 Regions with MJT from 23.0 to 24.9°C

2.4.1 WESTERN AUSTRALIA

SWAN DISTRICT (*ZONE: GREATER PERTH*)

Swan District is the most important region within the Greater Perth Zone (which also includes Peel and Perth Hills). Vineyards are concentrated in the Swan Valley subregion in the south-east of the state, 20 km east of the city of Perth (131.93°S, 115.98°E). This is the historical centre of grapegrowing in WA. The first vines were planted in 1830. By the 1850s, plantings had expanded and included table- and wine-grapes. The first dried fruit was produced in 1912. During the second half of the 20th century the planted area declined due to low yields and competition from alternative land-uses including urbanisation. The many small wineries of the region were traditionally producers of fortified wine but now table wines predominate. Smaller areas of vineyards are found in the north of the region near Gingin and Bindoon, and on the coastal strip. There are 1,689 ha of vineyards in the Greater Perth Zone and approximately 75% of the total area is found in the Swan Valley. The principal varieties of the Zone are Shiraz, Chenin Blanc, Chardonnay, Grenache, Verdelho and Cabernet Sauvignon for winemaking, Red Globe, Crimson Seedless, Sultana, Dawn Seedless and Flame Seedless for table use and Zante Currant and Muscat Gordo Blanco for drying.

Regional resources

The viticultural area of the Swan Valley is a generally flat river plain set between coastal sands on the west and the foothills of the Darling Scarp, rising to an elevation of about 60 m in the east. The climate is of pronounced Mediterranean type with a hot and dry summer, with very high solar radiation and evaporation and mild wet winters (**TABLE 2.1a**). Plantings in the Swan Valley subregion are mostly concentrated on recent alluvial deposits along the river and the surrounding older alluvial deposits along the foot of the Darling scarp. Recent alluvial soils include brown and red sandy earths (**Class 9.2**) and brown and red deep sands (**Class 9.1**). Soils on the older alluvial deposits include the less well drained grey and yellow brown deep sandy duplex (**Classes 6.2, 7.2**), grey shallow sandy duplex (**Classes 6.1, 7.1**) and yellow brown shallow loamy duplex (**Class 7.3**). At the foothills of the Darling Scarp, vines are planted on lateritic gravels (**Class 7.2**). Low yield and vigour are associated with drainage problems and/or summer water stress. Water resources in the region are restricted to artesian and sub-artesian bores of variable quality. Water from the Swan River is saline.

Management practices

The Swan Valley is not particularly prone to fungal diseases. Rootknot nematodes are widespread in the sandy soils; as a result, much of the area is on rootstocks, mainly Schwarzmann and 34 EM. East/west rows are common.

Row spacing is generally 3 to 3.5 m. The traditional single wire and T-trellises have been largely replaced by vertically shoot positioned trellis (VSP) in winegrape vineyards. Typical yields range between 2 and 4 t/ha for Chardonnay and 4 and 5 t/ha for Shiraz. Harvest commences in mid-February (Chardonnay).

Summary

The Swan Valley faces pressure from alternative land uses such as urbanisation and hobby farms. Expansion is also limited due to water shortage.

PEEL (*ZONE: GREATER PERTH*)

The Peel region extends from the southern suburbs of Perth to the northern border of the Geographe region. The first substantial plantings date from the mid-1970s. The planted area is approximately 150 ha. The economic centre of the region is Mandurah, 62 km south of Perth. Although the region is diverse in both climate and topography, most vineyards are located on a relatively narrow strip of coastal land near Mandurah, characterised by the so-called 'tuart sands'. These are deep, well drained, siliceous sands over limestone. They are suitable for viticulture but have low natural fertility. The climate is similar to that of the Swan Valley although cooler with less temperature variability due to earlier and more regular arrival of the south-westerly summer sea breeze (Gladstones 1992; **TABLE 2.1a**). Irrigation is essential and water is available from aquifers. Varieties and viticultural practices are similar to the Swan Valley. Harvest commences in mid- to late February (Chardonnay).

2.4.2 SOUTH AUSTRALIA

RIVERLAND (*ZONE: LOWER MURRAY*)

The Riverland region comprises a number of horticultural areas adjacent to the River Murray from Blanchetown to the Victorian border. The main centres are Waikerie (34.17°S, 139.98°E), Barmera, Berri, Loxton and Renmark (34.17°S, 140.75°E). The first major development of irrigated agriculture in the Riverland occurred at Renmark. The Chaffey brothers from California, under an agreement with the South Australian Government, commenced an irrigation scheme in 1887. Other small irrigation settlements followed from the 1890s until the First World War. These early settlements produced grapes mainly for drying, but distilleries were set up from 1917 to 1919 to utilise unwanted drying grapes, particularly Muscat Gordo Blanco. Soldier Settlement schemes were established after both World Wars with private holdings initially being 8 to 12 ha and each typically planted with several horticultural crops, mainly vines, citrus or stonefruit. The varieties planted before 1960 were generally either the 'drying' varieties such as Sultana and Muscat Gordo Blanco or varieties such as Doradillo, Pedro Ximenes and Grenache for spirit

or fortified wine production. As a result of the increased demand for table wine, there was extensive vineyard development by winery companies from the 1970s onwards. However, the wine industry is still very dependent on the independent growers who produce more than 85% of the total tonnes crushed. Of the 1,200 producers in the region, 60% have less than 10 ha of vineyard. The total area is 19,087 ha: the main varieties are Shiraz, Cabernet Sauvignon, Chardonnay, Muscat Gordo Blanco, Merlot, Ruby Cabernet and Colombard.

Regional resources

The climate in most respects is similar to that of the other inland regions with high summer temperatures, but it is the coolest of these regions during ripening (Gladstones 1992). The ripening mean temperature is 2°C less than that of the Riverina and rainfall is lower, mainly due to the drier summer and autumn (**TABLE 2.1a**). Spring frosts may be a hazard, their impact is lessened by soil management practices in the main. Two dominant landforms are used for horticulture in the Riverland; the river valley terraces ('river flats') and the mallee highlands (**FIGURES 1.5b, 1.7**). The river valley contains dissected terraces of various heights, occasional sandhills and stranded sandbars. Although the early viticultural plantings in the region were on the river flats, most development since the 1960s has been on the highland areas, particularly in the vicinity of Waikerie, Loxton and Berri. The mallee highlands consist of a gently rolling landscape superimposed with a series of discontinued east-west parallel sand dunes. These are formed on Murray Basin sediments with a limestone base overlain in turn by sand, clayey sand/sandy clay and heavy clay (the so-called Blanchetown Clay). Deposited on top of this sequence is a layer of wind-blown carbonate rich material (Woorinen Formation), capped by calcrete in places, and more recently, siliceous sands. The latter have generally been re-worked into longitudinal dunes. All highland soils are alkaline to neutral, with deep subsoils commonly strongly alkaline. Deep and gradational sandy soils (**Classes 8.1, 9.1, 9.2**) are characteristic of the dunes. Although infertile and prone to wind erosion, they are well drained with deep rootzones. Calcareous sandy loams (**Classes 8.3, 8.4, 8.6**) occur on the Woorinen Formation. Rootzone depth and drainage of these soils is dependent on the nature of the subsoil carbonate layer and the depth to the underlying Blanchetown Clay. This impedes deep drainage causing waterlogging and accumulation of salts in the subsoil. Lighter textured and rubbly carbonate layers with Blanchetown Clay deeper than 1.5 m are the most favourable. Soils of the river flats are generally heavier: sandy loams to sandy clay loams over brown to red clayey subsoils. Some of these are calcareous (**Class 8.5**), some are duplex with restrictive subsoils (**Class 6.3**), while others are gradational (**Classes 9.3, 9.4**).

There are also extensive areas of grey cracking clay (**Class 5.1**). Drainage problems and salt accumulation are widespread. In the depressions and down-slope areas, shallow water tables frequently develop requiring the installation of tile drains; drainage effluent is collected in sumps and pumped into evaporation basins or discharged into deep limestone strata.

Management practices

All vineyards are irrigated with water from the River Murray. Water-use is restricted by either water licence or entitlement from grower-owned schemes. In the early years furrow irrigation was the only system available. Today, overhead sprinklers (45% of the vineyard area), undervine sprinklers (30%) and drip irrigation (15% and increasing) are predominantly used. Typical amounts applied per annum have been 7 to 10 ML/ha by overhead sprinklers and 5 to 7 ML/ha by drip. However, since the late 1990s, irrigation amounts have decreased with increasing use of deficit irrigation strategies (see Volume II, Chapter 5). The older plantings were made with ungrafted vines but, since the 1980s, grafted vines have been increasingly used to overcome nematode problems. At present, as much as 30% of the area may be grafted, with Ramsey as the main rootstock. Typical yield ranges are 25 to 30 t/ha for Chardonnay and 18 to 24 t/ha for Shiraz. All vines are trellised. The majority of vineyards have a two-wire vertical trellis while the remainder have single wire (1.5 m high) or wide-T (about 1.2 m wide and 1.2 m high) trellises. Canopies are sprawling with an absence of shoot positioning. More than 90% of the area is mechanically pruned and mechanically harvested. Harvest commences in early to mid-February (Chardonnay). This region has a substantial area of non-pruned or minimally-pruned vineyards. Row width is usually 3.0 to 3.6 m and vine spacing 1.2 to 2.4 m, depending on the rootstock used. The most significant diseases are downy and powdery mildews which cause serious loss in about one year in three to five: the former is often associated with overhead sprinkler irrigation. Black spot (anthracnose) is seen occasionally in cool wet springs, particularly on Sultana. Rootknot (*Meloidogyne* spp.) and other nematodes reduce yields in ungrafted vineyards, sometimes seriously. Other pests include mites, lightbrown apple moth, mealy-bug and grapevine scale. Phylloxera is not present in the region. The soils are normally deficient in nitrogen and this is supplied to vines by growing cover crops or by light fertiliser applications. Zinc and manganese deficiencies occur and foliar sprays are routinely applied.

Summary

The Riverland is Australia's most productive winegrape-growing region, producing one-quarter of all grapes used for winemaking. It has become an important source of wine for Australia's export market. Innovative viticultural practices, particularly deficit irrigation, and a greater choice of varieties have resulted in significant improvements in the quality of its table wines.

SOUTHERN FLINDERS RANGES (*ZONE: FAR NORTH*)
One of the newest regions, Southern Flinders covers a large area from Georgetown (33.35°S, 138.38°E; 55 km north of Clare) in the south to Wilmington in the north. Vineyards have been established from close to sea level on the coastal plains of Spencer Gulf to 600 m or higher on the slopes of Mt Remarkable (963 m). Although tablegrapes have been produced on the coastal plain for many years, most winegrape vineyards were planted in the 1990s on elevated sites in the centre of the region. The total planted area is approximately 200 ha and the main varieties are Shiraz, Cabernet Sauvignon, Merlot and Grenache. The climate is variable, the major influences being elevation, topography and access to westerly sea-breezes in the summer. For example, annual rainfall ranges from 350 mm at Pt Germein (12 m elevation) to 473 mm at Georgetown (273 m; **TABLE 2.1a**) to 680 mm at Wirrabara (390 m). The winegrape harvest commences very early in late January (Chardonnay) on the coastal plain. The major restriction to future expansion is access to water for irrigation.

2.4.3 VICTORIA

MURRAY DARLING [FORMERLY SUNRAYSIA] (*ZONE: NORTH WEST VICTORIA*)
The Murray Darling region comprises areas on the Murray, Darling and Murrumbidgee Rivers, in north western Victoria and south-western New South Wales. The region extends for approximately 350 km along the River Murray from the South Australian border. It includes vineyards near Lake Cullulleraine, Mildura, Red Cliffs and Robinvale (Victoria) and Wentworth, Dareton, Buronga, Euston and Balranald (NSW). The major population centre is Mildura (34.18°S, 142.20°E; 450 km north-west of Melbourne). The Chaffey brothers commenced an irrigation settlement in the mid-1880s near Mildura and the First Mildura Irrigation Trust was formed in 1895. Blocks were allocated to soldier settlers after both World Wars. Dried fruit from the varieties Sultana, Zante Currant, Muscat Gordo Blanco and Waltham Cross was the most important product of these vineyards. Wine production increased significantly in the early 1980s being predominantly bulk wine for the cask market using multi-purpose varieties such as Sultana and Muscat Gordo Blanco. During the 1990s, there was a significant shift to the production of bottled wine using varieties such as Chardonnay, Shiraz, Cabernet Sauvignon and Merlot. Dried fruit production remains important. Grapes are also grown for the tablegrape market. This region has the largest vineyard area in Australia with approximately 25,000 ha (70% in

Victoria). The main varieties are Sultana, Cabernet Sauvignon, Chardonnay, Shiraz, Merlot and Muscat Gordo Blanco. Forty-six per cent and 11% of Sultana production was used for drying and table purposes respectively in 2001. Most grapes for wine are produced by independent growers.

Regional resources

The region is generally flat to gently undulating with occasional long sandy rises. Elevation is about 30 to 60 m. The climate is characterised by very high levels of solar radiation, temperature and evaporation, and low humidity (**TABLE 2.1a**). Both annual and growing season rainfall are very low. The soils preferred for vineyards are predominantly sandy loams that are calcareous throughout the soil horizon. The North West Victoria Zone is characterised by calcareous dunefields with generally east-west oriented sandhills and intervening swales. In some of the southern parts of the zone (i.e. Swan Hill region) hummocky dunes are more common. Calcareous soils are dominant in this zone. They vary considerably in terms of soil texture, ranging from those dominated by sands (mainly on dunes) to those that are clayey throughout. There is a general tendency for clay content to increase with depth. Coarse textured calcareous soils predominate in the north of the zone. Here, east-west dunes alternate with broad swales. The soils in the swales and broad north-south trending ridges generally have loamy surfaces overlying clay subsoils that are often sodic (**Classes 6.1, 6.2**). Sands (**Class 8.1**) are most common on the east-west dunes. The dunes can be fairly closely spaced in the central Mallee, and the different agronomic requirements of dunes and intervening loamy flats can pose difficulties for management. Heavier textured calcareous soils (**Classes 8.5, 8.6**) predominate in the south of the zone where east-west dunes are infrequent or replaced by sub-rounded hummocks. Soils on the crests and upper slopes of hummocks and stranded ridges have loamy surfaces (**Class 8.6**). The lower slopes and plains have clay loam to light clay surfaces (**Class 8.5**) and these may grade into cracking clay soils (**Classes 5.2, 5.1**). These heavier textured soils are often gilgai-ed on the plains and ridge slopes. Sands occur on the occasional east-west dunes further north. The heavier soils are relatively productive and stable. Cracking clay soils (**Class 5.1**) on the River Murray floodplain are used for viticulture to some extent. Many soils are prone to water table development making subsurface drainage necessary. Salt damage to vines may occur due to rising water tables resulting from poor irrigation management or poor water quality. Water is available for irrigation from the Murray, Darling and Murrumbidgee Rivers. The level of the River Murray is controlled by a series of locks. Growers require a water entitlement—which may be purchased on the open market—for irrigation water.

Management practices

The most significant pest is rootknot nematode on light-textured soils. This is managed by planting on rootstocks such as Ramsey and Schwarzmann. The absence of significant spring and summer rainfall ensures that the diseases downy mildew and black spot appear only sporadically. Powdery mildew is more serious from time to time. Australian Grapevine Yellows is a problem in some years, notably in Chardonnay and Riesling. Lime-induced chlorosis can also be a problem given the calcareous soils, and is mainly a consequence of poor irrigation management. Cover crops are usually sown in autumn after harvest as a means of adding organic content to the soil. In vineyards with sprinkler irrigation, cover crops may be retained (mown) over summer to assist with access. High risk of frost requires appropriate soil management in spring. Both overhead and undervine sprinklers, and drip have been installed for irrigation in many new plantings or redevelopments. Some flood/furrow irrigation remains although use is declining. In a benchmarking study undertaken in the Murray-Darling and Swan Hill regions between 1998 and 2002, the average irrigation amount applied was 5.5 ML/ha for both drip and overhead sprinklers (Giddings et al. 2002). Irrigation management practices such as regulated deficit irrigation (RDI) are being increasingly used by growers to control vigour and yield and to improve winegrape quality, particularly with the premium black varieties. The newer plantings tend to use two-wire vertical trellis. Narrow T trellis, 30 cm wide at 0.9 to 1.4 m high, is common in older plantings of varieties such as Sultana. Row x vine spacing is usually 3.0–3.3 m x 1.2–2.4 m. Vineyards that are flood irrigated typically have row widths of 3.6 m. Mechanical pruning is standard (except for Sultana), and minimal pruning is also commonly used. Mechanical harvesting, usually at night, is most common for winegrapes. Both vigour and yields are normally high: the latter may exceed 25 t/ha for varieties such as Chardonnay, Cabernet Sauvignon and Shiraz. However, target yields are more likely to be 18 to 20 t/ha for Shiraz, Cabernet Sauvignon and Merlot since the late 1990s. Hedging of vines in summer may occur, although it is not always necessary. Harvest commences in the second week of February (Chardonnay).

Summary

The early development of the Murray Darling region was closely associated with the dried vine fruit industry. More recently, there has been a significant shift to winegrape production. The reliable production of grapes suitable for wine for the export market is the key to the future success of grapegrowing in the region. Together with Swan Hill, this region produces 77% of the winegrapes in Victoria.

SWAN HILL (*ZONE: NORTH WEST VICTORIA*)

The Swan Hill region extends along the Murray for approximately 50 km. Swan Hill (35.34°S, 143.55°E; 300 km north-west of Melbourne) is the main population centre. Vineyards are found on both sides of the River in NSW and Victoria. The first irrigated vineyards were established at Nyah in 1900. The varieties planted before 1960 were either the 'drying' varieties such as Sultana and Muscat Gordo Blanco or varieties such as Doradillo, Pedro Ximenes and Grenache for spirit or fortified wine production. Since the 1980s there has been a greater emphasis on grapes for table wines. The total planted area is approximately 7,000 ha (more than 85% in Victoria). Principal varieties include Chardonnay, Colombard, Sultana, Muscat Gordo Blanco, Shiraz and Cabernet Sauvignon. The region is generally flat (elevation from 50 to 90 m). The climate has many similarities to the Murray Darling region but is slightly cooler and has more rain (**TABLE 2.1a**), and thus is less favourable for production of dried fruit. Water for irrigation is available from the River Murray under the water entitlement system. Management practices are similar to those in the Murray Darling region. Harvest commences in late February (Chardonnay).

RUTHERGLEN (*ZONE: NORTH EAST VICTORIA*)

The Rutherglen region is located along the River Murray. The first vines were planted near to the town of Rutherglen (36.05°S, 146.47°E; 240 km north-east of Melbourne) in the 1850s. This was followed by rapid expansion over the next 30 years. Many of the wineries currently operating in the region were established during that period. In the late 1890s two calamities befell the industry: the inadvertent introduction of phylloxera and economic depression. Despite the introduction of phylloxera-resistant rootstocks, many growers abandoned their vineyards. The region has experienced modest growth since 1960s. Collectively Rutherglen and the adjacent region of Beechworth have 1,070 ha with more than 80% in the former. The main varieties are Shiraz, Cabernet Sauvignon, Brown Frontignac and Muscadelle.

Regional resources

The countryside is largely flat at an elevation of 160 to 250 m (**FIGURE 2.3**). The climate is continental, very sunny and moderately arid (**TABLE 2.1a**). Spring frosts occur occasionally throughout the region. The outstanding feature of the climate of north-eastern Victoria in general is its more or less complete lack of afternoon sea breezes or other maritime influences because it is cut off from the coasts by the Australian Alps (Gladstones 1992). The North East Victoria Zone is characterised by steep mountains, wide valleys, and hilly plateaux. The dominant soils of the Zone have duplex profiles with hard setting sandy loam or clay loam topsoils commonly overlying red clay subsoils

Figure 2.3 A typical viticultural landscape in the Rutherglen region.

(Categories 6 and 7). Gentler hill slopes and river terraces often have gradational profiles (Category 9), which are favoured over duplex soils as they tend to have better subsoil drainage. These soils are usually well structured, friable when moist and usually moderately to strongly acidic throughout the profile. The Rutherglen region is characterised by older alluvial plains and younger alluvial areas associated with the River Murray. There are also hilly areas composed of sedimentary rocks and some granites. Common soils on the plains typically have fine sandy clay loam surfaces overlying subsurface horizons that grade into yellow and brown subsoil clays (**Classes 9.5, 9.6**). Surface horizons tend to be strongly acidic, but subsoils are usually alkaline. Large amounts of manganese segregations occur in the subsoils in some areas. Elsewhere, more strongly texture contrast soils can occur, with denser and more coarsely structured subsoils that are often sodic (**Classes 6.3, 6.4**). On the hills, soils often have large amounts of quartz gravel and stone, scattered both on the surface and in the surface horizons. These soils exhibit strong texture contrast, with sandy loam surfaces overlying red clayey subsoils that are slightly acidic to neutral (**Classes 7.3, 7.4**). The profiles usually merge with weathered rock before one metre depth on upper slopes and at about two metres on mid-slopes. On lower slopes the soils are typically more gradational in nature, with yellowish red to brown subsoil colours. Irrigation water is sourced from the River Murray or from dams. Drip irrigation is used in many vineyards.

Management practices

This region has two pests that are not commonly found in other parts of Australia: phylloxera, controlled by rootstocks, and *Xiphinema index*, the nematode vector of fanleaf virus, for which there is no adequate control. Traditionally, row spacing is 3.5 m and trellises are generally low, one- or two-wire trellises. Cane pruning is still common. Vine vigour and yields are generally low. Trellises and yields on newer vineyards are higher. Harvest commences in the second week of March (Chardonnay).

Summary

The Rutherglen region is acknowledged as a premium fortified wine region, notably for the styles traditionally known as 'Muscat' and 'Tokay'.

2.4.4 NEW SOUTH WALES

RIVERINA (*ZONE: BIG RIVERS*)

This region, formerly known as the Murrumbidgee Irrigation Area (MIA), is a large tract of irrigated land situated on the south-western plains of NSW at an elevation of 140 m. The township of Griffith (34.16°S, 146.03°E), central to the region, is 650 km south-west of Sydney. A large-scale public irrigation scheme was initiated in 1906. Winegrape production commenced in 1913, and the first winery was built in 1917. Production increased slowly at first but expanded considerably in the 1960s and 1970s. Further expansion in the 1990s has resulted in approximately 13,000 ha in the early 2000s. The main varieties are Semillon, Shiraz, Chardonnay, Cabernet Sauvignon, Merlot and Colombard. The Riverina remains the largest region in NSW, producing more than 60% of NSW's winegrapes. It is also an important producer of rice and other grains, vegetables and fruit. The main (and traditional) plantings are near Griffith and Leeton; newer developments are close to Wagga Wagga, Jerilderie, Coleambally, Hay and Hillston at elevations up to 230 m.

Regional Resources

The region is relatively flat which allows the extensive use of water reticulation and irrigation by gravity. The climate is characterised by high solar radiation, low rainfall uniformly spread throughout the year, and high evaporation with low relative humidity in summer (**TABLE 2.1a**). The Riverine plains were deposited by ancient streams and thus consist of highly variable alluvial soils with sands and gravel embedded in clays. The most common viticultural soils are red duplex types with hard surfaces. Both restrictive (**Classes 6.3, 6.4**) and non restrictive (**Classes 7.3, 7.4**) clayey subsoils occur. Gradational textured soils are also common: these include deep sandy surfaced profiles with mottled alkaline subsoils (**Class 9.2**), deep well structured loamy surfaced profiles (**Class 9.6**), and some less well structured loamy gradational soils, with or without calcareous subsoils (**Classes 9.3, 9.5**). Minor soils in the region include restrictive duplex types with yellow brown subsoil clays (**Classes 6.1, 6.2**), cracking clays (**Class 5.2**), and calcareous loams (**Class 8.6**). Many of the soils are prone to waterlogging. Salinity problems occur in areas of impeded drainage where salt has accumulated in the topsoil. Reclamation is achieved by leaching irrigations and tile drainage. Vines can only be grown economically with irrigation in this region. For most of the region, irrigation water is taken from the Murrumbidgee River and is of low salinity. The Lachlan River is the source of irrigation water at Hillston.

Management Practices

The Riverina is relatively free of pests and diseases although, in occasional years with summer rainfall, downy mildew and botrytis bunch rot can be of concern. With newer vineyard developments there has been a strong shift from the traditional practices of furrow and overhead sprinkler irrigation to undervine sprinkler and drip irrigation, with an estimated 20% of vineyards now using the latter. This change in irrigation practice has been driven by the desire to improve water use efficiency (primarily due to increasing water prices), reduced water security, environmental pressures and improved ability to manipulate fruit quality by irrigation strategy. With furrow irrigation, vineyards are irrigated up to 12 times each growing season (5 to 6 ML/ha/season). Prior to planting, new vineyards are carefully graded to ensure efficient flood irrigation. To overcome the problem of summer weeds created by furrow irrigation, the inter-row space is cultivated after every second or third irrigation. Soils were normally left undisturbed in autumn and winter, and the volunteer cover crop ploughed-under in early spring; however, winter cover crops are now being sown and herbicides are replacing under-vine cultivation. Although the Riverina is phylloxera free, there is nematode pressure and the use of rootstocks is widespread. The excellent growing conditions produce large, high-yielding vines. Pruning weights in excess of 1 kg per m row length and commercial yields as high as 10 kg per m row length (30 t/ha) are not uncommon. The regional average is approximately 17 t/ha. Most vineyards are planted to traditional spacings, with 3 m (row) and 2–3 m (vine) spacing. The main trellis types are single-wire and two-wire vertical. Approximately 90% of vineyards are mechanically pruned with hand cleanup and more than 50% are mechanically harvested. Hand-pruning is mostly to two-node spurs. Harvest commences in late February (Chardonnay).

Summary

The Riverina has developed steadily to become one of the major winegrape production regions in Australia with a significant shift from bulk and fortified wine production to commercial and sub-premium production in the 1990s.

MURRAY DARLING (*ZONE: BIG RIVERS*)
See 2.3.3 Murray Darling [formerly Sunraysia] (*ZONE: NORTH WEST VICTORIA*)

SWAN HILL (*ZONE: BIG RIVERS*)
See 2.3.3 Swan Hill (*ZONE: NORTH WEST VICTORIA*)

HUNTER (*ZONE: HUNTER VALLEY*)
The Hunter region extends north-west from Newcastle on the Pacific coast. There are two main viticultural areas: the 'Lower Hunter', nearer the coast and adjacent

to Cessnock (32.90°S, 151.35°E, 165 km north of Sydney), and the 'Upper Hunter', 70 km to the north-west, centred around Singleton, Denman and Muswellbrook. To date, the only designated subregion is Broke-Fordwich where most vineyards are found close to Broke, 25 km north-west of Cessnock. Settlement commenced in the Lower Hunter in 1826 and vineyards soon became part of mixed holdings, with the famous Kirkton vineyard of James Busby being planted in 1830. Modest expansion continued through the 1880s but the Depression of the 1890s caused major problems for the local wine industry. In the 20th century, expansion occurred slowly until the boom period of the 1960s and 1970s when winegrape production increased by 15 times. Much of this expansion took place in the Upper Hunter. However, in the 1990s, against the trend for the rest of Australia, the planted area declined as uneconomical vineyards, planted on poor sites in the 1970s, were removed. In 2001, there were 4,321 ha, mainly Chardonnay, Shiraz, Semillon, Verdelho and Cabernet Sauvignon. A large proportion of the vineyard area is owned by winery companies, and more than half is located in the Lower Hunter, where most vineyards are to the north and west of Cessnock.

Regional resources

The terrain is gently to markedly undulating, bordered to the north, west and south-west by the Great Dividing Range (**FIGURE 2.4**). Most vineyards are at elevations around 200 m but some are as high as 400 m. The Broke-Fordwich subregion is part of the catchment area of Wollombi Brook below the 200 m contour. The summer climate in the Hunter is humid, with high cloudiness and high rainfall (**TABLE 2.1a**). A break in the Great Dividing Range allows summer sea breezes to penetrate well up the valley before mid-afternoon. However, the northern arm from Muswellbrook to Scone (MJT = 24.6°C) is cut off from maritime influences by hills and mountains resulting in a more inland type of climate. The frequent cloud cover and relatively low sunshine hours explain why this region is purely a table wine area despite its high ripening mean temperatures (Gladstones 1992). Rainfall is often highest just prior to and during harvest in February; the summer falls are often intense and much runoff results. Although the long-term average water deficit during summer is small (due to high rainfall and low evaporation), the variation in rainfall is great and in some years non-irrigated vines may suffer water stress. The vintage period is one of the earliest and shortest in Australia: harvest commences in late January in the lower Hunter (Chardonnay), and two weeks later at Broke. In the Lower Hunter, duplex soils and cracking clays are the most widespread viticultural soils. Most of the duplex soils are hard surfaced, with either yellowish brown, acid-neutral restrictive subsoils (**Classes 6.3, 6.4**), or reddish, acid-neutral non-

Figure 2.4 A vineyard in the 'Lower' Hunter Valley

restrictive subsoils (**Classes 7.3, 7.4**). The cracking clays are mostly well structured, at least in the surface (**Classes 5.2, 5.3**). Other soils of the Lower Hunter include acid-neutral red duplex soils with well structured loamy surfaces and non restrictive subsoils (**Classes 7.1, 7.2**), deep, hard loamy soils with more clayey subsoils (**Class 9.5**), and deep well structured loams (**Class 9.6**). Deep alluvial loams (**Class 9.6**) and red duplex soils with variably structured alkaline subsoils (**Classes 6.3, 6.4, 7.3, 7.4**) are most common in the Upper Hunter. A range of yellow and brown duplex soils, mostly with hard surfaces and restrictive subsoils occur to a minor extent. Cracking clays, as for the Lower Hunter, are also minor components of the viticultural landscape. Water resources in the Lower Hunter were traditionally limited to farm dams and occasional bores. Those properties adjacent to rivers have a regular supply of good quality water as is common in the Upper Hunter. In 2000, a Private Irrigation District (PID) was established in the Lower Hunter. The PID has a 5,000 ML allocation from the Hunter River and this now supplies water to many vineyards and other agricultural and tourism operations in the Lower Hunter area.

Management practices

Downy mildew is the most serious grape disease in the Hunter due to the warm temperatures and high rainfall during the growing period. Six to 8 protective sprays are routinely applied per season, the number increasing to 15 in wet seasons. Bunch rot, caused by high rainfall near harvest, may cause substantial losses. The region has a unique viticultural pest, the fig longicorn borer, which causes significant economic damage to grapevines, mainly through the loss of cordons or trunk damage. The use of irrigation (mainly drip) has been extended to cover about three-quarters of the total vineyard area. Modest amounts of water are applied with the aim of minimising the effects of the short-term droughts. The traditional low single-wire trellis is increasingly giving way to the use of VSP, with fruiting wires at approximately 1.0–1.1 m. Cane pruning is most common on low vigour vineyards, with low node numbers per vine, e.g. 16–24. Spur pruning is increasingly used, mainly in newer vineyard developments where there is greater vine capacity due to better site preparation, the use of rootstocks and improvements in the control of pests and diseases. Vine vigour and yield vary from very low for old vines on poor soil without irrigation, to very high on deep alluvial soils with irrigation.

Summary

From the mid-1960s, the vineyards of the Hunter have changed from small family-owned estates to larger commercial enterprises. Extensive capital investment has been encouraged by the proximity to the large Sydney market. A reassessment of traditional practices has led to higher yields and the use of such labour-saving devices as mechanical harvesting. The climate of the region, with frequent summer droughts, high temperatures and humidity, and the prevalence of vintage-time storms, creates special problems.

GUNDAGAI (*ZONE: SOUTHERN NSW*)

This region includes riverine plains and western slopes of the Great Divide. It adjoins the Riverina region to the west, Hilltops (north), Canberra District (east) and Tumbarumba (south). The main population centres are Wagga Wagga, Junee and Cootamundra (34.64°S, 148.02°E; 290 km south-west of Sydney). The planted area is relatively small and the principal varieties include Chardonnay, Cabernet Sauvignon, Shiraz, Merlot and Sauvignon Blanc. The climate is similar to Riverina, but more humid and with higher rainfall (annual and growing season) and lower aridity (**TABLE 2.1a**).

COWRA (*ZONE: CENTRAL RANGES*)

The Cowra region has a history of wine production dating from the 1870s. The first modern plantings were in the early 1970s and by 1975 there were 36 ha. The second phase of planting took place from 1988. Today there are 1,600 ha. Most vineyards lie within 10 km of the town of Cowra (33.83°S, 148.68°E; 230 km west of Sydney), with a few near Canowindra to the north. The main varieties are Chardonnay, Shiraz, Cabernet Sauvignon, Semillon and Merlot. This region is the catchment area of the upper Lachlan River. Most vineyards are found between 250 and 350 m in undulating country. The climate is hot, continental and very sunny (**TABLE 2.1a**). There is moderate frost risk, with late spring frosts being a concern. Annual rainfall in the district is approximately 550 to 650 mm (50% falls during the growing season). The soils are variable but generally alluvial in origin. Hard duplex soils are dominant: the majority have non-restrictive neutral to

alkaline red clayey subsoils (**Classes 7.3, 7.4**), but profiles with poorly structured red or yellow brown subsoils (**Classes 6.3, 6.4**) are common. Loamy gradational soils (**Class 9.6**) are used to some extent. Good quality water is available, the Lachlan or Belabula Rivers being the main source, with less available from bores. The Wyangala Dam, upstream from Cowra, is a source of both high and low security water for viticultural use. Pest and disease pressure is low to moderate. Trellising is mainly single wire and VSP, with some modified Scott Henry and Smart-Dyson. Row and vine spacings are generally 3.0 m x 1.5–2 m. Mechanical pre-pruning followed by hand clean-up, and mechanical harvesting are most common. Although aridity is low, all vineyards are irrigated, most with drip systems, or sprinklers where frost is a concern. Yields are 8 and 12 t/ha for premium Shiraz and Chardonnay respectively. Harvest commences in mid-February (Chardonnay). The main problems include lightbrown apple moth and frost. Cowra has continued to grow and expand over the last three decades. The security of water supply is perhaps the greatest concern in terms of long-term viability and future expansion.

MUDGEE (*ZONE: CENTRAL RANGES*)

The Mudgee region is found on the western slopes of the Great Dividing Range, 260 km north-west of Sydney. Most vineyards are located in the vicinity of the township of Mudgee (32.60°S, 149.60°E). There are also some near Kandos to the south-east. The first plantings were made in 1858; by the 1880s there were 180 ha of vineyards producing grapes for 13 wineries. The industry declined in the 1890s, with only two wineries remaining by the 1930s. With the boom of the mid-1960s, interest in the area was revitalised such that by the late 1980s there were 450 ha of winegrape vineyards. As with many other viticultural regions there was a planting boom in the 1990s. This was driven by general industry expansion and the access to water and good soils, in addition to Mudgee's proximity to the Sydney market. There are now approximately 2,500 ha with the main varieties being Shiraz, Cabernet Sauvignon, Chardonnay, Semillon and Merlot.

Regional resources

The majority of the region's vines are planted on the slopes of gently rolling country at an elevation of 470 to 1,080 m (**FIGURE 2.5**). The region is a transitional zone between the western slopes of the Great Divide and the central tableland and western plains. Summers are hot and spring frosts can be a problem but few vineyards have any protection systems. Relative humidity during the growing season is moderate to high and both solar radiation and evaporation are high (**TABLE 2.1a**). Rainfall distribution is relatively uniform but shows a slight summer dominance. Risk of hail during the

Figure 2.5 A new vineyard near Mudgee

growing season is relatively high: there are several hail 'belts' in the region. The soils are generally suitable for viticulture. Duplex soils dominate the region. Most have hard surfaces, but subsoils vary from well structured red clays (**Classes 7.3, 7.4**), to restrictive yellowish brown or red clays (**Classes 6.3, 6.4**). Hard gradational loamy soils (**Class 9.5**), deep alluvial loams (**Class 9.6**), well structured cracking clays (**Class 5.3**) and well structured non cracking clays (**Class 9.8**) are significant, but less common. Water resources of the region are limited to the Cudgegong River, dams and private bores. The increasing salinity of some bores is becoming a concern, particularly in drought years. Many of the larger scale developments in the 1990s were made possible by the establishment of private pipelines from the Cudgegong River.

Management practices

Mudgee has moderate pest and disease pressure with late season bunch rots being the most significant problem, mainly in wet seasons. Row x vine spacing is 3.0–3.5 m x 1.5–2.4 m. VSP and single wire trellises are the most widely used. Spur pruning by hand or machine with hand clean-up are most common. More than 90% of vineyards are harvested by machine. Typical yields for Chardonnay and Shiraz are 10 to 12 t/ha. More than 80% of vineyards are irrigated, mostly by drip; 1.5 ML/ha is applied in normal years with up to 2.5 ML/ha in dry years. Harvest commences in late February (Chardonnay).

Summary

The Mudgee region has many suitable characteristics for viticulture and is representative of other areas of the central-west of NSW. The main limitation to production is water quantity and quality, and significant areas of good quality soils.

HASTINGS RIVER (*ZONE: NORTHERN RIVERS*)
The main population centre is Port Macquarie (31.50°S, 152.88°E, 400 km north of Sydney) located at the mouth of the Hastings River. The modern era of viticulture

commenced in 1980 and today there are approximately 140 ha. The main varieties are Chardonnay, Sauvignon Blanc, Shiraz, Cabernet Sauvignon and Chambourcin. The latter is a hybrid variety (see Chapters 5 and 6) with good resistance to foliar fungal diseases. Most vineyards are located within 15 km of the coast at elevations between 10 and 50 m. The climate is moderately maritime and very humid with a very high summer-dominant rainfall (**TABLE 2.1A**). Consequently disease pressure is high. Vintage is very early, typically starting in late January.

2.4.5 QUEENSLAND

SOUTH BURNETT (*ZONE: QUEENSLAND*)
This region includes much of the catchments of the Barambah and Barkers Creeks and the Stuart and Boyne Rivers, all tributaries of the Burnett River. It is Australia's most northerly wine region. Vineyards are concentrated around Lake Barambah near the town of Murgon (elevation 300 m) and the regional centre of Kingaroy (26.55°S, 151.85°E). The main planting of winegrapes has taken place since the mid-1990s. The current area of winegrapes is approximately 250 ha and the principal varieties include Shiraz, Cabernet Sauvignon, Merlot, Verdelho and Chardonnay.

Regional resources

Vineyards are found on gently to steeply undulating land, mainly between 250 and 550 m. Both distance from the sea and proximity of the Brisbane Range to the east influence the climate, which is characterised by hot summers and mild winters, summer dominant rainfall and high relative humidity (**TABLE 2.1A**). Frost risk is generally low. Highly variable rainfall combined with relatively high evaporation necessitates the use of irrigation for reliable production on most soil types. The most productive soils have formed from basaltic parent materials, 'soft' sedimentary rocks (sandstone and mudstone) and the alluvial material that has been deposited on floodplains and terraces. Soils formed on alluvium range from deep sandy loams (**Class 9.2**) on levees and lower terraces to dark cracking clays (**Classes 5.2, 5.3**) on the plains. hard setting restrictive duplex soils (**Classes 6.3, 6.4**) are common on higher terraces of old alluvium. Cracking clays are also associated with freshly exposed basalt and labile sedimentary rock. Red and brown non-cracking clays (**Class 9.8**) are widely distributed on deeply weathered basalt surfaces. Sandy surfaced restrictive duplex soils (**Classes 6.1, 6.2**) and occasionally deep loamy sands (**Class 9.1**) are associated with the extensive granite landscapes in the west of the region. Soil conservation measures are required on all sloping sites to reduce erosion. Irrigation water is sourced from dams or Lake Barambah (around Murgon) with 1.5 to 3 ML/ha applied (subject to availability) by drip.

Table 2.1b. Regions with mean January temperature (MJT) between 21.0 and 22.9°C.

Region	State	Station	Elevation (m)	MJT[y] °C	CTL °C	ARF mm	GSRF mm	GSRD	GSE mm	ARID mm	RH %	SSH
Geographe	WA	9534 Donnybrook	63	22.8[x]	11.1	991	168	36	1228[c]	446	51	8.9[b]
Northern Slopes	NSW	56018 Inverell Res.	584	22.8	13.6	807	525	52	1085	17	64	8.8
Hilltops	NSW	73056 Young	444	22.6	15.9	654	304	34	(1050)	(221)	58	9.9[a]
Adelaide Plains	SA	23020 Roseworthy	68	22.4	12.0	440	155	34	1289	490	46	9.4
Bendigo	Vic.	81003 Bendigo	225	21.6	13.8	551	224	37	1092[d]	322	57	9.2[a]
Clare Valley	SA	21014 Clare	385	21.5	13.3	632	199	36	1250[b]	426[b]	47	9.1[a]
McLaren Vale	SA	Composite[e]	210	21.4	10.9	656	182	39	1101[f]	323	54	8.7[a]
Blackwood Valley	WA	9510 Bridgetown	150	21.3[x]	10.9	835	170	39	(1000)	(330)	61	8.2[b]
Granite Belt	Qld	41095 Stanthorpe PO	792	21.5	13.7	770	488	55	977[g]	0	66	8.6[a]
Alpine Valleys	Vic.	82034 Myrtleford	222	21.3	13.9	905	363	41	880[h]	77	55	(8.8)
Barossa Valley	SA	23321Nuriootpa	274	21.2	12.4	502	163	38	1274	474	52	9.0
Goulburn Valley	Vic.	88053 Seymour	141	21.1	13.3	602	250	33	1044[i]	200	56	9.0[a]
Heathcote	Vic.	88029 Heathcote	320	21.0	13.1	574	236	32	1092[d]	310	65	(9.1)

[a] Gladstones (1992)
[b] Dry and Smart (1988)
[c] 9812 Harvey
[d] 81083 Eppalock Reservoir
[e] Average of 023703 Belair and 023031 Waite
[f] 23031 Waite

[g] 41175 Stanthorpe (Granite Belt HRS)
[h] 83079 Lake Buffalo
[i] 81019 Nagambie
[x] J. Gladstones (pers.comm.)
[y] See 2.1.1 and 2.1.2 in text for explanation of codes
( ) Denotes estimate

Management practices

Row x vine spacing is generally 3 m x 2 m. The main trellis systems are Smart-Dyson, VSP and Scott Henry. Mechanical pruning (with hand follow-up) and mechanical harvesting are used on more than 75% of the planted area. Yields vary according to soil type and water availability: 5 to 14 t/ha and 7 to 11 t/ha are typical for Chardonnay and Shiraz respectively. Harvest commences in late January (Chardonnay). Major problems include fungal diseases, birds and wind.

Summary

The South Burnett region is relatively young. Suitable land is available for expansion but the supply of water for irrigation is a likely constraint.

2.5 Regions with MJT from 21.0 to 22.9°C

2.5.1 WESTERN AUSTRALIA

GEOGRAPHE (*ZONE: SOUTH WEST AUSTRALIA*)
This region is named after the Bay that provides its western boundary. To the north, the region is bordered by the Peel region, to the south-west by the Margaret River region and to the south-east by the Blackwood Valley region. The main population centre is Bunbury (33.30°S, 115.63°E), 150 km south of Perth. Although there were a few small vineyards near Harvey prior to the Second World War, the first substantial plantings were not made until the 1970s, near Stratham and Capel. Now there are 83 vineyards with a total of 913 ha spread over the entire region. The main varieties for winemaking are Shiraz, Cabernet Sauvignon, Chardonnay and Semillon. The

major plantings are found near Harvey, Dardanup, Donnybrook and Busselton. The land rises gradually from the coastal plain in the west to the foothills of the Darling Range in the east (200–250 m). The climate of this region is quite variable (see Gladstones [1992] for a detailed description). The Busselton-Harvey coastal strip is strongly influenced by sea breezes, whereas the inland part near Donnybrook (**TABLE 2.1b**) is cut off from maritime influences by the Darling and Whicher Ranges. Only 17% of annual rainfall falls during the growing season. Risk of spring frosts is low near to the coast but much higher inland. The vineyards on the coastal plain are mostly found on recent alluvial soils including brown deep sand (**Class 9.1**), brown deep loamy duplex (**Classes 6.4, 7.4**) and brown loamy earth (**Class 9.5**). At the foot of the Darling Scarp the duplex sandy gravel (**Class 7.2**) and yellow deep sand (**Class 9.1**) have been planted. East of the scarp, loamy soils (**Classes 6.4, 7.3, 7.4, 9.5, 9.6**) dominate in the hills behind Harvey, the Ferguson Valley and at Donnybrook. Typical row x vine spacings are 3.0–3.3 m and 1.5–2.0 m. The majority of vines are on a VSP trellis system. Up to 80% of vineyards utilise mechanical pruning and harvesting. Soil management practices focus on undervine herbicide and mid-row covercrops. Drip irrigation is common: 80% of irrigation water is sourced from dams and the remainder from bores. Harvest commences in mid-February (Chardonnay). There is potential for further expansion.

BLACKWOOD VALLEY (*ZONE: SOUTH WEST AUSTRALIA*)
Although commercial viticulture commenced here in the late 1970s, it was not until the 1990s that significant expansion took place. This region is inland from the

Margaret River region and also shares boundaries with the Geographe, Manjimup and Great Southern regions. The major population centre is Bridgetown (34.95°S, 116.17°E), 212 km south-east of Perth. The topography is undulating and elevation varies from 100 m in the west (near Nannup) to 340 m in the centre and east (near Boyup Brook). This region has the same latitude as Margaret River but it is warmer and more continental (**TABLE 2.1b**). There is a severe risk of spring frosts. Rainfall ranges from 600 mm in the east to 1,100 mm in the south west. Vineyards are generally planted on well drained gravelly loams. The total planted area is approximately 500 ha. The main varieties are Shiraz, Cabernet Sauvignon and Chardonnay. Harvest commences in late February to early March (Chardonnay). Viticultural practices are similar to those of Manjimup (2.6.1).

2.5.2 SOUTH AUSTRALIA

ADELAIDE PLAINS (*ZONE: MOUNT LOFTY RANGES*)

Until the 1970s there were large areas of vineyards in what are now the suburbs of Adelaide. Apart from small remnants at Marion and Magill, these have been replaced by housing. The only significant areas are now found in the Angle Vale-Virginia area, a flat to very gently undulating tract of land on the flood plain of the Gawler River, along the northern fringe of metropolitan Adelaide (34.97°S, 138.63°E). There are 428 ha of vineyards with 29 producers (60% <10 ha). The main varieties are Shiraz, Cabernet Sauvignon, Chardonnay, Grenache and Sauvignon Blanc.

Regional resources

The climate is characterised by a hot and sunny growing season and low, winter-dominant rainfall (**TABLE 2.1b**). Soils are formed on alluvium, which varies from heavy clay through to fine sand and silt. The nature of the alluvium is the key determinant of soil characteristics. Sandy loam over restrictive red brown clay (**Classes 6.1-6.4**), formed on fine grained sediment is the most common soil. The better soils are formed on coarser grained alluvium: these have thick sandier surfaces over non-restrictive clayey subsoils (**Classes 7.2, 7.4, 9.2, 9.4**). The sandy material under the clayey subsoil provides deep drainage. Sixty percent of the vineyard area is irrigated from underlying aquifers; over-utilisation, causing a lowering of the water level and an increase in salinity, has led to legislated restrictions on water use. The remainder is irrigated with treated waste water.

Management practices

Drip irrigation is used almost exclusively with between 1.5 and 2.5 ML/ha applied per annum. The majority of vineyards have 3.0 to 3.3 m rows and 1.5 to 3.0 m vine spacing. The main trellis is a single wire with sprawling canopy. Yields are generally moderate: 10 to 12 t/ha are

Figure 2.6 Vineyards in the east of the Clare Valley region.

typical for both Chardonnay and Shiraz. Approximately 70% of the vineyard area is mechanically pruned, with close to 100% mechanically harvested. Less than 10% of the area is grafted. The region is characterised by an early harvest (from mid-February for Chardonnay) and low disease pressure.

Summary

Expansion in the region is unlikely due to lack of water resources.

CLARE VALLEY (*ZONE: MOUNT LOFTY RANGES*)

The region extends from north of Clare (33.84°S, 138.61°E; 115 km north of Adelaide) to the south of Auburn, but most vineyards are located between those towns (a distance of approximately 45 km). The first vineyards were planted in the 1840s around Clare and the area developed slowly to reach 2,200 ha in the mid-1980s. Until the 1960s, the main products were dried grapes (mainly currants) and fortified wine, but since that time most plantings have been made for table wine. Development by large winery companies was a feature of the latter part of the 20th century: today half of the production is winery-grown. Of the 214 producers in the late 1990s, 60% had fewer than 10 ha with 10% more than 50 ha. The vineyard area is 4,600 ha and the main varieties planted are Shiraz, Cabernet Sauvignon, Riesling, Chardonnay and Merlot.

Regional resources

The terrain is undulating to hilly (**FIGURE 2.6**). The north-south valley lies between low ranges to the west and east. The valley floor is at an elevation of 330 to 500m, but many vineyards are found on slopes between 450 and 500 m. The climate is similar to the more elevated parts of the Barossa Valley and the Eden Valley (the data recorded by the weather station located in the township of Clare (**TABLE 2.1b**) would be appropriate for the warmest parts of the region). That part of the region to the south of Watervale may be affected by afternoon sea breezes. Water resources from both aquifers and dams are limited. The ranges are formed on basement rocks which include siltstones, sandstones, dolomites and quartzites. Sandy loam to loam soils are most common, over red or brown clayey subsoils. Some of these duplex soils are restrictive (**Classes 6.3, 6.4**), while others are non restrictive (**Classes 7.3, 7.4**). In places, loamy topsoils directly overlie limestone or siltstone (**Classes 4.2, 4.3**). Profiles are invariably less than 100 cm deep. In the intervening valleys, sediments from the ranges underlie deeper soils which include duplex soils of loam over red or brown clay (as for the ranges, but deeper than 100 cm), deep clay loam (**Classes 9.4, 9.8**), deep sandy loam (**Class 9.6**) and cracking clay (**Classes 5.2, 5.3**). In the lower rainfall areas, accumulations of secondary carbonate are usual in the lower subsoil.

Management practices

Most vineyards are irrigated by drip; 0.6 to 1.0 ML/ha per annum is typical. Trellising, spacing and pruning are similar to the Barossa, for example, a two-wire vertical trellis or single wire trellis with 3.0 m rows. Less than 5% of the area is grafted. Yield varies from low to moderate, e.g. 8 to 10 t/ha for both Chardonnay and Shiraz. Up to 75% of the area is mechanically pruned (followed by hand regulation of node numbers) and mechanically harvested. Management of poor surface structure (and subsoil structure in many of the duplex soils) is a key issue. Erosion control is also required, as many vineyards are on moderate slopes. Other problems include frost and birds. Drip irrigation has permitted exploitation of shallow soils on slopes with good air drainage and thermal properties: traditional viticulture was restricted to the deeper soils on the valley floor. Harvest commences in early March (Chardonnay).

Summary

Clare has developed as an important wine-producing region since the 1960s, and now has a reputation for high quality table wines. Recent vineyard developments by large winery companies and others have offset the declining area controlled by independent growers. Further expansion is likely to be dependent on the availability of reticulated water sourced from the River Murray. Waterlogging and associated salt accumulation are the main hazards to sustainability.

MCLAREN VALE (*ZONE: FLEURIEU*)

The vineyards extend from Reynella in the north to Willunga in the south. The main concentration is found near to McLaren Vale township (35.23°S, 138.53°E; 35 km south of Adelaide). The first vines in the region appear to have been planted within a few years of the foundation of South Australia in 1836. Over the next 100 years or so, the vineyard area gradually increased and many wineries were established. Up until the 1950s, the area specialised in fortified wines. New vineyards

Figure 2.7 Looking south towards Willunga in the McLaren Vale region

and wineries developed during the table wine boom of the 1960s, particularly on the fringes of the established areas. The urban spread of Adelaide has considerably reduced the vineyard area, especially near Reynella; the present area is 5,723 ha. There are 355 producers and vineyard size is generally small, with 60% having fewer than 10 ha. The main varieties are Shiraz, Cabernet Sauvignon, Chardonnay, Grenache, Merlot and Semillon.

Regional resources

The majority of vineyards in the McLaren Vale-Willunga district are found on flat to gently undulating land within 12 km of the sea at elevations from 50 m to 200 m (**FIGURES 2.7, 2.8**). There are also vineyards at scattered sites in the Mt Lofty Ranges to the east, up to 350 m. The climate is characterised by warm summers, moderate winters and winter-dominant rainfall (**TABLE 2.1b**). It is cooler and more maritime than Adelaide city and afternoon sea breezes occur earlier and more regularly. Since less than 30% of annual rain falls in the growing season there is high likelihood of drought, especially on shallow soils. However, aridity is lower than in the Barossa Valley. The soils are formed over a mixture of Tertiary to early Quaternary age clayey sand to clay sediments, cemented in places, and overlain near the escarpment by younger silts, clays and gravels. Most viticultural soils are duplex with both restrictive subsoils (**Classes 6.2, 6.3, 6.4**) and non-restrictive subsoils (**Classes 7.3, 7.4**). Topsoils range from loose sands through to hard silty loams and sandy clay loams. Subsoils vary from friable yellow brown sandy clay loams through well structured red and brown clays to poorly structured sodic clays. Soil reaction varies from neutral to acidic at the surface, but except for deep sandy profiles, most are calcareous at depth. Irrigation management to minimise the accumulation of salts, especially on duplex soils with restrictive subsoils, is a key issue. On the better-structured soils, potential root zone depths exceed 100 cm. Other soils used for viticulture in the region include deep sands (**Class 9.1**),

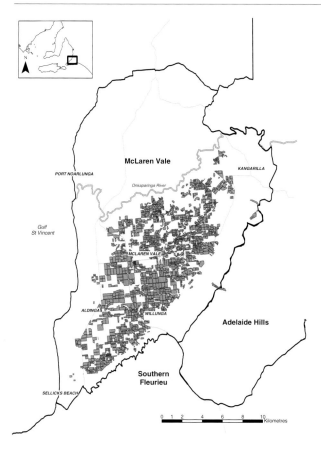

Figure 2.8 The distribution of vineyards in the McLaren Vale region of South Australia. This map has been produced using spatial information collected by the Phylloxera and Grape Industry Board of South Australia for use in its early detection programs, and 'ground-truthed' by means of the state-wide vineyard register. This map has been reproduced with the permission of the PGIBSA.

gradational loams and clay loams (**Classes 9.6, 9.8**), cracking clays (**Class 5.2**), calcareous loams (**Class 8.5**) and shallow loams over calcrete (**Class 4.2**). Sandy loams to loams over red or brown clay subsoils (**Class 7.3**) on weathering rock occur on the escarpment. Control of water erosion is a priority on these slopes. Supplies of underground water are available for irrigation but are variable in quantity and quality; up to 70% of the vineyard area is irrigated from these sources. The use of treated waste water for irrigation has increased since the 1990s (up to 15% of total area). The proportion of dryland vineyards may be as high as 10% of the total area.

Management practices

Row spacing varies from 2.7 to 3.3 m and vine spacing from 1.5 to 2.2 m. The most widely used trellises are 2-wire vertical with sprawl (50%), single wire and VSP: the latter is mainly found in newer plantings. Drip irrigation is by far the most common method of application with 0.8 to 1.5 ML/ha typically applied. The use of deficit irrigation strategies is increasing. Yields vary from very low to moderate, but large extremes exist depending on soil type and water availability; typical yields for Chardonnay and Shiraz are 8 to 18 t/ha and 4 to 20 t/ha respectively. Mechanical harvesting is used by 90% of the growers and mechanical pruning is now most common. However, there has been a recent trend back to hand pruning for vineyards producing premium fruit. Some areas of light-textured soils require the use of nematode-resistant rootstocks but less than 10% of the area is grafted. Harvest commences in early March (Chardonnay).

Summary

More than 90% of the vineyard area is now irrigated and new plantings of superior clonal material have increased average yield. It has emerged as an important region from the point of view of both wine quality and tourism, but there is limited scope for expansion due to urban development and lack of water.

BAROSSA VALLEY (*ZONE: BAROSSA*)

The Barossa Zone includes the Barossa Valley region (with the towns of Nuriootpa [34.48°S, 139.00°E], Tanunda and Lyndoch) and the Eden Valley region (with the towns of Eden Valley, Springton and Angaston—see 2.6.2). Nuriootpa is 62 km north-east of Adelaide. The first vineyard was planted in 1847 and further plantings followed up to the 1880s, fostered by the decline of the vineyard area in the eastern states. Development was further enhanced by Federation in 1900, since trade barriers between states were lifted and Barossa wines were shipped in large quantities to the eastern markets. Of the 468 producers in 2002, 50% had fewer than 10 ha of vines, and only 19% more than 25 ha. Traditionally the majority of holdings were mixed farms with other enterprises such as grazing or orchards but recently there has been more specialisation in viticulture. Many of the growers are descendants of the original German settlers. Until the 1960s, the major varieties grown in the region were Grenache, Shiraz, Doradillo and Pedro Ximenes for fortified wines and spirit. Table wine is now the most important product of the region, and the pattern of varieties has changed. The region has 8,089 ha and the main varieties are Shiraz, Cabernet Sauvignon, Semillon, Grenache, Chardonnay and Riesling.

Regional resources

The 'valley' consists of a plain running north-east/south-west at 180 to 300 m elevation. It is bounded to the west by small hills and gentle slopes and to the east by the steeper Barossa Ranges that rise to more than 600 m at the southern end (**FIGURE 2.9**). The climate is characterised by moderate rainfall with marked winter dominance and high summer evaporation and low relative humidity (**TABLE 2.1b**). Afternoon sea breezes may have a moderating effect, but the region is vulnerable to extreme temperature variability in summer. The warmest locations are found to the west and north-west of Nuriootpa, the coolest to the south near Williamstown. The foothills provide the best mesoclimates. There is a marked increase in rainfall, from 500 to 750 mm, from the northern to the southern extremities of the region. Vines suffer water stress in most parts of the region in most seasons, especially on shallow soils. There is occasional frost risk in low-lying vineyards. The soils of the Barossa Valley are extraordinarily diverse, due largely to the complex geology of the region. Low hills of basement rock provide the area's relief, and a source of sediment for the valley floor alluvial deposits. Significant areas are covered by Tertiary age deposits which vary from sands to heavy clays. Soils on the valley floor are mainly hard sandy loams to loams over red brown clay subsoils (**Class 7.3**). These are often sodic (**Class 6.3**). On the eastern side of the valley—which is defined by a pronounced escarpment—coarse textured alluvium from the rocks of the Eden Valley region gives rise to thick loamy sands with brown subsoil clays (**Class 7.2**). On the basement rock ranges, red brown loamy soils overlying red clay (**Class 7.3**), weathering rock (**Class 4.3**) or semi-hard carbonate (**Class 4.4**) are typical. On the gently undulating land covered by Tertiary deposits, the most widespread soils are sand over clay types (**Class 6.1**) and deep sands (**Class 9.1**) formed on coarse textured materials. Ironstone gravelly sandy loams with red clayey subsoils (**Class 7.4**) are also characteristic of these areas. Cracking clays (**Class 5.2**) occur on fine textured sediments mostly on elevated plains. Supplies of good underground water are limited. Where soil types are suitable, dams provide storage from local run-off or from non-permanent streams. New bores and surface dams are prohibited and present bores are metered.

Management practices

In general, the region is relatively untroubled by major pest and disease problems. Outbreaks of downy mildew are infrequent, only occurring in years with wet springs and summers. Powdery mildew is a problem for susceptible varieties in most seasons. Rootknot nematode, now recognised as a serious problem of sandy soils, can be overcome by using resistant rootstocks. Approximately 15% of the area is grafted, mainly to 1103 Paulsen, Ramsey, 140 Ruggeri and Schwarzmann. The widespread occurrences of poorly structured subsoils present the most significant soil management issue. The accumulation of salts in the rootzone must be avoided. This is particularly challenging given the relatively poor quality of ground water in the region. Other significant soil-related issues are management of poorly structured surface soils, and maintenance of optimum soil moisture and nutrient levels across vineyards often with mosaics of highly diverse soil types. Deterioration of soil structure and erosion in some areas is thought to be due to excessive cultivation during the growing season. The addition of organic matter, cover crops and reduction in cultivations have slowed the decline in soil structure. Minimum tillage systems have been adopted in some vineyards. To minimise frost damage, herbage is turned in early in spring and further cultivation is delayed until after the frost danger period. In 1978, only 12% of the vineyard area was irrigated (French et al. 1978); today most vineyards have limited irrigation, mainly by drip. The main source, from aquifers and dams, is restricted to 1.0 ML/ha. The traditional trellis is a single wire at 50 cm height, but higher trellises are now installed in both existing and new vineyards. The single wire at 1.0 m or higher is most common (75% of the area) followed by the two-wire vertical trellis. Small areas of untrellised 'bush' vines remain in some old plantings. Row width is usually 3.3 to 3.6 m and vine spacing 1.8 to 2.4 m. Traditionally, most vines were pruned to canes but spur pruning is now most popular. Node numbers on hand-pruned vines are usually low. Up to 80% of the vines are mechanically pruned followed by hand regulation of node numbers. More than three-quarters of the crop is picked by machine. Yields vary from very low to moderate, depending on soil type and water availability; typical yields for Chardonnay and Shiraz are 10 to 12 t/ha and 7 to 17 t/ha respectively but large extremes exist. Harvest commences in early March (Chardonnay).

Summary

The Barossa is probably the best-known wine-producing region in Australia. Clonally-selected planting material, rootstocks, better trellises and limited irrigation have resulted in large improvements; for example, average yield per hectare doubled between 1970 and 1990. Much of the recent development has taken place beyond the traditional viticultural boundaries, particularly on the lower rainfall land to the west. This has been made possible by reticulation of water sourced from the River Murray.

2.5.3 VICTORIA

BENDIGO (*ZONE: CENTRAL VICTORIA*)

There was a thriving wine industry near Bendigo from the 1860s to the 1890s. However, the introduction of phylloxera in 1893 caused a rapid demise. Vineyards were re-established near Bendigo from the late 1960s. The major plantings in the region are now found near Bridgewater, Bendigo and Castlemaine. This region is adjacent to the Pyrenees region (west), Heathcote region (east) and Macedon Ranges region (south-east). The major population centres are Bendigo (36.75°S, 144.28°E; 130 km north-west of Melbourne), Castlemaine, Maryborough, Dunolly and Bridgewater. The planted area is 788 ha and the main varieties are Shiraz, Cabernet Sauvignon and Chardonnay. Topography ranges from slightly undulating plains in the north to hilly in the south. Land available for viticulture is generally lower than 250 m. The climate of Bendigo is similar to that of the Goulburn Valley (**TABLE 2.1b**). Bendigo, like other regions in north-central Victoria, e.g. Pyrenees, has maximum temperatures during the ripening period favourably moderated as a result of a late southward extension of the north-east monsoonal influence (Gladstones 1992). West of the Loddon River, the main soils are duplex with hard setting sandy loam or clay loam topsoils, often containing ironstone gravel, and bleached subsurface horizons overlying mottled yellow (sometimes red) subsoils (**Classes 6.3, 6.4**). In the northern and western parts of the region, the clay subsoils are typically sodic, reddish in colour and have a neutral pH (which generally becomes more alkaline with depth). Subsurface horizons are more typically sporadically rather than conspicuously bleached (**Classes 6.3, 6.4**). To the south, yellow slightly acidic clay subsoils dominate. In the south east, along the northern slopes of the Great Dividing Range, soils are derived from granite/granodiorite, sandstone and shale. Established viticultural areas on granitic soils include Castlemaine, Mandurang and Harcourt. The soils in this landscape of low rolling hills are predominantly duplex (**Class 6.4**), with sandy loam topsoils overlying bleached sandy subsurface horizons. Subsoils occur at about 30-40 cm depth and are typically yellow, yellowish brown or reddish mottled clay (often sandy). On the steeper slopes and rocky crests, more uniform lighter textured soils occur (**Classes 4.1, 9.2**). In some areas siliceous hardpans up to a metre thick occur between the soil and the unweathered bedrock. This significantly restricts root and water movement. Soil depth over hard rock is variable. These soils are prone to sheet erosion. Gully erosion and minor salting may occur in drainage depressions. Irrigation water is available from the Loddon River and dams. Drip irrigation tends to be used although some vineyards are not irrigated. Harvest commences in early March (Chardonnay). Bendigo has a good reputation for red table wines.

GOULBURN VALLEY (*ZONE: CENTRAL VICTORIA*)

This region is adjacent to the Pericoota region (north-west), Heathcote region (west), Strathbogie Ranges region (south-east) and Glenrowan region (east). It extends from the town of Seymour (37.02°S, 145.15°E; 90 km north of Melbourne) in the south to the River Murray, its northern boundary. Other major population centres are Euroa, Shepparton, Echuca, Cobram and Yarrawonga. Winegrapes were first planted in the southern part of the region near Nagambie in 1860; some vines from these early plantings still survive. Those plantings near the River Murray date from the 1980s and 1990s. The main varieties include Shiraz, Cabernet Sauvignon, Chardonnay, Marsanne and Riesling. The total planted area of Goulburn Valley and Strathbogie

Figure 2.9 A typical viticultural landscape in the southern part of Barossa Valley region

Ranges combined is 2,530 ha with the largest proportion in the former region.

Regional resources

The region generally follows the northerly course of the Goulburn River, which rises near Mt Buller in the Victorian Alps. It is mostly flat, falling from an elevation of about 140 m in the south to about 50 m to 80 m in the north. The climate in the southern part of the Goulburn Valley is warm, moderately continental, moderately arid and sunny (**TABLE 2.1b**). It is hotter and drier in the north of the region near the River Murray (Yarrawonga: MJT = 23.6°C, annual rainfall = 516 mm). Frost is rarely a problem. This area is mainly an old alluvial plain (with prior streams), but has some areas of dissected uplands. A range of soils has developed on and near the prior stream channels. Some soils have developed as a result of over-bank flooding (e.g. lighter sandy loam soils on relict levees, grading to heavier clay soils on the more distant lower level plains), whilst coarser grained sands and gravels (**Class 9.1**) were deposited in prior stream channels. The dominant soil types in viticultural areas have strong texture contrast profiles (**Classes 6.4, 6.3**) with red, yellow and brown subsoils (depending on drainage status). Surface horizons are typically fine sandy clay loams, and bleached subsurface horizons often occur. Subsoils are usually alkaline and are often sodic and coarsely structured. In the southern part of the region, south of Nagambie, subsoils are not alkaline and often not sodic (**Classes 7.3, 7.4**). These soils are better drained. To the west of the region are the Colbinabbin (or Mt Elephant) Ranges. The upper slopes consist of well structured and friable red soils that lack strong texture contrast and have high amounts of free iron oxide (**Classes 9.6, 9.8**). These have developed on weathered greenstone deposits and are usually up to one metre in depth. On lower slopes, texture contrast soils (**Classes 6.3, 6.4**) are typical and subsoil drainage is slower than for the more friable soils on the upper slopes. Irrigation water is available from the Goulburn River, shallow aquifers and dams.

Management practices

In vineyards planted post-1990, row x vine spacing is typically 2.7–3 m x 1.5–1.8 m. The main trellis types are single wire and VSP. Approximately half of all vineyards are mechanically pruned, with over two-thirds mechanically harvested. Phylloxera is present in the areas near Nagambie and at Mooroopna, near Shepparton and is managed by using rootstocks. The main rootstocks are Schwarzmann, SO4, 110 Richter, 1103 Paulsen, 5C Teleki and 101-14. While phylloxera has not been detected in vineyards planted in the north of this region near the River Murray, its proximity to phylloxera-infested areas of the region's south and to Rutherglen indicate the need for careful quarantine procedures and the use of rootstocks. The most common form of irrigation is drip (approximately 70% of vineyards) followed by overhead sprinklers, undervine sprinklers and flood/furrow. There are a small number of non-irrigated vineyards. The typical volume of irrigation water used over the growing season in a drip-irrigated vineyard is 1–2 ML/ha/season. Yields for Chardonnay and Shiraz are typically 10 to 15 and 10 to 12 t/ha respectively. Harvest commences in early March (Chardonnay).

HEATHCOTE (*ZONE: CENTRAL VICTORIA*)

The Heathcote region is adjacent to the Bendigo region (west), Macedon Ranges region (south) and Goulburn Valley region (east). Most vineyards are currently found close to the town of Heathcote (36.95°S, 144.68°E; 120 km north-west of Melbourne) in the southern part of the region at an elevation of 160 to 320 m. The modern era of viticulture dates from the 1950s but most expansion has taken place since the 1980s. The main varieties are Shiraz, Cabernet Sauvignon and Merlot. The total planted area of Heathcote, Strathbogie Ranges and Central Victorian High Country regions combined is 367 ha. The climate is similar to that of the Goulburn Valley (**TABLE 2.1b**). The landscape comprises undulating rises and narrow alluvial floodplains. On the upper slopes, parent materials are either granodiorite or volcanic greenstone. Soils from both rock types are pH neutral and red in colour. Soils derived from granodiorite have duplex profiles with loamy sand topsoils and mottled yellow clay subsoils (**Classes 6.3, 6.4**), over bedrock at one metre. Soils formed from greenstone are gradational, loamier, and up to two m deep over bedrock (**Class 9.6**). The deeper gradational soils are preferred for viticulture as they have higher water holding capacity and are more fertile and easily worked. The lower colluvial slopes contain two main variations of relatively deep (2 m) duplex soils with bleached subsurface horizons that may also contain quartz gravel. In the northern part of the region, red clay subsoils are most common; these tend to be pH-neutral in the north-east, and alkaline in the north-west (**Class 7.3**). Yellow acidic

subsoils are more common on the south side of the Bendigo-Melbourne railway line (**Class 6.4**). The alluvial floodplains contain uniform sandy loam soils (**Class 9.5**) overlying older soils composed of either gradational black soils with yellow clay subsoils, or gravel; these are highly permeable to water, but may nevertheless be poorly drained. Erosion is a problem, especially on the steeper slopes. Compaction of the sandy loam topsoils can also be an issue. Many vineyards on favourable soils are non-irrigated; however most are irrigated from dams and bores. The Heathcote region has established a reputation for high quality red table wines. There is potential for further expansion. Harvest commences in mid-March (Chardonnay).

ALPINE VALLEYS (*ZONE: NORTH EAST VICTORIA*)

This region is located in the Great Dividing Ranges and includes the valleys of the Ovens, Buckland and Kiewa Rivers. It adjoins the Beechworth region to the north and King Valley region to the west. The major town, Myrtleford (36.57°S, 146.73°E), is 250 km north-east of Melbourne. Total planted area is 470 ha. The main varieties are Chardonnay, Sauvignon Blanc, Cabernet Sauvignon, Merlot and Shiraz. The region includes large areas of national park. Viticulture is confined to river terraces on the valley floors (elevation of 180 to 250 m) and upper slopes and hills (240 to 340 m). Although the climate of the north-western part of the region is relatively warm (**TABLE 2.1b**), it is cool in the more elevated south-eastern part near Bright (MJT= 20.2°C). Both growing season and annual rainfall are high leading to high disease pressure. The risk of spring frost is significant and, for this reason, vineyard site selection is critical in order to maximise cold air drainage. Red and brown gradational soils (Category 9) are widespread throughout the region. On lower terrace levels the soil profiles often have large amounts of unconsolidated river gravels, commonly layered. Along the floodplains, the soils are uniform brown sandy clay loams (**Classes 9.5, 9.6**) on the flats, with clay soils in wetland areas. They are well drained and relatively fertile. Duplex soils also occur in the region, typically on low hills, alluvial fans and older river terraces. These soils have strong texture contrast between clay loamy surface horizons and red clay subsoils (**Classes 7.3, 7.4**). Water for irrigation is available from the Ovens and Kiewa Rivers and their tributaries, and from dams and bores. Drip irrigation is common (1 ML/ha or less per season). Some vineyards are not irrigated. There is increasing use of regulated deficit irrigation for vigour control. Typical row x vine spacing is 3 m x 2 m. The main trellis systems are Scott Henry (50% of vineyards), Smart-Dyson and VSP. Most vineyards are mechanically harvested and mechanical pre-pruning is common. Yields are typically 15 to 16 t/ha for Chardonnay and 13.5 to 14 t/ha for Cabernet Sauvignon and Shiraz. The Alpine Valleys is located in a phylloxera zone: therefore planting on rootstocks is necessary. The most common rootstocks are Schwarzmann, 99 Richter, SO4, 5C Teleki, 5BB Kober and 101-14. Harvest commences in late March (Chardonnay). The major problems are frost, excessive shoot vigour, fungal diseases and birds.

2.5.4 NEW SOUTH WALES

PERRICOOTA (ZONE: BIG RIVERS)
This region lies just across the River Murray from the Victorian town of Echuca (36.15°S, 144.77°E), 200 km north-west of Melbourne. The climate (MJT = 22.95°C) is similar to Rutherglen. The modern era of viticulture in the Echuca area commenced in the early 1970s. The principal varieties include Chardonnay, Shiraz and Cabernet Sauvignon.

HILLTOPS (ZONE: SOUTHERN NSW)
The Hilltops region includes areas in the shires of Young, Harden and Boorowa in southern NSW. It is south-west and north-west of the Cowra and Canberra regions respectively. Best known for its fruit orchards particularly cherries, vineyards for wine production were not established until circa 1900 near Young (34.33°S, 148.30°E, 360 km south-west of Sydney). The current wave of vineyard plantings began in 1969, with the development of the 'Barwang' vineyard; however, significant expansion did not take place until the late 1990s to reach around 700 ha. The major varieties are Cabernet Sauvignon, Shiraz, Chardonnay, Semillon and Riesling. The region is hilly and undulating with vineyards being generally planted on hilltops and slopes in order to lessen the frost risk. Soils vary from fertile red soils derived from basalt to less fertile granitic soils. The climate is continental, very sunny, moderately arid and moderately humid (TABLE 2.1b). The main sources of water for irrigation are dams or bores and there are restrictions on such water use. Pest and disease pressure is low. Most vineyards are irrigated (mainly by drip). Production is limited by water supply. Trellising is

predominantly single wire or VSP. Pruning (generally spur) and harvesting have traditionally been carried out by hand, but they are rapidly moving to machine. Harvest commences in early March (Chardonnay). Typical yields for Chardonnay and Shiraz are 10 to 12 and 8 to 10 t/ha respectively. Birds and frost are the main problems. The Hilltops region is generally well suited to viticulture with the only major limitation to further development being security of water supply.

2.5.5 QUEENSLAND

GRANITE BELT (ZONE: QUEENSLAND)
This region, centred on Stanthorpe (28.62°S, 151.96°E; 180 km south-west of Brisbane), lies on either side of the New England Highway between Wallangarra and Dalveen and is bounded on the south and east by the NSW border. Vineyards are widespread throughout the region, which is also known for stone and pome fruit production. Grapegrowing and winemaking have been taking place, with reasonable continuity, since the 1820s. The planted area of winegrapes is approximately 640 ha and the principal varieties include Shiraz, Cabernet Sauvignon, Chardonnay, Semillon and Sauvignon Blanc.

Regional resources
Vineyards are planted on flat to undulating land, mainly at elevations between 750 and 800 m (FIGURE 2.10). The climate is characterised by warm summers, cool winters, summer-dominant rainfall, moderate relative humidity and low aridity (TABLE 2.1b). There is significant variation between day and night temperatures. The region is subject to hail storms during the growing season. Frosts can be a problem in early spring and are managed with a range of methods including late pruning. Vines are planted on granitic sandy soils with low water-holding capacity. The most productive soils are moderate to deep, bleached sandy soils with weak subsoil development (Classes 9.1, 9.2). These may overlay siliceous hardpans. Productive sandy textured, acidic duplex soils (Classes 7.1, 7.2) are found on elevated gentle rises and elevated plains, and less productive, less acidic and poorly drained sandy duplex soils (Classes 6.1, 6.2) on lower slopes, plains and alluvium. Soil conservation measures are required on all sloping sites to reduce erosion. Generally the soils need to be managed for acidity, poor nutrient status, low water holding capacity and waterlogging. Rooting depth may be restricted by impermeable subsoils, hardpans and shallow depth to rock.

Management practices
Row x vine spacing is 2.5–3 m x 1.2–1.8 m. The most widely used trellises are VSP and Scott Henry. Hand pruning is standard. Variability of rainfall plus the nature of the soils means that dryland vineyards are frequently

Figure 2.10 A vineyard in the Granite Belt region

Table 2.1c. Regions with mean January temperature (MJT) between 19.0 and 20.9°C.

Region	State	Station	Elevation (m)	MJT[y] °C	CTL °C	ARF mm	GSRF mm	GSRD	GSE mm	ARID mm	RH %	SSH
Shoalhaven Coast	NSW	68076 Nowra RAN	109	20.9	9.9	1135	639	74	1074	-102	72	6.9
Pyrenees	Vic.	81000 Avoca	242	20.8	13.3	543	216	35	(1000)	(284)	58	9.1[a]
Great Southern – Frankland River	WA	9843 Frankland	230	20.5[x]	10.2	611	165	50	1065	368	59	7.8[a]
Manjimup/Pemberton	WA	9573 Manjimup	280	20.5[x]	9.7	1023	220	51	793[c]	176	63	8.0[e]
Langhorne Creek	SA	23747 Strathalbyn	70	20.5	10.2	493	164	42	1072[d]	372	56	8.5[a]
Margaret River	WA	a	90	20.4	7.6[b]	1192	198	42	(910)	(257)	65e	7.9
Beechworth	Vic.	82001 Beechworth	580	20.4	14.2	954	375	46	(950)	(100)	49	(8.8)
Padthaway	SA	26091 Padthaway	37	20.3	10.5	509	159	47	1195	439	68	8.5
Canberra District	NSW/ACT	70015 Canberra Forestry	581	20.3	14.7	654	364	50	972	122	56	8.4
Wrattonbully	SA	26023 Naracoorte	58	20.2	10.6	578	188	44	1052[f]	338	63	8.0[f]
Great Southern – Mt Barker	WA	9581 Mt Barker	300	20.1[x]	9.3	738	226	62	(950)	(249)	66	7.3
Tumbarumba	NSW	72043 Tumbarumba	654	20.1	15.0	986	425	43	(900)	(25)	61	(8.5)
Sunbury	Vic.	86282 Melbourne Airport	113	19.8	10.7	548	293	59	1146	280	66	7.6
Orange	NSW	63254 Orange Agric.	922	19.6	14.4	949	468	49	1060	62	66	8.9
Coonawarra	SA	26091 Coonawarra	59	19.5	9.9	579	182	54	1057	347	62	7.8[a]
Southern Fleurieu	SA	Composite[g]	152	19.4	9.3	695	204	47	990[h]	291	66	8.1[a]
Southern Highlands	NSW	68005 Bowral	661	19.4	12.9	946	498	60	(950)	(-23)	69i	8.3[a]
Great Southern – Albany	WA	9500 Albany	18	19.3[x]	7.1	934	240	65	957[f]	239	70	7.3[j]
Eden Valley	SA	a	450	19.3	(11.5)	657[k]	183[k]	-	(950)	(384)	(58)	8.7
Yarra Valley	Vic.	Composite[l]	122	19.2	10.6	777	375	59	870[m]	60	71	7.5
Strathbogie Ranges	Vic.	82042 Strathbogie	520	19.2	13.5	986	358	39	902	93	65	(8.0)
Adelaide Hills	SA	23081 Lenswood	452	19.1	10.4	1029	276	54	935	192	65	8.8
Grampians	Vic.	89000 Ararat	332	19.1	11.7	616	251	46	1110[n]	304	56	8.7[a]
Geelong	Vic.	87025 Geelong	17	19.1	9.7	537	248	49	1014[o]	260	63	7.1[a]
Mornington Peninsula	Vic.	86079 Mornington	46	19.0	9.6	740	323	53	771[p]	62	67	7.0[a]
Gippsland	Vic.	85279 Bairnsdale Airport	49	19.0	10.0	672	361	63	891[q]	84	68	8.2[a]

[a] Gladstones (1992)
[b] Dry and Smart (1988)
[c] 9592 Pemberton
[d] 24558 Milang EWS
[e] 9574 Margaret River
[f] 26082 Struan
[g] Average of 023818 Kuitpo and 023751 Victor Harbour
[h] 23738 Myponga
[i] 68045 Moss Vale
[j] 9741 Albany Airport

[k] 23302 Collingrove
[l] Average of 086050 Healesville and 086282 Melbourne Airport
[m] 86363 Tarrawarra
[n] 79080 Stawell
[o] 87023 Geelong Salines
[p] 86357 Devil Bend Reservoir
[q] 84100 Bairnsdale Waterworks
[x] J. Gladstones (pers.comm.)
[y] See 2.1.1 and 2.1.2 in text for explanation of codes
( ) Denotes estimate

water-stressed. Where irrigation water is available from dams or creeks, it is applied by drip (1 to 3 ML/ha/season). The light-textured soils require the use of nematode-resistant rootstocks (approximately 30% of the area), mainly 1103 Paulsen, Ramsey and 5BB Kober. Yields vary from very low to moderate, but large extremes exist depending on soil type and water availability; typical yields for Chardonnay and Shiraz are 5 to 12 t/ha. Harvest commences in early March (Chardonnay). The main problems are fungal diseases, birds, lack of water for irrigation, frost and strong winds (for exposed sites).

Summary

The Granite Belt is an important region for wine tourism. In the past the region specialised in fortified wines but current emphasis is on table wines.

2.6 Regions with MJT from 19.0 to 20.9°C

2.6.1 WESTERN AUSTRALIA

GREAT SOUTHERN (*ZONE: SOUTH WEST AUSTRALIA*)
The Great Southern region adjoins the Blackwood Valley and Manjimup regions to the north-west. Five subregions have been recognised thus far within its boundaries: Frankland River, Mount Barker, Porongurup, Denmark and Albany. The initial trial plantings of winegrapes were made in the mid-to late 1960s near Mt Barker (34.60°S, 117.63°E, 350 km south-east of Perth) and Frankland (34.43°S, 116.98°E). More extensive plantings followed in the 1970s and 1980s. There are now approximately 1,200 ha planted in the region with the largest proportion in the Frankland River and Mount Barker subregions.

The main varieties are Cabernet Sauvignon, Shiraz, Merlot, Chardonnay, Sauvignon Blanc and Riesling.

Regional resources

Frankland River is the warmest subregion (**TABLE 2.1c**). Due to their close proximity to the coast, Albany (35.01°S, 117.70°E) and Denmark are the coolest and most maritime. Mt Barker and Porongurup are intermediate in terms of temperature (see Gladstones [1992] for a more detailed description of the regional climate). Wind exposure can be a problem in coastal areas of the Albany subregion. Proximity to the Southern Ocean brings warm humid winds with afternoon sea breezes and summer drizzle rarely experienced in other areas of the State. Frost is an issue in the Frankland, Mt Barker and Porongurup subregions. The topography is gently undulating with the exception of the Porongorup Ranges. Vineyards are found from close to sea level up to 400 m elevation. The soils are light-textured and acidic. Grapevines will have nutritional deficiencies, associated with low soil pH, if not managed correctly. The Frankland River subregion is characterised by undulating lateritic low hills and rises, overlying granite and gneiss. Lateritic gravelly sand and loam with clayey subsoil (**Classes 6.2, 7.2, 9.5**) are the most widely planted soils. Although many of these soils are like those at Margaret River—having formed on similar parent material—poorly structured, sodic clay subsoils are sometimes present due to the lower rainfall. Heavier soils with thin sandy loam topsoil and reddish clay subsoil are also common. Red shallow loamy duplex soil (**Class 7.3**) is found on areas where gneiss is exposed. On lower slopes plantings occur on yellow brown and grey deep and shallow sandy duplex soil (**Classes 6.1, 6.2, 7.1, 7.2**). Pale deep sand (**Class 9.1**) also occurs in mid-slope positions. The dominant landscape of the Mt Barker subregion is an undulating lateritic plain, with extensive areas of restricted drainage. Soils are similar to those in the Frankland River subregion: lateritic gravelly sand and loam with clayey subsoil (**Classes 6.2, 7.2, 9.5**). Most of the plantings in the Porongurup subregion lie on the footslopes of the granitic Porongurup ranges. Soils include yellow brown deep sandy duplex (**Classes 6.2, 7.2**), brown deep loamy duplex (**Classes 6.4, 7.4**), friable red brown loamy earth (**Class 9.6**) and duplex sandy gravel (**Class 7.2**). In the Albany subregion sedimentary rocks (siltstones and spongolite) overlie gneiss and granite. Soils include grey deep sandy duplex and yellow brown deep sandy duplex (**Classes 6.2, 7.2**), duplex sandy gravel (**Class 7.2**), pale deep sand (**Class 9.1**), pale shallow sand (**Class 4.1**) and shallow gravel (**Class 3.1**). Near Denmark there are brown deep loamy duplex (**Classes 6.4, 7.4**), friable red brown loamy earth (**Class 9.6**) and loamy gravel (**Classes 3.1, 9.5**) formed on hilly terrain over fresh gneiss. Ground water salinity is a problem in many parts of the region, particularly in the north. Most growers are reliant on surface water supplies and rising saline water tables threaten the future of irrigation supplies in the Mt Barker and Frankland River subregions. Some existing dams are becoming brackish and in some cases irrigation water salinity levels are beginning to have a detrimental effect on vine performance. Waterlogging is a more widespread problem, especially on lower slopes and broad flat areas where duplex profiles with restrictive subsoils are common. Poor inherent subsoil soil structure (or the presence of hardpans) on many of the inland soils not only affects drainage, but can limit root depth.

Management practices

Most vineyards are drip irrigated (0.5 to 1.0 ML/ha/season). Row x vine spacing is typically 3.0 m x 1.8–2.0 m. VSP trellising is most common. Approximately 50% of the area is mechanically pruned (with hand cleanup) and 85% is mechanically harvested. Canopy management practices such as shoot thinning, leaf plucking and trimming are commonly used throughout the region. Typical yield of Cabernet Sauvignon, Shiraz and Chardonnay is 6 to 12 t/ha. Harvest commences in early March (Chardonnay) at Mt Barker and Frankland, later in Albany and Denmark. The major problems are powdery mildew, bunch rot (particularly in the southern areas e.g. Denmark), spring frosts (Mt Barker, Frankland River), birds, high vigour (Albany, Denmark) and poor fruitset.

Summary

The major limitation to future expansion is a lack of good quality water for irrigation.

MANJIMUP[1] (*ZONE: SOUTH WEST AUSTRALIA*)

Timber and apples have been the major products of the Manjimup and Pemberton regions. A pilot vineyard was established midway between Manjimup and Pemberton by the WA Department of Agriculture in 1977 and commercial viticulture followed in the 1980s. The region is bordered by Blackwood region to the north, Pemberton region to the south and Great Southern region to the east. The town of Manjimup (34.23°S, 116.15°E) is 255 km south of Perth. The topography is undulating and most vineyards are found between 200 and 300 m. Vineyard plantings are approximately 1,200 ha for Manjimup and Pemberton combined with the largest proportion in the latter. The main varieties are Shiraz, Cabernet Sauvignon, Chardonnay, Verdelho and Sauvignon Blanc. The climate (**TABLE 2.1c**) has many similarities with that of the Mt Barker and Frankland subregions of Great Southern to the east with the advantages of a higher winter/spring rainfall and less temperature variability (Gladstones 1992). Spring frosts may be a problem in the northern parts. The region is

---

[1] Interim decision on GI at August 2004 (E. Sullivan, pers.comm.)

Figure 2.11 A vineyard in the Pemberton region

centred on a gently undulating lateritic plateau. Most vineyards have been established on the better drained crests, rises and the slopes of shallow minor valleys where the dominant soils are yellow brown 'jarrah' gravels (duplex sandy gravel (**Class 7.2**) and loamy gravel (**Classes 9.5, 9.6**). Vigour is generally high due to fertile soils and high soil moisture levels that often do not decline until mid-to late December. Cover crops may be used to reduce soil water availability after budburst. Row x vine spacing is 3 m x 1.5 m. VSP trellising is most common. Drip irrigation is standard (0.5–1.0 ML/ha/season). Water is sourced mainly from dams. The major problems are powdery mildew, botrytis bunch rot and birds. Typical yields are 8 to 12 t/ha for Shiraz, 7 to 11 t/ha for Cabernet Sauvignon and 6 to 12 t/ha for Chardonnay. Harvest commences in early to mid-March (Chardonnay).

PEMBERTON[2] (*ZONE: SOUTH WEST AUSTRALIA*)
This region has much in common with Manjimup, its neighbour to the north. However, there are distinct differences for both climate and soils. Most vineyards are located near to the town of Pemberton (34.45°S, 116.0°E; 280 km south of Perth) at an elevation of 60 to 200 m (**FIGURE 2.11**). The climate is cooler and more maritime than Manjimup with lower sunshine hours, higher rainfall (except January and February) and higher relative humidity (**TABLE 2.1c**). Around the boundary between the Manjimup and Pemberton regions, the plateau becomes increasingly stripped, passing through a transition zone into a series of undulating valleys (up to 100 m deep in places) and remnants of lateritic ridges. In this dissected terrain, where the underlying gneiss and granite have been exposed, many vineyards are planted on the 'karri' loams—red brown loamy gravel and brown loamy earth (**Class 9.5**), friable red brown loamy earth (**Class 9.6**), brown deep loamy duplex (**Classes 6.3, 7.3**) and red deep loamy duplex (**Class 7.4**). On the ridges, loamy gravels are more common than the duplex sandy gravels. The combination of the relatively fertile

'karri' loams with the moist spring climate may cause vigour problems. Viticultural practices are similar to those of Manjimup. Harvest commences in early to mid-March (Chardonnay).

MARGARET RIVER (*ZONE: SOUTH WEST AUSTRALIA*)
The potential for table wine production in Margaret River and Great Southern was first identified by Olmo (1956) and Gladstones (1965). The first commercial vineyards were established in the late 1960s and, by the late 1980s, there were around 350 ha. Major expansion took place during the 1990s and today the region has more than 4,000 ha, and produces more than 40% of Western Australia's winegrape tonnage. The main varieties are Cabernet Sauvignon, Shiraz, Chardonnay, Merlot, Sauvignon Blanc and Semillon. The first vineyards were planted 30 km north-west of the town of Margaret River (33.95°S, 115.07°E; 250 km south of Perth), but they now extend from Yallingup in the north to Karridale in the south.

Regional resources
A low ridge extends from Cape Naturaliste in the north to Cape Leeuwin at the southern tip of south-west Western Australia. Topography is undulating. There is a strong maritime influence on climate, with low temperature variability (**TABLE 2.1c**). Spring frosts are uncommon. Annual rainfall is high and very winter dominant. There is a downward gradient of temperature and sunshine hours from north to south (see Gladstones [1992] for a more detailed description of the regional climate). Chardonnay and Pinot Noir may burst as early as the beginning of July as a consequence of the relatively warm winter (mean temperature in July is 12.8°C). Strong winds in spring may cause severe shoot damage and crop loss. Underground water sources are limited; surface water catchment is the main source of irrigation water. The earliest sites to be selected for grapegrowing in the region were in undulating valleys such as that formed by the Willyabrup Brook (**FIGURE 2.12**). These valleys have been incised through a lateritic plateau overlying the granitic basement of the Leeuwin Block. Loamy ironstone gravel (**Classes 3.1, 9.5**) and ironstone gravelly sand over clay (**Class 7.2**) are the most common profiles, locally known as 'Forest Grove' soils. They consist of lateritic colluvium over clay derived from the deeply weathered mantle. The topsoil is typically a yellowish brown loamy sand to sandy loam with up to 60% rounded ironstone gravels. This overlies a mottled yellow clay at about 50 cm. Less common are friable red brown loamy earth (**Class 9.6**) and brown deep loamy duplex (**Class 7.4**) derived from freshly weathered basement rock (locally known as 'Keenan' soils). Small pockets of pale deep sand (**Class 9.1**) also occur in some plantings. Many vineyards are now established in other similar valleys and on the

---

[2] Interim decision on GI at August 2004 (E. Sullivan, pers.comm.)

Figure 2.12 A vineyard near Willyabrup in the Margaret River region

surrounding plateau surface. Here there is a mixture of the gravelly Forest Grove soils and 'Mungite' soils which include poorly drained sand grading to loam (**Class 9.2**), deep sandy duplex (**Class 6.2**) and shallow ironstone gravelly soil (**Class 4.1**). More recently the industry has spread to the undulating terrain east of the Bussell Highway: here there is a mixture of Forest Grove and Mungite soils. The region also includes the south-western edge of the Swan Coastal Plain, with plantings being centred around Jindong on red deep sand (**Class 9.1**), red sand grading to loam (**Class 9.2**) and friable red brown loamy earth (**Class 9.6**) formed on recent alluvium. Excess vigour may be a problem on some soil types, e.g. Keenan, where the subsoil remains moist throughout the growing season. This problem is most common in the higher rainfall district south of Margaret River.

Management practices

Canopy management, by means of divided canopy training systems, shoot positioning and summer pruning is widely practiced. Row x vine spacing is typically 3.0 m x 1.8–2.0 m. Approximately 70% of the region is machine harvested. Use of mechanical pruning (followed by hand cleanup) is increasing. Some vineyards are dry-grown but most are drip-irrigated (average application of 1 ML/ha/season). Cover-cropping is common; tall cereals such as oats and rye are sometimes sown in alternate rows to act as windbreaks during early spring. During the summer months, mid-row growth is regulated by mowing or by application of knockdown herbicides. The main problems are strong winds, fungal diseases (particularly powdery mildew), weevils and birds. The latter, particularly silvereyes, are a common pest especially for vineyards in close proximity to forests and bushland. Bird damage escalates when the season is not conducive to supporting the bird population, e.g. late forming and/or poor quantities of native gum blossom and extremely dry conditions. Vigour and yields are low to moderate, varying mainly with soil depth. Harvest commences at the end of February (Chardonnay).

Summary

This region has developed a good reputation for the quality of its table wines. The potential for expansion is limited by high land prices and a lack of suitable soil types and topography. Viticulture will face increasing pressure from alternative land uses, particularly housing and recreation.

2.6.2 SOUTH AUSTRALIA

LANGHORNE CREEK (*ZONE: FLEURIEU*)
The region is bounded by the Mt Lofty Ranges to the north and Lake Alexandrina to the south, and lies 60 km south-east of Adelaide. The first vineyard was planted in 1858 on the flats of the River Bremer. In the late 1980s, there were 400 ha of vineyards on the alluvial flats adjacent to the rivers, mainly owned by independent growers. Since that time, there has been major expansion, outside of the traditional boundaries, on lighter-textured soils. Today there are 5,043 ha and the major varieties are Cabernet Sauvignon, Shiraz, Merlot, Chardonnay and Riesling. Of the 91 producers, 26% have more than 50 ha and one-third of the production is winery-grown.

Regional resources

Vineyards are planted on a gently and slightly undulating plain with an average elevation of 20 m (range 0–50 m). Two rivers, the Bremer and the Angas, traverse the area. The climate is characterised by low winter-dominant rainfall and moderate temperatures during the growing season (**TABLE 2.1c**). A feature of this region is the limited daytime temperature rise caused by cooling sea breezes in the afternoon and the moderating effect of Lake Alexandrina. The comparison of rainfall with evaporation indicates the need for irrigation. Frost risk is low. Traditionally most vines were grown on deep alluvial soils; however, newer plantings have generally been made on shallower, lighter-textured soils with low readily available water (RAW) values. The alluvial plains are characterised by fine sandy and silty sediments, but textures tend to become more clayey at the eastern and western margins, and in the south. There is a well-defined boundary between the alluvial plains and the gently undulating landscapes to the east and west, where older sediments have significantly reduced drainage capacity. Typical viticultural soils are deep and coarse to medium textured (**Class 9.6**) with good drainage. However, there are considerable areas where more clayey sediments give rise to duplex soils with restrictive (**Classes 6.3, 6.4**) and non restrictive (**Class 7.4**) clayey subsoils, and to soils which are clayey throughout (**Classes 5.2, 9.7, 9.8**). Low rises produced by recent re-working of sandy surface soils are characterised by deep or gradational sandy soils with good to excessive drainage (**Classes 9.1, 9.2**). Duplex soils with sodic subsoils (**Classes 6.3, 6.4**) are typical of the more southerly parts of the region. Vineyards in the region were traditionally irrigated in winter by controlled flooding from the rivers, whose water was dammed and distributed through levee banks. One flooding to a height of 1.0 to 1.5 m supplied sufficient water to satisfy most of the vine requirements during the growing season. Today few vineyards are irrigated in this manner: 95% of the area is irrigated with water sourced from Lake Alexandrina, delivered by pipelines, the longest of which is 35 km. This water is licenced but there is no volumetric restriction.

Management practices
Row spacing varies from 2.5–3.0 m and vine spacing from 1.5–2.5 m. The most widely used trellises are VSP (50%) and single wire (30%): the latter is mainly found in older plantings. The majority of vineyards use mechanical pre-pruning followed by hand clean-up. Cane pruning is rare. Soil management is concerned with preventing waterlogging in heavier soils, with associated salt accumulation, and maintaining optimum soil moisture levels in vineyards characterised by high degrees of soil variability. Drip irrigation is mainly used with 1.0 to 2.5 ML/ha typically applied. The use of deficit irrigation strategies is increasing. More than 90% of production is mechanically harvested. Vigour and yields on traditional vineyards are high but less so for the newer plantings on the lower potential soils. Typical yields for Chardonnay and Shiraz are 10 to 15 t/ha. Less than 10% of the area is grafted to rootstocks. Powdery mildew is a serious problem in most years where vine canopies are dense; downy mildew and bunch rot are occasional problems. Harvest of Chardonnay commences in early to mid-March. Major problems are soil salinity and sodicity, saline irrigation water and wind.

Summary
The recent expansion in this region has been largely driven by its reputation for wine quality. Further expansion will be determined by availability of licenced water.

SOUTHERN FLEURIEU (*ZONE: FLEURIEU*)
The first vines were planted in the 1840s near Port Elliot but there was no serious production until the 1980s. Today there are more than 550 ha. Collectively the whole of the Fleurieu Zone, excluding Langhorne Creek and McLaren Vale regions, has 821 ha and 70 growers (63% <10 ha). The region embraces the southern part of the Fleurieu Peninsula including the towns of Myponga and Mt Compass on the higher land to the north and Yankalilla and Victor Harbour at lower elevations to the south. Vineyards are planted on coastal flats and slopes on undulating hills with elevations from 75 m to 300 m (**FIGURE 2.13**). The climate is strongly maritime (**TABLE 2.1c**). Annual rainfall ranges from 600 to 800

Figure 2.13 A vineyard near Normanville in the Southern Fleurieu region

mm. Strong southerly winds can be a limiting factor. Frost risk is generally low except for some sheltered sites. The gently rolling to moderately steep landscape of the southern Mt Lofty Range formed on weathering basement rocks, mainly siltstones and sandstones with dolomites/limestones in the south-west. Soils formed on these rocks are shallow to moderately deep with sandy loam to clay loam surfaces overlying clayey subsoils or weathering rock (**Classes 7.1, 7.3, 9.6**). Ancient glacial valleys within the range are characterised by variable sandy to sandy clay sediments. Typical soils in these areas have thick sandy surfaces over clayey subsoils (**Classes 6.2, 7.2**). Deep sands and thick sands over 'coffee rock' (iron/organic hardpan) are also common (**Class 9.1**). Ironstone soils (**Class 6.3**) occur on broad ridge tops. Deep black clayey soils (**Class 9.8**) are minor overall but locally significant. The soils formed on basement rocks are generally well suited to viticulture, although acidity must be managed. Waterlogging and occasional saline seepages are local problems on lower slopes. The sandy soils are infertile and strongly acidic, and prone to waterlogging where restrictive clayey subsoils are within 30 cm of the surface. Viticultural practices are similar to those in young vineyards in the McLaren Vale region immediately to the north. Irrigation is common, sourced from bores and dams. Birds are a major problem. The main varieties are Cabernet Sauvignon, Shiraz, Sauvignon Blanc and Chardonnay. Although this region has good potential for high quality wines, further expansion is limited by lack of suitable sites and water for irrigation.

CURRENCY CREEK (*ZONE: FLEURIEU*)
The first commercial vineyard was planted in 1969. There are now several hundred hectares from sea level to 50 m on flat to undulating land. The climate is similar to the adjacent Langhorne Creek region. Irrigation water is sourced from bores and dams.

KANGAROO ISLAND (*ZONE: FLEURIEU*)

The first commercial vineyard was established in the 1970s and major expansion took place from the mid-1990s. Today there are 20 vineyards at altitudes from 10–180 m on flat to undulating land. The major town Kingscote is 112 km south-east of Adelaide. The climate is similar to Southern Fleurieu. Most viticulture on the island is on the central plateau, an elevated ancient land surface underlain by highly weathered, kaolinized and ferruginized sandstones. Ironstone soils are characteristic of this landscape. The main soil types are **Classes 6.1-6.4, 9.5**. The main management issues on these soils are maintaining adequate nutrient levels (particularly phosphorus which is fixed by the ironstone), controlling acidity, and minimising the effects of waterlogging. Further expansion is limited by a serious lack of water resources.

PADTHAWAY (*ZONE: LIMESTONE COAST*)

This region is located in the south-east of South Australia. The vineyards are located near the small town of Padthaway (36.60°S, 140.49°E; 260 km south-east of Adelaide) and extend for 25 km in a narrow north-south strip. This was one of the few new areas developed in Australia during the 1970s. A trial planting of 20 ha was established in 1964, and by 1986 there were about 1,400 ha operated mainly by large wine companies. Today there are 3,351 ha and all major wine companies are represented in the region (70% of the crush is winery-grown). Average vineyard size is relatively large with 60% of producers having more than 50 ha. The main varieties planted are Shiraz, Cabernet Sauvignon, Chardonnay, Riesling and Pinot Noir.

Regional resources

The region is a narrow strip of land running along the western edge of the Naracoorte Range, an ancient coastal dune (**FIGURE 2.14**). Average vineyard elevation is 37 m. The upper layers of the dune sand are cemented to a hard carbonate rich material called calcarenite. The region extends across the gentle slopes abutting the range and on to the plains further to the west. The gentle slopes and plains are underlain by limestones and clayey sediments of an old lagoon floor. These materials are commonly capped by calcrete. The soils of the plains are generally non-restrictive duplex, thick loamy sand over clay (**Class 7.2**) or thin hard sandy loam to sandy clay loam over clay (**Class 7.3**), with some sand to sandy loam over restrictive clay (**Classes 6.2, 6.3**). Loamy to clay loamy gradational soils (**Classes 9.3, 9.4**) and shallow sandy loams to clay loams over calcrete (**Classes 4.2, 4.4**) also occur. Drainage problems and associated salt accumulation can develop where subsoil clays are restrictive (i.e. sodic or poorly structured). Root growth is generally impeded by the calcareous clay sediments underlying the soil at depths of less than 100 cm. On the rising ground to the east, there is a mixture of deep sandy soils (**Class 9.1**) and shallower sands to sandy loams (**Classes 4.1, 4.2**) on the calcarenite of the Naracoorte Range. The climate of the region is similar in many respects to Coonawarra (**TABLE 2.1c**). However, annual rainfall is lower, and both summer temperatures and sunshine hours are higher. In addition, maturity is earlier than Coonawarra: this decreases the risk of rain damage for late varieties. Spring frost can also be a problem. The aquifer is the only source of water for irrigation and salinity has increased to relatively high levels. The use of water is controlled by legislated water rights.

Management practices

These correspond in the main to those of the Coonawarra region, but as irrigation is more necessary, close to 100% of the area is irrigated, mainly by drip with 1 to 2 ML/ha. Row spacing varies from 2.75 to 3.0 m and vine spacing from 1.8 to 2.0 m. The most widely used trellises are high (up to 1.5 m) single wire and two-wire vertical; there is relatively little VSP. More than 90% of the area is mechanically pruned and harvested. Less than 5% of the area is grafted. Vigour and yields are generally high, reflecting good water availability. The mid-summer stress provides some control of shoot vigour. Typical yields are 15 to 20 t/ha for Chardonnay and 10 to 15 t/ha for Shiraz. Due to shallow soil, there is extensive undervine mounding. Both sprinklers and fans are used for frost control. Harvest commences in early March (Chardonnay).

Summary

The high land prices and limited areas of suitable soil at Coonawarra have influenced the rapid development of this region. The potential for further development appears to be limited by water entitlements and quality of the existing supply. Its reputation was established with white wine but the advent of deficit irrigation strategies has resulted in red wines of high quality.

Figure 2.14 A view towards the east in the Padthaway region

WRATTONBULLY (*ZONE: LIMESTONE COAST*)

The main population centre of this region is the town of Naracoorte (36.96°S, 140.74°E; 300 km south-east of Adelaide), which is adjacent to the region but not part of it. The first plantings were in 1968 but most vineyards have been developed since the early 1990s. Growers including wine companies were attracted by the good supply of water, the well drained limestone-based soils and similar climate to Coonawarra, its more famous neighbour to the south. The region extends from Naracoorte in the west to the Victorian border in the east, the main land use being grazing and forestry. Today there are 1,961 ha with 43 producers (42% >25 ha). The main varieties planted are Cabernet Sauvignon, Shiraz, Merlot and Chardonnay. Most vineyards are found at an elevation of 75 to 100 m on flat to undulating land. Climatically the region is similar to Padthaway and Coonawarra (**TABLE 2.1c**). Frost risk is lower than for Coonawarra. Management practices are very similar to those of the youngest vineyards of Coonawarra. The majority of vineyards have row x vine spacing of 2.75–3.0 m x 1.8 m and VSP trellis. Irrigation is used in all vineyards, mainly by drip. Typically application is 1.0 to 1.5 ML/ha, entirely sourced from an aquifer under licence. Typical yields are 8 to 12 t/ha for Chardonnay and 6 to 12 t/ha for Shiraz. The main problems are frost (controlled by sprinklers or fans) and birds. Because this region has such a large proportion of new plantings, its vineyards are good examples of modern design, for example, clonal planting material, extensive soil surveys prior to establishment and 100% mechanisation of pruning and harvesting. Harvest of Chardonnay commences in mid- to late March. Further expansion is limited by lack of well drained soils and water for irrigation.

COONAWARRA (*ZONE: LIMESTONE COAST*)

One of mainland Australia's most southerly wine-producing regions, it is located near to the village of Coonawarra (37.29°S, 140.82°E), 360 km south-east of Adelaide. The vineyards were traditionally restricted to a narrow north-south strip of land approximately 20 km long; since the 1990s the boundaries have expanded. The first vines were planted in the 1890s. Due to economic problems the area declined during the next fifty years, producing mainly grapes for distillation. From 1950 onwards (and particularly after the mid-1960s) winery companies expanded the plantings to 1,800 ha by the mid-1980s. Today, there are 5,120 ha of vineyards, mostly owned by winery companies. Of the 91 producers, 23% have 50 ha or more. The main varieties planted are Cabernet Sauvignon, Shiraz, Merlot, Chardonnay and Riesling. The total production from the Limestone Coast of South Australia is used almost exclusively for the production of table wine.

Figure 2.15 The favoured red soil of the Coonawarra region

Regional resources

The region is flat, at an elevation of 60 m (**FIGURE 2.15**). The climate is characterised by moderate, winter-dominant rainfall, moderate temperatures during the growing season, and moderate solar radiation (**TABLE 2.1c**). Rainfall is high (67 mm) during the vintage month of April and may cause problems with bunch rot. Although temperatures during the growing season are generally moderate, heat-waves may occur during January and February. Aridity is lower than for Padthaway. Maturity is in April when conditions are close to optimal for both Shiraz and Cabernet Sauvignon (Gladstones 1992). Frosts have been known to occur as late as December and the risk of frost damage is further exacerbated by the flat terrain. All vine plantings are found on the limited areas of well drained soil. The region spans several distinctive landscape features, all remnants of an ancient coastal dune/back-swamp system. On the eastern side is the Naracoorte Range, an undulating range formed on the cemented sands (calcarenites) of an old dune. Soils vary from deep sand (**Class 9.1**) to shallower sandy loam to sand (**Classes 4.2, 3.3**) over calcarenite. To the west of the range is a very gently undulating plain underlain by clayey sediments. Soils are mainly thick sand over restrictive or non restrictive brown clay (**Classes 6.2, 7.2**), with smaller areas of sandy loam to sandy clay loam over brown clay (**Classes 6.3, 6.4, 7.3, 7.4**). Further to the west is the north-south trending Coonawarra ridge, a very low elongate rise formed on fine grained calcarenite. Characteristic soils are shallow red clay loam to clay (**Class 4.4**) with a range of duplex and shallow sandier profiles. On the western side of the rise are flat plains with heavy black soils (often cracking) over limestone, calcreted clay or marl (**Classes 3.4, 4.4, 4.5, 5.2, 5.3**). The plains are naturally poorly drained (except for the areas of deep sand). However, the progressive installation of drains has alleviated the problem to a large extent. Nevertheless, waterlogging, either due to shallow water tables or restrictive clayey subsoils is a significant issue. On the Naracoorte Range and the Coonawarra ridge, drainage is good. Soil depth is variable, with calcarenite often shallower than 50 cm (except on the sand spreads of the range). Due to the limited areas of **Class 4.4** soil, most recent development has taken place on the other soil types, particularly in the west of the region. Aquifers underlying the region are recharged in winter. In summer, the water table may only be a few metres below the surface. There are no current restrictions on the amount that may be used for irrigation although it is likely that there will be a volumetric limit in future.

Management practices

Climatic conditions favour the development of fungal diseases such as downy mildew, bunch rot and powdery mildew. Consequently, protective sprays are applied regularly during the growing season. As roots of young vines have difficulty penetrating the limestone layer, deep ripping is usually carried out before planting. Maintenance of a bare, compacted, weed-free soil surface from budburst onwards is essential to reduce frost damage. Average spacings for the region are 2.7–3.0 m (row) and 2.0 m (vine). The most common trellis (80%) has a single wire at 1.2–1.5 m. Low output overhead sprinklers and fans are used for frost control (see Volume II, Chapter 8). Most vineyards are pre-pruned by machine. Vigour varies from moderate to high depending largely on soil and hence water-holding capacity. Most vineyards are irrigated with up to 1.5 ML/ha (60% by drip, 20% by fixed overhead sprinklers). All irrigation water is sourced from the aquifer. Typical yields are 8 to 14 t/ha for Chardonnay, 7 to 12 t/ha for Shiraz and 6 to 10 t/ha for Cabernet Sauvignon. Harvesting is mainly by machine. Less than 2% of the area is grafted to rootstocks. Harvest commences in late March (Chardonnay).

Summary

Recognition of the high quality of wines from this region has led to extensive development by large wine companies. A combination of modern techniques and reasonable yields has led to lower production costs than for most other areas. Potential for further vineyard development is limited by lack of suitable well-drained land. Other nearby parts of the Limestone Coast do, however, have good potential.

PENOLA[3] (*ZONE: LIMESTONE COAST*)
The history of this region is shared with that of the Coonawarra region, which it adjoins for most of its boundary from south-east to north-west. It has similar climate and soils to Coonawarra. There are relatively few vineyards at present.

EDEN VALLEY (*ZONE: BAROSSA*)
The Eden Valley is part of the Barossa Zone. The village of Eden Valley is 57 km north-east of Adelaide. Grapes have been grown since the 1840s but until 1960s there were relatively few, widely-dispersed vineyards. The main expansion in the region has taken place since the 1960s, mainly by winery companies, initially with Cabernet Sauvignon and Riesling, and more recently with Chardonnay, Semillon, Pinot Noir, Merlot and Viognier. Production is used exclusively for winemaking and approximately half of this is grown on winery-owned vineyards. There are 1,650 ha and, of the 102 producers, 60% have fewer than 10 ha. The main varieties planted are Shiraz, Riesling, Cabernet Sauvignon and Chardonnay.

Regional resources

In general the region includes the land higher than 400 m immediately to the east of the Barossa Valley. Elevation varies from 380 to 550 m. The valley is a natural drainage basin for the North Para River, which flows west into the Barossa Valley, and the Rhine River which flows east into the Murray. The climate is characterised by moderate rainfall with marked winter dominance and high summer evaporation (**TABLE 2.1c**). There is a marked increase in rainfall, from 500 to 800 mm, from the northern to the southern extremities of the region. Vines suffer water stress in most parts of the region in most seasons, especially on shallow soils. The mean temperature during the growing period is up to 2°C cooler in the Eden Valley than in the Barossa Valley (Boehm 1970) resulting in maturity up to three weeks later and ripening under cooler conditions. The northern part, for example, east and north-east of Angaston, is warmer than higher land to the south, particularly the High Eden subregion (480–550 m). There is occasional frost risk in low-lying vineyards. Like the Adelaide Hills, Eden Valley is in the Mount Lofty Ranges, but the underlying 'Kanmantoo Group' rocks give rise to a different suite of soils. These rocks are coarse grained and have been altered by heat and pressure during the development of the ranges to form highly micaceous schists and gneisses. The landscapes are undulating to rolling, and characterised by extensive rocky outcrops. Soil depth is highly variable over short distances, causing problems for efficient irrigation. Some soils simply consist of sandy to sandy loam topsoil overlying rock at shallow depth (**Classes 3.2, 4.1, 4.3**). On less rocky hills, lower slopes and valley flats, profiles are deeper. Some are duplex with sand to sandy loam topsoil over clayey subsoils. Non-restrictive forms are more common (**Classes 7.1 to 7.4**). Duplex soils with restrictive subsoils (**Classes 6.1-6.4**) are more prevalent in valleys. Deep sandy soils (**Class 9.1**) are common on creek flats. Most soils are naturally acidic. Saline seepages are scattered throughout this region, requiring

[3] Interim decision on GI at August 2004 (E. Sullivan, pers.comm.)

that deep drainage from irrigation is minimised, although over-use of water is generally not an issue, as suitable bore and surface supplies are limited. Where soil types are suitable, dams provide storage from local run-off or from non-permanent streams.

Management practices

Management practices in the northern part are similar to those of the Barossa Valley. Those in the southern part have more similarity with the Adelaide Hills to the south. Row width is usually 3.3–3.6 m and vine spacing 1.8-2.0 m. Plantings of less than 10 years are mainly VSP with the remainder having a single wire trellis (as in older plantings). Typical yields for Chardonnay, Shiraz and Riesling are 6 to 8, 6 to 8 and 4 to 5 t/ha respectively. Up to 15% of the area is grafted, mainly to 5BB Kober, 99 Richter, 1103 Paulsen and Schwarzmann. Irrigation is common, applied by drip at rates of 0.5-1.0 ML/ha, mainly sourced from dams. Control of water erosion on sloping land was traditionally achieved through the use of contour planting; however, most vineyards developed since the 1980s have rows at right angles to the contour combined with mown sward. There is increasing use of undervine straw mulch. Up to 90% of the area is mechanically pruned (followed by hand regulation of node numbers) and mechanically harvested. Disease risk is relatively low. The main problems are birds, strong winds, cool spring conditions leading to poor fruitset, vineyard variability due to variation in topsoil depth and low soil pH.

Summary

Recent development in this region has taken advantage of the good potential for quality table wine production. The exploitation of the shallow soils of the region has been made possible by the introduction of drip irrigation.

ADELAIDE HILLS (*ZONE: MOUNT LOFTY RANGES*)

This region extends from Mt Pleasant in the north to Macclesfield in the south. The north-south axis is 75 km long and it is 20 km wide. The region includes the highest parts of the Mt Lofty Ranges close to the city of Adelaide (34.97°S, 138.63°E). The first vineyard was established at Echunga in 1844 and by 1871 there were more than 500 ha. For many reasons the industry declined from the late 1800s with the result that, by 1930, no commercial plantings remained. The modern revival commenced in 1971 at Upper Hermitage, followed by Piccadilly Valley in the late 1970s. The major expansion occurred from the 1980s: today there are 2,691 ha. Of the 214 producers, 62% have fewer than 10 ha and only 15% have more than 25 ha. The main varieties planted are Chardonnay, Sauvignon Blanc, Pinot Noir, Cabernet Sauvignon and Shiraz.

Figure 2.16 A view of the Piccadilly Valley from Mt Lofty (Adelaide Hills region)

Regional resources

Most vineyards are planted on sloping land at elevations ranging from 300 to 560 m (average 400 m). The steepest land is generally on the west-facing steep scarps or tiers descending to Adelaide Plains. The climate is characterised by moderate growing season temperatures, high winter-dominant rainfall and moderate aridity. The coolest and wettest part of the region is to the north and north-east of Stirling extending to Uraidla and Lenswood. The warmest and driest are the western foothills, to the north of Gumeracha and the eastern foothills. There are two subregions that have been designated to date. The Lenswood subregion comprises land from 400 to 560 m (**TABLE 2.1c**). Vineyards are planted on east-facing slopes, close to tops of hills, for frost avoidance. Suitable sites are limited. It is cooler and wetter than the rest of the region with the exception of the adjacent Piccadilly Valley subregion. Vineyards in the Piccadilly Valley are mostly at 450 to 550 m (**TABLE 2.1d**; **FIGURE 2.16**). Annual rainfall is more than 1,000 mm. In this region, ripening is very sensitive to both aspect and altitude: a small difference in altitude, for example 50 m, may have a large effect on harvest date, for example, 10–12 days. There is also more season-to-season variation than in warmer regions. The chance of rain coinciding with ripening of late varieties is relatively high leading to a risk of fruit damage and bunch rot. Most soils are formed over basement rocks, but the variety of rock types and degree of weathering translates into a significant range of soils. Some are very shallow (**Class 3.2**) to shallow (**Class 4.3**), but most are deeper than 50 cm, and are duplex or gradational. Duplex soils with non-restrictive subsoils (**Classes 7.3 and 7.4**), and deep well structured gradational soils (**Class 9.6**) are most common. Duplex soils with restrictive subsoils (**Classes 6.2, 6.3, 6.4**) are limited to some lower slopes and flats, and hillslopes underlain by quartzitic rocks. Most topsoils are sandy loams to clay loams, and virtually all are naturally acidic. fine grained rocks (e.g. slates and siltstones) give rise to loamy soils, usually with clayey subsoils, while coarser grained rocks such as sandstones give rise to sandy or sandy loam soils. These generally have clayey subsoils as well. On upper slopes, ironstone gravelly variants of hillside soils are common. These overlie deeply weathered rocks that are kaolinitic and strongly acidic. On lower slopes and in valley floors, soils are deeper over alluvium. Clayey subsoils are typical (**Class 6.4**), but deep sandy gradational (**Class 9.2**) and deep loamy (**Class 9.6**) soils are not uncommon. Aquifers provide good quality water for irrigation in most parts of the region. The remainder is sourced from dams. There are no current restrictions on water use but construction of new dams is strictly controlled.

Management practices

This region has some of the highest planting densities in Australia: typical row x vine spacing is 2.1–2.8 m x 1.0–1.8 m. Trellising is VSP (80%) with divided systems such as Scott Henry and Smart-Dyson making up the rest. Typical yields for Chardonnay and Cabernet Sauvignon are 11 and 6.5 t/ha respectively. Most vineyards are mechanically pre-pruned with rigorous hand cleanup to regulate node numbers. More than half of the production is mechanically harvested. Less than 10% of the area is grafted (the main rootstock being 5C Teleki). The main soil management issues are control of acidity, and associated maintenance of general fertility in a high rainfall environment where leaching is accelerated. Management of waterlogging, particularly on lower slopes, is required at establishment (through mounding and drain installation). Erosion control is critical on steeper slopes, where severe damage can occur on inadequately managed sites. Limited irrigation (0.5 to 0.8 ML/ha) is widely used, exclusively applied by drip. The major problems are frost (controlled by sprinklers and fans), birds, disease, and poor set. Harvest of Chardonnay commences in late March to early April.

Summary

Viticulture in this region has expanded rapidly in recent times. It has become a source of premium fruit for winemaking, particularly sparkling wines. High land prices, competition with urban development and unpolluted catchment (this is the main source of water for the city of Adelaide) and environmental controls will limit future expansion.

2.6.3 Victoria

KING VALLEY[4] (*ZONE: NORTH EAST VICTORIA*)
The King Valley region bounds the Alpine Valleys region to the east. The main population centre Wangaratta (36.38°S, 146.31°E; 200 km north-east of Melbourne) lies at the northern end of the region where the King

Figure 2.17 A typical viticultural landscape in the King Valley region

River joins the Ovens River. Grapes were first grown at Milawa near Wangaratta in the 1880s. During the 1970s and 1980s, tobacco growers further up the valley changed to winegrapes. With grapevines planted near Whitfield at 800 m, the King Valley has some of the highest vineyards in Australia. The region has experienced substantial growth in recent years. There are 1,630 ha and the main varieties are Cabernet Sauvignon, Chardonnay, Shiraz, Merlot and Sauvignon Blanc.

Regional resources

Relatively flat land on the valley floor grades to steep and undulating country at elevations higher than 500 m (**FIGURE 2.17**). Temperature increases with elevation: for example, MJT at Milawa (200 m) is 21.7°C compared to 18.1°C for vineyards near Whitfield at 800 m (Gladstones 1992). As a result, maturity is up to 5 weeks later at Whitfield. Both growing season and annual rainfall are also relatively high. The latter ranges from 640 mm at Wangaratta up to 1,410 mm near Whitfield. At the higher elevations, the best sites are found on north-facing slopes with good air drainage and protection from incursion of cold air masses from nearby snowfields (Gladstones 1992). Red and brown gradational soils (**Classes 9.5, 9.6**) are widespread throughout the region. In the higher rainfall areas they are generally strongly acidic throughout. These soils can occur in many landscapes (from lower terraces to mountains) and have developed on a range of rock types. Fine grained gradational soils (**Class 9.8**) that are high in free iron oxide usually occur on deeply weathered basaltic parent materials and have only a limited distribution—they occur mainly on hilly country to the west of the King River, where they are limited to basalt residuals on broad plateaux and broad ridges.

Management practices

Phylloxera is present in the region and is spreading throughout the valley. Planting on rootstocks is therefore essential with Schwarzmann being the most common rootstock, followed by 99 Richter, 5C Teleki and SO4.

[4] Interim decision on GI at August 2004 (E. Sullivan, pers.comm.)

High summer rainfall results in high disease pressure. Bunch rots are the major disease problem, although downy mildew can also be a problem. Vigour is high. Divided trellises are used almost universally, to open up the canopy to assist with disease management and ripening. Approximately 50% of all vineyards use a two-wire 'ballerina' trellis with most of the remainder using a single wire 'ballerina'. Smart-Dyson, Scott Henry and VSP (with arched canes) trellises are also used. Most vineyards are mechanically pruned and harvested. Typical row x vine spacing in young vineyards is 2.8 x 2.2 m. Drip irrigation is widely used (approximately 0.8 ML/ha/season). Irrigation water is mainly sourced from streams, with a small amount from dams. Typical yields are 12 to 18 t/ha for both Chardonnay and Shiraz. Harvest of Chardonnay commences in late February in the warmest parts of the region. Frost, hail and bushfires are potential problems.

Summary

While this is a challenging region in many respects, it has experienced substantial growth in recent years to become a major producer of winegrapes.

PYRENEES (*ZONE: WESTERN VICTORIA*)

The Pyrenees region is bounded by the Bendigo region to the east and the Grampians region to the west. Although vineyards were first planted in this region during the mid-1800s they had largely disappeared by the turn of the century. The present vineyard development commenced in the early 1960s, initially for the production of grapes for brandy but the current emphasis is on table wine grapes, produced from 657 ha. The principal varieties include Shiraz, Cabernet Sauvignon, Pinot Noir and Chardonnay. Vineyards are planted near Avoca (37.08°S, 143.48°E; 175 km north-west of Melbourne), Moonambel and Landsborough on the slopes of the Pyrenees Ranges, mainly between 250 and 300 m elevation. The climate is similar to the Grampians with slightly higher temperatures and lower rainfall during the growing season (**TABLE 2.1c**). This region is characterised by alluvial valleys, sedimentary hills and the Pyrenees Ranges. The hills and mountains of the Pyrenees Ranges are composed of Cambrian sandstones and slates. Common soils on these slopes are shallow texture contrast types (**Class 7.3**), with stony fine sandy loam to loam surface soils and bleached sandy loam subsurface horizons, overlying slightly to moderately acidic red to yellowish red clay subsoils (at around 20-30 cm depth) that can often be stony. Yellow clay subsoils are more common in areas where site drainage is more restricted. Soil profile depths are usually less than one metre over weathered rock. On the steeper slopes and ridge tops shallow stony uniform textured loamy soils (**Class 4.3**) are most prevalent. On hills and rises composed of Ordovician sediments, more

Figure 2.18 A contour-planted vineyard on sloping ground at Great Western (Grampians region)

restrictive duplex soils (**Class 6.3**) are common. Most vineyards have limited irrigation, mainly drip, supplied from dams or underground sources. Trellis systems used include VSP. Harvest commences in mid-March (Chardonnay).

GRAMPIANS (*ZONE: WESTERN VICTORIA*)

The Grampians region lies between the Henty region (south-west) and the Pyrenees region (east). Major towns in the region include Ararat (37.28°S, 142.95°E) and Stawell. The Grampians region includes the subregion of Great Western (220 km north-west of Melbourne) at an elevation of 240 to 320 m. Great Western has a long history of grapegrowing: vines were first planted in 1868. By 1900, there were about 800 ha of vineyards. Although the area subsequently declined for economic reasons, Great Western continued to produce wine during the twentieth century, with up to 180 ha maintained until the mid-1980s. With modest expansion in the 1990s at Great Western and elsewhere in the region (particularly near Ararat), the planted area reached 726 ha by 2001. The principal varieties include Shiraz, Chardonnay, Riesling and Cabernet Sauvignon. The topography is moderately undulating (**FIGURE 2.18**). The early vineyards at Great Western were planted on the flat land but, in order to reduce frost risk, newer vineyards have been planted on slopes. Minimum temperatures are relatively low, leading to the likelihood of late spring frosts, a major problem in the region. The area around Ararat (**TABLE 2.1c**) is cooler than Great Western although rainfall is similar. The Grampians Range is a system of strike ridges, mountains and valleys. Surrounding areas to the east (Ararat, Great Western region) are mainly dissected uplands comprised of various sedimentary rocks. Soil profiles are generally texture contrast (mainly Category 7 with some Category 6) although there is a variety of other soils in the region, including sandy soils (**Class 9.1**) surrounding the Grampians Range to the east, and cracking clays (Category 5) mainly to the east of Stawell. Non-restrictive texture contrast soils (**Classes 7.3, 7.4**) are common on slopes of the undulating plains and hills around Great Western. Marginally sodic subsoils also exist in some areas (**Classes 6.3, 6.4**). Near Stawell and Ararat, texture contrast soils are common: **Class 7.4** (with some **6.4**) in the fomer and **Class 7.3** (with some **6.3**) in the latter. Irrigation water is sourced mainly from dams with some treated waste water available in the Ararat district. A range of trellis systems is used, mainly single wire and VSP. Cane pruning is still common. Harvest commences in mid-March (Chardonnay). Production is limited by frost, water stress and mediocre soils. The subregion of Great Western of the Grampians region has long been associated in Australia with sparkling wine. However, it is now better known for its table wines.

BEECHWORTH (ZONE: NORTH EAST VICTORIA)

Beechworth is a small region, adjoining the Alpine Valleys region to the south and the Rutherglen region to the north. A large proportion of the region is forest and included in national parks. It is centred on the historic gold-mining town of Beechworth (36.37°S, 146.71°E), 250 km north-east of Melbourne. Beechworth is distinguished from Rutherglen by being more elevated (vineyards are found at 300 to 600 metres) and much cooler (**TABLE 2.1c**). Beechworth also has higher rainfall. One outstanding feature of the climate of this region is the great variability of minimum temperatures resulting in very serious frost risk (Gladstones 1992). The region is typified by granite hills forming a plateau. The soils around the Beechworth plateau are generally high in coarse sand and fine gravel content and reasonably well drained (**Classes 7.3, 7.4**). Hill slopes and river terraces may have gradational profiles (**Class 9.6**)—these are favoured over duplex profiles as they are less prone to waterlogging. Vineyards in the region are small. The total area is less than 100 ha and the main varieties are Chardonnay, Cabernet Sauvignon, Shiraz and Pinot Noir.

SUNBURY (ZONE: PORT PHILLIP)

This region is situated on the north western outskirts of Melbourne. Vines were first planted at Sunbury (37.58°S, 144.73°E) in the late 1850s. While there has been some recent development within the region, plantings remain relatively small. Total planted area is 104 ha and the principal varieties include Chardonnay, Sauvignon Blanc, Cabernet Sauvignon and Shiraz. Topography is flat to undulating. Elevation ranges from 50 m to 400 m (the latter is the northern boundary with the Macedon Ranges region). The climate is similar to the Yarra Valley with only moderate rainfall (**TABLE 2.1c**). The region is located on part of an extensive undulating volcanic plain. Grey cracking clay soils (**Class 5.1**) are common—they are typically strongly sodic, alkaline and coarsely structured. Other soils in this region include **Classes 6.3** and **6.4**. Drip irrigation is

common and water is sourced from dams and creeks. Strong southerly winds may limit productivity. The potential for further expansion is limited due to competition with urban development.

YARRA VALLEY (ZONE: PORT PHILLIP)

Grapevines were first planted in the Yarra Valley in 1838 and by the 1870s there were 1,200 ha. Vineyards had largely disappeared by the 1920s for economic reasons. There was renewed interest in the region for table wine production from the late 1960s: the first wave of expansion resulted in 120 ha by the mid-1980s. However, the greatest growth of both vineyards and wineries took place during the 1990s. There are now 2,570 ha and the main varieties are Chardonnay, Pinot Noir, Cabernet Sauvignon, Sauvignon Blanc, Shiraz and Merlot. Vineyards are found around and to the north, east and south of Lilydale (35 km north-east of Melbourne), and near to Coldstream, Yarra Glen, Dixons Creek, Healesville (37.68°S, 145.53°E), St Andrews and Seville.

Regional resources

Most vineyards are planted on gentle to moderately steep slopes up to 200 m (**FIGURE 1.14**). The climate is moderately maritime with low radiation, high growing season rainfall and relative humidity (**TABLE 2.1c**), leading to problems with fungal diseases. Low-lying vineyards are susceptible to spring frost damage. The best sites are found on isolated or projecting hills. The region is characterised by alluvial flats associated with the Yarra River and surrounding low hills and hills of sedimentary origin. Texture contrast soils are common: they have very fine sandy clay loam surfaces with bleached subsurface horizons of similar texture, overlying mottled yellow and grey light to medium clay subsoils that are typically strongly acidic (**Classes 6.3, 6.4**). Related soils have a more gradual clay increase with depth (**Classes 9.7, 9.8**). Depth of surface horizons can be quite variable (typically 10–20 cm). In some of the more elevated areas on basalt-capped hillsides, soils are well structured, acidic, iron-rich with gradational texture profiles (**Class 9.8**). However, the presence of basalt is not always a guarantee of good drainage as perched water tables can occur, and profiles may remain waterlogged for several months. The basalt generally gives way to texture contrast soils further down the slope.

Management practices

Row x vine spacing is 3.0–3.25 x 1.5–1.8 m. The most common trellis is VSP (> 66% of vineyards). Mechanical pruning is not common although most fruit is mechanically harvested. Many vineyards use drip irrigation to counter the effects of mid-summer water-stress. Water is mainly sourced from dams. A small number of vineyards have access to irrigation water from the Yarra River and its tributaries. Excess vine vigour can occur on the deeper soils. Plantings are predominantly on own roots. Regular preventive spraying is essential for control of fungal diseases. Frost control methods include the use of helicopters, sprinklers and burning straw bales. Typical yields range from 7 to 11 t/ha for Chardonnay and Cabernet Sauvignon and 3 to 10 t/ha for Shiraz. Achieving adequate fruit maturity may be difficult in cool seasons. Harvest of Chardonnay commences in late March. Bird pests, particularly starlings, are a problem.

Figure 2.19 A vineyard in the Mornington Peninsula region

Summary

The region has a reputation for producing high quality wines. Its proximity to Melbourne has been of benefit to the development of the region by facilitating tourism, although in terms of future expansion for vineyards, there is competition with the residential use of land

GEELONG (*ZONE: PORT PHILLIP*)

Vineyards were established near Geelong (38.12°S, 144.37°E; 70 km south-west of Melbourne) on the western side of Port Phillip Bay in the early 1840s. By the 1870s there were several hundred hectares. However, by the turn of the century the industry had all but disappeared due to the combination of phylloxera and government-sponsored uprooting programs. The modern era of grapegrowing dates from the 1960s. Vineyards are now found in most parts of the region. There are 480 ha and the principal varieties include Chardonnay, Riesling, Sauvignon Blanc, Pinot Noir, Shiraz and Cabernet Sauvignon. The topography is generally moderately undulating at 20 to 300 m, with some steeper slopes in the north and north west up to 350 m. The climate is maritime and moderately sunny with relatively low rainfall, both growing season and annual (**TABLE 2.1c**). Spring frosts may be a problem in low-lying areas. The Bellarine Peninsula is characterised by alluvial plains and terraces surrounding a higher weakly dissected plateau. Dissected ranges, the Barrabool Hills, are also used for viticulture.

The main soils are texture contrast, with hard setting sandy loams overlying neutral to alkaline, often sodic, yellow clay subsoils (**Classes 6.3, 6.4**), or neutral, better-structured, red clay subsoils (**Classes 7.3, 7.4**). The coastal strip along Corio Bay and areas closer to Geelong, and extending westwards to Winchelsea, are more likely to have alkaline red clay subsoils. Dark cracking clays (**Classes 5.2, 5.3**) occur on parts of the larger hills. Most vineyards have limited irrigation (less than 1 ML/ha/season) sourced from surface storage. VSP is the most common trellis system. Both cane and spur pruning are used. Major problems are fungal diseases, light brown apple moth, birds and wind. Production is limited by water stress and poor fruit set. Harvest of Chardonnay commences in late March. Geelong has developed a reputation for the quality of wines produced from Pinot Noir and Chardonnay.

MORNINGTON PENINSULA (*ZONE: PORT PHILLIP*)

The Mornington Peninsula region lies immediately to the south of Melbourne, on the eastern side of Port Phillip Bay. Vines were first planted in the region in the 1890s. However, commercial viticulture did not commence, albeit on a small scale, until the 1970s. Major vineyard expansion took place during the late 1980s and 1990s. The average vineyard is small. Plantings total 520 ha and the main varieties are Chardonnay, Pinot Noir, Cabernet Sauvignon, Sauvignon Blanc and Riesling. Vineyards extend from Mornington (38.40°S, 145.04°E) in the north to the western shore of Western Port Bay in the south. The peninsula rises steeply from sea level at Dromana to a central ridge about 250 m high in the Red Hill district and then falls away to the coastal strip at Merricks and Balnarring. The climate is maritime, humid and moderately sunny. Mornington (46 m; **TABLE 2.1c**) is the warmest location on the Peninsula; the more elevated sites tend to be cooler and wetter. The region is relatively frost-free. Lack of continentality may lead to budburst and set problems with susceptible varieties. The Mornington Peninsula is a moderately dissected ridge comprising a mix of landforms, including undulating plains, rolling low hills and dunefields (**FIGURE 2.19**). Viticulture occurs most commonly on texture contrast soils developed on Tertiary sediments (mainly sandstone). Surface soils are commonly dark greyish brown fine sandy loams to fine sandy clay loams with bleached subsurface layers, which may also contain iron oxide concretions. Yellowish brown, often mottled with reddish brown and grey, medium clay appears abruptly below the bleached horizon, generally at around 35 cm (**Class 6.4**). Subsoil clays tend to be slightly acidic to neutral and well structured. Another major soil type used for viticulture occurs on the rolling low hills of Tertiary basalts (e.g. Red Hill). These soils are red, well structured, friable and earthy in appearance and are strongly acidic as well as having a high free iron oxide content (**Class 9.8**). Bunch rots can be a significant problem. Limited irrigation is relatively common. Vigour may be high on some soil types. A range of trellis systems is used including Scott Henry, VSP and lyre. Use of shelterbelts is desirable in exposed sites. Harvest of Chardonnay commences in late March.

VITICULTURE 1: RESOURCES

STRATHBOGIE RANGES (*ZONE: CENTRAL VICTORIA*)

The Strathbogie Ranges is a small region on the eastern side of the Hume Highway, from just north of Seymour (approximately 120 km to the north-east of Melbourne) to just north of Violet Town. It lies between the Goulburn Valley region and the proposed region of Central Victorian High Country. The region's modern wine history commenced with the planting of the Mt Helen vineyard in 1975. The principal varieties include Chardonnay, Riesling, Cabernet Sauvignon, Merlot and Shiraz. Vineyard sites can be found from 160 to 600 m. The more elevated area around Strathbogie (36.85°S, 145.73°E) is cool, with a high annual and growing season rainfall (**TABLE 2.1c**). The Strathbogie region is dominated by granite hills that are characterised by duplex soils (**Class 7.4**), with **Class 9.5** soils on steeper slopes and **Classes 6.3** and **6.4** on older alluvial plains. Phylloxera was discovered for the first time in the region in 2000. The major problems are spring frost, birds and fungal diseases.

(*ZONE: GIPPSLAND*)

The zone of Gippsland is in south-east Victoria (**FIGURE 1.1**). There has been slow growth since the first vineyards of the modern era were established in the 1970s. Vineyards are located near to Leongatha, Moe, Traralgon, Sale, Bairnsdale (37.88°S, 147.56°E) and Lakes Entrance. The total planted area is 185 ha and the main varieties are Pinot Noir, Chardonnay, Shiraz, Cabernet Sauvignon and Riesling. The climate is maritime and humid with moderate growing season rainfall (**TABLE 2.1c**). Soils are variable. In the area between Leongatha and Moe, friable red soils developed on Tertiary basalt are common: these soils are well drained, strongly acidic and high in free iron oxide. In the lower rainfall area to the east of Traralgon, texture contrast soils that have sodic subsoils are more common. Problems include poor set, fungal diseases, strong winds, frost (in more elevated locations) and birds.

2.6.4 NEW SOUTH WALES

SHOALHAVEN COAST (*ZONE: SOUTH COAST*)

This is a new and little-known region. It covers a relatively narrow coastal strip, extending from Kiama in the north to Batemans Bay in the south. There are fewer than 20 vineyards, mainly located in the north near Berry and Nowra (34.94°S, 150.55°E; 120 km south of Sydney). Total area is approximately 70 ha and the principal varieties include Chambourcin, Verdelho, Chardonnay, Semillon, Sauvignon Blanc, Shiraz and Cabernet Sauvignon. The climate is maritime, cloudy and very humid with a high, summer-dominant rainfall (**TABLE 2.1c**). Consequently, disease pressure is very high.

SOUTHERN HIGHLANDS (*ZONE: SOUTH COAST*)

The 20 or so vineyards in this region were mainly planted in the 1990s. It is north-west of, but not adjoining, the Shoalhaven Coast region. Bowral (35.50°S, 150.40°E), in the centre of the region, is 100 km south of Sydney. The principal varieties include Chardonnay and Cabernet Sauvignon. At this high elevation, the climate is cool and humid with a high summer-dominant rainfall (**TABLE 2.1c**). Disease pressure is very high. Harvest is very late (May).

TUMBARUMBA (*ZONE: SOUTHERN NSW*)

Tumbarumba is an emerging viticultural region, situated at the edge of the Australian Alps. The first vineyards were planted in the early 1980s, initially for the production of grapes for sparkling wine. Today there are approximately 200 ha. The main varieties are Pinot Noir, Chardonnay, Sauvignon Blanc, Merlot and Meunier. Most vineyards are found at an elevation of 550 to 800 m in close proximity to the township of Tumbarumba (32.76°S, 148.02°E; 375 km south-west of Sydney). The land is generally sloping and undulating, with most vineyards planted on hill slopes. The soils are derived from sedimentary shales and siltstones, granite-based materials or basalts. The climate is continental and sunny (**TABLE 2.1c**). Rainfall is evenly spread. The short growing season is limited by the occurrence of spring and autumn frosts. The main trellis types are VSP, Scott Henry and single wire. Vigour can be excessive due to the combination of good soils and high rainfall. Disease pressure is high in most seasons. Canopy management is generally more intensive than in most other Australian regions. Frost may have a significant impact on both yield and harvest date. Frost protection measures are widely used: these include overhead sprinklers and frost fans. Most vineyards are spur pruned by hand and harvesting is a combination of hand and machine, depending on winemaker requirements. Harvest commences in late March (Chardonnay). Tumbarumba is a challenging viticultural environment. However, it has proven to be a producer of high value fruit, particularly for sparkling wine.

CANBERRA DISTRICT (*ZONE: SOUTHERN NSW*)

The largest proportion of the vineyard area of this region is found to the north-west, north, north-east and east of the Australian Capital Territory boundary at an elevation of 500 to 800 m. The Hilltops region lies to the north-west. The first vineyards were planted in the early 1970s; there are now approximately 400 ha. The main varieties are Shiraz, Chardonnay, Riesling, Cabernet Sauvignon and Merlot. There is a concentration of vineyards close to the village of Murrumbateman, 40 km north of Canberra (35.30°S, 149.10°E) where the topography is undulating with open, flat valleys. The land to the east of the Yass River is more elevated. The climate is moderately continental and sunny (**TABLE 2.1c**). More than 50% of annual rainfall falls during the growing season but variability is high. There is a high risk of severe frost until November. Passive methods of frost control are most common (see Volume II, Chapter 8). Row x vine spacing is 2.75–3.0 m x 1.5–1.8 m and the main trellis systems are VSP and two-wire vertical. The majority of vineyards are mechanically pruned and harvested. Typical yields are 2 to 10 t/ha for Chardonnay and Cabernet Sauvignon. Less than 5% of the area is grafted to resistant rootstocks. Irrigation is common, mainly by drip (0.5 to 1.0 ML/ha/season). The main sources of water for irrigation are bores and dams (85%) and treated waste water (15%). The main problems are frost, birds and acid soils. Harvest commences in early March (Chardonnay).

ORANGE (*ZONE: CENTRAL RANGES*)

Although this region has always been an important centre for fruit production, including tablegrapes, it was not until the early 1980s that winegrape vineyards were first established on the slopes of Mount Canobolas (1,400 m). Today there are approximately 1,300 ha near to the town of Orange (33.32°S, 149.05°E; 270 km north-west of Sydney). The main varieties are Cabernet Sauvignon, Chardonnay, Merlot and Sauvignon Blanc with increasing interest in Pinot Gris and Sangiovese. Most vineyards are found on hilly and undulating country at 600 to 1,000 m elevation, making this the highest wine region in Australia. Temperature regime and variety choice are very dependent upon elevation. The climate is moderately continental, sunny, not arid and humid (**TABLE 2.1c**). The annual rainfall of 800–900 mm is reasonably uniformly distributed with the driest period being March–April when grapes ripen. Summer storms from the north may cause problems but they are usually brief. The relatively high humidity during ripening necessitates the use of good canopy management in order to reduce disease problems. Vineyard sites are mostly on hillsides to enable cold air to drain freely and minimise the risk of frost. The main soil types include deep red well structured medium to fine

textured soils of basalt origin (near Mt Canobolas), shallow sedimentary gravels, red and yellow loamy gradational soils, and red and brown texture contrast soils. Some shallow soils over calcareous rocks occur near 600–700 m elevation. Irrigation water is sourced mainly from bores and dams. Most vines have moderate to high vigour as a result of reasonable rainfall, fertile soils and mild summer temperatures. Canopy management (e.g. trellis system, shoot thinning, leaf removal) and crop control are important for disease control and optimisation of ripening. VSP and Smart-Dyson trellising are most common to carry moderate crops (8 to 12 t/ha). Harvest date is very dependent upon elevation: it commences in late March (Chardonnay) at 850 m and early May at 960 m (Beeston 2002). Most vineyards are irrigated by drip (0.5–2.0 ML/ha). The major problems are frost, hail, fungal diseases particularly botrytis bunch rot, and lightbrown apple moth. Climate is the major challenge to grape production in Orange, with site selection being vitally important. This impacts heavily on the ability to ripen fruit and also disease pressure.

2.7 Regions with MJT < 19.0°C

2.7.1 SOUTH AUSTRALIA

ADELAIDE HILLS (*ZONE: MOUNT LOFTY RANGES*)
Parts of this region at high elevations have an MJT less than 19°C (**TABLE 2.1d**). [See 2.5.2].

MOUNT BENSON (*ZONE: LIMESTONE COAST*)
A trial vineyard was established at Cape Jaffa in 1978 but commercial development did not take place until the late 1980s, with major expansion in the 1990s. Located 300 km south-east of Adelaide, today there are 500 ha. The main varieties planted are Cabernet Sauvignon, Shiraz, Chardonnay, Merlot and Sauvignon Blanc. The adjacent proposed region of Robe (37.16°S, 139.76°E), 10 km to the south, has 240 ha. The climate is very maritime,

Table 2.1d. Regions with mean January temperature (MJT) less than 19.0°C.

Region	State	Station	Elevation (m)	MJT[x] °C	CTL °C	ARF mm	GSRF mm	GSRD	GSE mm	ARID mm	RH %	SSH
Adelaide Hills	SA	23785 Stirling	496	18.7	10.7	1118	329	56	(900)	(121)	60	8.7[a]
Macedon Ranges	Vic.	88036 Kyneton	509	18.5	12.7	753	293	43	895[b]	154	58	(8.0)
Mount Benson	SA	26026 Robe	3	18.3	7.1	633	167	48	(980)	(323)	68	(7.8)
Henty	Vic	90048 Heywood	26	17.7	8.4	820	285	70	(850)	(140)	70	7.3[a]
Launceston*	Tas.	c	71	17.7	10.6	730	290	52	(850)	(135)	69	8.1[a]
St Helens*	Tas.	92033 St Helens	5	17.4	9.2	775	372	62	-	-	68	7.8
Hobart*	Tas.	94029 Hobart	50	16.7	8.6	619	308	65	709	47	60	7.0

[a] Gladstones (1992)
[b] 88042 Malmsbury Reservoir
[c] Composite of 91123 Launceston Mt Pleasant and 91237 Launceston Ti Tree

[x] See 2.1.1 and 2.1.2 in text for explanation of codes
* Not GI regions – see text for explanation
( ) Denotes estimate

similar to that of Coonawarra but with less diurnal variation (**TABLE 2.1d**). Budburst is earlier than Coonawarra but harvest is 7–10 days later. This is an undulating landscape formed on consolidated (lime-cemented) sands of old coastal dunes. This material is called calcarenite. Most of the soils are very shallow (**Classes 3.3, 3.4**) to shallow (**Classes 4.1, 4.2**) over calcarenite. Ripping of the calcarenite is required for vineyard establishment to enable the installation of trellises, and also to provide sufficient rooting depth for the vine. Substantial volumes of rock brought to the surface may need to be carted away following ripping. Deep sands (**Class 9.1**) and thick sandy duplex soils (**Class 7.2**) occur on accumulations of windblown sands, particularly on east-facing slopes. Protection from strong winds is desirable. Good quality water for irrigation is available from an aquifer: at present there are no restrictions. Management practices are similar to Wrattonbully. With 40% of the vineyard area grafted to rootstocks (mainly Schwarzmann, 5A Teleki, 5C Teleki, 1103 Paulsen and Ramsey) this is a relatively high proportion for South Australia. Also, the proportion of organic vineyards is high. Most vineyards are irrigated by drip at 0.8–1.5 ML/ha per annum. Typical yields for Chardonnay and Shiraz are 4 to 10 and 5 to 15 t/ha respectively. Disease risk is low. The main problems are frost (controlled by fans and soil management) and wind.

2.7.2 VICTORIA

MACEDON RANGES (*ZONE: PORT PHILLIP*)

This region lies between the Sunbury region (to the south) and the Bendigo and Heathcote regions (to the north). The modern era of viticulture dates from the late 1960s when a vineyard was established near Kyneton (37.27°S, 144.42°E; 85 km north-west of Melbourne) in the centre of the region. Further plantings followed in the 1970s; however major expansion did not take place until the 1990s. Today there are many small vineyards, mainly found near Gisborne, Macedon, Romsey, Lancefield and Kyneton. The total area is 377 ha and the principal varieties include Pinot Noir, Chardonnay, Cabernet Sauvignon and Shiraz. The land is undulating at 400 to 600 m elevation. The climate at Kyneton (509 m) is cool with only moderate growing season rainfall (348 mm during October to April) (**TABLE 2.1d**). The coolest sites are found near Kyneton and Romsey where most vineyards have been planted at elevations from 550 to 750 m, with elevation reaching 1,011 m at Mount Macedon; the climate is much cooler at these elevated sites. The strong, cold, prevailing winds from the south inhibit shoot growth, reduce yields and probably delay maturity: the use of windbreaks is strongly recommended on most sites. Vineyards are planted on a range of soil types from deep loams to granitic sandy-loams. Irrigation (drip) is required at many sites, due to

the combined effects of low growing season rainfall and poor soil water retention. Limited water is available from dams and bores. Yields are low due to the combined effects of wind and water stress. Canopy management practices (e.g. divided trellises, leaf and bunch removal) are widely used. Harvest is relatively late, even extending to mid-June in some years. Other problems include birds and frost. The region has developed a reputation for sparkling wine. Careful site selection is required because many areas within this region are only marginal for viticulture.

HENTY (*ZONE: WESTERN VICTORIA*)

The region of Henty in south-west Victoria shares its western border with South Australia. Bass Strait lies to the south. The main population centres are Warrnambool, Portland and Hamilton. The main land-use is grazing. A vineyard was established in 1964 by the Seppelt wine company at Drumborg near Heywood (38.14°S, 141.62°E, 280 km WSW of Melbourne). Today there are relatively few small vineyards totalling 223 ha dispersed throughout the region but mainly concentrated near Portland and Hamilton. The main varieties are Pinot Noir, Chardonnay, Meunier, Shiraz, Riesling, Cabernet Sauvignon and Sauvignon Blanc. The topography is flat to undulating. The climate in the south-west is very maritime (**TABLE 2.1D**). Annual rainfall is high and, although growing season rainfall is moderate, the number of raindays is high. Well drained red volcanic soils to the west of Portland and Heywood occur in association with texture contrast soils with yellow to brown subsoils. Texture contast soils with slightly acid to neutral brown to red clay subsoils are also common around Hamilton. The main problems are poor fruitset, frost (for inland sites), fungal diseases particularly bunch rot, birds and wind. The region has some of the latest maturing winegrapes in Australia: harvest of Chardonnay commences in mid-to late April.

2.7.3 TASMANIA

(*ZONE: TASMANIA*)

Grapegrowing commenced in this state in the 1820s but remained insignificant until the 1970s when the first of the present-day vineyards was planted. The industry developed rapidly from the 1980s. Vineyards are found in seven winegrowing areas within Tasmania (as defined by the Tasmanian Commissioner for Licencing). The three 'northern' areas, North West (20 ha), Tamar Valley (259 ha) and North East (243 ha) are largely found between Launceston (41.43°S, 147.16°E) and the north coast. The vineyards of the East Coast (52 ha) are located mainly between Bicheno and Swansea, a distance of approximately 30 km. The three 'southern' areas, Coal Valley (18 ha), Derwent Valley (49 ha) and Huon/Channel (40 ha) are confined to the south-east of

Figure 2.20 A vineyard on the Tamar River, Tasmania

the island within a 50 km radius of Hobart (42.89°S, 147.33°E). The average vineyard is small: of the 143 producers, 70% have fewer than 5 ha. Seventy-five per cent of grape production comes from the Tamar Valley and North East. The main varieties grown are Pinot Noir, Chardonnay, Riesling, Cabernet Sauvignon and Sauvignon Blanc.

Regional resources

All areas are very cool with rainfall varying from moderate (300 mm) to high (1,300 mm) (TABLE 2.1d). Most vineyards are located close to the coast and exposed to cold winds, however, frost risk is generally low. The preferred sites are at relatively low altitude (less than 100 m), 5 to 20 km inland or along river valleys (FIGURE 2.20), on ENE- to NNW-facing slopes with good wind protection and with well drained soils. Soils are predominantly uniform/gradational and duplex with restrictive subsoils (Classes 6.1-6.4). The most common of the uniform/gradational soils are deep well structured clayey types (Class 9.8) formed on basalts in the North East, on basaltic colluvium in the Tamar Valley, and on dolerites in the east coast, Derwent and Coal Valleys. Duplex soils form on sandstones in the North East and the Coal and Derwent Valleys, on Tertiary clay sediments in river basins, and on mudstones in the Huon Valley. Deep hard clayey (Class 9.7) and loamy (Class 9.5) soils occur on mudstones in the Huon Valley, and deep sandy gradational soils (Class 9.2) and deep bleached sands (Class 9.1) occur on windblown sand in the Tamar, Coal and Derwent Valleys. Cracking clays (Class 5.2) formed on dolerite or basalt occur in the Coal Valley, east coast and Tamar areas.

Management practices

Most vineyards have close row spacings, ranging from 1.2 to 2.4 m and vine spacings of 1 to 1.2 m; some vineyards have wide rows (3.6 m) with divided canopies, e.g. the 'lyre' system, Scott Henry. Excessive vegetative growth is a problem in many vineyards: canopy

management by summer pruning, shoot positioning and training system is essential. Regular spraying for fungal disease control is required. Cane pruning is most common. Most vineyards have drip irrigation to counter the effects of short-term droughts. Yields are low to moderate: the average yield (1998 to 2001) was 7 t/ha. The degree of exposure to cold winds during flowering and fruitset (mid-December to early January) has a large effect on yield; Cabernet Sauvignon and Merlot are particularly susceptible to poor set. Well-sheltered vineyards have recorded yields up to 15 t/ha. Harvest is very late, e.g. Chardonnay in early to mid-April, Cabernet Sauvignon in late May.

Summary

There has been considerable recent interest in grapegrowing in this state, particularly for the production of fruit for sparkling wine, premium pinot noir and aromatic white wines.

2.8 Concluding Remarks

In a relatively short time, the Australian wine industry has become a major player in the international export trade. This success has been largely based on 'branded, non-regional, commodity wine'. The time is now ripe for the industry to be more active in promoting the many and varied Australian wine regions and their 'regionally differentiated quality wine' products on the international stage (Croser 2004).

The following generalisations can be made about the viticultural regions of Australia:

(i)   Water supply is the major factor that limits yield. Most areas have winter-dominant rainfall, and soil depth is rarely adequate to store a full year's requirements. The highest yields are obtained under irrigation—84 per cent of Australian vineyards receive some irrigation.

(ii) The varietal spectrum is still relatively limited despite the large number of varieties now available (see Chapter 6). There is little regional specialisation of specific varieties.

(iii) Most traditional regions have a relatively low incidence of fungal diseases due to low rainfall and humidity during the growing season. The Hunter Valley is a notable exception.

(iv) Although the traditional regions are mainly in warm to hot climates, much of the recent vineyard expansion has taken place in warm to cool regions.

REFERENCES

Suggestions for further reading are marked (•).

Australian Bureau of Meteorology [Online, accessed July 2003]. URL: http://www.bom.gov.au

Australian Wine and Brandy Corporation [Online, accessed July 2003]. URL: http://www.awbc.com.au/winelaw/gi/index.asp#Section (a) Geographical Indications

- Beeston, J. (2002) The Wine Regions of Australia (Allen & Unwin: Crows Nest).

Boehm, E.W. (1970) Vine development and temperature in the Barossa, South Australia. Exp. Record, South Aust. Dept. Agric. **5**, 16-24.

Croser, B. (2004) Brand or authenticity? Aust. NZ Wine Industry J. **19** (2), 12-21.

- Dry, P.R. and Smart, R.E. (1988) The Grapegrowing Regions of Australia. In: Viticulture Vol. 1 Resources, 1st edn. Eds B.G. Coombe and P.R. Dry (Winetitles: Adelaide), pp. 37-60.

French, R.J., Armstrong, F.W. et al. (1978) Vineyards of the Barossa. Dep. Agric. South Aust., Soil Cons. Rep. 17/78.

Giddings, J., Kelly, S. et al. (2002) Winegrape irrigation benchmarking Murray Darling and Swan Hill 1998-2002. In: Proc. of a Seminar 'Managing Water', Mildura 2002 (Aust. Soc. Vitic. and Oen.: Adelaide), pp. 15-18.

Gladstones, J.S. (1965) The climate and soils of south western Western Australia in relation to vinegrowing. J. Aust. Inst. Agric. Sci. **31**, 275-88.

- Gladstones, J.S. (1992) Viticulture and Environment (Winetitles: Adelaide).

Maschmedt, D. J., Fitzpatrick, R. W. et al.(2002) Key for identifying categories of vineyard soils in Australia. CSIRO Land and Water Technical Report No. 30/02.

Olmo, H.P. (1956) A Survey of the Grape Industry of Western Australia (Vine Fruits Research Trust: Perth).

Smart, R.E. and Coombe. B.G. (1983) Water relations of grapevines. In: Water Deficits and Plant Growth, Vol. VII. Ed T.T. Kozlowski (Academic Press: New York), pp. 138-196.

Smart, R.E. and Dry, P.R. (1979) Vineyard Site Selection (Roseworthy Agric. College: South Australia), 163 pp.

Smart, R.E. and Dry, P.R. (1980) A climatic classification of Australian viticultural regions. Aust. Grapegrower & Winemaker No. 196, 8-16.

Winemakers Federation of Australia (2002) Vintage. The Australian Wine Industry Statistical Yearbook 2002 (Winetitles: Adelaide).

CHAPTER 3

Soils and Australian Viticulture

D. J. MASCHMEDT

The relationships between soil characteristics and grape and wine quality have traditionally received little attention in Australia. This contrasts with parts of Europe where great emphasis is placed on the concept of 'terroir' as espoused by Seguin (1986). This may in part be due to the widespread belief that grapevines will grow in a wide range of soils, and that climate and topography are the over-riding considerations. White (2003) challenges this view with a comprehensive account of soil-grape-wine relationships. Regardless of the adaptability of the grape vine, it only grows best when its requirements for nutrients and moisture are fully met (Northcote 1984). In Australia, the most important characteristic of a soil for growing grapevines is its capacity to supply moisture, whilst at the same time remaining sufficiently well drained to avoid periodic oxygen deficiency arising from waterlogging of the rootzone. Because of this, those properties that affect the water-holding status and the aeration of soil will be discussed in some detail.

Whilst managers of most commercial crop species aim for optimum production in terms of yield, the viticulturist commonly places quality considerations above tonnage. Enhancing quality at the expense of yield may be achieved through soil moisture control or reduced fertilizer application, but may also result from stress imposed on the vine by 'adverse' soil conditions. For example, a 'tight' clayey subsoil, hard pan or rock layer at shallow depth restricts root growth of most plants, including grapevines, causing moisture stress. Yields of virtually all plants are reduced under these conditions; but in grapevines, berry quality may also be enhanced. However, soil properties that induce stress on the vine may also signal potential longer term problems. For example, the tight clay, which may be linked to quality fruit, is also likely to prevent salt leaching, possibly resulting in a long term accumulation of undesirable sodium and chloride in the rootzone. These 'double-edged sword' characteristics of soils are complex and not well understood. For this reason, the focus in this chapter is on the soil as a medium for healthy vine

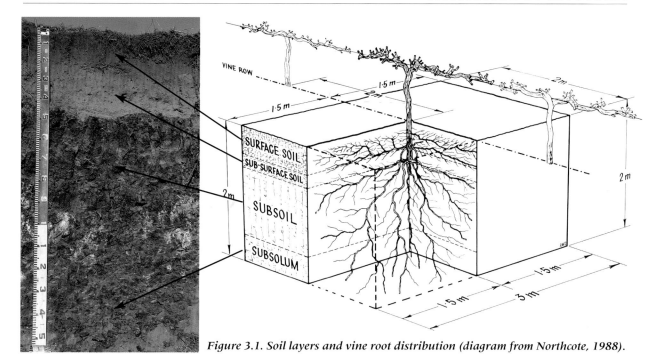

Figure 3.1. Soil layers and vine root distribution (diagram from Northcote, 1988).

growth; associations between restrictive soil properties and grape quality are not discussed.

In the vineyard, where grapevines are planted at a given spacing, there is a fixed area of soil available to each vine. The depth of the soil then determines the volume of soil available to each grapevine for root growth. All but the border vines in a vineyard have a finite volume of soil in which to grow; for those illustrated in **FIGURE** 3.1 the volume of soil is at least 12 m^3 per vine. A deep soil is one in which vine roots grow abundantly to a depth of 70 cm or more, whereas one in which roots are sparse below 30 cm is described as shallow. In some situations, where the aim is to ensure a supply of moisture to the roots for the longest possible time, deep soils are desirable. In other situations however, where the viticulturist wishes to exercise more control over rootzone moisture levels, a shallower soil may be required. Either way, the importance of soil depth, in providing a reservoir of water, and at the same time in supplying adequate oxygen for the growth of roots, is the best reason for studying soils and their effects on the growth of grapevines. Unfortunately such studies are difficult. In **FIGURE** 3.1 the soil has been divided into three more or less horizontal layers, the surface soil, subsurface soil, and subsoil, and a bottom layer termed the subsolum. The subsolum consists of the materials directly below the soil. These materials must be considered here, not only because vines are deep rooting, but also because they have a significant effect on deep drainage. In some more recently established vineyards—e.g. in the south-east of South Australia—soils are so shallow that the surface soil directly overlies the substrate. In these situations, the substrate must be ripped to provide sufficient depth. Generally however,

there is a surface layer overlying a subsoil layer; the subsurface soil layer does not always occur. In this chapter the physical and chemical properties of soils are considered in relation to the requirements of the grapevine followed by descriptions of the most important soils for grapegrowing.

3.1 Physical properties of grapegrowing soils

The physical properties of a soil affect entry, storage and drainage of water through the soil, aeration, the growth of plant roots and the liability of the soil to erosion. They also affect tillage operations that may be necessary during establishment and for inter-row management. Tillage, in turn, can alter the soil's physical properties. Penkov (1974) has shown that grapevines respond to good physical soil conditions by developing vigorous root systems that permeate the soil evenly and deeply. Conversely, Myburgh et al. (1998) highlighted the impact of restrictive layers on root distribution patterns. The physical and chemical properties of soil interact closely, and both are reflected in the morphological, or descriptive, features of the soil. Before a site for a new vineyard is selected (see Chapter 10), the physical properties of the soil should be given particularly careful consideration because most soil physical characteristics cannot be readily changed.

3.1.1 SOIL COLOUR
Colour is the most noticeable feature of soil (**FIGURES** 3.2-3.5). However, it is not always appreciated that it is often related to other factors affecting plant growth.

Surface soils

Generally, light coloured soils (such as bleached sands) reflect light and heat (**FIGURE 3.5**) whereas dark coloured soils (such as black cracking clays) absorb and radiate heat, and thus warm up and cool down readily. The reflectivity of soils depends mainly on the content of organic matter and water, the texture, and the angle of the incident light. Over the whole solar spectrum, reflection coefficients range from about 10% for dark soils rich in organic matter to about 30% for light desert sand. There is a broad relationship between the colour of surface soils and their organic matter content (**FIGURE 3.2**). For a given soil, the darker the surface soil, the higher is its organic matter content; this is generally indicative of a low level of soil disturbance. Higher organic matter levels are usually associated with improved aggregation of soil particles—this facilitates the entry of water and resistance to erosion.

Subsurface soils

Subsurface soils underlain by restrictive clayey subsoils are commonly light coloured (near white). This indicates that leaching has occurred and that the soil is periodically waterlogged. The amount of orange and rusty root-tracings and mottlings in the lower part of the subsurface layer increases with the frequency and duration of waterlogging (**FIGURE 3.4**).

Subsoils

Subsoil colour is a good indicator of the drainage and aeration status of the entire soil. Subsoil colours are commonly imparted by various oxides of iron and aluminium. Iron oxides in an aerobic soil (where they are fully oxygenated) tend to be red (**FIGURE 3.3**). With increasing periods of anaerobic (i.e. reducing) conditions caused by waterlogging, the iron oxides tend more toward grey colours. It can generally be inferred that aeration decreases and waterlogging becomes increasingly likely as soil colour changes from red to brown to yellow to grey to gley (light greys to bluish and greenish greys). 'Gley' is a soil colour referred to as such on standard charts (e.g. Munsell Soil Color Charts) and is a certain indicator of seasonal waterlogging. Mottling is a condition where the colouration of the soil is blotchy (**FIGURE 3.4**), for example blobs of grey and red colours in a brown matrix. Mottling is often an indicator of waterlogging, but care is needed to ensure that the colour blobs are not simply highly weathered stones or inclusions of another soil layer. Undoubtedly one reason why red soils are preferred for viticulture is that they are generally well drained and aerated. However, there are exceptions, because other properties, such as salinity and sodicity (sodium ion content), affect the capacity of soils to transmit water and air. For example, a non-sodic brown or yellow soil may be more permeable than a sodic red soil (see 3.1.8 and 3.2.5).

3.1.2 SOIL TEXTURE

Texture is a measure of the relative proportions of sand, silt and clay sized particles in the soil. It is probably the most important of all soil properties as it affects water holding capacity (3.1.6), nutrient retention (3.2.2 and 3.2.3) and erodibility, factors that are highly significant under Australian conditions. Because such a wide range

Figure 3.2 A dark well structured surface soil which has high fertility.

Figure 3.3 Soil with bright colours indicate good aeration and drainage.

Figure 3.4 Pale sub-surface soil and mottling in the subsoil indicate seasonal waterlogging.

Figure 3.5 Very pale or white colours indicate leaching and low organic matter.

of soils has been used for grapegrowing, almost all textures are found in Australian vineyards.

Virtually all soils consist of a mixture of grain sizes. Sands range from 2 to 0.02 mm in diameter, silts from 0.02 to 0.002 mm, and clay particles are smaller than 0.002 mm. The various combinations of grain sizes are given 'texture grades'. Some examples are sands, which contain 5% or less of clay-sized particles through loams, with about 25% of clay-sized particles, to heavy clays with more than 50% of clay-sized particles. Different texture grades feel different when a moist sample is manipulated with the fingers. Sands have almost no coherence, while heavy clays feel like plasticine. The amounts of organic matter, oxides of Fe and Al, Ca-Mg carbonates, the relative proportions of Ca to Mg and Na present on the clay-sized particles, and the type of clay minerals, all influence the behaviour and feel of the different texture grades.

Grits, gravels and stones (i.e. particles with grain size exceeding 2 mm) are not included in texture assessments, but are nevertheless significant. In the soil itself, these particles decrease its water holding capacity. On the soil surface, gravel or stone beds help to conserve moisture in the surface soil and reduce susceptibility to erosion. They also reflect light and heat onto the under parts of the canopy; lighter coloured stones or gravel reflect more than darker ones. Surface stones can also store heat, which is radiated back to the canopy during the evening.

3.1.3 SOIL FRIABILITY

Soil friability expresses the ease with which soil material crumbles and retains the aggregated (crumbly) condition. It is a complex attribute dependent on particle size (texture), the arrangement of particles and the spaces between them (structure) and the nature of bonding between the particles (affected by organic matter, oxides, carbonates etc). Organic matter improves friability while sodicity (3.2.5) adversely affects it for both surface soils and subsoils. Friability influences the rate of movement of water and air through the soil, the ease with which roots can penetrate the soil, and the efficiency of tillage. In short, the more friable the soil, the better is the growth of the grapevine; see also Wall (1987).

Surface and subsurface soils

Most surface and subsurface soils—except for sands (**FIGURE 3.6**), highly calcareous soils, soils naturally well supplied with organic matter (**FIGURE 3.7**), and self-mulching soils—set hard when dry (**FIGURE 3.8**). This hard setting property, common to many Australian soils, increases with increasing clay content. Root proliferation is restricted in these soils, as is water infiltration. Water ponds on flat ground, and on slopes it runs off, possibly initiating erosion. Hard setting soils should be cultivated while they contain optimum moisture. For most, this period is short, often the day

Figure 3.6 Loose sand with no root growth restrictions.

Figure 3.7 Crumbly surface loamy soil with no root growth restrictions.

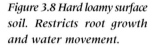

Figure 3.8 Hard loamy surface soil. Restricts root growth and water movement.

Figure 3.9 Coarsely structured subsoil, highly restrictive to roots and water movement.

following thorough wetting of the surface. Continued clean cultivation increases the strength of hard setting because organic matter is destroyed; conversely, a green manure crop, sod culture, or the introduction of a pasture phase provides extra organic matter and so ameliorates the hard setting condition. Where sodicity has influenced soil formation, or where the content of exchangeable calcium is less than about 50–60%, the application of gypsum makes the soil more friable, as does increasing the soil organic matter content. Self-mulching surface soils with high clay contents remain friable over only a limited moisture range and rapidly become sticky as moisture exceeds this range. This stickiness restricts the time available for cultivation and may impede the movement of machinery in the vineyard.

Subsoils

Friability in subsoils largely depends upon the size and strength of the aggregates or fragments resulting when the soil is disturbed. Friable to semi-friable subsoils break readily into small aggregates, 2 cm or less in size, which crumble easily between the fingers. Non-friable subsoils have larger aggregates (**FIGURE 3.9**) and even when moist, do not break up readily; they are usually sticky when moist. Poor friability may be found in sandy loam to loam subsoils, but is especially important in clay-textured ones. Friable subsoils allow water and air to move readily through the soil thus providing a good medium for root growth. Non-friable subsoils impede water and air movement and in extreme cases perched water tables may develop, thus creating conditions unfavourable for root growth. Both sodicity (3.2.5) and the content of fine carbonates (3.2.6) affect the friability of subsoils. Friability may be improved by applying gypsum directly into the subsoil. A quicker response will result from direct application compared with a surface application.

3.1.4 SURFACE SOIL THICKNESS

The thickness of surface soil is important because it influences the supply of nutrient elements; it is the layer that contains most nutrients to which fertilizers are often applied. Where it is thin, or where cultivation destroys surface feeding roots in the top 8–15 cm, the supply of nutrients may be limited. Thicker surface soils, of 15–30 cm or more with fertilizer placed within the layer, will usually support vigorous grapevines.

3.1.5 DEPTH TO IMPEDING LAYERS

Impeding layers obstruct both root growth and water movement, and (in the latter case) they can cause waterlogging. Unless an impeding layer occurs at depths greater than 150 cm, both the layer itself and its effect on the supply of water and oxygen will affect root growth. Under natural rainfall, grapevines should not be grown in soils with impeding layers at depths of less than 100 cm, and preferably 200 cm unless other favourable conditions prevail such as a gently sloping and naturally-draining topography. Where vines are grown under irrigation both soils and subsola should be free of impeding layers to a depth of at least 150 cm and preferably 300 cm unless drains have been installed. There are four kinds of layers that obstruct root growth and water penetration in Australian grapegrowing soils; these are country rock, calcrete, subsoil clays, and cemented pans.

Country rock

Country (or basement) rock underlies all land at some depth (**FIGURE 3.10**), and is generally an obvious feature in hilly landscapes. Weathering rock is usually apparent within 100 cm of the surface, but often shallower. There is usually some surface stone, and there may be isolated outcroppings. The denser rocks (some sandstones, quartzites and granites) almost totally restrict root and water penetration. Rocks in which fissures, cracks and cleavages occur (siltstones, slates, schists and phyllites) allow some root and water penetration and may prove satisfactory for grapegrowing, especially if they occur in close association with soils which are deeper than 100 cm. In some regions, such as the Adelaide Hills and Eden Valley, these cleaved rocks have been tilted so that the cracks are perpendicular to the ground surface. This allows significant water and root penetration, so even apparently shallow soils are satisfactory for viticulture. Where rocks outcrop and physically occupy land area, the establishment and maintenance of a vineyard may be hindered.

Calcrete

The term calcrete is used for all hardened to semi-hardened accumulations of calcium-magnesium carbonates (usually Ca-dominant) that occur either in subsoils or subsola of soils used for grapegrowing (**FIGURE 3.11**). Most calcretes, such as those of the Riverland region, occur where windblown carbonate-

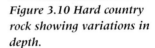

Figure 3.10 Hard country rock showing variations in depth.

Figure 3.11 Calcrete with few fissures allowing root penetration.

rich deposits have hardened due to prolonged seasonal wetting and drying cycles. Calcrete also occurs as a secondary capping on the aeolianite and calcarenite of ancient coastal sand dunes. The Coonawarra and Mount Benson calcretes are in this category. Calcretes may also form in subsoils or subsola due to the action of fluctuating ground water tables in calcareous soil materials. The main consideration is whether or not calcrete within 50 cm of the surface can be successfully ripped.

Pre-establishment ripping has two functions, viz. facilitating trellis and pipeline installation, and increasing rootzone depth. Some calcretes are simply too hard and/or too thick to rip. Many of the mallee (e.g. Riverland) calcretes can be ripped, but consist of several kinds of carbonate layers, each with different characteristics with respect to water movement and root growth (Wetherby and Oades 1975). These layers consist of hard calcretes and/or finely divided soft carbonates within the fine earth matrix (all soil particles less than 2 mm in size). Generally, the hard calcretes form a physical barrier to root and water penetration unless ripped, and may only soften slightly after many years of irrigation. However, the associated fine carbonates (unless sandy) commonly have adverse chemical properties, including high sodicity, alkalinity, salinity and toxic boron concentrations, such that an effective rootzone depth is not achieved. These materials also lose permeability over time. Detailed investigations of the calcrete and associated carbonate layers are necessary prior to vineyard development. The calcareous sands underlying the calcrete caps on old coastal dunes are not chemically hostile, so ripping to increase rootzone depth is standard procedure in these areas.

Subsoil clays

Impeding subsoil clays (claypans) occur in many texture contrast or duplex soils (3.3.6) and some other soils. Impeding subsoil clays are commonly sodic (3.2.5). Sodicity causes the individual clay particles to disperse, thereby clogging the fine pores of the soil (**FIGURE 3.12**). This results in increased bulk density and soil strength, and decreased porosity and hence permeability. Claypans therefore obstruct root and water penetration and are the main reason for waterlogging in duplex soils. Impermeability problems caused by subsoil clays are accentuated under irrigation because water applications promote more dispersion. Furthermore, the sodium in irrigation water increases the degree of sodicity. The thinner the depth of topsoil over the impeding layer, the more serious is the problem.

Subsolum clays also play a key role in vineyard performance. Impeding clay layers, even if below the rootzone, restrict deep drainage and contribute to the development of water tables and salt accumulation. The so-called Blanchetown Clay of the Murray Basin is a well known example of this type of impeding layer.

Cemented pans

These pans are mainly sands and gravels cemented by the infilling of coatings of clays and sesquioxides, but there is considerable variation in their thickness and composition (**FIGURE 3.13**). Many are related to subsola formed from layered deposits as in parts of the riverine plains of south-eastern Australia. Others occur below some of the sand over clay soils in the Swan Valley where ironstone gravels may be strongly cemented. Such pans prevent root and water penetration, and are a problem under irrigation. Although ripping breaks up these pans, amelioration is often difficult or impossible due to their depth.

3.1.6 AVAILABLE WATER CAPACITY

The available water capacity is an estimate of the soil's maximum store of water. It is the difference between field capacity and the wilting point, where the former is the upper limit of available water when the addition of more water is lost by drainage, and the latter is the lower limit of available water when water is so tightly held by soil that plant roots cannot extract it. The available water capacity represents the extreme of water availability and is a useful indication of the maximal amount of water that may be stored for plant use by a soil. Coarse sands have a low available water capacity of 8 cm/m (i.e. one metre depth of coarse sand can hold 8 cm of plant available water). More clayey soil materials have values between 10 and 20 cm/m (Salter and Williams 1967). The available water in a loamy fine sand over clay soil from the Barossa Valley is estimated to be 2,000 L for a 12 m³ volume (**FIGURE 3.1**). A similar volume of coarse sand is estimated to have only 1,000 L whereas the

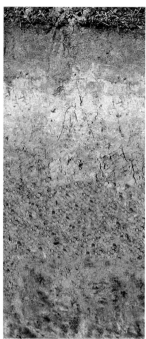

Figure 3.12 Poorly structured subsoil clay at shallow depth.

Figure 3.13 Cemented ironstone pan (granular appearance from half way down profile).

deeper cracking clays may have values from 1,300 L to 1,800 L. However, as the soil dries, stored water is held more tightly, and the vine must expend more energy to extract it, and so becomes stressed. Viticulturists wishing to minimize moisture stress use the 'readily available water' concept, or 'RAW'. This is the amount of water stored between field capacity and a suction of –60 kPa (wilting point is equivalent to a suction of –1500 kPa). The readily available water capacity is about 75% of total capacity in sandy soils, and about 40% in more clayey soils. Soil moisture monitoring is used as a tool in irrigation scheduling to ensure that the soil does not dry to the point where the vine begins to suffer stress.

3.1.7 SOIL PERMEABILITY

Soil permeability is a measure of the capacity of soil to transmit water vertically. Generally, soil permeability depends on the size and number of natural voids, and the amount of clay and its swelling properties. Sandy soils have many voids and little clay, so permeability remains high even when the soil is saturated. Conversely many clay soils, which have smaller and fewer voids, have low permeability when saturated. In the cracking clays, the initial rate of entry of water into the cracks is rapid but, as swelling closes the cracks, water either ponds on the surface or runs off depending on the topography. Permeability is related to the physical properties of texture, friability and impeding layers and to the chemical properties of salinity, sodicity and the contents of organic matter and carbonate.

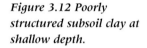

so amt of H₂O avail to plant fn of soil type

Fu same amt. of water in soil plant can access 90% fn sand & only 40% clayey

3.1.8 WATERLOGGING

Waterlogging is a serious potential problem as grapevines prefer soils that are well drained. Where stagnant water occurs, the roots of grapevines are weakened and may be attacked by root-rotting organisms causing loss of vigour and eventual loss of the vine. There are two main kinds of waterlogging; surface and subsurface.

Surface waterlogging

Surface waterlogging has two main causes. One is the slow permeability of surface soils in which water entry has become very slow as a result of the loss of friability (3.1.3). This is often due to poor soil management. Applications of gypsum and organic matter usually correct this condition. The second is due to thin surface soils overlying claypan subsoils (3.1.5). This condition can he corrected by incorporating gypsum into the claypan subsoil. Both types of surface waterlogging can be alleviated by mounding at the time of vineyard establishment.

Subsurface waterlogging

This occurs mostly in soils on low-lying or flat terrain where the surface soil is more than 20 cm thick and overlies claypan subsoil (3.1.5). Even on sloping ground, lateral movement of water along the top of the claypan is often insufficient to prevent waterlogging. Sandy soils with mottled and/or dispersive clay subsoils are the most severely affected, because their surfaces are highly permeable whereas their claypan subsoils are only very slowly permeable. Lateral water movement, although too slow to prevent waterlogging, nevertheless occurs.

This water eventually seeps into watercourses and if carrying nutrient or pesticide residues, can pollute streams. Another consequence of subsurface waterlogging is the formation of plough soles or traffic pans, which result from cultivating soil that is too wet or from the indiscriminate and frequent use of heavy equipment in the vineyard. In these circumstances, traffic and cultivation should be kept to a minimum when the soil is wet.

Remedial measures for subsurface waterlogging include mounding at establishment, deep ripping of the clay subsoil together with deep placement of gypsum, followed by cover cropping with deep-rooted species. These measures should help water to penetrate the subsoil and improve the moisture regime of the soil. **FIGURES 3.14** to **3.17** illustrate a range of soil waterlogging situations.

3.1.9 TOPOGRAPHY

The surface configuration of land influences, and is influenced by, the physical and chemical properties of the soil. Most of these relationships are fairly obvious. To the grapegrower, the topography is especially important as it affects water infiltration and drainage on the one hand and soil erosion on the other. In hilly country, slope aspect is an important consideration in terms of solar radiation and exposure. In steep country, machinery accessibility is also an issue.

The dune-swale topography that predominates throughout the Riverland, Murray Darling and Swan Hill regions is conducive to the development of seepage, waterlogging and attendant salinity problems. This,

Figure 3.14 Bleached sub-surface with rusty markings overlying a slowly-permeable mottled clay subsoil.

Figure 3.15 Soil consisting of low permeability heavy clay from the surface.

Figure 3.16 Permeable sandy soil prone to waterlogging due to shallow water table.

Figure 3.17 Sealed surface soil causes ponding of water.

together with the nature of the soils and the subsola, makes drainage with agricultural drains essential. The need for drains was recognized in the early years of these regions (Thomas 1939, Northcote and Boehm 1949) but disposal of the drainage water presents problems that are still receiving attention. The 'cliffs' or slopes between the highland dune-swale areas and the river terraces and flats are the only areas where artificial drainage may not be necessary. Elsewhere the general principle to follow is that seepage, waterlogging and salinity develop where slopes grade into or abut flats. The problems are accentuated by differences in the relative permeabilities of soil and/or subsola layers (Cockroft 1965). On flat or nearly flat land, the permeability of the surface soil is all-important.

3.1.10 SOIL EROSION

Erosion of surface soil is a serious threat to the sustainability of a vineyard. The bulk of the soil's nitrogen, phosphorus and organic matter is located in the upper few cm, as a casual glance at any set of down-profile soil analyses will demonstrate (see Appendix 1). Protection of the soil from erosion is perhaps the most fundamental requirement of a management system.

Water erosion in grapegrowing soils is of two types: the sheet removal of soil particles suspended in water as it flows over the soil surface, and the formation of gullies where water concentrates and 'knifes' through the soil. The degree of either form of erosion on any given soil type increases directly with increasing slope (Northcote et al. 1954). Often the most obvious effects of water erosion are found on duplex soils (3.3.2), even on slopes of only 1–1.5%. Where water infiltration is impeded, either by poorly structured surface soils or by restrictive subsoils, temporary saturation occurs in the soil surface following heavy rainfall. In this condition the soil has minimal strength, and is readily washed away on sloping ground. Sandy surfaces with less aggregation are more susceptible than finer grained soils. Erosion in vineyards has largely been curtailed through the adoption firstly of contour planting and more recently through the increasing use of ground cover vegetation and/or mulches. Establishment is generally the most sensitive period. Maintenance of vegetative cover is crucial, and on the steepest slopes, split establishments over two seasons can help minimize the risk.

Sandy soils, or soils which have been pulverized by excessive working, are poorly aggregated (i.e. individual particles are not bonded together into larger units). These particles have low mass and are readily moved by the wind. The problem tends to be worse on more exposed sites such as sandhills. In extreme wind events, sand blasting of foliage may accompany erosion. Although the sandy soils of the Riverland, Murray Darling and Swan Hill regions are potentially susceptible, management systems that maintain vegetative cover effectively control the problem.

3.2 Chemical properties of grapegrowing soils

The chemical properties of soil affect not only the nutrition of plants, but also the physical soil conditions and thus the moisture regimes. Since the grapevine can grow in a wide range of soils, it is able to obtain adequate moisture and nutrition under a variety of chemical soil conditions. However, some soils suit the grapevine better than others, and it is easier and cheaper to manage vineyards on the more suitable soils. The subjects discussed in this section include nutrition, salinity, sodicity and carbonate content. Some chemical properties of grape growing soils are set out in Tables in Section 3.3. These data are representative only and should be used as an indication of the range of chemical properties that exist in grapegrowing soils.

3.2.1 SOIL REACTION OR pH

pH is a measure of the soil's acidity or alkalinity. Soils that are neither acidic nor alkaline have pH 7.0 (neutral). Acidic soils have lower pH values and alkaline soils have higher values. Like most agricultural plants, grapevines prefer approximately neutral pH levels. There is an general tendency for soils to acidify under agricultural/horticultural land use, but local factors such as amount and type of fertilizer used, crop species, irrigation water quality and even proximity to lime-surfaced roads can have a marked impact.

Measurement of pH is probably the most commonly made soil test. The availability of colorimetric pH kits and portable electronic probes makes it one of the few chemical tests that can be easily undertaken in the field. It is not enough, however, to test the surface soil alone as pH can vary by as much as four units within the potential rootzone of the vine. Whilst grapevines are adaptable to variable pH values, extremes of pH affect the availability of most nutrient elements (**FIGURE. 3.18**), and are indicative of potentially significant problems such as sodicity and aluminium toxicity.

It is important to note that there are two methods commonly used to measure pH, and unfortunately they give different results. The traditional method is pH measured in water (pH_w), and the newer method is pH measured in 0.01M $CaCl_2$ (pH_{Ca}) both at a soil to solution ratio of 1:5. The pH_{Ca} method is commonly preferred because results show less seasonal variability caused by fluctuating soil moisture levels and solute concentrations. The difference between the two methods is not consistent, but as a very general rule of thumb, the pH_{Ca} value is 0.5–0.8 unit less than the pH_w value. It is common to use pH_{Ca} for assessing acidic soils, and pH_w for alkaline soils.

Soil pH is controlled by the cation exchange complex associated with the clay minerals and the organic fraction of the soil (refer to 3.2.2). Where a proportion of the base cations (calcium, magnesium, potassium and

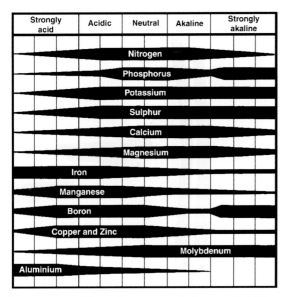

Figure. 3.18 Effect of pH on relative availability of nutrient elements.

sodium) has been leached from the soil and replaced by hydrogen and aluminium, an acidic reaction develops. This process of cation leaching is commonly triggered by excessive soil nitrates (e.g. from legume pastures or some nitrogenous fertilizers). For example, application of ammonium sulphate to the soil surface over 10 years can lower pH by about one unit to a depth of about 30 cm. Below that depth the effect decreases to 0.2–0.3 of a pH unit by 60 cm. Loss of cations of course means loss of fertility. Furthermore, low pH may induce aluminium and/or manganese toxicity, as availability of these elements increases with acidity (**FIGURE 3.18**). The acidification process must be arrested at an early stage, so lime or dolomite should be applied when pH_{Ca} reaches 5.5. Once pH_{Ca} falls below 4.5 the soil is strongly acidic, and vine performance will be significantly retarded.

At the other end of the scale, alkalinity is commonly caused by calcium carbonate in the soil. Calcium carbonate alone has a pH_w of around 8.3, quite acceptable for the growth of vine roots. Soils with higher pH, whilst commonly calcareous, are invariably sodic as well (refer to 3.2.5), with high levels of sodium carbonate and bicarbonate. Soils with pH_w exceeding 9.2 are strongly alkaline, and retard or prevent vine root growth. Elevated salinity and boron concentrations are frequently associated with these conditions. Amelioration is impractical. Strong alkalinity imposes a root depth restriction, so the drainage potential of the soil is critical in determining the likelihood of increasing sodicity and salinity further restricting rootzone depth.

3.2.2 EXCHANGEABLE CATIONS AND CATION EXCHANGE CAPACITY

Clay particles and organic matter have large surface areas with negatively charged sites that can attract and hold positively charged atoms called cations. The main cations are calcium, potassium, magnesium and sodium; these are important in plant nutrition. the greater the number of charged sites (measured by the cation exchange capacity or CEC), the greater is the nutrient retention potential of the soil and the better is its capacity to supply the major nutrient elements to plant roots. Nutrient retention capacity can be used to estimate inherent fertility – see below. Exchangeable cation and CEC values are measured in units called cmol+/kg. The proportions of the various cations on the exchange complex are also important. Soils in which exchangeable sodium accounts for more than 6% of the exchange complex commonly have poor structure (3.2.5). A high proportion of magnesium can have a similar effect. 'Magnesic' soils (Isbell 2002) with exchangeable Ca:Mg ratios of less than 0.1 are often structurally similar to sodic soils. The calcium, magnesium and potassium on the exchange complex are important sources of these essential macronutrients. Typical cation ratios in a 'well-balanced' soil are set out in **TABLE 3.1**. Some variation from these figures is generally acceptable as vine roots are able to maintain adequate balances through their absorption mechanisms.

Table 3.1 Ideal proportions of exchangeable cations. Source: South Australian Soil and Plant Analysis Service (1996).

Exchangeable cation	Proportion (%)
Calcium	65-75
Magnesium	10-15
Potassium	3-8
Sodium	Less than 6

In neutral to alkaline soils, the sum of exchangeable cations generally approximates the CEC value. Where this is the case, the soil is said to be base saturated, and the CEC provides a rough indication of inherent fertility. In acidic soils, the degree of base saturation decreases, as many of the exchange sites are occupied by hydrogen and aluminium ions. In these soils, a better indication of inherent fertility is gained from the base status. Exchangeable cation data for the upper subsoil, and in particular its base status is used in the Australian Soil Classification (Isbell 2002) to assess inherent nutrient retention capacity of soils, more or less independent of management. Base status is the sum of the exchangeable calcium, magnesium, sodium and potassium. In the classification, base status values of more than 15 cmol(+)/kg of clay in the upper subsoil are deemed to indicate an adequate nutrient retention capacity, more than 25 cmol(+)/kg being very high. Values of less than 5 cmol(+)/kg of clay indicate very low inherent fertility. The CEC of the surface soil is highly dependent on soil management as in sandy and sandy loam soils most of the CEC is associated with the organic matter. As surface soil CEC and base status values are largely management-dependent, they are not particularly useful for

Table 3.2 Variations in exchangeable cation properties between soil types. Source: DWLBC Soil and Land Information (2003).

Soil	Layer	Approx. clay %	pH$_{Ca}$	Organic carbon %	CEC cmol+/kg	Base sat'n %	Exchangeable cations (cmol+/kg)			
							Ca	Mg	Na	K
Acidic sand	Surface	5	4.2	0.1	1.7	70	0.91	0.18	<0.1	<0.1
	Subsoil	5	4.3	0.02	0.5	55	0.15	0.02	<0.1	<0.1
Alkaline sand	Surface	5	8.0	0.3	3.9	100	4.60	0.50	0.10	0.61
	Subsoil	5	8.3	0.1	3.5	100	3.93	0.77	0.09	0.19
Acidic sandy loam over clay	Surface sandy loam	15	4.6	2.6	4.8	82	2.91	0.71	0.12	0.18
	Subsoil clay	40	4.5	0.2	13.2	81	2.41	7.36	0.56	0.31
Neutral loam over clay	Surface loam	25	6.7	1.3	7.3	100	6.39	0.88	0.10	0.73
	Subsoil clay	45	6.7	0.7	28.5	82	16.9	4.73	0.42	1.33
Calcareous sandy loam	Surface sandy loam	15	8.0	1.1	16.4	95	11.4	2.07	0.23	1.96
	Subsoil sandy clay loam	30	8.8	0.1	14.1	100	1.53	6.04	6.14	1.46
Acidic clay loam over clay	Surface clay loam	35	4.5	7.7	18.0	65	7.17	3.90	0.19	0.50
	Subsoil clay	45	4.0	0.7	8.0	26	0.92	0.94	0.19	0.05
Cracking clay	Surface clay	45	7.1	2.0	34.8	100	30.7	5.41	0.33	1.53
	Subsoil clay	55	7.6	0.8	41.3	92	22.4	12.7	2.25	0.76

generalized assessments of inherent fertility. However, in soils with significant differences in base status between surface and subsoils (eg sand over clay soils), subsoil base status is a misleading indicator of inherent fertility. Consequently, although cation analyses are useful at the paddock/property level for estimating fertility status, they have limited application in broad scale land assessments, and should be used in conjunction with other parameters, as discussed below.

However, in soils with significant differences in base status between surface and subsoils (e.g. sand over clay soils), subsoil base status is a misleading indicator of inherent fertility. Surface soil CEC and base status are highly dependent on soil management, because in sandy and sandy loam soils most of the CEC is associated with the organic matter. Differences in exchangeable cation properties between soils can be extreme. The data in **TABLE 3.2** illustrate the effects of clay content, organic matter concentration and pH on cation exchange capacity, exchangeable cation ratios and base saturation. The nature of the constituent clay minerals also influences exchangeable cation properties. Measurements of cation exchange capacity and exchangeable cations are expensive, but desirable to determine relative deficiencies of these elements, to determine the most effective product for ameliorating acidity, to identify the cause of soil structural problems, and to assess the overall nutrient retention capacity of the soil.

3.2.3 NUTRIENT ELEMENTS

As indicated in 3.2.1 and 3.2.2, a guide to the reserves of mineral nutrients in soils may be obtained from the pH and exchangeable cation characteristics of the soil. Acidic soils have low cation exchange capacity with a predominance of hydrogen, while alkaline soils have relatively high cation exchange capacity with a predominance of metal ions (Ca, Mg, K and Na). The values for neutral soils lie between. Thus, in general, the

acidic soils have low nutrient element reserves, the neutral soils moderate reserves, and most alkaline soils have high reserves. Such comparisons should only be made between similar soils, that is, a sandy soil with other sandy soils and not with a cracking clay or a duplex soil. In acidic soils in particular, there is a delicate balance between nutrients, which is easily upset by over-cropping or continued applications of one fertilizer; such an imbalance can induce deficiencies of other nutrient elements. Soil ameliorants can also have adverse effects. Lime applications to correct acidity can induce manganese deficiency if too much is applied at once. Alkaline soils containing significant free calcium carbonate (calcareous soils - 3.3.8) also have a delicate nutrient balance that may be easily upset by heavy applications of fertilizer. For example, Zn deficiency may be induced by heavy applications of phosphatic fertilizers.

The nutrient elements required for plant growth are carbon, hydrogen, oxygen, nitrogen, phosphorus, potassium, sulphur, iron, calcium, magnesium, boron, manganese, copper, cobalt, zinc, molybdenum, and chlorine. Carbon is obtained by green plants from the carbon dioxide in the air, hydrogen and oxygen are obtained mainly from water and the remaining elements are obtained from the soil. Grapevine nutrition is discussed in detail in Volume II, Chapter 9. The purpose of this section is simply to tabulate (**TABLE 3.3**) some general relationships between soil properties and likely nutrient deficiencies.

3.2.4 SALINITY

A high concentration of soluble salts in the soil can limit plant growth, or even kill a crop, by creating an osmotic potential so high that plants have difficulty obtaining water and nutrients from the soil solution. Alkaline soils generally have higher surface and subsoil salinities than acidic and neutral soils as shown by their total soluble salt and sodium chloride (NaCl) contents. Generally,

Table 3.3 Most likely situations for nutrient deficiencies.

Element	Situation of likely deficiency
Nitrogen	Shallow soils, leached acidic soils and sandy soils Low rainfall environments Soils with low/nil legume content Waterlogged soils Frequently cultivated soils
Phosphorus	Almost universally deficient. More severe situations are: • sandy soils in high rainfall areas • alkaline soils • soils high in iron and/or aluminium
Potassium	Sandy soils in high rainfall areas
Calcium	Sandy soils in high rainfall areas, especially if prone to subsurface waterlogging
Magnesium	Deficiencies rare – possibly associated with high potassium levels
Sulphur	Sandy soils in high rainfall areas Soils low in organic matter
Copper	Mainly acidic and calcareous sands. Intermittently on a range of other soils types.
Manganese	Highly calcareous soils, particularly sands with more than 60% free carbonate Ironstone soils and some acidic sands Soils which have been over-limed or irrigated with alkaline water
Zinc	Calcareous soils of all texture ranges including clays Acidic sands and acidic to neutral sandy or loamy texture contrast soils
Molybdenum	Sandy, acidic or ironstone soils in high rainfall areas
Iron	Calcareous or poorly drained soils
Boron	Sandy acidic soils with low organic matter Boron toxicity is more serious problem than boron deficiency
Cobalt	High pH soils, soils low in copper

Figure 3.19 Damage caused by water table induced dryland salinity.

NaCl makes up two-thirds or more of the soluble salts, and bicarbonate, sulphate and other salts make up the rest. Three distinctive types of soil salinity are recognized in vineyards.

Dry saline land

This type of salinity is most common in low rainfall environments where soluble salts have accumulated in the soil (from wind-blown accessions or inherited from parent material or a former saline water table). Water tables are absent. Salt accumulation occurs either because rainfall is insufficient to leach salts below a particular depth, and/or a deep subsoil layer prevents leaching. Provided that the salts can be leached out with irrigation water, this type of salinity is not a major limitation to vineyard development or performance. However, where deep drainage is impeded and leaching is not effective, salt concentrations will increase with continued irrigation over time and production will eventually become unsustainable.

Water table induced (dryland) salinity

'Dryland' salinity (as distinct from irrigation-induced salinity - see below) is caused by rising saline ground water tables (**FIGURE 3.19**). Generally, water table rise

is a result of increased recharge following clearing of native vegetation and its replacement with shallower rooted annual crops and pastures that use less water. In most situations a regional or catchment water table is involved, so there is little chance of control of the problem from within a single vineyard. Consequently, development on land affected by or at risk of dryland salinity is inadvisable.

Irrigation induced salinity

As the name implies, this problem affects land where salt from applied irrigation water has accumulated in or immediately below the rootzone (**FIGURE 3.20**). This may be due to impeded deep drainage preventing the flushing of salts below the rootzone, or simply by poor irrigation practices. The latter situation is readily corrected, but the only way to overcome a deep drainage impediment is through the installation of artificial drains.

Soil salt concentrations were traditionally expressed as parts per million or the equivalent value as a percent. Salinity is now estimated from the electrical conductivity of the soil solution. The saturation extract method is a more reliable technique than the more commonly used 1:5 soil:water extract. Approximate soil salinity tolerances of grapevines are shown in **TABLE 3.4**.

Subsoils containing 0.3% total soluble salts have 40 tonnes of salts per hectare in each metre depth. Poor irrigation practice may cause a water table to develop in the soil which can concentrate much of this salt in the top of the water table zone causing severe salinity. In soils rich in fine earth carbonates (3.2.6), a significant proportion of the salts in the soil solution are sodium and bicarbonate. These salts intensify the osmotic potential, render the soil less permeable due to increased sodicity (3.2.5), raise the soil pH_w to 9 or higher, and decrease the availability of some nutrient elements. The relationship between salinity and irrigation, the effect of salinity on

Figure 3.20 Salinity in vineyard induced by irrigation.

Table 3.4 Approximate critical limits of soil salinity for grapevines.

Soil	Non saline		Marginally saline		Saline	
	ECe[*]	%TSS[#]	ECe[*]	%TSS[#]	ECe[*]	%TSS[#]
Topsoil - loamy sand	< 2.5	< 0.04	2.5 - 4	0.04 - 0.06	> 4	> 0.06
Topsoil - loam	< 2.5	< 0.05	2.5 - 4	0.05 - 0.10	> 4	> 0.10
Topsoil - clay	< 2.5	< 0.10	2.5 - 4	0.10 - 0.15	> 4	> 0.15
Subsoil - clay	< 2.5	< 0.10	2.5 - 8	0.10 - 0.30	> 8	> 0.30

[*] Electrical conductivity of saturation extract, expressed as dS/m
[#] Total soluble salts as percent of soil on a gravimetric basis

grapevines and the treatment of salinity problems in vineyards is discussed in Volume II, Chapter 7.

3.2.5 SODICITY

The friability and permeability of soils are strongly influenced by their sodium ion content, which if high enough will cause soil clay to disperse and block passage of water through the soil pores. The exchangeable sodium percentage is a measure of the sodium content or sodicity, of a soil. Exchangeable sodium percentages of 6 or more indicate that the soil is sodic, and 15 or greater that the soil is strongly sodic. Sodicity increases with pH. Sodicity in many surface soils is commonly less than 6, but if the exchangeable sodium percentage of the subsoil is 6 or more it is probable that the surface soil has been more sodic during its formation. Soils with sodic to strongly sodic surface soils are not usually used for grape growing. Magnesium ions are also thought to increase the dispersion of soil clay. This may be due either to the actual presence of high concentrations of Mg ions or to the low concentrations of Ca ions found in such soils. The importance of Ca ions in maintaining or improving soil friability and permeability by keeping soil clays flocculated and stable is well known. It is also clear that the content of Ca ions needs to be high in relation to combined total of Na and Mg ions.

Soil permeability (3.1.7) generally decreases as the exchangeable Na and Mg contents increase. This is particularly so in subsoils, where Na ions cause the clay to disperse as it wets. Thus sodic soils lose friability (3.1.3) rapidly when wetted. The surface soils of sodic soils, except where they are sands, also show low permeabilities and pronounced hard setting properties, even where their exchangeable sodium percentage is less than 6. Thus water entry is low and run-off high. Under Australian conditions, gypsum ($CaSO_4$) is the most useful improver of friability for both surface soils and subsoils.

Because gypsum is only slowly soluble it should be placed in the soil layer requiring treatment. About 16 tonnes/ha of gypsum are needed to remove 5 cmol(+)/kg of Na^+ ions from 30 cm of soil. Ca^{2+} ions released by the gypsum displace the Na^+ ions, which together with the sulphate (SO_4^{2-}) are leached from the soil. Sodicity also affects plant nutrition. Evidence has accumulated that for some plants (e.g. almonds), the availability of nutrient elements, and/or the ability of plants to take up nutrient elements from sodic soils, is restricted and causes some nutritional imbalance. Whether this is due to a chemical antagonism or to the poor physical state of sodic soils is not known. No data are available for grapevines.

3.2.6 SOIL CARBONATES

Carbonates are a feature of many viticultural soils in the lower rainfall areas of southern Australia. Soils containing detectable (on application of 1M hydrochloric acid) carbonates are termed calcareous. Some soils are calcareous throughout (commonly called 'mallee soils'), others only in the subsoil. Both calcium and magnesium carbonates occur, but $CaCO_3$ is predominant. Carbonates occur as finely divided material in the soil matrix, as nodules or concretions (rubble), or as sheet rock (calcrete). Wetherby and Oades (1975) and Wetherby (2003) developed a classification for subsoil carbonates. The classes and their drainage and root growth characteristics, are described in **TABLE 3.5**.

3.3 Soils used for grapegrowing in Australia

Grapevines are commercially grown on a wide range of soils. A thorough understanding of vineyard soils is essential for tailoring management practices to achieve optimal production. Whilst this understanding does not require knowledge of soil classification, communicating information and extrapolating from one situation to another is greatly assisted by a practical soil classification system. For example if the term 'sandy Sodosol' was mentioned, a person familiar with the Australian Soil Classification would immediately picture a sandy soil with

Table 3.5 Carbonate classes (adapted from Wetherby 2003).

Class	Description	Drainage / root growth
I	Fine soil carbonate in clay, few if any calcrete fragments present.	Drainage is impeded. Root growth is poor.
II	Sheet or boulder calcrete. Very hard, with slight softening only after prolonged irrigation.	Drainage is rapid in boulder form, but is restricted by sheets unless they are fractured. Root growth is good in boulder form, but is restricted by sheets and low water holding capacity.
III A	Compact mixture of loamy sand to light sandy clay loam (III AS) or sandy clay loam to light clay (III AL) and fine soil carbonate. Contains less than 30% calcrete fragments.	Drainage in III AS is good to medium and III AL medium. Root growth into III AS is medium and III AL fair.
III B	As for Class III A except that calcrete fragments account for 30-60% of the layer.	Drainage is moderate to good. Root growth is good, but coarse fragments limit moisture-holding capacity.
III C	As for Class III A except that calcrete fragments account for greater than 60% of the layer	Drainage is rapid. Root growth is good, but moisture holding capacity is severely limited due to fragments
IV	Weak accumulation of fine carbonate in a sand to sandy loam matrix.	Drainage is rapid. Root growth is good.

a poorly structured and probably dispersive clayey subsoil, prone to waterlogging and impeding healthy root growth.

Soil classification is continually being developed, in order to accommodate new knowledge, and to improve our capacity to differentiate soils that behave differently, and to group those that behave similarly. In Australia, soils have been traditionally classified using a system based on Great Soil Groups (Stace et al. 1968). Names such as red brown earth, terra rossa, solodized solonetz, kraznozem, podzol etc. are still widely used and provide an effective means of communication. Indeed, so entrenched did these terms become that some are still widely used today. However, the Great Soil Group names, for all their romantic appeal, provide an unsatisfactory basis for soil classification for two reasons. Firstly, the generalized nature of the system means that a range of soils with substantial differences can be classified into the same group. Secondly, there are many soils that do not fit into any group.

In 1960, the first of four editions of *A Factual Key for the Recognition of Australian Soils* (Northcote 1979) was published. This system put soil classification in Australia on a much more objective footing, by using a key for class allocation. It provided a significant improvement in terms of its capacity to differentiate a far greater number of soils. The most recent advance, the Australian Soil Classification (Isbell 1996, 2002), was tested on 14,000 soil profiles, and as a result, it is the most comprehensive system ever used in Australia. It combines many features of Northcote's system with a structure based on *Soil Taxonomy* (Soil Survey Staff 1999), the classification used in the USA. It has gained widespread acceptance across Australia as an easy-to-use generalized system, which accommodates virtually every Australian soil and discriminates between soils that were previously not separated.

However, an almost inevitable drawback with any generalized system is a poor capacity to cater for specialized applications. The need to recognize and understand viticultural soils is one such application. The *Australian Soil Classification*, whilst providing a sound framework for soil scientists to categorize soils and communicate with each other, is too complex for use in day-to-day viticulture. In the late 1990s, the Australian viticultural industry called for a user-friendly soil key that could be used by viticulturists to assist with rootstock selection and general vineyard soil management. A *Key for identifying categories of vineyard soils in Australia* (Maschmedt et al. 2002) was developed to address this concern. In the following pages, the soils used for grapegrowing in Australia are discussed in the context of the categories defined in Maschmedt et al. (2002).

CATEGORIES OF VINEYARD SOILS IN AUSTRALIA

The Key for identifying categories of vineyard soils in Australia identifies nine broad groupings. Within these categories, 36 sub-categories are defined. Soil depth and clay content are commonly used to differentiate classes because of the effects they have on water holding capacity, nutrition and rootzone depth.

3.3.1 CATEGORY 1: WET SOIL
Soil is saturated within the upper 50 cm for at least three months of the year, and cannot be feasibly drained. Problems of waterlogging, infrastructure installation and maintenance, and general accessibility prevent these soils from being used for commercial viticulture (FIGURE 3.21).

3.3.2 CATEGORY 2: VERY SHALLOW NON-RIPPABLE SOIL
Soil is formed over hard basement rock or hardpan (e.g. calcrete), which cannot be ripped. The profile is less than 15 cm deep (or less than 25 cm deep if sandy), and too shallow for sustainable production. Not only is the rootzone of the vine severely restricted, the installation of trellises and pipelines is extremely difficult (FIGURE 3.22).

3.3.3 CATEGORY 3: VERY SHALLOW OR STONY RIPPABLE SOIL
Soil is less than 15 cm deep over rippable rock or pan, or overlies unconsolidated soil material with more than 75% stones (TABLES 3.6, 3.7). Whilst an adequate rootzone depth can be achieved and underground works

Figure 3.21 Wet soil on low-lying ground with no prospect of drainage (Category 1).

Figure 3.22 Very shallow soil on non-rippable quartzite (Category 2).

Figure 3.23 Creek flat soil containing more than 75% coarse fragments in upper 100 cm (Sub-category 3.1).

Figure 3.24 Very shallow sandy loam over fragmented and rippable sandstone (Sub-category 3.2).

can be undertaken, consideration must be given to the nature of the material that is inevitably brought to the surface by ripping. For example, ripping calcrete will probably cause an increase in surface soil pH and carbonate content with implications for nutrition and pesticide efficacy. Sub-categories separate soils on the basis of clay content, and whether or not the underlying rock is calcareous.

Soils which are deep but have limited water holding capacity due to very high (more than 75%) stone content are most likely to occur in the ironstone gravelly areas of Western Australia, or on creek flats adjacent to rocky

ranges (**FIGURE 3.23**). They are generally well drained and have sufficient fine earth fraction to provide moisture retention, but usually constitute only a minor component of the vineyard. A problem with the alluvial forms of these soils is their susceptibility to flash flooding.

Very shallow soils over rippable non-calcareous rock invariably occur in hilly country. They are generally formed on more resistant variants of rocks underlying the deeper soils in the vineyard. Where the bedding of the rocks is more or less vertical as in the profile in **FIGURE 3.24**, ripping is unlikely to achieve any increase in water holding capacity. However, where the rocks have a

Table 3.6 Very shallow or stony rippable soils: sub-categories.

Sub-category	Name	Diagnostic features	Regional occurrence[a]	
			Common	Limited
3.1	Deep stony soil	Soil has more than 75% loose stone and gravel in the upper 100 cm	MR	GE, GS, MA, SW
3.2	Very shallow soil over rock	Underlying rock is non-calcareous	-	AH, EV, GR, GN
3.3	Very shallow sandy soil over calc-rock	Soil is sandy, underlain by calcareous rock or calcrete	-	MB, CC, CO
3.4	Very shallow loamy/clayey soil over calc-rock	Soil is loamy or clayey, underlain by calcareous rock or calcrete	-	MB, CC, CO

[a] Refer to the list of regional codes associated with Figure 2.2.

Table 3.7 Analytical data for some very shallow or stony rippable soils. Source: Soil and Land Information Group, Dept. of Water, Land and Biodiversity Conservation (SA).

Sub-category	Local name / Region	Depth (cm)	Texture / geology	pH CaCl$_2$	CO3 %	EC 1:5 dS/m	CEC cmol (+)/kg	Exchangeable cations			
								Ca	Mg	Na	K
3.3	Shallow loamy sand	0-8	Loamy sand	7.2	0	0.08	4.4	3.76	0.41	0.19	0.16
	South East of SA *	22-32	Calcrete	-	-	-	-	-	-	-	-
		90-142	Light sandy clay loam	8.7	19	0.11	2.0	1.55	0.85	0.27	0.10
3.4	Shallow sandy loam	0-7	Sandy loam	7.2	0	0.10	8.4	6.58	1.06	0.08	1.05
	South East of SA*	13-65	Calcrete	-	-	-	-	-	-	-	-
		65-100	Sandy clay loam	8.5	34	0.09	12.0	4.92	4.99	4.83	1.31

* Neither of these soils is from a viticultural region, but they are representative of very shallow soils in the Limestone Coast Zone.

Figure 3.25 Very shallow loamy sand over calcreted calcarenite (Sub-category 3.3).

Figure 3.26 Very shallow light sandy clay loam over calcreted limestone (Sub-category 3.4).

Figure 3.27 Shallow sandy soil with calcrete at 37 cm (Sub-category 4.1).

basis of clay content, presence of cracking clay (see also Category 5 below), and whether or not the underlying rock is calcareous (**TABLES 3.8, 3.9**).

Restricted water holding capacity is the key feature of these soils. Most are well drained, although some of the clayey types (4.4 and 4.5) may have shallow water tables. Provided adequate irrigation water supplies are available, shallow depth and good drainage can be used to advantage by the viticulturist as a means of controlling soil moisture content. Shallow sandy

flatter orientation, ripping will disrupt the uppermost layer, possibly exposing more highly weathered underlying material. Adjustments to irrigation scheduling will be needed to avoid overwatering of these soils, possibly causing downslope seepage.

Very shallow sandy and loamy soils over calcareous rock or calcrete are most likely to occur on old coastal features such as lagoons and dunes. These features are extensive in the Limestone Coast Zone (SA). In these situations, the shallow calcrete (**FIGURES 3.25, 3.26**) is generally underlain by softer marl or limestone (on flats), or semi-consolidated dune sands on rises. Ripping the calcrete cap exposes these softer materials, and increases the potential rootzone depth and water holding capacity of the soil. Where the cap is thick, disposal arrangements are needed for the large boulders, which are brought to the surface by the ripping operation.

3.3.4 CATEGORY 4: SHALLOW SOIL

Soil is between 15 and 50 cm deep over basement rock or hardpan. Texture contrast soils (refer to Categories 6 and 7 below) and calcareous soils (refer to Category 8 below) are excluded. Sub-categories separate soils on the

soils, with or without ironstone gravel (4.1) are mostly confined to the Margaret River, Swan District and Geographe regions of Western Australia. Probably the best known vineyards on shallow soils are those of Limestone Coast Zone (SA), where ancient coastal dunes have calcrete cappings at shallow depths. Sandier forms (4.1) are typical, especially in the coastal areas and at Padthaway, but at Coonawarra, more clayey forms are characteristic (4.2 and 4.4). These soils, commonly called *terra rossa*, have high calcium saturation, which promotes strong aggregation of soil particles. Consequently the soils are friable and well aerated. Similar soils occur in the Clare Valley and to a minor extent in the Adelaide Hills and Barossa Valley, but they are underlain by calcareous basement rock. Shallow cracking clays (4.5) on calcreted limestones and marls are common on lower lying land at Coonawarra. These soils are less well drained, and have reduced calcium saturation. They have particular impacts on viticulture including poor establishment (possibly due to soil cracking away from the young roots), difficulty in maintaining plant-available water, and excessive vigour caused by high natural fertility.

Table 3.8 Shallow soils: sub-categories.

Sub-category	Name	Diagnostic features	Regional occurrence[a]	
			Common	Limited
4.1	Shallow sandy soil	Soil is sandy, 25-50 cm thick	EV, GN	BE, CC, GS, MB, MR, PA, SW
4.2	Shallow loamy soil over calc-rock	Soil is loamy to clay loamy, underlain by calcareous rock or calcrete	CO, MB, WR	BV, CL, MV, PA, SF
4.3	Shallow loamy soil over rock/pan	Soil is loamy to clay loamy, underlain by non-calcareous rock or hardpan	EV	AH, CL, PY
4.4	Shallow clay over calc-rock	Soil is clayey, underlain by calcareous rock or calcrete	CO	PA
4.5	Shallow cracking clay over calc-rock	Soil is cracking clay, underlain by calcareous rock or calcrete	CO	-

[a] Refer to the list of regional codes associated with Figure 2.2.

Figure 3.28 Shallow clay loam over a thin calcrete band capping calcareous siltstone (Sub-category 4.2).

Figure 3.29 Shallow loamy soil over non-calcareous basement rock at 30 cm (Sub-category 4.3).

Figure 3.30 Shallow clayey soil over calcreted calcarenite at 37 cm (Sub-category 4.4).

Figure 3.31 Shallow cracking clay over calcreted marl at 20 cm (Sub-category 4.5).

Virtually all of the soils underlain by calcrete can be ripped to expose softer underlying material, thereby increasing rooting depth. Although the greater soil depth provides more buffering than in the case of the Category 3 soils (above), care is nevertheless needed to ensure that excessive calcareous material is not brought to the surface. Shallow soils over non-calcareous rock or hardpan (4.3) occur sporadically in hilly regions (e.g. Eden Valley, Adelaide Hills, Clare Valley, North East Victoria), where they are formed on basement rocks. These rocks tend to be less amenable to ripping than calcrete, so it is unlikely that they would be favoured for viticulture in their own right. However, a characteristic feature of basement rock landscapes is the intermingling of shallow soils with deeper types (usually Category 7 soils).

3.3.5 CATEGORY 5: CRACKING CLAY

Soil is clayey to at least 50 cm, and cracks on drying. Sub-categories separate soils on the basis of their structural condition, a measure of potential rootzone depth and susceptibility to waterlogging and deep drainage problems (TABLES 3.10, 3.11)

Table 3.9 Analytical data for some shallow soils. Source: Soil and Land Information Group, Dept. of Water, Land and Biodiversity Conservation (SA).

Sub-category	Local name / Region	Depth (cm)	Texture / geology	pH CaCl₂	CO3 %	EC 1:5 dS/m	CEC cmol (+)/kg	Exchangeable cations			
								Ca	Mg	Na	K
4.1	Shallow loamy sand on calcarenite	0-10	Loamy sand	6.9	0	0.09	5.5	6.32	0.90	0.17	0.67
	Currency Creek	15-28	Loamy sand	7.3	0	0.05	4.8	3.78	0.47	0.14	0.47
		28-50	Calcrete	-	-	-	-	-	-	-	-
		50-	Calcarenite	8.4	41.1	0.13	1.0	1.82	0.41	0.23	0.06
4.2	Terra rossa	0-9	Clay loam	7.3	0.5	0.17	15.5	11.48	2.26	0.11	1.26
	Clare Valley	9-34	Light clay	7.5	0.9	0.14	13.6	11.16	2.24	0.09	0.55
		34-36	Calcrete	-	-	-	-	-	-	-	-
		36-	Calcareous siltstone	7.8	74.9	0.29	1.6	3.33	0.54	0.19	0.08
4.3	Shallow sandy loam	0-20	Sandy loam	4.8	0	0.05	5.6	3.46	0.59	0.21	0.28
	Eden Valley	35-50	Loamy sand	5.1	0	0.03	2.9	1.42	1.10	0.15	0.06
		50-	Sandstone	5.7	0	0.03	2.4	1.09	3.27	0.77	0.05
4.4	Terra rossa	0-12	Light clay	7.4	3.0	0.12	25.6	21.5	1.6	0.19	0.94
	Coonawarra ridge	31-37	Light medium clay	7.7	19.0	0.15	24.7	23.1	0.6	0.47	0.34
		37-	Calcarenite	7.8	96.2	0.09	-	-	-	-	-
4.5	Rendzina	0-5	Light medium clay	6.7	0	0.27	24.6	13.3	9.7	1.49	1.29
	Coonawarra flat	7-17	Heavy clay	7.6	0	0.31	45.7	18.0	18.1	3.73	2.80
		17-55	Rubbly calcrete	8.1	33.6	0.55	30.4	10.5	13.2	3.99	2.78
		55-95	Calcareous clay (marl)	8.2	53.9	0.50	22.1	5.2	10.7	4.11	1.83

Table 3.10 Cracking clays: sub-categories.

Sub-category	Name	Diagnostic features	Regional occurrence[a]	
			Common	Limited
5.1	Poorly structured cracking clay	Hard settting, coarse blocky or massive surface	SU	MD, RL, SH
5.2	Well structured over restrictive cracking clay	Well structured within 80 cm of the surface over restrictive (coarse blocky or wet) layer	CO, HU, SB	AP, BV, CL, GL, LC, MD, MV, RI, RU, SH, TA
5.3	Well structured throughout cracking clay	Well structured surface, no coarse blocky structure within 80 cm of the surface	CO, HU, SB	AP, CL, GL, MU

[a] Refer to the list of regional codes associated with Figure 2.2.

Cracking clays are being increasingly used for viticulture despite their peculiar management problems. These relate to the difficulties of:

- maintaining adequate soil to root contact when the soil dries and shrinks;
- maintaining optimum soil moisture—clays have high wilting points, meaning that they hold large amounts of water too tightly for access by vine roots;
- controlling excessive vigour, a consequence of the high inherent fertility of many clay soils;
- managing waterlogging and deep drainage in poorer structured types;
- general accessibility on soils which can become very sticky when wet.

Frequently, cracking clays are formed on heavy clay deposits on alluvial flats and fans, old lake beds, colluvial slopes, plateaux (remnant land surfaces), and on hillslopes underlain by deeply weathered fine grained rock. These clays can severely impede deep drainage, so the thickness of overlying soil is critical to the performance of the vineyard. Ideally the impeding clay should be deeper than 150 cm; where shallower than 75 cm, the risk of water table development and salt accumulation is too great. Sub-category 5.3 soils are the most favourable in this regard.

Poorly structured cracking clay (Sub-category 5.1)

Some of the most extensive and oldest vineyard plantings along the River Murray flats and terraces are on poorly structured cracking clays. These soils are formed on fine grained alluvium, generally interbedded with sandier lenses which assist drainage. Waterlogging and salt accumulation are common, but improved irrigation efficiency should help to maintain the viability of these vineyards.

Well structured over restrictive cracking clay (Sub-category 5.2)

These soils are more commonly used for vineyards than the other two sub-categories of cracking clays. In the Hunter Valley they occur on colluvial slopes, in South Burnett, on alluvial plains, and at Coonawarra they occur on ancient lagoon floors. Elsewhere, they are scattered across the landscape, sometimes in characteristic topographical positions. For example, in the Barossa Valley, they generally occur on flat-topped rises. Surface soils are commonly self-mulching, or at least have well developed granular structure. They are

Table 3.11 Analytical data for some cracking clays. Source: Soil and Land Information Group, Dept. of Water, Land and Biodiversity Conservation (SA) and Dept. of Primary Industries, Water and Environ. (Tas.).

Sub-category	Local name / Region	Depth (cm)	Texture / geology	pH CaCl₂	CO3 %	EC 1:5 dS/m	CEC cmol (+)/kg	Exchangeable cations			
								Ca	Mg	Na	K
5.1	Grey clay	0-15	Light clay	7.1	-	0.78	-	-	-	-	-
	Riverland	30-70	Heavy clay	7.4	-	0.44	-	-	-	-	-
		70-100	Heavy clay	8.2	-	0.61	-	-	-	-	-
5.2	Black cracking clay	0-12	Light clay	7.4	0	0.16	nd	20	8.2	0.84	0.44
	Coal Valley, Tasmania	45-61	Medium clay	8.8	0	0.23	nd	21	17	3.1	0.29
		85-125	Medium clay	8.9	0	0.84	nd	18	27	7.3	0.30
5.2	Black cracking clay	0-10	Medium clay	7.7	1.7	0.15	40.0	34.2	4.9	0.32	1.85
	Barossa Valley	10-74	Heavy clay	7.8	1.0	0.18	32.6	30.8	5.8	0.93	1.35
		74-100	Heavy clay	8.2	8.2	0.31	32.6	18.6	9.3	4.57	0.74
5.2	Black cracking clay	0-10	Medium clay	7.1	0	0.42	34.8	30.71	5.41	0.33	1.53
	Clare Valley	20-40	Heavy clay	6.9	0	0.24	39.7	27.99	10.91	1.11	0.98
		85-140	Heavy clay	8.1	9.7	0.52	41.3	15.56	18.27	6.72	0.80
5.2	Black cracking clay	0-10	Medium clay	7.7	3.5	0.48	42.8	39.7	2.98	0.48	3.27
	McLaren Vale	30-70	Heavy clay	7.7	1.5	0.56	48.6	36.8	10.7	3.04	1.47
		100-130	Heavy clay	8.5	8.7	0.81	42.5	15.7	14.1	14.2	1.37
5.3	Black cracking clay	0-15	Medium clay	6.9	3.3	0.09	33.8	27.6	2.9	0.23	2.58
	Coonawarra	30-42	Light medium clay	6.7	1.4	0.05	32.0	24.5	3.0	0.31	2.19
		42-51	Light medium clay	7.0	2.1	0.09	32.5	24.5	3.0	0.33	2.01

Figure 3.32 Poorly structured cracking clay showing coarse structural aggregates to the surface. Little root growth likely below the brown subsurface layer (25 cm) (Sub-category 5.1).

Figure 3.33 Well structured over restrictive cracking clay showing impeding layer from 60 cm (Sub-category 5.2). Black Vertosol, Coal River Valley (Tas.); photograph by R. Doyle.

Figure 3.34 Well structured over restrictive cracking clay showing impeding layer from 30 cm (Sub-category 5.2).

Figure 3.35 Well structured throughout cracking clay showing non restrictive clay to 120 cm (grey brown layer near base) (Sub-category 5.3).

usually neutral, although mildly alkaline and even calcareous surfaces occur. There is a general tendency for the proportions of exchangeable magnesium and sodium to increase with depth and a corresponding decrease in exchangeable calcium (**TABLE 3.11**). This is reflected in the deterioration of structure, to the point where root growth is effectively impeded. The physically restrictive layer may also be chemically restrictive, due to high boron and sodium concentrations. Over-irrigation of these soils leads to an accumulation of salts at the top of the restrictive layer. Leaching is difficult because of the slow permeability of clayey soils.

Well structured throughout cracking clay (Sub-category 5.3)

These soils have no physical restrictions within 80 cm of the surface. In the Coonawarra region where they are common, limestone or marl below the soil profile will restrict root growth, but 80 cm provides ample rootzone depth. Controlling soil moisture over this depth range in a clayey soil is a significant management issue. Vigorous growth and high productivity are typical of these soils.

3.3.6 CATEGORY 6: DUPLEX SOIL WITH RESTRICTIVE SUBSOIL
This category has a clear to abrupt texture change (Isbell 1996) between the topsoil and subsoil. Root growth, water movement and aeration in the subsoil are significantly restricted by adverse physical characteristics. Sub-categories within each of the two categories separate soils on the basis of topsoil thickness

and hardness. The differences between restrictive and non-restrictive duplex soils (Category 7) lie in the structure of subsoil, so the two categories have many other features in common (**TABLES 3.12, 3.13**). These are discussed below.

General characteristics of duplex soils

Duplex soils are extensive throughout Australia, and are widespread in most viticultural areas, the most notable exception being the highland areas of the Riverland, Swan Hill and Murray Darling regions. The significance of 'duplex' character lies in the throttle imposed by the sudden increase in clay content at the topsoil-subsoil interface. This throttle is less marked where the subsoil is porous, and has relatively low bulk density and low strength (Soil Category 7), but there is nevertheless some impact on water movement and root growth. In the duplex soils with restrictive subsoils (Soil Category 6), this impact is accentuated, sometimes to the point where little effective root growth occurs at all in the subsoil. At best, root penetration of only about 20 cm can be expected in these materials (Wetherby 2003). Topsoil textures range from sand to clay loam (i.e. clay contents from 0% to 35%). The thickness of the topsoil is significant in duplex soils, especially those with restrictive subsoils. Thicker topsoils provide greater opportunities for root growth above the hard subsoil, or above the water table perching on the subsoil. The hardness of the topsoil is also significant, impacting on root growth, water infiltration and workability. Pre-plant ripping with gypsum incorporation is desirable with these soils, with on-going mulching to provide organic materials for aggregate stabilization.

Sandy topsoils generally do not impose physical restrictions on root growth, but they have other drawbacks. Natural fertility is low and severe deficiencies of phosphorus and nitrogen are common. Calcium, magnesium, copper, zinc and molybdenum deficiencies may also occur. Sandy soils are also susceptible to water repellence. Delving to bring subsoil clay to the surface can help improve nutrient retention capacity and ameliorate water repellence. However, delving becomes more difficult as clay depth increases. Where sandy topsoils are underlain by restrictive subsoils, mounding is an option to improve drainage along the planting rows, but sandy mounds tend to be short-lived. In duplex soils, the subsoil is easily distinguished from the topsoil. As well as having a significantly increased clay content, colour and structure contrasts are common. The change from topsoil to subsoil occurs over a vertical interval of less than 50 mm. The amount of clay increase that constitutes duplex is defined by Isbell (1996). Subsoil textures range from sandy clay loam to heavy clay (i.e. clay content as low as 20% and up to 80% or more). Typically, subsoil clay content lies between 35% and 60%.

Subsoil clays vary from red through yellowish brown and greyish brown to black. Where drainage is significantly impeded, subsoil colours are mottled, and distinctive bleaching of the subsurface layer immediately above the clay is characteristic (FIGURES 3.36-3.39). However, bleaching can be obliterated by cultivation, especially where topsoils are thin. Deeper subsoils are commonly calcareous and highly sodic. This can mean that soil pH can increase by up to four units in the upper metre of soil (e.g. from 5.5$_w$ to 9.5$_w$). Soil reaction varies widely, depending on rainfall, parent material, position in landscape, and quality of irrigation water. In higher rainfall areas soils may be acidic throughout, particularly on rising ground where leaching conditions are generally better than on flats. Even in high rainfall regions such as the Adelaide Hills and Clare Valley, deep subsoils can be alkaline due to poor drainage and/or the influence of alkaline ground water. In lower rainfall districts, there is a general tendency to higher alkalinity at depth (even though surface soils may still be acidic). Where annual rainfall is less than 500 mm, calcareous subsoils are common. In the poorly structured Category 6 soils, high sodicity may further increase alkalinity (e.g. pH$_{CaCl2}$ >8.0). Duplex soils formed on alkaline materials such as limestone or marl invariably have alkaline subsoils.

Characteristics of restrictive subsoils

The restrictive nature of subsoil is attributable to high strength, high bulk density and low porosity. Strength usually exceeds 2 MPa at field capacity, bulk density usually exceeds 1.3, and air filled porosity is usually less than 15% of soil volume. These properties are reflected in the observable ped structure of the soil. Columnar, prismatic, lenticular or angular blocky peds exceeding 20 mm across are typical of these subsoil materials. In soils without apparent pedality, restrictive subsoils are hard, dense and massive. Restrictive subsoils are commonly, but not always, sodic and dispersive. The impacts on root growth are essentially two-fold:
• roots have limited penetration capacity;
• water is likely to perch on top of the subsoil causing temporary waterlogging and possible salt accumulation.

Root growth in these subsoils is poor due to the high resistance imposed on the growing tips. It is common to observe roots on the surfaces of the peds, but few or none inside. Consequently water and nutrient uptake are inefficient. Wetherby (1998) suggests that vine roots are unlikely to penetrate more than 20 cm, indicating that restrictive subsoils only provide a maximum of about 10 mm of readily available water. This of course means that the nature and thickness of the topsoil are critical in determining viticultural potential. The thinner and sandier the topsoil, the lower the readily available water holding capacity, and the shorter the time to saturation. Waterlogging caused by a 'perched water table' sitting on top of the restrictive subsoil is a potentially serious constraint to the productivity and longevity of vineyards. Where water can flow laterally, as on sloping sites, the problem may be manageable (although water is lost to the rootzone), but on flatter

Table 3.12 Duplex soils with restrictive subsoils: sub-categories.

Sub-category	Name	Diagnostic features	Regional occurrence[a]	
			Common	Limited
6.1	Restrictive duplex soil with thin well structured topsoil	Topsoil is not hard and thinner than 30 cm	CC, EV, KI, GN, SW	AP, BV, GB, GS, HU, MD, RI, SB, SH, TA
6.2	Restrictive duplex soil with thick well structured topsoil	Topsoil is not hard and between 30 and 80 cm thick	AH, AP, BV, CC, CO, EV, GS, KI, GN, MV, SW, WR	GB, HU, MD, MR, PA, PB, RI, SB, SF, SH, TA
6.3	Restrictive duplex soil with thin hard topsoil	Topsoil is hard and thinner than 30 cm	AP, AV, BE, BV, CW, GL, GR, GV, HE, HU, LC, MU, MV, PA, PB, PY, RI, RU, SB, SU, YV	AH, CC, CL, CO, EV, KI, GN, RL, SF, SH, SR, TA, YV
6.4	Restrictive duplex soil with thick hard topsoil	Topsoil is hard and between 30 and 80 cm thick	AP, AV, BE, BV, CW, EV, GE, GL, GR, GV, HE, HU, LC, MO, MU, MV, PB, RI, RU, SB, SU, TA, WR, YV	AH, CC, CL, CO, GS, KI, GN, PY, SH, SR, YV

[a] Refer to the list of regional codes associated with Figure 2.2.

Figure 3.36 Duplex soil with thin sandy topsoil over a restrict-ive clay subsoil from 15 cm. Potential rootzone depth is 35 cm (Sub-category 6.1).

Figure 3.37 Duplex soil with thick sandy topsoil over a restrictive clay subsoil from 45 cm. Potential rootzone depth is 65 cm (Sub-category 6.2).

Figure 3.38 Duplex soil with thin hard sandy loam topsoil over a restrictive clay subsoil from 22 cm. Potential rootzone depth is 40-45 cm (Sub-category 6.3).

Figure 3.39 Duplex soil with thick hard light sandy clay loam topsoil over a restrictive clay subsoil from 60 cm. Potential rootzone depth is 80 cm (Sub-category 6.4).

ground agricultural drains and/or mounding will be required. During the growing season, saturation for periods exceeding one day can have detrimental effects on vine roots (Cass and Maschmedt 1998). This degree of waterlogging affects virtually all duplex soils with restrictive subsoils. Ripping with gypsum incorporation prior to planting is the best option for improving the structure of restrictive subsoils.

Restrictive duplex soil with well structured topsoil (Sub-categories 6.1, 6.2)

These soils are mostly 'sand over clay' types, although soft loamy sand to sandy loam, as well as crumbly loam to clay loam topsoils are included. The loamy types are better viticultural soils, having higher inherent fertility and water holding capacity, but sand to light sandy loam textures are more common in vineyards. The common feature of all texture grades is that they do not impose a physical restriction on root growth. The essential feature of these soils is the restriction imposed by the subsoil on both water movement and root growth. The severity of this restriction is largely determined by the topsoil thickness. In the illustrations below (**FIGURES 3.36, 3.37**), potential rootzone depths in the thin and thick sub-categories are 35 cm and 65 cm respectively, with corresponding RAW values of 15 mm and 25 mm. Increasing thickness of topsoil over the restrictive clayey subsoil provides greater buffering capacity against waterlogging, thereby improving the scope for irrigation flexibility. These soils are highly susceptible to water erosion on sloping sites, while the sandy-surfaced forms are also prone to wind erosion. Protection of the surface by mulch or grassy sward is necessary in most situations.

Restrictive duplex soil with hard topsoil (Sub-categories 6.3, 6.4)

These soils are sandy loam to clay loam over clay types. Topsoils are typically massive and dense. When dry, they form clods, which are sufficiently hard that they can not be broken by hand.

As is the case with the sub-category 6.1 and 6.2 soils, the thickness of the topsoil is significant in determining the potential rootzone depth and likely severity of waterlogging. In the illustrations (**FIGURES 3.38, 3.39**), potential rootzone depths vary from 40 cm to 80 cm, with corresponding RAW values of 25 mm and 50 mm. Gypsum is commonly applied to these soils, as both a surface conditioner, and as a flocculating agent to improve subsoil structure. In the latter situation, pre-plant ripping with gypsum incorporation is far more effective than post-establishment treatment. Mounding is a feasible technique for improving drainage of the upper rootzone along planting lines, and is clearly more effective in the thinner surfaced 6.3 soils. In sloping vineyards, water erosion is a real threat as these soils are highly erodible; therefore maintenance of an inter-row grassy sward or mulch is essential.

Table 3.13 Analytical data for some restrictive duplex soils. Source: Soil and Land Information Group, Dept. of Water, Land and Biodiversity Conservation (SA), Dept. of Primary Industries, Water and Environ. (Tas.) and Natural Resource Assessment Group, Agriculture WA.

Sub-category	Local name / Region	Depth (cm)	Texture / geology	pH CaCl$_2$	CO3 %	EC 1:5 dS/m	CEC cmol (+)/kg	Exchangeable cations			
								Ca	Mg	Na	K
6.1	Sand over sodic brown clay	0-15	Sand	7.3	0	0.04	2.0	1.15	0.41	0.05	0.11
	Barossa Valley	27-50	Sandy heavy clay	5.9	0	0.16	17.9	5.87	7.55	3.03	0.56
		110-135	Sandy medium clay	5.9	0	0.29	15.8	4.34	6.42	5.94	0.39
6.1	Sandy loam over clay	0-15	Sandy loam	6.1	0	0.06	nd	5.4	1.6	0.27	0.26
	Derwent Valley, Tasmania	29-50	Medium heavy clay	7.2	0	0.22	nd	1.8	14	3.0	0.58
		50-65	Medium clay	7.9	0	0.23	nd	0.71	15	3.5	0.67
6.2	Duplex sandy gravel	0-4	Loamy sand	5.2	0	0.06	5	2.2	1.0	0.2	0.1
	Margaret River	50-70	Light clay	5.1	0	0.03	1	0.2	0.7	<0.1	<0.1
		85-105	Light clay	5.1	0	0.03	<1	<0.1	0.7	<0.1	<0.1
6.2	Sand over clay	0-13	Loamy sand	4.7	0	0.21	4.2	2.72	0.37	0.17	0.35
	McLaren Vale	32-45	Medium clay	6.1	0	0.31	33.4	19.1	10.6	2.24	1.35
		90-125	Medium heavy clay	8.1	27	0.30	17.0	6.80	8.57	2.68	0.43
6.3	Sandy loam over red clay	0-21	Sandy loam	5.8	0	0.13	4.7	3.5	0.8	0.18	1.80
	Barossa Valley	21-50	Heavy clay	6.9	0	0.10	17.1	11.3	3.6	0.43	1.22
		90-100	Clay loam	7.9	0.5	0.28	10.2	6.6	3.0	0.42	0.57
6.3	Clay loam over brown clay	0-10	Clay loam	7.7	0	0.13	19.0	11.8	3.18	0.17	1.07
	Padthaway (plains)	24-36	Medium clay	7.4	0	0.12	41.1	24.6	7.85	1.51	2.31
		90-115	Light medium clay	8.0	60	0.20	18.3	13.5	3.38	1.62	1.04
6.4	Sandy loam over red clay	0-15	Fine sandy loam	6.3	0	0.13	9.3	8.13	1.29	0.14	0.56
	McLaren Vale	30-60	Medium clay	5.7	0	0.09	28.0	15.8	5.87	1.81	1.72
		90-130	Medium clay	7.9	9	0.28	20.3	14.8	4.37	1.45	0.99
6.4	Sandy loam over brown clay	0-15	Sandy loam	6.2	0	0.07	8.2	7.9	1.4	0.18	0.46
	Clare Valley	65-90	Heavy clay	6.5	0	0.08	31.0	16.9	10.9	0.53	1.07
		90-120	Heavy clay	6.8	0	0.10	30.2	17.8	12.4	0.73	0.98

3.3.7 CATEGORY 7: DUPLEX SOIL WITH NON-RESTRICTIVE SUBSOIL

This category has a clear to abrupt texture change (Isbell 1996) between the topsoil and subsoil. Root growth, water movement and aeration in the subsoil are not significantly restricted by adverse physical characteristics. Sub-categories separate soils on the basis of topsoil thickness and hardness (**TABLES 3.14, 3.15**). The differences between restrictive (Category 6) and non-restrictive duplex soils lie in the structure of subsoil, so the two categories have many other features in common (refer to the introductory paragraphs of 3.3.6).

Non-restrictive duplex soil with well structured topsoil (Sub-categories 7.1, 7.2)

These are soils with loose sandy to soft sandy loam surfaces over friable clayey subsoils. Physically, they are the best of the duplex soils, presenting minimal restrictions to root growth, water movement and aeration. They have a significantly greater rootzone depth and better leaching capacity than their Category 6 counterparts, thereby improving their long term viability under irrigation, and providing greater flexibility with regard to irrigation scheduling. They are not prone to the restricted infiltration and workability problems of the hard surfaced sub-categories of duplex soils, but in general have poorer nutrition status due to their lower clay contents.

Non-restrictive duplex soil with hard topsoil (Sub-categories 7.3, 7.4)

These soils include hard settting sandy loam to clay loam types over well structured clayey subsoils. Like the sub-category 7.1 and 7.2 soils, they have ample rootzones (except where underlain by basement rock or calcrete at depths of between 50 and 100 cm). Sub-optimal surface condition need not be a major problem, given that there are several ways of ameliorating poor structure. There is potential for water erosion in sloping vineyards, so effective cover must be maintained.

3.3.8 CATEGORY 8: CALCAREOUS SOIL

These soils are calcareous throughout, or at least from 20 cm depth. Differences within the category are linked to clay content, and form and amount of carbonate (**TABLES 3.16, 3.17**).

Carbonates in soil are easily detected by applying 1 M hydrochloric acid (HCl). The strength of the reaction (i.e. bubbling or fizzing) provides a rough indicator of carbonate content. Generally, a strong reaction in which bubble diameters exceed 5 mm, and the effervescence 'jumps up' indicates a carbonate content of more than 8%. At this level, nutrient fixation is likely to be a problem. Free carbonate in the soil reduces the availability of several nutrient elements including phosphorus, manganese, zinc and iron. The higher the carbonate content, the more severe these induced

Table 3.14 Duplex soils with non- restrictive subsoils: sub-categories.

Sub-category	Name	Diagnostic features	Regional occurrence[a]	
			Common	Limited
7.1	Non-restrictive duplex soil with thin well structured topsoil	Topsoil is not hard and thinner than 30 cm	EV, GB, SW	CC, GS, HU, SF
7.2	Non-restrictive duplex soil with thick well structured topsoil	Topsoil is not hard and between 30 and 80 cm thick	AP, BV, CC, CO, EV, GB, GS, MA, MR, PB, SF, SW	GE, HU, MB
7.3	Non-restrictive duplex soil with thin hard topsoil	Topsoil is hard and thinner than 30 cm	AH, BV, BW, CL, CW, GV, GR, HU, GN, MU, MV, PA, PY, RI, RU, SF, SW, UG	CC, CO, EV, GE, GL, HE, KI, MA, MD, SW
7.4	Non-restrictive duplex soil with thick hard topsoil	Topsoil is hard and between 30 and 80 cm thick	AH, AP, BV, BW, CL, CW, GE, GR, GV, HU, GN, LC, MU, MV, PB, PY, RI, RU, SR, UG	CC, CO, EV, GL, GS, KI, MR, WR

[a] Refer to the list of regional codes associated with Figure 2.2.

deficiencies become. High carbonate contents also affect the performance of some pesticides, particularly herbicides. Prolonged irrigation of calcareous soils can alter the concentration and nature of carbonates, for example by surface soil leaching and softening of sheet and rubbly subsoil calcrete layers.

The clay content and the amount of rubbly carbonate affect drainage and root growth (Wetherby and Oades 1975). In general, root growth and drainage are better in sandier and/or rubbly soils. Chemically-hostile layers tend to occur at shallower depth in the more clayey profiles, or those with less rubble. The potential vine rootzone is determined by the depth to either a hardpan (calcrete) or a chemically-hostile layer. Because calcareous soils tend to occur in drier areas where leaching is restricted, subsoil salinity and sodicity are common features. Boron toxicity is frequently associated with these conditions. All

calcareous soils are alkaline, and some are strongly alkaline at depth. Strong alkalinity is invariably associated with high sodicity, and commonly with high boron and electrolyte concentrations (**TABLE 3.17**). Root growth is severely restricted in heavier soils when pH (water) exceeds 9.2. Potential rootzone depth can be reduced to as little as 30 cm. Such conditions are common on flats and swales between sandy rises. Profiles with restricted drainage are at risk of salinization—deep subsoil salts are brought to the surface by rising water tables, and leaching of salts in applied irrigation water is impeded. The sandier forms are prone to wind erosion if exposed.

The calcareous soils are widespread in the irrigation areas of the River Murray from Mannum through to the Riverland in South Australia, throughout the Murray Darling region of Victoria to Swan Hill, and into New South Wales.

Table 3.15 Analytical data for some non-restrictive duplex soils. Source: Soil and Land Information Group, Dept. of Water, Land and Biodiversity Conservation (SA) and Natural Resource Assessment Group, Agriculture WA.

Sub-category	Local name / Region	Depth (cm)	Texture / geology	pH CaCl₂	CO3 %	EC 1:5 dS/m	CEC cmol (+)/kg	Exchangeable cations			
								Ca	Mg	Na	K
7.1	Sandy loam over brown clay	0-10	Sandy loam	4.2	0	0.08	9.0	4.6	0.9	0.10	0.15
	Southern Fleurieu	23-40	Medium clay	4.2	0	0.05	7.0	1.9	1.7	0.11	0.28
		70-130	Clay loam	4.8	0	0.04	1.9	<0.4	1.3	0.14	0.08
7.1	Sandy loam over brown clay	0-21	Sandy loam	5.1	0	0.05	2.6	1.8	0.5	0.12	0.12
	Eden Valley	21-65	Medium clay	5.0	0	0.07	4.2	1.4	2.0	0.20	0.12
		65-100	Weathered schist	5.1	0	0.08	3.0	0.7	2.3	0.17	0.08
7.2	Friable red brown loamy earth	0-10	Sandy loam	4.7	0	0.07	nd	6.05	1.05	0.11	0.28
	Manjimup	50-80	Clay loam	5.7	0	0.04	nd	2.91	0.80	0.10	0.19
		100-150	Clay loam	6.0	0	0.03	nd	2.46	1.09	0.10	0.12
7.2	Sand over red clay	0-12	Sand	7.3	0	0.35	3.7	1.90	0.50	0.53	0.41
	Adelaide Plains	44-61	Light clay	7.2	0	0.26	10.8	4.83	3.35	1.79	1.08
		100-160	Sandy loam	8.0	3.3	0.47	6.6	2.43	2.62	1.85	0.47
7.3	Sandy loam over red clay	0-15	Fine sandy loam	6.2	0	0.07	10.1	10.21	1.26	0.10	1.08
	Padthaway (plains)	28-45	Medium clay	6.9	0	0.09	35.2	22.01	4.52	1.03	2.02
		85-120	Medium clay	7.9	16	0.20	37.6	27.96	4.51	2.32	2.24
7.3	Clay loam over red clay	0-8	Clay loam	5.0	0	0.06	14.5	6.84	3.35	0.14	0.55
	Adelaide Hills	14-30	Heavy clay	4.4	0	0.04	14.4	4.36	6.50	0.21	0.56
		75-100	Medium clay	4.2	0	0.08	11.1	0.49	5.49	0.19	0.05
7.4	Loam over brown clay	0-15	Loam	4.4	0	0.07	nd	2.40	0.99	0.22	0.20
	Adelaide Hills	35-50	Medium clay	5.0	0	0.03	nd	2.90	6.18	0.20	0.27
		50-80	Light clay	4.9	0	0.03	nd	1.69	4.39	0.17	0.13
7.4	McLaren Vale	0-10	Fine sandy clay loam	6.1	0	0.20	11.3	8.4	1.0	0.25	0.90
		45-80	Medium heavy clay	5.6	0	0.15	18.8	8.7	7.2	0.78	0.75
		105-130	Heavy clay	7.0	0	0.18	23.2	12.0	6.6	0.97	0.73

Figure 3.40 Duplex soil with thin soft sandy loam topsoil over a friable clayey subsoil from 20 cm. Potential root zone depth is 70 cm (Sub-category 7.1).

Figure 3.41 Duplex soil with thick sandy topsoil over a well structured clayey subsoil from 45 cm, becoming sandier with depth. Potential root zone depth exceeds 150 cm (Sub-category 7.2).

Figure 3.42 Duplex soil with thin hard fine sandy loam topsoil over a non restrictive clayey subsoil from 15 cm. Potential root zone depth is 65 cm (Sub-category 7.3).

Figure 3.43 Duplex soil with thick clay loam topsoil over a non restrictive clay subsoil from 40 cm. Potential root zone depth is 90 cm (Sub-category 7.4).

Sandy calcareous soil (Sub-category 8.1)

These are typical of mallee sandhills and are commonly called 'mallee sands'. Past erosion of the sandhills has caused considerable depth variations, so whilst some profiles may be several metres deep, calcrete, other restrictive carbonate layers or clay layers can occur at any depth. The soils are commonly loamy sands (i.e. about 5% clay), often with a slight increase in clay content at depth (**FIGURE 3.44**). Carbonate concentrations are typically less than 5%, with surface pH$_{CaCl2}$ values of about 7.0-7.5. Inherent fertility is low: low clay and organic matter contents restrict the soil's capacity to retain nutrients, while free carbonate and elevated pH tend to 'tie up' phosphorus and trace elements to some extent. Drainage is rapid where there is no underlying restrictive layer (except at sites of

previous erosion - see above). Readily available water holding capacity is typically about 55 mm in a one metre deep profile. Wind erosion is a hazard if the soil surface is exposed, and occasionally water repellence is a problem preventing even wetting of the soil.

Shallow calcareous restrictive soil (Sub-category 8.2)

Calcrete pans, or cemented sheets of highly calcareous material, are common in mallee landscapes at variable depths below the soil surface. Sometimes the pans consist of weakly cemented nodules (rubble) in which case they are easily ripped to allow root penetration. However, some forms of calcrete are massive, dense and very hard (**FIGURE 3.45**). Ripping these materials is not practicable, because even if machinery can penetrate, the large loosened fragments cannot be crushed, and must be

Table 3.16 Calcareous soils: sub-categories.

Sub-category	Name	Diagnostic features	Regional occurrence[a] Common	Regional occurrence[a] Limited
8.1	Sandy calcareous soil	Sandy to at least 80 cm	-	MD, RL, SH
8.2	Shallow calcareous restrictive soil	Soil overlies non-rippable calcareous rock or calcrete between 15 and 50 cm	-	RL
8.3	Shallow calcareous non-restrictive soil	Soil over rippable calcareous rock or calcrete between 15 and 50 cm	-	RL
8.4	Rubbly calcareous soil	Soil has a layer with more than 30% carbonate rubble at least 20 cm thick	RL, MD, SH	-
8.5	Clayey calcareous soil	Clayey (> light clay) over carbonate layer within 80 cm	MD, RL, SH	MV
8.6	Loamy calcareous soil	Loamy, clay loamy or light clayey over carbonate layer within 80 cm	MD, RL, SH	RI, AP

[a] Refer to the list of regional codes associated with Figure 2.2.

Figure 3.44 Sandy calcareous soil showing unrestricted rootzone to 150 cm, and subsoil accumulation of Class IV carbonate (Sub-category 8.1).

Figure 3.45 Shallow calcareous restrictive soil showing massive Class II calcrete restricting root zone depth to 30 cm (Sub-category 8.2).

Figure 3.46 Shallow calcareous non restrictive soil showing rippable calcrete at 25 cm, and Pleistocene clay substrate at 170 cm (Sub-category 8.3).

Figure 3.47 Rubbly calcareous soil showing well defined Class III C nodular carbonate layer with Pleistocene clay at base (Sub-category 8.4).

removed from the site. The soil above the calcrete varies from loamy sand to clay loam (i.e. clay contents range from 5% to 35%) and contains variable amounts of carbonate nodules or fragments. Water holding capacity is determined by the depth to calcrete (which marks the lower extent of the rootzone), the concentration of coarse fragments, and the texture. RAW values therefore range from less than 10 mm to about 40 mm. Whilst 30–40 mm of RAW may be considered beneficial from a moisture management point of view, other development considerations such as the installation of trellising may determine the potential of these soils for viticulture.

Shallow calcareous non-restrictive soil (Sub-category 8.3)

These soils are similar to the shallow calcareous soils discussed above, except that the calcrete layer is rippable (**FIGURE 3.46**), providing additional rooting depth, and allowing easier installation of posts and irrigation hardware. Vine roots can generally penetrate about 50 cm into ripped calcrete, but this does not greatly increase the water holding capacity in the rootzone, because of the high proportion of rubble. About 5 to 10 mm of additional RAW can be achieved. The material underlying the calcrete has a significant bearing on the suitability of the soil for development. Generally the calcrete grades to a less rubbly very highly calcareous material, which in turn may overlie a heavy clay. In substantial areas of southern Australia's mallee landscapes, this is a hard, reddish coarsely structured

Pleistocene age (i.e. about one million years old) clay deposit, locally known as Blanchetown or Hindmarsh Clay. Being only slowly permeable, it prevents free drainage, and over time causes salts to accumulate in a perched water table, which eventually reaches into the rootzone. The Pleistocene clay has also prevented the leaching of toxic boron from the soil, and this can cause additional problems for vine root growth. As a general rule, careful irrigation design and management are needed where the clay is within 150 cm of the surface, and development is usually not recommended if the clay is shallower than 75 cm. The shallow calcareous soils are well suited to viticulture where the Pleistocene Clay is absent, soil texture is sandy loam to light sandy clay loam (10–25% clay), and readily available water holding capacities are in the 40–50 mm range. Otherwise, irrigation scheduling and/or future drainage problems are likely to downgrade site quality.

Rubbly calcareous soil (Sub-category 8.4)

These soils typically comprise a calcareous sandy loam surface, becoming slightly more clayey and calcareous with depth, over a well-defined layer of nodular (rubbly) carbonate at depths of between 20 and 50 cm (**FIGURE 3.47**). This rubble layer—described by Wetherby and Oades (1975) as Class III B or III C carbonate—grades to a very highly calcareous sandy loam to light clay with occasional nodules. This material in turn overlies older sediments. The rubble layer presents no barriers to vine roots, so effective rootzone depth in these soils is invariably more than 50 cm, and can be up to 100 cm. Even allowing for the rubble content, readily available water holding capacities are typically in the range 50 to 80 mm in the potential rootzone.

As is the case with all calcareous soils, there is a degree of nutrient fixation caused by the free carbonate content and alkaline pH of the soil, but only where there is a strong reaction to applied acid. Generally these soils are well suited to viticultural production—the main exception being when the soil is underlain by a restrictive clay layer, such as Pleistocene Clay, within 150 cm.

Clayey calcareous soil (Sub-category 8.5)

These soils are finer textured than the other calcareous sub-categories. This is at least partly a reflection of the materials underlying the soil (the 'substrate'). This is invariably a heavy clay sediment, and is often Pleistocene clay (Blanchetown Clay or equivalent). The profile consists of a calcareous loamy to clay loamy surface (20% to 35% clay), becoming more clayey and calcareous with depth. A well-defined highly calcareous clay layer (Wetherby and Oades (1975; Class I carbonate) occurs within 50 cm of the surface, usually shallower. The substrate layer is generally evident from depths of about 80 cm as the whitish carbonate layer gives way to the red or brown clay. The low permeability of the clay has caused salts and boron to accumulate in the lower soil profile over long periods of time, so it is common to record unacceptably high (for viticulture) levels of several soil properties within 50-75 cm of the surface. These include pH$_{CaCl2}$ values of more than 8.5, exchangeable sodium percentages (ESP) more than 25, extractable boron concentrations more than 15 mg/kg,

Figure 3.48 Clayey calcareous soil showing fine grained Class I carbonate at shallow depth, and Pleistocene clay from about 70 cm (Sub-category 8.5).

Figure 3.49 Loamy calcareous soil showing carbonate accumulation between 50 and 80 cm where high pH restricts root growth (Sub-category 8.6).

and electrical conductivities (saturation paste) more than 6 dS/m. Restricted drainage and the medium to long term impacts on rootzone salinity, sodicity and boron levels preclude these soils from most viticultural developments. However, they occur in association with other more favourable soils, so recognition is essential for successful vineyard development.

Table 3.17 Analytical data for some calcareous soils. Source: Soil and Land Information Group, Dept. of Water, Land and Biodiversity Conservation (SA).

Sub-category	Local name / Region	Depth (cm)	Texture / geology	pH CaCl₂	CO3 %	EC 1:5 dS/m	CEC cmol (+)/kg	Exchangeable cations			
								Ca	Mg	Na	K
8.1	Calcareous sand	0-10	Light loamy sand	8.0	1	0.11	4.4	4.7	0.57	0.08	0.87
		45-85	Light loamy sand	8.3	2	0.07	3.5	3.9	0.77	0.09	0.19
		85-150	Light loamy sand	8.2	2	0.07	3.2	4.4	0.60	0.09	0.21
8.3	Shallow calcareous sandy loam	0-10	Sandy loam	7.4	1	0.11	6.0	5.7	1.1	0.08	0.44
	(Lower Murray highlands)	18-81	Calcrete (scl matrix)	8.5	52	0.74	7.4	4.0	2.9	1.7	0.20
		81-120	Sandy clay loam	8.6	70	1.74	5.9	1.0	2.2	3.1	0.58
8.4	Rubbly calcareous sandy loam	0-10	Sandy loam	7.9	3	0.12	9.5	8.4	1.2	0.16	0.98
	(Lower Murray highlands)	27-43	Fine sandy clay loam	8.5	12	0.29	8.4	3.6	4.3	1.49	0.62
		75-121	Fine sandy clay loam	8.9	6	0.92	9.8	0.9	2.5	5.59	1.01
8.5	Calcareous loam of river flat	0-7	Lt sandy clay loam	8.4	5.0	0.69	13.5	7.8	4.7	2.2	1.7
	(Riverland)	30-65	Sandy light clay	8.6	22	0.38	9.8	4.1	4.9	3.6	0.76
		98-127	Medium clay	8.8	3	0.45	14.9	3.7	6.7	5.8	1.2
8.6	Calcareous sandy loam over	0-10	Sandy loam	8.0	3	0.15	17.3	11.9	3.2	0.60	1.9
	Pleistocene Clay (Riverland)	25-75	Sandy clay loam	8.8	24	1.57	14.1	1.5	6.0	6.1	1.5
		87-120	Medium clay	8.8	5	2.16	21.7	1.5	8.6	8.8	1.7
8.6	Calcareous sandy loam over	0-10	Heavy sandy loam	8.0	4	0.17	11.2	8.7	2.9	0.50	1.8
	calcrete (Riverland)	20-40	Sandy clay loam	8.1	12	0.14	9.0	9.8	2.9	0.59	0.80
		60-80	Sandy light clay	8.2	29	0.16	11.6	8.5	4.9	0.70	0.92

Table 3.18 Uniform or gradational soils: sub-categories.

Sub-category	Name	Diagnostic features	Regional occurrence[a]	
			Common	Limited
9.1	Deep sandy uniform soil	Sandy to at least 50 cm	CC, GB, GE, MV, RL, SW	AP, BV, EV, GR, GS, GV, LC, MB, MD, MR, PA, RU, SB, SF, SH, TA, WR
9.2	Deep sandy gradational soil	Sandy topsoil over loam to clay within 50 cm	GB, RI, SB, SW	AH, AP, BE, HU, LC, MD, MR, RL, SH, TA
9.3	Deep loamy calcareous unigrad* soil	Sandy loam to loam topsoil with calcareous subsoil	RI	MD, PA, RL, SH
9.4	Deep clayey calcareous unigrad* soil	Clay loam to clay topsoil with calcareous subsoil	CL	AP, MV, PA, RL
9.5	Deep hard loamy unigrad* soil	Firm to hard sandy loam to loam topsoil	GE, GS, KV, RI, MA, MR, PB, RU, SR, UG	BV, HE, HU, KI, MU, MV, SW, TA
9.6	Deep well structured loamy unigrad* soil	Sandy loam to loam topsoil well structured to at least 50 cm	AH, BW, HE, HU, KV, LC, MA, PB, RI, RU, UG	BV, CL, GS, GV, CW, MR, MU, MV, SF, SW
9.7	Deep hard clayey unigrad* soil	Firm to hard clay loam to clay topsoil	-	LC, TA, YV
9.8	Deep well structured clayey unigrad* soil	Clay loam to clay topsoil well structured to at least 50 cm	TA, HU, MO, SB	AP, CL, CO, GV, LC, KV, MU, MV, YV

* Unigrad implies 'uniform' or 'gradational' texture profile.
[a] Refer to the list of regional codes associated with Figure 2.2.

Loamy calcareous soil (Sub-category 8.6)

These soils consist of up to 50 cm moderately calcareous sandy loam (usually with some increase in clay and carbonate content over this depth), grading to a very highly calcareous light sandy clay loam to sandy light clay layer with minimal rubble, extending below 100 cm— this is the Class III A carbonate layer of Wetherby and Oades (1975). The more clayey types (Class III AL) allow vine roots to penetrate about 30 cm, while the sandier types (Class III AS) allow up to 50 cm penetration. Readily available water holding capacities therefore range from 50 to 80 mm. Salt accumulations in the carbonate layer are common, but these can be leached provided that the profile and the material below are free draining. Where the soils are underlain by restrictive clays, water tables and salt concentrations may build up over time. Carbonate contents of the topsoil are rarely high enough to cause significant nutrient fixation. Generally, these soils have high viticultural potential.

3.3.9 CATEGORY 9: UNIFORM OR GRADATIONAL SOIL

This category has a uniform clay content, or a gradual increase in clay content. A hard restrictive layer may occur anywhere in the profile. Because this category includes all the soils not classified elsewhere, there is a wide range. Soils may be sandy, loamy or clayey throughout, or may become more clayey with depth. Sub-categories separate soils on the basis of clay content, hardness and presence of subsoil carbonates (TABLES 3.18, 3.19).

The uniform or gradational soils are generally deep. The strength of sub-surface layer(s) may affect potential rootzone depth, but hard pan or hard basement rock does not occur in the upper 50 cm, and a clearly defined clayey subsoil (duplex) does not occur in the upper 80 cm. Clay content is important in determining water holding capacity, permeability and nutrient retention characteristics. Subsoil carbonates may be indicative of adverse chemical conditions.

Deep sandy uniform soil (Sub-category 9.1)

These soils have unrestricted root growth conditions to at least 50 cm, and commonly much deeper. However, water holding capacity per unit depth is less than in soils of higher clay content. For example, readily available water holding capacity of a sand is about 35 mm/m, compared with about 70 mm/m for a loam. Similarly, nutrient retention capacity is significantly lower for sands (compare the cation exchange values for the different texture classes in TABLE 3.19). Although the sands themselves are permeable, and sometimes excessively so, underlying materials affect overall site drainage. For example, a metre or so of sand on a dune may be underlain by an impervious clay which will either develop a water table, or direct drainage water laterally on to lower lying ground. This situation is not uncommon in the Riverland region. Similarly, deep sandy soils in valleys may be underlain by impeding clay layers, or even a water table; both cause a drainage restriction. This situation occurs for example in the Eden Valley and Margaret River regions on deep coarse textured alluvial soils

Deep sandy soils are common in the Riverland region, generally occurring on sand dunes. These are loose red sands with a neutral to alkaline reaction and often with free carbonate in the subsoil. They are highly susceptible to wind erosion, so inter-rows must be protected. Deep bleached sands are common in the Blewitt Springs area of the McLaren Vale region, on the slopes on the eastern side of the Padthaway region, on dunes at Currency Creek and in the Granite Belt. These tend to be acidic, and being more strongly leached than the red sands, have an even lower nutrient status. Similar sands occur to a more limited extent in the Barossa Valley. The variously coloured deep sands, which occur in all of the Western Australian regions, also fit into this sub-category.

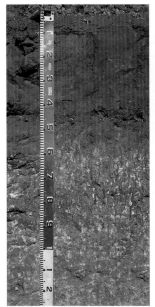

Figure 3.50 Deep sandy uniform soil showing unrestricted root zone to 200 cm. Note clayey lamellae from 150 cm – these help reduce deep drainage water loss (Sub-category 9.1).

Figure 3.51 Deep sandy gradational soil showing loamy sand topsoil over a non restrictive light sandy clay loam subsoil, calcareous from 85 cm (Sub-category 9.2).

Figure 3.52 Deep loamy calcareous unigrad soil with a light sandy loam topsoil becoming more clayey with depth and an unrestricted root zone to 90 cm (i.e. 30 cm into the calcareous sandy clay loam layer) (Sub-category 9.3).

Figure 3.53 Deep clayey calcareous unigrad soil showing well structured clayey topsoil and upper subsoil overlying a calcareous clayey layer allowing about 20 cm root penetration (Sub-category 9.4).

Deep sandy gradational soil (Sub-category 9.2)

In these soils, the sandy topsoil constitutes the main part of the rootzone, while the more clayey subsoil provides a reservoir of water. Depending on the friability of the subsoil, potential rootzone depths and available water holding capacities are moderate to high. Fertility is generally low, but superior to the deep sands of sub-category 9.1 by virtue of the more clayey subsoil. Surface soils are acidic to neutral, and subsoil pH can vary from acidic to alkaline. Most soils in the sub-category are permeable and well drained, although waterlogging can be a problem where clayey sediments occur at depth. Deep sandy gradational soils with alkaline subsoils are common in the Riverina region where they occur on gently undulating plains, sand spreads and low dunes. Some of these are prone to waterlogging. In the Riverland, Murray Darling and Swan Hill regions, these alkaline subsoil forms occur on low sand dunes and swales, and at Langhorne Creek and the Adelaide Plains, they occur on alluvial flats. Acidic forms occur on slopes and alluvial terraces and flats in the Swan District, Margaret River, Granite Belt and South Burnett regions.

Deep loamy calcareous soil (Sub-category 9.3)

These soils have a sandy loam to loam topsoil which grades to a subsoil which is calcareous at least in its lower part. Clay content often increases with depth.

Surface soils are neutral to alkaline, subsoils are always alkaline, sometimes strongly so. The potential rootzone extends into the calcareous subsoil layer—up to 50 cm where texture is coarser than sandy clay loam, and up to 30 cm for more clayey material. Readily available water holding capacities can consequently be high. Profiles are generally permeable, although the drainage characteristics of the more clayey carbonate layers tend to deteriorate after prolonged irrigation. Salt content may be moderate under dryland conditions, but provided deep drainage is adequate, this is quickly leached by irrigation water. These soils are most common in the Riverina, Riverland, Murray Darling, and Swan Hill regions.

Deep clayey calcareous unigrad soil (Sub-category 9.4)

These soils have a sandy clay loam to clayey topsoil which grades to a subsoil which is calcareous at least in its lower part. Surface soils are neutral to alkaline, subsoils are always alkaline, sometimes strongly so. Clay content generally increases with depth, so the carbonate layer is invariably clayey. This calcareous clayey material is a Class I carbonate layer, which only allows about 20 cm of vine root penetration—rootzone depths are consequently restricted where the carbonate is close to the surface. The profile in **FIGURE 3.53** has a readily

Figure 3.54 Deep hard loamy unigrad soil showing a massive loamy topsoil grading to a poorly structured clayey subsoil by 45 cm (maximum rootzone depth is 65 cm) (Sub-category 9.5).

Figure 3.55 Deep well structured loamy unigrad soil with a friable fine sandy loam topsoil grading to a well structured clayey subsoil by 40 cm. Potential rootzone depth is 100 cm or more (Sub-category 9.6).

Figure 3.56 Deep hard clayey unigrad soil with a light clay topsoil over a poorly structured medium heavy clay subsoil from 10 cm. Potential rootzone depth is 30 cm (Sub-category 9.7).

Figure 3.57 Deep well structured clayey unigrad soil with a friable clayey topsoil grading to a well structured clayey subsoil by 50 cm. Potential rootzone depth is 100 cm (Sub-category 9.8). Red Ferrosol, Pipers River (Tas.); photograph by D. Farquhar.

available water holding capacity of about 40 mm, but if the carbonate layer were at 20 cm depth, RAW would be little more than 20 mm. High clay content means high wilting point, so substantial volumes of water are needed to achieve field capacity. This can make irrigation management difficult, especially where these soils are mixed with sandier types. They are less permeable than their sandier counterparts of sub-category 9.3. Furthermore, they commonly overlie slowly permeable sediments that restrict deep drainage, thereby causing salts to accumulate in the root zone. These soils are inherently fertile and are generally excellent cropping soils, but their unfavourable moisture characteristics and useable depth restrict their use for viticulture. There are limited plantings in the Riverland, Adelaide Plains and McLaren Vale.

Deep hard loamy unigrad soil (Sub-category 9.5)

These soils have a sandy loam to loam topsoil which grades to a poorly structured subsoil which is generally more clayey. The topsoil is hard and massive, a condition commonly associated with a high proportion of fine sand and/or silt sized particles which pack tightly together thereby minimizing porosity. Surface soils are acidic to neutral, while subsoils can be acidic to alkaline, but not calcareous. Waterlogging is a common problem due to

poor subsoil structure. Where the subsoil is sodic, prolonged applications of salt in irrigation water will exacerbate this problem. Vine roots can only make use of the upper 20 cm of the subsoil, so rootzone depth is controlled by the depth to the subsoil. In the profile illustrated in **FIGURE 3.54**, maximum potential rootzone depth is 65 cm, with a readily available water holding capacity of about 45 mm. Ironstone gravel is widespread in these soils in the Western Australian regions and on Kangaroo Island. The gravel reduces available water holding capacity. These soils are common in all the Western Australian regions and are used to a limited extent for viticulture in the Riverina and Kangaroo Island regions.

Deep well structured loamy unigrad soil (Sub-category 9.6)

These soils have a sandy loam to loam topsoil which grades to a well structured subsoil. Clay content often increases with depth. Surface soils are acidic to neutral, subsoils may be acidic to alkaline, but not calcareous. The potential root zone extends 50 cm into a clayey subsoil and to the full thickness of a clay loamy or sandier subsoil. Consequently, water holding capacity can be high; about 75 mm for the profile in **FIGURE 3.55**. Profiles are generally permeable. These soils have

Table 3.19 Analytical data for some uniform or gradational soils. Source: Soil and Land Information Group, Dept. of Water, Land and Biodiversity Conservation (SA).

Sub-category	Local name / Region	Depth (cm)	Texture / geology	pH CaCl₂	CO3 %	EC 1:5 dS/m	CEC cmol (+)/kg	Exchangeable cations			
								Ca	Mg	Na	K
9.1	Deep sand	0-10	Fine sand	6.4	0	0.03	2.5	2.63	0.52	<0.1	<0.1
	Padthaway (dune slope)	50-60	Fine sand	7.2	0	0.02	1.0	0.88	0.21	<0.1	<0.1
		125-160	Lt. sandy clay loam	7.7	<1	0.16	7.8	4.80	1.90	0.66	0.36
9.1	Podzol	0-20	Sand	7.1	0	0.03	nd	3.4	0.45	0.03	0.11
	Derwent Valley, Tasmania	42-60	Sand	6.0	0	0.02	nd	0.88	0.15	0.05	0.08
		89-110	Loamy sand	5.5	0	0.02	nd	0.62	0.11	0.03	0.11
9.2 / 9.1	Pale sandy earth	0-5	Loamy sand	4.7	0	0.02	2	0.3	0.2	<0.1	<0.1
	Margaret River	18-40	Coarse sandy loam	4.7	0	0.02	1	0.1	0.3	<0.1	<0.1
		80-100	Coarse sandy loam	4.7	0	0.02	<1	<0.1	0.3	<0.1	<0.1
9.2	Sandy red gradational soil	0-15	Loamy sand	6.3	0	0.41	4.7	2.60	0.52	0.51	0.60
	Adelaide Plains	35-60	Lt. sandy clay loam	6.8	0	0.35	8.2	6.08	1.58	1.20	0.91
		60-85	Sandy clay loam	7.6	<1	0.38	14.7	7.99	3.63	1.53	1.41
9.3	Gradational sandy loam	0-10	Light sandy loam	6.8	0	0.11	6.7	5.0	1.3	0.11	1.3
	Southern Flinders Ranges	25-40	Sandy loam	7.8	<1	0.09	8.4	6.5	1.3	0.12	0.42
		60-80	Sandy clay loam	8.0	7	0.12	9.1	6.8	3.0	0.57	0.55
9.4	Gradational brown clay loam	0-10	Fine sandy clay loam	7.7	0	0.16	12.2	8.80	2.01	0.51	1.02
	Padthaway (plains)	22-43	Medium clay	7.0	0	0.13	38.0	22.61	7.19	2.10	2.44
		75-115	Medium clay	8.0	36	0.41	20.1	13.60	5.71	0.85	1.49
9.4	Deep gradational clay loam	0-10	Clay loam	6.8	0	0.11	13.5	8.21	1.68	0.08	1.26
	Clare Valley	25-40	Medium clay	6.7	0	0.08	30.2	18.17	9.01	0.29	1.50
		95-150	Heavy clay	7.8	12	0.19	27.6	13.78	9.83	0.42	1.04
9.5	Loamy gravel	0-10	Fine sandy loam	5.1	0	0.12	nd	7.8	1.6	0.34	0.19
	(25-70% ironstone gravel)	30-50	Fine sandy clay loam	4.9	0	0.03	nd	1.6	1.6	0.13	0.04
	Margaret River	65-110	Sandy light-med clay	5.3	0	0.02	nd	0.55	1.6	0.09	<0.02
9.5	Ironstone soil	0-10	Fine sandy loam	4.9	0	0.24	13.6	5.79	1.96	0.42	1.01
	(10-75% ironstone gravel)	10-25	Fine sandy clay loam	5.5	0	0.07	6.0	2.03	1.59	0.29	0.47
	Kangaroo Island	45-70	Medium clay	4.1	0	0.87	8.7	0.75	3.86	1.57	0.14
9.6	Gradational red sandy loam	0-12	Fine sandy loam	7.2	0	0.27	9.6	6.95	2.47	0.50	1.38
	Langhorne Creek	35-100	Fine sandy clay loam	8.1	0	0.21	6.2	3.53	1.61	1.21	0.69
		100-140	Loamy sand	7.6	0	0.05	3.3	1.36	0.95	0.63	0.27
9.6	Gradational loam	0-10	Loam	5.5	0	0.05	10.5	5.43	1.45	0.08	0.47
	Adelaide Hills	35-55	Medium clay	4.7	0	0.03	8.5	3.40	2.12	0.14	0.20
		80-120	Weathering siltstone	4.7	0	0.04	4.4	1.03	2.68	0.13	0.09
9.6	Loamy gravel	0-10	Fine sandy loam	5.0	0	0.12	nd	8.4	1.2	0.36	0.30
	Pemberton / Manjimup	25-40	Fine sandy clay loam	5.3	0	0.02	nd	3.0	1.1	0.12	0.05
		70-100	Light medium clay	5.8	0	0.04	nd	2.0	2.5	0.17	0.04
9.7	Brown clay	0-10	Light medium clay	6.8	0	0.28	25.9	23.9	6.35	1.24	1.73
	Langhorne Creek	27-40	Heavy clay	7.0	0	0.16	22.9	13.1	6.67	2.09	0.69
		65-115	Heavy clay	8.0	3	0.39	17.7	10.6	6.50	2.27	0.66
9.8	Kraznozem	0-20	Light clay	6.9	0	0.07	nd	11	3.2	0.15	0.77
	North East Tasmania	20-50	Light clay	6.1	0	0.05	nd	3.8	3.3	0.17	0.33
		50-96	Light clay	6.1	0	0.04	nd	1.9	4.6	0.32	0.14
9.8	Gradational red silty clay loam	0-15	Silty clay loam	7.4	0	0.22	13.0	8.6	3.2	0.33	0.65
	McLaren Vale	35-55	Light clay	6.0	0	0.11	8.4	4.6	1.4	2.34	0.24
		75-105	Medium clay	5.7	0	0.23	11.3	5.6	4.2	1.70	0.50

high viticultural potential. They are widely used in the Adelaide Hills, Langhorne Creek, Hunter, Margaret River, Geographe and Manjimup/Pemberton regions. They occur to a limited extent in the Barossa and Clare Valleys, McLaren Vale, Southern Fleurieu, Rutherglen, Great Southern, Swan District, Cowra and Mudgee regions.

Deep hard clayey unigrad soil (Sub-category 9.7)

These soils have a sandy clay loam to clayey topsoil which grades to a poorly structured clayey subsoil. The topsoil is hard and massive due to the combined effects of sub-optimal exchangeable calcium, and fine particle size of the sand fraction, and/or a high silt fraction. Surface soils are neutral to acidic, while subsoils can be acidic to alkaline but not calcareous. Clay content generally increases with depth. The clayey subsoil will only allow about 20 cm of vine root penetration, so potential rootzone depth is controlled by the depth to the subsoil clay. The profile illustrated in **FIGURE 3.56** has a restricted rootzone depth with a readily available water holding capacity of only about 15 mm. Being clayey, these soils are slow to wet up and useable moisture levels are difficult to maintain. Most soils are prone to waterlogging and restricted deep drainage. These are difficult viticultural soils, which are not widely developed. There are some plantings in Tasmania, and in the Langhorne Creek region.

Deep well structured clayey unigrad soil (Sub-category 9.8)

These soils have a sandy clay loam to clay topsoil which grades to a well structured subsoil. Clay content commonly increases with depth. Surface soils are acidic to neutral, subsoils may be acidic to alkaline, but not calcareous. The potential rootzone extends 50 cm into a clayey subsoil and to the full thickness of a clay loamy subsoil. Consequently, water holding capacity can be high; 60–70 mm for the profile in **FIGURE 3.57**. These soils are slow to wet up because of their clayey textures, and maintaining adequate levels of rootzone moisture can make irrigation difficult, especially where the soils are mixed with sandier types. Profiles are generally permeable, but underlying materials may be more restrictive leading to potential salt accumulation. These are potentially productive soils, although high inherent fertility in some may cause excessive vigour. They are common viticultural soils in the Henty, Hunter and South Burnett regions, and in Tasmania. They occur to a limited extent in the Clare Valley, Coonawarra, Langhorne Creek and Mudgee regions.

3.4 Soils used for grapevines in other countries

The world's oldest grape growing region extends from around the Mediterranean, north into Germany and the former Czechoslovakia and east into the former U.S.S.R around the Black and Caspian Seas. These vineyards cover more than 8.5 million hectares. In contrast, the rest of the world's vineyards cover less than 1 million hectares. They are widely distributed from the Americas, to South Africa, New Zealand, Australia and parts of Asia.

3.4.1 THE GENERAL NATURE OF THE SOILS

The considerable natural variation in the soil of European vineyards has been amplified by man's activities over the centuries: for example, terracing on 60° slopes of slate and granite along the hillsides above the Upper Douro River in Portugal has allowed soil to develop on the terraces between the walls. Even so it is possible to recognize five broad soil groupings, though it must be emphasized that these groupings do not cover all soil formations.

(i) In Western Europe there is a range of brown gradational loamy to clayey soils with long agricultural histories. They are thus highly artificial, are usually less than 2 m deep, have good drainage, range in pH from acidic to neutral and are underlain by acidic rocks, sediments, loess or calcareous rocks. These soils respond well to fertilizers and some acidic ones are liable to trace element deficiencies. No Australian soils satisfactorily fit in this grouping.

(ii) Leached, acidic, sandy soils derived from a great variety of siliceous rocks, sediments and aeolian deposits occur throughout Europe. A feature of the Bordeaux region is the thick gravel beds, some of which are regarded highly for grapevines. On the great plain in Hungary, grapevines were used to reclaim shifting dune sands, and in Rumania grapevines are planted in pockets 3 m down in sand so that their roots can more rapidly enter the underlying materials; the vines then have to grow up to ground level. These vines produce light wines where nothing grew before. The soils in this grouping often require drainage and fertilisers. These soils correspond to Australia's deep sandy uniform soils (Sub-category 9.1). Shallower forms are equivalent to shallow sandy soils (Sub-category 4.1).

(iii) Of very wide distribution are the various red brown and black, mostly loamy, sometimes clayey soils formed from limestones, and from some shales and volcanic rocks. They are generally of such variable depth that deep and shallow soils alternate within short distances. The content of metal cations in the subsoils varies from medium to high, and fertility is moderate. This grouping includes not only the better soils of Champagne but also the 'albarizas' of Jerez (Spain). The underlying limestone (chalk) is judged to be a most important feature for grapevines. Cracking clay soils (Category 5) are often associated with bottom lands, whereas the red, brown and black 'limestone' soils dominate the slopes. These are equivalent to very shallow to shallow loamy/clayey soils on calc-rock (Sub-categories 3.4, 4.2, 4.4 and 4.5). This pattern is similar to the associations of soils at Coonawarra.

(iv) In parts of eastern Europe, from lower Austria to the former U.S.S.R., there are a range of soils with black loamy to clayey, granular surfaces, that contain soft carbonates in their subsoils; they are easily worked productive soils, alkaline throughout their profiles and are largely derived from loess. Both shallow and deep forms are used for grapevines. The deep loamy and clayey unigrad soils (Sub-categories 9.6 and 9.8) of the Hunter River terraces could be placed in this grouping.

(v) A range of greyish-brown to yellowish-brown soils with dark loamy to clayey, granular surfaces, soft carbonates in the subsoil, generally alkaline and often developed on alluvial sediments occur in some vineyards of Eastern Europe, for example, in the Digomi and Mukharani plains of Georgia. A few Australian soils (e.g. deep clayey calcareous unigrad soil, Sub-category 9.4) fit satisfactorily into this grouping, while some duplex soils with non-restrictive subsoils (Sub-category 7.2) would if they did not have such pronounced texture contrast profiles.

The range of soils and soil properties found in Australian viticultural regions, as described in Section

3.3, illustrates the variability that may be encountered within one country. If the soils of all of the grapegrowing countries are considered in detail, the variation would be even greater.

3.4.2 PHYSICAL AND CHEMICAL PROPERTIES OF THE SOILS

Throughout the grapegrowing areas of the world, physical soil properties are universally recognized to be of major importance. The most important physical consideration is to have soils that are well drained, but which provide moisture throughout the growth cycle of the grapevine. Poor soil drainage and aeration affects not only the health of the vine, but also management of the vineyard, and the ease with which machinery can be moved. Soil depth is next in order of importance. As in Australia, soil depth must include not only the soil but also the subsola (often the parent materials in Europe and America). This is because the grapevine roots deeply, and growth will be restricted unless both soil and subsola can be easily penetrated by both roots and water.

The excellent performance of grapevines in some parts of Bordeaux, group (ii), is attributed to the subsola below the leached sand soils. The fame of vineyards on soils of group (iii) is due to the grapevine being able to penetrate the calcareous parent materials below the often thin soil. The success of grapevines on soils of groups (iv) and (v) can be attributed to the deep and friable nature of these soils. Finally, in the vineyards of Western Europe, gravels on the soil surface are especially esteemed for trapping sunlight and its warmth and directing these onto the underside of the vine and bunches of grapes, a factor of importance when growing grapes towards the cooler limits of their climatic range.

There are significant differences in the chemical properties of Australian grape soils and those used elsewhere. In general, more fertilizer is used in European vineyards, perhaps because of their long use for viticulture. In Australia, phosphorus is widely deficient and frequently applied. Elsewhere, fertilizing with potassium is widely practised, but in Australia K levels are generally adequate. But perhaps the most significant feature of Australian viticulture is the greater use of sodic soils. The calcareous soils (Category 8) and many duplex soils with restrictive subsoils (Category 6), for example, are more alkaline and have higher soluble salt contents than do soils used elsewhere, except in some parts of eastern Europe.

3.5 Assessing the potential of soils for grapegrowing

3.5.1 FINDING NEW VITICULTURAL AREAS

The art of gauging the viticultural potential of new areas depends on many factors besides land; climate, the kind of grape product wanted, and various economic considerations are all important. But assessment of the suitability of the soil is a fundamental starting point. Probably in the early stages of enquiry, soil-landscape maps such as the Atlas of Australian Soils (Northcote et al. 1960-68) provide a useful guide to soils and topography. After several areas have been chosen, a pedologist who specializes in soil-plant relationships should be consulted. The pedologist's task is to evaluate and rank the likely areas in order of their case of management from the standpoint of soils and topography. Aerial photographs and the information provided in this chapter would assist in this evaluation. When a final choice is made, the soil-topographic units of the proposed new vineyard should be defined, mapped and used as a basis for its management. This work can be carried out by vineyard personnel, under the guidance of the pedologist. Where this is done, the properties of the vineyard soils become better appreciated by those using them.

3.5.2 PLANTS AS INDICATORS OF SOIL CONDITIONS

Though not a substitute for examining the soil itself the study of native and exotic vegetation growing on an area can provide useful pointers to soil conditions and as a guide to vineyard site selection (Due 1979). The extent and mixing of plant species, especially of shrubs and trees, and variations in the growth of individual species may indicate strengths and weaknesses of a particular soil for the growing of grapes. Care is necessary, however. A species may give a good indication of viticultural potential in one locality but not in another, i.e. its adaptability to a range of soil conditions may be wider than that of the grapevine. Solitary individuals should also be regarded cautiously. As an example, the relationship between soils and the type of native vegetation found in the temperate semi-arid zone of the Murray Mallee highland areas of south-eastern Australia are listed below. The soils are described in Section 3.3.

(a) Dry Savannah (grassy) Forests to Dry Savannah Woodlands—both characterized by *Callitris* spp. (native pine)—occur on deep sandy gradational soils (Sub-category 9.2).

(b) Dry Savannah Woodlands—characterized by *Eucalyptus* spp. (large mallee) with native pine— occur on sandy calcareous soils (Sub-category 8.1).

(c) Dry Savannah Woodland to Dry Savannah Scrub— both characterized by *Casuarina* sp. (belar or belah)—occur on deep loamy calcareous unigrad soils (Sub-category 9.3), sandy, loamy and rubbly calcareous soils (Sub-categories 8.1, 8.6 and 8.4), and non restrictive duplex soils with thin hard topsoils (Sub-category 7.3).

(d) Dry Savannah Mallee Scrub—characterized by *Eucalyptus* spp. (mallee), sometimes with belar— occurs on sandy and loamy calcareous soils (Sub-categories 8.1 and 8.6).

(e) Grasslands—characterized by *Stipa* spp.—occur on non-restrictive duplex soils with thin hard topsoils (Sub-category 7.3).

In more general terms, it can be said that sclerophyllous plant communities (plants with hard leaves that minimize water loss, including heaths), are mostly confined to the more arid soils of lower fertility than those on which savannah woodland communities occur. Savannah woodlands, characterized by *Eucalyptus camaldulensis* (red gum) and/or *E. leucoxylon* (blue gum) often occur on non-sodic soils, whereas *E. odorata* (peppermint gum) savannah woodlands are often found on sodic sods. Sclerophyll mallee or mallee-broombush (*Eucalyptus* spp., often *E. incrassata, Melaleuca uncinata*) commonly occurs on restrictive duplex soils with well structured topsoils (Sub-categories 6.1 and 6.2). Open grassland communities occur on the cracking clays (Category 5), but savannah woodlands may develop on these soils also.

Data on relationships between vegetation and soils are progressively being compiled through State agency programs. Enquiries about data availability should be directed to agencies responsible for soils information. Refer to **TABLE 3.20** for contact details.

3.5.3 THE CRITERIA FOR GOOD GRAPEGROWING SOILS

Of the physical aspects, the principal requirements for good grapegrowing soils are an adequate supply of soil moisture, good soil drainage and aeration, and a stable non-eroding soil. The physical properties that influence these three requirements have been discussed in Section 3.1. A good physical soil system would be surface and subsurface soil of loamy fine sand, sandy loam, loam, silt loam, clay loam, or subplastic clay texture at least 15 cm thick and friable passing to a free-draining subsoil (which, if clay, must be friable) passing to free-draining subsola with no impeding layer to a depth of preferably 3m, especially if the vineyard is to be irrigated. Perhaps the best soils—soils where these requirements are most commonly met—are non-restrictive duplex soils with hard topsoils (Sub-categories 7.3 and 7.4), deep sandy and loamy calcareous unigrad soils (Sub-categories 9.2 and 9.3), deep well structured loamy and clayey unigrad soils (Sub-categories 9.6 and 9.8), deep sandy uniform soils (Sub-category 9.1), and shallow loamy to clayey soil over calc-rock (Sub-categories 4.2 and 4.4). In all cases, good soil management is necessary to maintain grapevine health, vigour and productivity.

From the chemical viewpoint, soils should be sufficient in nutrient elements and neither saline, sodic nor too high in soft carbonates. The soils listed above meet these requirements except for nutrients: phosphorus is deficient in most, and zinc deficiency occurs even in some of the best duplex soils. However, once properly diagnosed, nutrient deficiencies can be corrected and rarely do they seriously limit the use of a soil. On the other hand,

toxicities such as those due to aluminium and manganese in acidic soils can be serious limitations (see 3.2.1). It is important to have a satisfactory supply of water and oxygen at depth, and an absence of toxic substances, so that roots can grow vigorously and penetrate deeply.

3.6 Availability of soils information

Soils information is available in two forms. The basic type of information relates to a specific site, where a soil profile is described and possibly analysed for a range of properties. Where information is required across an area (a vineyard, catchment, region or entire continent), maps are used. Of course, the information from specific sites makes an important contribution to the compilation of a map.

The Atlas of Australian Soils (Northcote et al. 1960-68) provides the only consistent nation-wide coverage of soil description and distribution mapping. However, its continental scale makes it too generalized for most viticultural applications. Extensive local and regional

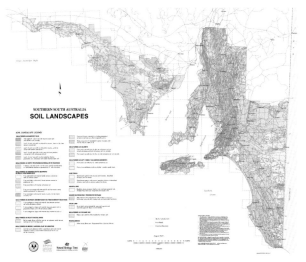

Figure 3.58 Seamless mapping coverage of 'soil landscapes' – southern South Australia.

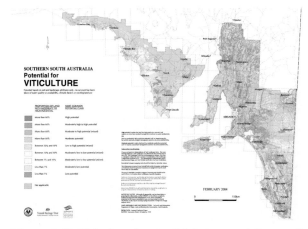

Figure 3.59 Viticultural potential interpreted from soil landscape data.

Table 3.20 Agency contacts for soil information.

State/Territory	Section/Agency	Address
Commonwealth	CSIRO Land and Water	GPO Box 1666 Canberra ACT 2601
New South Wales	Integrated Regional Knowledge NSW Dept. of Infrastructure, Planning and Natural Resources	PO Box 3720 Parramatta NSW 2124
Northern Territory	Resource Assessment Branch Dept. of Lands, Planning and Environment	PO Box 30 Palmerston NT 0830
Queensland	Land and Environmental Assessment, Natural Resource Sciences Dept. of Natural Resources	Block C, 80 Meiers Road Indooroopilly Qld 4068
South Australia	Soil and Land Information Dept. of Water, Land and Biodiversity Conservation	GPO Box 2834 Adelaide SA 5001
Tasmania	Land Resource Assessment Dept. of Primary Industries, Water and Environment	PO Box 46 Kings Meadows Tas 7249
Victoria	Land Resource Assessment State Chemistry Laboratory, Dept. of Natural Resources & Environment	621 Sneydes Road Werribee Vic 3030
Western Australia	Natural Resource Assessment Group Agriculture Western Australia	3 Baron-Hay Court South Perth WA 6151

mapping was undertaken by CSIRO Division of Soils, mainly during the 1950s and 1960s. Most of this work has subsequently been incorporated into State or Territory agency land resource assessment programs, which aim to improve the coverage and quality of soil mapping information (see **FIGURE 3.58**). The advent of sophisticated computer-based mapping facilities (e.g. geographic information systems) has enabled soil scientists to develop a range of data interpretation procedures, so that, for example, a soil map can be re-drawn in terms of viticultural potential. This is essentially achieved by matching the properties of each soil mapping unit with the requirements of the grapevine, and ranking the mapping units accordingly. An example of this type of interpretation is shown in **FIGURE 3.59**.

Most maps have accompanying reports including descriptions, analyses and possibly photographs of typical or representative soils. This detailed level of information can be very useful at the local scale. An example of a 'Soil Data Sheet' is presented in Appendix 1.

All States and Territories have databases including soil profile information, soil analyses, and various forms of mapping, where the focus is on the delineation of areas with specific associations of soils and soil properties. A summary of the range of soils information available across Australia is beyond the scope of this book. Enquiries relating to current information availability should be directed to the appropriate agency. To this end, contact details are provided in **TABLE 3.20**.

REFERENCES

Suggestions for further reading are marked (•).

Cockcroft, B. (1965) Pedology of the Goulburn Valley area. Victorian Dep. Agric. Vic. Tech. Bull. No. 19.

DWLBC Soil and Land Information (2003) Soil Data Sheets [CD ROM]. Soil and Land Information group, The Department of Water, Land and Biodiversity Conservation, South Australia.

Due, G. (1979) The use of vegetation as a guide to site selection. In: Vineyard Site Selection. Eds R.E. Smart and P.R. Dry (Roseworthy Agric. College), pp. 79-89.

Isbell, R.F. (1996) The Australian Soil Classification (CSIRO Publishing: Melbourne).

• Isbell, R.F. (2002) The Australian Soil Classification. Revised Edition (CSIRO Publishing: Melbourne).

• Maschmedt, D., Fitzpatrick, R. et al. (2002) Key for identifying categories of vineyard soils in Australia. Technical Report 30/02 (CSIRO Land and Water).

Munsell Soil Color Charts (Munsell Color Co. Inc., Baltimore 18, Maryland 21218, U.S.A.)

Myburgh, P., Cass, A. et al. (1998) A qualitative assessment of root systems in relation to soil physical conditions in Australian vineyard and orchard soils. Barossa Valley Rotary Foundation Fellowship Report.

• Nicholas, P.R. Ed (2004) Soil, Irrigation and Nutrition. Grape Production Series No. 2 (South Aust. Res. Dev. Inst.: Adelaide).

Northcote, K.H. (1979) A Factual Key for the Recognition of Australian Soils, 4th edn. (Rellim Tech. Publ.: Adelaide).

Northcote, K.H. (1984) Significance of soil properties in the agricultural context. In: Soils, Soil Morphology and Soil Classification. Training Course Lectures. Division of Soils CSIRO Australia (Rellim Tech. Publ.: Adelaide).

Northcote, K.H. and Boehm, E.W. (1949) The Soils and Horticultural Potential of the Coomealla Irrigation Area. CSIRO Division of Soils. Soils and Land Use Series No. 1.

Northcote, K.H. et al. (1960-68) Atlas of Australian Soils, Sheets 1-10, with explanatory booklets. CSIRO and Melbourne University Press: Melbourne).

• Northcote, K.H. (1988) Soils and Australian Viticulture. In: Viticulture Vol. 1, Edition 1. Eds B.G.Coombe and P.R.Dry (Australian Industrial Publishers: Adelaide), pp.

Penkov, M. (1974) Influence of the soil profile on the disposition of the root system of grapevine. Trans. 10th Int. Congress Soil Sci. Vol. 1, 246 (English Summary).

Salter, P.J. and Williams, J.B. (1967) The Influence of Texture on the Moisture Characteristics of Soils. J. Soil Sci. **18**(1), 174.

Seguin, G. (1986) 'Terroirs' and pedology of wine growing. Experientia 42 (1986), Birkhauser Verlag, CH4010 Basel, Switzerland.

Soil Survey Staff (1999) Soil Taxonomy: A Basic System of Soil Classification for Making and Interpreting Soil Surveys, 2nd edn, USDA Agric. Handbook No. 436 (Govt. Printer: Washington DC).

South Australian Soil and Plant Analysis Service (1996) Guidelines for the interpretation of soil results (Primary Industries, South Australia).

Stace, H.T.C., Hubble, G.D. et al. (1986) A Handbook of Australian Soils (Rellim Tech. Publ.: Adelaide).

Thomas, J.E. (1939) An investigation of the problems of salt accumulation on a mallee soil in the Murray Valley irrigation area. CSIRO Bull. 128.

Wall, P. (1987) Don't be misled by the vine's capacity for adaption. Australian Grapegrower & Winemaker No. 277, 23.

Wetherby, K.G. and Oades, J.M. (1975). Classification of carbonate layers in highland soils of the Northern Murray Mallee, South Australia. Aust. J. Soil Res. **13**, 119-132.

Wetherby, K.G. (2003) Soil Description Book. Revised edn. (K.G. & C.V. Wetherby, Soil Survey Specialists: Cleve SA).

• White, Robert E. (2003) Soils for Fine Wines (Oxford University Press: New York).

Appendix 1
Example of a Soils Data Sheet[1]

CLAY LOAM OVER BROWN CLAY

General Description: Greyish medium textured surface soil with a bleached A2 horizon, overlying a brown mottled clayey subsoil with minor carbonate at depth, formed in fine grained alluvium.

Landform: Outwash fans, lower slopes and alluvial flats.

Substrate: Fine grained, sometimes gravelly alluvium.

Vegetation: Red gum - blue gum woodland

Type Site: McLaren Vale Region. Midslope of a gently sloping pedimentalluvial fan. Hard setting surface with minor slate gravel. Average annual rainfall 625 mm

Soil Description:

Depth (cm)	Description
0-10	Dark greyish brown fine sandy clay loam. Clear to:
10-28	Dark greyish brown fine sandy clay loam with 20-50% slate gravel. Clear to:
28-45	Bleached clay loam with rusty mottles. Clear to:
45-80	Brown, yellowish and red mottled medium heavy clay with very coarse prismatic structure and slickensides. Gradual to:
80-105	Yellowish red and brown mottled weakly structured medium clay and 2-10% slate gravel. Clear to:
105-130	Dark brown and reddish mottled heavy clay with very coarse prismatic structure. Gradual to:
130-180	Brown and reddish mottled slightly calcareous weakly structured heavy clay.

Viticultural Soil Key: Restrictive duplex soil with thick hard topsoil (6.4)

Australian Soil Classification: Bleached-Vertic, Eutrophic, Brown Chromosol; thick, non-gravelly, clay loamy/clayey, deep

SUMMARY OF PROPERTIES

Drainage: Imperfectly drained. The tight clay subsoil has low permeability resulting in the "perching" of water in the bleached layer. This problem will be worse where the clay is at shallow depth. Avoidance of over watering is especially critical on this soil.

Fertility: The soil has a moderate level of inherent fertility, as indicated by the exchangeable cation data, although the bleached subsurface layer has a very low nutrient storage capacity (CEC less than 5 cmol). Concentrations of all tested elements (with the exception of magnesium) are adequate.

pH: Neutral (7.0) at the surface, alkaline (8.2) with depth.

Rooting depth: Some roots to 105 cm, although densities are low below 45 cm. Most growth is in the upper 30 cm.

BARRIERS TO ROOT GROWTH

Physical: The tight clay subsoil is the main physical barrier, along with potential waterlogging.

Chemical: There only unfavourable chemical conditions in the soil is salt accumulation from saline irrigation water. This is probably concentrated at the surface, where it is around double the desirable level of 0.25 d/m (1:5 soil:water). The boron and sodicity levels are within acceptable limits. There is possible manganese and iron imbalance resulting from waterlogging.

Water holding capacity: Approximately 150 mm, but not all is effectively available due to the low density of roots in the subsoil. Readily available water holding capacity in the upper 65 cm (i.e. topsoil plus 20 cm of subsoil) is approximately 45 mm.

Workability: Fair. The surface has a tendency to set hard when dry and become boggy when wet.

Erosion Potential: Low.

[1] The original data sheet has colour images.

Laboratory Chemical Data

Depth cm	pH H2O	pH CaCl2	CO3 %	EC1:5 dS/m	ECe dS/m	Org.C %	Avail. P mg/kg	Avail. K mg/kg	Boron mg/kg	Trace Elements mg/kg (DTPA) Cu	Fe	Mn	Zn	CEC cmol (+)/kg	Exchangeable Cations cmol(+)/kg Ca	Mg	Na	K	ESP
Row	7.0	6.9	0	0.60	4.01	2.1	97	403	1.5	10.9	43	10.7	6.1	na	13.0	1.3	0.39	1.05	2.5
0-10	6.3	6.1	0	0.20	1.45	2.0	29	390	1.0	2.6	47	14.1	4.3	11.3	8.4	1.0	0.25	0.90	2.2
10-28	5.4	4.9	0	0.07	0.63	1.1	6	285	0.6	0.6	91	9.4	0.5	8.9	6.1	1.3	0.23	0.51	2.6
28-45	5.0	4.4	0	0.04	0.34	0.2	<4	177	0.3	0.4	26	4.9	0.2	4.4	3.2	1.2	0.16	0.24	3.6
45-80	6.1	5.6	0	0.15	0.73	0.3	<4	236	1.7	1.1	13	7.0	0.2	18.8	8.7	7.2	0.78	0.75	4.1
80-105	6.8	6.3	0	0.12	0.69	0.2	<4	175	1.3	0.6	7	5.5	0.2	10.2	5.8	4.2	0.54	0.46	5.3
105-130	7.5	7.0	0.1	0.18	0.93	0.2	<4	243	3.4	0.7	7	2.4	0.1	23.2	12.0	6.6	0.97	0.73	4.2
130-180	8.2	7.9	0.3	0.24	1.43	0.1	<4	196	2.1	0.6	8	2.1	0.2	16.1	9.4	5.4	0.65	0.49	4.0

Note: Row sample bulked from 20 cores (0-10 cm) taken from along the planting lines. CEC (cation exchange capacity) is a measure of the soil's capacity to store and release major nutrient elements. ESP (exchangeable sodium percentage) is derived by dividing the exchangeable sodium value by the CEC.

CHAPTER FOUR

Climate and Australian Viticulture

J. S. GLADSTONES

4.1 Role and definitions of climate

Most accept that climate is crucial to viticulture. In cool continental climates of the Northern Hemisphere it limits winter survival. Elsewhere the decisive factor is usually warmth of the growing season. Soils and vineyard management play complementary roles, but climate alone decides what, if any, grape varieties can be grown and broadly the wine styles that can be made and how reliably.

4.1.1 DEFINITION BY TIME SCALE

Climate is not the same as weather. Weather prevails at an instant or over a short period: a day, a week, or perhaps up to a few months. Over a growing season or year we speak of it collectively as a season or vintage. Climate is long-term. It is only inferred reliably from the records of many years. The standard minimum for defining current climate is 30 years.

The long life-span of vines means that they can be affected by medium-term climatic changes such as that from the warm Middle Ages to the 'Little Ice Age' of the 15th to 19th centuries, from which recent warming may in part be only a natural recovery. This covered a range of perhaps 1.5°C, enough for quite drastic effects on viticulture at its cool margin. Lesser natural fluctuations occur from decade to decade as well as year to year. Gladstones (1992) documents their known history and possible causes.

Recent and future 'global warming' due to man-caused (anthropogenic) build-up of atmospheric gases may further affect viticultural climates. The reality of some such warming is now well established, but its size and impact remain controversial. Thus no measurement of climate is fully predictive, especially if based on short-term data (no matter how accurate or detailed). Good estimates must also allow for the particular locations and natures of the recording sites.

4.1.2 DEFINITION BY SPATIAL SCALE

Three spatial scales of climate are generally recognized.

Macroclimate

Also called regional climate, this broadly defines the climate of a region. Commonly it is from a major centre with long official records. Caution is needed in accepting such figures. Major centres are often coastal, or if inland at the bottoms of river valleys, and if large can have their own local effects on climate. Vineyards tend to be on slopes well removed from them, and to have significantly different climates.

Mesoclimate

This is the climate of a site as influenced by its particular location, altitude and topography. It can extend tens of metres or up to kilometres, depending on uniformity of the topography. 'Topoclimate' describes the same concept.

Apart from altitude the main determinant of mesoclimate is local air drainage, especially on still, cloudless nights. Free radiation of heat into space results in rapid night cooling of the ground surface and of air in contact with it. Surface-chilled air, being denser than the rest, trickles down slopes to collect on flat land or in depressions (**FIGURE** 4.1), forming a 'temperature inversion' in contrast to the normal temperature fall with altitude. This prevents convectional mixing with warmer upper air. In the absence of dispersing winds the stable cold air pool and any associated fog or frost remain until the morning sun heats the ground surface again.

Above the cold air pool and fog line, vertical air circulation can still take place. The descending surface-chilled air sets up a cycle bringing replacement warm upper air down on to the slopes above the fog line

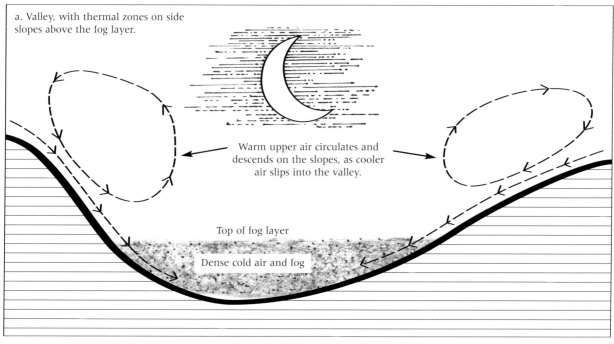

a. Valley, with thermal zones on side slopes above the fog layer.

Warm upper air circulates and descends on the slopes, as cooler air slips into the valley.

Top of fog layer

Dense cold air and fog

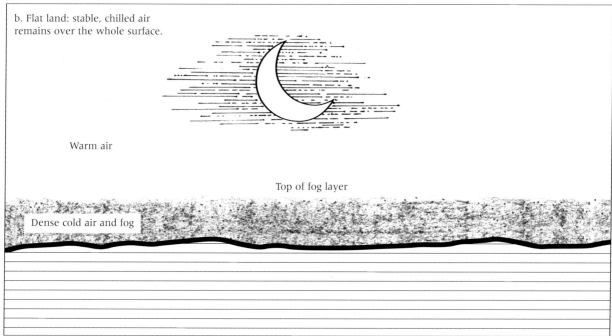

b. Flat land: stable, chilled air remains over the whole surface.

Warm air

Top of fog layer

Dense cold air and fog

Figure 4.1. Air drainage of slopes compared with hollows or flat land. From Gladstones (1992).

Surface-chilled air drifts down the hillsides and side valleys and away down the main valley floor, by-passing a projecting hill (A) and an isolated hill (B). Because the projecting and isolated hills have no external source of chilled air, they remain more or less entirely in the stable or circulating warm upper air as shown in Figure 1.

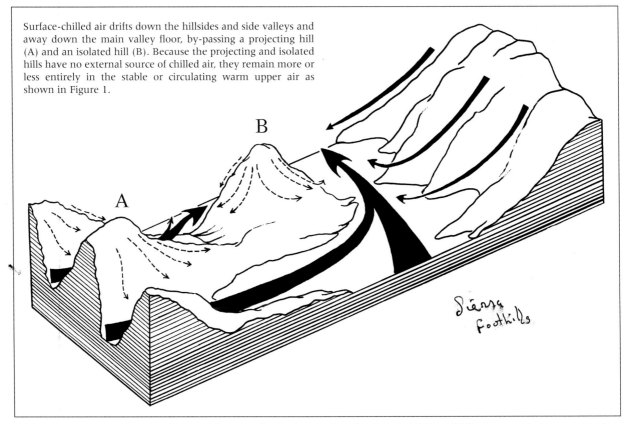

Figure 4.2 Cross-section of valley showing the air drainage of projecting and isolated hills. From Gladstones (1992).

(**FIGURE** 4.1), creating a 'thermal zone' there. This has higher night temperatures and, to a smaller extent, higher means than the valley floor or flat land, despite generally lower daytime maxima. Thermal zones are especially strong on the slopes of isolated hills, from which all surface-chilled air drains away, or else on projecting hills or ridges which externally sourced cold air by-passes (**FIGURE** 4.2).

Closeness to oceans or inland water bodies moderates both maximum and minimum temperatures, through the regular alternation of land and sea breezes or their more localized inland equivalents. Ocean characteristics have their own important effects. For instance the cold waters off the coasts of California and Chile influence adjacent land climates differently from the warmer waters surrounding Western Europe and Australasia.

Steepness and aspect of slopes have added significance through the duration, timing and intensity of sun exposure through the day and heating of the soil. The latter directly affects root function, and also climate close above-ground by radiative warming through cloudy periods and at night. Soil surface characteristics (4.2.5) play a complementary role in this through their influence on capacity to absorb and re-radiate heat. **TABLE** 4.1 sets out some estimated maximum adjustments to effective temperature for various topographic and soil factors.

Table 4.1 Temperature adjustments (°C) for topographic and soil factors[1]. From Gladstones (1992)

Factor	Minimum temp.	Maximum temp.	Variability Index[2]
Moderate slopes	+1.0	− 0.5	− 3.0
Steep slopes or isolated hills	+1.5	− 0.5	− 4.0
Slopes facing midday sun	+0.75	+0.25	− 1.0
Stony, rocky or calcareous soils	+1.0	− 0.5	− 3.0

1 Maximum adjustments relative to an assumed flat or valley recording site with non-rocky soil; part differences pro rata. Adjustments for different factors are assumed to apply uniformly through the season and are additive amongst themselves and to adjustments to mean temperature for altitude differences (0.6°C per 100m).

2 See Section 4.2.4.

Microclimate

This term applies strictly to the smallest scales of climate. Examples are local conditions behind windbreaks, embankments or terraces; between vine rows; or within vine canopies. Microclimates within grape bunches affect ripening processes and disease control, and are part of grape variety and clone differences. Unlike macroclimate and mesoclimate, which are fully determined by initial site selection, viticultural microclimates depend largely on vine and soil management.

4.2 Temperature: the primary climatic control

4.2.1 TEMPERATURE AND VINE PHENOLOGY

Phenology describes the processes and timing of a vine's development through dormancy, budburst, flowering, setting, veraison and ripening. It determines whether and when grape varieties can ripen in particular environments. Note that ripeness here refers primarily to 'flavour' ripening (see 4.4.5). The environmental controls over this differ from those governing vine photosynthesis, yield and to some degree berry sugar content at any ripening stage.

The evidence is now clear that vine phenology is controlled by temperature alone. Vine phenological processes respond more or less linearly from a mean temperature of about 10°C (below which no growth occurs) to perhaps 16–17°C, after which the response slows. Maximum rates in experiments have mostly been reached around 22–25°C mean temperature (Buttrose 1968, 1969, Buttrose and Hale 1973). Fastest node formation in the field at Geisenheim, Germany (Schultz 1993) was reached a little below 20°C mean temperature. All the studies indicated an effective plateau in phenological rates beyond these temperatures.

Consistent with these results, Gladstones (1992) found that average maturity dates of given grape varieties can be approximated from climatic data by assuming a linear phenological response from 10 to 19°C mean but a flat response beyond that. Such findings help explain, for instance, why in many environments seasonal maturation can be forecast from spring temperatures or flowering dates alone. Growth to flowering is in the highly responsive part of the temperature/phenology curve, while that from then on is mostly temperature-saturated (see also Chapter 7, 7.4.1).

4.2.2 TEMPERATURE AND VINE PRODUCTIVITY

Yield potential responds to temperature differently from phenology for two evident reasons. First, it depends directly on photosynthesis, which responds to daytime temperatures but also to light intensity and duration, leaf exposure to it, and the concentration of carbon dioxide (CO_2) in the air as well as sufficiency of water for the leaf stomata (pores) to stay open for CO_2 entry. Any or all of these can limit photosynthesis and hence dry matter production.

Second, all other growth processes such as assimilate transport, metabolism and cell division can continue at other times and may, in some cases, occur largely at night (Langridge and McWilliam 1967). Mean or day/night average temperatures are therefore the ones most relevant to phenology.

Daytime tests under non-limiting light have shown fastest assimilation (photosynthesis minus respiration) at vine leaf temperatures between about 25 and 30°C (Kriedemann 1968; Zuffery et al. 2000). Above that assimilation falls away, because whereas photosynthesis plateaus at an intermediate temperature, assimilate use by respiration continues to climb right to the highest temperatures short of cell death. However evidence exists (Schultz 2000) that the optimum leaf temperature for assimilation acclimates (adjusts) to some degree according to prior average temperatures.

Photosynthesizing leaf temperatures do not translate exactly into measured daytime or (still less) mean or day/night average air temperatures. Allowing for this, the findings agree well enough with those of Buttrose (1968, 1969) of an optimal mean air temperature for vine dry matter production around 20–22°C.

Vines in hot climates typically enjoy around optimum temperatures for assimilation through early growth to flowering and setting, encouraging both vegetative vigour and good bud fruitfulness and fruitset (see 4.4.3). The heavy crops set must then ripen under often above-optimum temperatures in mid summer. Resulting competition among the bunches for assimilate, commonly exacerbated by canopy shading (4.3.1), can cause delayed and uneven veraison, staggered ripening, low berry sugar contents and poor winemaking quality. Such climates with ample water and uncontrolled canopies are in general best suited to bulk wine production. However winemaking quality can be improved by careful water and crop limitation and appropriate canopy management.

Below the intermediate temperature optimum a contrasting situation obtains. Potential photosynthetic rate falls less with low temperatures than those of respiration and phenological development. Optimum to moderately low temperature therefore leaves a maximum 'surplus' of assimilate for processes such as stem thickening, build-up of assimilate reserves throughout the vine, and in time, transfer to the fruit. Moreover slower phenological development can be offset by a longer growth period where available, so that productivity is not necessarily affected.

Temperatures in this range can, however, limit yield by reducing either or both of fruitset and bud fruitfulness, which fall away with low temperatures around flowering (4.4.3). To a point this may be beneficial for fruit quality, but beyond it, can lead to vegetative rankness due to insufficient sink competition from the fruit. The optimum intermediate state is that of a naturally balanced vine. (Other environmental and management factors contribute to this, of course.)

4.2.3 CONTINENTALITY

In climatology this means the range between the average mean temperatures of the hottest and coldest months. It is often simplified to that between January and July. A 'continental' climate has a wide annual range, a

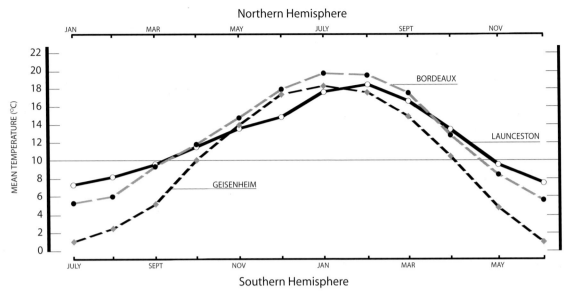

Figure 4.3 Continentality: annual march of monthly average mean temperatures at Launceston (Tasmania), Bordeaux (France) and Geisenheim (Germany). From Jackson and Spurling (1988).

'maritime' climate a narrow one.

The difference results from the land heating faster, and to higher temperatures, in spring-summer than the oceans, then cooling faster and further in autumn-winter. Thus the continent interiors have the widest annual range and coasts a narrower range, especially west-facing coasts. (Weather systems move mainly west to east, so west coasts are the most exposed to maritime influences and these can move well inland. East coasts are in the lee of the continents and thus more continental.)

The terminology breaks down in comparisons across the hemispheres. Even inland climates of Australia are 'maritime' by Northern Hemisphere standards (**FIGURE** 4.3). This is because the Southern Hemisphere has more ocean than the Northern Hemisphere, and because of Australia's low latitude.

Many assume that continental climates also have wide diurnal (day/night) temperature ranges, but this is not necessarily so. Central and eastern Europe and east Asia are highly continental, yet their growing seasons have narrow diurnal ranges (**TABLE** 4.2). That is because their summers are cloudy and humid, and because at high latitudes the sun stays low above the horizon resulting in only small hourly temperature changes.

Continental regions with very cold winters cannot support quality wine industries because *Vitis vinifera* is injured or killed by temperatures below about –15°C, even when dormant. With acceptable winter survival, however, a continental temperature regime has some benefits for viticulture. Release from winter dormancy and budburst are even, while rapid rise in spring temperatures reduces the period of post-budburst frost risk. Late spring-early summer warmth allows reliable flowering, setting and formation of fruitful buds for the

Table 4.2 Estimated average diurnal temperature ranges, °C, for the 7-month growing season. Adjusted for typical vineyard sites after Table 4.1.

Country/Region or location		Range °C	State/Region[a]		Range °C
Europe			*Australia*		
Germany	Rhine Valley	8.7	Queensland	Granite Belt	11.8
France	Alsace	8.0	NSW/ACT	Hunter	12.0
	Champagne	8.0		Mudgee	13.4
	Loire Valley	9.3		Orange	12.1
	Bordeaux	10.0		Riverina	14.7
	Burgundy	9.6		Canberra	12.6
	Upper Rhône	9.2	Victoria	Rutherglen	14.3
	Montpellier	11.0		Geelong	11.0
Austria	Vienna	7.4		Mornington	10.1
Hungary	Keszthely	8.0		Grampians	12.8
	Eger	9.6		Bendigo	13.1
Italy	Piedmont	9.0		Murray Darling	14.7
	Chianti	8.2	SA	McLaren Vale	10.1
Spain	Rioja	9.7		Adelaide Hills	10.9
Portugal	Douro Valley	12.0		Langhorne Ck	11.6
				Barossa Valley	13.9
USA				Clare	14.3
Oregon	Willamette V.	10.1		Riverland	15.5
Washington	Walla Walla	13.2		Coonawarra	13.6
	Prosser	15.4	WA	Margaret River	10.8
California	Salinas	11.6		Pemberton	10.8
	Napa	15.2		Great Southern	
	Fresno	16.8		(Mt Barker)	11.2
				Swan District	13.3
New Zealand			Tasmania	Tamar Valley*	9.0
N Island	Hawke's Bay	10.4		Derwent/	
S Island	Marlborough	10.1		Coal Valley*	10.4

a Geographical Indications (see Chapter 2) except where indicated by * following year (4.4.3), although the wet summers of some continental climates can counteract this. Then the rapid temperature fall in autumn probably enhances the ripening fruit's dominance over vegetative growth in competition for assimilates. Mostly these factors make for fruitful vines. Coolness late in ripening can help conserve delicate aromatics in the berries (4.4.5). Against this the margin between over-hot ripening and not ripening is narrow, leading to much vintage variation. In warm to hot continental climates the mid summers and ripening periods are nearly always too hot.

Warm maritime climates are benign in most respects, especially on west coasts, but cool maritime climates have limitations in their lack or irregularity of growing season warmth. Budburst can be uneven in the absence of well-defined winter dormancy and/or spring warmth, and spring frost risk is prolonged. Conditions at flowering are often unfavourable for both current setting and fruitful bud formation (4.4.3), leading to erratic cropping. However maritime climates that are not too cool have the advantage of a long autumn period with optimum temperatures for ripening (4.4.5).

4.2.4 SHORT-TERM TEMPERATURE VARIABILITY

This concept, proposed by Gladstones (1977, 1992), combines day/night (diurnal) temperature range with that from day to day or week to week within the season.

Most cold and heat injury to vines and their fruit results from temperature extremes. Average minima and maxima are seldom damaging. Also the vine, like other plants, can to some extent acclimate to progressive temperature changes in either direction.

The clearest example of harm from short-term temperature variability is post-budburst frost damage. Regularly low temperatures in spring protect by delaying budburst. The fact that grape varieties with early budburst such as Chasselas, Pinot Noir and Chardonnay grow in some of the coolest viticultural regions shows the effectiveness of this mechanism. The protection fails only where frosts return after periods warm and long enough to promote budburst and growth. Damage is worst when the preceding warmth has been enough to promote lush growth that lacks acclimation. Section 4.5.4 describes a new index of spring frost risk based on this principle. Comparable principles apply to cold injury during winter (4.4.1) and probably heat injury in summer (4.5.4).

The average diurnal temperature range at a site also has implications for vine growth, at least in spring in cool climates where budburst and early growth of deciduous plants appear primarily related to night temperatures (Geiger 1966). Thus site selection for narrow average diurnal range as well as least variability of the minimum is critical for making viticulture possible towards its cold limit.

4.2.5 SOIL TEMPERATURES

Soil temperature is part of the vine's microclimate in two ways. First, heat re-radiated from the soil contributes to the immediate above-ground thermal regime, most significantly at night and during the day under intermittent cloud. For trigonometrical reasons the absorption of heat depends on ground slope and aspect to the sun, and resulting differences are greatest early and late in the season and at high latitudes. Stony or rocky-surfaced, or bare, well firmed, dark-coloured soils absorb and re-radiate heat most readily, while damp soil stores more heat with a smaller temperature rise and releases it over a longer period. Dry, loose and mulch-covered surfaces insulate against both absorption and re-radiation. Waterlogged soils are slow to warm and more cooled by surface evaporation. The influence above ground is strongest for low-trained vines.

The second influence is directly on the vine's roots, the growing tips of which produce hormones that in part control above-ground growth. They include especially the cytokinins, which rise in the sap to promote budburst, growth, fruit set and formation of fruitful buds. Later they are important for resistance to stresses and senescence. Moderate soil warmth and good aeration promote cytokinin production (Woodham and Alexander 1966, Skene and Kerridge 1967). Optimum root temperature is probably around 20–25°C, much as for the above-ground parts. Thus well sun-exposed and quickly warming soil results in early and fruitful vine growth. However excessive topsoil temperatures and drying during summer can kill functional roots and curtail both root hormone production and nutrient uptake. Maintenance of functional roots is essential for continuing production of abscisic acid (ABA) to control top growth under partial root drying (4.3.2).

Key to localities on climatic maps

AR	Ararat	Vic
BE	Bendigo	Vic
BR	Berri	SA
CE	Cessnock	NSW
CL	Clare	SA
CO	Coonawarra	SA
GF	Griffith	NSW
KR	Kingaroy	Q
LA	Launceston	Tas
MB	Mt. Barker	WA
MR	Margaret River	WA
MU	Mildura	Vic
NU	Nuriootpa	SA
OR	Orange	NSW
RU	Rutherglen	Vic
ST	Stanthorpe	Q

4.3 Other elements of climate

4.3.1 LIGHT

There is little evidence that light or sunshine hours affect phenology except indirectly through temperature. Their main control is over photosynthesis and hence available assimilate for growth, build-up of carbohydrate reserves, and potentially fruit yield and sugar content.

Total requirement for light or sunshine hours depends on temperature, since high temperature accelerates respiratory loss of assimilate more than it does photosynthesis. Accelerated phenology at higher temperatures also limits the period of assimilation up to and during fruiting. Therefore vines in warm to hot areas need most sunshine duration and leaf exposure. The very warm Hunter Valley of New South Wales makes only table wines of generally moderate alcohol contents because its sunshine hours, more than ample for cool climates, are well below those of most other warm areas. **FIGURE** 4.4 shows the estimated averages of total growing season (October–April) sunshine hours across Australian viticultural regions.

Light intensity

Bright sunlight has an intensity of about 1500–2000 μmol/(m^2.s) (micromoles per square metre per second), or 10000–13000 foot candles, whereas grapevine leaves become photosynthetically-saturated around only a third of that intensity. Moreover inhibition of photosynthesis occurs as the intensity rises much above saturation, especially if accompanied by heat or moisture stress (Iacono and Sommer 1996).

It follows that leaves slanted obliquely to incoming light can still photosynthesize at a maximum rate while shading the underlying leaves less. This has implications for trellis design, row orientation and canopy management. It also means that cloudless skies and brilliant sunshine are not necessarily an asset. Haze and light cloud can still deliver photosynthetically optimal light intensities to the fully exposed leaves responsible for most photosynthesis, while reducing harmful heat and ultra-violet radiation (4.3.5). Also more of it reaches the canopy's shaded side and interior directly, by coming from many angles.

Nor do haze or light cloud necessarily bring rain, hail or other viticultural hazards. The fogs of California's coastal valleys bring no summer rain. Similarly Australia's south coast gets considerable cloud from summer afternoon onshore winds (**FIGURE** 4.5), mostly with little or no rain (**FIGURE** 4.6a).

Light duration

Daylength has been widely accepted as a factor in defining the northern limit of viticulture in Europe (e.g. Huglin 1983). However results such as those of Buttrose (1969) and Schultz (1993) suggest that any relationship to phenology is only indirect. Its most likely basis (Gladstones 1992) lies in the effect of day versus night length on average air temperature over the 24 hours. This might be expected to increase relative to the mean (which is strictly half way between the maximum and minimum, and often the only statistic available) in some proportion to the length of the light period. Perhaps more importantly, long days and short nights increase relatively the period when leaf and other growing tissues can be warmed above air temperature, and reduce that during which radiation cools them below air temperature. Either way, the effect on phenology is mediated by temperature rather than directly by light.

Short-term or transient light effects, as well as total exposure, can influence photosynthesis and hence potential for yield. Exterior leaves exposed to continuous sunshine soon become photosynthetically-saturated, especially at low temperatures which limit how fast assimilates can be carried away and utilized. Broken sunshine and intermittent or flecked bright light within the canopy can therefore be used more effectively per unit of light energy than continuous bright light (Kriedemann et al. 1973, Poni et al. 1993), though less so than continuous low-intensity light. This has implications for canopy structure and management, and for the effects of wind (4.3.4).

Light spectral quality

Visible light comprises the wavelengths between 400 and 730 nm, ranging from violet and blue at about 400–500 nm, through green and orange to red, merging into invisible infrared heat radiation beyond 730–740 nm. Leaves very largely absorb and use the blue and red wavelengths for photosynthesis, transmitting or reflecting those of intermediate green wavelengths (hence the perceived colour of leaves etc.). Also very largely transmitted or reflected are the far-red and near-infrared wavelengths above about 720 nm. Ultraviolet radiation, with wavelengths below 400 nm, can have important effects as discussed in 4.3.5.

The spectral composition of light from the sky varies little with weather. Cloud affects light intensity and directionality, but not greatly its wavelengths. But once inside the canopy the selective absorption of photosynthetically-active wavelengths reduces their proportion to commonly a tenth or less compared with normal light. To a smaller extent the same applies to external light reflected from neighbouring canopies or green ground cover.

More or less regardless of light intensity, an ample proportion of red wavelengths around 660 nm, as in pure natural light, locally evokes bud fruitfulness, short internodes, lateral branching and high leaf chlorophyll content, the same response as from cytokinins produced by warm and well aerated roots (4.2.5). Depletion of the photosynthetically active wavelengths evokes the

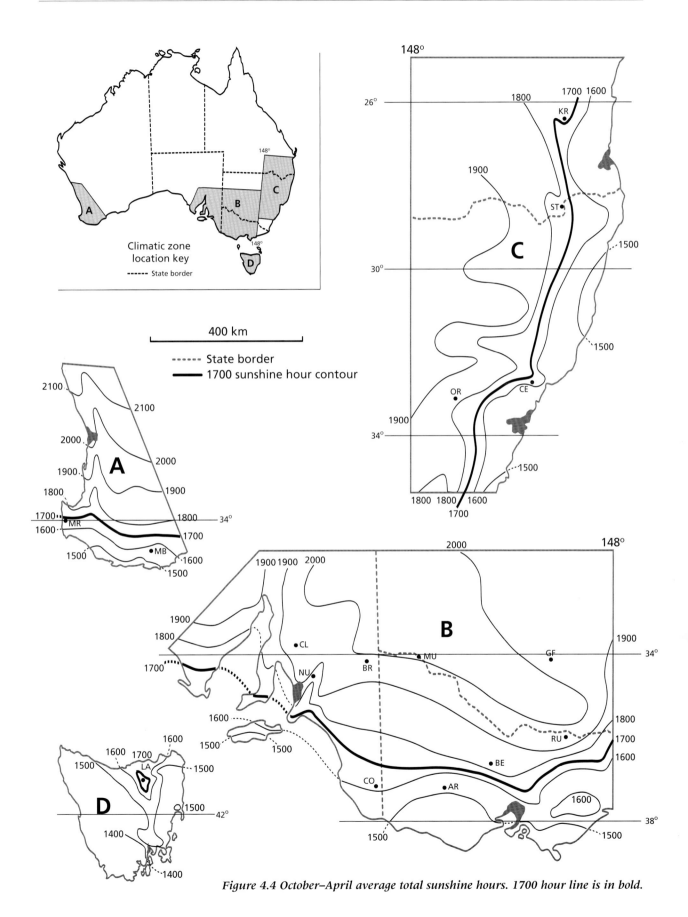

Figure 4.4 October–April average total sunshine hours. 1700 hour line is in bold.

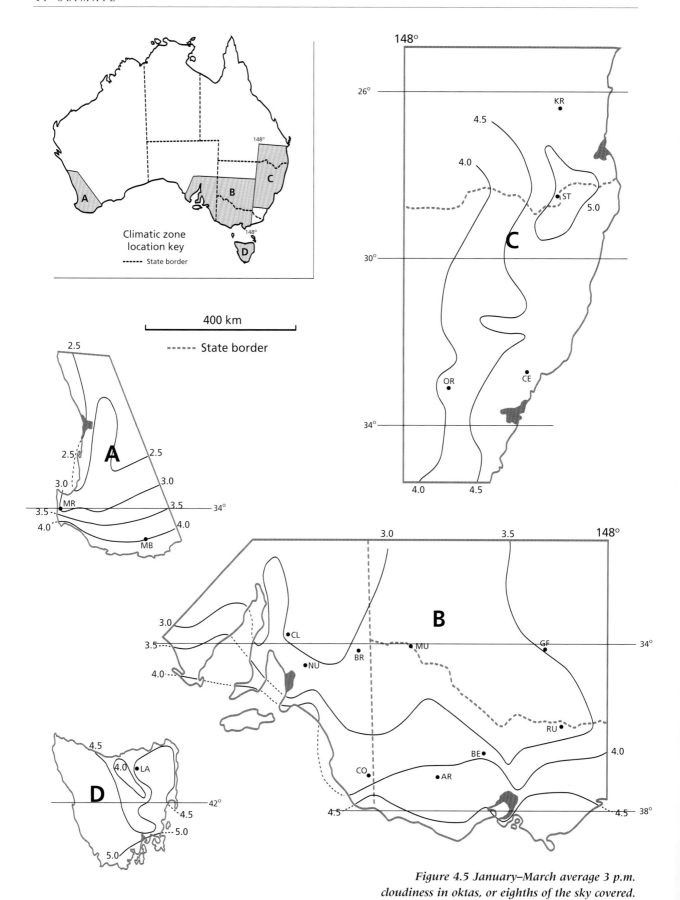

Figure 4.5 January–March average 3 p.m. cloudiness in oktas, or eighths of the sky covered.

opposite response of internode elongation, little branching, reduced chlorophyll and poor bud fruitfulness. The ratio of red to far red wavelengths (R:FR) gives a measure of this spectral depletion and is a critical statistic of canopy microclimate.

An aspect so far little studied in viticulture is that of reflection from the ground or from artificial reflectants. Light quality around the bunches directly affects the ripening biochemistry of the fruit (Smart 1987; Smart et al. 1988). The practice of leaf plucking in the fruit zone is partly a response to this. Limited reports suggest further positive quality responses from reflective ground covers, while conceivably some of the reported natural associations between soil surface colour and wine qualities could be related to soil-reflected light.

4.3.2 RAINFALL AND HAIL

Rainfall and its distribution directly limit viticulture where there is no irrigation. Productive dryland vineyards in cool areas need at least about 500 mm annually, distributed through the growing season or available from soil storage. Warm climates need 750 mm or more for high productivity, but many quality regions get much less than that. **FIGURE** 4.6b shows annual rainfall averages for Australian viticultural regions.

Traditional mediterranean viticulture accommodates to growing season rainfall shortage by restricting vine numbers per hectare together with shoot numbers per vine by hard pruning. On deep enough soils this allows each vine and shoot access to the stored winter-spring rainfall in a large soil volume. Most Australian dryland viticulture uses limited drip irrigation for commercially viable yields, and to avoid stresses at times critical to fruit quality. The new management technique of partial rootzone drying (PRD) (Dry and Loveys 1998) promises to develop further this management in future, both reducing water needs and potentially improving fruit quality. This works by controlled moderate root drying on alternate sides of the vine, resulting in a more or less continuous supply of root-produced ABA which controls vegetative vigour and transpiration without significantly reducing yield or harming the roots (see Volume 2, Chapter 6).

Rainfall is also important for its harmful effects when excessive or untimely. Winter–spring waterlogging is common on shallow soils in Australia's winter-rainfall regions. Vines tolerate temporary waterlogging when fully dormant, but not after the start of new root growth following budburst in spring. Section 4.4.3 below deals with the problems of rain around flowering.

Prolonged wet weather at any time of season, but especially through summer and ripening, increases the risk from diseases such as downy mildew and botrytis rots. **FIGURE** 4.6a gives a general idea of relative risks.

Direct rain damage to ripening berries results from their rapid swelling due to water intake, which is related to the osmotic pressure developed in the juice with rising sugar content (Considine and Kriedemann 1972). It can come both from the roots and directly through the leaves or berry skin. Cracking, compression and sometimes ejection from the bunch then occurs and is readily followed by botrytis and other rotting. It is worst when previous conditions have been dry, because the berry skins are then more brittle and relative swelling may be greater. Bunches may also be more compact. The problem is accentuated on shallow soils that drought readily and where free water accumulates within a confined root zone. Deep and well drained soils absorb rain without excessive wetting, and also encourage water-absorbing roots beyond the depth most immediately affected. This is why in Bordeaux the best terroirs maintain wine quality through wet vintages that can be disastrous for lesser terroirs.

Heavy rain at harvest time creates special problems for those dependent on mechanical harvesting, since boggy ground can preclude harvest for long periods or even altogether. Later harvest, if possible, is likely to be beyond optimum maturity and cannot exclude diseased fruit. Hand pickers can operate under most conditions and may be able to pick before the worst damage is done. Later they can select what healthy crop remains.

Rain in mid to late autumn, rather than temperature, often defines the end of the practical ripening season in areas of predominantly winter rainfall and some with summer or uniform rainfall. As noted above this can differ for mechanically versus hand-picked fruit.

Hail

This is damaging at any time during growth and even during dormancy. Canes are most injured while young, tender and exposed. Severe damage destroys current crop potential and can compromise that for the following year or more. Losses close to harvest are not uncommonly total. Hail netting can prevent them, but in most Australian environments the occasional risk does not warrant the cost.

Devastating hail forms most typically in the strong updrafts of thunderstorms. Proximity to sun-heated escarpments of hills or plateaus is a risk factor for the necessary updrafts, but once triggered the storms can wander haphazardly or in some areas along preferred trails.

Summer hail risk is only partly related to summer rainfall (**FIGURE** 4.7a versus **FIGURE** 4.6a). It is greater where wet summers are also cool, as in the higher tablelands of eastern Australia. Burgundy in France is a notorious example.

Rain fronts in spring also form thunderstorms and hail where forced upwards over a coast or scarp. Such hail extends into the most vulnerable period for young vine growth and is the main source of damage in winter-rainfall areas (**FIGURE** 4.7b).

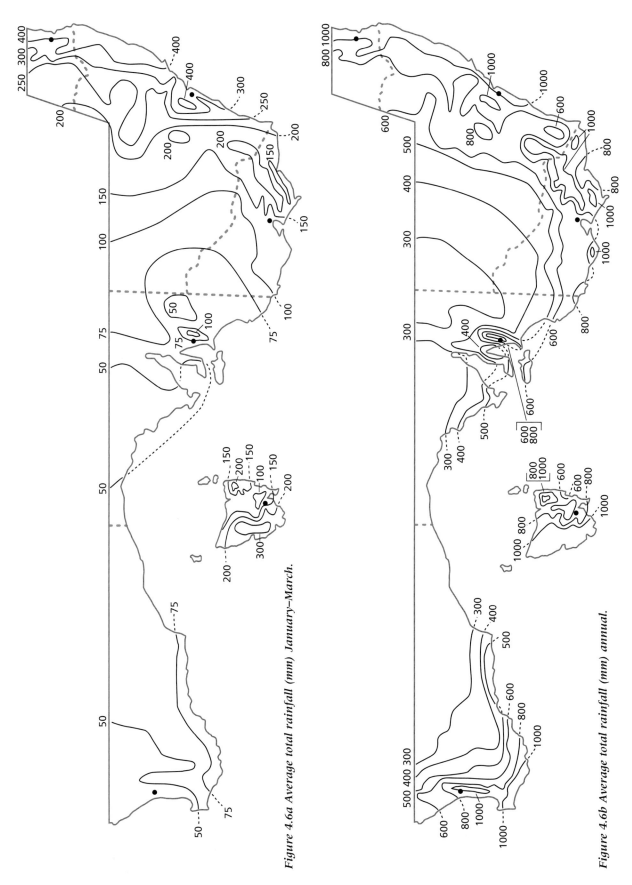

Figure 4.6a Average total rainfall (mm) January–March.

Figure 4.6b Average total rainfall (mm) annual.

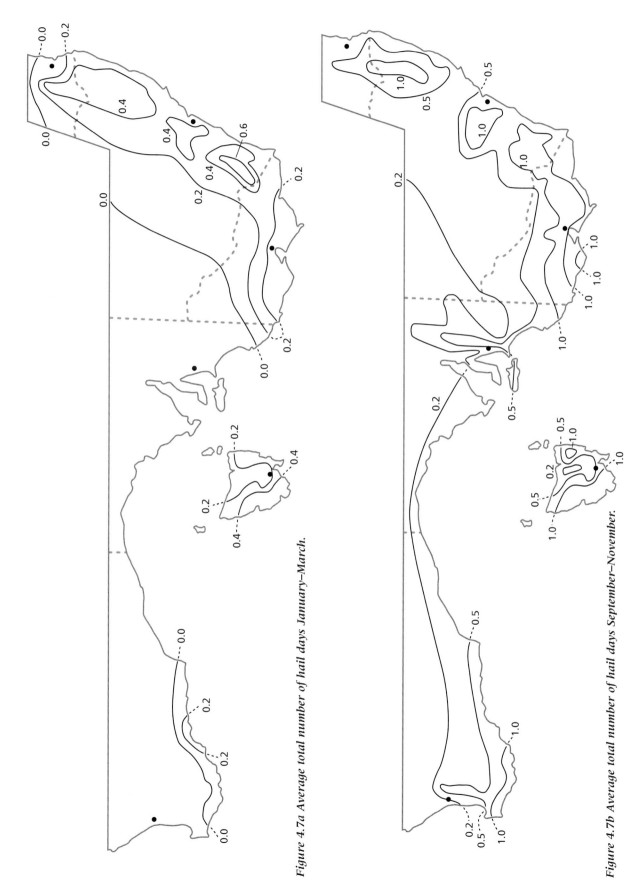

Figure 4.7a Average total number of hail days January–March.

Figure 4.7b Average total number of hail days September–November.

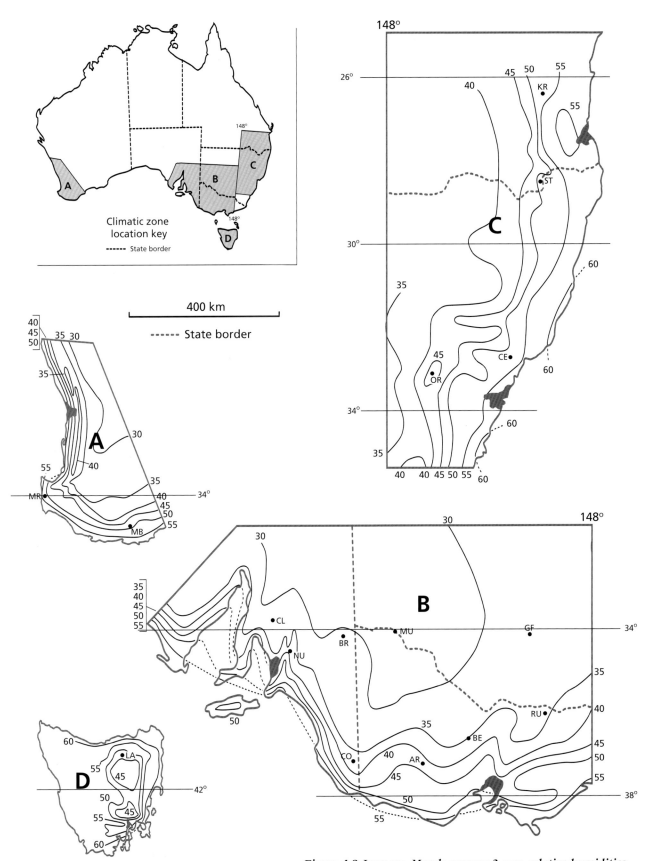

Figure 4.8 January–March average 3 p.m. relative humidities.

4.3.3 HUMIDITY

Atmospheric humidity is very significant for viticulture. It is usually expressed as *relative humidity* (RH), which is the amount of water vapour in the air as a percentage of what it would hold when fully saturated at the same temperature. Capacity to hold water vapour rises with temperature, so with no change in absolute water content the RH falls as temperature rises and rises as temperature falls. The temperature at which a cooling air body's RH reaches 100% is its *dew point*.

Another useful measure is *saturation deficit* which is the amount of water vapour, as partial pressure in millibars, by which an air body falls short of saturation at its current temperature. It directly indicates evaporative power and potential plant stress. *Vapour pressure deficit* is an alternative term for the same thing.

High RH is conducive to fungal diseases, especially if high enough to reach dew point at night which provides the leaf dampness needed to germinate fungal spores. The higher the temperature at which this occurs the greater in general is the danger, depending on fungal species. Risk estimates are thus possible, which can be based on long-term climate data for regions or on short-term or immediate weather data for current risks (see Volume 2, Chapter 11).

The standard Australian climatic data specify RH at 9 am and 3 pm The 9 am figures vary only a little across viticultural regions, but more when local topography is taken into account, e.g. the morning collection of cool, foggy air on valley floors and flats. Therefore while generalized mapping gives some indication of fungal disease risks, individual vineyard mesoclimates play a big role as well.

The 3 pm relative humidities (**FIGURE** 4.8) vary more across viticultural regions and less with individual sites. Together with 3 pm or maximum temperatures they indicate regional stresses important to wine quality.

Typically in warm and sunny areas the leaf stomata (pores) close and photosynthesis stops through the middle of the day. Partly this is due to build-up of assimilates, but to the extent that it is caused by stress, much then depends on milder conditions in mid to late afternoon for recovery of photosynthetic and perhaps other functions. In this context afternoon sea breezes play a major role in near-coastal areas, where average relative humidities at 3 pm in summer largely reflect the timing and regularity of sea breeze arrival.

Atmospheric humidity during those times the stomata are open is a prime determinant of the vine's economy of water use. High humidity results in greater water use efficiency because less evaporates out of the leaves as transpiration for the same amount of CO_2 passing in (Bierhuizen and Slatyer 1965). Thus in general both rain and applied water are used more efficiently in humid and coastal climates than in the arid inland.

4.3.4 WIND

Strong winds particularly damage young growth in spring, when the shoots are weak, brittle and not developed enough to act as mutual windbreaks. Worst affected in Australia are immediate coastal (particularly south coastal) areas, followed by exposed inland hills and plateaus. In all areas much depends on shelter by local topography and vegetation.

Even moderate winds in spring can reduce vine vigour and yield. Working in South Australia's Eden Valley, Dry and Botting (1993) found yield responses to a sheltering windbreak which resulted mainly from better initiation and development of bud inflorescence primordia in October-December of the year prior to bearing. Likely explanations were higher temperatures of the sheltered vines (see 4.4.3) and stronger growth from more continuous stomatal opening and photosynthesis.

Other damage comes from hot, dry winds from the continental interior during summer heatwaves. Worst effects are in mainland south coastal and adjacent areas, partly because heatwaves there tend to last longer than on east and west coasts, and partly because the hot northerlies alternate with cool southerlies so that vines acclimate less and the onset of stress is more sudden.

Not all effects of wind are negative. The ventilation of vine canopies by moderate winds helps minimize disease, and moving leaves give better intermittent sunlight penetration for photosynthesis (4.3.1) and moderate fruit exposure without over-heating (4.4.5).

A regular summer pattern of coastal and near-coastal land/sea breezes gives arguably the best combination in Australia, of dry land air in the morning and mild, humid sea breezes in mid to late afternoon. Temperatures and humidities are close to optimum for vine function through much of the day and evening, giving effectively a cooler and more equable climate than the simple maxima and minima might indicate. Local lore places great stress on such breezes for making good table wines in otherwise hot areas such as the Hunter Valley in New South Wales and the Swan District in Western Australia.

4.3.5 ATMOSPHERIC CO_2 AND UV-B RADIATION

Both of these factors have changed over time and will continue to do so.

Atmospheric CO_2

Anthropogenic (man-caused) rises in atmospheric CO_2 concentration are well documented and world-wide. From a pre-1800 concentration of around 270 parts per million (ppm) it has risen already to 370 ppm as a result of burning fossil fuels, forest clearing and breakdown of soil organic matter under cultivation. The figure is expected (e.g. Schultz 2000) to reach 600 ppm late in the 21st century.

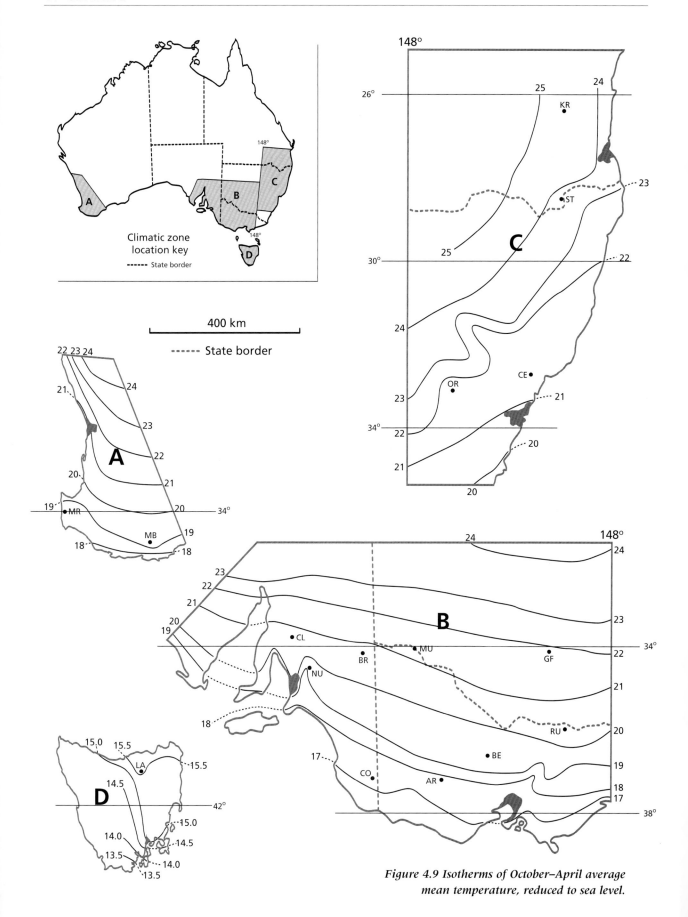

Figure 4.9 Isotherms of October–April average
mean temperature, reduced to sea level.

One effect (along with that of certain other gases) is a global increase in temperature. The thermophysics are clear on this, but the amount remains in doubt although early catastrophic fears are now greatly tempered. Measured temperatures have suggested a rise of about 0.6°C since the mid–19th century, but not all of this is necessarily due to 'greenhouse' effects since natural fluctuations could also be an arguable cause. For further discussion see Gladstones (1992), Chapter 23.

'Forecasts' of temperatures over the next 50 or 100 years are thus very speculative. A recent review of Barlow (2002) suggested a 'mid-range' scenario for vines in Australia of around 1.0°C rise by 2050. This would result in a southwards migration of the temperature belts averaging 80–100 km (**FIGURE** 4.9). However, the record and theory point to more of the change being in winter than in summer, and from night rather than day temperatures, which minimizes harmful effects and could in fact be beneficial.

The direct effects of CO_2 concentration on crop growth are well documented both from experiments (Bowes 1993) and commercial greenhouse culture (Mortensen 1987). The main effect is increased assimilation especially at higher temperatures, which is maintained across all light intensities. The evidence suggests an optimum CO_2 concentration for most crops around 700–900 ppm, or as is believed to have been present when modern plants were evolving some tens of millions of years ago. Full yield response to these concentrations requires increased temperature, but quality effects remain uncertain.

A suggested result (Gladstones 1992) is that the best sites for commercial viticulture could for the next few decades stay much as now. Undoubtedly any temperature rise will enable a significant poleward expansion of viticulture, which may be needed to maintain true cool climate wine styles, but these vines will benefit least from the extra CO_2.

UV-B radiation
Damaging ultra violet radiation in the wavelength range 290–320 nm, known as UV-B, can reach the earth's surface but is mostly absorbed and blocked selectively by ozone in the stratosphere. In recent decades there has been progressive destruction of the ozone layer by synthetic halocarbons released through their use as spray propellants and in airconditioning. Schultz (2000) cites evidence that this has increased UV-B penetration to the earth's surface in the Northern Hemisphere by 4–8% per decade, and also shifted its spectrum towards the more damaging shorter wavelengths. The effect has, however, probably peaked and should return to 1980 levels over 50 or so years under international agreements to phase out the offending compounds.

The intensity of incident UV-B radiation on any vineyard depends on its latitude, the time of season and especially the time of day. Highest intensity is when the sun is vertically overhead, so that its radiation has the shortest possible passage through the ozone layer and hence least UV absorption. Lower sun angles, for whatever reason, correspondingly increase the length of passage and UV absorption. Clouds in the lower atmosphere do not block UV selectively, but reflect away part of all solar radiation including UV. It follows that Australia's sunny, low-latitude vineyards have particular reason to be concerned with UV-B effects, especially for grape varieties that ripen early.

Described effects of UV-B radiation include the presence (or increase) of phenolic and other UV-absorbing compounds in leaves and grape skins; reduced carotenoids and certain of the amino acids important in fermentation; less chlorophyll, and damage to photosynthetic enzymes, hence reduced growth; and thicker and more waxy leaves, enhancing disease resistance. Some plant compounds affected are important for wine flavour. All these factors influence the optimum sunlight/UV-B exposure of leaves and especially the fruit, and hence optimum canopy management across environments.

4.4 Climatic effects at different growth stages

4.4.1 THE DORMANT PERIOD

Forms of dormancy
Writers use a variety of terms for the stages of vine and bud dormancy. Here I use those most commonly used in Australia and in the authoritative text of Mullins et al. (1992). Lavee and May (1997) review bud dormancy using somewhat different terminology, as indicated below in brackets.

Conditional dormancy (pre-dormancy) is that of the newly formed latent buds during active growth. The growing tips of both main and lateral shoots export hormones that suppress lateral buds below them. Loss of a shoot tip removes the source of this suppression, allowing latent buds below it on that shoot to develop.

When the canes mature from mid to late summer the buds enter *organic* dormancy (dormancy). Even with no suppressor from growing points their activation is delayed or (in *deep* dormancy) prevented despite otherwise suitable conditions for growth. Bud water contents and respiration fall to low levels and starch grains build up in them, as also in the cane's phloem and cambial tissues.

Organic dormancy dissipates as temperatures fall in late autumn and early winter, and is replaced by *enforced* dormancy (post-dormancy), during which buds are ready to grow as soon as temperatures rise enough. In this state the buds and other still-living tissues can undergo acclimation (or hardening) to low winter temperatures.

Full entry into organic and enforced dormancy depends on proper cane maturation and build-up of carbohydrate reserves, which can be impeded by over-cropping, late crop maturation, or loss of leaves through drought, disease or harvest damage. Premature budburst may then follow. The same can happen where winters are not cold enough to bring about full dormancy, as sometimes occurs in south-west coastal areas of Western Australia with grape varieties of low natural dormancy such as Chardonnay.

Winter killing

Vitis vinifera withstands temperatures down to about –15°C if fully dormant and adequately hardened, but with some varietal differences, e.g. the relative resistance of cv. Riesling. Native American *Vitis* species withstand lower temperatures. Rogiers (1999) and Howell (2001) give fuller accounts.

Hardening depends on progressive exposure to falling temperatures. It entails conversion of starch and sucrose to the soluble monosaccharides glucose and fructose, and in some cases the oligosaccharides raffinose and stachyose. These and certain soluble 'anti-freeze'proteins lower tissue freezing points and prevent the growth of large, cell-lacerating ice crystals. Young, heavy-cropping or otherwise stressed vines with low carbohydrate reserves suffer most.

Warmer temperatures bring deacclimation, which involves the opposite processes and can happen over a matter of days or at most weeks. Variability of winter temperatures is therefore an important factor in winter killing and injury, especially in North America where arctic air masses often penetrate well south.

Despite having higher winter temperatures there is now evidence of a sporadic winter injury problem in southeastern Australia as well, leading (or at least contributing) to a syndrome known as restricted spring growth or RSG (Mattschoss 1994, Wilson 1997, Vagnarelli 1998, Whiting and Pascoe 1999). Bark and trunk splitting are common features, preceded by stem phloem discolouration that is readily seen on dissection. Characteristically these occur on the northwest side, which receives greatest winter heating and therefore presumably acclimates least or deacclimates most. Low carbohydrate reserves and incomplete entry into dormancy appear to contribute here as elsewhere.

4.4.2 THE BUDBURST PERIOD

Cold resistance irrevocably disappears once the spring growth stimulus has registered and bud swelling starts. Woolly buds withstand no lower than about –3°C. Young, fast-growing shoots have greatest frost susceptibility, with injury if temperatures at shoot height fall below about –1°C.

Grape varieties differ in their degrees of winter dormancy and time of bud burst, with late-bursting varieties requiring higher temperatures to break dormancy. All budburst in warm, maritime climates is at temperatures above those absolutely needed, but varietal differences in timing appear largely preserved.

4.4.3 THE PERIOD AROUND FLOWERING

Flowering time is crucial for vine fruitfulness and yield. Buttrose (1974) has reviewed early work in this area, since largely confirmed.

Effects in the current season

Vines need warmth and sunshine during and around flowering for best fruit set. Wet, cold and cloudy weather results (to varying degrees according to grape variety) in either or both of two conditions: poor set or *coulure*, where many of the berries fall off when small, and 'hen and chicken' or *millerandage*, in which small, seedless berries or berries with incompletely formed seeds accompany normally-seeded larger berries on the same bunch.

Coulure appears to be caused by lack of assimilate within the bunch, often from competition by vigorous growth under ample water and nitrogen supply as well as low sunshine. *Millerandage*, by contrast, results directly from low air temperature just before and during flowering. This interferes with ovule development and pollen function, and with normal development of the resulting seeds and hence berries (Ebadi et al. 1996).

Most cell divisions of a grape's fleshy tissue (pericarp) occur before flowering, with just one to two more generations in the three weeks or so after (Coombe 1976) during which the berries are sensitive to environmental stresses. High temperatures (Hale and Buttrose 1974) and water stress (McCarthy 2000) at this time both irrevocably reduce potential for final berry size. Ojeda et al. (2001) present evidence that this is due to reduced extensibility of the newly forming cell walls, rather than to curtailment of the final cell divisions.

Effects on the following season

Flowering coincides in part with bud formation for the next season's cropping shoots, including the primordia of the bunches they will carry. The process continues for as long as the current shoot develops, with buds closest to its base forming earlier and under generally cooler conditions than those further out.

There is now ample evidence that temperatures during individual bud formation influence their fruitfulness the following season, i.e. the proportion of the shoots developed from them carrying bunches and the number of bunches on each (Baldwin 1965, Buttrose 1970, 1974, Sommer et al. 2000, MacGregor 2002). Some evidence (Dunn and Martin 2000) suggests a further influence on bunch size. Fruitfulness and large bunch size result from warmth during bud formation and an ample supply of cytokinins from warm, well aerated roots.

Grape varieties differ greatly in their fruitfulness and the temperatures during bud initiation needed to achieve it. Riesling forms fruitful buds at low temperatures (Buttrose 1970), and can be pruned short anywhere. Sultana and Ohanez are fruitful only well out on the canes even in hot climates, and must always be pruned long.

Light exposure of the buds is also involved, although how much through bud warming by sunlight remains unclear. Photosynthesis by the nearest leaves evidently plays a part, since a bud's carbohydrate content can partly predict its fruitfulness (Sommer et al. 2000). Such differences in light exposure stem largely from canopy management, as Dry (2000) discusses. Experienced pruners know to select 'sun' canes for their fruitfulness, in preference to those developed in canopy shade.

4.4.4 Post-setting to veraison

Stage 1 of berry growth (Winkler 1962) encompasses the end of pericarp cell division and subsequent cell growth of the pericarp and seed initials. In Stage 2 the seeds develop but the berries remain small and hard. The duration of this stage largely determines variety differences in maturity. It can last only a week or so in seedless varieties and six weeks or more in those maturing late. Environment and management can also influence the duration of this stage. Both low and especially very high temperatures tend to prolong Stage 2 (Hale and Buttrose 1974), as do heavy crop load or factors leading to it. During this stage, however, the berries and vines in other respects most tolerate heat and drought.

This is a time when growth is often profitably limited by moderate stress. Desirable effects include vine hardening and better light penetration to the renewal and fruit zone.

4.4.5 Veraison to harvest

Weather and the course of ripening

Stage 3 and berry ripening start at veraison. There is a sudden softening of berries followed by intake of water and expansion of the berries, which become translucent. Hexose sugar accumulation starts, followed shortly by the appearance of skin anthocyanins in black varieties.

Veraison and soon after is a time of renewed heat sensitivity for the berries. Prolonged heat and sun exposure readily cause collapse and shrivelling of those fully exposed. This sensitivity diminishes as berry sugar and skin phenolics build up.

Coombe (2000) describes observations suggesting a critical stage during veraison for each berry, at which some form of heat can interrupt or completely block further ripening and lead to berries ranging from green to ripe on the same bunch. He proposes differing degrees of phloem damage and its repair as a possible

mechanism. This condition appears distinct from that caused by later sunburn, which brings about general collapse of the most exposed berries.

Sugar and pigments can peak four to five weeks from veraison in a warm and sunny environment, after which flavour ripening, or 'engustment', starts (Coombe and McCarthy 1997, 2000). Engustment in such an environment takes perhaps a further three weeks to flavour maturity. In more cloudy climates it seems that engustment and final sugar accumulation can be roughly synchronous, while in still more cloudy climates such as in Northern Europe the build-up of sugar can lag, leading to flavour maturity at low sugar levels.

Sunshine and phosynthesis presumably play a part in this relationship, but new evidence suggests atmospheric evaporative power as a major control. Water carries sugar and other solutes to post-veraison berries via the phloem, and without berry stomata the rate of movement appears limited by that of evaporation directly through the cuticle and its surface wax layer (Rebucci et al. 1997; Dreier et al. 2000). Barring sugar source limitation, high atmospheric saturation deficits would thus promote rapid sugaring and early high baumés. This is a process independent of engustment and other non-sugar components of ripening.

The same presumably applies to potassium. Its build-up in berries would be enhanced relative to sugar where canopies have many shaded leaves that contribute little sugar, but have stored potassium to unload. The combination helps to explain the excess potassium often found in grapes from hot, irrigated areas.

Shiraz and some other grape varieties are prone to a breakdown of the phloem connections to the berries before full ripeness (McCarthy 1999, Coombe and McCarthy 2000). Sugar and water access to the berries is then blocked, but engustment can continue; so does evaporative water loss, which can lead to berry shrivelling and loss of yield. This happens independently of water supply to the vine, and in evident response to current evaporative conditions. Skin injury by sunburn or disease could be expected to accelerate water loss, as might insufficient prior acclimation and cuticular wax build-up in mainly cool or humid climates (see 4.5.4: Heat stressfulness index).

Although engustment takes place only late in ripening, there is evidence that conditions earlier are crucial for it. French lore says, "C'est Août qui fait le gout" (It's August that makes the flavour). Benign conditions at veraison with uninterrupted early sugar and (in black varieties) anthocynanin accumulation seem related to final high quality (Pirie and Mullins 1977; Carbonneau and Huglin 1982). See also Chapter 11.

Apart from temperature and evaporative conditions, the influence of weather during engustment is complex. Photosynthesis and sugar accumulation probably limit only in cloudy climates or in heavily shaded canopies.

Table 4.3 Suggested optimal averages in the final 30 days of ripening[1] for different wine styles. From Gladstones (1992), slightly modified.

| | Sparkling wines | Table wines | | | Fortified wines |
		Light	Med-full	Full[2]	
Av. mean, °C	12-15	15-18	18-21	21-24	21-24
Av. max, °C	< 21	< 24	< 27	< 30	< 30
Av. highest max, °C	< 27	< 30	< 33	< 36	< 39
TVI[3]	< 30	< 33	< 36	< 39	< 42
Sunshine hours	150-180	180-210	210-240	240-270	> 270
Rainfall mm	< 50	< 50	< 40	<30	< 20
Early p.m. RH %	60-65	60-65	55-60	50-55	40-50

1 Final 30 days to average date of full maturity and start of vintage for dry table wines, assuming moderate yields.

2 Suited to large-scale commercial production for everyday wines; high quality attainable with strictly controlled growth and yields, especially in near-coastal areas with sea breezes.

3 Temperature variability index: see 4.5.4 of text.

Rain and water uptake influence more as sugar builds up and the danger of berry splitting and flavour dilution grows. High temperatures favour rapid malic acid loss by respiration, and low temperatures its retention. Low temperatures during engustment favour the retention of aromatic flavour components.

In summary, all considerations point to the desirability for table wines of equable temperatures and moderately high relative humidities throughout ripening, and especially during engustment. Ideal conditions do, however, differ according to wine style, as we will now discuss.

Macroclimate, wine styles and quality

Traditional northern European opinion holds that the best table wines come from cool areas where grapes only just ripen, with periodic failure to ripen accepted as the price for outstanding quality in successful vintages. Jackson and Lombard (1993), Jackson and Schuster (2001) and in part Happ (1999a,b 2000) adopt this position. Happ lays particular emphasis on 'heat load' from high day temperatures during late ripening as an adverse factor for quality across all table wine styles.

Due (1988) has argued cogently against this view, maintaining that preference for cool-climate wines largely reflects the historical bias of northern European markets for their domestic product, combined with technical limitations to making good wine in warm climates which have now been overcome.

Gladstones (1977, 1992) agrees with much of Due's argument but also argues that very high day temperatures at veraison and during ripening are damaging. He suggests instead a range of mean temperature optima through ripening depending on wine style, with as little as possible daily and weekly variation around them. High day temperatures, especially extremes, are thought to damage through both injury and pigment degradation, and through evaporative or degradative losses of flavour and aroma compounds. By contrast *relatively* warm nights promote quality by maximizing sugar transport to the berries and the berry metabolism responsible for colour, flavour and aroma formation. Equability of temperatures during ripening is the ideal.

The result is a spectrum of potential wine styles for which optimum ripening conditions can be defined (TABLE 4.3). Delicate, fresh and aromatic (especially white) table and sparkling wines need cool, equable late ripening to maximize and conserve the more volatile components in the grapes, and retain acid, with only moderate sunshine hours and high humidities to keep alcohol low. Full-bodied, red table wines need ample total flavourants, pigments, tannins and alcohol, but usually less acids, and hence more ripening warmth and sunshine. Their essential quality constituents are more temperature-stable and less fugitive than in delicate white wines, so temperature equability is less critical if still important. Fortified wines have the requirements of full-bodied table wines but with still more sunshine to maximize berry sugar content. All styles (except concentrated fortified wines that depend on berry raisining) benefit from moderately high afternoon relative humidities as discussed in 4.3.3. These differences are in turn subject to the individual temperature sensitivities of grape varieties and their distinctive flavourants.

The contribution of mesoclimate

Mesoclimates resulting from local topography contribute much to the ripening-period temperature equability thought to contribute to grape and wine quality, as well as to making viticulture possible at its cold limit (4.1.2). Factors of slope and air drainage, proximity to the coast or inland water bodies, heat-absorbent rocky soils and slopes facing the sun all modify local climate chiefly by raising effective evening and to a lesser extent night temperatures (TABLE 4.1). Such conditions characterize the greatest quality vineyards of the Old World, as is clear from evidence such as that of Johnson and Robinson (2001), and can be expected to do so elsewhere as well.

Microclimate during ripening

Microclimates around and within the bunches contribute a final dimension to ripening. The berry constituents most influenced are the phenolics, i.e. non-volatile cyclic compounds built up from or around the 6-carbon benzene ring, with phenol (C_6H_5OH) as the basic building block. Flavonoid phenolics in grapes include the tannins together with flavonols such as the anthocyanins and quercetin. Important non-phenolics also affected are the volatile isoprenoids, based on the C_5H_8 isoprene unit, which include the mono- and sesquiterpenes and carotenoid-derived C_{13}-norisoprenoids that contribute much to grape flavours and aromas.

As well as existing in their free volatile states, the isoprenoids, together with the flavonols, also combine in the engusting grape with glucose molecules to form non-volatile (and therefore odourless and relatively stable) glycosides. These can later hydrolyze in the must and wine, especially at low pH, to release again the free, volatile flavourants. Ample available sugar in the berry skin throughout ripening favours both their initial formation and their conjugation with glucose to give stable reserve forms. A common dependence on sugar availability for the synthesis of all these compounds explains the remarkable correlation between colour and quality in red wines from a given grape variety (Pirie and Mullins 1977, Somers 1998).

Phenolic compounds form most in berry skins at least partly exposed to the sun, and especially to UV-B radiation (section 4.3.5), against which they act as a natural sunscreen. In the case of the anthocyanins only moderate light intensities are needed for maximum synthesis, together with suggested intermediate mean air temperatures around 20°C (Pirie 1979, Haselgrove et al. 2000). The evidence also strongly suggests a role of the light's spectral quality (Smart et al. 1988), with a high R:FR ratio needed for synthesis. Strong sun exposure can degrade anthocyanins, however, so that in sunny climates the highest contents at maturity tend to be under partial canopy shade (Mabrouk and Sinoquet 1998; Haselgrove et al. 2000).

Further work (Bergqvist et al. 2001, Spayd et al. 2002) has now shown that anthocyanin degradation in exposed bunches results specifically from high berry temperature, which can reach 15°C above that of the air, not from light itself which only promotes anthocyanin formation. This underlines a further advantage of intermittent, or 'dappled' light as under broken cloud or moderate leaf canopies. It can allow the fruit enough direct sunlight for the quick-acting light-dependent processes of optimum ripening, while mostly avoiding the cumulative over-heating that results when high air temperature and continuous sun exposure combine.

Isoprenoids likewise form more in sun-exposed than in shaded bunches and berries. However I speculate (Gladstones 1992) that their accumulation in free and glycoside forms is complicated by evaporative as well as likely degradative losses from exposed skins under high temperature (for instance, see Reynolds and Wardle 1988, Macaulay and Morris 1993, Belancic et al. 1997). Greatest aromatic intensity and varietal typicity in sunny climates result from partial or reduced-intensity sunlight exposure combined with moderate air temperatures.

A further class of compound, the methoxypyrazines, have a similar basic ring structure to the phenolics but with two of its six carbon atoms replaced by nitrogen atoms. Methoxypyrazines give the wines from certain grape varieties herbaceous aromas and a potentially harsh, disagreeable taste if present at more than very low levels. Highest contents are in bunches heavily shaded by dense, leafy canopies. It might be speculated that their synthesis rather than phenolics is favoured by a high ratio of available nitrogen to carbon. Exposure to direct sunlight late in ripening results in their loss by photodecomposition (Hashizume and Samuta 1999).

A consistent picture emerges on light microclimate in the vine's fruiting zone, analogous to and interacting with that for temperature. There is an intermediate optimum of moderate or intermittent direct illumination of the fruit, depending on grape variety and desired wine style. Attaining it requires the right canopy management for each environment.

Effects of row direction

The above discussion has implications for optimum row direction, particularly with vertical types of canopy training. In a cold climate where the fruit barely ripens under limiting low temperatures, direct bunch illumination is essential and benefits most in the warmer times of day; only then are temperatures high enough for ripening metabolism, and further fruit warming helps. Rows running north–south achieve this best, with leaf trimming in the fruit zone and all fruit fully illuminated either in mid to late morning or early to mid afternoon. In moderately cool climates a north–south row direction is still probably appropriate, but with less or no leaf trimming on the west side. Full shading up to early afternoon reduces heat acclimation of the west-exposed fruit, and makes it liable to damage from even moderate heat when suddenly and fully exposed at the hottest time of day.

In hot, sunny, low-latitude climates even full leaf cover gives insufficient protection on the west side of vertical canopies. Rows approximately east–west seem desirable in this situation, allowing leaf trimming along the south side (Southern Hemisphere) to give exposure to sun shining along the row in early morning or late afternoon, together with maximum indirect illumination. Untrimmed foliage on the north side protects most fruit from the near-vertical midday sun.

For a wide range of intermediate climates, logic suggests a best row orientation of about north-west to south-east in the Southern Hemisphere, or north-east to south-west in the Northern Hemisphere. This allows fruit illumination on one side through much of the morning and on the other in late afternoon, when temperatures are closest to optimal for it and UV-B intensities mostly not excessive (4.3.5). Greatest fruit shading, regardless of latitude and sun angle above the horizon, is when it is most needed in early and mid afternoon as the sun shines directly along the rows. Scope is still left for fine tuning through leaf trimming (or lack of it) on either side. Other features will, of course, come into decisions on row direction, including topography and perhaps diversity of fruit exposure to give wine complexity.

4.4.6 SOME GENERAL CONCLUSIONS ON CLIMATE

We saw earlier (4.1.2, 4.4.1–2) how viticulture at its cool limit demands mesoclimates with the warmest nights and least variability of the minimum temperature. The same factors as help avoid frost also advance the vine's phenology, both through raising mean temperatures and probably through faster development at the same mean temperature. The combination allows later-maturing and better quality varieties to be grown (e.g. Riesling in Germany), and to ripen under lower daytime heat loads. At the same time relatively warm nights (or perhaps more critically warm evenings as discussed in 4.5.4 below) are also thought to favour sugar transport to the berries and flavourant biosynthesis. Thus necessary site selection for low temperature variability and frost avoidance in cool climates automatically selects for best wine quality.

Such considerations help to explain the old belief that great wines come from 'the warmest sites in the coolest climates'; also the paradoxical fact that despite all belief in cool climates, the great vintages in them come disproportionately from warmer than average, early-ripening seasons.

We can deduce that warmth of climate, within reason, is not in itself a bar to the highest wine quality. The same can be achieved in warm climates, albeit in different styles, *provided* that similar principles of site selection are employed as are mandatory for survival in cool climates. Principally in Australia this means selection of coastal or near-coastal areas subject to humid afternoon sea breezes in summer; or marginally sub-tropical inland areas with summer afternoon humidity and cloudiness, although this may bring unwanted ripening and harvest period rain and there is often a high risk from spring frosts. In all cases it means a regional climate and local topography and soils most conducive to temperature equability for the vines in spring and especially during ripening.

Average ripening dates can now be acceptably estimated for any site and major grape variety from existing adequate climatic records, as described fully by Gladstones (1992) and briefly in 4.5.3 below; and thence, average ripening-period temperatures and other conditions. This in turn allows a broad prediction for a new site or area of prospective wine styles, best grape varieties, and to some extent potential wine quality. Importantly in commerce it becomes possible to estimate risks from detrimental ripening period factors such as heat, rain, hail or disease, or from frost and other hazards through the rest of the season. Various existing indices (4.5 below) can help, and more will be needed as knowledge grows. This goes beyond merely finding

equivalents of Old World viticultural areas. It potentially finds better ones and identifies reasons why.

New low-cost, automated technology for detailed climate recording is adding to present understanding: perhaps not greatly as to the major climatic controls of viticulture, but more in defining local climatic differences and individual site climates. Examples include the nature and arrival timing of sea breezes, cloud or fog in coastal and near-coastal areas. Likewise the way diurnal temperature curves are affected by slope, air drainage, aspect, soil and nearby water bodies could be especially important for otherwise unfavourable inland climates of the dry continents. We can predict from research on many other crops that the starch built up in vine leaves during the day, surplus to what can be transported out of the leaves and utilized at the time, only starts to hydrolyse and move to fruit and other sinks after sundown. It could thus well prove that evening (as opposed to night) temperatures have a special importance for ripening processes. They are the temperatures most affected by local site factors that experience suggests are related to grape and wine qualities.

None of this will ever fully explain terroir, but it brings us closer to an understanding of it.

4.5 Climate measures and indices

No single or simple measure can fully describe viticultural climate. Yet simple measures and indices still have a role.

4.5.1 SIMPLE TEMPERATURE-BASED INDICES

Degree day summations

These date historically from the work of A.P. de Candolle (1855), who observed that budburst in French vines occurs about the time spring mean temperatures reach 10°C. He reasoned that useful heat for vines could be measured by the seasonal summation of excesses above that base.

The most used such system is that of Amerine and Winkler (1944) in California. In Celsius form this measures monthly degree days (i.e. monthly average mean temperature minus 10, multiplied by the number of days in the month) summated over an assumed 7–month growing season of April–October (Northern Hemisphere) or October–April (Southern Hemisphere). It succeeds in California because temperature there also predicts other important factors such as sunshine hours and aridity. Elsewhere the method has been less successful, particularly in warm summer-rainfall areas such as sub-tropical New South Wales and Queensland, where summer rain and cloud can counteract or overshadow temperature effects on fruit qualities.

Table 4.4 Thermal regions for viticulture as measured by 7–month growing season average mean temperature[1]

Temp. °C	Wine styles	Typical locations/regions
14-15	Very light and sparkling wines from the earliest- maturing grape varieties	S. England; Seattle, USA; Christchurch, NZ
15-16	Cool-climate still and sparkling wines from early- maturing grape varieties	Champagne,Burgundy, Fr.; Rhine V, Ger.; Willamette V, USA; Tasmania; Marlborough, NZ
16-17	Light to medium-bodied wines from early to midseason grape varieties	Loire V, Fr; Yarra V, Vic.; Eden V, Coonawarra, SA
17-18	Medium to full-bodied wines from early to late-midseason grape varieties	Bordeaux, N Rhône, Fr.; Napa V, USA; Barossa V, SA; Margaret River, WA
18-20	Full-bodied table wines; fortified sweet wines[2]. All grape maturities	S France; NE Victoria; Mudgee, NSW; McLaren Vale, SA
20-22	Full-bodied table wines[3]; fortified sweet wines[2]. All grape maturities	Douro V, Port.; Riverland, SA; Riverina, Hunter V, NSW; Swan V, WA

[1] As adjusted for latitude (see text 4.5.1) and topography (text 4.2.2-3, Table 4.1).

[2] Fortified sweet wines only with enough sunshine hours.

[3] Best quality with coastal sea breezes and/or cloud; bulk wine inland under full irrigation.

Warmest month mean temperature

Prescott (1969) suggested that the average mean temperature of the warmest month (MTWM) indicates effective seasonal warmth just as well as any temperature summation. It ignores differences in continentality (4.2.3) and thus over-estimates the ripening capacity of continental relative to maritime climates. Nevertheless the MTWM has the practical virtue of simplicity. It remains widely used either in its original form or still more simply as average January (or July) mean temperature, MJT.

Seasonal average mean temperature

Average mean temperature over the same 7–month growing season expresses much the same as temperature summation, but in a some ways more usable form. For instance if reduced to sea level by adding 0.6°C per 100 metres of recording site altitude it can depict underlying cross-country temperature trends. FIGURE 4.9 shows these for Australian viticultural regions. Actual growing season average mean temperature for any site of known altitude is readily estimated by interpolation from its map position and subtracting 0.6°C per 100 metres of altitude. This achieves the same as the computer modelling of Kirk and Hutchinson (1994).

Further refinement is possible by allowing for site characteristics as in TABLE 4.1, and for latitude/daylength as discussed under 4.3.1. The latter can be approximated by adding 0.03°C to mean temperature for each degree of latitude above 40° or subtracting 0.03° for each degree below 40°. The adjusted growing season average mean temperature can then be matched against TABLE 4.4.

4.5.2 TEMPERATURE-LATITUDE INDICES

The Heliothermic Index of Branas

Branas (1946) used the summation of monthly average mean temperatures over 10°C, multiplied by a photosynthesis factor proportional to average growing season daylength at the site latitude, to give a 'heliothermic index' defining the northern limit of

viticulture in western Europe. As discussed in 4.3.1, in phenological terms the index remains essentially a temperature summation, adjusted for latitude. However in northern Europe photosynthesis and sugar can also limit directly, so the concepts behind the index remain appropriate there.

The LTI of Jackson and Cherry

Jackson and Cherry (1988) describe a statistically-derived latitude-temperature index (LTI) which uses the average mean temperature of the warmest month, multiplied by 60 minus site latitude in degrees. The negative latitude factor weighs opposite to that in the heliothermic and other indices, obstensibly to allow for reduced continentality and longer available growth periods at low latitudes. The latitude factor over-compensates, however, for instance equating the ripening capacity of Hobart (latitude 43°) with that of Bordeaux (latitude 45°), and placing Launceston, Tasmania and Blenheim, New Zealand, as effectively warmer than Bordeaux. The over-estimation is still greater at lower latitudes, giving a degree of temperature three times the weighting at latitude 30 as compared with latitude 50°. Clearly the LTI is misleading and has no application to Australia.

4.5.3 MULTI-FACTORIAL MEASURES

Smart and Dry's climate classification

Smart and Dry (1980) proposed a multi-factor classification of viticultural climates by the following criteria.

- Mean January temperature (five categories)
- Continentality (five categories)
- October–March sunshine hours/day (four categories)
- Aridity, or 0.5 of annual pan evaporation in mm minus annual rainfall in mm (four categories)
- January 9 a.m. relative humidity (four categories)

Taken together these provide a fair descriptive overview of viticultural climate, but the classifications

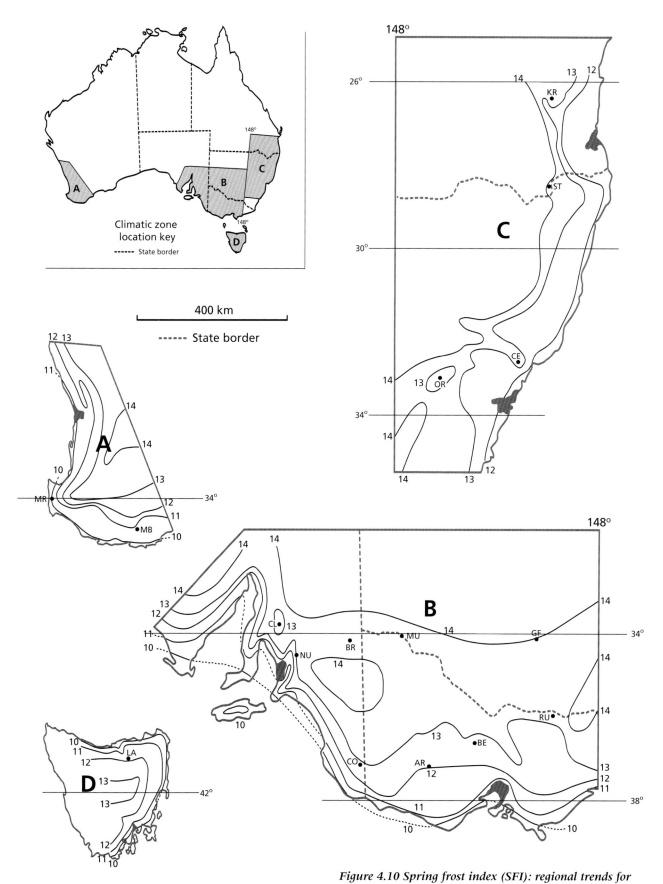

Figure 4.10 Spring frost index (SFI): regional trends for September–October, unadjusted for vineyard site characteristics.

Table 4.5 Grape maturity groups, with biologically effective °C days[1] to maturity and representative varieties. From Gladstones (1992), slightly modified.

Maturity group	Effective °C days	Varieties
1	1050 or less	Madeleine Angevin
2	1100	Chasselas, Müller-Thurgau
3	1150	Pinot Noir, Chardonnay
4	1200	Semillon, Riesling
5	1250	Cabernet Franc, Shiraz
6	1300	Colombard, Cabernet Sauvignon
7	1350	Grenache, Petit Verdot
8	1400	Trebbiano, Mataro
9	1450 or more	Doradillo, Biancone, Tarrango

[1]See text, Section 4.5.3.

remain very broad for practical use. Most citations have been confined to the first two criteria.

Weather during ripening

Gladstones (1977, 1992) argued that ripening and harvest are the critical time for fruit and wine quality, and selected the final 30 days leading up to a variety's average date of harvest commencement for dry table wines as the criterion for comparing climates or sites.

The approach requires climate-based prediction of such dates for grape varieties as classified into maturity groups (**TABLE** 4.5). This entails refining the temperature summation method (4.5.1) by adjusting for latitude/daylength and making a further allowance for diurnal temperature range. The adjusted monthly means are finally capped at 19°C as discussed 4.2.1. Resulting 'biologically effective degree days' are counted cumulatively from 1 October (1 April in the Northern Hemisphere) up to the dates their totals meet the requirements of each maturity group. This assumes normal commercial cropping levels for quality fruit: dates may be advanced marginally by low cropping levels or retarded by over-cropping, extreme heat in berry Stage 2, or heavy rain or irrigation. Back-interpolation within the original climate statistics gives long-term average conditions for all recorded climatic elements during each maturity group's final 30 days to ripeness, to compare either against postulated ideals (**TABLE** 4.3) or against other sites or maturity groups.

Smart's homoclime approach

Smart (1977) proposed seeking closest possible matches (homoclimes) of proven existing viticultural climates, an approach made feasible by growing computer power. Problems include (as in other methods) the selection of truly representative climate data and of sites and periods for matching, together with choice of sorting criteria and their weighting. Some of these problems can be overcome, but not all. Also, the method does not identify still better environments. Homoclime studies will undoubtedly become more prominent as models develop

and viticultural environments are better documented.

4.5.4 MEASURES OF TEMPERATURE VARIABILITY AND VINE STRESS

Sections 4.2.4, 4.4.2 and 4.4.5 describe how irregular extremes of cold in winter-spring, and of heat during fruiting, are the prime causes of vine and fruit temperature injury. Here we discuss some indices of the risks.

Temperature variability index, TVI

Proposed by Gladstones (1977, 1992) this is a measure of a site's short-term temperature variability, as distinct from continentality. For any month it is the average diurnal temperature range plus that between its average lowest minimum and average highest maximum. A low figure indicates equability that should favour vine growth and flavour ripening processes. The spring frost and heat stressfulness indices described below are separate and largely independent components, but as a comprehensive macroclimatic or mesoclimatic descriptor the TVI remains useful.

Spring frost index, SFI

Frost after budburst is a common hazard for which variability of the minimum temperature forms the strongest predictor (4.2.4). The spring frost index (SFI) of Gladstones (2000) is the range for a given spring month between its average mean and its average lowest minimum. Both statistics are available from long-term records. For comparing regions I use the combined average of April–May in the Northern Hemisphere and October–November in the Southern Hemisphere. **TABLE** 4.6 compares SFIs for some Australasian versus Northern Hemisphere viticultural areas, adjusted for typical vineyard sites, while **FIGURE** 4.10 shows the trends of unadjusted values across southern Australia. Values below 11 indicate a low risk, 11–13 intermediate risk, and above 13 a high risk, other than in climates warm enough for there to be little frost risk at any time.

Three points emerge. First, the SFI has least relevance to the radiative frosts associated with local mesoclimates (4.1.2). Instead it appears mainly to be a macroclimatic or regional feature, controlled by the dispositions of oceans, continents and mountain ranges via factors such as humidity, wind systems and regional air masses and their drainage. That is, it measures primarily the risk of advective frosts, such as described by Cashman (2000) for southeastern Australia. These result from the migration of extensive cold air masses and are the main cause of widespread frost damage from which local site selection and measures such as wind machines provide least protection. Second, the SFI stays fairly constant from month to month, in contrast to absolute temperature averages. Therefore selection of a standard two months does not create serious bias in regional comparisons. Comparable indices for the winter months

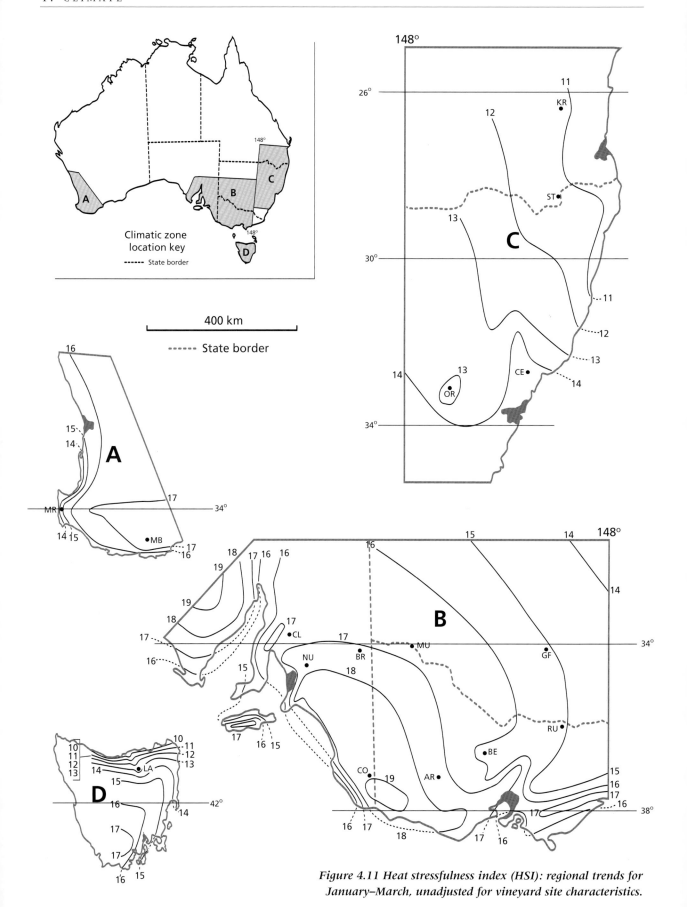

Figure 4.11 Heat stressfulness index (HSI): regional trends for January–March, unadjusted for vineyard site characteristics.

would be useful in continental climates subject to winter killing (4.4.1), although to the extent that both stem from constant landform factors the spring indices will in many cases be a pointer to these as well. Third, general climatic warming or cooling has only a minor effect on spring frost risk for vines at any site (other than when warming is sufficient to remove all frost risk or cooling enough to introduce it *de novo*) because of offsetting shifts in the time of budburst. The SFI is thus a robust index for long-term regional comparisons.

Measures of heat load

Happ (1999a,b; 2000) emphasised minimizing daytime heat load for table wine quality. As a measure he proposed the accumulations of degree hours above an arbitrary threshold of 22°C, as measured at 20–minute or hourly intervals across Australian and French viticultural environments. The results showed a good relationship for all grape varieties between low heat load, so defined, during the final 30 days of ripening and

Table 4.6 Estimated spring frost indices (SFI)[1], adjusted for typical vineyard sites after Table 4.1.

Country/Region or location		SFI	State/Region[2]		SFI
Europe			*Australia*		
Germany	Rhine Valley	10.4	Queensland	Granite Belt	13.8
France	Alsace	9.8	NSW/ACT	Hunter	13.3
	Champagne	10.8		Mudgee	13.8
	Loire Valley	11.1		Orange	12.2
	Bordeaux	10.6		Riverina	13.8
	Burgundy	11.3		Canberra	13.3
	Upper Rhône	11.7	Victoria	Rutherglen	13.7
	Montpellier	10.5		Geelong	10.8
Austria	Vienna	10.2		Mornington	9.5
Hungary	Keszthely	10.3		Grampians	12.7
	Eger	11.3		Bendigo	12.0
Italy	Piedmont	8.6		Murray Darling	13.7
	Chianti	9.7	SA	McLaren Vale	10.3
Spain	Rioja	9.9		Adelaide Hills	10.3
Portugal	Douro Valley	10.3		Langhorne Ck	11.9
				Barossa Valley	13.2
USA				Clare	12.8
Oregon	Willamette V	10.0		Riverland	13.9
Washington	Walla Walla	11.5		Coonawarra	13.0
	Prosser	14.1	WA	Margaret River	9.9
California	Salinas	10.5		Pemberton	10.2
	Napa	11.5		Great Southern	
	Fresno	12.2		(Mt Barker)	10.0
				Swan District	12.1
New Zealand			Tasmania	Tamar Valley*	10.1
N Island	Hawkes Bay	11.1		Derwent/	
S Island	Marlborough	11.7		Coal V*	10.6

1 See text, Section 4.5.4. Averages for October-November (Southern Hemisphere) or April-May (Northern Hemisphere)

2 Geographical Indications (see Chapter 2) except where indicated by *

high quality as judged by established wine repute. Corresponding relationships to ripening-month mean temperatures were poor. On the other hand heat load correlated reasonably well with average maximum temperatures (Happ 1999a). The latter therefore gives a useful approximation to heat load for broad climatic comparisons. Average highest maximum temperatures for each summer or ripening month (e.g. Gladstones 1992, 2000) directly indicate damaging extremes.

Heat stressfulness index (HSI): a proposed new index

An aspect not allowed for above, or in any absolute temperature measure, is acclimation. Thus, vines or fruit should be less damaged by a given heat load or extreme if previously and fairly continuously exposed to non-damaging temperatures nearly as high. Comparable acclimation is known for grapevine photosynthesis (Schultz 2000), and in adaptation to sunlight and UV-B intensity through the formation of flavonoids and other compounds that absorb or reflect harmful radiations (Price et al.1995; Schultz 2000). This suggests that an index of heat variability analogous to that for spring frost risk might be a useful adjunct to absolute heat measures. The heat stressfulness index (HSI) proposed here measures the range between a month's average mean temperature and its average highest maximum, averaged for regional comparisons over July–September in the Northern Hemisphere and January–March in the Southern Hemisphere.

TABLE 4.7 shows representative HSIs for Australasian and Northern Hemisphere viticultural areas, and **FIGURE** 4.11 its trends across southern Australia. Two things stand out. First, the range among viticultural areas is large. Second, its trends across Australia are distinctive and clearly meaningful. Even more than the Spring Frost Index, HSI is a macroclimatic element that depends on the dispositions of the coasts, mountain ranges and prevailing winds.

Mainland south coastal Australian HSIs are high compared with Europe, which undoubtedly limits potential here for delicate 'European'-style wines. However the limitation is not absolute. Coonawarra, for instance, has a very high January–March HSI. The practical effect is to restrict its well adapted varieties to those ripening late in autumn, when temperatures are both lower and more equable. This brings risks of ripening failure in cool or wet autumns. A low summer HSI allows adaptation of a wider varietal maturity range. In this respect it complements a maritime seasonal temperature pattern (4.2.3). Also grape varieties can be selected that tolerate high temperatures well. Chenin Blanc, Verdelho and to a large degree Chardonnay appear to do so, whereas Pinot Noir is notoriously sensitive.

Values along mainland Australia's south coast are high because most summer winds are either northerlies from

Table 4.7 Estimated heat stressfulness indices (HSI)[1], adjusted for typical vineyard sites after Table 4.1.

Country/Region or location		HSI	State/Region[2]		HSI
Europe			*Australia*		
Germany	Rhine Valley	12.4	Queensland	Granite Belt	11.0
France	Alsace	12.6	NSW/ACT	Hunter	13.9
	Champagne	11.7		Mudgee	12.9
	Loire Valley	12.9		Orange	12.4
	Bordeaux	12.9		Riverina	15.1
	Burgundy	12.7		Canberra	13.8
	Upper Rhône	11.5	Victoria	Rutherglen	15.1
	Montpellier	11.9		Geelong	17.8
Austria	Vienna	11.4		Mornington	14.9
Hungary	Keszthely	10.9		Grampians	17.3
	Eger	11.1		Bendigo	15.6
Italy	Piedmont	10.2		Murray Darling	16.4
	Chianti	9.9	SA	McLaren Vale	15.9
Spain	Rioja	13.5		Adelaide Hills	16.4
Portugal	Douro Valley	14.9		Langhorne Ck	17.9
				Barossa Valley	17.3
USA				Clare	16.1
Oregon	Willamette V.	13.5		Riverland	17.7
Washington	Walla Walla	15.3		Coonawarra	18.4
	Prosser	15.4	WA	Margaret River	15.0
California	Salinas	13.2		Pemberton	16.4
	Napa	15.4		Great Southern	
	Fresno	14.4		(Mt Barker)	17.6
				Swan District	15.9
New Zealand			Tasmania	Tamar Valley*	11.2
N Island	Hawkes Bay	11.9		Derwent, Coal V.*	15.9
S Island	Marlborough	12.3			

1 See text, Section 4.5.4. Averages for January–March (Southern Hemisphere) or July–September (Northern Hemisphere)

2 Geographical Indications (see Chapter 2) except where indicated by *

the heated interior or southerlies from the cool Southern Ocean. The Tasmanian north coast is conversely equable, with northerlies moderated by passage across Bass Strait while daytime southerlies are warmed by passage across land. This is clearly an area of choice in Australia for producing European-style cool-climate wines from heat-sensitive varieties, having conditions comparable to those of New Zealand. Gladstones (2000) and Iland and Fetzmann (2002) present more detailed analyses for Pinot Noir. Some cool locations of southern mainland Australia have advantages of less ripening-period rain, but the risk from excessive heat, UV-B radiation and in some cases moisture stress is much greater.

Also of interest is the trend in southeastern Australia of lower summer HSI to the north-east, reaching European levels in northern New South Wales and southeast Queensland. Comparable trends are apparent in falling sunshine hours (**FIGURE** 4.4), greater 3 pm cloudiness (**FIGURE** 4.5) and in part greater 3 pm relative humidity (**FIGURE** 4.8). All these impact on wine style, and in themselves are arguably positive for table wine quality. The main offsetting problems are

summer rain and hail (**FIGURES** 4.6a and 4.7) together with spring frosts, particularly on the western slopes of the Great Dividing Range (**FIGURE** 4.10). More than anywhere else in Australia, successful viticulture here hinges on site and locality selection to minimize viticultural risks. Western spurs and isolated hills of the Range appear to have some of the best prospects. Advantages of the Orange area surrounding Mt Canobolas in New South Wales, and of the semi-isolated plateau immediately around Beechworth in Victoria, show clearly in the climatic statistics and maps. Other like localities doubtless exist and can be identified.

DATA SOURCES

All Australian climatic data used to prepare the maps and tables of this chapter were supplied by the Severe Weather Section Regional Office of the Commonwealth Bureau of Meteorology, Perth, and are from the period 1957–2000. Overseas data in **TABLES** 4.2, 4.6 and 4.7 are from Gladstones (1992), where source details are listed in Appendix 2.

REFERENCES

Suggestions for further reading are marked (•).

Amerine, M.A. and Winkler, A.J. (1944) Composition and quality of musts and wines of California grapes. Hilgardia 15, 493-675.

Baldwin, J.G. (1965) The relation between weather and fruitfulness of the Sultana vine. Aust. J. Agric. Res. 15, 902-908.

Barlow, S. (2002) Global climate change and impact on regional temperature patterns and rainfall seasonality. Proceedings, Colloquium on Climate Change, Melbourne 2000 in CD-ROM Cool Climate Viticulture and Oenology (Winetitles: Adelaide).

Belancic, A., Agosin, E. et al. (1997) Influence of sun exposure on the aromatic composition of Chilean Muscat cultivars Moscatel de Alejandria and Moscatel rosada. Amer. J. Enol. Vitic. 48, 181-186.

Bergqvist, J., Dokoozlian, N. et al. (2001) Sunlight exposure and temperature effects on berry growth and composition of Cabernet Sauvignon and Grenache in the central San Joaquin Valley of California. Amer. J. Enol. Vitic. 52, 1-7.

Bierhuizen, J.F. and Slatyer, R.O. (1965) Effect of atmospheric concentration of water vapour and CO_2 in determining transpiration-photosynthesis relationships in cotton leaves. Agric. Meteorol. 2, 259-270.

Bowes, G. (1993) Facing the inevitable: plants and increasing atmospheric CO_2. Ann. Rev. Plant Physiol. and Plant Molecular Biol. 44, 309-332.

Branas, J. (1946) In Branas, J., Bernon, G. and Levadoux L. Elements de Viticulture Générale. Montpellier.

Buttrose, M.S. (1968) Some effects of light intensity and temperature on dry weight and shoot growth of grape vine. Ann. Bot. 32, 753-765.

Buttrose, M.S. (1969) Vegetative growth of grapevine varieties under controlled temperature and light intensity. Vitis 8, 280-285.

Buttrose, M.S. (1970) Fruitfulness in grape vines: the response of different cultivars to light, temperature and daylength. Vitis 9, 121-125.

• Buttrose, M.S. (1974) Climatic factors and fruitfulness in grapevines. CAB Horticultural Abstracts 44, 319-326.

Buttrose, M.S. and Hale C.R. (1973) Effect of temperature on development of the grapevine inflorescence after bud burst. Amer. J. Enol. Vitic. 24, 14-16.

Carbonneau, A.P. and Huglin, P (1982) Adaptation of training systems to French regions. Proc. Grape and Wine Centennial Symposium, University of California, Davis 1980, pp. 376-385.

Cashman, G. (2000) Advection frost: a case study of the freeze of 27-28 October 1998 and its effects on the vineyards of the Canberra district. Part 1. Meteorological aspects. Aust. Grapegrower & Winemaker No. 438, 74-84.

Considine, J.A. and Kriedemann, P.E. (1972) Fruit splitting in grapes: determination of the critical turgor pressure. Aust. J. Agric. Res. 23, 17-24.

Coombe, B.G. (1976) The development of fleshy fruits. Ann. Rev. Plant Physiol. 27, 507-528.

Coombe, B.G. (2000) Hen and chicken vs sweet and sour. Aust. NZ Wine Industry J. 15 (2), 13.

Coombe, B.G. and McCarthy, M.G. (1997) Identification and naming of the inception of aroma development in ripening grape berries. Aust. J. Grape and Wine Res. 3, 18-20.

Coombe, B.G. and McCarthy, M.G. (2000) Dynamics of grape berry growth and physiology of ripening. Aust. J. Grape and Wine Res. 6, 131-135.

De Candolle, A.P. (1855) Géographie Botanique Raisonée (Paris, 2 vols).

Dreier, L.C., Stoll, G.S. et al. (2000) Berry ripening and evapotranspiration in Vitis vinifera L. Amer. J. Enol. Vitic. 51, 340-346.

• Dry, P.R. (2000) Canopy management for fruitfulness. Aust. J. Grape and Wine Res. 6, 109-115.

Dry, P.R. and Botting, D.G. (1993) The effect of wind on the performance of Cabernet Franc grapevines. 1. Shoot growth and fruit yield components. Aust. NZ Wine Industry J. 8, 347-352.

• Dry, P.R. and Loveys, B.R. (1998) Factors influencing grapevine vigour and the potential for control with partial rootzone drying. Aust. J. Grape and Wine Res. 4, 140-148.

• Due, G. (1988) History, geography and the 'cool climate' dogma. Aust. and NZ Wine Industry J. 2 (4), 42-44.

Dunn, G.M. and Martin, S.R. (2000) Do temperature conditions at budburst affect flower number in Vitis vinifera L. cv. Cabernet Sauvignon? Aust. J. Grape and Wine Res. 6, 116-124.

Ebadi, A., May, P. et al. (1996) Effect of short-term temperature and shading on fruit-set, seed and berry development in model vines of V. vinifera, cvs. Chardonnay and Shiraz. Aust. J. Grape and Wine Res. 2, 2-9.

• Geiger, R. (1966) The Climate near the Ground. English translation of 4th German Ed. 1961 (Harvard University Press: Cambridge, Mass).

Gladstones, J. (1977) Temperature and wine grape quality in European vineyards. In: Proc. 3rd Aust. Wine Industry Tech. Conf., Albury 1977 (Aust Wine Res. Inst.), pp. 7-11.

• Gladstones, J. (1992) Viticulture and Environment (Winetitles: Adelaide).

Gladstones, J. (2000) Past and future climatic indices for viticulture. Aust. NZ Wine Industry J. 15 (2), 67-71.

Hale, C.R. and Buttrose, M.S. (1974) Effect of temperature on ontogeny of berries of Vitis vinifera cv. Cabernet Sauvignon. J. Amer. Soc. Hortic. Sci. 99, 390-394.

Happ, E. (1999a) Indices for exploring the relationship between temperature and grape and wine flavour. Aust. NZ Wine Industry J. 14 (4), 68-75.

Happ, E. (1999b) Story time: no grape needs heat in the ripening cycle. Aust. NZ Wine Industry J. 14 (6), 68-73.

Happ, E. (2000) Site and varietal choices for full flavour outcomes in a warm continent. Aust. NZ Wine Industry J. 15 (1), 54-64.

Haselgrove, L., Botting, D. et al. (2000) Canopy microclimate and berry composition: the effect of bunch exposure on the phenolic composition of Vitis vinifera L. cv. Shiraz grape berries. Aust. J. Grape and Wine Res. 6, 141-149.

Hashizume, K. and Samuta, T. (1999) Grape maturity and light exposure affect berry methoxypyrazine concentration. Amer. J. Enol. Vitic. 50, 194-198.

Howell G.S. (2001) Grapevine cold hardiness: mechanisms of cold acclimation, mid-winter hardiness maintenance, and spring deacclimation. Proc. ASEV 50th Anniversary Annual Meeting, Seattle 2000, pp. 35-48.

Huglin, P. (1983) Possibilités d'appréciation objective du milieu viticole. Bulletin de l'O.I.V. 56, 823-833.

Iacono, F. and Sommer, K.J. (1996) Photoinhibition of photosynthesis and photorespiration in Vitis vinifera under field conditions: effects of light climate and leaf position. Aust. J. Grape and Wine Res. 2, 10-20.

• Iland, P.G. and Fetzmann, D. (2002) Cool climate Pinot Noir wine styles - what, where and why? Proc. 5th Int. Symp. Cool Climate Vitic. and Oenol., Melbourne 2000 in CD-ROM Cool Climate Viticulture and Oenology (Winetitles: Adelaide).

Jackson, D.I. and Cherry, N.J. (1988) Prediction of a district's grape-ripening capacity using a latitude-temperature index (LTI). Amer. J. Enol. Vitic. 39, 19-26.

Jackson, D.I. and Lombard, P.B. (1993) Environmental and management practices affecting grape composition and wine quality- a review. Amer. J. Enol. Vitic. 44, 409-430.

Jackson, D.I. and Schuster, D. (2001) The Production of Grapes and Wine in Cool Climates, 3rd Ed. (Brassell Assoc. and Gypsum Press: Wellington).

Jackson D.I. and Spurling, M.B. (1988) Climate and viticulture in Australia. In: Viticulture Vol. 1, Edition 1. Eds B.G.Coombe and P.R.Dry (Australian Industrial Publishers: Adelaide), pp. 91-106.

Johnson, H. and Robinson, J. (2001) The World Atlas of Wine, 5th Ed. (Mitchell Beazley: London).

Kirk, J.T.O. and Hutchinson, M.F. (1994) Mapping of grapevine growing season temperature summation. Aust. NZ Wine Industry J. 9, 247-251.

Kriedemann, P.E. (1968) Photosynthesis in vine leaves as a function of light intensity, temperature and leaf age. Vitis 7, 213-220.

Kriedemann, P.E., Torokfalvy, E. et al. (1973) Natural occurrence and photosynthetic utilization of sun-flecks by grapevine leaves. Photosynthetica 7, 18-27.

Langridge, J and McWilliam, J.R. (1967) Heat responses of higher plants. In: Thermobiology. Ed A.H. Rose (Academic Press: London), pp. 231-292.

Lavcc, S. and May, P. (1997) Dormancy of grapevine budsÑfacts and speculation. Aust. J. Grape and Wine Res. 3, 31-46.

Mabrouk, H. and Sinoquet, H. (1998) Indices of light microclimate and canopy structure of grapevines determined by 3D digitising and image analysis, and their relationship to grape quality. Aust. J. Grape and Wine Res. 4, 2-13.

Macaulay, L.E. and Morris, J.R. (1993) Influence of cluster exposure and winemaking processes on monoterpenes and wine olfactory evaluation of Golden Muscat. Amer. J. Enol. Vitic. 44, 198-204.

MacGregor, C.A. (2002) Cool climate crop estimation. Proc. 5th Int. Symp. Cool Climate Vitic. and Oenol., Melbourne 2000 in CD-ROM Cool Climate Viticulture and Oenology (Winetitles: Adelaide).

McCarthy, M.G. (1999) Weight loss from ripening berries of Shiraz grapes (Vitis vinifera L. cv. Shiraz). Aust. J. Grape and Wine Res. 5, 10-16.

McCarthy, M.G. (2000) Developmental variation in sensitivity of Vitis vinifera L. (Shiraz) berries to soil water deficit. Aust. J. Grape and Wine Res. 6, 136-140.

Mattschoss, R. (1994) Restricted spring growth - the hidden cause. Aust. Grapegrower & Winemaker No. 372, 65-66.

Mortensen, L.M. (1987) Review: CO2 enrichment in glasshouses. Crop responses. Scientia Hortic. 33, 1-25.

Mullins, M.G., Bouquet, A. et al. (1992) Biology of the Grapevine. Cambridge University Press, Cambridge, UK.

Ojeda, H., Deloire, A. et al. (2001) Influence of water deficits on grape berry growth. Vitis 40, 141-145.

Pirie, A.J.G. (1979) Red pigment content of wine grapes. Aust. Grapegrower & Winemaker No. 189, 10-12.

Pirie, A.J.G. and Mullins, M.G. (1977) Inter-relationships of sugars, anthocyanins, total phenols and dry weight in the skin of grape berries during ripening. Amer. J. Enol. Vitic. 28, 204-209.

Poni, S., Marchiol, L. et al. (1993) Gas exchange response of grapevine leaves under fluctuating light. Vitis 32, 137-143.

Prescott, J.A. (1969) The climatology of the vine (Vitis vinifera L.). 3. A comparison of France and Australia on the basis of the warmest month. Trans. Roy. Soc. South Aust. 93, 7-15.

Price, S.F., Breen, P.J. et al. (1995) Cluster sun exposure and quercetin in Pinot Noir grapes and wine. Amer. J. Enol. Vitic. 46, 187-194.

Rebucci, B., Poni, S. et al. (1997) Effects of manipulated grape berry transpiration on post-veraison sugar accumulation. Aust. J. Grape and Wine Res. 3, 57-65.

Reynolds, A.G. and Wardle, D.A. (1988) Canopy microclimate of Gerwürztraminer and monoterpene levels. Proc. 2nd Int. Symp. Cool Climate Vitic. and Oenol., Auckland 1988, pp. 116-122.

• Rogiers, S.Y. (1999) Frost injury and cold hardiness in grapes. Aust. Grapegrower & Winemaker No. 432, 13-19.

Schultz, H.R. (1993) Photosynthesis of sun and shade leaves of field grown grapevine (Vitis vinifera L.) in relation to leaf age. Suitability of the plastochron concept for expression of physiological age. Vitis 32, 197-205.

Schultz, H.R. (2000) Climate change and viticulture: a European perspective on climatology, carbon dioxide and UV-B effects. Aust. J. Grape and Wine Res. 6, 2-12.

Skene, K.G.M. and Kerridge, G.H. (1967) Effect of root temperature on cytokinin activity in root exudates of Vitis vinifera L. Plant Physiol. 42, 1131-1139.

Smart, R.E. (1977) In: Proc. 3rd Aust. Wine Industry Tech. Conf., Albury 1977 (Aust Wine Res. Inst.), pp. 12-18.

Smart. R.E. (1987) Influence of light on composition and quality of grapes. Acta Hortic. 206, 37-47.

• Smart, R.E. and Dry, P.R. (1980) A climate classification for Australian viticultural regions. Aust. Grapegrower & Winemaker No.196, 8-16.

Smart, R.E., Smith, S.M. et al. (1988) Light quality and quantity effects on fruit ripening for Cabernet Sauvignon. Amer. J. Enol. Vitic. 39, 250-258.

Somers, C. (1998) The Wine Spectrum: an Approach towards Objective Definition of Wine Quality (Winetitles: Adelaide).

Sommer, K.J., Islam, M.T. et al. (2000) Light and temperature effects on shoot fruitfulness in Vitis vinifera L. cv. Sultana: Influence of trellis type and grafting. Aust. J. Grape and Wine Res. 6, 99-108.

Spayd, S.E., Tarara, J.M. et al. (2002) Separation of sunlight and temperature effects on the composition of Vitis vinifera cv. Merlot berries. Amer. J. Enol. Vitic. 53, 171-182.

Vagnarelli, B. (1998) Restricted spring growth (RSG) in spring 1997. Aust. Grapegrower & Winemaker No. 413, 22-24.

Whiting, J. and Pascoe, I. (1999) Frost damage on young grapevines. Aust. Grapegrower & Winemaker No. 430, 48-54.

Wilson, Y. (1997) Winter chilling injury. Aust. Grapegrower & Winemaker No. 402a, 157-158.

Winkler, A.J. (1962) General Viticulture (University of California Press: Berkeley) (Australian edition 1963, Jacaranda Press: Brisbane).

Woodham, R.C. and Alexander, D. McE. (1966) The effect of root temperature on development of small fruiting Sultana vines. Vitis 5, 345-350.

Zufferey, V., Murisier, F. et al. (2000) A model analysis of the photosynthetic response of Vitis vinifera L. cvs Riesling and Chasselas leaves in the field. 1. Interaction of age, light and temperature. Vitis 39, 19-26.

CHAPTER FIVE

Classification of Grapevines and their Interrelationships

M. R. THOMAS AND R. VAN HEESWIJCK

5.1 Origin of the grapevine

The grapevine *Vitis vinifera* as we know it today is a product of both natural evolution and domestication by humans. Despite its long historical association with the rise of civilisation, the grapevine has changed little in both form and genotype compared to many other crops such as wheat where breeding has had a major impact. This is largely due to vegetative propagation.

5.1.1 EVOLUTIONARY HISTORY

Fossil records indicate that grapevines were present on earth long before modern man (*Homo sapiens*). Fossilised leaves suggest that ancestors of grapevine were present during the Jurassic period, 181 million years ago, when dinosaurs dominated the earth and flowering plants (Angiosperms) were beginning to out-compete non-flowering plants (Gymnosperms) such as ferns (**TABLE 5.1**). One of the main advantages Angiosperms had over Gymnosperms was the ability to attract other organisms such as insects and birds to assist in pollination and the spread of seed. It is thought that the development of attractive and nutritious fruit was a major factor in assisting the dispersal of grapevine seed by birds (Hardie 2000). The separation into distinct grapevine species occurred over a long period of time as a result of multiple instances of regional isolation and adaptation to changes in climate, pests, diseases and environment. This speciation was essentially complete by the time human civilisation appeared.

5.1.2 TAXONOMIC CLASSIFICATION

Scientists have developed naming and classification systems for animals and plants which are intended to reveal inter-relationships and to allow each to be referred to without ambiguity. The basic unit is the species whose members have similar characteristics and interbreed. Related species are grouped into genera and related genera into families. To refer to a species, the name of the genus is given first, followed by the name of the species. As an example, the domestic cat is *Felis domestica*; lion and tiger are other species of the genus *Felis*, lynx and cheetah belong to other genera in the family Felidae. Sometimes the same species has been described under different names by different people, or the same name has been given to different species. When essential for accuracy the authority is given after the name of the species e.g. *Vitis vinifera* L. where the L. stands for the botanist, Linnaeus.

Table 5.1. The History of Vitis: relation with the geological time scale and the history of life.[1]

Era	Period	Epoch	Millions of years from start to present	Significant events
PRECAMBRIAN			4,500	Presumptive origin of life.
PALEOZOIC	Cambrian		600	Marine invertebrates; primitive algae.
	Ordovician		500	First agnathan (jawless fish) vertebrates.
SILURIAN			425	Invasion of land by primitive organisms.
	Devonian		405	First amphibians and insects.
	Carboniferous		345	Extensive forests of early vascular plants.
	Permian		280	Continents aggregated into Pangaea.
MESOZOIC	Triassic		230	First dinosaurs. Gymnosperms dominant. Continents begin to drift apart to form Laurasia and Gondwana.
	Jurassic		181	First land 'bird' (*Archaeopteryx*) and mammals. Angiosperms appear in tropics. *Vitaceae* evolves from *Cissus*-like progenitors. Ancestral (Labruscoid) forms of *Vitis* presumed to have arisen in North America; presumed dispersal largely by birds over Laurasia.
	Cretaceous		135	Continents drifting. Angiosperms become dominant over gymnosperms. Labruscoid forms similar to *V. aestivalis* and *V. riparia* inhabited cooler, northern regions of North America and N.E. Asia.
CENOZOIC	Tertiary	Palaeocene	63	Separation of North America and Eurasian continents by Atlantic Gulf gives rise to the evolution of two distinct races of *Vitis*, i.e. the American and Eurasian.
		Eocene	58	*Vitis* acquires a creeping habit better adapted to light seeking in the forest habitats that became more extensive with the more humid conditions of this epoch. *V. sezannensis*, earliest (Lower Eocene) fossil representative of *Vitis*, inhabited sub-tropical forest in Eastern France. *Vitis* distributed over northerly parts of Northern Hemisphere as climate becomes warmer. Continents in approximately modern positions.
		Oligocene	36	
		Miocene	25	Lower Miocene species, e.g. *V. islandica*, *V. teutonica* morphologically similar to present day representatives of the genus *Muscadinia*, e.g. *M. rotundifolia*, *M. munsoniana*, which inhabit the warm regions around the Gulf of Mexico.
		Pliocene	12	*Vitis proevinifera*, near-Labruscoid form present on warm, southern slopes of Central Massif, France. Intermediate forms of *V. takeyensis* and *V. vinifera*.
	Quaternary	Pleistocene Holocene	2	Repeated glaciations. Speciation or eco-speciation in refuge habitats.
(RECENT)			0.01	Rise of civilisation. Man begins cultivation. Earliest hypothesised date of *Vitis* cultivation.

1 Adapted from Hardie (2000).

Taxonomy of plants has traditionally been based on similarities or differences in physical characters such as leaf and flower anatomy. The application of molecular biology to plant taxonomy is having a significant impact and it is now possible to compare DNA sequences from different species and develop more accurate phylogenetic relationships than previously possible.

For flowering plants a number of different classification systems exist and the Flowering Plant Gateway (2001) lists the major ones as; Cronquist system (1988), Thorne system (1992), Takhtajan system (1997) and the APG (Angiosperm Phylogeny Group) system (1998). The differences between the systems result from the use of different methods to infer past evolutionary relationships from present day species. A cladistic classification system like the APG system is likely to become increasingly dominant in the future

with DNA sequence information complementing morphology for determining genetic relatedness. This type of plant classification system is used by the largest public DNA sequence database, managed by NCBI (National Center for Biotechnology Information), for linking information from DNA and protein sequences to plant names and a taxonomy database is available on the internet (http://www.ncbi.nlm.nih.gov/Taxonomy/taxonomyhome.html). The NCBI classification for the grapevine species Vitis vinifera is as follows: eudicotyledons (Dicots); core eudicots; rosids; rosids incertae sedis; Vitaceae; Vitis.

The *Vitaceae* family has up to 14 genera with about 700 species worldwide. This would be a conservative estimate as it is thought, for example, that up to a third of the northern Australian species have not as yet been botanically described and similar situations no doubt exist elsewhere. It is a very widely spread family represented throughout the tropical and temperate zones around the world. Characteristically the plants are woody shrubs or climbers with leaf-opposed tendrils, the grapevine being a typical member in this respect.

5.2 The Family Vitaceae

Six of the genera contained within this family feature in the flora of the Australia continent: *Cissus*, *Cayratia*, *Clematicissus*, *Tetrastigma*, *Leea* and *Ampelocissus*. However, whilst a few Australian species have been exploited as a food source by aborigines or, more recently, by European settlers, their potential as ornamental vines or as a genetic resource for plant breeding remains essentially untapped.

The genus *Vitis* is not native to Australia, but it is the member of the family Vitaceae of most importance to commercial viticulture. In some taxonomic classifications the genus has been further split into the subgenera Vitis (Euvitis) and Muscadinia. However, as early as 1903, Small proposed that Vitis and Muscadinia be classified as distinct genera. Significant differences in morphology, anatomy, DNA and chemical composition all lend weight to this distinction, so they will be treated as separate genera in the information presented here.

5.2.1 VITIS

The genus *Vitis* is distinguished from most of the other genera of the family Vitaceae by having petals which remain joined at the top and detach from the base to fall together as a calyptra or 'cap'. All species of Vitis in the wild are normally dioecious i.e. they have separate male and female plants with flowers all of one sex (**FIGURE 5.1**). Under domestication, varieties with perfect flowers (hermaphrodites) appear to have been selected, otherwise a number of unproductive male vines would be required in a planting to pollinate female vines. The exact number of species in the genus Vitis is not certain, the species in Asia in particular being poorly defined. Estimates range from 40 to more than 60, most of which are found in the temperate regions of the northern hemisphere with a few in the tropics.

Vitis species have 38 chromosomes (n=19) while *Muscadinia*, *Ampelocissus*, *Parthenocissus* and *Ampelopsis* have 40 chromosomes (n = 20) and *Cissus* has 24 chromosomes (n = 12). More detail on the different *Vitis* species and their importance to viticulture is provided below in sections 5.3, 5.4 and 5.5.

5.2.2 MUSCADINIA

The genus *Muscadinia* is characterised by vines with smooth, persistent bark, many and small bunches, and berries that have very thick, tough skins and drop as they ripen. Many of these features are also found in *Ampelocissus*. There are only two or three species

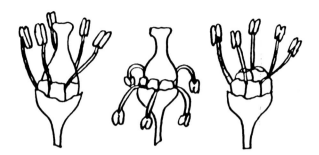

Figure 5.1 Types of grape flowers: A. Hermaphrodite; B. Functionally female, due to the reflexed stamens; C. Male, due to the lack of an ovary. (From Galet, 1979).

recognised in the genus *Muscadinia* depending upon the classification system used. The best known is the muscadine grape *Muscadinia rotundifolia* (classified as *Vitis rotundifolia* var. *rotundifolia* by Moore (1991)), a native of the south eastern United States where the climate is warm and humid during most of the year. It was domesticated by the European settlers when they found that European grapes (*Vitis vinifera*) were too susceptible to local diseases such as Pierce's disease to be grown in the region. The well-known variety Scuppernong was one of the earliest selections but, as with most wild *Muscadinia* it is dioecious. The selection of hermaphroditic mutants early in the 1900's was important for the development of higher-yielding varieties such as Carlos and Noble. The very thick skins and musky flavour are sometimes unattractive to those used to eating European grapes. Nevertheless, the fruit of muscadines has been eaten fresh, dried, or made into juice, wine, pies, jam etc. for hundreds of years, by Native Americans as well as European settlers. Today, the muscadines remain central to commercial viticulture on the coastal plains of south eastern USA.

M. munsoniana (classified as *Vitis rotundifolia* var. *munsoniana* by Moore (1991)), is found in Florida and the Bahamas, has more slender canes and is more evergreen than *M. rotundifolia*. Its bunches are made up of a larger number of smaller berries that are not so thick skinned and have a less musky flavour. Another species, *M. popenoei*, is a little known vine found in Mexico.

Some members of the genus *Muscadinia* are of great interest to vine breeders because of their excellent resistance to many of the pests and diseases which affect *Vitis* spp. such as Pierce's disease, phylloxera, rootknot nematodes, dagger nematode (*Xiphinema index*), downy and powdery mildews. The difference in chromosome number, amongst other factors, has limited the number of fertile, or partly fertile intergeneric hybrids (so-called VR hybrids) obtained from crosses between *Muscadinia* and *Vitis*. However in a few rare cases successful backcrossing of VR hybrids to *V. vinifera* has been achieved (Bouquet 1986, Olmo 1971).

5.2.3 CISSUS

By far the largest genus in the family *Vitaceae* is *Cissus*, with about 350 species. It includes what are thought to be the most primitive members of the family, some with terminal inflorescences like *Leea*. However, the pattern of two nodes with a tendril followed by one without, characteristic of cultivated grapes (*Vitis vinifera*), is already evident in some species. There is a wide range of plant types, from succulent species resembling cacti to lianas in tropical jungles.

Ten species are known in Australia. Some are perennial vines of the rain forests; one of these, *C. antarctica*, known as the Kangaroo Vine, has attractive simple leaves and has been adopted internationally as an ornamental plant. Being adapted to deep shade it can be readily grown indoors. Other species develop a rhizome, or underground stem, from which new shoots are produced in each growth cycle. The shoots are in some cases small and upright, in others long and trailing over trees. Species in areas with well defined wet and dry seasons have a very regular phenology. Shoots appear shortly before the start of the wet season and complete their growth and fruiting before dying back in the next dry season. Others, such as *C. opaca* of the brigalow regions, are more erratic. The rhizomes can be quite large, perhaps up to 50 cm in length and 20 cm in diameter.

All Australian species have purple-black berries, ranging from about 1 to 2 cm in diameter, but the fruit is rather dry and unattractive, often with an unpleasant pungent taste and irritating crystals in the flesh. Tubers, when present, seem to be more attractive as food. The aborigines ate them either raw or roasted and pigs like them well enough to dig for them. One species, *C. repens*, with succulent young stems and heart-shaped leaves, is said to have been a source of edible leaves, used perhaps in the way that vine leaves are used in Mediterranean countries.

5.2.4 CAYRATIA

Members of this genus were formerly included in *Cissus* but usually have five rather than four petals, compound rather than simple leaves, and more than one seed per berry. Of the 45 species described, most are found in Asia, with 8 species in Australia, all of which have rhizomes with ephemeral shoots. **FIGURE 5.2** shows a shoot of *C. saponaria* with a simple, an unequally-trifoliate, and an equally-trifoliate leaf. This sort of variability is very common in Australian *Vitaceae* and makes for difficulties in distinguishing between them. The berries of the *Cayratia* species, although small, seem to be somewhat juicier and more palatable than those of the *Cissus* species but again irritating crystals are present.

5.2.5 CLEMATICISSUS AND TETRASTIGMA

The genus *Clematicissus* contains several species of importance to ornamental horticulture. The only species in Australia, *C. angustissima*, is confined to the Murchison area of Western Australia and grows each year from rhizomes which are also attractive to pigs. *Tetrastigma* is a

Figure 5.2. **Cayratia saponaria,** *an Australian member of the family Vitaceae, is a rhizomatous plant with deciduous shoots. Leaf structure varies from simple to trifoliate.*

genus of about 90 species, extending from S.E. Asia to Australia. The only Australian species, *T. nitens*, known as the three-leafed water grape or shining grape, is a vigorous climber with trifoliate leaves found in the rain forests of Eastern Australia. Its fruit is said to be easily the most palatable of the native grapes, approaching the cultivated grape in flavour.

5.2.6 AMPELOCISSUS

Another genus represented in Australia is *Ampelocissus*, which has 95 species altogether extending throughout the tropics. It is thought to be the genus most closely related to the true grapes (*Vitis* and *Muscadinia*), some species having edible berries. The Australian plants are mostly referred to as *A. acetosa* but may consist of several species. They occur in the northern tropical areas and have rather soft, herbaceous shoots which grow in the wet season each year from rhizomes. These rhizomes have been roasted and eaten by the Australian aborigines.

5.2.7 OTHER GENERA

Two other genera, *Pterisanthes* with 20 species in south east Asia and *Rhoicissus* with 12 species in tropical and southern Africa, are thought to be closely related to *Ampelocissus* and *Vitis*. *Pterisanthes* is unusual in having its flowers borne on curious leaf-like structures. *Ampelopsis* (20 species) and *Parthenocissus* (15 species) are closely related to each other and include the Boston Ivy (*P.*

Figure 5.3. **Leea rubra**, *a species of the family Leeaceae, which is related to Vitaceae, grows in the monsoonal areas of Australia. Note its compound leaves and terminal clusters.*

tricuspidata) and the Virginia Creeper (*P. quinquefolia*). They are found in the temperate regions of North America and Eastern Asia and some *Ampelopsis* extend into sub-tropical areas. Finally, there are two genera with a single species each; *Acareosperma* in Laos, related to *Cissus*, and *Cyphostemma* in Africa. The small *Leea* genus, placed in the *Leeaceae* family under the Cronquist system but in the family *Vitaceae* in the NCBI database, consists of shrubs with terminal flower clusters and no tendrils. The Australian species, *Leea rubra* (**FIGURE 5.3**), is common in the northern monsoonal areas. The soft woody shoots grow from a large woody underground organ to which they may die back under unfavourable conditions. However, in monsoonal rainforest it maintains a permanent bushy structure, interweaving through adjacent trees, and can reach a height of 5 m. Although different in anatomical detail, the black berries are reminiscent of grapes and have grape-like seeds.

5.3 The Genus Vitis

The species of genus *Vitis* occur in widely different geographical areas and show a great diversity of form. They are however sufficiently closely related to allow easy interbreeding and the resultant interspecific hybrids are invariably fertile and vigorous. Thus the concept of a species is less well defined here than in most other plant

families and instead represents more likely the identification of different ecotypes which have evolved in distinct geographical and environmental circumstances.

Most Vitis species are found in the temperate regions of the Northern Hemisphere in America and Asia. *Vitis vinifera*, discussed in detail in Section 5.4, is the only species originating in Eurasia, but is now spread around the world as the main species of cultivated grape. Whilst little is known about *Vitis* species from Asia, those from North America have been relatively well characterised. The early European settlers tried to domesticate them, as with *M. rotundifolia*, when the vines brought from Europe succumbed to local pests and diseases. The native American *Vitis* species were generally not found to be satisfactory, however, because of characteristics such as very small berries, extreme seediness, and overpowering or pungent flavours. More successful varieties such as Concord, Delaware and Catawba were obtained through hybridisation with *V. vinifera* and other *Vitis* species. Some of these hybrids were taken to Europe as curiosities and unfortunately carried with them diseases and pests such as mildews and phylloxera which proved subsequently very damaging to European vines. As a result, the native American species have been studied further in search of genetic sources of resistance, highlighting the need for collection and preservation of *Vitis* germplasm. The following describes some of the better known North American *Vitis* species using the nomenclature suggested in Moore (1991) which is the most recent study of their systematics. Where other names have been commonly used in viticultural literature, they will also be provided, in brackets.

5.3.1 VITIS SPECIES

V. labrusca

This species has large berries with a distinctive 'foxy' aroma due to the presence of methyl anthranilate and other volatile substances. It is native to the eastern USA and is involved in the parentage of most American hybrids (section 5.5). It is a strongly growing vine with large, thick, almost entire leaves, dull green above, with the lower surface densely covered with white to brownish or reddish hairs. It differs from the other species of *Vitis* in having tendrils at all nodes beyond the base of the shoot, instead of every third node being without a tendril. The fruit is most often black, but vines with red or white fruit can also be found. The bunches are usually short, with fewer than 20 berries. The berries fall easily when ripe and the flesh can readily be squeezed out of the skin without being crushed. The juice is likely to be lower in both sugar and acid than that of other North American species. Selections of *V. labrusca* root and graft well but are insufficiently resistant to lime and phylloxera for use as a rootstock. They can have good resistance to cold, crown gall (*Agrobacterium*) and powdery mildew, but can be susceptible to downy mildew, black rot and Pierce's disease. Varieties of *V. labrusca* include Isabella and Concord, the latter being very important in commercial viticulture in the eastern USA. The discontinuous pattern of tendrils on Concord shoots suggests that it is a hybrid.

V. aestivalis

Native to the eastern USA, *V. aestivalis* is another strongly growing species which by natural and deliberate crossing forms part of the make-up of many American hybrids including Norton (syn. Cynthiana; Reisch et al. 1993) which is a natural hybrid of *V. labrusca* and *V. aestivalis*. Its leaves resemble those of *V. labrusca* except that the hairs on the lower surface tend to be in tufts and are rusty or red-brown in colour. The fruit is always black, does not have the intense flavour of *V. labrusca*, and can be quite juicy and sweet. The bunches are longer but the berries more numerous and smaller. Selections of *V. aestivalis* root poorly and are insufficiently resistant to lime and phylloxera for use as a rootstock but they have good resistance to downy and powdery mildews. Good resistance or tolerance to Pierce's disease was reported by Loomis (1958).

V. riparia

This is a diverse, wide-ranging and commonly found species in the northern USA west of New England, extending north into Canada and south almost to the Gulf of Mexico. It is a vigorous, tall-growing vine preferring moist habitats and usually occurring along rivers or streams. The leaves are generally long and 3-lobed, of a brighter green and thinner than those of the two preceding species and hairless on the lower surface. The bunches are medium in size with numerous small black berries, high in acid but free of objectionable flavours. The most well known variety is Riparia Gloire de Montpellier which has been used widely as a rootstock in Europe. The roots of some selections of *V. riparia* are very resistant to phylloxera. Resistance to cold and fungal diseases is good, but not to lime, drought or Pierce's disease. Natural hybrids of *V. riparia* and *V. labrusca* are common to parts of north-eastern USA.

V. rupestris

This species is a sprawling, much-branched vine which sometimes becomes low-climbing. The tendrils are small and usually do not persist. It occurs in a rather narrow band running north-east from south-west Texas, preferring the gravelly banks of mountain streams or the rocky beds of dry watercourses. The roots tend to penetrate vertically instead of spreading laterally as in other species. The leaves are small and kidney shaped, wider than they are long, light silvery-green, smooth and glossy above and below. The bunches are small with only a few small black berries, again free of disagreeable

flavours. The most well-known variety is the rootstock Rupestris St. George (syn. du Lot). The roots of some *V. rupestris* selections are very resistant to phylloxera. Cuttings root and graft well and resistance to downy and powdery mildews is good, but most varieties are susceptible to lime. Good resistance to Pierce's disease was reported by Loomis (1958).

V. cinerea var. helleri (V. berlandieri)

A stocky, moderately climbing vine, *V. cinerea* var. *helleri* is found on the limestone soils of south-west Texas and adjacent areas of Mexico. In some classifications it is accorded species status as *Vitis berlandieri*. It has medium to large, slightly 3-lobed leaves, glossy above and becoming hairless below as they expand to full size. The bunches are more branched than those of the species previously mentioned and carry numerous small black berries. The fruit ripens very late, is high in both sugar and acid, and is juicy with a pleasant taste. Selections have good resistance to phylloxera, lime, fungal diseases and Pierce's disease. They are an excellent source of rootstock material but only as hybrids with other *Vitis* species since they are notoriously difficult to root from cuttings. *V. cinerea* var. *helleri* has the ability to exclude chloride which is useful in breeding for salinity tolerance (Newman and Antcliff 1984).

V. cinerea var. cinerea

This species is similar to *V. cinerea* var. *helleri* but its range extends further north and it grows in more moist habitats. Its leaves are similar, but duller on the upper surface and remain hairy below when fully expanded. The bunches are large and loose, with numerous small black berries. The fruit ripens late, becoming sweet and pleasant after frost. Selections of *V. cinerea* var. *cinerea* have very good resistance to phylloxera but are sensitive to lime and difficult to root. As for *V. cinerea* var. *helleri*, they are most useful after hybridisation with other *Vitis* species.

V. mustangensis (V. candicans)

The original description of *V. candicans* is ambiguous, therefore Moore (1991) suggests that the correct name for this species is *V. mustangensis*. It is a vigorous, climbing vine, notable for the disagreeable, pungent flavour of the fruit. It occurs on limestone soils in a rather limited area of the south-central USA. It has leaves that are dull green above but covered with dense white hairs below and on the petiole. It has short bunches with less than 20, large berries. The berries remain firmly attached to bunches after they are fully ripe and range from dark red to black in colour. Selections of *V. mustangensis* (*V. candicans*) are resistant to phylloxera, drought, Pierce's disease, downy mildew and powdery mildew. They are difficult to root and sensitive to lime and are most important as progenitors of hybrid rootstock varieties.

V. acerifolia (V. longii, V. solonis)

The species *V. longii* and *V. solonis* have been reclassified together as *V. acerifolia* by Moore (1991). They grow typically as stocky, erect, much-branched shrubs which can also become a high-climbing vine. They are vigorous, resembling *V. riparia*, but with slightly rounder leaves, often hairy on the lower surface. Bunches are shorter and compact with many small black berries.

V. champinii

This species is considered to be a natural hybrid between *V. rupestris* and *V. mustangensis* (*V. candicans*) (Moore, 1991). It occurs in the well drained calcareous soils in south central Texas and has short bunches with a few relatively large black berries. The variety Ramsey has been an important rootstock in Australia with good resistance to rootknot and citrus nematodes, phylloxera, drought and salinity (May 1994).

V. vulpina (V. cordifolia)

One of the most vigorous species, *V. vulpina* (*V. cordifolia*) can climb to the top of very tall trees and develop a trunk up to 50 cm in diameter. It is found over a wide area of the eastern USA. It has medium to large, entire, heart-shaped leaves, bright green and glossy above and with at most only a few hairs on the lower surface. Bunches are medium to large and loose with numerous small black berries. The berries have thick skins and little pulp and are often sour and astringent. This species is extremely difficult to root and is sensitive to lime and powdery mildew, but not downy mildew.

Other species

Also of interest to viticulturists have been *V. lincecumii* and *V. rufotomentosa*, both reclassified as sub-groups of *V. aestivalis* (Moore, 1991). *V. californica* and *V. girdiana*, native to California, have been of less practical interest; having developed in the absence of the pests and diseases found east of the Rocky Mountains, they show little resistance to them. As mentioned above, variations on species names have been proposed for some cultivated American grapes; *V. labruscana* for those with *labrusca-vinifera* parentage (e.g. Concord) and *V. bourquiniana* for those with *aestivalis-vinifera* parentage. These cannot however be considered as different species in the true sense of the word.

Vitis species from Eurasia seem to show an interesting parallelism with the American species - e.g. *V. coignetii* resembles *V. labrusca*, and *V. vinifera* resembles *V. californica*. Some Asian species have been used occasionally as ornamentals but the only species to attract viticultural attention is *V. amurensis*. This is the most northerly species and has been used in hybridisations to introduce winter cold resistance and early maturity into cultivated grapes.

5.4 The Species *Vitis vinifera*

The European grape is *Vitis vinifera* and, apart from rootstocks, this species comprises the majority of the genetic material used for viticulture in Australia, as in many grape growing countries.

5.4.1 WILD VINES

In Europe and Western Asia, where *V. vinifera* has been cultivated for many centuries, wild vines also occur. One school of thought has seen the wild vines as related to, and possibly ancestors of, the cultivated vines but now distinct from them. At the beginning of the nineteenth century Gmelin (quoted by Levadoux 1956) described the wild vines of the middle Rhine as a separate species, *V. silvestris*. This name has been extended to the wild vines in general, although sometimes the distinction has been reported as only sub-specific—*V. vinifera silvestris* as distinct from *V. vinifera sativa*, the cultivated grape. The opposing and more likely view is that the wild vines are simply *V. vinifera* with the differences between the wild and cultivated vines being merely the effect of domestication.

The differences thought to distinguish the primordial wild vines from cultivated vines mostly tend to disappear when both are grown under the same conditions. Trials in several countries have shown that when looked after in the same way the best of the wild vines of the region have fruit comparable in size and composition with some cultivated varieties. Indeed, in leaf, fruit and seed characters the differences are not as great as the differences among the cultivated varieties themselves.

A fundamental difference would appear to be that the primordial wild vines are dioecious, that is they have distinct male and female flowers borne on separate vines, as in the American species. Most cultivated varieties have perfect flowers, a very desirable character when they are to be grown in pure plantings. However, as already mentioned, a perfect-flowered form of *M. rotundifolia* was ultimately found when the species was grown under domestication. There can be little doubt that perfect-flowered forms of wild *Vitis vinifera* would also have arisen in the past and be selected for cultivation due to their better fruit set.

Thus there does not seem to be a case for separating the primordial wild vines as a distinct species or subspecies of *Vitis*. They can be regarded simply as the original form of *V. vinifera* to which cultivated varieties would revert if allowed to run wild.

5.4.2 CULTIVATED VINES

The cultivated varieties of *Vitis vinifera* (see chapter 6) show a much greater range of variation than any of the wild species of *Vitis*. There are large differences in the size and shape of leaves, berries and seeds and in other characters such as the degree of hairiness. Although the

Figure 5.4. The three proles of Vitis vinifera. Left to right: Clairette, proles pontica; Riesling, proles occidentalis; Sultana, proles orientalis.

position has been somewhat confused by the widespread movement and deliberate crossing of varieties it is possible to recognise various groups that are characteristic of particular regions. The differences between these groups may be not entirely a matter of response to environment but partly due to human selection. Thus in Western Europe the selection would have been mainly for grapes for winemaking while in the Middle East it would have been for fruit for eating fresh. The traditional scheme of classification based on morphological characters recognises three major groups, called proles. Some differences in the shoots of proles are illustrated in **FIGURE 5.4**.

Proles pontica

This group comprises varieties native to the countries around the Aegean and Black Seas. Varieties grown in Australia include Zante Currant, Clairette, Chaouch and Furmint. They are characterised by a dense white hairiness on the growing shoot tips and the lower surface of mature leaves. Bunches are medium to compact, berries are usually round, medium to small, and juicy.

There is a fairly high proportion of fruitful shoots, with more than one bunch per fruitful shoot. The greatest resistance to cold in winter is found in this group.

Proles occidentalis

These are the varieties native to Western Europe. Many of the winegrape varieties of high quality belong here, some well known examples being Riesling, Cabernet Sauvignon, Traminer, Chardonnay, Semillon and Mataro. The development of hairs on the shoot tips and

leaves is less dense than in the proles pontica and the leaves often tend to turn or fold back to give a convex upper surface. The bunches are usually small and compact, and the berries usually round, small and juicy. The proportion of fruitful shoots is high with two or more bunches per fruitful shoot. The varieties are adapted to long days and a short growing and ripening season, and are fairly resistant to cold.

Proles orientalis

The varieties of this group are native to the Middle East, Iran, Afghanistan and nearby areas. This group provides most of the table and raisin varieties and includes Sultana, Muscat Gordo Blanco, Waltham Cross, Cinsaut and Ohanez. The young shoot tips are hairless and shiny and the leaves have at most a few bristly hairs on the lower surface. Leaves tend to fold inwards to give a concave upper surface. Bunches are large, often loose and branching. Berries are usually oval to elliptical and large unless seedless. There is a strong tendency to seedlessness in many varieties so that bunches may have both large berries with seeds and smaller seedless berries. The flesh of the berries is usually firm, often crisp, and the juice tends to be lower in both sugar and acid than it is in the other two proles. The proportion of fruitful shoots is lower and there is often only one bunch per fruitful shoot. A long growing season is generally needed and there is very little resistance to cold.

The differences between the proles are not as clear cut as the above descriptions might suggest and exceptions in particular features are not hard to find. DNA analysis has given some support to the proles grouping of

126

varieties but again many exceptions exist and the power of the DNA technology to determine inter-relationships between varieties (Thomas et al. 1994) may eventually see the proposal of a new classification system with the assignment of the geographical origin of varieties determined by DNA. Some promising results have already been reported in this area with Austrian, French, Portuguese, Greek, Croatian, Spanish and Italian varieties correctly assigned to specific European regions (Sefc et al. 2001).

At the other end of the scale it is also possible using DNA analysis to determine the exact parentage of varieties whose origins have been lost by the passage of time (Sefc et al. 2001; see **TABLE 5.2**). Investigations of some of our most popular wine varieties using DNA markers have revealed that the parents of Cabernet Sauvignon are Cabernet Franc and Sauvignon Blanc and that Pinot Noir and Gouais Blanc are the parents of at least 16 French varieties including Chardonnay, Melon and Gamay Noir. It is also possible to determine which variety was the female parent by examination of the DNA from the chloroplast as these organelles in grapevine are passed to the progeny by the mother. In this way it has been shown that Sauvignon Blanc was the female parent of Cabernet Sauvignon. The uncertain pedigree of Müller-Thurgau has also been solved by DNA analysis. It was previously believed that Riesling and Silvaner were the parents of Müller-Thurgau but it is now known that Riesling and Madeleine Royale are the true parents.

The details which can now be uncovered by DNA analysis suggests that it will now not be too long before accurate genetic relationships for most of the important varieties are determined. The information gained from these types of studies will also allow better breeding strategies to be adopted by selectively choosing superior parents and avoiding the negative effects of inbreeding.

5.4.3 VINIFERA BREEDING PROGRAMS

Until the early 19th century all cultivated varieties appear to have come from natural chance crosses with new varieties arising as seedlings or later by bud mutation. The wine, table grape and dried fruit industries have depended heavily on production from these old established varieties. This is especially true of varieties used in wine production where only relatively few varieties dominate world production. An early example of selective *V. vinifera* breeding was that of Louis Bouschet who in 1824 became interested in varieties with red juice as a possible means of improving the colour of the red wines of the Midi of France. When none of the varieties available proved to yield well enough he crossed the most highly coloured, Teinturier du Cher, with the local varieties Aramon, Carignan and Grenache to try to combine colour with yield. His selection Petit Bouschet (Aramon × Teinturier) was widely planted by 1865. His son, Henri Bouschet, used Petit Bouschet as a parent in further crosses and obtained Grand Noir de la Calmette with Aramon, Alicante Bouschet with Grenache, and Morrastel Bouschet with Morrastel. Although Petit Bouschet has almost disappeared from France, Henri Bouschet's varieties have also been grown in other countries and the most successful one, Alicante Bouschet, occupied ~9,000 ha in France in 1998.

Breeding efforts received a boost in the late 19th and early 20th centuries with the spread of pathogens such as powdery mildew and phylloxera from America to Europe. Most of the effort was directed towards interspecific hybrids as *V. vinifera* lacked natural resistance to these pathogens. Unfortunately adoption of these new varieties was low due to poor fruit quality. However, despite setbacks, the breeding and release of new *vinifera* varieties has gradually increased over the course of the 20th century. Breeding activity in the table grape and dried fruit industries throughout the world

Table 5.2. *Proposed parentage of grapevine varieties as determined by DNA profiling.*[1]

Parents	Progeny
Sauvignon Blanc and Cabernet Franc	Cabernet Sauvignon
Riesling and Madeleine Royale	Müller-Thurgau
Gouais Blanc (Heunisch Weiss) and Pinot Noir	Chardonnay, Gamay Noir, Aligoté, Auxerrois, Melon, Aligoté, Aubin Vert, Bachet Noir, Beaunoir, Dameron, Franc Noir de la Haute Saône, Gamay Blanc Gloriod, Kipperlé, Peurion, Romorantin, Roublot, Sacy
Peloursin and Syrah (Shiraz)	Durif
Traminer and Österreichisch Weiss	Silvaner
Silvaner and Roter Veltliner	Neuburger
Grauer Portugieser and Frühroter Veltliner	Jubiläumsrebe
Malvasia Fina and Síria	Boal Ratinho

1 Adapted from Sefc (2001).

has resulted in the establishment of both public and private breeding programs with rapid adoption by growers of newly released varieties. This is similar to other plant-based industries where conventional breeding of new varieties has proved to be the basis of increased quality and reduced cost of production. In contrast, the wine industry has been conservative in adopting new varieties largely because industry and market forces and, in some countries, governmental controls discourage plantings of new varieties from breeding programs. This situation appears to be slowly changing, especially in the New World wine countries.

The significant advantage of breeding is the ability to produce improved varieties which display better performance and berry quality characters under local conditions. This is the opposite to the situation with the traditional varieties where viticulturalists are often restricted in trying to find a similar environment to that of the region from which the variety originated.

In Germany the variety Müller-Thurgau, raised from a cross in 1882, has become a leading variety because of its reliable maturation in the short growing season. At the other extreme, breeding may provide better wine grape varieties for the inland areas of California and Australia where temperatures are much higher than those natural to the popular varieties originating from Western Europe. Of the major 16 varieties used for red wine production in Australia, two varieties have been derived from breeding programs. Ruby Cabernet, a cross between Carignan and Cabernet Sauvignon, was bred in California by Olmo and released in 1948 and for the Australian 2002 vintage was the fourth major red-wine variety contributing 5.9% to the total red-wine grape crush. Tarrango, a cross between Touriga and Sultana, was bred in Australia by Antcliff and released in 1975 and contributed 0.3% to the total red-wine grape crush in 2002 (Australian Bureau of Statistics, 2003). Tarrango was selected by CSIRO to suit Australian conditions through its later maturity and higher natural acidity. In 2000, four new wine grape varieties; Tyrian, Cienna, Vermilion and Rubienne were also released by CSIRO to the Australian industry after extensive evaluation. These varieties are the product of a cross made in 1972 between the Spanish wine variety Sumoll and Cabernet Sauvignon and were selected for both wine quality and plant performance under Australian growing conditions.

The adoption of Müller-Thurgau, Ruby Cabernet and the Bouschet varieties by the respective German, Australian and French wine industries illustrate the significant lag period between production of a new wine grape variety by conventional breeding and acceptance by industry. Advances in the field of plant biotechnology since the early 1980s has seen the recent development of an alternative strategy for grapevine improvement known as molecular or transgenic breeding (Kikkert et al. 2001). The attraction of this approach is that genes responsible for improved characters like disease resistance can be directly inserted into established varieties such as Chardonnay in a process taking little more than a year. In theory, this approach appears to be a good compromise between wine marketing where varietal labelling is important and the need for improved plant performance and berry quality in the vineyard. In practice, the technology for grapevine still has to prove itself in the vineyard. In addition, adoption of these transgenic vines by industry will only occur if there is world-wide public acceptance of the cultivation and use of GMO (Genetically Modified Organism) plants.

5.5 Interspecific hybrids

As mentioned earlier, the *Vitis* species will interbreed quite readily and after repeated crossings hybrids have been produced which can have eight or more species in their ancestry. The first commercially important interspecific hybrids worldwide were those which enabled the growing of grapes in the difficult conditions of the eastern USA. Later, with the spread of diseases and pests from North America to Europe, the use of hybrids became important in Europe also. The main use of hybrids nowadays is as rootstocks for *V. vinifera* varieties, but they are still very important as fruiting varieties in parts of eastern North America, Asia, South America and eastern Europe.

Interspecific *Vitis* hybrids have not been as important in Australia as they have in other parts of the world, primarily because the absence of phylloxera from most Australian viticultural regions has allowed the continued predominance of own-rooted *Vitis vinifera* vines.

Incorporation of *Muscadinia* genotypes into *Vitis* hybrids has long been desired because of the many superior pest and disease resistance characters contained within this genus. This has proved difficult because, amongst other things, the first generation hybrids are often sterile due to the differences in chromosome number. Where fertile, or partly fertile hybrids have been obtained their use in viticulture remains limited by the presence of a range of unwanted characters. In some cases, they are most promising as a source of *Muscadinia* genes that will probably require gene mapping and transgenic breeding strategies to introduce them into the *Vitis* gene pool. An extensive backcrossing program by Bouquet over many years has been undertaken in France to produce plants containing disease resistance from *Muscadinia* and fruit quality from *V. vinifera* (Bouquet 1986, Pauquet 2001). Recently, the successful production of fertile progeny from the hybridisation of *M. rotundifolia* with *V. rupestris* has been reported and provides new opportunities for the introduction of *Muscadinia* genes into *Vitis* hybrids for rootstock breeding (Walker and Jin 2000).

5.5.1 AMERICAN HYBRIDS

This term is generally reserved for hybrids from eastern North America (Hedrick 1908) in which the species *V. labrusca*, *V. aestivalis* and *V. vinifera* are the most important components. Originally selected to cope with the difficult growing conditions of the eastern USA, some of the early American hybrids were also tried as replacements for *V. vinifera* in France when the vineyards began to succumb to powdery mildew, downy mildew and phylloxera in the second half of the 19th Century. They gave wines of very poor quality, with undesirable flavours such as the 'foxy' flavour characteristic of *V. labrusca* and since 1934 it has been illegal to plant them in France. They remain commercially important in eastern North America where they are used for producing grape juice, wine, table grapes, preserves and food additives. Many varieties have highly flavoured fruit reminiscent of raspberries, strawberries, passionfruit or pineapples, and make a more attractive juice than the sweet and rather insipid juices from *V. vinifera* varieties. Many are insufficiently resistant to phylloxera to be grown as own-rooted vines and require rootstocks in infested areas.

By far the most important variety is Concord, a black labrusca type, first introduced into cultivation in north eastern USA around 1850 and now producing over 300,000 tonnes of fruit in that region. Other well known varieties grown on a smaller scale include Ives and Isabella (black), Catawba, Delaware and Norton (syn. Cynthiana) (red), and Niagara (white). Delaware is an important table grape in Japan. Varieties such as Jacquez and Noah can still be found in parts of Europe. In Australia, Canada Muscat (an aromatic white labrusca type) is grown on a very small scale.

5.5.2 FRENCH HYBRIDS

Despite the failure of American hybrids, French breeders such as Baco, Couderc, Seibel, and the Seyves continued their efforts during the late 1800s and early 1900s to breed 'direct producers'— hybrids that would combine good fruit quality with adequate disease and pest resistance, obviating the need for grafting to rootstocks. They concentrated on the more productive *V. vinifera* varieties, made some use of American hybrids, and brought in species such as *V. rupestris*, *V. riparia* and *V. berlandieri* which had excellent disease and pest resistance and were free of the undesirable flavours of *V. labrusca*. The pedigree of two of the better hybrids, Villard Blanc and Villard Noir, is highly complex and covers eight generations, involving 51 known crosses and at least eight different species (see Boubals 1956 and Antcliff 1988).

By 1955 an area of just over 400,000 ha, or nearly one third of the French vineyards, was planted to French hybrids. Wine quality, particularly for some of the earlier releases, was often below standard, although in some cases the wines could be described as unusual rather than unpleasant. At that time, new planting regulations that aimed to eliminate or discourage the planting of inferior varieties were brought into force and by 1968 the area of hybrids had declined to about 300,000 ha and by 1988 to less than 35,000 ha, representing only 3.5% of the total. The area of a few of the better hybrids actually increased during this period. Baco 22A is still used in Armagnac, however hybrids are otherwise no longer allowed to be planted in AOC regions in France.

Many French hybrids have been tested in other countries and breeding of newer versions with attributes of cold hardiness and disease resistance continues in North America and eastern Europe. Some varieties e.g. Vidal, Seyval, Chambourcin and Cayuga are grown on a commercially important, albeit sometimes small scale in Australia, North America, South America and Asia.

The ability to obtain acceptable wine quality from the French hybrids Chambourcin and Rubired has recently been acknowledged through their addition to the list of varieties permitted for export to Europe from Australia and the USA respectively (EC regulation 160/2000). Chambourcin, bred in France and released in 1963, has good tolerance to downy and powdery mildews but, as with some other French hybrids, is insufficiently resistant to phylloxera to be reliably grown on own-roots in infested vineyards.

The greatest impact of French hybrids may be in table grape production. Carolina Blackrose, descended from Villard Blanc by successive back crosses to Chaouch and Blackrose, has performed well in Australia and was used as one of the parents of the tablegrape Marroo Seedless, released in the early 1980s by CSIRO, Merbein (Clingeleffer and Possingham 1988).

5.5.3 NEWER EUROPEAN HYBRIDS

Efforts to breed disease resistant hybrids with improved wine quality have continued in a few countries, most notably Germany where a new series of varieties were released during the 1990s. The variety Regent [(Sylvaner × Müller-Thurgau) × Chambourcin], bred at the Institut für Rebenzüchtung, Geilweilerhof has been authorised for use in Germany since 1996 and is accepted as being indistinguishable from *V. vinifera* varieties by traditional ampelographic and sensory analysis. Present trends suggest that a combination of improved varieties and mounting pressure to reduce pesticide contamination of the environment will lead to increased acceptance of the use of hybrids in wine production. These newer hybrids have not been bred to be 'direct producers' and, as with many of the earlier hybrids, grafting to phylloxera resistant or tolerant rootstocks is still required in phylloxera-infested regions.

5.5.4 ROOTSTOCKS

The use of rootstocks was the second, but ultimately the preferred method of dealing with the phylloxera problem in France (see chapter 8). The first varieties used, apart from some of the American hybrids which gave some protection when used as rootstocks, were varieties of a single species e.g. *V. rupestris* var. du Lot (syn. St. George) and *V. riparia* vars. Gloire de Montpellier and Grand Glabre. It was soon found advantageous to use hybrids of the American species to combine their desirable features such as tolerance of moist conditions (*V. riparia*), of dry conditions (*V. rupestris*) and of calcareous soils (*V. berlandieri*).

Hybridisation was particularly important in the case of *V. berlandieri*, which could not be used as the pure species because of the difficulty of rooting its cuttings. Notable early successes in France were 3309 Couderc and 101-14 Millardet (*V. riparia* × *V. rupestris*), 161-49 Couderc and 420A Millardet (*V. riparia* × *V. berlandieri*) and 99 Richter and 110 Richter (*V. rupestris* × *V. berlandieri*). As phylloxera spread to other European countries local hybrid rootstocks were produced, such as the *V. rupestris*–*V. berlandieri* hybrids 140 Ruggeri and 1103 Paulsen in Italy and the *V. riparia*–*V. berlandieri* selections of Teleki in Hungary. Other species such as *V. champini* and *V. cinerea* have also been incorporated into rootstocks such as Boerner (Becker 1988) but the three species mentioned above have proved to be the most important.

M. rotundifola is highly resistant to phylloxera but is not suitable for use as a rootstock itself due to graft incompatibility with *V. vinifera*, poor rooting ability and high susceptibility to lime induced chlorosis. *M. rotundifolia* × *V. vinifera* (VR) hybrids can be successfully grafted to *V. vinifera* scions, but their development as rootstocks has been hampered by their lack of fertility and poor propagation characteristics. In addition, some have been shown to be insufficiently resistant to phylloxera, suggesting a dominant genetic trait might be involved in phylloxera susceptibility. Similarly, hybrids of *V. vinifera* with any one of the American *Vitis* species do not generally give sufficient long-term protection against phylloxera. The most striking illustration of this was the decline of Californian vineyards planted on ARG1 (*V. vinifera* × *V. rupestris*) during the 1980s and 1990s, due to emergence of the so-called biotype B phylloxera (Granett et al. 1985). The full range of phylloxera biotypes present in vineyards world-wide and their interaction with different rootstocks is only now being explored.

Another root pest which can debilitate *V. vinifera* vines is rootknot nematode. This is a problem in sandy soils, in contrast to phylloxera which is most serious in clay soils. Fortunately, some of the phylloxera-resistant rootstocks will also give protection against rootknot nematode. The species which appears to be most effective in both respects is *V. champini* leading to extensive use of the variety Ramsey in Australia. The dagger nematode *Xiphinema index* continues to threaten viticultural

production world-wide because of its transmission of the grape fan leaf virus (GFLV). No *Vitis* rootstock capable of preventing GFLV infection has yet been developed. *M. rotundifolia* is highly resistant to *X. index* and GFLV transmission and *M. rotundifolia* × *V. vinifera* (VR) hybrid rootstocks have been shown to delay, but not prevent, transmission of the virus, and apparently confer some tolerance to its effects (Walker et al., 1994). The recent production of fertile *M. rotundifolia* × *V. rupestris* hybrids mentioned above, may facilitate introduction of the very good nematode resistance of *Muscadinia* into existing rootstock varieties. It is possible however that good resistance to both the nematode and to the virus is required for effective control. In this case, transgenic breeding could be used to provide virus resistance.

5.5.5 GLORY VINES

The red juice character in varieties such as those with which the Bouschets worked is accompanied by a brilliant red colouration of the foliage in autumn, making them attractive ornamental plants. Glory vines are selected for this colouration, as well as male flowers, or production of very small bunches with very small berries. This allows vigorous vegetative development capable of covering large structures, without the mess that dropping of mature fruit can cause. The use of hybrids with American species also ensures healthy foliage without the need for protective sprays. One of the most popular varieties of glory vine in Australia is ARG9 (*V. vinifera* × *V. rupestris*); a fitting cultivar name could be 'Ganzin Glory'.

5.6 Concluding remarks

The ability to accurately determine genetic relationships for all taxonomic classification levels is improving with the increasing use of DNA sequence information in combination with physical character descriptions. For grapevines this should eventually provide a definitive number of species within the genus *Vitis* and the evolutionary relationship of *Vitis* to other members of the *Vitaceae* family. The morphological and physiological differences between varieties, species and genera is due to genetic variation which has arisen during evolution as a result of adaptation to different environmental conditions including both abiotic and biotic stresses. The main mechanisms responsible for producing this variation is DNA recombination during sexual crossing and DNA mutation. The genetic diversity existing within the *Vitis* and *Muscadinia* genera is a valuable resource for improving vineyard material and has already proved especially useful in rootstock breeding. Apart from a few exceptions, since the late 1800s adoption of new winegrape scion varieties has not been extensive. Marketing forces and perceived grape quality appear to be the main reasons why Old World varieties such as

Chardonnay and Cabernet Sauvignon bred by accident hundreds of years ago still dominate today's vineyards. We now know through the use of DNA technology the parents of these varieties and the increased use of DNA technology to identify important genes controlling berry quality and pathogen resistance, e.g. powdery mildew resistance (Donald et al. 2002) may lead to the production of new superior scion varieties, through marker-assisted breeding or transgenic breeding, which have higher industry adoption rates.

REFERENCES

Suggestions for further reading are marked (•).

• Alleweldt, G. and Possingham, J.V. (1988) Progress in grapevine breeding. Theor. Appl. Genet. 75, 669-673.

• Antcliff, A.J. (1988) Taxonomy. In: Viticulture Vol. 1, Edition 1. Eds B.G.Coombe and P.R.Dry (Australian Industrial Publishers: Adelaide), pp. 107-108

APG (1998) An ordinal classification for the families of flowering plants. Annals of the Missouri Botanical Garden 85, 531-553.

Australian Bureau of Statistics (2003) Australian Wine and Grape Industry. Document 1329.0.

• Basiouny, F.M. and Himelrick, D.G. (2001) Muscadine Grapes (ASHS Press: USA).

Becker, H. (1988) Boerner: The first rootstock immune to all phylloxera biotypes. Proc. 2nd Int. Cool Climate Vit. & Oenol. Symp., Auckland, NZ 1988. Eds R.E. Smart, R.J. Thornton et al. (N Z Soc. Vitic. and Oenol.: Auckland), pp. 51-52.

Boubals, D. (1956) Amelioration de la resistance de la vigne au mildiou (Plasmopara viticola (B. et C.) Berlese et de Toni. Recherche de géniteurs de résistance. Ann. Amelior. Plantes 6, 481-525.

Bouquet, A. (1986) Introduction dans l'espèce Vitis vinifera L. d'un caractere de résistance à l'oidium (Uncinula necator Schw. Burr.) issu de l'espèce Muscadinia rotundifolia (Michx.) Small. Vignevini 12 (suppl), 141-146.

Clingeleffer, P.R, and Possingham, J.V. (1988) Marroo Seedless. A new table grape variety. Agric. Science (Aust). 1, 18-19.

• Cribb, A.B. and Cribb, J.W. (1975) Wild Food in Australia (Collins: Sydney).

Cronquist, A. (1988) The evolution and classification of flowering plants, 2nd Ed. (Nelson: London)

Donald, T.M., Pellerone, F. et al. (2002). Identification of resistance gene analogs linked to a powdery mildew resistance locus in grapevine. Theor. Appl. Genet. 104, 610-618.

Flowering Plant Gateway (2001) at http://www.csdl.tamu.edu/FLORA/newgate/gateopen.htm

• Galet, P. (1956) Cepages et vignobles de France. I. Les vignes americaines (Ecole Nat. Sup. Agric.: Montpellier).

• Galet, P. (1979) A Practical Ampelography. Grapevine Identification (Comstock Publishing Assoc. and Cornell University Press: Ithaca).

Granett, J., Timper, P. et al. (1985) Grape phylloxera (Daktulosphaira vitifoliae Fitch) (Homoptera: Phylloxeridae) biotypes in California. J. Econ. Entomol. 78, 1463-1467.

Hardie, W.J. (2000) Grapevine biology and adaptation to viticulture. Aust. J. Grape Wine Res. 6, 74-81.

Hedrick, U.P. (1908) The Grapes of New York (J.A. Lyon Co.: Albany).

• Jackson, R.S. (2000) Grape species and varieties. In: Wine Science. Principles, practice, perception (Academic Press: San Diego), pp. 13-44.

Kikkert, J.R., Thomas, M.R. et al. (2001) Grapevine genetic engineering. In: Molecular Biology and Biotechnology of Grapevine. Ed K.A. Roubelakis-Angelakis (Kluwer Academic Publishers: Netherlands), pp 393-410.

Levadoux, L. (1956) Les populations sauvages et cultivées de Vitis vinifera L.. Ann. Amelior. Plantes. 6, 59-118.

Loomis, N.H. (1958) Performance of Vitis species in the South as an indication of their relative resistance to Pierce's disease. Plant Dis. Rep. 42, 83-86.

May, P. (1994) Using grapevine rootstocks. The Australian perspective (Winetitles: Adelaide).

Moore, M.O. (1991) Classification and systematics of eastern North American Vitis L (Vitaceae) north of Mexico. Sida 14, 339-367.

• NCBI taxonomy browser at http://www.ncbi.nlm.nih.gov/Taxonomy/taxonomyhome.html

Newman, H.P. and Antcliff, A.J. (1984) Chloride accumulation in some hybrids and backcrosses of Vitis berlandieri and Vitis vinifera. Vitis 23, 106-112.

• Olien, W.C. (1990) The muscadine grape: Botany, viticulture, history and current industry. HortSci. 25, 732-739.

• Olmo, H.P. (1976) Grapes. In: Evolution of Crop Plants. Ed N.W. Simmonds (Longman: London), pp. 294-298.

Olmo, H.P. (1971) Vinifera rotundifolia hybrids as wine grapes. Amer. J. Enol. Vitic. 22, 87-91.

Pauquet, J., Bouquet, A. et al. (2001) Establishment of a local map of AFLP markers around the powdery mildew resistance gene Run1 in grapevine and assessment of their usefulness for marker assisted selection. Theor. Appl. Genet. 103, 1201-1210.

Reisch, B.I., Goodman, R.N. et al. (1993) The relationship between Norton and Cynthiana, red wine cultivars derived from Vitis aestivalis. Amer. J. Enol. Vitic. 44, 441-444.

Sefc, K.M., Lefort, F. et al. (2001) Microsatellite markers for grapevine: a state of the art. In: Molecular Biology and Biotechnology of Grapevine. Ed K.A. Roubelakis-Angelakis (Kluwer Academic Publishers: Netherlands), pp. 433-463.

Small, J.K. (1903) Flora of the southeastern United States (Published by the author: New York).

Takhtajan, A. (1997) Diversity and classification of flowering plants (Columbia University Press: New York).

Thomas, M.R., Cain, P. et al. (1994) DNA typing of grapevines: A universal methodology and database for describing cultivars and evaluating genetic relatedness. Plant Mol. Biol. 25, 939-949.

Thorne, R.F. (1992) Classification and geography of the flowering plants. Bot. Review 58, 225-348.

• Viala, P. and Vermorel, V. (1901-09) Ampelographie. Traité général de viticulture Vol. 1-7 (Masson: Paris).

Walker, M.A., Wolpert, J.A. et al. (1994) Viticultural characteristics of VR hybrid rootstocks in a vineyard site infected with grapevine fanleaf virus. Vitis 33, 19-23.

Walker, M.A. and Jin, Y. (2000) Breeding Vitis rupestris x Muscadinia rotundifolia rootstocks to control Xiphinema index and fanleaf degeneration. Proc. VII Int. Symp. Grapevine Genetics and Breeding. Eds A. Bouquet and J-M. Boursiquot. Acta Hort. 528, 511-515.

CHAPTER SIX

Grapevine Varieties

P. R. DRY

6.1 Varieties with more than 1,000 ha
    1. White-berried varieties
    2. Black- and red-berried varieties

6.2 Varieties with 100 to 1,000 ha
    1. White-berried varieties
    2. Black- and red-berried varieties

6.3 Varieties with less than 100 ha
    1. White-berried varieties
    2. Black- and red-berried varieties

6.4 Concluding remarks

Nearly all commercial grapevines grown in Australia are varieties of *Vitis vinifera* which originated in Asia Minor (see Chapter 5). Apart from its susceptibility to phylloxera and downy mildew, *V. vinifera* will not survive in very cold climates where freezing temperatures can kill vines. Under these conditions, it is necessary to rely on native grapes and hybrids of *V. vinifera* and American species of *Vitis* that are far more tolerant of cold injury. Winter conditions of this kind are rare in Australia.

Although about 24,000 varieties of *V. vinifera* have been named, it is likely that only 5,000 or so are genuinely different varieties (Truel et al. 1980) and only a small proportion of these are used commercially. In France, the official statistics list 216 varieties of 10 ha or more, of which 179 are *V. vinifera* and 37 are hybrids. The number of varieties of commercial importance in Australia is much smaller. Until the early 1960s, the total number of known varieties in Australia was less than 100; the early emphasis on fortified wines did not create a demand for a wide array of table wine varieties. Even now there may be fewer than 80 varieties with more than 20 ha, which is a small number considering that there are no planting restrictions in Australia. Most European countries have restrictions on the varieties which may be planted in each district: for example, Grenache is widely-grown in the south of France but is not permitted in the Bordeaux region. The 20 most

important winegrape varieties in the world are listed in **TABLE** 6.1. It is interesting that some of these varieties (e.g. Airen, Bobal) are not known at all in Australia, and others such as Rkaziteli, Carignan and Barbera have been introduced relatively recently.

Selection of the correct varieties, both for environmental conditions and end-use, is fundamental for the success of any viticultural enterprise. This applies especially for wine as there is such a large number from which to choose. Varieties suitable for drying, on the other hand, are fewer, being largely limited in Australia to Sultana, Muscat Gordo Blanco, Waltham Cross, Zante Currant and Carina although some wine varieties such as Shiraz have been dried in the past. The genetic characteristics of winegrapes, more than any other factor, predetermine the style and quality of a wine. While climate influences the levels of sugar, acid, pigments, tannin and the intensity of aromas and flavours, the relative winemaking quality of different varieties is relatively consistent from region to region. Accordingly the performance of a variety in one region may be quite a good guide to its suitability for another.

The 94 varieties described in this text include all of the varieties used commercially for winemaking in Australia at the beginning of this millennium. They have been divided into 'white' and 'black or red': 'white' varieties may have ripe berry colours ranging from green to yellow to pink; 'black or red' varieties may have ripe berry colours ranging from red to purple to black and, if used for winemaking, are normally used for red wine. Of the 42 white varieties, 3 are multipurpose, that is, used for wine, table and drying, and 5 are used as tablegrapes (see Volume II, Chapters 12 and 14). Of the 52 black or red varieties, one is multipurpose and 8 are used for drying or table. They have been further subdivided based on the national 2002 planting statistics, i.e. those with a total planted area (bearing plus non-bearing) greater than 1,000 ha; those with more than 100 ha but less than 1,000 ha; and those with fewer than 100 ha. Within each category, all varieties are listed alphabetically. **FIGURE** 6.1 shows tonnages of grapes used for all purposes from 1980 to 2002 for the major varieties of each berry colour.

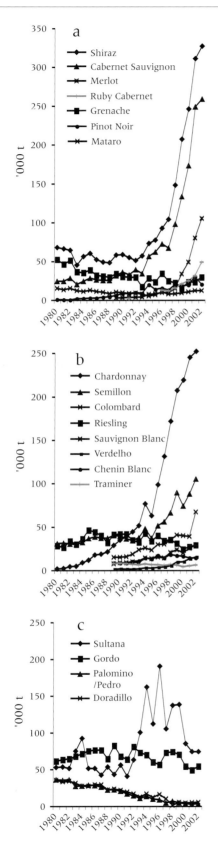

Figure 6.1. Grape varieties for winemaking ('000 tonnes) in Australia, 1980 to 2002. a) Black varieties. b) 'Premium' white varieties. c) Multipurpose and 'non-premium' white varieties.

Table 6.1. The top 20 winegrape varieties in the world[1]

Variety	Area ('000 ha)	Principal countries
Airén (W)	423	Spain
Grenache (B)	318	Spain, France
Carignan (B)	244	France
Trebbiano (W)	203	France, Italy
Merlot (B)	162	France, Italy
Cabernet Sauvignon (B)	146	France, Bulgaria, USA
Rkaziteli (W)	129	Georgia, Russia, Ukraine, Bulgaria
Mataro (B)	118	Spain, France
Bobal (B)	106	Spain
Tempranillo (B)	102	Spain, Portugal
Chardonnay (W)	99	USA, France, Australia, Italy
Sangiovese (B)	99	Italy, France (Corsica)
Cinsaut (B)	86	France, South Africa
Welschriesling (W)	76	Former Yugoslavia, Hungary, Romania
Catarratto (W)	75	Italy (Sicily)
Aligoté (W)	72	Russia, Ukraine, Moldova, Bulgaria
Muscat Gordo Blanco (W)	67	Spain, Australia, South Africa
Pinot Noir (B)	63	France, Moldova, Germany, USA
Sauvignon Blanc (W)	61	France, Moldova, Ukraine
Chenin Blanc (W)	54	South Africa, USA, France

1. Modified from a table on page 753 of the *Oxford Companion to Wine* 2nd ed. The preferred names for Australia have been used.

Unless otherwise stated in the text, the planting and production statistics for Australia are given for 2001–02 (Winemakers Federation of Australia 2003). The percentage figures in parentheses refer to the total planted area (bearing plus non-bearing) for that zone[2] as a percentage of the total planted area for Australia for that variety. For other countries, the statistics are less current and data have been used from various sources including Clarke and Rand (2001). For more details on the varietal names used in Australia (valid and invalid synonyms), the reader should consult Dry and Gregory (1988). The descriptions attempt to outline the significance of each variety in Australia and elsewhere. This chapter is not intended as an ampelography and for this reason has been cross-referenced with Kerridge and Antcliff (1999). Some morphological characters of the 60 most-important varieties are summarised in **TABLE 6.2**

2. The zones used are those of the Geographical Index system (described in Chapter 2).

Table 6.2 Characteristics of grape varieties used in Australia

Page No.	Variety	End use	Colour	Berry Size	Shape	Bunch Size	Compactness	Phenology Budburst	Ripening	Yield
142	Barbera	W(t)	B	M	O	M	WC	M	M	H
146	Bastardo	W(f)	B	S	R	S	C	M	E	M
144	Biancone	W(t,d)	W	M	R	ML	W	M	L	H
142	Cabernet Franc	W(t)	B	S	R	S	LW	E	M	M
137	Cabernet Sauvignon	W(t)	B	S	R	S	LW	M	M	L
146	Carignan	W(t)	B	M	R	M	C	L	L	H
146	Carina	D	B	S	R	S	L	E	E	M
146	Chambourcin	W(t)	B	M	R	M	W	E	E	H
135	Chardonnay	W(t)	W	S	R	S	C	E	E	M
144	Chasselas	W(t)	W	M	R	M	C	E	E	M
139	Chenin Blanc	W(t)	W	S	O	M	C	E	M	H
147	Cinsaut	W(t,f)	B	M	O	M	WC	L	M	M
144	Clairette	W(t)	W	M	O	M	W	L	L	M
135	Colombard	W(t,d)	W	SM	R	M	W	E	M	H
140	Crouchen	W(t)	W	S	R	SM	C	M	M	H
147	Dolcetto	W(t)	B	SM	R	SM	W	M	E	M
140	Doradillo	W(t,f,d)	W	L	R	L	W	M	L	H
142	Durif	W(t,f)	B	S	R	M	C	M	M	M
142	Frontignac (syn. Muscat apg)	W(t,f)	W,R,B	S	R	M	WC	E	E	M
147	Gamay	W(t)	B	S	O	M	C	E	E	M
147	Graciano	W(t)	B	S	R	M	C	L	L	LM
137	Grenache	W(t,f)	B	M	R	M	C	M	L	H
142	Malbec	W(t)	B	S	R	M	LW	M	M	M
140	Marsanne	W(t)	W	S	R	M	W	L	M	M
138	Mataro	W(t,f)	B	SM	R	M	WC	L	L	M
138	Merlot	W(t)	B	S	R	S	LW	E	M	M
143	Meunier	W(t)	B	S	R	S	C	E	E	M
148	Mondeuse	W(t)	B	M	R	M	C	E	M	H
145	Mueller-Thurgau	W(t)	W	M	O	M	W	M	E	H
140	Muscadelle	W(t,f)	W	S	R	M	WC	M	M	M
	Muscat apg (see Frontignac)									
135	Muscat Gordo Blanco	W,T,D	W	L	O	L	L	M	L	H
143	Nebbiolo	W(t)	B	S	R	S	W	M	M	M
145	Ondenc	W(t)	W	M	O	S	W	M	E	M
140	Palomino	W(t,f)	W	M	R	L	LW	M	M	H
141	Pedro Ximenes	W(t,f)	W	M	R	L	W	M	E	H
138	Petit Verdot	W(t)	B	S	R	M	W	M	L	LM
138	Pinot Noir	W(t)	B	S	R	S	C	E	E	L
136	Riesling	W(t)	W	S	R	S	C	M	M	L
145	Roussanne	W(t)	W	S	R	SM	C	M	M	L
148	Rubired	W(t,f)	B	S	R	M	L	M	M	H
139	Ruby Cabernet	W(t)	B	M	O	M	W	L	M	MH
143	Sangiovese	W(t)	B	M	R	SM	W	M	M	M
136	Sauvignon Blanc	W(t)	W	S	R	S	C	M	M	L
136	Semillon	W(t)	W	S	R	M	C	M	M	M
139	Shiraz	W(t,f)	B	S	O	M	LW	M	M	M
148	Souzao	W(t,f)	B	M	R	SM	C	M	L	M
136	Sultana	W,T,D	W	SM	O	L	W	M	E	M
146	Taminga	W(t)	W	M	R	M	W	M	M	H
148	Tannat	W(t)	B	M	R	ML	C	L	M	H
143	Tarrango	W(t)	B	M	O	L	W	M	L	H
143	Tempranillo	W(t)	B	M	R	L	WC	M	M	MH
148	Tinta Amarella	W(f)	B	M	R	M	W	M	E	M
148	Touriga	W(t,f)	B	S	O	SM	W	M	M	M
141	Traminer	W(t)	W	S	R	S	C	E	E	LM
141	Trebbiano	W(t,d)	W	M	R	ML	W	L	L	M
137	Verdelho	W(t,f)	W	S	O	S	L	E	M	M
141	Viognier	W(t)	W	S	R	S	S	E	M	L
141	Waltham Cross	W,T,D	W	L	O	L	L	L	M	H
144	Zante Currant	D	B	S	R	S	W	E	E	M
149	Zinfandel	W(t)	B	M	R	M	C	M	M	M

Explanatory notes:
End use: W = winemaking, (t,f,d) = table wines, fortified wines, distillation respectively; T = tablegrape; D = drying grape
Berry colour: B = black; R = red; W = white
Berry size, bunch size: S = small; M = medium; L = large
Berry shape: R = round; O = slightly oval to oval; E = elongated
Bunch compactness: C = compact; W = well-filled; L = loose
Budburst, ripening: E = early; M = mid-season; L = late
Yield: L = low; M = moderate; H = high

but the reader should keep in mind that the characters listed in the table may be affected by both cultural and environmental factors.

This chapter includes most of the varieties that are currently grown in Australia for commercial purposes. Those varieties that exist as odd vines in old mixed plantings are not described: these include Alvarelhão, Bourboulenc, Calitor, Folle Blanche, Furmint, Gouais, Grec Rose, Mammolo, Mauzac, Monbadon, Montils, Moschata Paradisa, Peloursin, Piquepoul Noir, Solvorino, Troyen and Terret Noir (see mentions in Antcliff [1983] or Kerridge and Antcliff [1999]). Other varieties such as Emerald Riesling, Flora, Melon, Muscat Ottonel, Siegerrebe and Valdiguie were introduced into Australia in the 1960s (Kerridge and Antcliff 1999); they were evaluated commercially on a small scale, but so far have not proved to be viable.

6.1 Varieties with more than 1,000 ha

6.1.1 WHITE-BERRIED VARIETIES

Chardonnay

Chardonnay was the single most sought-after grape variety in the 1980s in Australia and elsewhere and large areas were planted in many different parts of the world. Chardonnay probably originated in the northern part of France where it is an important variety. In Burgundy (13,000 ha), it is the preferred of the two white varieties (the other is Aligoté) permitted for white wines. In Champagne (8,600 ha) it is normally blended with Pinot Noir. Since the 1970s it has spread to the south of France, e.g. 8,000 ha in Languedoc-Roussillon. It is widely planted throughout the rest of Europe, particularly Italy (12,000 ha) and Moldova (5,000 ha). California has more than 37,000 ha, the area having increased five-fold since 1980. Chile and South Africa each have around 6,000 ha. It is the main variety of New Zealand.

In Australia, Chardonnay has been grown since the 1900s, but despite its overseas reputation, the area remained small until the early 1970s. Over the next 2 decades the planted area increased from less than 100 ha to 3,700 ha as the demand increased for its high quality table wines. During the 1990s, the area increased by almost 5 times to become Australia's most important white winegrape with 21,724 ha. It is widely grown with the largest areas in North West Victoria (14%), Big Rivers (NSW) (14%) and Lower Murray (SA) (13%). Chardonnay is a relatively easy variety to grow, with good yields and few problems; it ripens well in all climatic regions in Australia, is not readily damaged by rain before harvest, and is easily harvested by machine. Early budburst is its major disadvantage, making it prone to spring frost damage. It is also susceptible to powdery mildew (oidium). Although traditionally cane-pruned, many Chardonnay vines in Australia are successfully spur-pruned. Good, well-balanced wines can be produced under a wide range of climatic conditions. [Kerridge and Antcliff 1999, p. 35].

Colombard

Colombard is a comparatively recent introduction to Australia from California where its 18,000 ha are mainly found in the hot Central Valley. Colombard originated in the southwest and west of France; it is one of the varieties used for Cognac and there are also plantings in the Bordeaux area where it is used as an accessory variety in white table wines. The total area in France decreased from 13,000 ha in 1958 to around 5,000 ha in the 1980s; it has been largely static since that time. It is also important in South Africa (11,600 ha).

In Australia, the area (2,631 ha) has more than doubled since 1990. It is grown almost exclusively in the hot inland regions, e.g. Lower Murray (SA) (39%), Big Rivers (NSW) (32%). Colombard is vigorous and high-yielding. Young shoots are liable to be damaged by strong winds in spring. It is susceptible to powdery mildew but moderately tolerant of downy mildew and bunch rot. Fruit hangs well on the vine after it is ripe. The main feature of the variety is its high acid content: because of this, it is considered satisfactory in California and Australia for blending to produce good quality still and sparkling wines. It can also have a distinctive varietal character but is rarely used as a varietal wine. [Kerridge and Antcliff 1999, p. 45].

Muscat Gordo Blanco

Muscat Gordo Blanco was Australia's most important winegrape in the mid-1980s. Best known internationally as Muscat of Alexandria, it has been grown in the Mediterranean basin for many centuries. It is now widely grown throughout the world, with large plantings in Chile, South Africa, Morocco, France and Spain.

Gordo, as it is most often known in Australia, is a true multipurpose grape, being used as a tablegrape, dried for raisins, and crushed for unfermented grape juice and wine. However, in Australia, 95% of the production is now used for winemaking (mainly bulk table wine and fortified sweet wines). The Australian total area is 2,530 ha: it is grown almost exclusively in the hot inland regions, e.g. Lower Murray (SA) (43%), North West Victoria (30%) and Big Rivers (NSW) (24%). Gordo vines lack vigour but they can produce good yields. In warm areas the fruit can attain a high sugar content but is then low in acid with high pH. The fruit has a strong muscat flavour. The variety is susceptible to erinose and nematodes. Poor berry setting can be a problem impairing its usefulness as a tablegrape. It is best pruned to one-node spurs. [Kerridge and Antcliff 1999, p. 113]

Riesling

Riesling is widely grown throughout the world. It has many synonyms and possesses the ability to produce wines with recognisable varietal character in most situations. Riesling appears to have originated in Germany where it is planted on 22,350 ha (22% of the total vineyard area), just ahead of Müller-Thurgau (21%). In the Rheingau and Mosel, it comprises 82% and 55% of the planted area respectively. In France, 3,000 ha are grown in Alsace. Smaller areas are found in Austria, northern Italy, and eastern European countries. Outside of Europe, the largest areas are found in Australia, South Africa and USA.

In Australia, it has been called Rhine Riesling to avoid confusion with other varieties which have been incorrectly called Riesling in the past, e.g. 'Hunter River Riesling', an invalid synonym for Semillon: however, this undesirable practice is declining. The area of Riesling increased in the 1970s and early 1980s, peaking at 4,800 ha in the early 1980s. Over-supply resulted in removal of plantings, particularly in hot regions, reducing the area to 3,600 ha by the late 1980s (when it was still Australia's second-most important white winegrape, after Gordo). Since that time, the area has stabilised to be 3,962 ha. Most plantings (67%) are found in South Australia, mainly the Barossa (25%), Mount Lofty Ranges (18%) and Limestone Coast (12%). The South West of WA also has a significant area (9%). Riesling is only moderately productive and ripens well in all regions in Australia in most seasons. Well-balanced musts can be produced in hot regions. It is susceptible to bunch rot (due to its compact bunches) and erinose. Traditionally cane-pruned, it has been successfully spur-pruned in Australia. In cool climates, it is one of the best varieties because it is relatively cold tolerant. It is used for both dry and sweet table wines that possess a definite varietal character. [Kerridge and Antcliff 1999, p. 131].

Sauvignon Blanc

Sauvignon Blanc has increased in popularity in Australia, California, France, New Zealand and South Africa since the 1980s. The main plantings in France have traditionally been near Bordeaux (5,000 ha) where it is used as a minor but important partner of Semillon. However, at the present time it is likely that the largest area is found in the Loire Valley (7,500 ha), where it is used on its own. It is now also extensively planted in the south of France, e.g. 4,000 ha in Languedoc-Roussillon. After France, Moldova, California, South Africa and Italy probably have the largest areas. The so-called Sauvignon in Chile (6,500 ha) is a closely-related variety, known as Sauvignonasse in France and Tocai Friulano in Italy. New Zealand has 3,086 ha where it is the second-most important variety.

In Australia, the area increased from about 100 ha in the mid-1970s to 900 ha in the late 1980s. However, during the 1990s, the area increased three-fold to 2,914 ha. It is widely distributed with the largest areas in the South West of WA (25%) and Mt Lofty Ranges (SA) (10%). Sauvignon Blanc is a vigorous variety with a large leaf area-to-fruit weight ratio. Although classed as unproductive in France, yields from locally-selected clones in Australia have been good. It has responded well to light pruning. In cool climates, Sauvignon Blanc gives wines with a strong varietal character. This character is less developed in warmer areas where fresh, well-balanced table wines can be produced. [Kerridge and Antcliff 1999, p. 141].

Semillon

Semillon is widely used throughout the world for white table wine. It was Australia's second-most important white wine variety in the late 1990s. There has been confusion between Semillon and several other varieties in Australia in the past, particularly Chenin Blanc and Crouchen. It was incorrectly known as Hunter River Riesling in NSW. Semillon is a major white variety in France where it is particularly important in Bordeaux (9,000 ha) for both dry and sweet table wines. It is also important in Chile (2,300 ha), and other significant areas are found in California, Argentina and South Africa (each with about 1,000 ha).

The Australian area of Semillon has steadily increased since the 1970s to reach 6,610 ha. The largest areas are found in Big Rivers (NSW) (32%), Barossa (SA) (13%) and Hunter Valley (NSW) (11%). It is a reasonably vigorous variety with clones showing growth habits varying from spreading to upright. Yields are good but the berries tend to split in wet weather when ripe, leading to bunch rot problems. It is one of the most susceptible varieties to rootknot nematode and is a difficult variety to harvest by machine. Spur pruning is most common. In Australia it is used for dry white table wines which, although fairly neutral when young, develop distinctive and desirable varietal characters with ageing. [Kerridge and Antcliff 1999, p. 143].

Sultana

Sultana is an important grape variety in Australia with 10,906 ha. It is primarily a drying grape but, in some years, nearly half of the total production may be crushed for wine. For example, in 1999, 47% was used for winemaking, 42% was dried and 11% was used as tablegrapes. The proportion of the crop that is dried will vary from season to season depending on the international trade for dried fruit and domestic demand for bulk white wine. It is the world's most important drying and tablegrape variety. Sultana appears to have originated in Asia Minor or the Middle East, and is grown for dried fruit from Greece to northwest China. California has the largest area: there, Thompson Seedless, as it is known, is used for wine, drying and table. South Africa also has a large area (11,500 ha).

Almost the entire planted area of Sultana is found in the hot inland regions of Australia, principally North West Victoria (77%). Sultana requires cane pruning due to the low fruitfulness of basal nodes. 'Minimal pruning', originally developed for this variety, has been most successful (Clingeleffer 1983). It is very susceptible to the fungal diseases downy mildew, powdery mildew and black spot (anthracnose) and the berries are prone to rain damage when ripe. These factors combine to limit its commercial culture to regions of low summer rainfall. Both fresh and trellis-dried fruit is readily harvested by machine. Sultana is ideally suited to drying by virtue of its tender skin, capacity to develop high sugar levels and readiness with which the berries shatter from pedicels after drying. The lack of seeds and firm flesh make Sultana attractive as a tablegrape despite its natural small size and tendency to shatter in transit; however, both problems can be overcome by various cultural treatments (see Volume 2, Chapter 12). Sultana musts have moderate acid levels and can produce fresh, neutral table wines, most often used for blending. It is also used for fortifying wine and distillation, thus making it a most versatile grape variety. [Kerridge and Antcliff 1999, p. 153].

Verdelho

Verdelho is a Portuguese variety, grown on the island of Madeira and in the Douro Valley, where it is known as Gouveio: in both regions it is used for fortified wines. There is a small area in the Loire region of France. In Australia, the area increased substantially during the 1990s: the current 1,645 ha is mainly grown in Big Rivers (NSW) (25%), Hunter Valley (NSW) (21%) and South West of WA (9%). The name Madeira has been incorrectly used for this variety in NSW. It is moderately vigorous and productive. Budburst, flowering and ripening are early. It is very susceptible to powdery mildew and is suitable for mechanical harvesting. In Australia, Verdelho is generally used for full-bodied table wines with distinctive varietal character. [Kerridge and Antcliff 1999, p. 177].

6.1.2 BLACK- AND RED-BERRIED VARIETIES

Cabernet Sauvignon

Cabernet Sauvignon is widely regarded as the world's premium variety for red wine. It is also probably the most widely planted. Recent research has established that Cabernet Sauvignon is the result of a chance crossing of Cabernet Franc and Sauvignon Blanc (see Chapter 5) that took place many centuries ago. It came to prominence in the Bordeaux region of France from the 18th century where it is the major variety in the best wines of the Medoc and is typically blended with Cabernet Franc, Merlot and several minor varieties. Total

area in France (around 40,000 ha) has doubled since the 1970s: approximately two-thirds are found in Bordeaux with most of the remainder in Languedoc-Roussillon. It has always been important in Chile (26,000 ha) but in countries such as USA, Bulgaria, Romania, Moldova, Argentina and South Africa, the increase in plantings has been more recent. California has one of the largest areas with 21,000 ha. It is important in New Zealand (727 ha).

In Australia, the planted area increased from a few hundred hectares in the late 1960s to around 4,000 ha by the late 1980s. During the planting boom of the 1990s, Cabernet Sauvignon was one of the favoured varieties and the area increased to 29,573 ha by 2002. Almost 60% of the planted area is in South Australia, for example, Limestone Coast (19%) and Lower Murray (14%). North West Victoria (10%) and Big Rivers (NSW) (9%) also have large areas. Cabernet Sauvignon has been generally regarded as a low-yielding variety; however, yields have been improved by the use of selected virus-free clones. Traditionally it is cane-pruned, but spur-pruning has been successful in Australia and large areas are now mechanically pruned. Poor set can be a problem, particularly in cool regions in vineyards of high vigour. It is quite susceptible to powdery mildew and bunch-stem necrosis. The bunches have good tolerance of rain damage and bunch rot. The small, tough berries are readily mechanically harvested. The wines of Cabernet Sauvignon have a recognisable varietal character in all climatic regions but this is usually most intense when vines are grown under cool conditions. [Kerridge and Antcliff 1999, p. 25].

Grenache

Grenache is a very important variety in southern Europe. In Spain, where it is known as Garnacha, it is the most important red-wine grape, covering about 15% of the planted area (170,000 ha); the largest areas are in Aragon and Castilla-La Mancha. The area in France (92,000 ha) tripled in the 1960s and 1970s, mainly at the expense of the lesser-quality variety Aramon, so that it is now the second most widely planted black variety after Carignan. Grenache is concentrated in the south of France, where it is often blended with other varieties such as Carignan and Mataro. For example, Languedoc-Roussillon and the Rhone each have around 40,000 ha. Some of the most prized wines of the Rhone are blends of Grenache and Shiraz. It is also found in Corsica, Sardinia (under another name) and in the south of Italy (where it is known as Granaccia or Alicante). Outside of Europe, the largest areas are found in Tunisia, California and Australia.

In Australia, the area of Grenache increased during the 1960s to reach a peak of nearly 7,000 ha in the early 1970s. At that time it was Australia's most important black winegrape. Since the 1970s, the area has declined to 2,528 ha: in the 1990s this was mainly due to a preference by wineries for Shiraz, Cabernet Sauvignon and Merlot. However the area has stabilised since the late 1990s. More than 80% of the plantings are found in South Australia, mainly the Lower Murray (28%), Barossa (27%) and Fleurieu (23%). Grenache yields well but the amount of fruit colour is more sensitive to crop level than for most black varieties. Experience in South Australia and Europe has shown that it is one of the best varieties in hot, dry conditions. It is susceptible to poor set, bunch rot, downy mildew and powdery mildew. Pruning is generally to spurs. Most of the Grenache vines throughout the world are untrellised 'bush vines', a training method facilitated by the erect growth habit. The wines of Grenache are often low in colour (by Australian standards) and age rapidly. It is the principal rosé variety and is also used for tawny port. For red table wines it is usually combined with other varieties such as Shiraz and Mataro. There are also forms of Grenache with white, pink and 'grey' fruit that are extensively used for white wine in the south of France. [Kerridge and Antcliff 1999, p. 77] .

Mataro/Mourvèdre

Mataro was the fourth most important red wine variety in Australia in the 1980s. Although widely distributed throughout the world (TABLE 6.1), it is only an important variety in Spain where there are 110,000 ha (it is also known as Monastrell or Morastell). The area in France (7,000 ha) increased substantially during the 1970s and 1980s, mainly in Provence where it is known as Mourvèdre. There is also increasing interest in Mataro in California but the area is relatively small (180 ha).

Seventy per cent of the 1,238 ha grown in Australia is found in South Australia, mainly the Lower Murray (49%) and Barossa (14%). After suffering a significant decline in planted area during the 1970s and 1980s, Mataro has made a modest recovery during the 1990s. Mataro has a late budburst and recovers well after frost; for this reason it was originally planted in frost-prone sites in South Australia instead of Shiraz or Grenache. Growth habit is strongly erect and yields are potentially high. It is a hardy, drought-tolerant variety requiring warmer sites than Grenache in order to ripen fruit adequately. The wines of Mataro are neutral and often astringent, usually blended with Shiraz and/or Grenache for table or fortified wine. [Kerridge and Antcliff 1999, p. 89].

Merlot

Merlot appears to have originated in the Bordeaux region of France where it is the principal variety (60,000 ha). This is another variety that has seen significant international expansion in the late 20th century, for example, Italy (32,000 ha), the south of France (23,000 ha in Languedoc-Roussillon), USA (California and Washington), Bulgaria, Moldova and Romania. In California there were fewer than 800 ha in 1985; today there are 17,000 ha. It is also important in Chile but it is likely that more than 50% of the area designated as Merlot is actually Carmenère, a rare old minor variety from Bordeaux. The area in South Africa increased four-fold in the 1990s to reach 3,700 ha. It is the second-most important red wine variety in New Zealand with 960 ha.

The growth in Australia has been no less spectacular in recent times. During the 1990s the area increased by more than 30 times to 10,101 ha. In the late 1990s, half of the vines were non-bearing. It is now widely planted, with the largest areas in Big Rivers (NSW) (15%), North West Victoria (13%), Lower Murray (SA) (12%) and Limestone Coast (SA) (11%). Merlot is more productive than Cabernet Sauvignon or Cabernet Franc in Bordeaux but this has not always been the experience in Australia because it may be susceptible to poor set. However, this problem can be largely overcome by grafting onto a rootstock and may be related to a deficiency of molybdenum. It is also particularly sensitive to salinity. Merlot ripens earlier than Cabernet Sauvignon. It may be subject to bunch rot. It is often blended with Cabernet Sauvignon and/or Cabernet Franc. [Kerridge and Antcliff 1999, p. 95].

Petit Verdot

Petit Verdot is a minor variety in the Bordeaux region of France where it is one of the permitted varieties in the best red wines of the Medoc. It is also grown in California (150 ha), Argentina and Chile. With 1,313 ha, Australia may have one of the largest areas internationally: most of this was planted in the 1990s (in 2001, 40% was non-bearing). It is mainly grown in South Australia (70%), principally the Lower Murray (48%). It is a vigorous and potentially productive variety, although some clones have setting problems. Petit Verdot ripens later than Cabernet Sauvignon and has some resistance to bunch rot. Wines are well-coloured with high levels of acid and tannins. It is usually blended with other Bordeaux varieties for table wine (Kerridge et al. 1987a). [Kerridge and Antcliff 1999, p. 187].

Pinot Noir

Pinot Noir is the variety used for the red wines of Burgundy and one of the principal varieties for the white sparkling wines of Champagne. France has the world's largest area of Pinot Noir: 26,000 ha is equally divided between the two regions. It is one of the few red wine varieties ripening early enough for Germany (8,600 ha as Spätburgunder or Blauburgunder) and Switzerland. It is grown in Italy and most eastern European countries, particularly in Moldova and Romania. There are 5,000 ha in the coolest parts of California and 2,600 ha in Oregon (USA). It is the most important red-wine grape of New Zealand (1,716 ha).

The area in Australia has increased from less than 50 ha in the early 1970s to 4,414 ha in 2002. The largest areas are found in the relatively cool zones: Port Phillip (Vic.) (28%), Limestone Coast (SA) (10% and Mount Lofty Ranges (SA) (10%). Pinot Noir is an old and variable variety with hundreds of different clones (see Chapter 9). Amongst the 20 or so different clones in Australia there are recognisable differences in growth habit, berry size, bunch compactness and leaf shape. The results from clonal comparisons suggest that some clones are better adapted to particular areas than others. Budburst is early, thus predisposing the vines to spring frost damage. The compact bunches are very susceptible to bunch rot but clones with less compact bunches are now available in Australia. The colour of Pinot Noir wines is not intense and fruit from hot areas usually makes uninteresting wines lacking in colour and flavour. However, in cool areas, the wines can be of excellent quality with a distinctive varietal character. [Kerridge and Antcliff 1999, p. 129].

Ruby Cabernet

Ruby Cabernet is a cross between Carignan and Cabernet Sauvignon, bred in California and released in 1948. Designed for producing quality red wines in hot areas, it has achieved significance in California (3,200 ha), mostly grown in the San Joaquin Valley. In Australia, where it is grown almost exclusively in the hot inland regions, the planted area (2,817 ha) increased four-fold during the 1990s. It is susceptible to fungal diseases and unfavourable soil conditions but has performed well on nematode-resistant rootstocks in the Riverland and elsewhere (Nicholas 1985). It is productive, responds well to minimal pruning and is readily harvested by machine. An outstanding feature of the variety is the deep red colour of its wine; it is typically blended with other varieties. [Kerridge and Antcliff 1999, p. 137].

Shiraz

Shiraz is Australia's most important grape variety. Until the end of the 20th century, it was unimportant in other wine-producing countries, including France where its traditional home is the northern Rhone. In recent times, the area in France (where it is known as Syrah) has greatly increased, particularly in the Rhone and Languedoc-Roussillon; there may be as many as 45,000 ha in France compared with just 3,000 ha in the 1960s. It is now grown widely e.g. USA (California, Washington), Argentina, South Africa (3,400 ha), Mexico and Italy. Recent interest in the variety in California has resulted in a planted area of 3,000 ha. The Petite Sirah of California is a different variety (see Durif). New Zealand has 101 ha, mainly grown in Hawkes Bay.

The area of Shiraz in Australia increased greatly during the 1960s and 1970s, reaching a peak of about 10,000 ha in the mid- to late 1970s. Over the ensuing 10 years the area halved as the demand for red wine decreased. However, since the early 1990s, more Shiraz has been planted than any other variety: by 2001 there were 37,030 ha (23% of the total Australian vineyard area). Although it is widely distributed, more than half of Shiraz plantings are found in South Australia, particularly the Lower Murray (16%), Fleurieu (13%) and Barossa (12%). Big Rivers (NSW) also has a large area (13%). Shiraz has become Australia's most important red wine variety because it yields well under a range of climatic conditions with relatively few problems and may produce excellent wine. The bunches stand up to wet weather near harvest better than most varieties (this accounts for its popularity in the Hunter Valley), but the berries tend to wilt when ripe and become more difficult to harvest mechanically. Shiraz wines are of good colour, contain moderate amounts of acid and tannin and possess a positive though mild fruit flavour. [Kerridge and Antcliff 1999, p. 145].

6.2 Varieties with 100 to 1,000 ha

6.2.1 WHITE-BERRIED VARIETIES

Chenin Blanc

Chenin Blanc is the main variety in the Loire Valley of France (9,000 ha) where it is used for both still and sparkling wines. The largest area (25,000 ha) of this variety is found in South Africa (where it has been known as Steen or Stein), occupying about one-quarter of total vineyard area (but losing ground to Chardonnay, Sauvignon Blanc and Colombard). California (8,600 ha) and Argentina (4,300 ha) also have large areas. Chenin Blanc appears to have been grown in Australia for a long time but under different names: in the 1970s, much of the Semillon in Western Australia and all of the so-called Albillo and Sherry in South Australia was found to be Chenin Blanc. The planted area (820 ha) has doubled since the late 1980s: the main plantings are in the Lower Murray (SA) (24%), North West Victoria (13%) and Barossa (SA) (11%). Chenin Blanc is a vigorous variety with early budburst making it prone to spring frost damage. Shoots adhere firmly and are not readily detached by strong winds in spring. Yields are high but it is susceptible to fungal diseases; there is clonal variation in bunch compactness and time of ripening and at least some clones are susceptible to splitting by rain and bunch rot at harvest. Pruning is mainly to spurs. Chenin Blanc has good acidity and hence is used for well-balanced table wines in hot regions in Australia, California and South Africa. It also provides good material for sparkling wines. [Kerridge and Antcliff 1999, p. 39].

Crouchen

Crouchen is a variety from the south-west of France. It has now almost disappeared from that country because of its susceptibility to foliar fungal diseases and bunch rot. The variety now appears to be grown only in South Africa (2,800 ha) and Australia. In South Africa it is still known as Cape Riesling and appears to have been introduced under that name to South Australia. Until correctly identified, Crouchen was known as Clare Riesling in Australia (Antcliff 1975). Also, because of morphological similarity, some Crouchen was mistakenly known as Semillon in the Barossa. The area of Crouchen in Australia (114 ha) has declined by more than 90% since the late 1970s as it has fallen out of favour with winemakers. Most of the plantings are in the hot inland regions, e.g. North West Victoria (58%). Crouchen is a high-yielding variety used for dry white table wines. It is susceptible to fungal diseases and rootknot nematode. In cool areas it may not ripen adequately. [Kerridge and Antcliff 1999, p. 47].

Doradillo

Doradillo has been Australia's traditional distillation variety. However, when demand for white table wine base material outstripped supply, the neutral wines of Doradillo were blended with more aromatic varieties, such as Gordo, for the cask market. A decrease in the demand for brandy, fortifying spirit and sherry resulted in a significant reduction of the planted area from the 1970s with only 247 ha remaining in the late 1990s. The largest area is found in the Lower Murray (SA) (72%). Although originally imported from Spain, Doradillo is not recorded separately in Spanish plantings and may perhaps be included under the name Jaen, said to have been used for more than one variety in Spain (Kerridge and Antcliff 1999); however, Jaen is morphologically different. Neither is it Airen, another Spanish variety (TABLE 6.1). Doradillo is moderately vigorous with a relatively shallow and weak root system that is sensitive to poor drainage. Yields may be high and the fruit ripens late. [Kerridge and Antcliff 1999, p. 51].

Frontignac

(see 6.2.2)

Marsanne

Marsanne is a minor variety from the Rhone Valley where it is sometimes blended with Roussanne. There have been increased plantings in Languedoc-Roussillon in recent times. It is relatively unknown in the rest of Europe and little is planted in the New World.

Australia has some of the oldest Marsanne vines in the world. From fewer than 30 ha nationally, the area increased to 275 ha during the 1990s. It is mainly grown in Big Rivers (NSW) (29%) and Central Victoria (29%). Marsanne is vigorous and productive. Table wines typically have little varietal character and tend to age rapidly, but there are some exceptions. [Kerridge and Antcliff 1999, p. 87].

Muscadelle

Muscadelle was formerly known as Tokay in Australia and hence assumed to have originated from the Tokay-Hegyalja district of Hungary. However, in 1976, it was identified as Muscadelle (Antcliff 1976), a variety of the Bordeaux region where it forms a minor component in the dry and sweet white table wines of Graves, Barsac, Sauternes, etc. France has around 2,000 ha but the area has decreased by almost two-thirds since the late 1960s. There are also small plantings in California (where it is incorrectly known as Sauvignon Vert) and in eastern Europe. It should not be confused with the so-called Muskadel of South Africa which is actually Muscat à Petit Grains. Most of the Australian area (183 ha) is in South Australia, mainly the Barossa (30%) and Lower Murray (14%), followed by North East Victoria (27%). Muscadelle is a fairly vigorous and productive variety. The fruit ripens early and can attain a very high sugar content: for this reason it has traditionally been used for sweet fortified wines, traditionally known as 'tokay' in Australia where the use of Muscadelle for this wine style appears to be unique; some of these wines are highly regarded. It has also been used for dry white table wines. [Kerridge and Antcliff 1999, p. 109].

Palomino

Palomino and Pedro Ximenes were formerly grouped together for statistical purposes: they were Australia's sixth most important winegrapes in the 1980s in terms of tonnes crushed and traditionally have been used for fortified wines, particularly sherries. They have also been used for bulk table wine. Since the 1980s, the planted area has greatly decreased due to decreased demand for fortified wine and the need for better table wine varieties. In 2002 there were only 104 ha of Palomino, mostly in the Lower Murray (SA) (49%), Big Rivers (NSW) (24%) and Barossa (SA) (20%). Palomino is an important variety in Spain (57,000 ha), providing almost 90% of the grapes used for sherry, and is still important in South Africa (2,500 ha) (where it may be called 'White French') although the area more than halved in the 1990s. Smaller areas are found in France (where it is known as Listan), California and Argentina. Palomino yields well and when ripe has high sugar content but low acid and high pH, with neutral flavour. It is better suited to fortified wines than table wines. It is susceptible to sunburn and recovers poorly after frost. Although susceptible to powdery mildew and black spot, the bunches stand up well to wet weather near vintage. [Kerridge and Antcliff 1999, p. 121].

Pedro Ximenes

Pedro Ximenes (also spelt Ximenez) comes from Spain where there are about 27,000 ha: it is one of the permitted varieties in Jerez for sherry production but only a small proportion of the total plantings are in this region. It is an important white variety in Argentina. In Australia, there are 104 ha, mainly in South Australia, e.g. Barossa (34%) and Lower Murray (21%). Pedro Ximenes is a productive variety but the berries have a tender skin that is susceptible to rain damage and consequently bunch rot. It is also more susceptible to downy mildew and powdery mildew than most varieties, and recovery from spring frost damage is poor. Although most suited to the production of fortified wines, the neutral table wines are suitable for blending. [Kerridge and Antcliff 1999, p. 123].

Traminer

Traminer produces table wines with a distinctive varietal character. The best-known Traminer wines are probably from the Alsace region of France where there are about 2,500 ha, making it the most important variety in that region. Moldova may have the largest area (around 4,000 ha) followed by Germany and Austria which each have fewer than 1,000 ha. It is also grown in California (680 ha), Bulgaria, Italy and Romania. New Zealand has 159 ha. Traminer has been grown in Australia for some time, mainly in NSW; however, the area increased from less than 100 ha in the early 1970s to peak at 750 ha in 1987. Since that time it has declined slightly to 614 ha. Although generally considered to be a variety most suited to cool climatic regions, it is mainly planted in the hot inland regions of Australia, e.g. Big Rivers (NSW) (49%) and Lower Murray (SA) (12%). Yield is usually low although good yields have been reported from hot regions with intensive irrigation. The small compact bunches have a short peduncle and are borne close to the base of the shoot, making hand-harvest difficult. There is marked clonal variation within the variety with respect to aromatic character and berry colour, which ranges from white to red. The pink and red clones tend to be more aromatic and, in Alsace, were originally distinguished as Gewürztraminer (although gewürz is German for 'spice', it really means 'perfumed' in this context [Robinson 1986]). Today, Gewürztraminer is more commonly used as a synonym for Traminer, irrespective of clone. [Kerridge and Antcliff 1999, p. 171].

Trebbiano

Trebbiano is the leading white winegrape in Italy (60,000 ha) where it is more specifically known as Trebbiano Toscano to distinguish it from several other varieties also called Trebbiano. Recent DNA research has indicated that all varieties named Trebbiano are genetically different. It is also the most important white variety in France (95,000 ha), and is mainly planted in Cognac (where it is known as St Emilion), Provence, Bordeaux and Armagnac. The official French name is Ugni Blanc. Elsewhere in the world it is a relatively minor variety, with plantings in South Africa, California and Argentina. Saint Emilion, White Hermitage and White Shiraz are invalid synonyms in Australia. In Australia, the planted area (677 ha) halved during the 1990s: 77% is found in Big Rivers (NSW). Trebbiano is a productive variety that bursts late. Young shoots are susceptible to wind damage. The thick-skinned berries resist rain damage but it juices badly when machine-harvested. Pruning is normally to spurs. It is very susceptible to rootknot nematodes. In Australia, Trebbiano is mainly used for the production of well-balanced, neutral table wines suitable for blending with more fruity types, and for fortified wines. It is also used for good quality brandy spirit. [Kerridge and Antcliff 1999, p. 173].

Viognier

Viognier is a minor variety of the northern Rhone (France). In Condrieu it is used alone for a dry white table wine, but in the red wine of Cote Rotie it may be blended with Shiraz. During the 1990s it has become one of the world's most fashionable varieties. Within France, it has spread to the south where there are now more than 1,000 ha in Languedoc-Roussillon alone. In California, the state total increased from a few hectares in 1988 to more than 500 ha by the late 1990s. Australia has been no exception to this international trend and by 2002 there were 458 ha, mainly in South Australia. It has low to moderate vigour and productivity. Budburst is early and ripening is midseason. It is more tolerant of berry splitting and bunch rot than most varieties. Although traditionally cane-pruned, it has been successfully spur-pruned in Australia. It appears to be very sensitive to magnesium deficiency and primary bud necrosis. The wine is potentially of high quality with a distinct varietal character of apricot and peach so long as fruit is harvested when fully ripe. [Kerridge and Antcliff 1999, p. 179].

Waltham Cross (Rosaki)

Waltham Cross is principally a tablegrape although it is also dried for raisins. It is widely grown throughout the world including the south of France (where it is called Dattier de Beyrouth), Italy (as Regina), the Middle East, South Africa and California. The preferred international name is Rosaki. About 40% of production is dried in Australia: 20% is used as tablegrapes and the remainder used for winemaking, mainly distillation. In Australia (287 ha), it is mainly grown in North West Victoria (64%). The large, oval berries have a crisp, firm texture with a neutral but pleasant flavour and, although seeded, the seed number per berry is low. The presence of small seedless ('chicken') berries and the tendency to shatter are disadvantages (see Volume II, Chapter 12).

6.2.2 BLACK- AND RED-BERRIED VARIETIES

Barbera

Barbera is one of the world's most widely planted grape varieties. It is one of the most important black winegrape varieties in Italy (50,000 ha), with production centred in Piedmont where it accounts for about 50% of the planted area. In the north of Italy it is likely to be the major component of a wine but in central and southern Italy it is likely to be blended with two or more other varieties. It is also important in California (4,900 ha), particularly in the hot San Joaquin Valley, and there are several thousand hectares in Argentina. The Australian area is 182 ha, with the largest plantings in Big Rivers (NSW) (29%) and North East Victoria (19%). The fruit hangs well on the vine, retaining a high acidity even under hot conditions (Kerridge et al. 1987a). Barbera wines from moderately cropped vines are usually modestly well coloured and astringent. In hot climates in Australia wines tend to lack colour and age rapidly, and in cool regions acid may be excessively high (Kerridge et al. 1987a). It may be spur- or cane-pruned, readily mechanically harvested and shows some sensitivity to bunch rot (McKay et al. 1999). [Kerridge and Antcliff 1999, p. 11].

Cabernet Franc

Cabernet Franc is an important variety in France (31,000 ha) but it has been overshadowed by the growth of Cabernet Sauvignon during the past three decades. In the Loire, it is still the most important variety. However, in Bordeaux, there are now more than two vines of Cabernet Sauvignon for every one of Cabernet Franc. In Italy (6,000 ha), it is more highly regarded than Cabernet Sauvignon and planted in more regions. It is also important in eastern Europe. There are 1,100 ha in California (mainly Napa and Sonoma). Since the early 1990s it has been increasingly planted in Argentina and Chile. New Zealand has 156 ha. In Australia, prior to the 1970s, Cabernet Franc was mostly found as odd vines in blocks of Cabernet Sauvignon, a situation common in North Eastern Victoria. The area more than doubled during the 1990s: there are now 873 ha. It is widely grown with the largest areas in South West (WA) (24%) and Limestone Coast (SA) (13%). Cabernet Franc is better suited to cool climates than Cabernet Sauvignon: budburst and ripening are earlier. It is also more tolerant of winter injury than most vinifera varieties and for this reason has become popular in New York (USA) and Canada. Cabernet Franc is more productive than Cabernet Sauvignon, but does not always attain the yields of Merlot, to which it bears a strong morphological resemblance. The wines of Cabernet Franc are of high quality with a distinct varietal character and are softer than Cabernet Sauvignon, with which it is often blended (Kerridge et al. 1987a). [Kerridge and Antcliff 1999, p. 23]

Durif

Durif originates from the Rhone Valley of France; however it is no longer recommended and the area is declining. It appears to be a seedling of Peloursin, the male parent being Shiraz (Meredith et al. 1999). In fact, the old plantings of Durif in North East Victoria were a mix of Durif and Peloursin; this is also the case for the so-called Petite Sirah of California (1,100 ha). In Australia (463 ha), it is mainly grown in Big Rivers (NSW) (57%) and North East Victoria (27%). Durif produces wines of intense colour and high tannin In Australia it is used for red table wine and port. [Kerridge and Antcliff 1999, p. 55].

Frontignac

Frontignac has many synonyms in commercial use throughout the world. Muscat à Petits Grains is the official name for this variety and means 'muscat with small berries'. Both words Frontignan and Frontignac have been widely used in Australia as synonyms and while the former is unacceptable to the Office International de la Vigne et du Vin, the latter is not and hence is recommended. It is one of the oldest varieties, being well known to the Romans. Three colour variants exist: white, red and black. The variants mutate readily from one to the other and there seems to be two types of white, one which is stable and one which mutates readily to the coloured forms (Antcliff 1979). The stable white form is most common in Europe. In France (6,000 ha), where the white form predominates, it is grown in the south (Frontignan, Banyuls, etc.) where it is used for sweet fortified wine, and in Alsace for table wine. It is widespread in Italy (14,000 ha) as Moscato Bianco, and its end-uses include Asti Spumante. It is also grown in other European countries, for example, Greece. Most of the Muskadel, as the variety is known in South Africa, is the red form (Orffer 1979) but only the white form seems to be grown in California and Argentina. In Australia, 35% of the total area of 650 ha comprises the white form. During the 1990s, the area of the white form decreased while that of the coloured forms increased. Sixty per cent of the white form is grown in South Australia, particularly the Barossa (25%) and Lower Murray (24%). The coloured forms are most common in North East Victoria (34%) where the variety is known as Brown Muscat. It has moderate vigour and yield. Spur pruning is most common. If left on the vine, the fruit wilts to give a very high sugar concentration: this is no doubt one of the reasons for its use for sweet fortified wines, known as 'muscats'. It is also used for white table wine with a distinctive muscat flavour. [Kerridge and Antcliff 1999, p. 111].

Malbec

Malbec comes from the west of France where it is known as Cot. The area in France (5,000 ha) has more than halved since the early 1960s, mainly because of low productivity. It is grown near and to the east of Bordeaux, and in the Loire Valley. Argentina has the largest area of Malbec (10,000 ha): there it is the most important black variety in terms of wine quality. Chile has 640 ha and there are small areas in California (150 ha), northern Italy and New Zealand (110 ha). The Australian area (496 ha) more than doubled during the 1990s. More than 60% is found in South Australia, particularly Lower Murray (17%), Limestone Coast (16%) and Fleurieu (11%). There is also a significant area in the South West of WA (15%). The situation in Australia has been confused because at least two other varieties, Dolcetto and Tinta Amarella, have sometimes been incorrectly called Malbec in the past. Malbec is notorious for its irregular cropping due to poor set; however, this problem has been partly overcome by the use of improved clones and appropriate choice of rootstocks. It is easily harvested by machine. Malbec usually has good colour and tannin, and is often blended with Cabernet Sauvignon and/or Shiraz. [Kerridge and Antcliff 1999, p. 83].

Meunier

Meunier is a 'sport' (mutation) of Pinot Noir. Commercial plantings in Australia are often a mix of the two varieties due to the genetic instability of Meunier. The greatest area of the variety is in France (11,000 ha), and mainly in the Champagne region where it makes up 40% of the planted area. It is one of the few black winegrapes grown in Germany (2,300 ha) where it is called Schwarzriesling or Müllerrebe. In Australia (169 ha), where it is often known as Pinot Meunier, it is mainly confined to cool zones, for example, Mount Lofty Ranges (SA) (20%), Western Victoria (15%) and parts of North East Victoria (14%). It is preferred to Pinot Noir in frost-prone sites because it has slightly later budburst. Fruitset and yield may be higher than Pinot Noir. In France, Meunier is blended with Pinot Noir and Chardonnay for champagne. In Australia it is used for sparkling wine in the same way, but traditionally has also been used for attractive, light, dry red wines. [Kerridge and Antcliff 1999, p. 97].

Nebbiolo

Nebbiolo originated in Piedmont, Italy where it is used for the high quality wines of Barolo and Barbaresco. There are small areas in Switzerland, Argentina, Mexico, California and Australia (102 ha). It has not been successful in cool regions in Australia because productivity may be low and ripening is late. It is susceptible to poor set but moderately productive. Due to poor basal bud fruitfulness, it is best cane-pruned. There are many clones in Italy with a high degree of variability (McKay et al. 1999). In Australia it is mainly grown in Fleurieu (SA) (14%), Barossa (SA) (12%) and North West Victoria (10%). Wines may have high

alcohol and tannin but often only moderate colour (this variety has low malvidin pigment content relative to Cabernet Sauvignon or Shiraz). [Kerridge and Antcliff 1999, p. 185].

Sangiovese

Sangiovese is perhaps the leading wine grape of Italy. Probably indigenous to Tuscany (42,000 ha), it is now grown throughout Italy (including Sicily) where it is used in many red wines of controlled appellation, sometimes alone (for example, Brunello di Montalcino) but more often blended with other varieties (for example, Chianti). There are several thousand hectares in Argentina. The plantings in both USA (mainly California with 1,175 ha) and Australia (660 ha) increased significantly during the 1990s. It is mainly grown in North West Victoria (19%), Fleurieu (SA) (14%) and Big Rivers (NSW) (13%). It is a vigorous variety that ripens at about the same time as Shiraz. Wine colour is sensitive to cropping level. It is suitable for mechanical harvesting and may be either spur- or cane-pruned. There is considerable morphological variability between clones (McKay et al. 1999). [Kerridge and Antcliff 1999, p. 139].

Tarrango

Tarrango was bred in Australia by the CSIRO and released in 1975. A cross of Touriga and Sultana, it is used for light-bodied, fast-maturing red table wines. The Australian area is 151 ha, mainly grown in the hot regions along the River Murray. It is productive and the fruit ripens late with good acidity and low pH (Kerridge et al. 1987b). Cane or minimal pruning should be used due to the low fruitfulness of basal buds. [Kerridge and Antcliff 1999, p. 159].

Tempranillo

Tempranillo is widely grown throughout Spain where there may be more than 70,000 ha. It is the major component of the best red wines of Rioja and Ribera del Duero. In Portugal, where it is known as Tinta Roriz, it is one of the favoured port varieties. There are more than 2,000 ha in the south of France, and it may be grown in Italy as Negretto. Argentina has a large area as Tempranilla. In California (220 ha) it was formerly called Valdepenas. There is increasing interest in Australia: fifty per cent of the 163 ha were non-bearing in 2002. The largest areas are found in North West Victoria (14%), Big Rivers (NSW) (14%), Central Victoria (13%) and Fleurieu (SA) (12%). Because maturity is early midseason, it can ripen successfully in many cool regions. It has relatively large berries for a black winegrape variety and yield control may be necessary to achieve good wine quality. It may be spur-pruned and has good drought tolerance. [Kerridge and Antcliff 1999, p. 161].

Zante Currant (Currant)

Currant is a traditional drying variety. However, up to 15% of the production may be used for other purposes: for example, 1,600 tonnes were crushed for wine in 2001 in Australia. Despite its very small berry size, it is also occasionally used as a tablegrape because it has very early maturity and is seedless. It is an important variety in the Mediterranean region: Greece produces most of the world's dried currants followed by Australia, California (where it is known as Black Corinth) and South Africa. About half of Australia's plantings (879 ha) are found in North West Victoria. In the past there were significant plantings in the Barossa, Adelaide Plains, Clare, McLaren Vale (SA) and Swan Valley (WA) regions. The planted area has declined substantially since the 1970s. Moderately productive, it is spur-pruned, and is susceptible to poor set, powdery mildew, sunburn and berry splitting after rain (see Volume II, Chapter 14).

6.3 Varieties with less than 100 ha

6.3.1 WHITE-BERRIED VARIETIES

Arneis

Arneis is a minor variety of Piedmont, Italy where it has undergone a modest revival since the 1970s. It has low yield and is very susceptible to powdery mildew. The white table wines have low acidity and a distinctive aroma of almonds and peaches (McKay et al. 1999).

Biancone

Biancone is a high yielding variety from Corsica, mainly grown in the Riverland (SA). Previously known as White Grenache, it was correctly identified in the 1970s. Apart from its high yield, it has no great merit even though some winemakers claim it is useful for dry white wine. [Kerridge and Antcliff 1999, p. 17].

Calmeria

Calmeria is a late ripening, white, seeded tablegrape. It was selected from a seedling of Ohanez (Almeria) in California in 1939. Mainly grown in the Sunraysia (Vic. and NSW) and Swan Hill-Kerang (Vic.) regions, it is suitable for export (see Volume II, Chapter 12).

Canada Muscat

Canada Muscat is a *vinifera-labrusca* hybrid (Muscat Hamburg x Hubbard), first grown commercially in Ontario, Canada. In Australia (83 ha), it is mainly grown in the hot inland regions. It is moderately productive and early ripening. An excellent juice variety, it is also used for wine as a blender. If harvested early, it has a pleasant flavour of tropical fruit (Kerridge et al. 1987c).

Cañocazo

Cañocazo was known for many years as False Pedro in South Australia and Common Palomino in Victoria before being identified as Cañocazo. A minor Spanish variety, it is no longer authorised for planting in that country. It produces neutral wine and has mainly been used in Australia for fortified wines and distillation. [Kerridge and Antcliff 1999, p. 29].

Cannon Hall Muscat

Cannon Hall Muscat is grown almost exclusively in the Swan Valley (WA). Originally an English greenhouse variety it is mostly used as a tablegrape for both the local and export markets. It is a seeded, early to mid-season grape, with a distinctive muscat character (see Volume II, Chapter 12).

Chasselas

Chasselas is the principal variety in Switzerland where it is mainly used for white table wine. It is also used for winemaking in Alsace (France), Germany, Austria, Romania, Hungary, Moldova, Ukraine and New Zealand. It is an important tablegrape in Europe, particularly in France and Italy. The Australian area is small: in Victoria it is used for white table wine and in NSW and WA as a tablegrape. Although its quality as a tablegrape is not high, it matures very early and thereby attracts reasonable prices. In cool regions, Chasselas is used to produce table wine without pronounced varietal character. In hot regions, the fruit is too low in both sugar and acid to be satisfactory for winemaking. [Kerridge and Antcliff 1999, p. 37].

Clairette

Clairette is an important variety in the south of France (3,500 ha) where much of the white table wine is a blend of this variety and Trebbiano. It is also grown in South Africa (1,400 ha). In France it is sometimes known as Blanquette and this name has been used in NSW. In Australia, most plantings are found in the Hunter Valley (NSW) and in North East Victoria. Clairette is a vigorous variety with the young shoots susceptible to wind damage in spring. Although prone to poor set, it is tolerant of powdery mildew and bunch rot. [Kerridge and Antcliff 1999, p. 43].

Dourado

Dourado originates from Portugal. It appears to be the same as the variety known as 'False Pedro' in South Africa. In Australia, it has been variously known as Pedro, Rutherglen Pedro or Pedro Ximenes in error. Small plantings are found in the Riverina (NSW) and Rutherglen (Vic.) regions where it has been mainly used for fortified wines. It is productive but susceptible to downy mildew and bunch rot. [Kerridge and Antcliff 1999, p. 53].

Farana

Farana is a variety of Mediterranean origin, known as Planta Pedralba in Spain, Mayorquin in France, Damaschino in Sicily and Farana in Algeria. In Australia, a little is grown in the Barossa (SA) where it was formerly known as False Trebbiano. Yield is very high. It is used for both table and fortified wine. [Kerridge and Antcliff 1999, p. 59].

Italia

Italia is a tablegrape variety derived from a cross between Bicane and Muscat Hamburg. It has been planted widely in southern Europe and California. In Australia the largest plantings are in the Swan Valley (WA) and in Queensland. The berries are large, attractive, yellow-white with a pleasant muscat flavour. It is susceptible to fungal diseases (see Volume 2, Chapter 12).

Müller-Thurgau

Müller-Thurgau is the second most important winegrape of Germany with 20,600 ha. Although grown elsewhere in Europe (Hungary 8,000 ha; Austria 4,400 ha; Czechoslovakia 5,000 ha), it is not important in France. It was the major winegrape in New Zealand, in spite of its susceptibility to bunch rot, but the area declined substantially in the 1990s. For many years Müller-Thurgau was thought to be a hybrid of Riesling and Sylvaner (hence the use of the synonym Riesling Sylvaner in New Zealand) but recent DNA research suggests that it may be a cross of Riesling and Chasselas de Courtillier. It is not grown extensively in Australia. It is well suited to cool regions because it ripens very early, and recovers well after frost (the secondary buds are fruitful). However, it is very susceptible to fungal diseases and winter freeze damage. The table wines of Müller-Thurgau are pleasant and fruity, but not distinguished. [Kerridge and Antcliff 1999, p. 107].

Ohanez

Ohanez is a late-maturing, white tablegrape suitable for cold-storage and export. Also known as Almeria, it has male-sterile flowers and adequate pollination is necessary to produce a crop (see Calmeria). Spain produces and exports large quantities of Ohanez but it appears to be of minor importance elsewhere. In Australia, it is mainly grown at Swan Hill (Vic.): smaller plantings are found in other tablegrape producing regions. It is a vigorous variety, often grown on an overhead (pergola) trellis. Cropping is more reliable when cane-pruned (see Volume II, Chapter 12).

Ondenc

Ondenc is a minor French variety grown in the south-west of France under different names which were not recognised as belonging to the same variety until relatively recently, e.g. Piquepoul de Moissac in Armagnac

and Blanquette in Bordeaux. The situation in Australia has been similarly confused because, until recently, it was known as Irvine's White in Victoria and Sercial in South Australia (Antcliff 1976). In the mid-1970s there were about 250 ha planted but today the area is probably only 20 ha or so. It has been used successfully for sparkling wine in Australia. [Kerridge and Antcliff 1999, p. 117].

Orange Muscat

Said to be the Moscato Fior d'Arancio of Italy, it was introduced to Australia in the late 20th century via California. The berries have a distinctive orange colour and strong muscat character at maturity. It is grown in some regions in preference to Muscat Gordo Blanco because the fruit is less susceptible to sunburn, it ripens earlier and the table wine is better.

Perlette

Perlette is an early, white, seedless tablegrape. It is a hybrid of Muscat Reine des Vignes and Thompson Seedless (Sultana) from California where it is grown on a large scale. Most of the Australian plantings are found in NSW. Cane pruning is usually required to obtain satisfactory yields (see Volume II, Chapter 12).

Pinot Blanc

Pinot Blanc is a white-fruited form of Pinot Noir. It is a minor but widespread variety in central and eastern Europe, grown as Weisser Burgunder in Germany (2,396 ha) and Pinot Bianco in north-eastern Italy. It is not important in the New World. In some countries it has been confused with Chardonnay and Melon. The small area in Australia is restricted to the cool regions.

Rkaziteli (Rkatsiteli)

In terms of world production, this is a major variety (**TABLE** 6.1) as a result of extensive plantings in eastern Europe. It is said to originate from Georgia. There is a small area in North West Victoria and Lower Murray (SA). Only moderately productive, it is generally used for table wine (Kerridge et al. 1987d). [Kerridge and Antcliff 1999, p. 133].

Roussanne

A minor variety from the Rhone Valley, it is often blended with Marsanne. In France (300 ha) it is now mainly grown in Herault and Vaucluse. There are also small areas in Italy, California and Australia. Neither vigorous nor productive, it is sensitive to powdery mildew and bunch rot. It ripens mid- to late season and the full-bodied wines have distinctive honey, floral and apricot flavours. [Kerridge and Antcliff 1999, p. 189].

Sylvaner

Sylvaner is widely grown throughout central and eastern Europe: Germany has the largest area (6,900 ha). It is not widely grown in the New World. There are a few small plantings in Australia but the variety has not been accepted to any extent because of the indifferent quality of its wines here (Kerridge et al. 1988). It is high yielding but susceptible to fungal diseases. [Kerridge and Antcliff 1999, p. 155]

Taminga

Taminga is an Australian variety bred by the CSIRO at Merbein. A cross of (Planta Pedralba x Sultana) x Traminer, it is a high yielding, aromatic white winegrape, particularly suited to hot climatic regions. [Kerridge and Antcliff 1999, p. 157]

Tocai Friulano

Although this variety probably originated in France (where it is known as Sauvignonasse), it has almost disappeared in that country. The largest plantings are now found in Chile (more than 5,000 ha) where it has been erroneously called Sauvignon Blanc. This confusion is not surprising because it appears to be related to Sauvignon Blanc. The preferred synonym, Tocai Friulano, is the name by which it is known in Italy where it is important in the northeast. It is widespread in Australia but mainly in old plantings of other varieties in NSW and Victoria. [Kerridge and Antcliff 1999, p. 167]

Vernaccia di San Gimignano

This is the best known of the 'family' of Vernaccia varieties found in Italy. It is used for white wines in Tuscany (McKay et al. 1999). However, limited Australian experience indicates that the variety is difficult to grow and the wines lack character.

6.3.2 BLACK- AND RED-BERRIED VARIETIES

Alicante Bouschet

Alicante Bouschet is a cross of Petit Bouschet and Grenache. It has red juice, and has been used to improve the colour of low-priced red wines in the Mediterranean basin since the 19th century. It is no longer recommended in France and the area continues to decline.

Bastardo

Bastardo is considered one of the better port varieties in Portugal, although it is not as widely grown as Touriga or Tinta Amarella. It is also grown in the east of France under the name Trousseau. The area in Australia is small: there is some in South Australia where it was previously called Cabernet Gros and a little in northeast Victoria. The fruit attains a high sugar concentration as the berries wilt. It is susceptible to rain damage. Although Bastardo has been used in Australia for red table wine it is best suited for fortified wines. [Kerridge and Antcliff 1999, p. 13]

Bonvedro

Bonvedro was incorrectly called Carignan in Australia until the 1970s. It is a Portuguese variety also grown in northeast Spain as Cuatendra. In Australia, all but a few hectares are located in South Australia, mostly in the Barossa. The area has declined since the 1970s. It is more susceptible to disease, frost and drought than comparable varieties such as Mataro. Table wines from Bonvedro are low in colour and tannin. [Kerridge and Antcliff 1999, p. 19].

Cardinal

Cardinal is a tablegrape from California. A hybrid of Flame Tokay and Ribier, it is important in California, France, Spain, Italy, Romania and Bulgaria. It is one of the earliest coloured tablegrapes (see Volume II, Chapter 12). Curiously, it is reputed to be the basis of the wine industries of Thailand and Vietnam.

Carignan

Carignan is one of the most important winegrapes in the world (**TABLE** 6.1). In France, it still occupies more than 10% of the planted area even though large areas have been removed since the 1970s. It is planted entirely in the south: in Languedoc-Roussillon, one-third of all vines are Carignan. It is also an important variety in Spain (8,000 ha) and in Algeria. Outside of Europe and North Africa, the only significant plantings are found in California (3,100 ha) and Chile. The Australian area is small (73 ha) and mainly confined to the Lower Murray (SA) (75%). It has an erect growth habit and is often grown without trellising in France and Spain (see Grenache). Carignan is more susceptible to fungal diseases, particularly powdery mildew, than most varieties, and does best in a hot, sunny, dry climate where high yields are possible. Carignan gives wines of moderate colour, good tannin and no pronounced varietal character (Kerridge et al. 1987b). [Kerridge and Antcliff 1999, p. 31].

Carina

Carina was bred in Australia by the CSIRO and released for commercial use in 1975. It is a small black seedless grape, suitable for drying into currants. It has the distinct advantage over Zante Currant in that it is resistant to rain damage when the fruit is ripening (see Volume II, Chapter 14).

Chambourcin

Chambourcin is a complex 'French hybrid', released in France in 1963. Although there is still a small area in France, it is more extensively grown elsewhere, e.g. eastern USA. The area in Australia is small but it does have potential in regions with high growing-season rainfall, e.g. northern NSW and Qld. It is very productive, has good resistance to fungal diseases and moderate resistance to phylloxera. The wine is more *vinifera*-like than most hybrids with good colour and varietal character. [Kerridge and Antcliff 1999, p. 33].

Cienna

Cienna is a black winegrape variety bred in Australia by the CSIRO. A cross of Sumoll and Cabernet Sauvignon, it was released for commercial evaluation in the late 1990s.

Cinsaut

Cinsaut is a variety from the south of France (45,000 ha). Sometimes spelt Cinsault, it is often confused with another distinct variety Oeillade. Occasionally used as a tablegrape, it is regarded as a good winegrape in the south where it is recommended for blending with Carignan. Formerly known as Hermitage in South Africa (3,700 ha), it was the principal red wine variety until the mid-1990s (see Cabernet Sauvignon) but the planted area has declined since the late 1980s. There are 3,000 ha in southern Italy as Ottavianello. Cinsaut has declined in importance in Australia: most of the remaining vines are located in the Barossa (SA), North East Victoria and Big Rivers (NSW). It is well adapted to hot, dry conditions. Although susceptible to fungal diseases, the fruit is not easily split by rain when ripe. In Australia it is used for red table wine and port of average quality, often blended with more tannic varieties. [Kerridge and Antcliff 1999, p. 41].

Cornichon

Cornichon is more correctly known as Olivette Noire. In the tablegrape trade in Australia it is more commonly called Purple Cornichon or Black Lady's Fingers. It is grown in the hottest areas of France and is the last black tablegrape on the market. The bunches are very attractive with deep purple berries with thick tough skins. While the berries stand up well to transport they are predisposed to shattering. It is very susceptible to downy mildew (see Volume II, Chapter 12).

Dolcetto

Dolcetto is an important variety in the Piedmont region of Italy (10,000 ha). Little is grown in other parts of Italy or in other countries. The area in Australia is small but was larger in the past. Some old plantings of Dolcetto in Victoria were incorrectly called 'Malbec'. It is an early-ripening variety used for red table wine (McKay et al. 1999). [Kerridge and Antcliff 1999, p. 49].

Emperor

Emperor is a late-ripening red tablegrape suitable for cold storage and export. Although not particularly important in Europe, it is a major tablegrape in California where 90% of production comes from the San Joaquin Valley. Sometimes known as Red Emperor, the berries are light red to reddish-purple with firm texture and tough skins. It is the main storage variety in California, being kept in cold storage for up to six months (See Volume II, Chapter 12).

Gamay

Gamay is an important variety in France (34,000 ha). More than half is grown in Beaujolais where it is the only variety permitted in the red wine of that appellation. The remainder is in other parts of Burgundy and in the Loire. It is also grown in the north of Italy, Slovenia and Croatia. The area in Australia is very small. It should not be confused with Napa Gamay (see Valdiguie) nor the so-called 'Gamay Beaujolais' (a clone of Pinot Noir introduced from California). It is very fruitful, recovers well after frost, but prone to overcropping and bunch rot. Gamay is used for light-bodied red table wine, usually consumed early (Kerridge et al. 1987b). [Kerridge and Antcliff 1999, p. 69].

Graciano

A variety of Spanish origin, it is an important component in the high quality red wines of Rioja and Navarra. Although the production is small, there has been renewed interest in recent times stimulated by high prices. In France, where it is known as Morrastel, it is recommended in the south. The area in Australia is small. It has erect growth, late budburst, and is tolerant of both drought and powdery mildew. The wine has good colour and tannin. [Kerridge and Antcliff 1999, p. 73].

Jacquez

This appears to be a natural hybrid of *Vitis aestivalis* and *Vitis vinifera*. It is thought to have originated in southeast USA but it is not widely grown in that country. Due to its phylloxera resistance, it has been used as a rootstock in both France and South Africa. Usually known as Troya in Australia, there are small plantings in Big Rivers (NSW). It is resistant to fungal diseases. [Kerridge and Antcliff 1999, p. 81].

Lagrein

Lagrein is a minor variety from the Trentino-Alto Adige region of Italy where it is used to produce well-coloured wines with low tannin. There is a small area in Victoria (Kerridge et al. 1987a).

Marroo Seedless

Marroo Seedless is a black, seedless tablegrape bred in Australia by the CSIRO. A cross of Carolina Blackrose and Ruby Seedless, it was released for commercial evaluation in the early 1980s. It has medium berries (produced without the use of gibberellic acid; see Volume II, Chapter 12) and is resistant to downy mildew.

Marzemino

A variety originating from north-east Italy, it is used for early-drinking red table wines (Kerridge et al. 1987a). There is a small area in the King Valley.

Mondeuse

A minor variety from eastern France, there is a small area in North East Victoria. It is productive, ripens late, has good acid in hot climates, and is tolerant of fungal diseases and rain damage. Wines have good colour and tannin. [Kerridge and Antcliff 1999, p. 101].

Muscat Hamburg

Muscat Hamburg is a specialist tablegrape with a strong muscat flavour. Grown widely throughout southern Europe, it is the second most popular tablegrape in France. In Australia, it is most important in Queensland where it is popular with growers because it is tolerant of rain damage. Not a particularly good shipping variety, it is mostly grown fairly close to the principal market outlets (see Volume II Chapter 12).

Pinot Gris

This variety differs from Pinot Noir only in that it has less pigment in the skin. However it is normally used to make white table wine with a golden colour. There are 1,000 ha in France, mainly in Alsace (where the wine is labelled 'Tokay'). It is more important in Germany (2,600 ha) as Ruländer and in northern Italy (2,200 ha) as Pinot Grigio, and widely distributed in central and southeastern Europe. There are 219 ha in New Zealand. [Kerridge and Antcliff 1999, p. 127].

Red Prince

Red Prince is a table variety, mainly grown in Western Australia. The berries are large, red and firm-fleshed. Berry thinning is necessary to produce an export-quality product (see Volume II, Chapter 12).

Ribier

Ribier is a table variety grown in most of the tablegrape-producing regions of Australia. It performs well in Queensland. The berries are large and black (see Volume II, Chapter 12).

Rubienne

Rubienne is a black, winegrape variety bred in Australia by the CSIRO. A cross of Sumoll and Cabernet Sauvignon, it was released for commercial evaluation in the late 1990s.

Rubired

Rubired is a hybrid of Tinta Cao and Alicante Ganzin. It was bred in California and released in 1958; there, by the late 1990s, it had reached 4,300 ha. Having red juice, it produces wines of intense colour. This has prompted its use as colouring material for table wines. The *Vitis rupestris* ancestry of Alicante Ganzin has resulted in Rubired possessing some resistance to fungal diseases. [Kerridge and Antcliff 1999, p. 135].

Saperavi

Saperavi is a variety from the Russian Federation where it is the main red wine variety. There are small areas in north-east Victoria and the Adelaide Hills. The juice is coloured. It can potentially produce high quality wines of good colour and tannin (Kerridge et al. 1987a).

Souzao

Souzão (or Sousão) is a Portugese variety. In the Douro Valley, it is used for port and for dry table wine in other regions. One of its chief characteristics is the intense colour of its wines, usually blended with other varieties. It has moderate yield, and ripens late. [Kerridge and Antcliff 1999, p. 101].

Tannat

Tannat is a minor French variety from the southwest where it is typically blended with other varieties. Outside of France it is only important in Uruguay. As its name suggests, the well-coloured wines are characterised by high levels of tannins (Kerridge et al. 1987a). Wine quality is potentially high.

Tinta Amarella

Tinta Amarella is grown in the Douro Valley, Portugal where it is regarded as a good variety for port. It is also used in southern Portugal for red table wine. There is a small area in South Australia (mainly the Barossa, where it has been known as Portugal in the past). It is usually blended with other varieties for port production. [Kerridge and Antcliff 1999, p. 165].

Touriga

Touriga Nacional is the most widely planted, and most favoured, of the port varieties of the Douro Valley, Portugal. Known as Touriga in Australia (77 ha), it is principally grown in the Barossa (SA) (24%) and North East Victoria (14%). It produces fortified wines of excellent quality and shows promise as a table wine variety. [Kerridge and Antcliff 1999, p. 169].

Tyrian

Tyrian is a black, winegrape variety bred in Australia by the CSIRO. A cross of Sumoll and Cabernet Sauvignon, it was released for commercial evaluation in the late 1990s.

Vermilion

Vermilion is a black, winegrape variety bred in Australia by the CSIRO. A cross of Sumoll and Cabernet Sauvignon, it was released for commercial evaluation in the late 1990s.

Zinfandel

Zinfandel is the most widely-planted black winegrape in California (20,350 ha) where it is grown in all regions. DNA research has established that it is identical to a minor variety of Croatia known as Crljenak. From Croatia, it appears to have spread to Italy within the past 300 years where it became known as Primitivo (17,000 ha) and grown principally in Apulia. It is very susceptible to rain damage and bunch rot, hence its usefulness in Australia is likely to be limited to the low autumn rainfall areas. Although yields are good, it ripens unevenly and is difficult to harvest by machine. It is prone to second-cropping and the exposed fruit is likely to sunburn. Zinfandel can produce good quality red wines with a distinct varietal character. [Kerridge and Antcliff 1999, p. 181].

6.3 Concluding remarks

For the first 150 years Australia's viticulture was primarily based on initial introductions of varieties from southern France and Spain. These suited the predominant use of grapes during this time, that is, fortified wine production and dried fruit. The advent of phylloxera forced the introduction of resistant rootstocks at the end of the nineteenth century, but no significant change was made to the range of *vinifera* varieties. The big shift in demand to table wines from the 1960s led to the diversion of some varieties from their former use and the planting of available table wine varieties, often unsuited for this purpose. Further introduction of many varieties during this period led to the evaluation and adoption of a significant number which have proved well-suited to Australian conditions, both for table wine and as tablegrapes. During the 1990s there has been a further wave of introductions as interest in varieties from Italy, Spain and eastern European countries has increased. It is likely that one or more of the following varieties will become commercially important in Australia in the future: Aghiorghitiko, Aglianico, Albariño, Areni, Bogazkerei, Cortese, Corvina, Fiano, Gargenega, Godello, Grechetto, Grüner Veltliner, Limnio, Louriero, Montepulciano, Nero d'Avola, Petit Manseng, Prosecco, Sagrantino, Teroldego, Torrontes, Trajadura, Verdejo, Veronese, Verdicchio, Verduzzo, Xynomavro.

REFERENCES

Suggestions for further reading are marked (•).

Antcliff, A.J. (1975) A probable identification of Clare Riesling. Aust. Grapegrower & Winemaker No. 141, 16-17.

Antcliff, A.J. (1976) Variety identification in Australia. A French expert looks at our vines. Aust. Grapegrower & Winemaker No. 153, 10-11.

Antcliff, A.J. (1979) Major Wine Grape Varieties of Australia (CSIRO: Adelaide).

Antcliff, A.J. (1983) Minor Wine Grape Varieties of Australia (CSIRO: Adelaide).

• Boehm, E.W. and Tulloch, H.W. (1967) Grape varieties of South Australia (SA Dept. of Agric.: Adelaide).

• Clarke, O. and Rand, M. (2001) Grapes and Wines (Websters Int. Publ.: London).

Clingeleffer, P.R. (1983) Sultana vine management. Aust. Grapegrower & Winemaker No. 232, 7-17.

Dry, P.R., and Gregory, G.R. (1988) Grapevine Varieties. In: Viticulture Volume 1. Resources. 1st edition. Eds B.G. Coombe and P.R. Dry (Australian Industrial Publishers: Adelaide).

• Galet, P. (1979) A Practical Ampelography. Translated by L.T. Morton (Comstock Publishing Assoc.: Ithaca).

• Kerridge, G. and Antcliff, A.J. (1999) Wine Grape Varieties (CSIRO Publishing: Melbourne).

Kerridge, G.H., Clingeleffer, P.R. et al. (1987a) Varieties and varietal wines from the Merbein grape germplasm collection. I. Varieties producing full-bodied red wines. Aust. Grapegrower & Winemaker No.277, 14-18.

Kerridge, G.H., Clingeleffer, P.R. et al. (1987b) Varieties and varietal wines from the Merbein grape germplasm collection. II. Varieties producing light-bodied red wines. Aust. Grapegrower & Winemaker No. 279, 14-19.

Kerridge, G.H., Clingeleffer, P.R. et al. (1987c) Varieties and varietal wines from the Merbein grape germplasm collection. II. Varieties producing aromatic white wines. Aust. Grapegrower & Winemaker No. 280, 29-34.

Kerridge, G.H., Clingeleffer, P.R. et al. (1987d) Varieties and varietal wines from the Merbein grape germplasm collection. IV. Varieties producing delicate white wines. Aust. Grapegrower & Winemaker No. 283, 17-23.

Kerridge, G.H., Clingeleffer, P.R. et al. (1988) Varieties and varietal wines from the Merbein grape germplasm collection. V. Varieties producing full-bodied white wines Aust. Grapegrower & Winemaker No. 292, 31-35.

Meredith, C.P., Bowers, J.E. et al. (1999) The identity and parentage of the variety known in California as Petite Sirah. Am. J. Enol. Vitic. 50(3), 236-242

McKay, A.D., Crittenden, G.J. et al. (1999) Italian Winegrape Varieties in Australia - exploring the potential of Barbera, Nebbiolo, Sangiovese, Vernaccia di San Gimignano, Dolcetto and Arneis (Winetitles: Adelaide).

Nicholas, P.R. (1985) Selection of varieties and rootstocks for quality cask wine production in the Riverland. In: Irrigation, Salinity and Grape Quality: proceedings of a seminar, 1984. Eds D.C. Lester and T.D. Lee, T.D (Aust. Soc. Vitic. Oenol.: Adelaide), pp. 51-60.

Orffer, C. Ed (1979) Wine Grape Cultivars in South Africa (Human and Rousseau: Cape Town and Pretoria).

• Robinson, J. (1986) Vines, Grapes and Wines (Mitchell Beazley: UK).

Robinson, J. Ed (1999) Oxford Companion to Wine 2nd edition (Oxford University Press: UK).

Truel, P., Rennes, C. et al. (1980) Identifications in collections of grapevines. In: Proc. 3rd Int. Symp. on Grape Breeding, Davis, CA, USA (Univ. Calif.: Davis), pp. 78-86.

Winemakers Federation of Australia (2003) Vintage: The Australian Wine Industry Statistical Yearbook 2003 (Winetitles: Adelaide).

CHAPTER SEVEN

Grapevine Phenology

I. PEARCE and B.G. COOMBE

Phenology is the study of the timing of natural phenomena that recur periodically in plants and animals. It deals with records of timing and dimensions of events. The word 'phenology' is derived from the term 'phenomenon' which is defined as being anything that appears. Examples of phenological studies are investigations of the timing of stages in plant growth or in the migrations or development of insects or other animals. For grapevines, phenology refers to the timing of growth stages and the influence of climate and weather on them.

The aim of phenological studies is to describe the causes of variation in timing and duration of natural phenomena by seeking correlations with weather indices. Such information helps in the understanding of how living things react to the weather and in predicting their behaviour in new environments. From a climatological viewpoint, phenological events are considered to integrate the effect of important bioclimatic factors, and therefore act as a foundation for the interpretation of local seasons and climatic zones. In fact, phenological events recorded by man represent the oldest climatic data and predate by many centuries records from meterological instruments.

For species of plants cultivated by man for a desired end use, such as the grapevine, it is also important to understand the impact viticultural practices, in addition to climate and seasonal changes, can have on phenology. Phenological data are essential for making best practice decisions during vineyard establishment and operation, for example:

(a) vineyard establishment: including site selection, vineyard design, individual block (or patch) design within a vineyard and selection of varieties to plant.

(b) timing of routine vineyard practices: for example, pruning, soil management, irrigation, canopy and nutrition management, pest and disease monitoring, agrochemical application, harvesting etc.

(c) operating and capital budget management: for example, planning labour, equipment and cash flow requirements for the current and future seasons.

This chapter aims, first, to provide an outline of the annual growth cycle of the grapevine and to recommend a scheme to identify grapevine growth stages as development progresses, second, to present data showing variations in phenology and finally, to review current literature that examines the relationship between phenology and weather.

7.1 Annual growth cycle

The annual growth cycle of the grapevine comprises a vegetative and reproductive cycle; the sequences of events are shown in a generalised timeline in **FIGURE 7.1** and are described below.

Spring
Buds progress from post-dormancy, with visible leaf tissue marking the beginning of budburst. Following an initially slow growth of shoots after budburst there is a massive growth of vegetative tissues during late spring, which has been termed the 'grand period of growth'. Lateral shoots form readily on vigorous shoots.

150

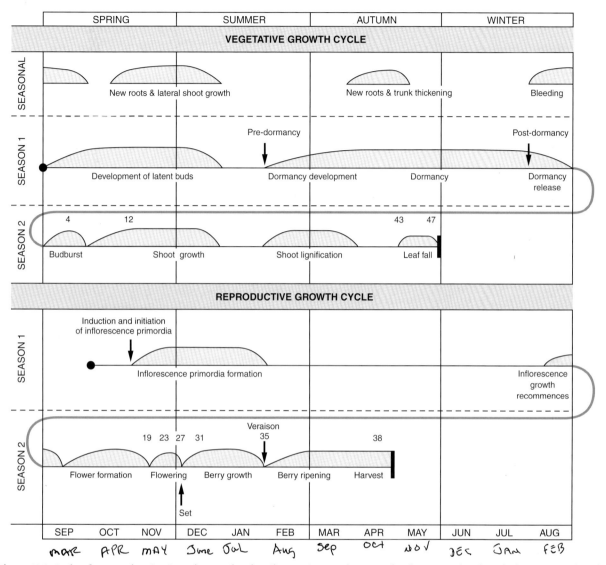

Figure 7.1 Cycle of vegetative (top) and reproductive (bottom) growth events in the grapevine in relation to months of the year (southern hemisphere). Each cycle begins at the circle and ends at the rectangle. The numbers 4 to 38 refer to the major growth stages described in FIGURE 7.3.

At budswell, and during budburst, inflorescence primordia growth resumes with further branching, branch elongation and flower formation (May 2000, May 2004). Inflorescences become visible on shoots several weeks after budburst. The inflorescences develop and single flowers form compact groups, then become separated before the flower caps begin to fade in colour. The flower caps loosen as the base of the petals detach and roll backwards. This results in the caps falling off and the stamens being released, and is termed flowering. Flowering culminates a long and slow development of the inflorescences and flowers, which begins at a similar time one year before when latent buds are formed (late spring and early summer). After induction occurs, floral initiation proceeds as anlage differentiate and undergo extensive branching over many months to form

inflorescence primordia (May 2000). Berry setting occurs late in spring in the middle of the grand period of shoot growth, and signifies the beginning of berry formation. The first major flush of root growth coincides with flowering and set.

Summer

Berry development is divided into two growth stages, which are separated by a lag phase. The first stage, *berry formation*, involves an increase in the size of the hard green berries, through cell division and enlargement, occupying 5–7 weeks. Berry growth rate then slows during the lag phase which ends with the onset of veraison and thus beginning the second growth phase, *berry ripening*. During berry ripening cell enlargement increases berry size, and sugar, anthocyanins (in coloured varieties) and aroma and flavour compounds accumulate, whilst the acid level declines (see Chapter 11, **FIGURE 11.3**). Concurrent with berry development is the slowing of shoot lengthening with the cessation of shoot tip growth during mid-summer. Latent buds, which will produce next season's shoots, enter a pre-dormant state late in summer when active bud growth is prevented mostly by correlative inhibition.

Autumn

The berry ripening period continues into autumn and coincides with the lignification of shoot stems to form canes and the abscission of some basal leaves. Harvest commences when the fruit reaches a desired composition. Latent buds progress from pre-dormancy to dormancy; this transition occurrs over a 2–3 week period coinciding with the lignification of shoots. The woody tissues, trunks and roots expand in girth, and a second flush of root growth occurs. Finally, leaves fall as winter approaches.

Winter

Buds remain dormant through winter, with the transition from dormancy to post-dormancy occurring late in winter. Lavee and May (1997) provide a detailed review of the stages of and influences on grapevine bud dormancy. They recommended that the Bugnon and Bessis (1968) naming system for parts arising from latent buds be adopted. In this system, N is the main shoot, N+1 is the lateral shoot, N+2 is the latent bud which normally produces next years shoot (but if this fails a shoot from an N+3 bud takes over) (May 2004).

These growth cycles result in large mass changes in the vine during the course of each year. The nature of fresh weight changes is illustrated in **FIGURE 7.2**; Conradie (1980) has published a similar figure based on measured values of dry mass. Castelan-Estrada et al. (2002) describe a non-destructive technique for estimating above ground vegetative and reproductive mass, using allometric regression equations. The ranges of quantities of different grapevine organs per square metre of commercial vineyards are given in **TABLE 7.1**. Over and above the annual changes, there are also long-term ageing changes in the structural roots and tops which have not been recorded.

7.2 Definition of growth stages

The identification of growth stages is critical to the study of grapevine phenology, viticulture research and vineyard operations. Four descriptive systems have been developed for grapevines to date, and are listed in chronological order.

Table 7.1 Quantities of different grapevine parts in commercial vineyards (expressed per square metre of total land surface[1]).

Part	Units	Range of commercial values		
		Low	Median	High
Pruning weight	kg per m^2	0.03	0.3	1.0
Nodes retained at pruning	nodes per m^2	3	10	30
Number of shoots	shoots per m^2	2.5	8	25
Total leaf area	m^2 per m^2	0.5	2	5
Number of bunches	bunches per m^2	5	25	50
Crop weight	kg per m^2	0.2	1.3	5
Equivalent volume of table wine	L per m^2	0.12	0.8	3

[1] *Multiplication factors to convert from amount per m^2:*
(a) x (space per vine in m^2) gives amount per vine, e.g. x 7 gives
 amount per vine in a vineyard spaced 2 x 3.5m
(b) x 4047 gives amount per acre
(c) x 10,000 gives amount per hectare

Some approximate conversion factors:

kg per m^2	x 4	gives tonnes per acre
	x 10	gives tonnes per hectare
	x 100	gives quintals per hectare (used in Italy)
L per m^2	x 4	gives kilolitres per acre
	x 10	gives kilolitres per hectare
	x 100	gives hectolitres per hectare (used in France)
hL per ha	÷ 6 to 7	gives tonnes per hectare

1. Baggiolini (1952) described 10 readily identifiable growth stages, labelled A to J, between budburst and set. The primary purpose of this scheme was to assist with the timing of agrochemical applications. The lack of descriptions for growth stages after set, prompted Baillod and Baggiolini (1993) to revise the scheme and add 6 more stages, labelled K to P. However, the successive numbering (A to P) of the 16 major stages does not allow intermediate stages to be included.

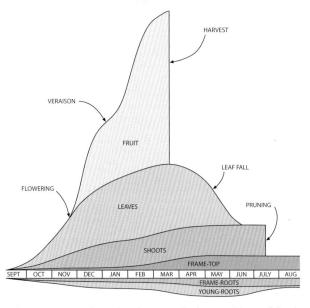

Figure 7.2 Yearly cycle of accumulation and loss of fresh matter on a mature grapevine.

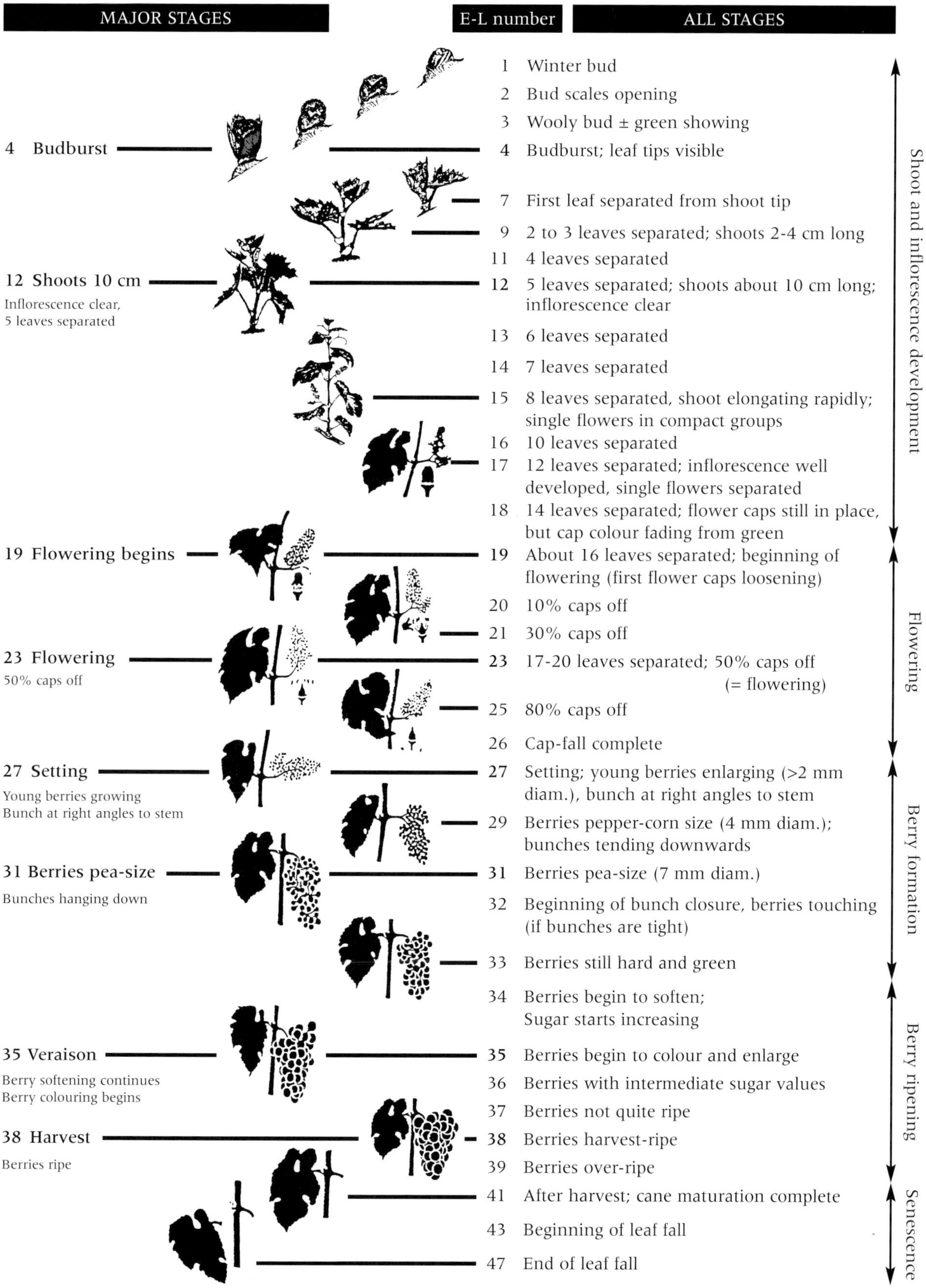
MAJOR STAGES
E-L number
ALL STAGES
4 Budburst
12 Shoots 10 cm
Inflorescence clear,
5 leaves separated
19 Flowering begins
23 Flowering
50% caps off
27 Setting
Young berries growing
Bunch at right angles to stem
31 Berries pea-size
Bunches hanging down
35 Veraison
Berry softening continues
Berry colouring begins
38 Harvest
Berries ripe
1 Winter bud
2 Bud scales opening
3 Wooly bud ± green showing
4 Budburst; leaf tips visible
7 First leaf separated from shoot tip
9 2 to 3 leaves separated; shoots 2-4 cm long
11 4 leaves separated
12 5 leaves separated; shoots about 10 cm long; inflorescence clear
13 6 leaves separated
14 7 leaves separated
15 8 leaves separated, shoot elongating rapidly; single flowers in compact groups
16 10 leaves separated
17 12 leaves separated; inflorescence well developed, single flowers separated
18 14 leaves separated; flower caps still in place, but cap colour fading from green
19 About 16 leaves separated; beginning of flowering (first flower caps loosening)
20 10% caps off
21 30% caps off
23 17-20 leaves separated; 50% caps off (= flowering)
25 80% caps off
26 Cap-fall complete
27 Setting; young berries enlarging (>2 mm diam.), bunch at right angles to stem
29 Berries pepper-corn size (4 mm diam.); bunches tending downwards
31 Berries pea-size (7 mm diam.)
32 Beginning of bunch closure, berries touching (if bunches are tight)
33 Berries still hard and green
34 Berries begin to soften; Sugar starts increasing
35 Berries begin to colour and enlarge
36 Berries with intermediate sugar values
37 Berries not quite ripe
38 Berries harvest-ripe
39 Berries over-ripe
41 After harvest; cane maturation complete
43 Beginning of leaf fall
47 End of leaf fall
Shoot and inflorescence development
Flowering
Berry formation
Berry ripening
Senescence

Figure 7.3 Modified E-L system for identifying major and intermediate grapevine growth stages (revised from Coombe 1995). Note that not all varieties show a woolly bud or a green tip stage (May 2000) hence the five budburst stages in the modified original 1995 system have been changed slightly by removing stage 4 and allocating the definition of budburst to what was formerly stage 5.

2. Eichhorn and Lorenz (1977) developed a more comprehensive scheme detailing 22 growth stages between winter bud and the end of leaf fall. The 47 number coding used in the scheme provides the opportunity to include additional intermediate stages if required.

3. Lorenz et al. (1994) adapted the General BBCH scale (Hack et al. 1992) to produce the Extended BBCH scale for the grapevine. The General BBCH scheme was developed to provide uniform descriptions of growth stages for monocot and dicot crops, and thus assist agrochemical application timing and research.

4. Coombe (1995) modified Eichhorn and Lorenz's (1977) scheme to develop the Modified E-L system (FIGURE 7.3). This scheme has recently been revised by Coombe and May to include minor changes in the way the progression of budburst is described. Stage 5 has been removed and the descriptions for stages 3 and 4 have been modified to account for the fact that not all varieties show a woolly bud or green tip stage. The revised Modified E-L system meets the five attributes of a growth stage scheme that Coombe (1995) identified as being critical to its success: these are (a) provision of both major and intermediate stages, (b) continuous sequence of stages, (c) clearly identifiable stages, (d) stages that have wide applicability and (e) have low variability. The latter four requirements were not met by the Extended BBCH scheme. Some practical considerations for assessing the growth stage of a vineyard block, using the Modified E-L scheme are provided by Coombe (1995). The visual assessment of percent capfall (E-L number 20, 21, 23 and 25) is difficult due to the variation in flower opening within and between inflorescences. To assist in the estimation of percent capfall, May (2003 unpubl.) recommends counting the total number of flowers with and without caps off, for the third bunch lateral (i.e. % capfall = {number of flowers with caps off ÷ total number of flowers} x 100). For grapevine growth stages that are not defined by a percentage, for example E-L number 16 (10 leaves separated) compared to E-L number 25 (80% caps off), it is accepted that 50% of a vine must be at that or a higher E-L number. For example, to say that a vineyard block is at E-L number 16, 50% of the shoots in that vineyard block have an E-L number equal to or greater than 16.

The existence of 4 different schemes necessitates the requirement for a conversion table between schemes (TABLE 7.2). The Modified E-L system is the recommended scheme for Australian vineyards and has been widely adopted by the Australian wine industry for vineyard operations and viticulture research. In the booklet titled 'Agrochemicals registered for use in Australian viticulture', produced yearly by The Australian Wine Research Institute, E-L numbers are used to advise grape growers of the correct times for agrochemical applications. Such support for the Modified E-L scheme is critical to the integration and use of this system in Australian viticulture.

Table 7.2 Comparison of the lettering or numbering used to identify grapevine growth stages in the four schemes (taken from Coombe 1995).

	Baillod & Baggiolini	Eichhorn & Lorenz	Extended BBCH	Modified E-L
	A	01	00	1
		02	01	2
	B		03	
		03	05	3
Budburst	C	05	07	4
	D		09	
	E	07	11	7
			12	
		09	13	9
			14	11
Shoots 10 cm	F	12	15 53	12
			16	13
				14
	G	15	19 55	15
				16
	H	17	57	17
				18
Flowering begins		19	60	19
			61	20
		21	63	21
Full bloom	I	23	65	23
		25	68	25
		26	69	26
Setting	J	27	71	27
		29	73	29
	K	31	75	31
			77	32
	L	33	79	33
				34
Veraison	M	35	81	35
				36
				37
Harvest	N	38	89	38
				39
	O	41	91	41
			92	
	P	43	93	43
			95	
		47	97	47

7.3 Timing of and interval between major growth stages

Progression through the annual growth cycle is influenced by a complex interaction of variables including, (1) variety, (2) region, (3) season and (4) viticultural practices (McIntyre et al. 1982). Coombe (1988) highlighted that there are no extensive and detailed data on grapevine phenology in Australia; unfortunately, such studies have yet to be undertaken. The majority of information on phenology in Australia is an indirect result of research into viticultural practices, such as irrigation, nutrition, canopy management and winegrape quality. McIntyre (1982) reviewed the limited published work, mostly being recordings of budburst, flowering and harvest in specific grape regions. In evaluating procedures used by researchers, McIntyre (1982) observed that medians are more useful than

Table 7.3 Dates of budburst, flowering and harvest of 11 grape varieties in 12 locations/11 regions of Australia[1]

Location	(Region[2])	State	Sultana	Riesling	Semillon	Shiraz	Palomino	Cabernet Sauvignon	Grenache	Muscat Gordo	Waltham Cross	Trebbiano	Doradillo	Median date
Budburst date (days after 31 August)														
Cessnock	(HU)	NSW		16	12	15		19				15	18	16-Sep
Upper Swan	(SW)	WA	9	6	1	8		16	12	18	16			11-Sep
Adelaide	(–)	SA		5	14	5	4	21	5			5	7	5-Sep
Griffith	(RI)	NSW	9	16	20	19	18	20	21	26	25	27	23	20-Sep
Rutherglen	(RU)	Vic.		24		25	29	28	31		33	32		29-Sep
Mildura	(MD)	Vic.	1	11	7	12	14		10	8	14		16	11-Sep
Nuriootpa	(BV)	SA		7	21	8	16	20	13	24		25	14	16-Sep
Loxton	(RL)	SA	3		16	8	13	13	8	18	23	18	17	15-Sep
Coonawarra	(CO)	SA		26	24	16	20	31	26				31	26-Sep
Swan Hill	(SH)	Vic.	12			17	16		10	20	28		19	17-Sep
Eden Valley	(EV)	SA	6	18		20								18-Sep
Tabilk	(GV)	Vic.		11		28		16				17		17-Sep
Median date			8-Sep	14-Sep	15-Sep	16-Sep	16-Sep	20-Sep	12-Sep	19-Sep	24-Sep	18-Sep	18-Sep	16-Sep
Flowering date (days after 31 October)														
Cessnock	(HU)	NSW		4	6	6		8				12		6-Nov
Upper Swan	(SW)	WA	15	10	8	9		12	14	16	19			13-Nov
Adelaide	(–)	SA		18	20	21	21	20	20			21	20	20-Nov
Griffith	(RI)	NSW	8	10	10	13	11	18	11	18	8	21	13	11-Nov
Rutherglen	(RU)	Vic.		28		23	28	24	26		35	32		28-Nov
Mildura	(MD)	Vic.	8		4	5	11		7	13	11	m	11	10-Nov
Nuriootpa	(BV)	SA		20	20	20	23	21	21	24		27	20	21-Nov
Loxton	(RL)	SA	11	1	8	3	14	6	5	12	14	19	12	11-Nov
Coonawarra	(CO)	SA		26	28	30	28	33	29				30	29-Nov
Swan Hill	(SH)	Vic.	18			16	19		15	20	24		20	19-Nov
Eden Valley	(EV)	SA		26		35								1-Dec
Tabilk	(GV)	Vic.		34		31		30					33	2-Dec
Median date			11-Nov	19-Nov	9-Nov	18-Nov	20-Nov	20-Nov	15-Nov	17-Nov	17-Nov	21-Nov	20-Nov	19-Nov
Harvest date (days after 31 January)														
Cessnock	(HU)	NSW		18	16	26						57		22-Feb
Upper Swan	(SW)	WA		39	41	51		56		31	29			11-Mar
Adelaide	(–)	SA		30	46	38	33	33	62			46	67	13-Mar
Griffith	(RI)	NSW	17		22	32	36	55	51	58	38	49	66	15-Mar
Rutherglen	(RU)	Vic.		48	49	44	63	31	55					20-Mar
Mildura	(MD)	Vic.	24			30	55		45	50	62		85	21-Mar
Nuriootpa	(BV)	SA		61	55	36	52	51	52	63		74	53	24-Mar
Loxton	(RL)	SA	36		42		47		52	71	76	66	88	30-Mar
Coonawarra	(CO)	SA		50	63	71	59	54	89					1-Apr
Swan Hill	(SH)	Vic.	24			38				50	74	85	89	2-Apr
Eden Valley	(EV)	SA		65		68								7-Apr
Tabilk	(GV)	Vic.		65		65		81				83		13-Apr
Median date			24-Feb	20-Mar	15-Mar	9-Mar	23-Mar	25-Mar	23-Mar	25-Mar	2-Apr	6-Apr	16-Apr	22-Mar

[1] Compiled from records collected during 1966 to 1970 by 12 cooperators organised and guided by P. May, CSIRO Division of Horticultural Research. The values presented are medians of the year values and those at the base and right-hand side are medians of medians. The order of regions is based on the median harvest dates. [2] Refer to Chapter 2 for explanation of regional codes.

means, as they reduce the influence of extreme values.

One survey, organised by May and reported by Coombe (1988), collated phenological information for 11 varieties from 12 Australian regions over 5 years; median dates for budburst, flowering and harvest are presented in **TABLE 7.3**. A second study, was conducted on the Primary Industries of South Australia (PIRSA) Nuriootpa germplasm collection over 5 years (1982 – 1987). The dates of budburst, flowering and veraison were recorded by D.G. Furkaliev for 25 varieties, the management of the vines being the same for each variety. In the last 3 years of the study, 50-berry samples were collected weekly during the ripening period, and the total soluble solids (TSS), expressed as °Brix, titratable acidity and pH determined (**TABLE 7.4**). These data represent the first report in Australian literature of the dates of veraison which has been a serious omission since it represents the beginning of berry ripening.

The Brix index columns in **TABLE 7.4** are new phenological stages which may help unravel causes of

Table 7.4 Dates of budburst, flowering, veraison, 15°Brix and 20°Brix for 23 grape varieties grown in the Primary Industries of South Australia (PIRSA) germplasm collection at Nuriootpa. Data presented for budburst, flowering and veraison are the medians of four years (1982-1986), for 15°Brix, 1-2 years (1984-1985) and for 20°Brix, 3 years (1984-1987). Dates for 15°Brix and 20°Brix were determined from maturity graphs provided by PIRSA for each variety. Data is sorted by 20°Brix date. The four unheaded columns are the intervals in days between the adjacent pair of phenological dates. From McCarthy and Furkaliev (1999) PIRSA Internal Report.

Variety	Budburst		Flowering		Veraison		15°Brix		20°Brix
Gamay	15-Sep	59	13-Nov	74	26-Jan	15	10-Feb	17	27-Feb
Traminer	19-Sep	58	16-Nov	66	21-Jan	16	6-Feb	21	27-Feb
Shiraz	22-Sep	61	21-Nov	72	1-Feb	12	13-Feb	15	28-Feb
Meunier	13-Sep	64	16-Nov	69	23-Jan	15	7-Feb	22	29-Feb
Pinot Noir	17-Sep	58	14-Nov	75	27-Jan	19	15-Feb	14	29-Feb
Crouchen	30-Sep	56	25-Nov	66	29-Jan	18	16-Feb	15	2-Mar
Chardonnay	11-Sep	60	10-Nov	74	23-Jan	26	15-Feb	17	3-Mar
Cabernet Sauvignon	2-Oct	50	21-Nov	74	3-Feb	11	14-Feb	18	3-Mar
Merlot	16-Sep	61	16-Nov	78	1-Feb	17	18-Feb	15	4-Mar
Riesling	24-Sep	53	16-Nov	75	29-Jan	21	19-Feb	14	4-Mar
Tinta Maderia	27-Sep	55	20-Nov	70	29-Jan	16	14-Feb	19	4-Mar
Grenache	19-Sep	58	16-Nov	79	3-Feb	14	17-Feb	17	5-Mar
Barbera	19-Sep	64	22-Nov	78	7-Feb	17	24-Feb	11	6-Mar
Cabernet Franc	27-Sep	54	20-Nov	90	18-Feb	6	23-Feb	12	6-Mar
Colombard	24-Sep	57	20-Nov	72	31-Jan	26	23-Feb	13	7-Mar
Carignan	19-Sep	67	25-Nov	75	8-Feb	17	25-Feb	12	8-Mar
Semillon	22-Sep	61	21-Nov	72	1-Feb	17	18-Feb	19	8-Mar
Muscadelle	29-Sep	57	25-Nov	64	28-Jan	27	24-Feb	13	8-Mar
Malbec 1056	16-Sep	61	15-Nov	71	25-Jan	24	18-Feb	20	9-Mar
Touriga	23-Sep	53	15-Nov	83	6-Feb	19	25-Feb	13	9-Mar
Ruby Cabernet	17-Sep	66	22-Nov	68	29-Jan	20	18-Feb	21	10-Mar
Chenin Blanc	18-Sep	65	22-Nov	71	1-Feb	19	20-Feb	19	10-Mar
Biancone	26-Sep	61	26-Nov	76	10-Feb	31	12-Mar	22	3-Apr
Mean	21-Sep	59	19-Nov	73	31-Jan	18	18-Feb	15	4-Mar
Standard Deviation	5.43	4.34	4.20	5.66	6.33	5.35	7.17	4.27	7.98

variation in berry ripening. While growers measure °Brix changes during ripening, the discipline of determining and recording a single key point would permit broader comparisons between seasons, varieties and of treatments in viticultural experiments. The value 15°Brix is suitable as it occurs after the initial steep rise in °Brix and hence indicates the basis of timing and degree of sugaring.

Three aspects of the methodology are important for interpreting phenological data and making comparisons between studies:

1. The scheme used to identify growth stages.

2. The definition of when a particular growth stage is reached. The proportion of a grapevine required to be at that particular growth stage, varies from 10%, 50% to 70% and as high as 80%. Variation between individuals in determining the proportions can be significant.

3. The interpretation of the description for a growth stage on the different schemes. In particular, the definition of 'berries ripe for harvest' or 'berries harvest-ripe' is dependent on the wine style to be produced. Wine style may vary from sparkling wine, to light, medium or full-bodied table wines, to dessert wines or fortified wines. For example, a standard total TSS of 19.8°Brix is targeted for Semillon in Griffith for the

production of medium-bodied table wines, and it reaches this TSS from mid-February to mid-March. In contrast, Semillon harvested for dessert wine in Griffith, and thus a significantly higher TSS of 45 °Brix, is harvested from late May to mid-June (E. McLachlan, pers. comm.). Averaging or comparing such data, can lead to erroneous interpretations.

7.3.1 VARIETY

In most Australian vineyards, and for most varieties, budburst occurs during September, flowering during November and December, veraison in January and February and harvest from February through to May. The median dates for the varieties listed in **TABLE 7.3** and **TABLE 7.4**, show a range between varieties (across all regions and years) of approximately 3 weeks for budburst, 2 weeks for flowering, 4 weeks for veraison and 7 weeks for harvest. The reported 3-week variation in budburst date for the PIRSA collection is a result of Cabernet Sauvignon bursting 22 days after Chardonnay, the earliest variety in the data set. Early budburst can present a significant risk in regions where spring frosts occur. The relative timing of budburst between varieties is also detailed in **TABLE 6.2**, Chapter 6. Flowering date

Table 7.5 Harvest dates of 4 varieties in 12 locations in 10 regions of Australia. Harvest date calculated as the weighted (tonnes) average delivery date for all deliveries to Orlando Wyndham Group wineries between 1995 and 2001, and represents over 50,000 tonnes of fruit. A narrow TSS range of 22.5 to 23.4°Brix was used to define harvest for Chardonnay, Shiraz and Cabernet Sauvignon, and 19.8 to 20.7°Brix for Semillon.

Region	(Location)	State	Semillon	Chardonnay	Shiraz	Cabernet Sauvignon	Median date
Hunter	(Lower)	NSW	7-Feb	15-Feb	19-Feb		17-Feb
Hunter	(Upper)	NSW	9-Feb	19-Feb	21-Feb		20-Feb
Riverina		NSW	23-Feb	25-Feb	8-Mar	25-Mar	8-Mar
Riverland	(Waikerie)	SA		2-Mar	27-Mar		14-Mar
Riverland	(Barmera)	SA	24-Feb	8-Mar	17-Mar	26-Mar	17-Mar
Barossa Valley		SA	24-Mar	5-Mar	26-Mar	23-Mar	23-Mar
Mudgee		NSW	21-Mar	4-Mar	28-Mar	7-Apr	28-Mar
McLaren Vale		SA	16-Mar	15-Mar	6-Apr	9-Apr	6-Apr
Padthaway		SA		29-Mar	19-Apr	7-Apr	7-Apr
Cowra		NSW	6-Mar	2-Mar	8-Apr	18-Apr	8-Apr
Langhorne Creek		SA		16-Mar	9-Apr	20-Apr	9-Apr
Coonawarra		SA		3-Apr	19-Apr	27-Apr	19-Apr
Median date			1-Mar	4-Mar	27-Mar	7-Apr	25-Mar

within a region and year is relatively constant between varieties. McIntyre et al. (1982) similarly reported a narrow range for flowering date between varieties at Davis, California. This synchronisation phenomenon is probably caused by the rising daytime temperatures that occur as spring progresses, a feature of Mediterranean climates. The interval between budburst and flowering is approximately 60 days, with variation in the duration of this interval between varieties being up to 16 days. The consistency of flowering date between varieties suggests that this variation can be largely attributed to the varying date of budburst between varieties, such that shorter intervals represent varieties with a late budburst (e.g. Cabernet Sauvignon).

Given the relative uniformity of flowering, the wide variations reported in harvest date between varieties of up to 7 weeks may be attributed to the differences in the interval from flowering to veraison. This interval can vary between varieties, from 3 weeks within a region (TABLE 7.4) to 7 weeks (TABLE 7.3) when averaged across 12 regions. Coombe (1988) concluded that for most varieties in Australia the interval from flowering to harvest is 125 ± 15 days. The PIRSA data allow us to divide this long interval further: the ranges in duration of the intervals, flowering to veraison, veraison to 15°Brix and 15°Brix to 20°Brix, are 73, 18 and 15 days, respectively. This suggests that the variation in the interval of flowering to veraison is the greatest contributor to the 6-week variation reported between varieties in harvest date. The order of the varieties in TABLE 7.4, from earliest to latest (20°Brix), display similarities between the 5 stages but there are sufficient differences between them to show that each growth event reacts in an individual way to the weather. This reflects the different physiological controls operating for each variety. The results for the variety Biancone, with

lateness at all stages, suggest an overriding genetic difference.

The weighted average harvest dates for 4 varieties from 10 regions over 7 years are presented in TABLE 7.5. Chardonnay was harvested 3 and 5 weeks earlier than Shiraz and Cabernet Sauvignon respectively, with the harvest of the latter 2 varieties being within 2 weeks of each other. For the PIRSA collection, the first variety to reach 20°Brix was Gamay (27 Feb) and the latest Biancone (3 April), a difference of 39 days.

Varieties differ in the stability of their phenology under different conditions. For example, the date of harvest for Cabernet Sauvignon in the Barossa Valley and Padthaway is earlier than Shiraz, but later than Shiraz for the 7 other regions listed in TABLE 7.5. Riesling ripens earlier than Shiraz in warm regions (MJT of 21-23°C) but later than Shiraz in cool regions (MJT of 18-20°C) (Dry 1984). Calo et al. (1975) have calculated 'stability indices' for 80 varieties in Conegliano, Northern Italy. No such study has been conducted in Australia.

The timing of intermediate growth stages of 11 varieties at Griffith, in relation to budburst, flowering and harvest is displayed in FIGURE 7.4. The uniformity of flowering amongst varieties is evident, as is leaf coloration and leaf fall. Not all varieties behave uniformly; Malbec has an early veraison but the latest harvest. McIntyre et al. (1982) similarly report, for example, that in Davis (California), Cabernet Sauvignon had a later than average budburst but an early harvest, whilst Almeria (Ohanez) had an earlier than average budburst but a later harvest.

Boursiquot et al. (1995) use a 'reference' variety, Chasselas, to make comparisons of budburst and ripeness dates between a large number of varieties in the Domaine de Vassal collection in France. Similarly, McIntyre et al. (1982) plotted the relative onset of budburst, flowering and harvest between varieties as the days from the average; Semillon had the closest dates to the average for each event.

7.3.2 REGION

The variation in phenology between regions is shown in TABLE 7.3 and FIGURE 7.5. For the regions listed in TABLE 7.3, averaged over all varieties and years, budburst occurred during 3 weeks in September, flowering during 4 weeks from early November to early December and harvest occupied a 7-week period from late February to mid-April. These ranges would be extended further if the more extreme locations of Alice Springs, Northern Territory and Pipers Brook, Tasmania

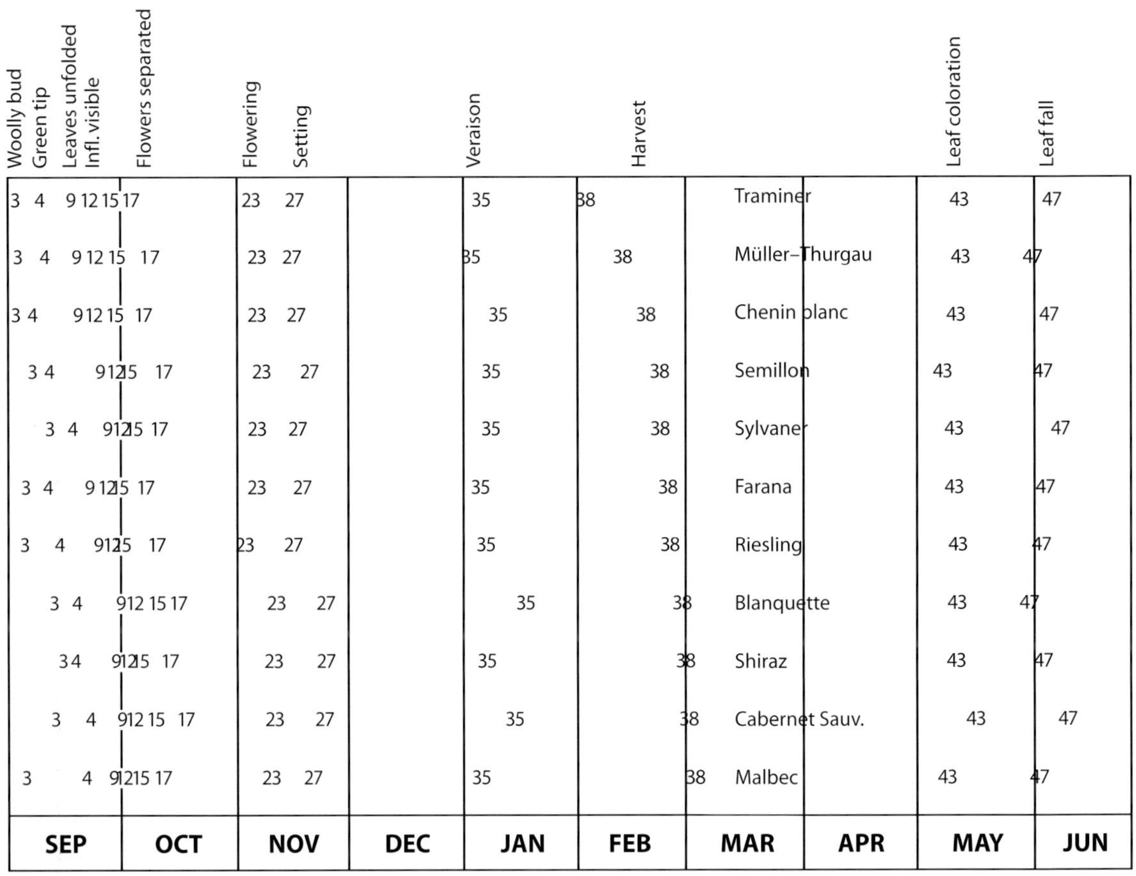

Woolly bud / Green tip	Leaves unfolded / Infl. visible	Flowers separated	Flowering	Setting	Veraison	Harvest	Variety	Leaf coloration	Leaf fall	
3 4	9 12 15	17	23	27	35	38	Traminer	43	47	
3 4	9 12 15	17	23	27	35	38	Müller–Thurgau	43	47	
3 4	9 12 15	17	23	27	35	38	Chenin blanc	43	47	
3 4	9 12	15 17	23	27	35	38	Semillon	43	47	
3 4	9 12	15 17	23	27	35	38	Sylvaner	43	47	
3 4	9 12	15 17	23	27	35	38	Farana	43	47	
3 4	9 12	15 17	23	27	35	38	Riesling	43	47	
3 4	9 12	15 17	23	27	35	38	Blanquette	43	47	
3 4	9 12	15 17	23	27	35	38	Shiraz	43	47	
3 4	9 12	15 17	23	27	35	38	Cabernet Sauv.	43	47	
3 4	9 12	15 17	23	27	35	38	Malbec	43	47	

SEP	OCT	NOV	DEC	JAN	FEB	MAR	APR	MAY	JUN

Figure 7.4 Dates of 12 E-L growth stages (Figure 7.3) for 11 grape varieties growing at Griffith Viticultural Station (Riverina NSW), recorded during three seasons (1970-71, 1972-73 and 1983-84). From Coombe (1988).

were included (**FIGURE 7.5**). Similarly, a greater range of 9 weeks for harvest, between 10 regions (averaged over 4 varieties) is shown in **TABLE 7.5**. The wide range of 4 weeks in flowering date between regions, contrasts sharply with the narrow range in flowering date between varieties within a region.

Interestingly, for those regions represented in both **TABLE 7.4** and **FIGURE 7.5**, the order by harvest date is the same: the earliest being the Hunter (Upper Hunter and Lower Hunter) then, Riverina, Riverland (Barmera and Waikerie), Barossa Valley and the latest being Coonawarra. The early harvest in Hunter and Alice Springs (extreme) is not due to an early budburst but to the shorter intervals from budburst to flowering and flowering to harvest (**FIGURE 7.5**). Lateness of harvest has a number of causes: late budburst (Rutherglen and Pipers Brook, Tas.), a long interval between budburst and flowering (Drumborg, Henty) and a long interval between flowering and harvest (Hobart, Tas.). The interval between flowering and harvest between regions is less variable by 3 weeks compared with that between varieties; the range shown in **FIGURE 7.5** (excluding the earliest and latest) is from 107 to 137 days. The inclusion of Alice Springs would extend this range by 3 weeks. In northern parts of Europe, where budburst and flowering are later, this

interval is shorter, for example, 100 days in Bordeaux.

The progression of grapevines through key growth stages does not follow in strict proportion under all conditions. For example, the order of regions by budburst date does not match the order of regions by flowering or harvest date (**TABLE 7.3** right-hand-side and **FIGURE 7.5**). Another example is provided by the differences in amount of development of Shiraz shoots in different districts on the same day, compared with the average date of harvest (**TABLE 7.6**). Despite general similarities in order, especially in the warmer regions in the top half of the table, there are notable discrepancies; Mudgee and Nuriootpa (Barossa Valley) have earlier harvests than their 1 November shoot growth might indicate while Coonawarra and Drumborg (Henty) have later harvests.

Given the vast differences between regions in the way the weather unfolds, these variations between regions are not surprising.

7.3.3 YEARS (SEASONS)
The majority of phenological data recorded in Australia over a number of sites and varieties is collected for only a short period of predominantly 5 or less years. Therefore long term trends in phenology in Australia are anecdotal or unknown.

Table 7.6 Number of visible internodes[1] on shoots of Shiraz grapevines on 1 November, 1975, compared with harvest dates[2] (long-term regional averages).

Region (location)	Number of internodes	Harvest date
Hunter NSW	19[3]	20-Feb
Riverina NSW	13.5	1-Mar
Swan District WA		1-Mar
Murray Darling (Mildura) Vic.		1-Mar
Murray Darling (Robinvale) Vic.	13	3-Mar
Swan Hill Vic.		9-Mar
– (Adelaide) SA	11.5	9-Mar
McLaren Vale SA		12-Mar
– (Barooga) NSW		18-Mar
Margaret River WA	11	2-Apr
Mudgee NSW	10.5	9-Mar
Coonawarra SA		8-Apr
King Valley Vic.		20-Mar
Great Southern (Frankland) WA	10	-
Henty Vic.		24-Apr
Barossa Valley SA	9.5	12-Mar
Goulburn Valley Vic.		5-Apr
Grampians Vic.	9	1-Apr
Clare Valley SA		1-Apr

[1] Numbers of internodes longer than 7 mm (pencil thickness) on the majority of shoots of winter pruned vines.
[2] Data collected by B.G.Coombe plus some harvest dates from P.R. Dry, R.E. Smart and A.J.G Pirie.
[3] These vines were flowering.

From short term data sets, it can be concluded that budburst, flowering and veraison dates may vary between years by up to 2.5 weeks. In contrast, harvest date between years displays considerable variation of up to 8 weeks. Interestingly a similar variation of 3 weeks in harvest date exists between years for Chardonnay and Cabernet Sauvignon, despite a large difference of 5 weeks in actual harvest date between the 2 varieties (TABLE 7.5). Another example of this variation in harvest date between years is provided by ripeness data of the same Grenache vines; juice samples reached 21°Brix on 14 April, 22 February, 15 March and 11 March in the 4 successive years 1975 to 1978 (Coombe and Iland 1987). The authors suggest that much of this variation was due to varied veraison date.

For Shiraz grown at Waikerie (Riverland), the number of days between any interval that combines any 2 of the growth stages, budburst, flowering, veraison, 10°Brix and 15°Brix, varies by less than 2 weeks between years (McCarthy 1997). There is a greater variation between years for intervals from any of the above stages through to 20°Brix and harvest (defined as 23-24°Brix); the lowest being 10 days for the interval 15°Brix to 20°Brix and the highest 5 weeks for budburst to 23.5°Brix (FIGURE 7.6). Of particular interest is that, over the 4 years, the intervals flowering to 10°Brix and flowering to

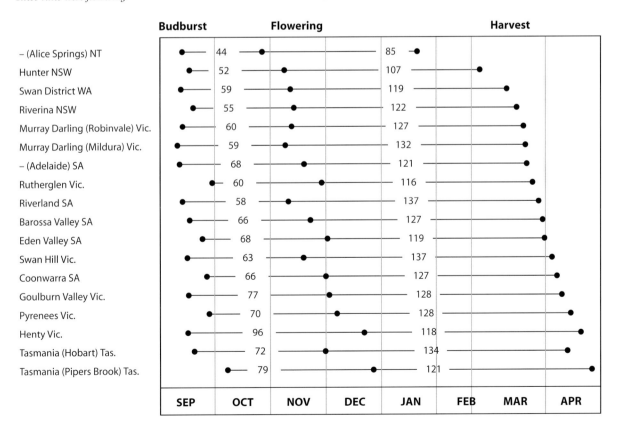

Figure 7.5 Generalised dates of budburst, flowering and harvest, together with the intervening days, for 18 locations representing a wide array of Australian grapegrowing environments. The data include information from TABLE 7.3, A.J.G Pirie (pers. comm.), and Smart et al. (1980).

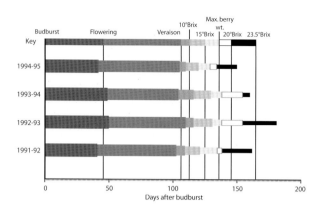

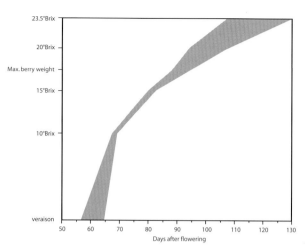

Figure 7.6 Schematic presentation of the duration (days) between growth stages for irrigated Shiraz vines grown at Waikerie, (Riverland SA), recorded over four seasons (1991-92, 1992-93, 1993-94, 1994-95). Vertical lines indicate the average number of days after budburst for the indicated growth stage (from McCarthy 1997).

Figure 7.7 Variation in the number of days between flowering and key growth stages of irrigated Shiraz vines grown at Waikerie, (Riverland SA), recorded over four seasons (1991-92, 1992-93, 1993-94, 1994-95). Y axis is not to scale (from McCarthy 1997).

15°Brix, varied by only 2 and 3 days, respectively, suggesting a genotypic control of berry development during this period (**FIGURE 7.7**). A 3-day range between years for the interval from flowering to 15°Brix was also noted for the PIRSA collection (**TABLE 7.4**). This is supported by Calo et al. (1998) who reported that the interval from flowering to veraison is largely dependent on the genetic characteristics of a variety rather than the environment. This phenomenon deserves further study.

A long term (1952-1997) study of Cabernet Sauvignon and Merlot grown in Bordeaux, France, reported a greater variation of 5 weeks in both flowering and veraison dates, and a 6-week range in harvest date (no

budburst observations) (Jones and Davis 2000). Over the 46-year observation period, the harvest date was found to change significantly, being 13 days earlier in 1997 than in the 1950s (**FIGURE 7.8**). Harvest was defined as the '...point at which, due to optimum sugar levels, the harvest commences', rather than a specific TSS level. Therefore, the earlier harvest date noted may simply be due to the fact that harvest over time is occurring at a lower sugar level, and thus earlier. Warmer growing seasons were also suggested as a possible explanation. The average interval lengths over the 46 years for flowering to veraison, flowering to harvest, and veraison to harvest were 67, 112 and 45 days respectively. A decrease in the length of these intervals over the observation period of 4, 10 and 6 days respectively was noted. The general pattern of each time series for flowering, veraison and harvest were similar, and Jones and Davis (2000) report that the timing for each of these stages is dependent on the timing of the previous stage (**FIGURE 7.8**). This conclusion is supported by Due et al. (1993) although exceptions will occur.

7.3.4 VITICULTURAL PRACTICES

Pruning

Late pruning, whether late in winter during dormancy or early in spring after the onset of budburst, will influence phenology. A 6-week difference (7 July cf. 17 August) in winter pruning time of Cabernet Sauvignon vines in Victoria, delayed the onset and mean date of budburst by four and five days respectively (Martin and Dunn 2000), and this difference persisted at flowering, veraison and maturity. Late pruning in the spring, after budburst has commenced, may delay the bursting of the buds left after spur pruning by up to 3 weeks and

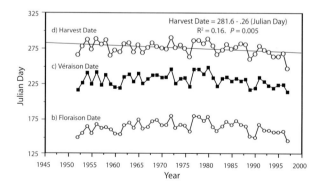

Figure 7.8 Time series for flowering, veraison and harvest for Cabernet Sauvignon and Merlot reference vineyards in Bordeaux, France, from 1952 to 1997 (adapted from Jones and Davis 2000). Data points represent the average of values for both varieties and all reference vineyards. Harvest date is the only time series that significantly changed over time.

flowering by 1 week, compared with normal mid-winter pruning (Coombe 1964). Late pruning may be used for early bursting varieties, such as Chardonnay, to reduce the risk of damage in frost prone areas.

Double pruning has a large effect on phenology, the purpose being to shift the ripening of grapes in hot areas into late autumn when temperatures are lower compared with late summer. For instance Shiraz vines repruned on 14 December, when berries were about 8 mm diameter, resulted in budburst, flowering and harvest dates of 21 December, 25 January and 6 May compared with normal dates of 12 September, 6 November and 14 February. Note that double pruning reduced the interval from budburst to flowering from 55 days to 35 days but had no effect on that from flowering to harvest (Dry 1987). Double pruning is not commonly used in Australian viticulture.

Irrigation practices

The effect of soil water deficit at different grapevine growth stages can be either positive or negative. Severe water stress at any time during the annual growth cycle, such as in unirrigated vineyards which depend on stored soil water from winter rainfall, will restrict shoot and root growth and significantly reduce yields. This in turn will affect the timing of major growth stages, with early budburst and veraison dates but delayed maturity (Smart and Coombe 1983). Irrigation strategies, such as regulated deficit and partial rootzone drying, have been developed to control the timing and level of water stress, and thus manipulate vegetative growth and berry size and improve water use efficiency, whilst maintaining or augmenting grape quality. Deficit irrigation strategies are normally applied between setting and harvest, the duration and extent determined by the current season and vineyard conditions, stored soil water and the reason for applying stress.

The dates of budburst, flowering and veraison, and the intervals between these stages were not influenced by seven irrigation deficit treatments applied to Shiraz between flowering and harvest (McCarthy 1997). The harvest date, however, was influenced by deficit irrigation. Unirrigated vines were harvested 2–3 weeks earlier in 3 of the 4 seasons, with yield being reduced by approximately 30%. In the final season yield was reduced in unirrigated vines by 70%, with harvest being one week later compared to fully irrigated vines. This suggests that the unirrigated vines experienced severe soil water deficit, compounded by low seasonal rainfall, which negatively impacted on yield and ripening. The relationship between irrigation deficit, yield and the timing of harvest does not always follow the same pattern. For example, irrigation deficit between flowering and veraison resulted in vines being harvested 1 to 2.5 weeks earlier than fully irrigated vines, despite yield being significantly lower in only one of the 4

seasons. Additionally, post-veraison deficit resulted in a similar yield in 1993-94 but a 16% lower yield in 1994-95 than fully irrigated, however, harvest date was approximately 1 week later than fully irrigated vines in both seasons. The general conclusion by McCarthy (1997) is that water deficit during berry development, whether in part or wholly induced by regulated irrigation, will reduce yield. The extent of this yield reduction will determine the impact on harvest date.

Yield

Under normal conditions, yield will influence the timing of harvest date such that, in general, vines with high yields will reach a desired maturity level later compared to vines with lower yields; quantification of this relationship is shown for Shiraz in **FIGURE 7.9**. However, if the low yield is due to significant stress placed on the vine then harvest may be delayed.

7.3.5 SPECIAL GROWING CONDITIONS

Glasshouse grapes

The culture of some early tablegrape varieties in glasshouses with early pruning and cyanamide treatment may bring about budburst in June, flowering in September and harvest in November in contrast with 'outside' vines where the corresponding dates are September, November and February. Similar behaviour is being found in hot, northerly regions in Queensland and Northern Territory.

Tropical grapes

In tropical environments, with an absence of cold temperatures, plants like the grapevine behave as

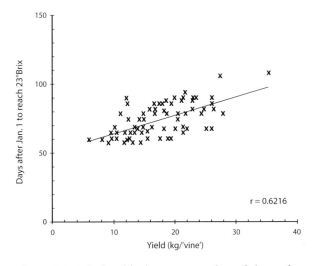

Figure 7.9 Relationship between number of days after January 1 to reach 23.0 ± 0.5°Brix and yield, for Shiraz vines grown in the Riverland, SA, during the 1994-95 season (taken from Botting et al. 1996). Correlation coefficient 'r' significant at 0.1% level.

evergreens with a continuous but desultory emergence of shoots and production of fruit throughout the year. If such vines are defoliated or pruned there is a synchronisation of budburst, flowering and cropping with a timing predetermined by the date of the initial treatment. In this way, 2 or more crops can be obtained every 12 months. In an Australian example (Anon. 1987), tablegrapes near Townsville, Queensland, are harvested in September.

7.4 Relationship between phenology and weather

In view of the many examples that point to a relationship between the weather and grapevine development, it is understandable that attempts have been made to seek correlations between them. Correlations can be made between dates and durations, on the one hand, and selected climatic or weather factors on the other. Similar studies have sought correlations between climatic factors and yield, grape composition, quality and vintage ratings. Significant correlations, even excellent ones, do not prove anything; they only indicate associations.

It should always be borne in mind that the particular growth event being measured may itself be correlated with another event, which may be the one being influenced by the weather factor. For example, the formation of new nodes on shoots is closely correlated with the development of flowers such that flowering occurs when the shoot has 17 to 18 visible internodes (Pratt and Coombe 1978). Does a correlation between, say, flowering date and a temperature index indicate that temperature influences flowering, or is it node formation that is being influenced?

The reverse problem also occurs, namely that the particular weather factor being quantified may be correlated with another factor that may in fact be the more realistic controller. Nevertheless, correlations are worth seeking since they lead to ideas that may be investigated by other methods, and because they may help in predicting vine behaviour in different seasons and regions.

Most of the work correlating grape phenology with weather has dealt with the timing of the major growth events—budburst, flowering, veraison and harvest. Temperature is stated as being a key climatic factor that controls the developmental rate of grapevines (Coombe 1988, Gladstones 1992 and Schultz 1993). It is argued that associations between other climatic factors and phenology, for example sunshine duration and day-length, are via an indirect effect on temperature (Gladstones 1992; see also Chapter 4). Given this, it is not surprising that most correlative work undertaken has involved various temperature indices; these, and some non-temperature indices are discussed below.

7.4.1 TEMPERATURE

Heat degree days

Degree days (also called heat units) are units calculated to indicate the amount of heat required, between upper and lower temperature thresholds, for a plant to progress from one stage to the next. Summation of degree day units over time may be used to predict when a particular growth stage will be reached.

The degree day concept was developed to calculate the interval between planting and harvest of annual crops. When applied to winegrapes in California heat degree days gave a useful correlation with wine styles (Amerine and Winkler 1944) and the system has since become widely adopted in many countries for the classification of regions (refer to Chapters 4 and 10). However the value of degree days in predicting the time of, or duration between growth stages is limited.

The method used to calculate degree days has been the subject of much debate, in particular: (1) the use, or lack thereof, of an upper temperature threshold, (2) the base threshold temperature used, (3) the interval over which degree days are summed, and (4) the calculation of mean temperatures for a period e.g. daily or monthly.

Winkler et al. (1974) used degree days to model harvest date and the interval between flowering and harvest. Under Californian conditions, specific varieties in different seasons and regions were found to have a constant number of heat units (mean temperature > 10°C) accumulated between flowering and harvest; 900°C units for early varieties and 1650°C for late. However, number of days (date) is reported to be as accurate as degree days as a measure of this interval in California (McIntyre et al. 1987) and of harvest date in South Australia (Coombe 1973). In addition Coombe and Iland (1987) found that heat units are not constant for this interval.

By adjusting the base temperature to 8°C rather than 10°C, Boehm (1970) found heat degree day summations for the interval budburst to flowering to be more constant, however degree day summations proved to have no application in interpreting the 3-week difference in maturity between 2 regions (Eden Valley and Barossa Valley).

The regression of simple heat or temperature accumulations against phenological dates produces models that account for over 97% of the variation in the data; procedural error is generally associated with such high percentages (Due et al. 1993, Jones and Davis 2000). The inevitable link between accumulations and elapsed time, and thus an inherent positive relationship between their relative values and interval length, lessens the ability of accumulations to accurately predict or describe phenological dates (Due et al. 1993, Jones and Davis 2000).

Gladstones (1992; Chapter 4) continues to use the degree day concept to predict maturity dates and thus evaluate the potential of new viticultural areas. Importantly, however, he incorporates modifications to improve the accuracy of this technique. These adjustments account for, (1) the non-linear response of vine growth to temperature, (2) variations in daylength for a particular month and latitude, (3) variations in diurnal temperature range, and (4) differences in altitude, topography and soil type between the weather station and the actual vineyard site (refer to Gladstones 1992, 1994 and Chapter 4 for detailed explanations). The adjusted degree days are termed 'biologically-effective degree days' (BEDD), and are used to group grape varieties into eight groups based on the number of BEDD required over the seven month growing season to reach maturity (dry or semi-sweet table wines). For existing regions, Gladstones (1992) reports that the average maturity date, plus or minus a week, can be predicted for a variety in one of the 8 groups.

Maximum and minimum temperature

The most commonly used functions of temperature are (1) daily maximum, (2) daily minimum, (3) mean daily temperature ((maximum + minimum) / 2), and (4) daily temperature range (maximum – minimum). The method by which these temperature functions are used to model phenology is important. Averages of functions, although relying on simple data and successfully being used to predict phenology, may conceal the effects of short-term weather events; these may be accommodated by time series data collection and modeling (Due et al. 1993).

The use of these temperature functions to explain the timing of, and interval between growth stages will be explored in four parts relating to the work on budburst, flowering, veraison and harvest. Reference is made to a paper by Due et al. (1993); the basic data set used is similar to that in **TABLE 7.3** (with some minor exceptions e.g. inclusion of Currant and omission of Eden Valley and Coonawarra).

Budburst

There is ample evidence that higher temperatures during the latter part of winter hasten budburst date, with temperatures calculated either as daily maximum (Antcliff and Webster 1955, Baldwin 1966, McIntyre 1982) or as daily means (Alleweldt and Hofäcker 1975, Pouget 1967). Similarly, Due et al. (1993) reported that, over 4 years, 11 regions and 12 varieties, most of the variation in budburst date was accounted for by the average maximum temperature between 1 August and 10 days prior to budburst and, to a lesser extent the minimum temperatures during the 10 days prior to budburst. The importance of long-term warmth is supported by the finding that the onset of budburst is earlier when soil temperatures at 20 cm depth are warmer (Alleweldt and Hofäcker 1975). The number of buds bursting per day, after the first bud has burst, is

strongly correlated with the mean air temperature on the day the buds burst, but inherently limited by the number of remaining buds to burst (Martin and Dunn 2000).

Comparing 5 Australian districts, Heinze (1977) considers that altitude and proximity to the sea are more influential than latitude. Varieties which burst early are considered by Pouget (1968) to be those with a low temperature threshold.

The reproductive potential of buds on an individual vine is reported to affect the relative timing of budburst, with a tendency of primary shoots with higher bunch numbers to burst earlier (Martin and Dunn 2000). Given this, and the significant effect of pruning time on budburst date (see 7.3.4), Martin and Dunn (2000) suggest that the inclusion of parameters to account for these influences may improve models to predict budburst and subsequent phenology.

Flowering

The fact that flowering of most varieties is quite uniform within a region, although it varies between regions and years (see 7.3.2 and 7.3.3), is probably attributable to the unifying effect of the onset of spring heat in each region and year.

Winkler et al. (1974) state that flowering in California occurs when mean daily temperature rises to 20°C; but this is not the case in Australia where mean temperature at flowering has been found to range from 15.5°C at Drumborg (Henty, Vic.) to 18.5°C at Qualco (Riverland, SA) (Heinze 1977). Note, however, that temperature averages depend on the interval over which they were calculated.

The close link between the rate of node formation at the shoot tip and of the development of flowers, referred to in section 7.4, suggests that it is likely that both growth processes are influenced together over a long period. Evidence for this is provided by Due et al. (1993). Variety, year, region and the long-term weather variate, average of the maximum temperature, accounted for 77% of the variation in flowering date. Considering that weather factors are already inherently incorporated in the year and region term, this finding provides support for a link between temperature and flowering date. Heinze (1977) and McIntyre (1982) also highlight the dominant effect of maximum temperature on the length of the interval between budburst and flowering. Similarly, exposure to low day/night temperatures of 12°C / 9°C for one week immediately prior to flowering delayed flowering of Chardonnay and Shiraz potted vines by 5 and 7 days, respectively (Ebadi et al. 1995).

In addition to the effects of temperature on budburst date, May (2004)[1] has discussed the European work showing that higher temperatures during budburst may

[1] The reference May (2004) is listed at the end of this Chapter. It is an important source of information and ideas on grape flowering and setting but, due to the timing of its publication, this information could not be properly integrated here (see also Chapter 11, section 11.1.1).

reduce the numbers of flowers initiated on each bunch. May compiled a valuable table of mean daily maximum and minimum temperatures (plus 86 and 14 percentiles) for the months of August, September and October from 45 recording stations covering the main Australian viticultural regions. He concluded that in none of these regions is flower initiation likely to be inhibited by budburst temperatures.

Veraison and Sugaring

The transformation of a bunch of grapes from the lag phase into the ripening berry stage is as dramatic as the hatching of a batch of eggs in an incubator. For each individual berry (or egg), the change occurs during one day and independently of its neighbours. Day one for the grape berry marks the beginning of changes involving softening, sugaring, colouring and a host of others which are discussed in Chapter 11, section 11.1.2. Softening and sugaring appear to be among the earliest events and are concurrent. It is proposed that the linkage between them results from an unusual happening involving the development of leakiness in the membranes surrounding the vacuoles of the berry's flesh cells. This leakiness results in pressure changes that permit flow of sugary phloem sap into that berry. Once started, sugaring progresses in each berry so that the °Brix of its juice rises regularly, i.e. that berry is ripening.

Unfortunately records of veraison date are rather rare and subject to uncertainty because of differences between recorders in the method of its determination. The dates of veraison listed in **TABLE 7.4** have provided one general guide showing that veraison occurred between 21 January and 10 February during four years comparing 25 varieties in the PIRSA germplasm collection at Nuriootpa. Similarly in the collection at Griffith Viticultural Station, comparing 11 varieties over three years (**FIGURE 7.4**), veraison occurred during the first 18 days of January. These dates are not as focussed as are the respective dates of flowering. Season-to-season comparisons of juice °Brix curves extrapolated back in time suggest that veraison date greatly influences harvest date (Coombe and Iland 1987).

The poor understanding of the physiological events associated with the triggering of veraison have made difficult the development of methods for its investigation and routine recording in the field. Research is needed on these matters.

Harvest

The large variation in harvest date between regions and years has led to researchers investigating the link with temperature functions. The results, although somewhat confusing, are summarised as follows:

(i) mean January (southern hemisphere) temperature correlated with the harvest date of 4 varieties (Smart 1979);

(ii) mean November-December (southern hemisphere) temperatures predicted veraison date and hence harvest date of Grenache in 4 years (Coombe and Iland 1987);

(iii) temperature predicted harvest date for late varieties but not for early varieties;

(iv) cumulative daily air temperature difference was the most reliable predictor of the interval flowering to harvest (McIntyre 1982);

(v) the greater the number of days above 25°C and 30°C for the intervals flowering to veraison and veraison to harvest, respectively, the earlier the harvest (Jones and Davis 2000); and

(vi) variety, year and region accounted for 57% of the variation in harvest date; the inclusion of the minimum temperatures for the epochs, (1) 1 January to 11 of January prior to harvest, (2) 10 days prior to harvest and (3) flowering to harvest, and the maximum temperature 10 days prior to harvest, accounted for a further 32% of the variation in harvest date (Due et al. 1993).

Due et al. (1993) concluded that temperature accounted for little of the variation in harvest date, citing that region and year effects have a far greater influence. Gladstones (1994, 1996) argues that Due et al. (1993) provides no evidence for such a conclusion given that (1) region and year terms inherently incorporate averages of weather for a given region across years, in addition to soil and vineyard management differences and (2) that harvest was defined by end-use which varied significantly from fresh tablegrapes to table wine to fortified wine.

Attention is drawn to the large body of literature on the relationship between temperature and grape composition. Refer to 4.2.2. for a discussion of this link.

7.4.2 WATER AND RADIATION

Although temperature is the major factor influencing grapevine phenology, additional influences arise from other climatic and growth factors. Water stress arising from low soil water status and/or high atmospheric deficit, has inhibitory effects on growth and alters phenology (Smart and Coombe 1983).

McIntyre's (1982) study of grapevine phenology in the Hunter region showed that available soil water became an increasingly important determinant of development as the season progressed. Using the Waite Index ($P/E^{0.75}$) as a long term indicator of available soil water (in the absence of irrigation), McIntyre (1982) found that the higher the index, i.e. the lower the water stress, the longer the interval from budburst to flowering and from flowering to veraison and harvest.

The difference between wet and dry bulb temperatures at 9 am was included by Due et al. (1993) as a variable in the last of the four years: the regressions show that this indicator of vapour pressure deficit had a small but significant association with the intervals from 1 July to budburst and budburst to flowering. Relative humidity has been considered as a factor influencing winegrape quality in different grapegrowing regions (Pirie 1978, Gladstones 1977, Dry and Smart - Chapters 2 and 10). These studies suggest that the relationship between water and grape phenology deserves more research.

Solar radiation is another key climatic factor determining plant growth and it would be expected that lack of radiation incidence would affect grape phenology. In Europe, and suggested in Gladstones (1992), the contribution of daylength is recognised in the use of heliothermic indices to delineate grape areas, but in the present context, radiation intensity is of interest. High light favours high bunch numbers, shorter internodes and high content of phenolics, which in turn may inhibit the growth of plant organs (Buttrose 1970, Kliewer 1982, Smart 1987). However, from the work thus far it seems that radiation is not a major contributor to the determination of grapevine phenology; however the matter has yet to be investigated thoroughly.

McIntyre (1982) has suggested that an ideal indicator might be one which accommodates shifts in the levels of soil moisture, air temperature and solar radiation.

7.5 Concluding remarks

Phenological data are important for the design and operation of a vineyard. This chapter summarises the present limited information on grapevine phenology in Australia. Examination of the association of weather with phenological events suggests that the best correlations are between temperature functions and budburst and flowering: those with harvest are variable and hence give poor predictions. Much more information is needed, however, before conclusions can be drawn. It is disappointing that 16 years after the first edition of this chapter, there is still an urgent need for better data on this subject documenting both vegetative and reproductive stages, preferably concurrently in diverse regions. However, of significance during this period has been the development and adoption by the Australian wine industry of the Modified E-L scheme for identifying grapevine growth stages. With the aid of this scheme and methodical recording, phenological data can be readily obtained. Modern methods of data recording and handling have simplified this job and the main requirement now is for an organised, Australia-wide program of phenological observation. This should be coupled with parallel records of weather factors, preferably with instruments adjacent to the recorded vines.

REFERENCES

Suggestions for further reading are marked (•).

Alleweldt, G. and Hofäcker, W. (1975) Einfluss von Umweltfaktoren auf Austrieb,

Blüte, Fruchtbarkeit und Triebwachstum bei der Rebe. Vitis **14**, 103-115.

Amerine, M.A. and Winkler, A.J. (1944) Composition and quality of musts and wine of Californian grapes. Hilgardia **15**, 493-675.

Anon. (1987) Unique North Queensland vineyard plans major expansion. Aust. Grapegrower & Winemaker No. 284, 16-17.

Antcliff, A.J. and Webster, W.J. (1955) Studies on the Sultana vine. II. The course of bud burst. Aust. J. Agric. Res. **6**, 713-24.

Baggiolini, M. (1952) Les stades repères dans le développement annuel de la vigne et leur utilisation pratique. Rev. Rom. Agric. Vitic. Arboric. **8**, 4-6.

Baillod, M. and Baggiolini, M. (1993) Les stades repères de la vigne. Rev. Suisse Vitic. Arboric. Hortic. **25**, 7-9.

Baldwin, J.G. (1966) Dormancy and time of budburst in the sultana vine. Aust. J. Agric. Res. **17**, 55-68.

Boehm, W.E. (1970) Vine development and temperature in the Barossa district, SA. South Aust. Dept. Agric. Experimental Record **4**, 16-24.

Botting, D.G., Dry, P.R. et al. (1996) Canopy architecture — implications for Shiraz grown in a hot, arid climate. Aust. Grapegrower & Winemaker No. 390a, 53-57.

Boursiquot, J.M., Dessup, M. et al. (1995) Distribution des principaux caractères phénologiques, argonomiques et technologiques chez Vitis vinifera L. Vitis **34**, 31-35.

Bugnon, F. and Bessis, R. (1968) Biology de la Vigne (Masson et Cie: Paris).

Buttrose, M.S. (1970) Fruitfulness in grapevines: the response of different cultivars to light, temperature and daylength. Vitis 9, 121-125.

Calò, A., Costacurta, A. et al. (1998) La stabilità all'ambiente dei caratteri della vite: l'esempio della fenologia. Riv. Vitic. Enol. **1**, 3-16.

Calò, A., Costacurta, A. et al. (1975) Stabilita ambientale di alcune caratteristiche fenologiche in varietá di Vitis vinifera. Estr. Riv. Vitic. Enol. Conegliano 11-12, 3-33.

Castelan-Estrada, M., Vivin, P. et al. (2002) Allometric relationships to estimate seasonal above-ground vegetative and reproductive biomass of Vitis vinifera L. Ann. Bot. **89**, 401-408.

Conradie, W.J. (1980) Seasonal uptake of nutrients by Chenin Blanc in sand culture. I. Nitrogen. S. Afr. J. Enol. Vitic. **1**, 59-65.

• Coombe, B.G. (1995) Adoption of a system for identifying grapevine growth stages. Aust. J. Grape Wine Res. **1**, 104-110.

Coombe, B.G. (1964) The winter treatment of grape vines with zinc and its interaction with time of pruning. Aust. J. Exp. Agric. Anim. Husb. **4**, 241-6.

Coombe, B.G. (1973) The regulation of set and development in the grape berry. Acta Hort. **34**, 261-273.

Coombe, B.G. (1987) Influence of temperature on composition and quality of grapes. Acta Hort. **206**, 23-35.

Coombe, B.G. (1988) Grape phenology. In B.G. Coombe and P.R. Dry (editors). Viticulture Vol. 1; Resources. Winetitles, Adelaide pp. 139-158.

Coombe, B.G. and Iland, P.G. (1987) Grape berry development. In: Proc. 6th Aust. Wine Industry Tech. Conf., Adelaide 1986. Ed T.H. Lee (Aust. Industrial Publ.: Adelaide), pp. 50-54.

Dry, P.R. (1984) Recent advances in Australian viticulture. In: Proc. 5th Aust. Wine Industry Tech. Conf., Perth 1983. Eds T.H Lee and T.C Somers (Australian Wine Research Institute: Adelaide), pp. 9-21.

Dry, P.R. (1987) How to grow 'cool climate' grapes in hot regions. Aust. Grapegrower & Winemaker No. 283, 25-26.

• Due, G., Morris, M. et al. (1993) Modelling grapevine phenology against weather: considerations based on a large data set. Agric. Forest Meteorol. **65**, 91-106.

Ebadi, E., Coombe, B.G. et al. (1995) Fruit-set on small Chardonnay and Shiraz vines grown under varying temperature regimes between budburst and flowering. Aust. J. Grape Wine Res. **1**, 3-10.

Eichorn, K.W. and Lorenz, D.H. (1977) Phäenologische Entwicklungsstadien der Rebe. Nachrichtenbl. Deut. Pflanzenschutzd. (Braunschweig) **29**, 119-120.

Gladstones, J. (1977) Temperature and wine grape quality in European vineyards. In: Proc. 3rd Aust. Wine Ind. Tech. Conf., Albury 1977 (Australian Wine Research Institute: Adelaide), pp. 7-11.

• Gladstones, J. (1992) Viticulture and Environment (Winetitles: Adelaide).

Gladstones, J. (1994) Climatology of cool viticultural environments: Reply to criticism and a further examination of Tasmania and New Zealand. Aust. NZ Wine Ind. J. **9**, 349-361.

Gladstones, J. (1996) The Due model — The last word. Aust. NZ Wine Ind. J. **11**, 134-139.

Hack, H., Bleiholder, H. et al. (1992) Einheitliche Codierung der phäenologischen Entwicklungsstadien mono- und dikotyler Pflanzen. — Erweiterte BBCH-Skala, Allgemein . Nachrichtenbl. Deut. Pflanzenschutzd. **44**, 265-270.

Heinze, R.A. (1977) Regional effects on vine development and must composition. In: Proc. 3rd Aust. Wine Ind. Tech. Conf., Albury 1977 (Australian Wine Research Institute: Adelaide), pp. 18-24.

• Jones, G.V. and Davis, R.E. (2000) Climate influences on grapevine phenology, grape composition, and wine production and quality for Bordeaux, France. Amer. J. Enol. Vitic. **51**, 249-261.

Kliewer, W.M. (1982) Vineyard canopy management — a review. In: Proc. Int. Symp. Grapes and Wine, Davis 1980. Ed A. D. Webb (Univ. of Calif.: Davis), pp.132-136.

• Lavee, S and May, P (1997) Dormancy of grapevine buds — facts and speculation. Aust. J. Grape Wine Res. 3, 31-46.

Lorenz, D.H., Eichhorn, K.W. et al. (1995) Phenological growth stages of the grapevine (Vitis vinifera L. ssp. vinifera) — Codes and descriptions according to the extended BBCH scale. Aust. J. Grape Wine Res. 1, 100-103 (translation by P. May of an original paper in German by the same authors in Vitic. Enol. Sci. **49**, 66-70 (1994)).

Martin, S.R. and Dunn, G.M. (2000) Effect of pruning time and hydrogen cyanamide on budburst and subsequent phenology of Vitis vinifera L. variety Cabernet Sauvignon in central Victoria. Aust. J. Grape Wine Res. **6**, 31-39.

• May, P. (2000) From bud to berry, with special reference to inflorescence and bunch morphology in Vitis vinifera L. Aust. J. Grape Wine Res. **6**, 82-98.

• May, P. (2004) Flowering and Fruitset in Grapevines (Phylloxera and Grape Industry Board of South Australia and Lythrum Press).

McCarthy, M.G. (1997) Effect of timing of water deficit on fruit development and composition of Vitis vinifera cv. Shiraz. PhD thesis, Univ. of Adelaide.

• McIntyre, G. N. (1982) Grapevine phenology. PhD thesis, Univ. of Newcastle.

• McIntyre, G.N, Kliewer, W.M. et al. (1987) Some limitations of the day degree system as used in viticulture in California. Amer. J. Enol. Vitic. **38**, 128-133.

McIntyre, G.N., Lider, L.A. et al. (1982) The chronological classification of grapevine phenology. Amer. J. Enol. Vitic. **33**, 80-85.

Pirie, A.J.G. (1978) Comparison of the climates of selected Australian, French and Californian wine producing areas. Aust. Grapegrower & Winemaker No. 15, 74-78.

Pouget, R. (1967) Methode d'appreciation de l'évolution physiologique des bourgeons pendant la phase de pré-débourrement de la vigne: Application à l'etude comparée du débourrement de la vigne. Vitis **6**, 294-302.

Pouget, R. (1968) Nouvelle conception du seuil de croissance chez la vigne. Vitis **7**, 201-205.

Pratt, C. and Coombe, B.G. (1978) Shoot growth and anthesis in Vitis. Vitis **17**, 125-133.

Schultz, H.R. (1993) Photosynthesis of sun and shade leaves of field-grown grapevine (Vitis vinifera L.) in relation to leaf age. Suitability of the plastochron concept for the expression of physiological age. Vitis **32**, 197-205.

Smart, R.E. (1987) Influence of light on composition and quality of grapes. Acta Hort. **206**, 37-47.

Smart, R.E. and Coombe, B.G. (1983) Water relations of grapevines. In: Water deficit and plant growth. Ed T.T. Kozlowski (Academic Press: New York), pp. 138-196.

Smart, R.E., Alcorso, C. et al. (1980) A comparison of winegrape performance at the present limits of Australian viticultural climates — Alice Springs and Hobart. Aust. Grapegrower & Winemaker No. 196, 28-30.

Winkler, A.J., Cook, J.A. et al. (1974) 'General Viticulture' (Univ. Calif. Press: Berkeley).

CHAPTER EIGHT

Grapevine Rootstocks

J.R.WHITING

Viticulture in Australia is based on varieties of the European vine, *Vitis vinifera* L., the predominant species of commercial grape production throughout the world. This species is particularly prone to attack by two soil-borne pests, the grape phylloxera and plant parasitic nematodes. The European vine can be protected from these pests by grafting to rootstock varieties derived from other vine species and hybrids that are resistant. Many of the rootstocks used for this purpose are adapted to particular soil types and some may also be used to overcome vineyard problems such as drought and salinity.

8.1 Resistance

Nematodes and phylloxera attack the vine by quite different and distinct mechanisms. Immunity to either pest is considered to be rare and is found in the genus *Muscadinia* (see 5.2.2). However, the rootstocks commonly used to protect against nematodes and phylloxera possess heritable characteristics that permit relatively less retardation of total growth compared to other varieties at the same level of infestation. A rootstock that displays such traits is termed resistant, relative to other susceptible varieties. Resistance to insects or nematodes may involve any of the following properties (Painter 1951):

(i) Non-preference: when the rootstock possesses characteristics that are unattractive to soil-borne pests for reproduction, feeding or shelter.

(ii) Antibiosis: when the pest is able to establish feeding sites but the rootstock adversely affects the growth and reproduction of the pest.

(iii) Tolerance: when the rootstock can live and thrive, suffering little permanent damage, despite supporting a pest population capable of severely damaging more susceptible varieties. Tolerant varieties may even be more conducive to the buildup of a pest population than susceptible varieties.

The advantage of this concept of resistance is that it distinguishes between the total growth of the plant and the inherent protective properties that contribute to this growth. It is the *effectiveness* of the protective properties rather than their mere presence that is of practical importance. It follows that resistance is properly measured as *the fractional reduction in total growth, over a specified period of time, in the presence of a pest, disease or debilitating condition*. Such an expression of resistance on a proportional basis, with respect to the healthy condition of that particular rootstock, standardises the differences in absolute growth that exist between different rootstocks.

Commonly used measures of resistance are based either on evidence of the protective properties alone (e.g. evidence of root damage, or differences in the size and fecundity of the pest population), or, alternatively, on the growth of the rootstock in the presence of the pest compared to that of some standard type, e.g. *V. vinifera*, under the same conditions. In some situations it is not just the direct pest attack that causes the plant to suffer. With phylloxera, for example, secondary fungal infections following insect damage produce more root damage and less vine growth than when fungi are excluded (Omer *et al.* 1995). Micro-propagated grapevines have been used to determine resistance. There are advantages in using this approach: experimental conditions are easily controlled, secondary pathogens can be eliminated, response to single cultures of pests can be evaluated and time periods are shorter. Techniques such as egg mass staining (Cousins and Walker 2000) allow more rapid evaluation of the nematode reproductive ability and greater capacity to screen large numbers of hybrids. However, these approaches allow no distinction between the benefits due to resistance and those due to other physiological characteristics of the rootstock. Studies on resistant rootstocks at the genetic level have identified genes or groups of genes responsible for conferring resistance (Walker and Jin 2000). Transgenic plants offer a potential way of conferring resistance in susceptible plants and progress is being made with some of the techniques available (Nicol *et al.* 1999). With nematodes, resistance is commonly defined as the plant's ability to inhibit nematode reproduction, while tolerance describes the plant's ability to grow and produce satisfactory yields despite relatively high nematode populations. While it seems that existing measures of resistance have served their purpose in a general sense, it is also apparent that the lack of clear distinction between resistance and other physiological characteristics, such as absolute growth or rate of growth, has clouded the assessment of rootstock performance and recommendations based thereon. The situation in the vineyard is even more complex. As this chapter unfolds it will become apparent that vineyard performance of a grafted vine depends not only on resistance and other inherent properties of the rootstock but also on factors such as stock-scion relationships, cultural conditions and activity of specific pests.

8.1.1 RESISTANCE TO PHYLLOXERA

The life cycle of phylloxera is described in Volume II, Chapter 10. Under Australian conditions, phylloxera is frequently found on roots and occasionally on leaves of some of the most popular rootstocks. The occurrence and extent of leaf galling and root symptoms is closely related to the species origin of the rootstock (Boubals 1966, Buchanan and Hardie 1978). Economic losses are only

Figure 8.1: Impact of phylloxera on Cabernet Sauvignon: own-rooted (middle), grafted to Freedom (near left) and 140 Ruggeri (far right).

caused when a virulent soil-inhabiting form of the insect feeds upon the root tissue of non-resistant vines (**FIGURE 8.1**). It should be noted that some 'strains' of phylloxera feed and reproduce on excised roots of some rootstocks better than on *V. vinifera* (Viduka *et al.* 2003), but the practical significance of this has not been determined.

The lesions caused by feeding are of two kinds; *nodosities*, characteristic hook-shaped galls that develop on young roots, and *tuberosities*, rounded swellings, which occur, on older tissue giving the root a 'warty' appearance. The initial damage to grapevine roots, especially abnormal growth and disturbance of metabolism in the affected tissues, is primarily due to the activity of phylloxera itself (Rilling 1975). Decay of the root lesions caused by soil-borne microorganisms is considered to be largely responsible for the subsequent decline of the vine. Anatomical differences between the roots of *V. vinifera* and the American species have been used to account for differences in the root damage caused by phylloxera (Pratt 1974). According to Boubals (1966), it is only susceptibility to the formation of tuberosities that has practical significance as to whether or not a rootstock will succumb to phylloxera. Certain resistant rootstocks, such as Rupestris du Lot, form numerous nodosities without showing marked diminution in growth. However, it has been shown that high numbers of nodosities on the roots of 5C Teleki rootstock [*V. cinerea* var. *helleri* (herein referred to by the more commonly used *V. berlandieri*; see Chapter 5) x *V. riparia*], combined with environmental stress, results in depressed growth and yield in Germany (Porten *et al.* 2000).

Boubals (1966) studied the behaviour of phylloxera on the roots of numerous representatives of Vitaceae and found two types of resistance:
(i)   Resistance by tolerance, brought about by the formation of a layer of cork tissue (periderm) around the root lesion, which is the type found in all resistant *Vitis* species; the periderm limits the spread

of decay into the root or may cause abscission of all or part of the lesion (Niklowitz 1955).

(ii) Resistance by repulsion of the insect by the root, which is found in *Muscadinia rotundifolia* (also known as *Vitis rotundifolia*) and to a lesser extent in *V. berlandieri, V. rupestris* and *V. riparia*. Boubals (1966) regarded this as evidence of antibiosis, however non-preference may have been involved. The same type of resistance was also found in several other vine genera not exploited commercially, such as *Cissus* and *Leea* (see 5.2.3, 5.2.7).

Studies on feeding by the virulent phylloxera clone G4 on susceptible plants have shown that it feeds on parenchyma cells within the root and generally only one or a few at a time (Kellow *et al.* 2004). In susceptible roots, only single stylet tracks are observed within the galls and starch and amino acids accumulate in the cortical cells due to increased phloem unloading. In association with this there is a loss of suberisation of the endodermis, thus movement of nutrients from the phloem to the cortex is uninhibited. The swelling of the root (galling) is believed to result from an inductive agent (possibly an auxin or a precursor thereof) injected by the insect. In resistant rootstocks, multiple and branched feeding tracks are observed, possibly representing aborted feeding attempts (Kellow *et al.* 2000). Where phylloxera penetrate with their stylet, there appears to be a rapid oxidative browning response in the neighbouring tissue without phloem nutrient unloading, and phylloxera are unable to feed properly. It seems that susceptible roots do not react quickly enough or at all to inhibit phylloxera feeding. Immune plants (*M. rotundifolia*) in these studies did not show any feeding attempts by phylloxera. Rootstocks differ in their responses to phylloxera. In Ramsey (*V. champinii*), small nodosities are formed and insects feed and reproduce, albeit at a greatly reduced rate. In *V. riparia* phylloxera attempts to feed, nodosities were initiated but they quickly became necrotic and the phylloxera dies. With Schwarzmann (*V. riparia* x *V. rupestris*) and Börner (*V. riparia* x *V. cinerea*) phylloxera attempt to feed, but are unable to become established, with necrosis of the tissue and death of the phylloxera. Thus the resistance mechanism of Ramsey is by antibiosis and that of Schwarzmann, Börner and *V. riparia* is by non-preference.

Several attempts have been made to rank the phylloxera rootstocks according to numerical ratings of resistance, e.g. Viala and Ravaz (1901), Boubals (1966), Granett et al. (1983), Forneck *et al.* (1996), using either field grown vines, open-potted vines, excised cultured roots or micro-propagated vines. Different reactions occur on roots of *Vitis* spp., including: i) large yellow nodosities showing no browning or necrosis on susceptible *V. vinifera*, ii) smaller nodosities with brown, necrotic tissue at abandoned feeding sites, eg. Ramsey, iii) no nodosities with necrosis of the tissue surrounding

feeding sites and death of phylloxera, e.g. *V. riparia* and Börner, and iv) no attempt to feed, e.g. *M. rotundifolia* (Kellow *et al.* 2002). Similar responses were recorded on micro-propagated *in vitro* cultured vines and on potted vines. These ratings are generally subject to the limitations associated with existing measures of resistance, viz. some rootstocks perform well with reproducing phylloxera on the roots, and, in early work, the rootstocks were screened with un-defined 'biotypes' of phylloxera. Since the early 1900s, phylloxera biotypes have been reported in many countries, such as France, Germany, Canada, South Africa and USA, and inconsistent reactions noted with rootstocks. Phylloxera biotypes have also been studied in Australia, initially using random amplified polymorphic DNA (RAPD) analysis (Corrie *et al.* 1997). These studies were further refined by using microsatellite DNA markers with biotypes now defined as genotypes or clones (Corrie *et al.* 2002). The importance of the interaction of phylloxera clone with the rootstock Schwarzmann has demonstrated that one genotype of phylloxera (SRU-1) caused extensive nodosity development and another genotype (VWL-1, syn. clone G4) did not feed at all on excised roots (Kellow *et al.* 2002). Thus ratings based on insect development or galling reaction using single clones of phylloxera may provide an incomplete guide to the resistance of rootstocks (see also Viduka *et al.* 2003).

As noted previously, vine performance in the vineyard is also governed by factors that influence the activity of the insect or the growth of the vine. For example, in coarse textured soils where phylloxera activity is low, infested vines, even on their own roots, can survive for longer than in soils of finer texture (Nougaret and Lapham 1928). Phylloxera has been recorded as surviving in soils up to 70% sand (Buchanan and Whiting 1991). ARG1, a rootstock with low phylloxera resistance, was used satisfactorily for many years in north eastern Victoria, and in New Zealand. It was also recommended for phylloxera control in fertile, moist soils in California (Lider *et al.* 1978). Conversely, this rootstock failed to resist phylloxera in the field when used in South Africa and Sicily (Perold 1927). At the time, Perold (1927) explained the decline of vines grafted to this rootstock in South Africa to the possible evolution of a new biological race of phylloxera. The situation was manifested in California with the description of two biotypes of phylloxera, types A and B, and the finding that some rootstocks with *V. vinifera* in their parentage were susceptible to biotype B, e.g. ARG1 (Granett *et al.* 1987). This resulted in a huge replanting program in California to replace ARG1 with more resistant rootstocks. These experiences show the importance of field evaluation to determine rootstock performance under specific viticultural conditions and concurrent examination of the biology of phylloxera under the same conditions.

8.1.2 RESISTANCE TO NEMATODES

The nature of rootstock resistance to nematodes is not well understood, and the question of immunity is disputed. Rootknot nematodes have been found associated with some of the most resistant rootstocks (Lider 1960, Sauer 1972) and this suggests that resistance is largely achieved by tolerance, although other properties cannot be discounted. It is also clear that the resistance of a particular rootstock is generally, though not necessarily, specific, in that it is confined to one nematode species or a group of closely related species. Thus Kunde *et al.* (1968) found that Ramsey (tested under the incorrect name Salt Creek, see 8.3.1) and Dog Ridge, rootstocks that are highly resistant to rootknot nematodes (*Meloidogyne* spp.), were susceptible to dagger nematode (*Xiphinema index*). Similarly many of the commonly used rootstocks for rootknot nematodes are susceptible to *Pratylenchus* spp. This could be due to different feeding mechanisms between nematode species.

The mechanisms of resistance are not well known. Ferris *et al.* (1982) demonstrated that the resistance of Harmony, Ramsey and Dog Ridge to *M. arenaria* was expressed primarily through reduced stylet penetration of the root system, in combination with a failure of the nematodes to establish feeding sites and/or induction of host biochemical defences. In most situations, nematode resistance genes elicit a hypersensitive response or localised necrosis leading to a breakdown of the feeding site, and natural resistance genes are specific to one nematode species or pathotype (Heinrich *et al.* 1998). With the resistant rootstock RS-9 (Ramsey x Schwarzmann), feeding by *M. arenaria* induced necrosis within the root, either in the cortical cells, which delays movement of juveniles to the vascular system, or in the vascular tissue, which prevents feeding (Anwar and McKenry 2000). However, in the resistant rootstock 10-23B (*V. doaniana*), no hypersensitive reaction was evident but juveniles were starved during development resulting in non-reproducing females. Caution must be used in accepting the identification of *Meloidogyne* spp. where they have been described based on perineal pattern in conjunction with rootstock resistance in early publications. A more accurate method based on DNA analysis has demonstrated that species identified by perineal pattern may not always match that determined by mitochondrial DNA testing (McLeod and Steel 1999). The latter report concludes that *M. arenaria* and *M. javanica* are common in NSW vineyards, but doubts the existence of *M. incognita* therein based on DNA analysis.

Little is known of the resistance of rootstocks to nematodes of other genera. Sauer (1977) monitored the relationships of citrus nematode (*Tylenchulus semipenetrans*) and rootlesion nematode (*Pratylenchus spp.*) with a number of rootstocks in a field study lasting five years. Population size of both nematode species appeared to be related to rootstock host. This may reflect differences in rootstock resistance, however, in the trials associated with these observations, there was no indication that either nematode species had any effect on crop productivity (Sauer 1974). Root lesion nematode has been shown to cause extensive root damage to 1613 and Harmony in experiments conducted in pots (Sauer 1977). While there is no evidence of yield loss in the vineyard, the use of these rootstocks on sites infested with this species may create unnecessary risks.

8.2 Phylloxera-resistant rootstocks

8.2.1 DEVELOPMENT OF PHYLLOXERA-RESISTANT ROOTSTOCKS

The grape phylloxera is indigenous to North America where its native habitat is the region to the east of the Rocky Mountains. Many of the wild vine species of this region have acquired inherent resistance to this aphid-like pest. In 1863, phylloxera, undoubtedly introduced with American vines, appeared in France. The subsequent spread of the insect through Europe and elsewhere is recounted in Volume II, Chapter 10. In the early 1880s, rootstocks derived from resistant American species were developed. These and their successors have been adopted as the principal long-term counter to phylloxera in the vineyards of the world. A well-documented account of the impact of phylloxera on European viticulture and the subsequent development of resistant rootstocks is presented by Ordish (1972). Alternative methods of control have been less satisfactory. The principal species used in the development of phylloxera-resistant rootstocks were *V. aestivalis*, *V. berlandieri*, *V. vulpina* (*V. cordifolia*), *V. monticola*, *V. riparia* and *V. rupestris*. Breeding and evaluation programs continue in many parts of the world. A summary of information on evaluation of rootstocks from France, South Africa, Australia and USA is compiled in Wolpert *et al.* (1992).

Two species, *Muscadinia rotundifolia* and *M. munsoniana*, are immune to phylloxera. Unfortunately morphological and botanical differences between these species and vines of the Euvitis or true vine section, to which most other species belong, prevent satisfactory grafting and make hybridization difficult (see Chapter 5). However, Jelenkovic and Olmo (1968) reported successful hybridization between *V. vinifera* and *M. rotundifolia*, and, hybrids of *V. rupestris* and *M. rotundifolia* have been screened for resistance to *Xiphinema index* (Walker and Jin 2000). This suggests that, in future, it may be possible to further exploit species of the Muscadine genus as a breeding source of rootstock varieties. Other attempts to combine the resistance of the American vine species with the desirable fruit characteristics of the *V. vinifera* varieties through hybridization have met with considerable success. The culture of varieties of this nature, the so-called American and French-American hybrids, was considerable at one time, with over 400,000 hectares grown in France and large areas in eastern Europe.

8.2.2 PHYLLOXERA-RESISTANT ROOTSTOCKS IN AUSTRALIA

Phylloxera was first identified in Victoria in 1877 and in New South Wales in 1884. Resistant rootstocks have been used extensively in the infested areas of both states. Experience with rootstocks in Victorian vineyards commenced in 1900 when over 100,000 resistant vines and cuttings, mainly selections and hybrids of *V. rupestris* and *V. riparia*, were distributed to growers and nurseries throughout the state. A summary of the history of attempts to eradicate phylloxera and the eventual move to the use of rootstocks is presented in Hardie and Cirami (1988). By 1920 most vineyards were fully reconstituted with rootstocks using Rupestris du Lot, 1202 Couderc, 3306 Couderc, 3309 Couderc and ARG1 (de Castella 1920). In 1924, Richter's *V. berlandieri* x *V. rupestris* hybrids 99 Richter and 110 Richter were imported by the Victorian Department of Agriculture. The rootstock 99 Richter subsequently performed very favourably in comparison with other rootstocks popular at that time (see 8.5.6). The next period of field rootstock trials in phylloxera-infested sites in Victoria were assessed in the 1980s. These trials included some previously used rootstocks as well as more recent imports from California and Europe. In contrast to earlier work, ARG1 did not yield well and high populations of phylloxera became established on the roots in the field. The rootstocks that yielded consistently well included hybrids of *V. berlandieri* x *V. riparia* (5BB Kober/5A Teleki and 5C Teleki), *V. berlandieri* x *V. rupestris* (99 Richter, 110 Richter and 140 Ruggeri), *V. riparia* x *V. rupestris* (Schwarzmann), and *V. champinii* (Ramsey) (Whiting and Buchanan 1992, Whiting 2003).

In New South Wales, phylloxera outbreaks were confined to two separate regions; the Counties of Camden and Cumberland near Sydney, and a small area near Corowa. In addition to the rootstocks adopted by Victoria in the early 1900s, Riparia Gloire, 106-8 and 101-14 performed satisfactorily. Phylloxera was found in Queensland, in the Brisbane suburb of Enoggera in 1910 and reappeared at Myrtletown, another Brisbane suburb, in 1932. From the rootstock experiments that followed, 1202 and ARG1 gained most widespread acceptance, not only to combat phylloxera but also to improve the growth of vines planted in infertile soils (Hardie and Cirami 1988). Tablegrape growers at Stanthorpe, Queensland, commenced using rootstocks in 1910 in preparation for the possible appearance of phylloxera. Despite the absence of the pest, rootstocks such as Rupestris du Lot, 3309 and ARG1 have been used to improve vine growth and productivity in infertile soils (Taylor and Bowen 1955). Subsequently, Rupestris du Lot, 3306 and to a lesser extent Isabella were recommended for this purpose, and recently Ramsey and Schwarzmann have been used. In sub-tropical Central Queensland, the rootstocks Freedom, 5BB Kober, 1103 Paulsen, K51-32 and 1613 were considered satisfactory with Maroo Seedless and Flame Seedless (Oag 1995).

It is probable that the vineyards of South Australia, Western Australia, Tasmania, the Victorian and New South Wales Sunraysia regions, the mid-Murray horticultural areas around Robinvale and Swan Hill, and the Riverina region in NSW have been protected from phylloxera by regulations that control the introduction of grapevines into those areas, thus avoiding the possibility of the pest entering on infested material. Additional safeguards exist in the form of laws in New South Wales, Victoria and Queensland that isolate affected localities and prohibit the transfer of vines from within them (Proclaimed Vine Disease Districts or Phylloxera Infested Zones (PIZs)). According to Coombe (1963) the introduction of resistant rootstocks into South Australia was also opposed on the grounds that, if phylloxera was inadvertently introduced, rootstocks might assist in its spread. The reasons were twofold. The winged form of phylloxera initiates a sexual cycle that results in the formation of leaf galls. The establishment of viable leaf galls occurs only on certain American vines and their hybrids. Hence the use of American rootstocks provides the potential for spread of phylloxera by means of the winged form. The other possibility was that the roots of American vines, whether in a grafted vineyard or a mother vine planting, could harbour the root-living form of phylloxera without showing symptoms and so provide a source for the unwitting infestation of clean areas.

Over the years several cases of misnaming of rootstocks have occurred. Ramsey was incorrectly named Salt Creek in many early publications, and Schwarzmann was incorrectly known as Teleki in Western Australia. The rootstock imported in 1964 from California as 99 Richter (Australian Accession Code I.V.64.2083) is, in fact, 110 Richter (Hardie *et al.* 1981). It seems likely that much of the Californian experience purportedly with 99 Richter has actually been with 110 Richter (see 'Letter to the Editor' American Journal of Enology and Viticulture, by C.J. Alley and H.P. Olmo, Vol. 32, issue 1, 1981). Similarly a rootstock imported as SO4 (I.V.66.2136) from California has been identified as 5C Teleki; by comparison, SO4 (I.C.80.8341) imported from Europe is correct. Also 5A Teleki (I.V.66.2133) from California has been shown by DNA fingerprinting to be the same as 5BB Kober.

One could argue that the benefit of having rootstocks that are readily available, and can also be used for other purposes, overrides the risk of phylloxera infestation. In recent years therefore, South Australia and Western Australia, along with most other states, have established source plantings of important, virus-tested, rootstock varieties. A survey of rootstock use in Australia, confined to the varieties Shiraz, Cabernet Sauvignon, Chardonnay and Semillon (these varieties comprised 45% of the total planted area in Australia in 1996), showed that 28% of those varieties were planted on rootstock (Anon. 1996). In South Australia, a non-phylloxera state, around 18% of the plantings were on rootstock in 2004 (N. Dry, Phylloxera and Grape Industry Board of SA, pers. comm.).

8.3 Nematode-resistant rootstocks

8.3.1 DEVELOPMENT OF NEMATODE RESISTANT ROOTSTOCKS

Rootstocks that resist rootknot nematode

Nematode resistance in *Vitis* species was first recognised in Florida, USA, by Neal (1889). He was also the first to suggest that rootstocks might be used for grafting in commercial vineyards. Snyder (1936) reported the first comprehensive study of the commercial application of nematode resistant grapevines in the San Joaquin Valley, California. A large number (154) of varieties of *V. vinifera*, as well as other grape species selections and hybrid rootstocks, were examined in soils infested with rootknot nematodes. In these studies all *V. vinifera* varieties were heavily infested. Most of the American species selections and hybrids were likewise infested; a few, however, exhibited moderate to high resistance. Among the latter were 1613, 1616 and three *V. champinii* varieties: Dog Ridge, Barnes and de Grasset. Similar resistance was also found in a variety tested under the name *V. doaniana* Salt Creek; however it now seems probable that this was actually a fourth *V. champinii* variety, Ramsey, the error apparently having been made before this study commenced. The incorrect name (Salt Creek) was used in studies subsequent to Snyder's in both California and Australia but Loomis and Lider (1971) re-established its correct identity. The name Ramsey is used for the variety in this chapter.

The grape species considered by Snyder to have the most potential for resistance were *V. champinii*, *V. acerifolia* (syn. *V. longii*, *V. solonis*) and *V. cinerea* var. *cinerea* (herein referred to as *V. cinerea*). This work laid the foundation for future nematode rootstock investigations. The succeeding studies, which took place in California and which ultimately aroused world-wide interest in rootstocks as a means of combating the nematode problem, have been reviewed by Lider (1960). More recently Walker *et al.* (1994a) tested rootstocks with *M. incognita* and found good resistance (based on nematode reproduction) in *V. aestivalis*, *V. cinerea*, *V. rufotomentosa*, *V. champinii*, *M. rotundifolia*, and some selections of *V. rupestris* and *V. californica*. The two rootstocks of particular importance with respect to rootknot nematode control are both vigorously-growing selections of *V. champinii*, namely Ramsey and Dog Ridge. Both possess a high degree of resistance to rootknot nematode and are capable of producing high-yielding, vigorously-growing scions in sandy, relatively infertile vineyards. In California, the less vigorous 1613 performed satisfactorily on fertile soils infested with rootknot nematode, although some instances of susceptibility were recorded.

In an attempt to combine the high nematode resistance of Dog Ridge with the more easily controlled vigour of 1613, Weinberger and Harmon (1966) produced Harmony, a rootstock derived from the hybridization of open-pollinated seedlings selected from each of these rootstocks. Harmony seems well suited to all but the most severely rootknot nematode-infested and infertile soils in California (Winkler *et al.* 1974). Similarly *V. champinii* was crossed with *V. riparia* to produce rootstocks with more manageable vigour, i.e. K51-32 and K51-40. Several other rootstocks resist rootknot nematodes. These include 99 Richter, 34 EM, 5BB Kober and Schwarzmann (Galet 1956, Lider 1960, Goss and Cameron 1977a). In general, none of these provides the resistance of the *V. champinii* hybrids, but it is likely that some could be suited to particular vineyard conditions where other factors such as soil type or stock-scion interaction necessitate some compromise in this property.

The occurrence of virulent strains of *M. incognita* has been reported in California and in Australia. McKenry (1992) reported the rootstocks Ramsey, Dog Ridge, 1613, Freedom and Harmony to be susceptible to a virulent population of *M. incognita*. In Australia, the resistant rootstock Ramsey showed root galling, high nematode reproduction rates and reduced growth with a virulent strain of *M. incognita* (Walker 1997). Virulent strains of nematodes appear rare at this stage but vigilance is required to prevent further spread of these strains. Hybrids of *M. rotundifolia* x *V. vinifera*, which have been reported as immune to *Meloidogyne* spp., have been produced and tested. Limited adoption has taken place perhaps due to the concern that their partial *V. vinifera* parentage will impact on phylloxera resistance.

Rootstocks that resist dagger nematode

In preliminary trials in which resistance of some commonly used rootstocks was rated on visible root damage and changes in the population of the dagger nematode (*Xiphinema index*), Kunde *et al.* (1968) found that 1613 and Riparia Gloire were moderately resistant. *V. vinifera* and 25 other rootstocks out of a total of 35 tested were quite susceptible. The important aspect of these trials was an indication of resistance in several American vine species tested, namely *V. mustangensis* (*V. candicans*), *V. acerifolia*, *V. arizonica*, *V. rufotomentosa* and *V. smalliana*. L.A. Lider made crosses with the most resistant species identified by Kunde *et al.* (1968) and established them, along with selections of *V. vinifera* x *M. rotundifolia* (known as VR hybrids bred by H.P. Olmo in 1948) and several susceptible rootstocks, in a field trial with the nematode-fanleaf virus complex. Early reports after 9 years showed only one hybrid, VR O39-16, did not have fanleaf virus, but after 12 years it was also detected with the virus (Walker *et al.* 1994c). Even though the VR hybrids are deemed resistant to *X. index*, transfer of fanleaf was occurring presumably by *X. index* attempting to feed on the roots. Two VR hybrids, O39-16 and O43-43, maintained normal crop yields during the

12 years of the trial whereas other susceptible rootstocks (ARG1, Harmony, Rupestris du Lot) and a promising resistant rootstock (Lider 171-6, a *V. rufotomentosa* x *V. vinifera* hybrid) yielded poorly (Walker et al. 1994b).

Even though there is some degree of resistance to *X. index* in 1613, Dog Ridge, Ramsey, Freedom and Harmony, grapevine fanleaf can be transferred to those rootstocks. Despite the caution with respect to phylloxera susceptibility, VR O39-16 has been recommended for areas where *X. index* is likely to carry grapevine fanleaf. McKenry *et al.* (2001a), using potted vines, concluded that Freedom, VR O39-16, Schwarzmann and 171-6 displayed resistance to *X. index*. *V. cinerea* hybrids, such as Börner, have been reported to be immune to *X. index* and to prevent transmission of grapevine fanleaf (Becker 1989, cited in Nicol *et al.* 1999), but further testing is required under a broader range of conditions. Coiro *et al.* (1990) found that *X. index* sourced from different countries had different reproduction rates on the same rootstocks, potentially producing different resistance classifications depending on the nematode source. This work needs to be substantiated but suggests that local testing is required and questions the reliance on non-local testing results.

Rootstocks that resist other nematodes

A number of other nematode species have been shown to damage grapevine roots, e.g. *Tylenchulus semipenetrans* and *Pratylenchus* spp., and several more have been found associated with grapevine roots without showing specific feeding damage, e.g. *Criconemella xenoplax*, *Longidorus* spp., and *Paralongidorus* spp.. The latter two genera have been identified as vectors of virus-like diseases in Europe and North America (Krake *et al.* 1999) and it would be advantageous to have resistant rootstocks available. No rootstocks tested were classed as having any resistance to *Criconemella xenoplax* by McKenry *et al.* (2001a) in small pot trials. With *Tylenchulus semipenetrans*, not all rootstocks tested in Australia are resistant. Edwards (1988, 1989) found high levels of *T. semipenetrans* associated with the rootstock Harmony but with no obvious effect on yield. Harmony was classed as tolerant and all other rootstocks surveyed were classed as at least moderately resistant. Wachtel (1986) cautioned against using K51-32 where *T. semipenetrans* is present due to a significant reduction in root growth in pot experiments.

8.3.2 NEMATODE-RESISTANT ROOTSTOCKS IN AUSTRALIA
One of the earliest reports of plant-parasitic nematode attack on vines in Australia was that of Quinn (1947) who noted an occurrence in a vineyard with sandy soil at Geelong, Victoria. Although this report did not specify the particular type of nematode encountered, there are two species of nematode that are cause for particular concern in the vineyards of this country; rootknot nematode (*Meloidogyne* spp.) and dagger nematode (*X.*

index). The biological characteristics of these and other nematode species that occur in Australian vineyards are discussed in Volume II, Chapter 11.

Rootstocks that resist rootknot nematode
Rootknot nematodes occur in most vineyard areas in Australia. However, serious infestation is confined to soils of coarse texture. Rootknot nematode seldom causes serious problems in fine-textured soils. The testing of rootstocks as a control measure commenced in the 1950s. Early research was based on readily available phylloxera resistant rootstocks. In Western Australia the rootstocks Schwarzmann (erroneously known then as 'Teleki') and 34 EM (erroneously thought to be 161-49) achieved early popularity. In Victoria, Sauer (1967) demonstrated that 101-14 and Rupestris du Lot could be used to improve the yield of Sultana vines grown in nematode-infested replant vineyards in the Sunraysia region. However, it has been the studies that commenced with the introduction in the early 1960s of Ramsey, Dog Ridge and 1613 from the University of California, Davis, that have produced the most progress in this field.

In 1966, the then CSIRO Division of Horticultural Research included these rootstocks in a series of trials designed specifically to solve the rootknot nematode problem for Sultana growers. These trials, which were confined to sand and sandy loam soils, showed conclusively that Ramsey was the best available rootstock for Sultana under these conditions. Worthwhile yield increases were achieved whether nematode infestation of these soils was severe, moderate or absent (Sauer 1972, May *et al.* 1973, Sauer 1974). In the Sunraysia region, other varieties, which have shown a similar response when grafted to this rootstock, even on sites where nematodes cause no obvious damage, include Palomino, Cabernet Sauvignon, Shiraz, Colombard, Chenin Blanc, Barbera and Carignan.

Trials on coarse-textured soils infested with rootknot nematode in New South Wales, Victoria, South Australia and Western Australia have all shown similar responses, with both Ramsey and Dog Ridge commonly inducing superior productivity (Stannard 1976, Goss and Cameron 1977b, Cirami *et al.* 1984, May 1994). Both rootstocks are recommended for nematode-infested soils in Queensland. In north eastern Victoria the rootstocks 5C Teleki, 5BB Kober, Harmony and 110 Richter yielded as well as Ramsey in a trial with Cabernet Sauvignon in a site with high levels of rootknot and low levels of citrus nematode (Edwards 1989, Whiting 2003). In another two trials in north-east Victoria, with a lower proportion of sand and moderate levels of rootknot and citrus nematode, the rootstocks listed above and Schwarzmann yielded well. In a trial in the Barossa Valley, in a site described as heavily infested with *Meloidogyne* spp., 5C Teleki (reported as SO4), K51-32, Schwarzmann, 101-14, 5BB Kober and 1616 yielded as well as Ramsey (McCarthy and Cirami 1990).

Rootstocks that resist dagger nematode

In Australia, the dagger nematode appears to be confined to a few vineyards within a small area close to Rutherglen in north-eastern Victoria (Meagher *et al.* 1976). This nematode not only damages vine roots, causing replant failure and decline of mature vines, but is also the vector of grape fanleaf virus. The effects of fanleaf virus are described in Volume II, Chapter 11. Rootstocks developed in California to combat the effects of this nematode were screened in pots and then tested in north east Victoria in a loamy sand soil with low numbers of *X. index* and other nematodes. Good yields and growth were obtained with the easily propagated Lider seedlings 171-13 (*V. rufotomentosa* x *V. vinifera*), 122-16 (*V. rupestris* Metallique x 1613), 88-113 (*V. slavini* x *V. rupestris* Metallique), 171-52 (*V. rufotomentosa* x *V. vinifera*), 106-38 (*V. acerifolia* x (*V. riparia* Gloire x *V. champinii* Ramsey)) and 116-11 (*V. mustangensis* x 1613), as well as Dog Ridge, 101-14, 5C Teleki and Ramsey (Harris 1988). Due to a complex of pests at this site and that some of the better performing rootstocks have *V. vinifera* parentage, further work is required before firm conclusions can be drawn on *X. index* resistant rootstocks in Australia.

8.4 Rootstock adaptation

Some of the American species from which modern rootstocks are derived have their origins in quite distinct geographical regions of North America (Bailey 1934). Rootstocks derived from these species often display the traits of their parents in terms of adaptation to certain soil types and conditions. The corollary of this feature is that some rootstocks tolerate adverse soil conditions more readily than do others, although rootstocks do not necessarily tolerate some soil conditions better than ungrafted *V. vinifera*. Several countries rank rootstock performance primarily against various soil types or descriptors. May (1994) has suggested a need for such an approach in Australia. A step towards this has been made by defining the soil types in which rootstock evaluations have been conducted (Cass *et al.* 2002), but further work is required to link the viticultural performance of the rootstocks with the soil classifications. This interpretation will need to be undertaken with care because factors other than soil classification will influence results, e.g. soil pest status, use of irrigation water and the wide range of climates associated with some soil classifications.

Some of the characteristics of soils likely to influence rootstock performance are covered in the following sections. The examples that follow illustrate the importance of adaptation with respect to the choice of rootstock.

8.4.1 LIMESTONE SOILS

Unlike *Vitis vinifera*, many American vine species are particularly intolerant of lime. In soils rich in this constituent there is reduced availability of iron and the grafted vines show yellowing of leaves (chlorosis), symptoms typical of iron deficiency. This trait is present in many rootstocks, and the tolerance of rootstocks to such conditions has been ranked by Viala and Ravaz (1901) and Galet (1956). *V. vulpina* and *V. riparia* have a low tolerance while *V. berlandieri* has a high tolerance. This is apparent also in the rootstocks derived from the *V. berlandieri* species, for example, 420A, 99 Richter and 5BB Kober. Elsewhere, 101-14 (*V. riparia* x *V. rupestris*) showed chlorosis symptoms in potted calcareous soil whereas 140 Ruggeri (*V. berlandieri* x *V. rupestris*) did not.

Thus far in Australia, tolerance to lime has not been an important criterion for the choice of rootstock because the use of rootstocks has been mainly confined to phylloxera or rootknot nematode control. Phylloxera is presently confined to regions with non-calcareous soils and rootknot nematode is a serious problem only on deeper sandy soils. However, if it becomes necessary to use rootstocks on calcareous soils, lime tolerance is likely to be an important consideration. Chlorosis has been associated with the use of certain rootstocks on the finer textured loam or clay loam soils of the Sunraysia region. Limestone occurs in these soils usually as a loosely aggregated sub-stratum (see Chapter 3) and the calcium carbonate content of the topsoils range from zero to 21.6 per cent (Penman *et al.* 1940). In two successive seasons, Colombard vines grafted to Ramsey in an experiment established on sandy loam at the Department of Primary Industries, Mildura, showed 62% and 29% incidence of chlorosis symptoms respectively, while ungrafted Colombard vines, randomly interplanted, displayed no symptoms.

Similar observations have been made with grafted Muscat Gordo Blanco vines grown on moderate-to-heavy textured soils in two trials in the same region (**FIGURE 8.2**). Vines grafted to K51-32, Dog Ridge and

Figure 8.2: Chlorosis symptoms on Muscat Gordo Blanco grafted to Schwarzmann (near left) compared with own-rooted vines (far right).

Schwarzmann consistently showed symptoms of chlorosis, whilst 110 Richter and Harmony showed less symptoms. Own-rooted vines of Muscat Gordo Blanco and grafted to 5BB Kober (5A Teleki) and 1613 did not display symptoms on two sites where it was possible to make this comparison (Whiting *et al.* 1987). The symptoms are usually transient and observation suggests that this condition is likely to appear with excessively high soil moisture during spring and that growth made later in the season is usually unaffected. The testing of Fercal, a highly regarded rootstock in France for lime tolerance, in high lime conditions in Australia has not been undertaken.

8.4.2. COMPACT CLAY SOILS

Hybrids of *V. vulpina* are particularly well suited to fine-textured clay soils. Australian experience with these rootstocks has been limited. The only *V. vulpina* hybrid grown in commercial vineyards in this country is 106-8. Muscat Hamburg grafted to this rootstock was superior to own-rooted vines and those on other phylloxera-resistant rootstocks in a trial established on heavy volcanic clay loam at Orchard Hills, NSW (Hardie and Cirami 1988). This rootstock warrants further testing.

8.4.3 POORLY-DRAINED SOILS

Interpretation of reports on waterlogging tolerance of rootstocks can be confounded because the consequences of waterlogging may include reduced oxygen concentration to roots and alterations to root physiology, as well as an interaction with root diseases. These differences are often not clearly defined in reports, and, combined with the sometimes mis-identification of rootstocks, could contribute to conflicting conclusions by different authors.

Some rootstocks, particularly those derived from *V. berlandieri*, will not tolerate the waterlogged conditions that are frequently encountered in poorly drained soils. This is likely to be, at least partly, a consequence of poor root aeration, but root rot caused by *Phytophthora cinnamomi* (a fungal organism which thrives in waterlogged soils) has been isolated as the cause of decline of vines grafted to some *V. berlandieri* and *V. rupestris*-derived rootstocks in South Africa (see 8.6.1). The rootstock 99 Richter has a reputation for not being suited to waterlogged soils. At a waterlogged site in Victoria, 99 Richter and 101-14 failed to establish, but rootstocks that survived included 420A, 110 Richter, Schwarzmann, 3306, Fercal, and ungrafted Pinot Noir (Whiting and Orr 1990). The rootstock 3306 has been used for poorly drained soils in some vineyards in north eastern Victoria. It should be noted that there is no indication that any rootstock is more tolerant of waterlogged soils than own-rooted *V. vinifera* varieties. In any case it is preferable to drain waterlogged soils rather than rely on rootstocks to overcome the problem.

8.4.4 SALINE SOILS

Whilst *V. vinifera* varieties are moderately tolerant of salinity (i.e. high total salts), there is a wide range of tolerance between other *Vitis* spp. (Downton 1977a). The lessened ability of *V. vinifera* to tolerate salinity may result from excessive intake of chloride rather than sodium. Certain rootstocks reduce the accumulation of chloride in the scion variety (Sauer 1968, Bernstein et al. 1969). For example, Sauer (1968) reported that, using Murray River water for irrigation, the level of chloride in the leaf petioles of field grown Sultana vines grafted to eight rootstocks was 68 to 82% lower than that of own-rooted vines (even those that had been self-grafted to Sultana to determine whether the graft itself affected chloride status). Downton (1977b), working with Ramsey, Harmony and Schwarzmann, reported similar reductions in petiole chloride. He also found that the magnitude of the chloride reduction depended on the scion variety. Despite variations between rootstocks and ungrafted vines, high salinity reduces vegetative biomass of both grafted and ungrafted vines. The leaves of Shiraz vines grafted to 1103 Paulsen and 140 Ruggeri had lower chloride concentrations than Ramsey, 101-14 and ungrafted Shiraz at a low salinity site (0.43 dS/m) whilst at a high salinity site (2.3 dS/m) only 140 Ruggeri had lower leaf chloride than other rootstocks (Walker *et al.* 2000).

The performance of field vines to drip irrigation with saline water has been examined in several trials in Australia (Walker *et al.* 2002 and refs. therein). Whilst not consistent across all trials, the general responses to increasing salinity are lower yields, lower bunch numbers per vine, lower berry weights and less growth. Sultana grafted to Ramsey rootstock had larger canopies, lower lamina leaf chloride and was able to maintain CO_2 assimilation rates under a high salinity treatment (3.4 dS/m irrigation water) whereas own-rooted Sultana was not able to do so (Walker *et al.* 1997). In the study by Walker *et al.* (2002), the rootstocks Ramsey, 1103 Paulsen and R2 imparted higher growth and yields than other rootstocks and ungrafted vines at irrigation salinity concentrations of 3.5 dS/m which was around 10 fold greater than average River Murray water salinity during the trial period (0.32 dS/m). Francois and Clark (1979) have noted that rootstocks that reduce chloride uptake by the roots would be of little benefit with over-vine sprinkler irrigation because chloride is readily absorbed directly by the leaves.

The relationship between rootstocks and soil salinity has been determined for a number of sites in Australia. In numerous trials the salinity of the water used to irrigate the vines has been reported, however, the soil salinity is often higher due to the effects of evapotranspiration concentrating the salts in the soil. Grapevines usually show no yield loss up to a threshold salinity concentration and as the soil salinity increases further, yield declines at a linear rate. Zhang *et al.* (2002) reported

Table 8.1 Guide to salt-tolerance of grapevines. Source: Tee et al. (2004).

Classification of salt-tolerance	Type	Approximate threshold soil saturation paste salinity (dS/m)
Sensitive	Most *V. vinifera* varieties, 3309, 1202, K51-40	1.8
Moderately sensitive	Colombard, 101-14, 5BB Kober, 5C Teleki, 110 Richter, 99 Richter, K51-32	2.5
Moderately tolerant	Rupestris du Lot, 140 Ruggeri, Schwarzmann, Ramsey	3.3
Tolerant	1103 Paulsen	5.6

threshold soil salinity concentrations for Sultana at two sites of 2.1 and 2.3 dS/m compared with Sultana grafted to Ramsey at one site at 3.8 dS/m. No threshold value could be determined for Sultana grafted to the rootstocks 1103 Paulsen and R2 (a non specified hybrid of *V. champinii*, *V. berlandieri*, and *V. vinifera*) within the range of soil salinities studied. Above the threshold value, Sultana yields declined by 8.9 and 15.0 % per 1.0 dS/m increase in soil salinity at two sites. By comparison the yield of Sultana grafted to Ramsey declined at 5.6% per 1.0 dS/m increase. A summary of rootstock salt-tolerance from these trials and other results is provided in **TABLE 8.1**. Grape juice chloride and sodium concentrations were consistently lower on Shiraz grafted to rootstocks compared to ungrafted vines (Walker *et al.* 2000) and this trend was also reflected in the finished wine. In the first instance it is best to avoid saline soil situations or, failing that, take steps to ameliorate the effects of saline situations, e.g. installing drainage, lowering water tables, and leaching salt from the rootzone.

8.4.5 ACIDIC SOILS

In highly acidic soils vines become susceptible to the toxic effects of excesses of aluminium and/or manganese. Rootstocks derived from species such as *V. riparia*, *V. vulpina* and *V. labrusca*, which are native to regions with acid soils, seem likely to best tolerate such conditions. This may explain why Branas (1974) found Rupestris du Lot (*V. rupestris*) and the *V. berlandieri* x *V. rupestris* hybrid 99 Richter to be unsuited to acidic soils. However, in a study of the growth responses of potted Chenin Blanc grafted to a range of rootstocks (Conradie 1983), those on the *V. berlandieri* x x *V. rupestris* hybrids 140 Ruggeri, 110 Richter and 99 Richter were more suited to acidic (pH 4.1) conditions, and vines grafted to the rootstocks 101-14, SO4 and Rupestris du Lot were least suited. Growth of the less well-suited rootstocks was significantly improved by liming the soil to pH 6.0. Cirami (1993) tested a limited range of rootstocks in a moderately acid soil in the Adelaide Hills region, and found equally good yields from 1616, 106-8 and own-rooted Pinot Noir, and lower yields from 34 EM. The evaluation of

Gravesac, a rootstock regarded as suitable for acid soils in France, has not been reported in Australia. Soil acidity can be corrected by the addition of lime and it is recommended that this approach is used rather than relying on selecting a rootstock tolerant of an acid soil.

8.4.6 DROUGHT

The ability to withstand drought varies among *Vitis* species and reflects their adaptation to the water regimes of their natural habitats. Variation can be observed in traits associated with water uptake, e.g. the density and distribution of the root system, and those associated with water use, e.g. leaf size and indument, and the structure and density of the stomata. Most situations in Australia have the capacity for irrigation to be used to alleviate water stress and it is only in a relatively few situations that a highly drought tolerant rootstock is required. Rootstocks generally retain the drought tolerant traits in accordance with their species of origin. For example, those derived from *V. riparia* are, in common with this species, notably poor in regard to drought tolerance. It was largely for this reason that de Castella (1935) recommended against the use of Riparia Gloire and 101-14 in north eastern Victoria. Goss and Cameron (1977a) reached a similar conclusion regarding the use of Schwarzmann and 34 EM in non-irrigated vineyards in Western Australia. However, the ability of the grafted vine to withstand dry conditions will also depend on the specific soil type, the climate and the physiological interaction between the rootstock and scion variety. An example is that of vines grafted to Rupestris du Lot, which tolerate drought well, but only when grown on deep penetrable soils which allow the development of the characteristically plunging root system capable of fully utilising soil moisture (de Castella 1921b).

Factors that influence water-use through effects on the size and structure of the foliar canopy, such as scion/rootstock interaction and cultural practices, are likely to exert a major influence on the drought tolerance of specific graft combinations. Efficient water use will be of increasing interest to grape growers in many situations to maximise production per unit of water. Also, techniques such as Regulated Deficit Irrigation, which impose water stress on vines to manipulate vine growth, berry development and consequent grape quality, may require rootstocks with greater drought tolerance. A drought tolerance rating of some rootstocks of interest in Australia is presented in **TABLE 8.2**. The ratings are based on a transpiration index of potted, grafted Cabernet Sauvignon vines under limited water supply (Carbonneau 1985) and generally correspond with vineyard observations. Tolerant rootstocks were able to maintain transpiration better than susceptible rootstocks under water stress conditions. All the rootstocks listed are primarily used for phylloxera resistance. Other methods of assessing drought tolerance have been described. Leaf water potential monitored through the season varied between dryland, field grown grafted rootstocks, with 1103 Paulsen and 41B showing less negative values than Rupestris du Lot and 110 Richter (Ezzahouani and Williams 1995). However this did not translate into greater yields on the less stressed vines since 1103 Paulsen yielded significantly less than 110 Richter and 41B.

Leaf water use efficiency was evaluated for a range of rootstocks in the field by assessing the ratio of the rate of carbon dioxide assimilation to stomatal conductance in well-watered vines (Walker *et al.* 2000). Under low salinity conditions (0.43 dS/m irrigation water) there were no differences in water use efficiency between rootstocks yet there were significant yield differences. With higher salinity (2.3 dS/m irrigation water), 140 Ruggeri demonstrated better water use efficiency than 101-14 and Ramsey, but this did not translate into any significant differences in yield. In non-saline conditions, rootstock effects on transpiration efficiency are small compared to environmental effects and scion genotype (Gibberd *et al.* 2001). The ratings based on water use (**TABLE 8.2**) are not always reflected in yield results from field evaluations of rootstocks under 'dryland' conditions in Australia. In a shallow, sandy soil without phylloxera or nematodes, McCarthy *et al.* (1997) found Shiraz grafted to 110 Richter, K51-40, 1103 Paulsen and Freedom yielded significantly less than own-rooted Shiraz. There were no significant differences in yield between own-rooted Shiraz and Shiraz grafted to Ramsey, 140 Ruggeri and 99 Richter. In another trial in a dryland shallow, sandy duplex soil site with phylloxera present, Brown Muscat grafted to the rootstocks 1202, Ramsey and 5BB Kober yielded significantly better, and 5C Teleki significantly less, than own-rooted Brown Muscat (Whiting 2003). It is clear that inherent differences in the efficiency of water use for growth and grape production between rootstocks may not be related to field performance in every site nor provide a significant advantage over ungrafted *V. vinifera* varieties. Further work is required on this issue.

8.5 Stock-scion relationships

It has been noted in many reports that there are contradictions in rootstock performance (May 1994) and these inconsistencies could relate to interactions between the rootstocks, scions, cultural management strategies and the environment. There have however been cases of mistaken identity of rootstocks, which contributes to some extent to these inconsistencies. Very little referencing to 'authentic' rootstock sources or DNA databases are made in the literature. The development of DNA testing is advanced enough to determine the specific rootstock parentage and the identification of rootstocks should be confirmed through tissue samples and compared to registered databases.

Table 8.2 Grapevine drought tolerance based on a plant transpiration index. Source: Carbonneau (1985).

Rating	Rootstock
Highly tolerant	110 Richter, 140 Ruggeri
Tolerant	1103 Paulsen, SO4, 99 Richter
Less tolerant	3309, 420A, Fercal, 5BB Kober, 161-49, 41B, Rupestris du Lot, 101-14
Susceptible	Riparia Gloire

8.5.1 COMPATIBILITY

Successful grafting depends on the formation of a sound union between rootstock and scion variety. The inability of parts of two different plants, when grafted together, to produce such a union, and of the resulting single plant to develop satisfactorily, is termed 'incompatibility' (Hartmann and Kester 1968). The compatibility of *V. vinifera* varieties grafted onto resistant rootstocks has been studied extensively in California, e.g. Snyder and Harmon (1948), Harmon (1949), and in Australia, e.g. Anon. (1928), Manuel (1948). Incompatibility was not a serious problem in any of these experiments.

In some instances repeated problems have been encountered. In France an incompatible combination of Shiraz clone 101 and SO4 clone 5 has been detected and studies demonstrated a graft-transmitted 'viral' agent as the likely cause (D'Khili *et al.* 1996). In another combination of concern, Jaoumet and 57 Richter, a hormonal imbalance was implicated. The rootstock 5BB Kober has been consistently reported as inducing negative reactions with some clones and varieties in Europe and has encountered problems with Chardonnay in Australia. Indexing and ELISA testing in Sardinia failed to link the stunting and bushy growth syndrome in 5BB Kober with ten virus-like diseases, and it was concluded that an unknown factor was responsible (Garau *et al.* 1994).

Australian experience has shown that most varieties can be matched with suitable rootstocks, but for some, such as Muscat Gordo Blanco, Muscadelle, Muscat Rouge (syn. Brown Muscat, Brown Frontignac), Zante Currant, Cardinal, Barlinka and Ohanez, care in the choice of rootstock has been suggested. Sarooshi and Bevington (1976) reported that the combination of Muscat Gordo Blanco and Ramsey was incompatible, the symptoms being die-back of shoot tips, stunted growth, poor fruitset and eventual death of the vine. Similar effects (**FIGURE 8.3**) have been encountered in an experiment at the Department of Primary Industries, Mildura. The cause of this condition is unclear, but Sarooshi and Bevington reported symptoms of legno riccio virus (apparently transmitted from the scion) on Rupestris du Lot vines included in their experiment. A selection of the tablegrape variety Barlinka, which is grown in Western Australia, is incompatible with Ramsey. Decline of the scion occurs one to four years after grafting (Hardie and Cirami 1988). Also, in Western

Figure 8.3: Stunted growth of Muscat Gordo Blanco grafted to Ramsey (foreground) compared with own-rooted vines (background).

Australia, vines of Cardinal grafted to Schwarzmann have declined with weak growth following the production of the first crop (Goss and Cameron 1977a). Leaf roll disease of the scion is suspected as the cause (Hardie and Cirami 1988). Muscat Gordo Blanco was also incompatible with 34 EM in rootstock experiments conducted in the Swan Valley, WA, from 1965 to 1977.

Bioletti *et al.* (1921) suggested that growth abnormalities of the graft union, either overgrowth of the rootstock by the scion or the size of the swelling, could be used as measures of an incompatible condition. The former characteristic, expressed as the percentage ratio of the diameter of the rootstock to that of the scion, was favoured as it was less dependent on other factors such as cultural conditions or vine age. Percentages greater than 100 or less than 75 were associated with weak vines. Ratios of 80 to 100 were considered excellent and normal. This relationship has been considered to apply in a general sense. For example, severe overgrowth of the rootstock by the scion was a factor correlated with the abandonment of *V. riparia* rootstocks in Victoria (de Castella 1921a). However, Wilkinson and Burney (1921) cite a European example of 40-year-old vines grafted to Riparia Gloire that displayed no signs of deterioration despite very marked scion overgrowth.

The percentage difference between rootstock and scion trunk diameters does seem to fail as a method for predicting yield performance. In a compatibility study of Muscat Gordo Blanco on nine rootstocks, yield of any given rootstock-scion combination was not correlated with the relative diameters of the rootstock and scion below and above the graft union. In Western Australia there is significant scion overgrowth with Schwarzmann, but there is no apparent ill-effect on vines at least 20 years old. The difference in rootstock and scion trunk diameter on vines that grow and yield well suggests variations in the conducting capacity of the trunk tissue of the rootstock and scion.

May (1994) summarised numerous reports of incompatibility and concluded that incompatibility is probably not genetically based but is due to the use of infected grafting material. An association between rugose wood disease complex with gross swelling of graft unions and vine decline has been described for Muscat Gordo Blanco, Moss Sultana, Malta Seedless and Menindee Seedless (Krake *et al.* 1999).

8.5.2 AFFINITY

In early studies the terms *compatibility* and *affinity* were often used interchangeably to indicate the harmony existing between rootstock and scion after grafting. However, Rives (1971) has made a distinction between these terms. He showed that the potential vegetative 'vigour' (measured as the weight of prunings) of grafted vines depends on three factors, namely, the vigour of the rootstock, the vigour of the scion variety (both genetically fixed), and the complex interaction or combining ability of the rootstock and scion. It is the effect of the interaction between the rootstock and scion in a particular graft combination that Rives calls *affinity*. Affinity may well encompass a number of factors within a graft combination including nutrient uptake, and the impact on vigour, fruitset, and fruit development. For example, a variety like Cabernet Sauvignon is susceptible to magnesium deficiency and it would be unwise to graft it onto a rootstock such as SO4, which has a poor ability to take up magnesium where that nutrient is limiting. Yields from a long-term rootstock trial at Wahgunyah, Victoria, with eight rootstocks and eight scion varieties showed a significant interaction between rootstock and variety, illustrating that the rootstocks did not have the same effect on each variety.

8.5.3 LONGEVITY

Grafted vineyards are sometimes considered to have a shorter life than ungrafted vineyards. This has been attributed to weaknesses arising from the graft union and/or infestation of the union by insects or decay organisms. It has been suggested that failure of grafted vines may occur from the time of vineyard establishment, but these failures are now more commonly attributed to infectious agents, e.g. *Phaeomoniella chlamydospora*. Husmann *et al.* (1939) reported the results of trials involving 311 *vinifera* grape varieties grafted to 105 nematode and phylloxera resistant rootstocks. It was ascertained that 1,903 *vinifera* rootstock combinations comprising 6,966 vines maintained an average growth rating considered as satisfactory or excellent for a 20-year period or more. Some were still growing satisfactorily after 32 years, although the tests had not run long enough to determine the actual longevity of grafted vines. De Castella (1920) estimated that the useful life of a grafted vineyard under Australian conditions could range from 30-40 years. Experience supports this claim.

8.5.4 ROOTSTOCK EFFECTS ON GROWTH

The vegetative growth of a grapevine is clearly seen in the shoots, but there is also annual growth in the trunk and cordons, and the root system. Total shoot growth can be influenced by budburst percentage, rate of shoot growth, mass of each shoot, available vine reserves, leaf photosynthetic capacity, and length of growing cycle. The primary function of rootstocks in problem soils or where nematodes or phylloxera are present is to maintain, if not increase, the total growth of the vine. Across many published reports there are not always consistent growth responses with rootstocks, and differences in growth may only be expressed under particular circumstances. For example, in non-saline conditions there were no differences in budburst between ungrafted and grafted potted vines, but when sodium chloride was added, ungrafted vines burst earlier than the grafted vines (Downton and Crompton 1979).

Some reports on vine growth in situations where there are no impediments to growth show that there may be no differences between rootstocks. In situations where impediments to growth are apparent then there can be distinct differences between rootstocks (May 1994 and references cited therein). In general, rootstocks with *V. riparia* parentage have lower vigour than vines with *V. rupestris* parentage. A relationship between vigour conferred by the rootstock, and the growth period of shoots and fruit maturation has been determined under European conditions (Delas 1992). It is claimed that 'high vigour' rootstocks prolong the growth period of the shoots and this reduces sugar accumulation in the fruit, whereas 'low vigour' rootstocks shorten the growth period and induce early maturation of the crop. However in Australia where there are often situations of greater stress on the vines than in Europe, 'low vigour' rootstocks can have less sugar and berry colour at harvest compared to well-balanced grafted vines with more vigour (Whiting 2003). In the deep, sandy soils of the hot, irrigated regions, it is commonly recognised that some rootstocks have a significant impact on growth. Whilst Ramsey produces significantly greater pruning weights than other rootstocks in the deep, sandy soils of the warm-hot, irrigated regions (e.g. May *et al.* 1973, Walker *et al.* 2002), in cooler regions with heavier soils Ramsey may not produce any more growth than ungrafted vines (Whiting 1988). The high vigour of Ramsey in some situations has led to unbalanced vines and consequent negative impacts on yield and fruit quality. Any increase in vegetative growth if adequately managed can contribute directly to improved productivity by allowing the retention of more fruiting units at pruning. Vigour management strategies are available to contain the excess growth of shoots to produce better-balanced vines. Keller *et al.* (2001a) reported higher rates of photosynthesis with 5BB Kober and SO4, and lower with 3309 and 140 Ruggeri. In some reports, rootstocks in the field have higher rates of photosynthesis than ungrafted vines (Düring 1994, Walker *et al.* 1997) but not in other reports (Walker *et al.* 2000, Gibberd *et al.* 2001). The latter authors concluded that the response depends on the scion x rootstock combination and soil-water status.

Differences in root growth between rootstocks have been noted by several authors. Southey and Archer (1988) concluded that the spatial arrangement of roots in the soil profile was determined by the soil environment, but the density of roots was determined by the rootstock. They found that 140 Ruggeri had the greatest root density and 1103 Paulsen the lowest in one site, but the converse was found in another site, hence there can be a site x rootstock interaction. In Australia limited studies have been undertaken. Nagarajah (1987) determined that Sultana grafted to Ramsey had a more extensive root system than ungrafted Sultana, with more fine roots, higher root density and greater total root length with Ramsey.

8.5.5 ROOTSTOCK EFFECTS ON NUTRITION

There are many reports in the literature on the impact of rootstocks on mineral nutrient uptake. Whilst May (1994) concluded that the magnitude of the differences in most reports was often much less than seasonal variation, there are some significant interactions between rootstocks and nutrients. Many plantings of grafted vines have been treated with similar fertiliser (and water) applications as determined for ungrafted vines and this may have contributed to excessive vigour problems. The main nutrients of concern in Australia are nitrogen and potassium. Leaf petiole surveys have shown differences between rootstocks illustrating differential uptake that may necessitate different nutrient management strategies for different rootstocks. Whilst there are often significant and consistent differences between rootstocks within a site, across different trial sites rootstocks rarely produce consistent trends. Variations in soil nutrient levels, soil moisture availability, soil chemistry, soil pest populations and climate influence rootstock performance. There have been attempts to correlate petiole and berry results; and with potassium, for example, the results show positive relationships in some trials but not others.

In reviewing several rootstock trials Kliewer (1991) concluded that the rootstocks with the greatest amount of growth generally have the highest concentrations of nitrogenous compounds in the leaves and fruit, perhaps due to their more extensive root system. In non-fruiting potted Cabernet Sauvignon vines grafted to a range of rootstocks there were significant differences in the concentration of total nitrogen in the leaves, possibly associated with differences in nitrate reductase activity, but only small differences in total nitrogen in the roots (Zerihun and Treeby 2002). The high nitrogen concentration in the leaf was not related to rootstock mass. In field-grown grafted Müller-Thurgau grapevines, rootstocks had a significant impact on nitrogenous compounds in the extracted sap (Keller *et al.* 2001a). The *V. berlandieri* x *V. riparia* hybrids 5BB Kober, 5C Teleki, 8B Teleki and SO4 had higher sap concentrations of nitrate nitrogen than 3309 and 140 Ruggeri. 5BB Kober had the highest total nitrogen concentration mainly due to high glutamine. Keller *et al.* (*loc. cit.*) suggested the *V. berlandieri* x *V. riparia* hybrids (excluding SO4) were better suited to soils with low nitrogen status. Free amino acids have a role as nitrogen sources for yeast during fermentation, as well as links to ethyl carbamate and higher alcohol formation in wine. Total free amino nitrogen concentrations were categorised from highest to lowest as: ungrafted Chardonnay = Schwarzmann = K51-40 > Ramsey = Freedom = K51-32 > 140 Ruggeri = 101-14 (Treeby *et al.* 1998), and different rootstocks produced significant differences within individual amino acids. The differences between rootstocks were not related to petiole nitrate-nitrogen concentrations obtained at flowering.

Rootstocks have a strong influence on the concentration of potassium uptake as expressed by petiole analysis. Ungrafted rootstocks show a wide variation in petiole potassium concentrations (Rühl 1989) as do scion varieties grafted to a range of rootstocks. Experience has shown that the rootstocks Freedom, Dog Ridge, Rupestris du Lot, Ramsey and Schwarzmann regularly have higher petiole potassium. However, values for potassium concentration in the petioles in Australia may not be excessive in comparison with overseas observations (May 1994). Mechanisms that may influence potassium concentrations in rootstocks include rooting morphology and density, root physiology, vigour of scion growth, crop load, and leaf shading.

8.5.6 ROOTSTOCK EFFECTS ON YIELD

In addition to vegetative growth, rootstocks influence reproductive growth of the grapevine. In some cases, crop production effects can be attributed to the direct influence of rootstocks on bud fruitfulness, fruitset or berry size. For example, de Castella (1920) noted that grafting often improved fruitset, particularly in varieties poor in this respect. He suggested that this improvement was due to the graft union behaving like a cincture. Keller *et al.* (2001b) has shown that rootstocks can influence the number of flowers per inflorescence, percent fruitset and consequent number of berries per cluster. Whilst some rootstocks had a greater percent set than others, they did not necessarily end up with highest number of berries per bunch because other rootstocks had more flowers per inflorescence.

The long-term influence of rootstocks on productivity was demonstrated by an experiment conducted at Wahgunyah, in north-eastern Victoria, in which the yield

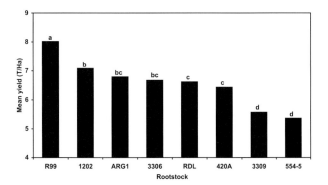

Figure 8.4: Mean annual yield of eight scion varieties grafted to rootstocks at Wahgunyah, Victoria. Rootstocks with differing letters indicate significant differences at P = 0.05. (99R = 99 Richter, RDL = Rupestris du Lot). Source: S. Martin (unpublished).

of eight scion varieties, each grafted to eight rootstocks, was compared for 35 years. The outstanding rootstock from this experiment was 99 Richter (**FIGURE 8.4**). All scion varieties grafted to 99 Richter outyielded those grafted to ARG1, which at that time was the most widely used rootstock in north-eastern Victoria. Sampling at the trial site indicated the presence of dagger nematode, rootknot nematode, root lesion nematode, stubbyroot nematode (*Paratrichodorus* spp.), and phylloxera. The soil was a deep loam overlain with silty alluvium deposited by successive flooding of the adjacent Murray River.

Low yields may be encountered when rootstocks induce excessive vegetative growth. This problem occasionally occurs in the Sunraysia region when Dog Ridge and Ramsey are planted in deep and/or fertile soils. Typically, the number of bunches is low and fruitset is poor. Sommer *et al.* (2001) showed that grafting of Sultana to Ramsey rootstock conferred lower bud fruitfulness than on ungrafted vines but yields remained higher on the grafted vines through more canes per vine and greater bunch weights. Dense foliage during the inflorescence initiation period may reduce bud fruitfulness by preventing adequate light penetration for optimum initiation of fruitful buds. Cultural practices aimed at slowing shoot growth during these critical periods such as application of growth retardants, withholding irrigation and nutrients or pruning to induce relatively higher cropping levels, offer scope for alleviating this problem and, where vine vigour of Ramsey can be decreased, fruitfulness is improved.

Poor fruitset has also been associated with excessive levels of nitrate in leaf petioles at flowering (Cook and Kishaba 1956). Cook and Lider (1964) found that scions grafted to Rupestris du Lot (syn. Rupestris St George) consistently accumulated high levels of nitrate in the petioles. In north-eastern Victoria the use of this rootstock has been associated with poor set, particularly in the scion variety Malbec, a variety notorious in this respect (de Castella 1921a). Merlot is another variety susceptible to poor set and bunch weights were improved by using the rootstocks SO4, 3309 and Riparia Gloire in France (Delas *et al.* 1991), but decreased when generous amounts of nitrogen were added. Consideration of the problem induced by excessive shoot growth and that associated with high levels of nitrate leads to the conclusion that nitrogenous fertiliser should only be applied sparingly, if at all, in vineyards established with vigorous rootstocks.

8.5.7 ROOTSTOCK EFFECTS ON FRUIT AND WINE COMPOSITION

The effect of rootstock on fruit composition has been the subject of much speculation since the practice of grafting commenced. Early experience revealed that European varieties did not acquire the distinctive flavour characteristics of the American species to which they were grafted, and reciprocal grafting of bunches of grapes showed that aromas and flavours were made within the berry and not imported from elsewhere in the vine. However, as early as 1904, it was reported that rootstocks modified the weight and colour of berries and their content of sugar, acid and minerals (Curtel 1904). Bénard *et al.* (1963) found that rootstocks could influence the mineral composition of berries but concluded that other variables such as climate, soil and fertilizer should have more influence on wine composition than rootstocks. Nevertheless recent investigations suggest a more critical role of rootstocks in modifying grape composition, and greater emphasis should be given to this feature in the selection of rootstocks, particularly those used in winegrape production. For example, in California, Ough *et al.* (1968a) compared the quality and composition of fruit of ten varieties grown on two different rootstocks, Rupestris du Lot and 99 Richter, and found large and easily detected differences. Most scion varieties grafted to the more vigorous Rupestris du Lot rootstock yielded fruit with higher concentrations of total nitrogen, titratable acid, tannin, potassium, phosphorous, ammonia, biotin and a higher pH. The changes in the mineral composition of the fruit were closely related to the influence of rootstock on the ratio of leaf area to crop load. These authors also showed that the composition and quality of wine produced differed significantly according to rootstock (Ough *et al.* 1968b).

In Australia, Hale (1977) and Hale and Brien (1978) found that berries produced in experimental plots in the Sunraysia region on Shiraz vines grafted to Ramsey and Dog Ridge had higher concentrations of potassium and malic acid, higher pH and less colour (in black varieties) than on ungrafted vines. Wine produced from fruit of the ungrafted vines was preferred to that of the grafted vines, although no adjustments were made to juice acidity, as would be done with commercial winemaking

procedures. These results and those of Downton (1977b) suggest that the extent of the effect depends upon scion variety. From extensive cooperative trials in South Australia and Victoria (Rühl *et al.* 1988), four rootstocks were found to give high juice pH, associated with high K content and low tartrate/malate ratio (Harmony, Dog Ridge, Freedom and Rupestris du Lot), and five rootstocks gave low juice pH: 140 Ruggeri, 1202, 5BB Kober (incorrectly named 5A Teleki in this case; see 8.2.2), 5C Teleki and 101-14). This work does not support the view that all juices from vines grafted to Ramsey have high potassium, and the ratio of tartrate to malate was also important. In one trial no significant differences in juice potassium were reported between rootstock treatments yet there were significant differences in potassium concentration in the wine, with Ramsey and 1103 Paulsen higher than 101-14 and ungrafted Shiraz (Walker *et al.* 2000). In another trial there was a good correlation between juice and wine potassium concentrations. Juice analysis may not always reflect concentrations in resultant wine due to differential extraction of potassium from the skin.

The different capacities of rootstocks to absorb potassium have been linked with different mechanisms being present in vine roots. 'Active transport', where energy is used to upload potassium into the root tissue, is present in low- and high-absorbing rootstocks, whereas 'passive transport' tied to the transpiration stream only operates in the high-absorbing rootstocks (Rühl 1992). A rootstock such as 140 Ruggeri, which provides relatively little potassium to the scion, retains potassium in the vacuoles of root cells (Rühl 1993). Vigorous rootstocks are known to cause shading of the fruit and lower sugar concentrations. Mpelasoka *et al.* (2003) speculate that increased potassium translocation to the berries may adjust the osmotic potential to maintain turgor and water potential gradients, and berry growth, when less sugar is imported into the berry. In some varieties only, the rootstock Ramsey induced higher skin and pulp potassium concentrations compared with ungrafted vines, but after fermentation without pH adjustment all varieties on Ramsey had higher wine potassium (Walker *et al.* 1998).

Aspects of wine colour may be influenced by rootstock but inconsistent results have been obtained. In one trial (low salinity irrigation water) ungrafted Shiraz had a greater wine colour density than Shiraz grafted to 1103 Paulsen or 140 Ruggeri, but, in another trial (high salinity irrigation water), Shiraz grafted to 140 Ruggeri or 101-14 had greater wine colour density than ungrafted Shiraz (Walker *et al.* 2000). The authors attributed some of the lack of differences in total phenolics, total anthocyanins and ionised anthocyanins in the latter trial to a narrow range of berry weights across the rootstock treatments. The impact of rootstock on wine score has had minimal attention. Whilst Walker *et al.* (2000) showed some rootstocks had a better wine score than ungrafted Shiraz in one trial but not in another, the wines were produced without adjusting juice pH (as would be done for commercial wines) and resulted in high wine pH and low wine scores.

Rootstocks may also influence the harvest date of the scion. This is particularly important to tablegrape producers seeking economic benefits associated with early markets. The popularity of the rootstock Riparia Gloire in the Cumberland region of New South Wales was due primarily to the early ripening and desirable colouration that it imparts to Muscat Hamburg. Conversely, rootstocks that induce profuse growth, e.g. Ramsey, Dog Ridge and Rupestris du Lot, have been associated with delayed ripening and poor colouration. These rootstocks should be avoided for tablegrapes, particularly red and black types.

The effects of rootstock on grape composition may thus be considered the result of a physiological interaction between soil, roots and scion, which affects crop load, vegetative growth and the nutritional status of the vine. Ough et al. (1968a) suggested that such an influence may only be detected under conditions that allow full expression of the growth differences due to different rootstocks. Some of the effects on fruit composition attributed to rootstocks, such as high pH, low titratable acid and low colour, may even be encountered in own-rooted vines when the ratio of crop to leaf area is low and/or the fruit develops in shade (Jackson 1986, Smart 1982).

8.6 Influence on diseases and disorders

8.6.1 SUSCEPTIBILITY TO DISEASE

Bunch rot (primarily Botrytis cinerea)

Increased bunch rot has been associated with some rootstocks. Ferreira and Marais (1987) showed that with spur pruning, Ramsey, 110 Richter and 101-14 had high levels of bunch rot and they associated the response with bunch compactness. The incidence of botrytis bunch rot was reduced by cane pruning, and the lowest incidence was on 99 Richter and 101-14. Whiting (2002) has described differences in the incidence of bunch rot of Chardonnay, being greatest in the rootstocks 161-49 and 5BB Kober, and associated with a greater number of berries per bunch.

Phytophthora cinnamomi

This fungal organism can cause root rot and sudden decline of grapevines (Volume II, Chapter 11). The first record of this disease in grapevines was from a planting of Rupestris du Lot rootlings in New South Wales in 1964 (McGechan 1966). Resistance to *P. cinnamomi* has been investigated by Marais (1979). *Vitis vinifera* varieties appeared strongly resistant; however, there were notable

Table 8.3 Grapevine susceptibility to Phytophthora cinnamomi. Source: Marais (1979).

Susceptibility	Rootstock
High	Rupestris du Lot, 99 Richter, 1103 Paulsen
Moderate	110 Richter, 140 Ruggeri, 101-14, 3306
Low	Ramsey, SO4, 420A, *V. vinifera*

differences among rootstocks. The results pertaining to rootstocks of interest in Australia are summarised in **TABLE 8.3**. The use of rootstocks with high susceptibility should be avoided in vineyards where *P. cinnamomi* is present. These differences in susceptibility to *P. cinnamomi* do not necessarily relate to tolerance of waterlogging (see 8.4.3).

Rhizoctonia solani

Ramsey (*V. champinii*) is more susceptible to *Rhizoctonia solani* than Colombard (*V. vinifera*) (Walker 1997).

Crown gall (Agrobacterium tumefaciens)

This bacterial disease occurs worldwide and can cause severe damage on *V. vinifera*, especially in cool climate regions. In an experiment where rootstocks were inoculated with different strains of crown gall, Ferreira and van Zyl (1986) reported Ramsey, 99 Richter and 110 Richter as susceptible rootstocks, with 5BB Kober, 101-14, Harmony, 3309, Freedom and 125AA Kober as resistant. SO4, 1103 Paulsen and 5C Teleki were moderately susceptible. When planting into problem areas susceptible rootstocks should be avoided. The incidence of crown gall in the field in Australia is quite low, but at times nurseries have reported a very high incidence of galls on young grafted vines. This has been correlated with the increased use of rootstocks (Ophel *et al.* 1988). These authors surveyed a range of rootstock and scion propagation material and found that the bacterium survives systemically in grapevines. Levels of contamination in two of the most used rootstocks in South Australia (Ramsey and K51-40) were very high (50 to 100% of cuttings infected), low or undetectable in other rootstocks and moderate (10 to 40% of cuttings infected) in almost all scions tested. Studies indicate that hot water dipping at 50°C for 30 minutes can eradicate the bacterium or reduce it to below the level of detection (Burr *et al.* 1989). Hot water treatment had variable effects on graft take but had a positive or nil effect on subsequent vine growth in the nursery (Ophel *et al.* 1990).

8.6.2 VIRUS-LIKE DISEASES

Many rootstocks are symptomless carriers of virus-like diseases. The use of infected rootstocks has undoubtedly contributed greatly to the spread of such diseases throughout the world. Luhn and Goheen (1970) noted

Table 8.4 Rootstock suitability according to soil depth and soil water status. Source: modified from Whiting (2003).

Soil Depth	Soil water status	Rootstock
Shallow (<20cm)	Dry	110 Richter, 140 Ruggeri
e.g. shallow sand, loam and clay; restrictive duplex	Irrigated	110 Richter, 99 Richter, 140 Ruggeri, 1103 Paulsen, 5BB Kober, 5C Teleki, SO4, Teleki 'C', Ramsey
Medium (20-75cm)	Dry	110 Richter, 99 Richter, 140 Ruggeri, 1103 Paulsen, Teleki 'C', 5BB Kober
e.g. calcareous sand, loam and clay; non-restrictive duplex	Irrigated	110 Richter, 99 Richter, 140 Ruggeri, 1103 Paulsen, Teleki 'C', 5BB Kober, 101-14, Schwarzmann, 3309, K51-40, 3306
Deep (>75cm)	Dry	110 Richter, 99 Richter, 140 Ruggeri, 1103 Paulsen, 5BB Kober
e.g. uniform or gradational, deep sand, loam and clay	Irrigated	110 Richter, 140 Ruggeri, 1103 Paulsen, 101-14, Schwarzmann, 3309, 5C Teleki, Riparia Gloire, Ramsey, Dog Ridge

that vines in an old vineyard established in California prior to the introduction of rootstocks were relatively free of virus-like diseases. This is in contrast to the subsequent widespread occurrence of virus-like diseases in grafted vines and those propagated therefrom. In California the rootstock ARG1 appears to be resistant to many viruses. Scion varieties carrying latent viruses do not show symptoms when grafted to this rootstock, however when the same varieties are grafted onto susceptible rootstocks, symptoms are expressed (Golino 1993). For example, the severity of fanleaf virus symptoms on Chenin Blanc vines, grafted on ARG1, 1613, Harmony and Ramsey and established as replants in a vineyard infested with the dagger nematode (*X. index*), was strongly correlated with the rootstock type (Hardie and Cirami 1988). The vines grafted on ARG1, 1613 and Harmony showed slight leaf-deforming symptoms but those on Ramsey were severe. Yields of vines on Ramsey were significantly less than those from the other three rootstocks. This response was attributed to a difference in susceptibility of the rootstocks to the virus rather than to nematode resistance.

There seems little doubt that rootstocks were a primary source of virus-like diseases in Australian vineyards. It is imperative that only virus-tested rootstocks be used in future plantings. The extent to which infection with virus-like diseases has influenced the evaluation of rootstocks in the past is not clear. However this is a factor that warrants consideration (see also Volume II, Chapter 11).

8.6.3 GRAPEVINE DISORDERS

Keller *et al.* (2001b) reported no significant rootstock effects on inflorescence necrosis, bunch-stem necrosis and bunch rot. However, Theiler (1976, cited in Keller *et al.* 2001b) has classified 5BB Kober, 5C Teleki and SO4 as promoting bunch-stem necrosis, and 3309 as not promoting it. Holzapfel (1993, cited in May 1994) concluded that 5BB Kober, 8B Teleki, SO4, 5C Teleki and 34 EM are likely to increase the incidence of the disorder, and 125AA Kober, 1103 Paulsen and Schwarzmann less likely to do so.

8.7 Choice of rootstock

In Australia, rootstocks are most commonly used to avoid the problems of rootknot nematode and/or phylloxera. Situations have been described where rootstocks provide benefits even in the absence of these pests. In general, however, economics determine that rootstocks are used only as a matter of necessity. The successful choice of a rootstock requires careful consideration of the purpose for which it is required and conditions under which it is to be grown. Obviously, rootstocks for control of nematodes or phylloxera must have adequate resistance. In Australia, the soils that favour phylloxera are generally unfavourable to rootknot nematode, the most common nematode problem, and the choice of rootstock may be straightforward. There are, however, a number of soils where both pests occur and fortunately there are a number of rootstocks that have a high level of resistance to both. Some examples are Ramsey, 5C Teleki, 5BB Kober and 99 Richter. The coincidence of phylloxera and the dagger nematode in the soils of north eastern Victoria is cause for concern; rootstocks that will resist both are required in this region.

With an understanding of the basic characteristics of the site and of the traits of the major rootstock species used in rootstock breeding (see 5.3.1), the selection of a range of suitable rootstocks can be determined:

- deep soils or ample soil moisture in cool climates are suited to *V. riparia* x *V. rupestris* rootstocks (e.g. 3309, 3306, 101-14, Schwarzmann)
- medium depth soils with moderate soil moisture in cool climates are suited to *V. berlandieri* x *V. riparia* rootstocks (e.g. SO4, 5BB Kober, 5C Teleki)
- shallow soils or limited soil moisture in warm to hot climates are suited to *V. berlandieri* x *V. rupestris* rootstocks (e.g. 1103 Paulsen, 99 Richter, 110 Richter, 140 Ruggeri).

A further classification of rootstocks based on soil depth and soil water status is provided in **TABLE 8.4**. Additional characteristics, such as nematode resistance, tolerance of salinity and potassium uptake need to be considered before making an appropriate choice.

Table 8.5 Characteristics of important rootstocks for Australian vineyards[1]

Rootstock	Species origin	Relative scion vigour	Nematode resistance		
			Rootknot	Dagger	Root lesion
Ramsey	V. champinii	high	high	low	high
Dog Ridge	V. champinii	very high	high	low	moderate to high
K51-32	V. champinii x V. riparia	high	moderate to high	low to moderate	high
K51-40	V. champinii x V. riparia	high	high	na	na
Freedom	V. champinii x 1613	high	high	high	moderate
Harmony	V. champinii x 1613 (open pollinated)	moderate to high	moderate to high	moderate to low	low
1616 Couderc	V. acerifolia x V. riparia	moderate	high	low	na
1613 Couderc	V. acerifolia x [V. vinifera x (V. riparia x V. labrusca)]	moderate	moderate	moderate	low
Rupestris du Lot	V. rupestris	moderate to high	low	low	moderate
Aramon x Rupestris Ganzin No 1 ARG1	V. vinifera x V. rupestris	moderate	none	low	low
1202 Couderc	V. vinifera x V. rupestris	moderate to high	none	low	low
Riparia Gloire	V. riparia	moderate to low	low	moderate	na
Schwarzmann	V. riparia x V. rupestris	moderate	high	high	low
101-14 Millardet and de Grasset	V. riparia x V. rupestris	moderate	high	low to moderate	low
3309 Couderc	V. riparia x V. rupestris	moderate	low	moderate	moderate
3306 Couderc	V. riparia x V. rupestris	moderate	low	low to moderate	moderate
106-8 Millardet and de Grasset	V. riparia x (V. vulpina x V. rupestris)	moderate	moderate	na	na
99 Richter	V. berlandieri x V. rupestris	moderate to high	moderate to high	low	low
110 Richter	V. berlandieri x V. rupestris	low to moderate	moderate	low	low
140 Ruggeri	V. berlandieri x V. rupestris	moderate to high	high	low	low
1103 Paulsen	V. berlandieri x V. rupestris	moderate	moderate to high	low	moderate
34 EM Foex	V. berlandieri x V. rupestris	moderate	moderate	low	na
Selection Oppenheim No. 4 SO4	V. berlandieri x V. riparia	moderate to high	moderate to high	low	moderate
5BB Kober (5A Teleki)	V. berlandieri x V. riparia	moderate to high	high	low	low
420A Millardet and de Grasset	V. berlandieri x V. riparia	low to moderate	moderate	low	low
5C Teleki 2	V. berlandieri x V. riparia	moderate	moderate	low	moderate

[1] Information based on Hardie and Cirami (1988) and modified using the following additional sources: Cirami (1999), Delas (1992), Hannah and Krstic (2003), May (1994), McKenry et al. (2001b), Nicol et al. (1999), Whiting (2003).

Phylloxera resistance	Lime tolerance	Drought tolerance	Root strike	General comments
high	moderate	moderate to high	poor	**Ramsey** is well suited to coarse-textured soils of low fertility. It has yielded well with a wide range of scions. It is well suited for Sultana in sandy soils in the Murray River irrigation districts. Caution is required where it may produce excess vigour and where excess potassium uptake may increase juice pH. Unless managed particularly well, it can reduce red wine colour and quality. Moderately tolerant of soil salinity. Susceptible to zinc deficiency. Some incompatibilities have been recorded.
moderate	moderate	moderate to high	poor	**Dog Ridge** is suited only to very coarse-textured, infertile soils. Excessive vigour and low productivity result from its use in more fertile soils. Excess potassium uptake may increase juice pH. Susceptible to zinc deficiency. May be suited to scion varieties of low vigour such as Muscat Gordo Blanco.
moderate	moderate	low to moderate	good	**K51-32** was developed for resistance to rootknot nematode with similar vigour to Ramsey but more easily propagated. High potassium uptake. Susceptible to citrus nematode and does not tolerate drought or saline conditions. Other rootstocks better.
na	moderate	moderate	good	**K51-40** was developed for resistance to rootknot nematode with similar vigour to Ramsey but more easily propagated. Quite sensitive to soil salinity. High potassium uptake. Other rootstocks better.
high	na	moderate	good	**Freedom** is more vigorous and has greater yields than Harmony. Not widely tested. Has high potassium uptake.
moderate	moderate	moderate	good	**Harmony** performed well in early trials with Muscat Gordo Blanco and some table grape varieties. Suited to medium to coarse textured soils. High levels of citrus nematode build up on its root system. Has high potassium uptake. Other rootstocks better.
high	low to moderate	low	good	**1616** grows poorly in infertile and light sandy soils. On better soil it produces scions of moderate vigour, with good crops of high quality fruit. Tolerates wet soil conditions and saline soils.
moderate	low	low to moderate	good	**1613** is best suited to moist, fertile sandy/sandy loam soils. Not suited to finer textured soils in cooler climates. Outperformed by many other rootstocks.
moderate to high	moderate	moderate	good	**Rupestris du Lot**, when planted on deep, well-drained soils that allow unrestricted root development imparts drought tolerance to the scion. Poor set and reduced yield can occur with shy-bearing varieties. Lacks nematode resistance and has moderate tolerance of soil salinity. High potassium uptake.
low	moderate	low	good	**ARG1** is not a rootstock for dry, infertile soils. Used successfully for many years in north eastern Victoria with a wide range of scions. In recent trials its phylloxera resistance has been insufficient. Does not tolerate saline soils and has low nematode resistance.
moderate	moderate	low	good	**1202** requires deep, fertile soils, although scion vigour can be high where soils remain moist. It demonstrates good resistance to local phylloxera genotypes, but is not recommended for planting in case virulent genotypes develop. Lacks nematode resistance and sensitive to soil salinity.
high	low	low	good	**Riparia Gloire** is the only pure *riparia* selection still in commercial use in Australia. Suited only to deep, moist, and fertile loams with good drainage, and does not tolerate drought. Has induced early ripening in table grapes. Tends to over-bear. Sensitive to nematodes.
high	moderate	low to moderate	good	**Schwarzmann** has been used with a broad range of varieties and sites in Australia. Does best on deep, moist soils and suffers from drought. Advances fruit maturity and has moderate uptake of potassium. Moderately tolerant of soil salinity. Not recommended for fine textured soils.
high	moderate	low to moderate	good	**101-14** requires deep, moist soils and does not tolerate drought. Performed well in hot, irrigated regions, with moderate yields and good colour in black varieties. Early ripening but with high juice pH. Moderate sensitivity to soil salinity. Some incompatibility problems reported.
high	moderate	low to moderate	good	**3309** was widely grown in north east Victoria in the past, and is widely grown in the north east of USA. Suited to deep, moist soils. Sensitive to soil salinity. Other rootstocks usually better.
high	moderate	low to moderate	good	**3306** was widely grown in north east Victoria in the past. Reputedly better than 3309 in moist, fine textured soils. Does not tolerate saline soils. Other rootstocks better.
high	low	low	good	**106-8** is suited to lime free, compact soils. Has been used around Sydney for Muscat Hamburg table grapes and some wine varieties.
high	moderate	high	fair	**99 Richter** is suited to a wide range of soil types, but not wet, poorly-drained situations. Scion varieties grafted to this rootstock may develop slowly but will deliver consistently good crops. Drought tolerant but moderate sensitivity to soil salinity. Performed well at Wahgunyah, Victoria, and in the Barossa Valley.
high	moderate	very high	fair	**110 Richter** is less vigorous, more drought tolerant and grapes are later maturing than 99 Richter. Suited to hillsides and dry-farmed sites. Consistently low juice pH. Moderate sensitivity to soil salinity.
high	high	very high	fair	**140 Ruggeri** imparts considerable drought tolerance to scions. Quite vigorous and high yielding. Performs well in shallow, dry, calcareous soils and is suited to acid soils. Moderately tolerant of soil salinity.
high	moderate	high	fair	**1103 Paulsen** imparts good drought tolerance and is suited to acid soils. Quite tolerant of soil salinity. Some variation in performance with good growth and yields in the Barossa Valley and in the hot, irrigated regions, but lower vigour and yields in cooler regions of Victoria.
high	moderate	low to moderate	poor	**34 EM** has been used with good success in Western Australia (was known earlier as 161-49) and performed well with Cardinal and Muscat Gordo Blanco. Minimal experience in other states. Not for use where drought is prevalent.
high	moderate	moderate	good	**SO4** is suited to a range of soils but does best in well-drained soils of low fertility in cool regions. Widely used in Germany and France. Some problems with low fruitset, poor magnesium uptake and high inflorescence necrosis have been reported in France.
high	moderate	moderate	good	**5BB Kober** is best suited to cooler climates, but can be too vigorous in deep, moist, fertile soils. Performed well in sandy nematode infested soils in north east Victoria. Moderately sensitive to soil salinity. Sensitive to phytophthora root rot.
high	moderate	moderate	fair	**420A** is suited to poorer, fine textured soils. Does not withstand waterlogging. Overcropping may be a problem in the early years of vine development. Susceptible to drought. Other rootstocks better.
high	moderate	low to moderate	good	**5C Teleki** is widely used in Germany where it is reported to advance grape maturity. Its moderate vigour is suited to well drained, fertile soils, and it tolerates lime. Has performed well in a wide range of sites in Victoria and South Australia. Moderately sensitive to soil salinity.

[2] Described as SO4 in Hardie and Cirami (1988)
na indicates that reliable information is not available

Consideration must be given to all factors that influence the performance of the grafted vine, viz. adaptation to location, soil type and soil chemical properties; compatibility and affinity between rootstock and scion; and susceptibility to soil diseases and bacteria. It is clear that vegetative growth, yield and fruit composition are directly influenced by each of these factors, along with the rootstock. For the economical production of grafted vines the propagation success rate must also be considered. A summary of the important characteristics of rootstocks currently used in Australia is presented in **TABLE 8.5.**

8.8 Concluding remarks

Rootstocks derived from American vine species have been used in grape culture since the early 1880s when they were introduced into Europe to counter the effects of phylloxera. The subsequent discovery of nematode resistance, also possessed by certain American vine species, has led to the increasing use of rootstocks. Historically, the use of rootstocks has been confined primarily to these two aspects of pest control.

The other attributes of rootstocks described herein, e.g. drought tolerance and lime tolerance, have been regarded as secondary factors, which aid in the selection of a rootstock to suit a particular soil type or vineyard condition. However, it is becoming increasingly apparent that rootstocks may be used to improve productivity in situations free of phylloxera or parasitic nematodes. The extent of the range of conditions under which these advantages occur and the extent to which economics will allow the establishment of grafted vineyards under such conditions remain to be determined.

REFERENCES

Suggestions for further reading are marked (•).

Anon. (1928) Guide, Field Day, Viticultural Station, Rutherglen. (Dept. Agric.: Victoria).

Anon. (1996) Australian Wine and Grape Industry. Aust. Bureau of Statistics Cat. No. 1329.0.

Anwar, S.A. and McKenry, M.V. (2000) Penetration, development and reproduction of *Meloidogyne arenaria* on two new resistant *Vitis* spp.. Nematropica **30**, 9-16.

Bailey, L.H. (1934) The species of grape peculiar to North America. Genres Herbarum 3, 151-244.

Bénard, P., Jouret, C. et al. (1963) Influence des porte-greffes sur la composition minéral des vins. Ann. Technol. Agric. **12**, 277-285.

Bernstein, L., Ehlig, C.F. et al. (1969) Effect of grape rootstocks on chloride accumulation in leaves. J. Amer. Soc. Hortic. Sci. **94**, 584-590.

Bioletti, F.T., Flossfeder, F.C.H. et al. (1921) Phylloxera resistant stocks. Calif. Agric. Exp. Stn. Bull. No. 331.

Boubals, D. (1966) Etude de la distribution et des causes de la résistance au Phylloxéra radicole chez les Vitacées. Ann. Amélior. Plantes **16**, 145-183.

Branas, J. (1974) Viticulture. (Dehan: Montpellier).

Buchanan, G.A. and Hardie, W.J. (1978) Phylloxera: the implications of D.C. Swan's observations to viticulture in Victoria. J. Aust. Inst. Agric. Sci. **44**, 77-81.

Buchanan, G.A. and Whiting, J.R. (1991) Phylloxera management: prevention is better than cure. Aust. N.Z. Wine Industry J. **6**, 223-227, 230.

Burr, T.J., Ophel, K. et al. (1989) Effect of hot water treatment on systemic *Agrobacterium tumefaciens* biovar 3 in dormant grape cuttings. Plant Disease

73, 242-245.

Carbonneau, A. (1985) The early selection of grapevine rootstocks for resistance to drought conditions. Amer. J. Enol. Vitic. **36**, 195-198.

Cass, A., Fitzpatrick, R. et al. (2002) Soils of the Australian rootstock trials. Aust. NZ Grapegrower & Winemaker No. 461a, 40-42, 44-45, 47, 49.

Cirami, R. M. (1993) Assessing rootstocks for cool climate vineyards with acid soils. Aust. Grapegrower & Winemaker No. 352, 155-156.

• Cirami, R.M. (1999) Guide to selection of phylloxera resistant rootstocks. (Phylloxera and Grape Industry Board of SA: Adelaide).

Cirami, R.M., McCarthy, M.G. et al. (1984) Comparison of the effects of rootstock on crop, juice and wine composition in a replanted, nematode infested Barossa Valley vineyard. Aust. J. Exp. Agric. & Anim. Husb. **24**, 283-289.

Coiro, M.I., Taylor, C.E. et al. (1990) Resistance of grapevine rootstocks to *Xiphinema index*. Nematol. Medit. **18**, 119-121.

Conradie, W.J. (1983) Liming and choice of rootstocks as cultural techniques for vines in acid soils. S. Afr. J. Enol. Vitic. **4**, 39-44.

Cook, J.A. and Kishaba, T. (1956) Petiole nitrate analysis as a criterion of nitrogen needs in California vineyards. Proc. Amer. Soc. Hort. Sci. **68**, 131-140.

Cook, J.A. and Lider, L.A. (1964) Mineral composition of bloomtime grape petiole in relation to rootstock and scion variety behavior. Proc. Amer. Soc. Hort. Sci. **84**, 243-254.

Coombe, B.G. (1963) Phylloxera and its relation to South Australian viticulture. Dept. Agric. South Australia Tech. Bull. No. 31.

Corrie, A.M., Buchanan, G.A. et al. (1997) DNA typing of populations of phylloxera (*Daktulosphaira vitifoliae* (Fitch)) from Australian vineyards. Aust. J. Grape and Wine Res. **3**, 50-56.

• Corrie, A.M., Crozier, R.H. et al. (2002) Clonal reproduction and population genetic structure of grape phylloxera, *Daktulosphaira vitifoliae*, in Australia. Heredity **88**, 203-211.

Cousins, P. and Walker, M.A. (2000) Improved techniques for evaluating rootknot nematode resistance in *Vitis* rootstocks. Acta Hortic. No. 528, 575-577.

Curtel, M.G. (1904) De l'influence de la greffe sur la composition du raison. C.R. Seances Acad. Agric. Fr. **139**, 491.

de Castella, F. (1920) Twenty years of reconstitution. J. Dept. Agric. Vic. **18**, 481-492.

de Castella, F. (1921a) Resistant stocks. J. Dept. Agric. Vic. **19**, 278-289.

de Castella, F. (1921b) Resistant stocks. J. Dept. Agric. Vic. **19**, 490-499.

• de Castella, F. (1935) Phylloxera-resistant vine stocks. J. Dept. Agric. Vic. **33**, 281-288, 303.

Delas, J.J. (1992) Criteria used for rootstock selection in France. In: Proc. Rootstock Seminar: A worldwide perspective, Reno, 1992. Eds J.A. Wolpert, M.A. Walker et al. (American Society for Enology and Viticulture: Davis), pp 1-14.

Delas, J., Molot, C. et al. (1991) Effects of nitrogen fertilization and grafting on the yield and quality of the crop of *Vitis vinifera* cv. Merlot. In: Proc. Int. Symp. on Nitrogen in Grapes and Wine, Seattle 1991. Ed J.M. Rantz (American Society for Enology and Viticulture: Davis), pp. 242-248.

D'Khili, B., Boubals, D. et al. (1996) Étude de l'incompatibilité au greffage chez la vigne. Bull. O.I.V. No. 787-8, 757-780

Downton, W.J.S. (1977a) Chloride accumulation in different species of grapevines. Scientia Hortic. **7**, 249-253.

Downton, W.J.S. (1977b) Influence of rootstocks on the accumulation of chloride, sodium and potassium in grapevines. Aust. J. Agric. Res. **28**, 879-889.

Downton, W.J.S. and Crompton, A.W. (1979) Budburst in Sultana grapevine as influenced by salinity and rootstock. Aust. J. Exp. Agric. & Anim. Husb. **19**, 749-752.

Düring, H. (1994) Photosynthesis of ungrafted and grafted grapevines: Effects of rootstock genotype and plant age. Amer. J. Enol. Vitic. **45**, 297-299.

Edwards, M.E. (1988) Effect of type of rootstock on yields of Carina grapevines (*Vitis vinifera*) and levels of citrus nematode (*Tylenchulus semipenetrans* Cobb.). Aust. J. Exp. Agric. **28**, 283-286.

Edwards, M. (1989) Resistance and tolerance of grapevine rootstocks to plant parasitic nematodes in vineyards in North-East Victoria. Aust. J. Exp. Agric. **29**, 129-131.

Ezzahouani, A. and Williams, L.E. (1995) The influence of rootstock on leaf water potential, yield, and berry composition of Ruby Seedless grapevines. Amer. J. Enol. Vitic. **46**, 559-563.

Ferriera, J.H.S. and van Zyl, F.G.H. (1986) Susceptibility of grape-vine rootstocks to strains of *Agrobacterium tumefacians* biovar 3. S. Afr. J. Enol. Vitic. **7**, 101-104.

Ferreira, J.H.S. and Marais, P.G. (1987) Effect of rootstock cultivar, pruning method and crop load on *Botrytis* cinerea rot of *Vitis vinifera* cv. Chenin blanc grapes. S. Afr. J. Enol. Vitic. **8**, 41-44.

Ferris, H., Schnieder, S.M. et al. (1982) Probability of penetration and infection by rootknot nematode, *Meloidogyne arenaria*, in grape cultivars. Amer. J. Enol. Vitic. **33**, 31-35.

Forneck, A., Walker, M.A. et al. (1996) Aseptic dual culture of grape (*Vitis* spp) and grape phylloxera (*Daktulosphaira vitifoliae* Fitch). Vitis **35**, 95-97.

Francois, L.A. and Clark, R.A. (1979) Accumulation of sodium and chloride in leaves of sprinkler-irrigated grapes. J. Amer. Soc. Hort. Sci. **104**, 11-13.

Galet, P. (1956). Cépages et vignobles de France. Tome 1: Les vignes américaines (Déhan: Montpellier).

• Galet, P. (1979) A Practical Ampelography: Grapevine identification. (Cornell University Press: Ithaca).

Garau, R., Prota, V.A. et al. (1994) Investigations on a stunting factor in *Vitis vinifera* L. transmissible by grafting to 'Kober 5BB'. Phytopath. Medit. **33**, 113-118.

Gibberd, M.R., Walker, R.R. et al. (2001) Transpiration efficiency and carbon-isotope discrimination of grapevines grown under well-watered conditions in either glasshouse or vineyard. Aust. J. Grape and Wine Res. **7**, 110-117

Golino, D. (1993) Potential interactions between rootstocks and grapevine latent viruses. Amer. J. Enol. Vitic. **44**, 148-152.

Goss, O.M. and Cameron, I.J. (1977a) Grapevine rootstocks for use in Western Australia. Dept. Agric. Western Australia Bull. No. 4008.

Goss, O.M. and Cameron, I.J. (1977b) Rootstocks for Currants. Aust. Dried Fruits News, New Series No. 4(4), 9-10.

Granett, J., Bisabri-Ershadi, B. et al. (1983) Life tables of phylloxera on resistant and susceptible grape rootstocks. Entomol. Exp. Appl. **34**, 13-19.

Granett, J., Goheen, A.C. et al. (1987) Evaluation of grape rootstocks for resistance to type A and type B grape phylloxera. Amer. J. Enol. Vitic. **38**, 298-300.

Hale, C.R. (1977) Relation between potassium and the malate and tartrate contents of grape berries. Vitis **16**, 9-19.

Hale, C.R. and Brien, C.J. (1978) Influence of Salt Creek rootstock on composition and quality of Shiraz grapes and wine. Vitis **17**, 139-146.

Hannah, R. and Krstic, M. (2003) Matching rootstock and scion combinations in Sunraysia. Final report to GWRDC, Project No. RT 02/19-3 (Dept. Primary Industries: Mildura).

Hardie, W.J. and Cirami, R.M. (1988) Grapevine rootstocks. In: Viticulture Vol. 1, Resources. 1st edition. Eds B.G. Coombe and P.R. Dry (Winetitles: Adelaide), pp 154-176.

Hardie, W.J., Whiting, J. R. et al. (1981) The identity of an imported selection of 99R rootstock. Aust. Grapegrower & Winemaker No. 210, 6, 8, 10.

Harmon, F.N. (1949) Comparative value of thirteen rootstocks for ten *vinifera* grape varieties in the Napa Valley in California. Proc. Am. Soc. Hortic. Sci. **54**, 157-162.

Harris, A.R. (1988) *Xiphinema index*-resistant *Vitis* rootstocks screened for comparative field performance in a Chasselas vineyard replant site. Vitis **27**, 243-251.

Hartmann, H.T. and Kester, D.E. (1968) Plant Propagation; Principles and Practice 2nd Edition. (PrenticeHall: Englewood Cliffs).

Heinrich, T., Bartlem, D. et al. (1998) Molecular aspects of plant-nematode interactions and their exploitation for resistance strategies. Australasian Plant Path. **27**, 59-72.

Husmann, G.C., Snyder, E. et al. (1939) Testing *vinifera* grape varieties grafted on phylloxera-resistant rootstocks in California. U.S. Dept. Agric. Tech. Bull. No. 697.

Jackson, D.I. (1986) Factors affecting soluble solids, acid, pH and color in grapes. Amer. J. Enol. Vitic. **37**, 179-83.

Jelenkovic, G. and Olmo, H.P. (1968) Cytogenetics of *Vitis* III. Partially fertile F1 diploid hybrids between *V. vinifera* L. x *V. rotundifolia* Michx. Vitis **7**, 281-293.

Keller, M., Kummer, M. et al. (2001a) Soil nitrogen utilisation for growth and gas exchange by grapevines in response to nitrogen supply and rootstock. Aust. J. Grape and Wine Res. **7**, 2-11.

Keller, M., Kummer, M. et al. (2001b) Reproductive growth of grapevines in response to nitrogen supply and rootstock. Aust. J. Grape and Wine Res. **7**, 12-18.

Kellow, A.V., McDonald, G. et al. (2002) *In vitro* assessment of grapevine resistance to two populations of phylloxera from Australian vineyards. Aust. J. Grape and Wine Res. **8**, 109-116.

Kellow, A.V., Sedgley, M. et al. (2000) Analysis of the interaction of phylloxera with susceptible and resistant grapevines using *in vitro* bioassays, microscopy and molecular biology. In: Proc. Int. Symp. on Grapevine Phylloxera Management, Melbourne 2000. Eds K.S. Powell and J. Whiting (Dept. Natural Resources & Environment: Rutherglen), pp. 21-30.

• Kellow, A.V., Sedgley, M. et al. (2004) Interaction between *Vitis vinifera* and grape phylloxera: Changes in root tissue during nodosity formation. Ann. Bot. **93**, 581-590.

Kliewer, W.M. (1991) Methods for determining the nitrogen status of vineyards. In: Proc. Int. Symp. on Nitrogen in Grapes and Wine, Seattle 1991. Ed J.M. Rantz (American Society for Enology and Viticulture: Davis), pp. 133-147.

Krake, L.R., Steele Scott, N. et al. (1999) Graft-transmitted diseases of grapevines (CSIRO Publishing: Collingwood).

Kunde, R.M., Lider, L.A. et al. (1968) A test of *Vitis* resistance to *Xiphinema index*. Amer. J. Enol. Vitic. **19**, 30-36.

• Lider, L.A. (1960) Vineyard trials in California with nematode-resistant grape rootstocks. Hilgardia **30**(4), 123-152.

Lider, L.A., Ferrari, N.L. et al. (1978) A study of longevity of graft combinations in California vineyards with special interest in the *vinifera x rupestris* hybrids. Amer. J. Enol. Vitic. **29**, 18-24.

Loomis, N.H. and Lider, L.A. (1971) Nomenclature of the 'Salt Creek' grape. Fruit Var. Hortic. Dig. **25**, 41-43.

Luhn, C.F. and Goheen, A.C. (1970) Viruses in early California grapevines. Plant Dis. Rep. **54**, 1055-1056.

Manuel, H.L. (1948) Phylloxera resistant grapevine stocks - experiments at Griffith Viticultural Nursery, 1929-47 (Govt. Printer: Sydney).

Marais, P.G. (1979) Situation des porte-greffes résistants a *Phytophthora cinnamomi*. Bull. O.I.V. **52**, 357-376.

• May, P. (1994) Using grapevine rootstocks: the Australian perspective (Winetitles: Adelaide).

May, P., Sauer, M.R. et al. (1973) Effect of various combinations of trellis, pruning and rootstock on vigorous Sultana vines. Vitis **12**, 192-206.

McCarthy, M.G. and Cirami, R.M. (1990) The effect of rootstocks on the performance of Chardonnay from a nematode-infested Barossa Valley vineyard. Amer. J. Enol. Vitic. **41**, 126-130.

McCarthy, M.G., Cirami, R.M. et al. (1997) Rootstock response of Shiraz (*Vitis vinifera*) grapevines to dry and drip-irrigated conditions. Aust. J. Grape and Wine Res. **3**, 95-98.

McGechan, I.K. (1966) *Phytophthora cinnamomi* responsible for a root rot of grapevines Aust. J. Sci. **28**(9), 354.

McKenry, M.V. (1992) Monitoring guidelines: All nematodes. In: Grape Pest Management. Ed D.L. Flaherty et al. (University of California: Oakland), pp. 285-293.

McKenry, M.V., Kretsch, J.O. et al. (2001a) Interactions of selected rootstocks with ectoparasitic nematodes. Amer. J. Enol. Vitic. **52**, 304-309.

McKenry, M.V., Kretsch, J.O. et al. (2001b) Interactions of selected *Vitis* cultivars with endoparasitic nematodes. Amer. J. Enol. Vitic. **52**, 310-316.

McLeod, R.W. and Steel, C.C. (1999) Rootknot nematodes from vineyards and comparisons between crop species as hosts for *Meloidogyne* spp. Aust. J. Grape and Wine Res. **5**, 104-108.

Meagher, J.W., Brown, R.H. et al. (1976) The distribution of *Xiphinema index* and other parasitic nematodes associated with grapevines in north-eastern Victoria. Aust. J. Exp. Agric. & Anim. Husb. **16**, 932-936.

Mpelasoka, B.S., Schachtman, D.P. et al. (2003) A review of potassium nutrition in grapevines with special emphasis on berry accumulation. Aust. J. Grape and Wine Res. **9**, 154-168.

Nagarajah, S. (1987) Effect of soil texture on the rooting patterns of Thompson Seedless vines on own roots and on Ramsey rootstock in irrigated vineyards. Amer. J. Enol. Vitic. **38**, 54-59.

Neal, J.C. (1889) The rootknot disease of the peach, orange and other plants in Florida, due to the work of *Anguillula*. Division of Entomology, U.S. Dept Agric. Bull. No. 20, 1-31.

• Nicol, J.M., Stirling, G.R. et al. (1999) Impact of nematodes on grapevine growth and productivity: current knowledge and future directions, with special reference to Australian viticulture. Aust. J. Grape and Wine Res. **5**, 109-127.

Niklowitz, W. (1955) Histologische Studien an Reblausgallen und Reblausabwehrnekrosen (*Viteus vulpinae* CB. auf *Vitis vinifera* und *Vitis riparia*). Phytopathol. Z. **24**, 299-340.

Nougaret, R.L. and Lapham, M.H. (1928) A study of phylloxera infestation in California as related to types of soils. U.S. Dept. Agric. Tech. Bull. No. 20, 1-38.

Oag, D. (1995) Rootstock evaluation for table grapes in sub-tropical areas of Queensland. Aust. Grapegrower & Winemaker. No.384, 77, 79-80.

Ophel, K., Burr, T.J. et al. (1988). Detection of *Agrobacterium tumefaciens* biovar 3 in South Australian grapevine propagation material. Australasian Plant Pathol. **17**, 61-66.

Ophel, K., Nicholas, P.R. et al. (1990) Hot water treatment of dormant grape cuttings reduces crown gall incidence in a field nursery. Amer. J. Enol. Vitic. **41**, 325-329.

Omer, A.D., Granett, J. et al. (1995) Effects of fungal root infections on the vigor of grapevines infested by root-feeding grape phylloxera. Vitis **34**, 165-170.

• Ordish, G. (1972) The Great Wine Blight. (Dent: London).

Ough, C.S., Lider, L.A. et al. (1968a) Rootstock-scion interactions concerning wine making. I. Juice composition changes and effects on fermentation rate with St. George and 99-R rootstocks at two nitrogen fertilizer levels. Amer. J. Enol. Vitic. **19**, 213-227.

Ough, C.S., Cook, J.A. et al. (1968b). Rootstock-scion interactions concerning wine making. II. Wine compositional and sensory changes attributed to rootstocks and fertilizer level differences. Amer. J. Enol. Vitic. **19**, 254-265.

• Painter, R.H. (1951) Insect Resistance in Crop Plants. (Macmillan: New York).

Penman, F., Hubble, G.D. et al. (1940). A soil survey of the Mildura Irrigation Settlement, Victoria. CSIRO Bull. No. 133.

Perold, A.I. (1927) A Treatise on Viticulture (Macmillan: London).

• Pongracz, D.P. (1983) Rootstocks for Grapevines (David Philip: Capetown).

Porten, M., Schmid, J. et al. (2000) Current problems with phylloxera on grafted vines in Germany and ways to fight them. In: Proc. Int. Symp. on Grapevine Phylloxera Management, Melbourne 2000. Eds K.S. Powell and J. Whiting (Dept. Natural Resources & Environment: Rutherglen), pp. 89-98.

Pratt, C. (1974) Vegetative anatomy of cultivated grapes - a review. Amer. J. Enol. Vitic. **25**, 131-150.

Quinn, D.G. (1947) Current news of vine stocks - report to Federal Viticultural Congress, Melbourne 1947.

Rilling, G. (1975) Zur Frage der direkten oder inderekten Schädigung van Rebenwurzeln bei Befall durch die Reblaus (Dactylosphaera vitifolii Shimer). Vitis **14**, 40-42.

Rives M. (1971) Statistical analysis of rootstock experiments as providing a definition of the terms vigour and affinity in grapes. Vitis **9**, 280-290.

Rühl, E. (1989) Uptake and distribution of potassium by grapevine rootstocks and its implication for grape juice pH of scion varieties. Aust. J. Exp. Agric. **29**, 707-712.

Rühl, E. (1992) Effect of K supply and relative humidity on ion uptake and distribution on two grapevine rootstock varieties. Vitis **31**, 23-33.

Rühl, E. (1993) Effect of K^+ supply on ion uptake and concentration in expressed root sap and xylem sap of several grapevine rootstock varieties. Wein-Wiss. **48**, 61-68.

Rühl, E.H., Clingeleffer, P.R. et al. (1988). Effect of rootstocks on berry weight and pH, mineral content and organic acid concentrations of grape juice of some wine varieties. Aust. J. Exp. Agric. **28**, 119-125.

Sarooshi, R.A. and Bevington, K.B. (1976). Graft incompatibility in a Gordo Blanco rootstock trial. Aust. Grapegrower & Winemaker No. 148, 11-12.

Sauer, M.R. (1967) Rootknot tolerance in some grapevine rootstocks. Aust. J. Exp. Agric. & Anim. Husb. 7, 580-583.

Sauer, M.R. (1968) Effects of vine rootstocks on chloride concentration in Sultana scions. Vitis **7**, 223-226.

• Sauer, M.R. (1972) Rootstock trials for Sultana grapes on light textured soils. Aust. J. Exp. Agric. & Anim. Husb. 12, 107-111.

Sauer, M.R. (1974) Yield of Sultanas on rootstocks. J. Aust. Inst. Agric. Sci. **40**, 84-85.

Sauer, M.R. (1977) Nematode resistant grape rootstocks. Aust. Dried Fruit News, New Series No. 5(1), 10-14.

Smart, R.E. (1982) Vine manipulation to improve wine grape quality. In: Proc. Symp. Grapes and Wine Centennial, Davis 1980. Ed A.D. Webb (University of California: Davis), pp. 362-375.

Snyder, E. (1936) Susceptibility of grape rootstocks to rootknot nematode. U.S. Dept. Agric. Circ. No. 405, 1-15.

Snyder, E. and Harmon, F.N. (1948) Comparative value of nine rootstocks for ten Vinifera grape varieties. Proc. Amer. Soc. Hortic. Sci. **51**, 237-294.

Sommer, K.J., Islam, M.T. et al. (2001) Sultana fruitfulness and yield as influenced by season, rootstock and trellis type. Aust. J. Grape and Wine Res. 7, 19-26.

Southey, J. M. and Archer, E. (1988) The effect of rootstock cultivar on grapevine root distribution and density. In: The grapevine root and its environment. Ed J.L. van Zyl (Dept. Agric. Water Supply: Pretoria) Tech. Bull. No. 215, 57-73.

Stannard, M.C. (1976) Research for the fruit industries viticulture. Dept. Agric. New South Wales 61 pp.

Taylor D. and Bowen, T.J. (1955) Resistant stocks for grapes at Stanthorpe. Queensl. Agric. J. **81**, 15-18.

Tee, E., Burrows, D. et al. (2004) Best irrigation management practices for viticulture in the Murray-Darling Basin (Cooperative Research Centre for Viticulture: Glen Osmond).

Treeby, M.T., Holzapfel, B.P. et al. (1998) Profiles of free amino acids in grapes of grafted Chardonnay grapevines. Aust. J. Grape and Wine Res. **4**, 121-126.

Viala, P. and Ravaz, L. (1901) American Vines. (Trans. by R. Dubois and W.P. Wilkinson). (Government Printer: Melbourne).

Viduka, K., Mitrosvki, P. et al. (2003) Can phylloxera grow on your rootstocks? Part 2. Aust. N.Z. Grapegrower & Winemaker No. 476, 55-59.

Wachtel, M.F. (1986) Resistance and tolerance of grapevine rootstocks to citrus nematode (Tylenchulus semipenetrans). Aust. J. Exp. Agric. **26**, 517-521.

Walker, G.E. (1997) Effects of Meloidogyne spp. and Rhizoctonia solani on the growth of grapevine rootlings. J. Nematology **29**, 1-9.

Walker, M.A. and Jin, Y. (2000) Breeding Vitis rupestris x Muscadinia rotundifolia rootstocks to control Xiphenema index and fanleaf degeneration. Acta Hortic. No. 528, 511-515.

Walker, M.A., Ferris, H. et al. (1994a) Resistance in Vitis and Muscadinia species to Meloidogyne incognita. Plant Disease **78**, 1055-1058.

Walker, M.A., Wolpert, J.A. et al. (1994b) Viticultural characteristics of VR hybrid rootstocks in a vineyard site infected by grapevine fanleaf virus. Vitis **33**, 19-23.

Walker, M.A., Wolpert, J.A. et al. (1994c) Field screening of grape rootstock selections for resistance to fanleaf degeneration. Plant Disease **78**, 134-136.

Walker, R.R., Blackmore, D.H. et al. (1997) Effect of salinity and Ramsey rootstock on ion concentrations and carbon dioxide assimilation in leaves of drip-irrigated, field-grown grapevines (Vitis vinifera L. cv. Sultana). Aust. J. Grape and Wine Res. **3**, 66-74.

Walker, R.R., Clingeleffer, P.R. et al. (1998) Effects of rootstock Ramsey (Vitis champini) on ion and organic acid composition of grapes and wine, and on wine spectral characteristics. Aust. J. Grape and Wine Res. **4**, 100-110.

Walker, R.R., Read, P.E. et al. (2000) Rootstock and salinity effects on rates of berry maturation, ion accumulation and colour development in Shiraz grapes. Aust. J. Grape and Wine Res. 6, 227-239.

Walker, R.R., Blackmore, D.H. et al. (2002) Rootstock effects on salt tolerance of irrigated field-grown grapevines (Vitis vinifera L. cv. Sultana). 1. Yield and vigour inter-relationships. Aust. J. Grape and Wine Res. **8**, 3-14.

Weinberger, H.J. and Harmon, F.N. (1966) Harmony, a new nematode and phylloxera resistant rootstock for vinifera grapes. Fruit Var. Hortic. Dig. **20**, 63-65.

Whiting, J. (1988) Influences of rootstocks on yield, juice composition and growth of Chardonnay. In: Proc. 2nd Int. Symp. for Cool Climate Viticulture and Oenology, Auckland 1988. Eds R.E. Smart, R.T. Thornton et al. (NZ Soc. Vitic. Oenol.: Auckland), pp. 48-50.

Whiting, J.R. (2002) Influence of rootstock on bunch rot. Viticare News No. 3(10), 1-2.

• Whiting, J. (2003) Selection of grapevine rootstocks and clones for Greater Victoria. (Dept. Primary Industries: East Melbourne).

Whiting, J.R. and Buchanan, G.A. (1992) Evaluation of rootstocks for phylloxera infested vineyards in Australia. In: Proc. Rootstock Seminar: A worldwide perspective, Reno, 1992. Eds J.A. Wolpert, M.A. Walker et al. (American Society for Enology and Viticulture), pp. 15-26.

Whiting, J. and Orr, K. (1990) 99 Richter and 101-14 rootstocks susceptible to waterlogging. Aust. Grapegrower & Winemaker No. 321, 60.

Whiting, J.R., Buchanan, G.A. et al. (1987) Assessment of rootstocks for wine grape production. In: Proc. 6th Aust. Wine Industry Tech. Conf., Adelaide 1986. Ed T.H. Lee (Aust. Industrial Publ.: Adelaide), pp. 184-190.

Wilkinson, H.H. and Burney, M. d'A. (1921). Affinity. Aust. Brewers J. **39**, 379-387.

Winkler, A.J., Cook, J.A. et al. (1974) General Viticulture (University of California Press: Berkeley).

• Wolpert, J.A., Walker, M.A. et al. (1992) Rootstock seminar: A worldwide perspective. (Amer. Society Enology & Viticulture: Davis).

• Zang, X., Walker, R.R. et al. (2002) Yield-salinity relationships of different grapevine (Vitis vinifera L.) scion-rootstock combinations. Aust. J. Grape and Wine Res. **8**, 150-156.

Zerihun, A. and Treeby, M.T. (2002) Biomass distribution and nitrate assimilation in response to N supply for Vitis vinifera L. cv. Cabernet Sauvignon on five Vitis rootstock genotypes. Aust. J. Grape and Wine Res. **8**, 157-162.

CHAPTER NINE

Grapevine Planting Material

P.R. NICHOLAS

Considering the high cost of establishing a vineyard, which is then expected to last 30 or more years, it is crucial that the best-available planting material is used. In particular, it should be disease-free, genetically-uniform and true-to-type. Vine improvement programs have been established in each Australian state to provide certified planting material in sufficient quantities to satisfy grower requirements. These programs have greatly benefited by recent advances from world-wide cooperative research efforts, which have developed new methods for detecting grapevine viruses and have increased our understanding of the deleterious effects of these viruses on vine productivity and grape quality. The long list of references at the end of this chapter attests the extent of this international research effort.

9.1 Genetic resources

9.1.1 INTRODUCED MATERIAL
Grapevine planting material was first introduced into Australia with the First Fleet in 1788. Subsequent introductions have been documented by Krake et al.

(1999), but of particular interest is the wide range of varieties introduced into New South Wales by James Busby in 1832. These early introductions were soon distributed to other states. Phylloxera was first found in Australia in Victoria in 1875—it devastated plantings in that state and necessitated replanting onto resistant rootstocks. However, quarantine restrictions allowed other plantings such as those in South Australia to continue to be of ungrafted vines (Boehm 1996). As a result, the early introductions into Australia are a valuable source of material, which has not been contaminated by the transfer of viruses from infected rootstocks to scions, as has occurred in other countries. In France, for example, the spread of fanleaf virus from the phylloxera-resistant rootstock Rupestris du Lot has been a particular problem (Boidron 1995). Some of the varieties originally introduced to Australia were misnamed, but later correctly identified by French ampelographer Paul Truel (Antcliff 1976; Chapter 6).

A major expansion of grapevine genetic resources has occurred in Australia with introductions from the 1960s to the present time. Much of this material has come from Foundation Plant Services at the University of California, Davis; the history of this agency has been described by Alley and Golino (2000). Other sources have included the Centre for Plant Health in Canada and clonal selection programs in France (Boidron 1995), Italy (Mannini 1995) and Germany (Schmidt et al. 1995).

Although cooperative exchange of planting material continues on a world-wide basis, there has been an increased tendency in recent years for availability of some planting material to become more restricted. Golino (2000) has reviewed these new developments. There has been an increase in patented grape varieties. Where material cannot be patented, such as with clones of traditional varieties, trademarks may be used. An example is the marketing of the French ENTAV/INRA® selections. Also, proprietary programs may be developed in which valuable selections are marketed exclusively and are not available to all growers.

9.1.2 GENETIC RESOURCE COLLECTIONS

Many early introductions into Australia—and most of the more recent ones—are now in genetic resource collections (deLaine and Nicholas 1999). The largest of these are held by CSIRO at Merbein and SARDI at Nuriootpa. These collections are maintained to retain genetic diversity of those varieties currently used commercially and to preserve those varieties not used at the present time. The varieties held are also useful for ampelographical comparisons and for breeding (see Chapter 5).

9.2 Clonal selection

Early methods used to obtain improved planting material were by mass selection. Initially this involved taking cuttings for propagation from 'good plantings'. This was later improved by negative selection, i.e. avoidance of undesirable vines, and then further refined by positive selection only from desirable vines (McCarthy 1988b). Clonal selection programs followed and most new vineyards are now planted with clones of *V. vinifera* varieties, derived from vine improvement schemes by this method. A clone can be defined as *a population of plants, all members of which are descendants by vegetative propagation from a single individual* (Mullins et al. 1992). Clonal selection began in Germany in 1876, in France in 1946, and in Italy in the 1960s (Walter and Martelli 1997). In Australia, clonal selection began in the late 1950s in South Australia (McCarthy 1988b, Cirami and Ewart 1995) and these early trials soon led to its adoption in other states.

Clones assessed may be local selections or come from overseas programs. Local selections are made from old vineyards of proven performance and quality, by observing vines for desirable characteristics prior to harvest for two or more years and visually checking them for freedom from disease symptoms. In early vine improvement programs in Australia, many selections were not virus-tested prior to their establishment in clonal comparison trials. With the development of rapid, laboratory-based methods for virus detection, candidate clones can now go through sanitary selection and, if necessary, disease elimination procedures may be implemented before they are included in comparison trials.

9.2.1 SANITARY SELECTION

Sanitary selection involves eliminating clones with detrimental viruses and other disease agents (Martelli 1999). In Australia, candidate clones are rapidly screened for viruses using both ELISA serological and RT-PCR laboratory methods and the remaining ones are then biologically indexed.

The laboratory methods are usually based on scrapings of the cortex of dormant (woody) cuttings (Habili and Randles 2002). Although green tissue can be sampled, timing is important as test reliability varies for different viruses at different times of the year.

Table 9.1 Virus detection methods commonly used in sanitary selection in Australia.

Virus diseases	ELISA tests for pathogen	RT-PCR tests for pathogen	Biological indexing indicator
Leafroll			
Grapevine leafroll	GLRaV-1, GLRaV-3	GLRaV-1, GLRaV-2, GLRaV-3, GLRaV-4, GLRaV-5, GLRaV-9, GRSLaV	Cabernet Franc
Rugose wood complex			
Rupestris stem pitting		RSPaV	Rupestris St George
Kober stem grooving	GVA	GVA	5BB Kober
Grapevine corky-bark		GVB	LN33
LN33 stem grooving			LN33
Fleck			
Grapevine fleck	GFkV	GFkV-A, GFkV-B	Rupestris St George
Fan leaf			
Grapevine fanleaf		GFLV	Rupestris St George

Boscia et al. (1997) have reviewed ELISA testing procedures. Each test uses antiserum produced from an immunisation reaction, which occurs when an animal—usually a rabbit—is injected with the virus. ELISA tests are relatively cheap and easy to perform, provided high quality antiserum for the virus is available (**FIGURE 9.1**). The use of RT-PCR methods has been reviewed by Minafra et al. (1997). RT-PCR involves amplification and detection of a small part of the genome of the virus, making the test far more sensitive than ELISA. The ELISA and RT-PCR tests, which are commonly used in Australia, are shown in **TABLE 9.1**.

Biological indexing with woody indicators was used

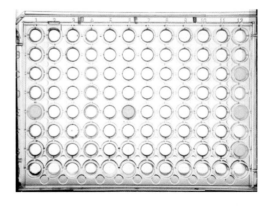

Figure 9.1 An ELISA plate showing the positive reaction to Grapevine leafroll-associated virus 3 in yellow. Out of 96 grapevine samples loaded in this plate, 5 tested positive to this virus (N. Habili, Waite Diagnostics).

prior to the availability of laboratory methods. Indexing conducted in Australia involves grafting candidates and indicators together and the resultant vines are then grown for several years in the field to observe any virus symptoms. Therefore, this test detects the disease rather than the associated virus. The indicators used are shown in **TABLE 9.1**. A description of indexing procedures can be found in Martelli (1993) and Garau et al. (1997). The early indexing work in Australia was reported by Shanmuganathan and Fletcher (1980) and Cirami et al. (1988). Indexing with woody indicators is still considered to be essential in sanitary selection.

The effect of virus diseases on grapevine yield and quality was reviewed by Walter and Martelli (1997) and Mannini (2003). Further general information on grapevine viruses can be found in the monographs by Bovey et al. (1980), Pearson and Goheen (1988), Frison and Ikin (1991), Martelli (1993) and Krake et al. (1999), and in Volume II, Chapter 11.

Leafroll viruses

Leafroll-associated viruses are limited to the phloem. They are considered the most detrimental of the grapevine viruses. An example of the effect of leafroll virus on yield is shown in **TABLE 9.2** where the low yielding clone was shown by indexing to be infected with the virus. Reported yield losses due to leafroll viruses generally vary from minor to more than 50%. Average yield loss has been estimated to be 20% in California (Goheen 1982). Leafroll viruses can also affect grape quality by causing delayed maturity, and reduced fruit colour of black varieties. Symptoms of the disease are displayed in autumn as a downward rolling of the margins of leaf blades and premature interveinal colouration (red with black varieties and yellow with white varieties).

The most common leafroll-associated virus detected in diagnostic RT-PCR tests in Australia is GLRaV-3 followed by GLRaV-1 and GLRaV-9 (Habili and Symons 2000, Habili and Rowhani 2002). GLRaV-2, which is less common, is reported to be involved with the incompatibility of scions grafted onto 5BB Kober (Greif et al. 1995). Grapevine rootstock stem lesion-associated virus (GRSLaV), found in the tablegrape Red Globe, is closely related to GLRaV-2: it can cause death of vines grafted to 5BB Kober, 5C Teleki, 3309 and 1103 Paulsen after two years (Uyemoto et al. 2001, Golino 2003). Other leafroll viruses that are less common are GLRaV-4, which is found in the Sultana clones H4 and H5 (Habili et al. 1996,) and GLRaV-5 found in a clone of Tempranillo and in clone 3A of Emperor.

The mealybug *Pseudococcus longispinus*—also found in Australia—has been reported to transmit GLRaV-3, GLRaV-5 and GLRaV-9 in California (Golino et al. 2002, Sim et al. 2003). GLRaV-1 can be transmitted by scale insects in Italy (Fortusini et al. 1997). The mealybug *Planococcus ficus*, which can colonise vine roots to a depth of 30 cm and is implicated in wide-scale spread of leafroll virus in South Africa (Walton and Pringle 2004), has not been found in Australia.

Rugose wood complex viruses

Rugose wood is a complex disease characterised by symptoms on the woody cylinder beneath the bark of the trunk. Symptoms are uncommon on ungrafted rootstocks and scions, but may appear following grafting. They include: swelling above the graft union, with a marked difference in diameter between the scion and rootstock; and pits or grooves on the woody cylinder. Vine yield and vigour are often reduced. Budburst may be delayed and vines may decline or even die. Water stress in combination with rugose wood and leafroll viruses will increase the severity of symptoms.

Four different rugose wood disorders can be distinguished by biological indexing (Garau et al. 1997). These are Rupestris stem pitting, Kober stem grooving, corky bark and LN33 stem grooving. Rupestris stem pitting symptoms have been associated with the *Foveavirus* RSPaV, which is present in most Australian vineyards— this may not be of major economic significance for vines on their own roots (Reynolds et al. 1997).

The phloem-limited *Vitivirus* Grapevine virus A (GVA) is the agent of Kober stem grooving (Garau et al. 1994, Chevalier et al. 1995). It can be symptomless in some varieties (Garau et al. 1991), but has been associated with Shiraz disease in South Africa (Goszczynski and Jooste 2003) and Australia (Habili and Randles 2004). Symptoms of Shiraz disease include: delayed budburst; stunted growth; canes which never mature; and leaves with leafroll-virus-like symptoms that do not drop in winter. GVA can be spread by the mealybug *Pseudococcus longispinus* (La Notte et al. 1997).

Corky bark symptoms are characterised by atypical production of corky tissues above the graft union. The phloem-limited *Vitivirus* Grapevine virus B (GVB) has been associated with corky bark symptoms, but its presence is not always consistent with symptoms (Bonavia et al. 1996). There is a large sequence variation in the genome of GVB isolates (Shi et al. 2004). Although GVB has been detected in some Australian vineyards, corky bark is not known to occur in Australia (Whattam 2001).

Table 9.2 The effect of a leafroll virus on the yield of Muscat Gordo Blanco at Loxton Research Centre (1972-1978).

Clone	Average yield kg/vine	Leafroll virus
131	33.9	Negative
173	32.7	Negative
19	32.4	Negative
15	31.7	Negative
138	31.2	Negative
103	20.3	Positive
LSD p=0.05	2.4	

Fleck

Grapevine fleck virus is common in Australia, but it is often unrecognised because varieties of *V. vinifera* and most rootstocks are symptomless. Translucent leaf spots are characteristic symptoms when Rupestris St George is used as the indicator. At least two variants of the virus exist (Shi et al. 2003) and they can be detected by a single RT-PCR assay. The detrimental effects of fleck have been described in a review by Walter and Martelli (1997). In particular, it can reduce graft take. There are no known vectors of fleck.

Fanleaf

Grapevine fanleaf virus is commonly found throughout the world, but not so in Australia (Habili et al. 2001) because the nematode vector *Xiphinema index* is confined to a small area near Rutherglen, Victoria. Fanleaf is very rarely seen in other regions in Australia. Symptoms of fanleaf include: malformed fan-shaped leaves; canes with zigzag growth; foliage with chlorotic discolourations; fewer and smaller bunches; poor fruitset and shot berries; and greatly reduced yield.

Australian grapevine yellows

Several phytoplasmas have been associated with Australian grapevine yellows disease (Gibb et al. 1999, Constable 2002), which predominantly affects Chardonnay and Riesling (Krake et al. 1999). A leafhopper vector is suspected. Symptoms appear as yellow, down-curled leaves, bunches which wither and fall from flowering onwards and shoots that fail to lignify over winter. A nested PCR assay is available for their detection, but the level of infection is very low in dormant cuttings taken from infected vines—at most it is 1/1000 (P. Magarey, pers. comm.). Nevertheless, as a precaution, planting material should be taken from symptomless vines and hot-water-treated before propagation.

9.2.2 DISEASE ELIMINATION

In the past, thermotherapy was the only method available to eliminate viruses from grapevines (Nyland and Goheen 1969). This involves growing potted vines in heated cabinets at 38°C. Under these conditions replication of viruses is inhibited and new shoot tips may be virus-free. These are removed and mist-propagated. The period of heat treatment required to eliminate different viruses varies, e.g. fanleaf may be eliminated within 30 days, whereas it may take 6 months or longer to eliminate leafroll virus. The removal of leafroll virus by thermotherapy can increase yield (**TABLE 9.3**).

Meristem tip culture was found to be a more successful method of removing leafroll virus (Savino et al. 1990). This involves cutting 0.5 mm of shoot tip—which includes the meristem and a few leaf primordia— followed by culture *in vitro* on a sterile medium. The

Table 9.3 Effect of removal of leafroll virus by vine thermotherapy on the performance of clone 32 of Muscadelle; 1985-1988 (McCarthy et al. 1989).

| Clone | Average yield kg/vine | | | | Leafroll virus |
	1985	1986	1987	1988	
32	5.7	9.6	9.9	16.5	Positive
HT32	8.0	13.5	12.0	20.2	Negative
LSD p=0.05	1.2	1.3	1.5	1.6	

procedure has been refined to the extent that the method is now considered to be reliable (Golino et al. 1998), although vine thermotherapy may still be used prior to meristem tip culture (Buciumeanu and Visoiu 2000, Mannini and Credi 2000).

Fragmented shoot apex culture has been used in Australia to remove grapevine viruses (Barlass et al. 1982). The procedure involves fragmenting one mm sections of shoot apices and growing them *in vitro* in a sterile liquid nutrient medium at 27°C and 35°C. This method can remove leafroll and fleck at either temperature, but yellow speckle (a viroid) and fanleaf will only be removed at 27°C and 35°C respectively.

Other methods that have been used to remove viruses in grapevines include: *in vitro* thermotherapy of whole plants (Grenan and Valac 1992, Leonhardt et al. 1998); somatic embryogenesis (Goussard et al. 1991, Gribaudo et al. 2003); and cryopreservation (Wang et al. 2003).

9.2.3 GENETIC SELECTION

Genetic differences between clones may originate from somatic mutations, which occasionally occur in dividing cells and give rise to chimera tissue (a mixture of normal and mutant cells). Any bud arising from mutant cells will develop a shoot carrying those cells. If the shoot has obvious debilitating changes, it will normally be rejected for propagation. However, some variants have been selected as being useful, such as the selections Pinot Gris and Pinot Blanc, which are colour mutants of the long-cultivated variety Pinot Noir. The variety Meunier is another mutation of Pinot Noir, which can be differentiated from Pinot Noir on the basis of the felty appearance of its growing tip and young leaves (Galet 1998). A large degree of clonal variation also exists within Pinot Noir with respect to growth habit (sprawling and upright growth) and bunch characteristics (tight and loose bunches). Flavour variants exist in some varieties: for example, there are clones of Chardonnay that produce a slight muscat character in wines (Galet 1998), and Sauvignon Musque is an aromatic clone of Sauvignon Blanc (Meredith 2000). However, the existence of genetic divergence is highly unlikely with most rootstocks and fruiting varieties such as Ruby Cabernet, which have resulted from historically-recent breeding programs (see Chapter 5).

It is uncertain whether differences between variants of

some old varieties are due to somatic mutations or to their 'polyclonal' origin, i.e. the variants may have originated from genetically-related seedlings. For example, the variety Sangiovese has six distinct variants, which have been designated as 'biotypes' (Calo et al. 1995).

9.2.4 CLONAL COMPARISON

Clones found to be free of important viruses by sanitary selection or disease elimination procedures can then be compared in trials in clonal selection programs. These trials must be well-designed with adequate replication to convincingly establish the often small differences between clones (Nicholas 2003). In clonal trials conducted following sanitary selection, clonal differences may be genetic or due to some other factor, such as the presence of unknown pathogens. Genetic fingerprinting techniques are generally unable to distinguish clones within a variety.

In early trials in Australia, clones were mainly selected on the basis of yield, although the analytical measures of fruit composition (Brix, pH, titratable acidity, colour) were also used. In the 1980s, greater importance was placed on evaluation of wine quality—as a result, small-lot winemaking was integrated into many Australian selection programs.

Clonal comparison trials conducted in Australia have included: Cabernet Sauvignon (Whiting and Hardie 1981, McCarthy and Ewart 1988, Cirami et al. 1993); Chardonnay (Cirami 1993a, Ewart et al. 1994, Whiting 2003); Merlot (Whiting 2003); Pinot Noir (Ewart and Sitters 1987, McCarthy 1988a, Ewart and Sitters 1989, Whiting and Hardie 1990, Whiting 2003, Farquhar 2003); Riesling (Cirami et al. 1985, Cirami et al. 1988, Ewart and Sitters 1988, McCarthy 1988a, Whiting 2003); Sauvignon Blanc (Cirami 1993b, Ewart et al. 1993, Ewart et al. 1994); Semillon (Cirami et al. 1985, Ewart et al. 1994); and Shiraz (Cirami et al. 1985). A catalogue of information on the clones available in Australia, from these trials and other sources, is in preparation by the author. Information is also available on clones distributed in many overseas schemes, including those in California (Bettiga et al. 2003), France (Boidron et al. 1995) and Italy (Calo 2000).

9.3 Certification

It is crucial that a certification program is in place to ensure that the best-available planting material is used (Martelli 1992). The critical situations where grapevine planting material must be certified are in post-entry quarantine and vine improvement schemes.

9.3.1 POST-ENTRY QUARANTINE

Australia is kept free of many devastating pests, which occur in other countries, by strict quarantine controls on imported planting material. A quarantinable pest is

Table 9.4 Quarantinable diseases on imported grapevines.

Pathogen	Disease
Fungi	
Guignardia bidwellii	black rot
Mycosphaerella angulata	angular leafspot
Physopella ampelopsidis	grapevine rust
Pseudopezicula tetraspora	angular leaf scorch
Pseudopeziula tracheiphila	rotbrenner
Bacteria	
Xylella fastidiosa	Pierce's disease
Xylophilus ampelinus	bacterial necrosis
Viruses	
Arabis mosaic virus	arabis mosaic
Corky bark associated virus	corky bark
Grapevine ajinashika luteovirus	Ajinashika disease
Grapevine Bulgarian latent virus	Bulgarian latent
Grapevine chrome mosaic virus	chrome mosaic
Grapevine fanleaf virus	fanleaf
Grapevine Joannes Seyve virus	Joannes Seyve
Tomato ringspot virus	tomato ringspot
Phytoplasma	
Flavescence dorée	Flavescence dorée

defined as a pest of potential economic importance to the area endangered thereby and not yet present there, or present but not widely distributed and under official control. Quarantinable pathogens of grapevines imported into Australia (as dormant canes) are listed in **TABLE 9.4**. One of the most important of these is Pierce's Disease, which is now seriously threatening Californian vineyards. Post-entry quarantine protocols for grapevine cuttings include inspection for insect and disease symptoms, fumigation with methyl bromide (to destroy insect pests), hot-water-treatment and sodium hypochlorite dip (to eradicate various phytoplasmas and bacteria), followed by pathogen testing using woody indexing, herbaceous indexing and ELISA methods. In future, RT-PCR methods are also likely to be used (Sivapalan et al. 2001).

9.3.2 VINE IMPROVEMENT SCHEMES

Vine improvement schemes are organised on a state-by-state basis in Australia. An account of the historical development of these schemes can be found in McCarthy (1988b). There are generally three stages in the multiplication of propagation material in these schemes. The first stage is the establishment of a field planting of nuclear stock vines of elite clones, which have been certified to be free of important viruses and other disease agents. This is established in an area not previously planted to grapevines and away from possible sources of infection. Several vines are usually planted of each clone. Pre-multiplication rows are then established using material taken from the nuclear stock planting. These are preferably sited in soil that has not been planted to grapevines for at least five years, and there may be 50 or more vines planted of each clone. The final stage is the establishment of larger 'increase' blocks, typically one-third to a half hectare in size. These are planted with material propagated from nuclear plantings or pre-multiplication rows.

There are certain protocols required for the certification of each stage, which cover the establishment and maintenance of the plantings. Nuclear stock vines must be checked by a recognised ampelographer to ensure that they are true-to-type. Sanitary protocols specify periodic visual inspections and laboratory tests for viruses, which must be conducted to check for any possible new infection. Cuttings for propagation from 'increase' blocks are supplied to nurseries with a specified type of label. The final stage of certification requires nurseries to satisfy an accreditation process.

9.4 Concluding remarks

It is fortunate that there has not been the wide-scale spread of either phylloxera or fanleaf virus in Australia, which have caused additional complications in vine improvement programs in many other countries. Also, although there is some spread of leafroll virus by vectors in the field in Australia, there is, fortunately, not the extensive spread of this virus as has occurred in South Africa. Australia has a heritage of many good locally-selected clones on which to base its industry. The availability in recent years of RT-PCR methods to detect viruses has enabled rapid screening of clones, thereby reducing the number of clones that need to be indexed, and this has greatly assisted progress in the development of new nuclear collections. There has been considerable recent progress in the certification of vine improvement programs in Australia. It is imperative that vigilance and quarantine procedures be maintained to keep out many unwanted pests and diseases, particularly Pierce's Disease.

REFERENCES

Suggestions for further reading are marked (•).

Alley, L. and Golino, D.A. (2000) The origins of the grape program at Foundation Plant Materials Service. In: Proc. ASEV 50th Anniversary Annual Meeting, Seattle (ASEV: Davis), pp. 222-229.

Antcliff, A.J. (1976) Variety identification in Australia. A French expert looks at our vines. Aust. Grapegrower & Winemaker No. 153, 10-11.

Barlass, M., Skene, K.G.M. et al. (1982) Regeneration of virus-free grapevines using in vitro apical culture Ann. Appl. Biol. **101**, 291-295.

• Bettiga, L.J., Christensen, L.P. et al. (2003) Wine Grape Varieties in California (Univ. California Agric. and Natural Res.: Oakland).

Boehm, W. (1996) The Phylloxera Fight (Winetitles: Adelaide).

Boidron, R. (1995) Clonal selection in France. Methods, organization, and use. In: Proc. Int. Symp. Clonal Selection, Portland 1995. Ed J.M. Rantz (ASEV: Davis), pp. 1-7.

• Boidron, R., Boursiquot, J.M. et al. (1995) Catalogue of Selected Wine Grape Varieties and Clones Cultivated in France (ENTAV: Le Grau Du Roi).

Bonavia, M., Digiaro, M. et al. (1996) Studies on 'corky rugose wood' of grapevine and on the diagnosis of grapevine virus B. Vitis **35**, 53-58.

Boscia, D., Digiaro, M. et al. (1997) ELISA for the detection and identification of grapevine viruses. In: Sanitary Selection of the Grapevine. Ed B. Walter (INRA Editions: Colmar).

• Bovey, R., Gartel, W. et al. (1980) Virus and Virus-like Diseases of Grapevines (Editions Payot: Lausanne).

Buciumeanu, E. and Visoiu E. (2000) Elimination of grapevine viruses in Vitis vinifera L. cultivars. In: Extended Abstracts 13th Meeting ICVG Adelaide (University of Adelaide and CSIRO: Adelaide), pp. 169-170.

Calo, A. (2000) Catalogo dei cloni del nucleo di premoltiplicazione delle Venezie (Istituto Sperimentale per la Viticoltura: Susegana, Italy).

Calo, A., Costacurta et al. (1995) Characterization of biotypes of Sangiovese as a basis for clonal selection. In: Proc. Int. Symp. Clonal Selection, Portland 1995. Ed J.M. Rantz (ASEV: Davis), pp. 99-104.

Chevalier, S., Greif, C. et al. (1995) Use of an immunocapture-polymerase chain reaction for the detection of grapevine virus A in Kober stem grooving-infected grapevines. J. Phytopath. **143**, 369-373.

Cirami, R.M. (1993a) Clonal selection of Chardonnay grapevines. Aust. Grapegrower & Winemaker No. 352, 61, 63-65, 67.

Cirami, R.M. (1993b) Fine tuning of Sauvignon Blanc clonal selections for South Australia. Aust. Grapegrower & Winemaker No. 352, 113-114.

• Cirami, R.M. and Ewart, A.J.W. (1995) Clonal selection, evaluation, and multiplication in Australia. In: Proc. Int. Symp. Clonal Selection, Portland 1995. Ed J.M. Rantz (ASEV: Davis), pp. 52-59.

Cirami, R.M., McCarthy, M.G. et al. (1985) Clonal selection and comparison in South Australia. Aust. Grapegrower & Winemaker No. 262, 18-19.

Cirami, R.M., McCarthy, M.G. et al. (1988) Clonal selection of Riesling in South Australia. Aust. Grapegrower & Winemaker No. 290, 17-18.

Cirami, R.M., McCarthy, M.G. et al. (1993) Clonal selection and evaluation to improve production of Cabernet Sauvignon grapevines in South Australia. Aust. J. Exp. Agric. **33**, 213-220.

Cirami, R.M., van Velsen, R.J. et al. (1988) Grapevine virus indexing in the South Australian Vine Improvement Scheme, 1974-1987. Aust. J. Exp. Agric. **28**, 645-649.

Constable, F.E. (2002) The Biology and Epidemiology of Australian Grapevine Yellows Phytoplasmas. PhD Thesis, University of Adelaide.

• deLaine, A.M. and Nicholas, P.R. (1999) National Register of Grapevine Varieties and Clones (AVIA: Mildura)

Ewart, A.J.W., Gawel, R. et al. (1993) Evaluation of must composition and wine quality of six clones of Vitis vinifera cv. Sauvignon Blanc. Aust. J. Exp. Agric. **33**, 945-951.

Ewart, A.J.W. and Sitters, J.H. (1987) Oenological parameters for the selection of Pinot Noir and Chardonnay. In: Proc. Seminar Aspects of Grapevine Improvement in Australia, Canberra 1986. Ed T.H. Lee (ASVO: Glen Osmond), pp. 77-84.

Ewart A.J.W. and Sitters, J.H. (1988) Wine assessment of Pinot Noir, Chardonnay and Riesling clones. In: Proc. 2nd Int. Symp. for Cool Climate Vitic. and Oen., Auckland. Eds R. Smart, R. Thornton, et al. (NZSVO: Auckland) pp. 201-205.

Ewart, A.J.W. and Sitters, J.H. (1989) Latest results on Pinot Noir clones for dry red wines. Aust. Grapegrower & Winemaker No. 304, 115-117.

Ewart, A.J.W., Sitters, J.H. et al. (1994) Wine evaluations of Chardonnay, Sauvignon Blanc and Semillon clones from the Barossa Valley, SA. Aust. Grapegrower & Winemaker No. 366a, 76-78, 80.

Farquhar, D. (2003) Evaluation of the Quality Performance of the Clones of Pinot Noir. Final Report to Grape and Wine Research and Development Corporation. (DPIWE: Tasmania).

Fortusini, A., Scattini, G. et al. (1997) Transmission of grapevine leafroll virus 1 (GLRV-1) and grapevine virus A (GVA) by scale insects. In: Extended Abstracts 12th meeting ICVG, Lisbon, pp. 121-122.

Frison, E.A. and Ikin, R. (1991) Technical Guidelines for the Safe Movement of Grapevine Germplasm (FAO/IBPGRI: Rome).

• Galet, P. (1998) Grape varieties and rootstock varieties (Oenoplurimedia: France).

Garau, R., Padilla, V. et al. (1997) Indexing for the identification of virus and virus-like diseases of the grapevine. In: Sanitary Selection of the Grapevine. Ed B. Walter (INRA Editions: Colmar).

Garau, R., Prota, V.A. et al. (1991) Distribution of Kober stem grooving and Rupestris stem pitting of grapevine in symptomless cv. Torbato scions. In: Proc. 10th meeting ICVG, Volos, Greece. Eds I.C. Rumbos, R. Bovey et al. (Ores Publishing: Volos), pp. 175-181.

Garau, R., Prota, V.A et al. (1994) On the possible relationship between Kober stem grooving and grapevine virus A. Vitis **33**, 161-163.

Gibb, K.S., Constable, F.E. et al. (1999) Phytoplasmas in Australian grapevines - detection, differentiation and associated diseases. Vitis **38**, 107-114.

Goheen, A.C. (1982) Grape pathogens and prospects for controlling grape diseases. In: Proc. Grape and Wine Centennial Symposium, Davis. (University of California: Davis), pp. 24-27.

Golino, D.A. (2000) Trade in grapevine plant materials: local, national, and worldwide perspectives. In: Proc. ASEV 50th Anniv. Ann. Meeting, Seattle, Washington (ASEV: Davis), pp. 216-221.

Golino, D.A. (2003) Emerging grapevine diseases. In: Extended Abstracts 14th meeting ICVG, Locorotondo, Italy (University of Bari), pp. 136-138.

Golino, D.A., Sim, S. et al. (1998) Optimising tissue culture protocols used for virus elimination in grapevines. Phytopath. 88(9), S32.

Golino, D.A., Sim, S.T. et al. (2002) California mealybugs can spread grapevine leafroll disease. Calif. Agric. 56(6), 196-201.

Goszczynski, D.E. and Jooste, A.E.C. (2003) Shiraz disease (SD) is transmitted by mealybug *Planococcus ficus* and associated with *Grapevine virus A*. Extended Abstracts 14th meeting ICVG, Locorotondo, Italy (University of Bari), p. 219.

Goussard, P.G., Wiid, J. et al.. (1991) The effectiveness of *in vitro* somatic embryogenesis in eliminating fanleaf virus and leafroll associated viruses from grapevines. S. Afr. J. Enol. Vitic. 12, 77-81.

Greif, C., Garau, R., et al. (1995) The relationship of grapevine leafroll-associated closterovirus 2 with a graft incompatibility condition of grapevines. Phytopathologia Mediterranea 34, 167-173.

Grenan, S. and Valac, C. (1992) Consequences of *in vitro* thermotherapy on the production characteristics of some varieties of Vitis vinifera. J. Int. Sci. Vigne Vin 26(3), 155-162.

Gribaudo, I., Bondaz, J. et al. (2003) Elimination of grapevine leafroll-associated virus 3 from the wine grapevine Muller-Thurgau (Vitis vinifera L.) through somatic embryogenesis. Extended Abstracts 14th meeting ICVG, Locorotondo, Italy (University of Bari), pp. 240-241.

Habili, N. and Randles, J.W. (2002) Developing a standardised sampling protocol for consistent detection of grapevine viruses by the PCR assay. Aust. NZ Grapegrower & Winemaker No. 464, 88-91.

Habili, N. and Randles, J.W. (2004) Descriptors for Grapevine virus A associated syndrome in Shiraz, Merlot and Ruby Cabernet in Australia and its similarity to Shiraz Disease in South Africa. Aust. NZ Grapegrower & Winemaker No. 488, 71-74.

Habili, N. and Rowhani, A. (2002) First detection of a new virus, Grapevine leafroll-associated virus type 9, in a popular clone of Cabernet Sauvignon in Australia. Aust. NZ Grapegrower & Winemaker No. 461a, 102-103.

Habili, N., Rowhani, A. et al. (2001) Grapevine fanleaf virus: a potential threat to the viticultural industry. Aust. Grapegrower & Winemaker No. 449a, 141,143,145.

Habili, N. and Symons, R.H. (2000) Grapevine viruses detected by Waite Diagnostics in Australia. Extended Abstracts 13th Meeting ICVG Adelaide (University of Adelaide and CSIRO: Adelaide), p. 124.

• Krake, L.R., Steele Scott, N. et al. (1999) Graft-transmitted diseases of grapevines (CSIRO: Collingwood).

La Notte, P., Buzkan, N. et al. (1997) Acquisition and transmission of Grapevine virus A by the mealybug *Pseudococcus longispinus*. J. Plant Path. 79, 79-85.

Leonhardt, W., Wawrosch, C., et al. (1998) Monitoring of virus disease in Austrian grapevine varieties and virus elimination using *in vitro* thermotherapy. Plant Cell Tissue and Organ Culture 52(1-2), 71-74.

Mannini, F. (1995) Grapevine clonal selection in Piedmont (Northwest Italy): focus on Nebbiolo and Barbera. In: Proc. Int. Symp. Clonal Selection, Portland 1995. Ed J.M. Rantz (ASEV: Davis), pp. 20-32.

Mannini, F. (2003) Virus elimination in grapevine and crop performance. Extended Abstracts 14th meeting ICVG, Locorotondo, Italy (University of Bari), pp. 234-239.

Mannini, F. and Credi, R. (2000) Appraisal of agronomic and enological modifications in the performances of grapevine clones after virus eradication. Extended Abstracts 13th Meeting ICVG Adelaide (University of Adelaide and CSIRO: Adelaide), pp. 151-154.

Martelli, G.P. (1992). Grapevine Viruses and Certification in EEC Countries: State of the Art (CIHEAM: Bari, Italy).

• Martelli, G.P. (1993). Graft-Transmissible Diseases of Grapevines (FAO: Rome).

Martelli, G.P. (1999) The impact of propagation material on vine health - a European perspective. In: Proc. 10th Aust. Wine Industry Technical Conference, Sydney (Winetitles: Adelaide), pp. 197-207.

McCarthy, M.G. (1988a) Clonal comparisons with Pinot Noir, Chardonnay and Riesling clones. In: Proc. 2nd Int. Symp. for Cool Climate Viticulture and Oenology, Auckland. Eds R. Smart, R. Thornton, et al. (NZSVO: Auckland), pp. 285-286.

McCarthy, M.G. (1988b) Grapevine planting material. In: Viticulture Volume 1. Resources in Australia. Eds B. G. Coombe and P. R. Dry (Winetitles: Adelaide), pp. 177-189.

McCarthy, M.G., Cirami, R.M. et al. (1989) Virus thermotherapy effects on the performance of a Muscadelle selection. Vitis 28, 13-19.

McCarthy, M.G. and Ewart, A.J.W. (1988) Clonal evaluation for quality

winegrape production. In: Proc. 2nd Int. Symp. for Cool Climate Viticulture and Oenology, Auckland. Eds R. Smart, R. Thornton, et al. (NZSVO: Auckland), pp. 34-36.

Meredith, C. (2000) Keeping it all in the family. Identifying grape varieties with DNA typing. Grape Grower May 2000, 19-20.

Minafra, A., Greif, C. et al. (1997) Molecular tools for the detection of grapevine viruses. In: Sanitary Selection of the Grapevine. Ed B. Walter (INRA Editions: Colmar).

Mullins, M.G., Bouquet, A. et al. (1992). Biology of the Grapevine (Cambridge University Press: Cambridge).

Nicholas, P.R. (2003). Standardised Protocols for Conducting Grapevine Improvement Trials in Australia. Final Report to Grape and Wine Research and Development Corporation (SARDI: Loxton).

Nyland, G. and Goheen, A.C. (1969) Heat therapy of virus diseases of perennial plants. Ann. Rev. Phytopathol. 7, 331-354.

• Pearson, R.C. and Goheen, A.C. (1988) Compendium of grape diseases (American Phytopathological Society: St. Paul, Minnesota).

Reynolds, A.G., Lanterman, W.S. et al. (1997) Yield and berry composition of five *Vitis* cultivars as affected by Rupestris stem pitting virus. Amer. J. Enol. Vitic. 48, 449-458.

Savino, V., Boscia, D. et al. (1990) Effect of heat therapy and meristem tip culture on the elimination of grapevine leafroll-associated closterovirus type III. In: Proc. 10th meeting ICVG, Volos, Greece. Eds I.C. Rumbos, R. Bovey, et al. (Ores Publishing: Volos), pp. 433-436.

Schmid, J., Ries, R. et al. (1995) Aims and achievements of clonal selection at Geisenheim. In: Proc. Int. Symp. Clonal Selection, Portland 1995. Ed. J.M. Rantz, (ASEV: Davis), pp. 70-73.

Shanmuganathan, N. and Fletcher, G. (1980) Indexing grapevine clones in the fruit variety foundation of Australia for virus and virus-like diseases. Aust. J. Exp. Agric. & Anim. Husb. 20, 115-118.

Shi, B.J., Habili, N. et al. (2003) Necleotide sequence variation in a small region of the *Grapevine fleck virus* replicase provides evidence for two sequence variants of the virus. Ann. Appl. Biol. 142, 349-355.

Shi, B.J., Habili, N. et al. (2004) Extensive variation of sequence within isolates of grapevine virus B. Virus Genes 29(2), 279-285.

Sim, S.T., Rowhani, A. et al. (2003) Experimental transmission of Grapevine leafroll-associated virus 5 and 9 by longtailed mealybugs. Extended Abstracts 14th meeting ICVG, Locorotondo, Italy (University of Bari), pp. 211.

Sivapalan, S., Whattam, M. et al. (2001). Review of Post Entry Quarantine Protocols for the Importation of Grapevine (Vitis) into Australia (Australian Quarantine and Inspection Service: Knoxfield).

Uyemoto, J.K., Rowhani, A. et al. (2001) New closterovirus in Redglobe grape causes decline of grafted plants. Calif. Agric. 55(5), 28-31.

• Walter, B. and Martelli, G.P. (1997) Clonal and sanitary selection of the grapevine. In: Sanitary Selection of the Grapevine. Ed B. Walter (INRA Editions: Colmar).

Walton, V.M. and Pringle, K.L. (2004) A survey of mealybugs and associated natural enemies in vineyards in the Western Cape Province, South Africa. S. Afric. J. Enol. Vitic. 25, 23-25.

Wang, Q., Gafny, R. et al. (2003) Elimination of *grapevine virus A* by cryopreservation. Extended Abstracts 14th meeting ICVG, Locorotondo, Italy (University of Bari), p. 242.

Whattam, M. (2001) Grapevine corky bark disease: a serious quarantine threat of grapevines for Australia. Aust. Plant Pathology 30, 379-380.

Whiting, J.R. (2003). Selection of Grapevine Rootstocks and Clones, for Greater Victoria (Department of Primary Industries: Victoria).

Whiting, J.R. and Hardie, W.J. (1981) Yield and compositional differences between selections of grapevine cv. Cabernet Sauvignon. Amer. J. Enol. Vitic. 32, 212-218.

Whiting, J.R. and Hardie, W.J. (1990) Comparison of selections of *Vitis vinifera* cv. Pinot Noir at Great Western, Victoria. Aust. J. Exp. Agric. 30, 281-285.

CHAPTER TEN

Vineyard Site Selection

R.E. SMART and P.R. DRY

European viticulture has long recognized the importance of site selection, having gone through centuries of trial and error evaluation. Since early Roman times viticulturists have been interested in the proper location of vineyards for producing the best grapes; the proverb *Bacchus amat colles* (Bacchus loves the hills) was the result of their experience. Sites prone to freezing or frost injury were avoided, as were those giving inadequate ripening in cold regions. Perhaps this sentiment also arose from bad experiences with deep and too-fertile soils in valley bottoms negatively impacting on quality.

Since the first European settlement in Australia, most vineyard regions, and indeed vineyard sites, have been selected almost by chance. It is only since 1960 that

scientific site selection has been employed; examples of this will follow relating mainly to winegrapes, although many of the principles relate equally to table and drying grapes. This chapter has drawn heavily on the booklet produced for the Vineyard Site Selection short course held at Roseworthy Agricultural College in December 1979 (Smart and Dry 1979).

10.1 Definitions

10.1.1 MACROCLIMATE, MESOCLIMATE AND MICROCLIMATE
The three levels of climate were defined by Smart (1984) [see also Chapter 4.1.2]:

Macroclimate (or regional climate) describes the general climate pattern as may be determined from a central recording station. The appropriate scale is from tens to hundreds of kilometres.

Mesoclimate (or topoclimate or site climate) can vary from the general macroclimate due to differences in elevation, slope, aspect or distance from large bodies of water (tens of metres up to kilometres).

Microclimate (or canopy climate) is the climate within and immediately surrounding a plant canopy (millimetres to metres).

10.1.2 WHAT IS SITE SELECTION?
Site selection is simply the choice of a vineyard site, normally done to optimize some aspect of vineyard performance. It involves considerations of location, topography and soils. This Chapter will emphasise climate factors in particular, soils being covered in Chapter 3. However we recognise that soil evaluation is an integral part of site selection.

The vineyard performance to be optimised typically is in terms of projected yield, wine quality or costs of production, but there are many important non-viticultural factors affecting the appropriateness of a vineyard site, e.g. reputation of the region, previous land-use, proximity to markets, labour and services. In Australia, where the majority of regions are not used for grapegrowing, site selection often involves selection of 'new' regions and is thus macroclimate selection. In regions where vineyards are already established, site selection may also involve mesoclimatic evaluation.

Although the concept of *'terroir'* is not as well appreciated in New World countries as it is in France, it does impact on site selection philosophy. Given that arguments are made about the virtues of and differences between *terroirs*, this concept can be incorporated into site selection by recognition of topographic and soil features.

10.1.3 Sources of mesoclimatic variation

Elevation
Mean temperature decreases by 0.5 to 0.6°C for every 100 m increase in elevation — the so-called lapse rate. Also exposure to wind generally increases with elevation, especially on escarpments. Vineyards in the Eden Valley (SA) experience lower growing season temperatures (approximately 1.5°C) than those on the floor of the nearby Barossa Valley and consequently ripen about three weeks later (Boehm 1970) — this is associated with an elevation difference of 200 m or more. Similarly, Shiraz vineyards in central Victoria with an elevation difference of 250 m are harvested 17 days apart (Dry 1984).

Proximity to large bodies of water
Large bodies of water store heat and reduce both diurnal and seasonal temperature range. For maximum effect the water body must be large. The vineyards near Australia's coastline experience this moderating influence, as also do those near the Tamar estuary (Tas.).

Slope and aspect
Vineyards on slopes have many advantages over those on flat land, particularly in cool climates. In the coolest regions of Europe, grapegrowing may sometimes be successful only on sloping land. A slope facing the sun will intercept more solar radiation than flat land. Aspect is also important: a slope facing the sunny part of the sky will be warmer than one on the opposite side of the hill. Generally, slopes are important only as far as radiation interception is concerned at high latitudes (i.e. far from the equator), at 47° and higher, when temperatures are limiting and when the sky is mostly cloud-free. Most Australian regions do not satisfy the first two criteria, although this can be important in Tasmania or at high elevations on the mainland.

Therefore, in mainland Australia, slope and aspect are mainly important from the point-of-view of protection from frost and wind. Slopes can be warmer and have a longer frost-free period than flat land due to the downward flow of cold air. Differences in minimum temperature can be large: a gradient of 10°C was recorded by Spurling and Jennings (1956) over a horizontal distance of 1,500 m during frost conditions in the relatively flat Riverland (SA). Because of the lower

energy gain from the morning sun, the intense night cooling in the lower terrains produces an after-effect which extends well into the late morning.

Aspect and adjacent topography affect the degree of exposure to wind. Wind not only affects grapevine physiology (Chapter 4) but also affects the heat budget of a site (10.4.2). This is particularly important in cool areas where cold winds may occur during sunny weather. Examples of areas in Australia where selection of the appropriate aspect for shelter from cold winds has been an important consideration include Geelong, Macedon Ranges, Mornington Peninsula (Vic.), Adelaide Hills, Eden Valley, Southern Fleurieu (SA) and Tasmania.

Rainfall can also be affected by aspect and is generally higher on the windward side of hills. Where high rainfall during the growing season promotes fungal disease problems, rain-shadows may be deliberately chosen as a method of reducing disease pressure.

FIGURE 10.1 shows the different temperature zones (mesoclimates) in a hypothetical landscape in the southern hemisphere. This figure shows how slope and aspect affect temperature and wind exposure. Becker (1977) studied the performance of Pinot Gris grapevines in southern Germany, planted on sites corresponding to a slope facing south (a) and a high plateau (g) in **FIGURE 10.1**. The former had 14% more heat days from March to October and 57% more during the ripening period: flowering and ripening commenced nine and six days earlier respectively, the fruit had higher sugar and lower acidity, and the wine was improved. Such results might be expected in regions where vine performance is limited by low temperatures. This however is infrequently the case in Australia.

10.2 History of site selection in Australia

10.2.1 The first vineyards
TABLE 1.2 shows the decade of first plantings in major Australian viticultural regions. Their location in most instances was an historical accident - vineyards were usually planted to provide wine and fresh fruit for the local population. Gold mining, in particular, provided the stimulus for vineyard development in many cases, e.g. Mudgee (NSW), Avoca, Bendigo, Great Western, Ballarat and Rutherglen (Vic.).

There were few, if any, weather records available at that time, so which factors guided these early vignerons in their site selection? A study of the early accounts of Australian viticulture by Busby (1825), Kelly (1861), Belperroud (1859), Ward (1862) and de Castella (1891) reveals a good understanding of the important roles that soil type, aspect and topography play in European viticulture. However, the summer drought in most Australian regions required

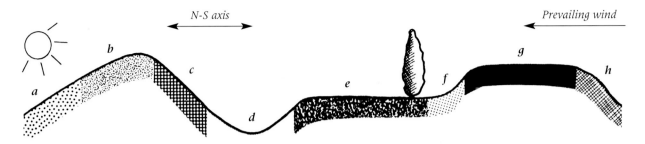

Figure 10.1. Association of mesoclimates with topography in the southern hemisphere (from Jackson and Schuster 1987).
(a) A warm site catching more sun owing to the lie of the land — it misses late spring and early autumn frosts, since the cold air will drain to low-lying areas.
(b) The advantages of (a) will be counteracted by the cold which comes with altitude.
(c) A cold site: although it may miss frosts in spring and autumn, it will accumulate much less heat in summer due to exposure to wind and a poor angle to sun.
(d) Very cold and the area most susceptible to frost — cold air from surrounding districts will drain into this area.
(e) Still frosty but less than (d). Some shelter from wind may be obtained by the hill and trees behind.
(f) The trees densely planted at the base of the hill prevent cold air draining away and a potentially frost free site has been lost
(g) Less frost than (e), but a prevailing cold wind and altitude may prevent the accumulation of warm air in summer.
(h) Cold, like (c) above.

an essential change in their European-influenced attitudes. Whereas Busby (1825) recommended calcareous soils for winegrapes in preference to fertile clay soils, just a few years later Kelly (1861) wrote:

"The vine in our drier climate requires soils more retentive of moisture than in Europe ... from ignorance of the great difference between climates of the northern and southern hemisphere, many vineyards planted according to the general practice of France or Germany on the sunny slopes of calcareous hills have proved failures, while many damp situations where there is a subsoil permeated by water from higher ground which would be considered unfit for the vine in Europe have proved excellent vineyard sites in Australia."

Hence the predominance of early vineyards on the deep alluvial soils of the valleys (Swan Valley (WA), Clare Valley, Barossa Valley (SA), Hunter (NSW), Yarra Valley (Vic.)) and plains. Vineyards on more elevated sites on shallow soils were tried but abandoned due to a combination of water stress and wind, but Sutherland (1892) clearly recognized their potential for producing quality wines. Since the widespread adoption of drip irrigation in the 1970s it has been possible to plant vineyards on the shallower soils of slopes.

The importance of shelter from hot northerly and cold southerly winds was recognized at an early stage; another reason for the tendency to plant in the more sheltered valleys. Where natural shelter was not provided, most early vineyards were protected by windbreaks planted at the time of vineyard establishment. In many parts of South Australia, the windbreaks of olives still remain even though the vineyards have long since gone.

10.2.2 IRRIGATION SETTLEMENTS

The first vineyards to be irrigated from the River Murray were planted in the 1890s; however, the major expansion in the Riverland (SA), Murray Darling (Vic., NSW) and Riverina (NSW) regions did not take place until after the World Wars when the government instituted a policy of settling repatriated soldiers on the land (see Chapter 1). Site selection was governed more by the proximity of towns and water reticulation than any other factors. Most soil types were planted indiscriminately prior to the advent of CSIR (later the CSIRO) soil surveys (see Chapters 2 and 3). Frost is a major problem, but more so for the evergreen citrus orchards than the winter-dormant vineyards.

Today the dried fruit industry is centred in the Murray Darling (Vic., NSW) and Riverland (SA) regions, due to a combination of high yields and good drying conditions in late summer and autumn. By comparison, grape drying was tried in the equally productive Riverina (NSW), but later abandoned because the drying season was found to be shorter and less reliable. In the past, dried fruit has been an important product in dryland areas with dry, sunny autumns, e.g. Swan District (WA), Clare Valley, Barossa Valley, McLaren Vale and Adelaide Plains (SA).

10.2.3 THE 1960s TO THE 2000s

Consumption of wine per head of population in Australia almost doubled in the 1960s. Most of this increase comprised table wines rather than the more traditional fortified wines. To satisfy this increased demand new vineyards were planted, generally in regions with a long-established wine industry. Others however were planted in regions that had supported a thriving wine industry in the past but were virtually vine-free in the early 1960s (e.g. Yarra Valley), and some were planted in regions with no previous history of commercial viticulture. With few exceptions, it is likely that factors such as proximity to markets and prior reputation were more important in site selection than assessment of climate, soils and water resources.

In the rush to plant new vineyards the experience of the previous 150 years was often ignored: the Hunter is just one of many examples. The early vineyards in the southern Hunter (and most of those vineyards that had survived to the 1960s) were generally planted on fertile sandy loams and red loams of volcanic origin (see Chapters 2 and 3): these soils have good depth and drainage. Many of the vineyards established after 1960 were planted on shallow, acidic, poorly-drained clay soils with no provision for irrigation to counter the occasional summer drought. Despite limited irrigation, most of these vineyards with an average yield of 1 to 3 tonnes/ha have since been removed.

In many cases there was an attempt to maximize water availability to new vineyards to improve yields and profitability. To this end, vineyards were established beyond what were regarded as the traditional boundaries for grapegrowing in regions such as the Barossa Valley, Clare Valley, Riverland (SA) and Hunter (NSW). For example, new vineyards were established in the Eden Valley (SA): previous attempts here had usually failed due to lack of water, but modern developments in dam construction and drip irrigation systems allowed commercially viable grapegrowing, even on relatively shallow soils. Many of the new sites in the Hunter (mainly the northern Hunter) were chosen so that the vineyards could be irrigated from the Hunter River and its tributaries: a stark contrast to the non-irrigated vineyards of the traditional southern Hunter.

The initial impetus for new vineyard development was fuelled by a demand for table wine, including bulk wine; hence the diversion of large quantities of Sultana and Muscat Gordo Blanco from drying to winemaking and the establishment of large plantings of traditional winegrapes in the Riverland, SA (near Waikerie, Morgan and Renmark) and Murray Darling (Vic., NSW). Subsequently, there was recognition that the best table wines from 'noble' varieties such as Cabernet Sauvignon and Riesling would be produced from sites that were cooler than the traditional hot areas. Such sites could be found at higher elevations, e.g. Eden Valley, Adelaide Hills (SA), the slopes of the Great Dividing Range in Victoria and NSW, or in more southerly locations, e.g. south-west of WA, Padthaway (SA), Henty, Mornington Peninsula, Gippsland (Vic.), and Launceston and Coal River (Tas.). At the same time, pressure of urban development was decreasing the availability of fruit from traditional areas, e.g. Swan District (WA), McLaren Vale (SA). Similarly, suitable land was in short supply at Coonawarra (SA) and Grampians (Vic.). These factors

also promoted the search for new vineyard sites (Smart 1977, Gladstones 1977, Smart and Dry 1979).

For many of these new areas, grapegrowing has been successful where it would have failed miserably a century ago; modern irrigation technology, land preparation and disease and pest control have made this possible. Nevertheless, some of the current problems of these new areas were not foreseen when they were originally selected, e.g. wind, excess vigour and acid soils.

The following examples are representative of some of the developments in Australian viticulture since the early 1960s where there appears to have been a deliberate attempt to assess macro- and mesoclimatic suitability, soils, water resources and other factors. Other examples, not covered in this discussion, include Pipers Brook (Tas.), the environs of Canberra (ACT), Mornington Peninsula, Henty and other areas close to Melbourne (Vic.) Further opportunities exist to find new vineyard areas, especially with the application of detailed homoclime studies. Formerly limited to analysis of data from the network of climate stations maintained by the Bureau of Meteorology (see www.bom.gov.au), analysis can be applied to 'gridded' data which is available down to scale of about 2 km cells. Thus, modern site selection may be conducted at almost the vineyard level rather than at the regional level (Smart 2003).

South west of Western Australia
Viticulture in WA has traditionally been centred on the Swan Valley because of its close proximity to Perth and suitability for the production of grapes for fortified wine and for table and drying. Olmo (1956) concluded that the cooler southern parts of the state were better suited to table wine production than the Swan Valley; in particular, he selected the Mt Barker and Frankland sub-regions. Gladstones (1965, 1966) later extended Olmo's work, using a temperature basis modified to allow for the lower latitude of south-western Australia compared with Europe and California and also taking into account frost risk, ripening period, rain and hail risk, sunshine hours and susceptibility to high temperature extremes in middle and late summer. He suggested that the slightly warmer and sunnier areas near to Busselton and Margaret River could have advantages over Mt Barker and Frankland for table wine production. Subsequently Gladstones (1987) recommended further locations in the south-west including areas near to the towns of Manjimup, Pemberton, Nannup, Albany and Denmark.

Padthaway (SA)
In the early 1960s, the Seppelt wine company was looking for new areas suitable for Riesling and Cabernet Sauvignon. Using Coonawarra as a standard, a search was conducted in the south east of SA. The area near Padthaway was found to have well-drained soils and plentiful supplies of underground water. The frost

liability of the region was determined using temperature records from nearby meteorological stations (M.B. Spurling, pers. comm.); despite limitations, the frost risk was predicted to be lower than that for Coonawarra and this has subsequently proved correct. Experience has also shown that the early predictions of good yields and good wine quality were justified.

Drumborg

A lack of suitable land and inadequate water resources at Great Western (Grampians, Vic.) led the Seppelt wine company to search for alternative sites suitable for early-maturing winegrapes. An area of well-drained fertile, volcanic soil (see Chapters 2 and 3) at Drumborg (Henty) near the southern Victoria coast was planted in 1964. The low temperatures (Chapter 2; Heinze 1977) and low sunshine during the growing season result in delayed flowering and ripening (**TABLE 10.1**), with inadequate ripening for all but the earliest varieties. The high number of raindays (almost one day in two from budburst to harvest) causes fungal disease problems. Although vine growth is slow for the first three to four years, subsequent excessive vegetative growth creates problems. Cold weather during flowering causes poor set (Heinze 1977).

Eden Valley and Adelaide Hills (SA)

Until the 1960s the vineyard area in the Eden Valley was small compared to that on the floor and lower slopes of the Barossa Valley. Recognition of the relationship between elevation and temperature and consequent effects on fruit composition and wine quality led to the establishment of vineyards comprising premium table wine varieties such as Riesling and Cabernet Sauvignon initially and Chardonnay and Pinot Noir later. Modern technology of dam construction, contour banking, water reticulation and drip irrigation made possible the establishment of vineyards on shallow soils susceptible to summer drought; such sites had been tried in the past but abandoned because of low yields.

The first vineyard of the modern era was planted in 1961 at Pewsey Vale and further development has continued. Many vineyards are found at 450 m elevation or higher. The grapevines were slow to establish on these sites due to a combination of water stress (not all vineyards were irrigated at first), wind and soil problems (acid soils are common: Dundon et al. (1984) reported surface soil pH ranging from 4.2 to 4.7). The importance of wind as a factor limiting productivity on these elevated and generally exposed sites has now been recognized (Ewart et al. 1987, Hamilton 1988, Dry et al. 1988).

Until the late 1970s there were few vineyards in the Adelaide Hills. Planting in the Piccadilly-Summertown area commenced in the late 1970s and this was followed

Table 10.1 Phenology and composition of Riesling at Drumborg (Henty, Vic.), Padthaway, Barossa, Riverland (SA) - average of five seasons[1]

Location	Date of:			Juice composition		
	Budburst[2]	Flowering[3]	Harvest	Sugar (°Be)	Acid (g/L)	pH
Drumborg	18 Sept	21 Dec	11 Apr	11.8	9.4	3.20
Padthaway	9 Sept	23 Nov	29 Mar	12.0	8.0	3.38
Barossa	9 Sept	23 Nov	12 Mar	11.5	8.0	3.38
Riverland	9 Sept	3 Nov	20 Feb	11.3	7.9	3.48

[1] 1971/72 to 1975/76; [2] 75% woolly bud; [3] 75% flowering. Adapted from Heinze (1977).

by vineyard development at Mt Pleasant, Lenswood and Gumeracha in the 1980s and Lobethal, Forreston, Birdwood and Mt Barker in the 1990s (see Chapter 2). Steep slopes have been planted for frost avoidance and the recent tendency to run rows up and down the slope (rather than following the contour as practised in the earlier vineyards) requires the use of sod culture to decrease erosion. In turn vines need to be irrigated to avoid water stress, the risk being exacerbated by the presence of actively-growing swards during the growing season. Winds from the south and south east appear to significantly reduce fruit-set.

Around Launceston

In early 2003 a program was initiated by Tamar Ridge Wines to search for homoclimes of prestigious New Zealand vineyard areas around Launceston, Tasmania. That they existed could be anticipated because of similarity in latitude and island influence. Very close temperature homoclimes of Marlborough, Martinborough and Central Otago in New Zealand were located near to Launceston, and also on the east coast. This search was made using gridded climatic data with a resolution of around 2 km. Hazard analysis was also carried out by calculating and mapping frost incidence and the likelihood of autumn rains.

10.3 VINEYARD SITE SELECTION IN OTHER COUNTRIES

The examples described below have delineated optimal areas for grapegrowing by mapping climatic or soil indices and using an overlay approach. For each region it is necessary to use a limited number of critical yet quantifiable criteria. For a review of site selection in cool regions, refer to Becker (1985).

Rheingau, Germany

A viticultural atlas for site selection in the Rheingau region was first published in 1967 and was followed by more detailed maps (Zakosek et al. 1972-1985, 1979). The maps include information on soil type with recommendations on rootstocks and soil amendments. In addition, three climatic zones are mapped: the warmest zones have a long vegetation period suitable for Riesling and similar varieties (Becker 1988).

Oregon, USA

Optimal areas in Oregon for *Vitis vinifera* varieties were delineated by the mapping and overlaying of four climatic indices: expected 20-year minimum temperatures, heat summation, Thornthwaite's potential evapotranspiration index and length of growing season (Aney 1974).

British Columbia, Canada

An atlas based on climate and soil characteristics was developed in British Columbia to assist in the identification of suitable sites for economical grape production in the Okanagan and Similkameen valleys (Anon. 1984, Vielvoye 1988a). Solar radiation, degree days (base 10°C) over the growing season and autumn freeze risk data were each grouped into four classes for the purpose of mapping. Similarly, 87 soil classifications were reduced to four suitability classes based on limitations for viticulture. The final suitability maps were developed by overlaying all of the climatic and soil themes: five suitability classes were derived. Land areas in Class 1 are the most desirable and the least restrictive for grape production: they have the highest number of growing season heat units, a long frost-free season, high solar radiation and desirable soil characteristics and are capable of growing the widest range of grape varieties. A more recent study has utilised modern GIS (Geographic Information System) technology (P. Bowen, pers. comm.)

Virginia, USA

Site selection in this eastern USA state is largely based on avoidance of spring frost and winter freeze injury. Both of these hazards can be avoided by selection of a thermal belt at high elevation with good cold air drainage (Wolf and Boyer 2001). This work was done using GIS and included development of a vineyard site attribute classification. A 100 point ranking included elevation (30 points), soils (25), land use (20), slope (15) and aspect (10). The best sites were assessed with 85 points or better, and unsuitable ones with less than 55. The study showed a strong correlation with historically successful fruit production, especially apples, and sites highly rated for grape production. Such studies can have output as maps showing desirable vineyard sites. This work has been further extended (Wolf and Boyer 2003) to include assessment of soil effects, and consideration of pest and disease hazards along with atmospheric pollution.

New York State, USA

Researchers at Cornell University have developed a similar system which is based on use of GIS (McCandless 1999). They produced maps with resolution of one square kilometre to show site suitability for viticulture. The maps incorporated climate, soil and land use information. In particular, maps showed hazards of winter freezing temperatures and a growing season length of 160 frost-free days.

Figure 10.2 A contour-planned vineyard on sloping ground at Great Western, Victoria. Vineyards on the flats in this region are prone to frost damage.

10.4 Components of site selection

Some of the following aspects concerning vineyard sites are illustrated in **FIGURES 10.2** to **10.5**.

10.4.1 WATER SUPPLY

The overriding importance of water supply in vineyard site selection in Australia has already been emphasized in this chapter. The need for an assured supply of water for irrigation is obvious even for high rainfall districts. With few exceptions, Australian grapegrowing is practiced in regions with low summer rainfall (**TABLE 2.1**) and Australian grapegrowing soils are generally unable to store enough of the winter rainfall for the full growing-season requirements; therefore water-stress occurs. In many instances this problem is exacerbated by shallow rootzones; subsoils are not conducive to root growth because of poor aeration, acidity, physical strength, etc. (see Chapter 3). Even sites with an annual rainfall of 1,000 mm or more may require irrigation from midsummer onwards, e.g. Adelaide Hills (SA), Margaret River (WA). Moreover, rainfall is often unreliable and reliance on average data in site selection is dangerous; for example, although the Hunter (NSW) has a small surplus of rainfall over estimated vineyard water use based on long-term averages (**TABLE 2.1**), the reality is that this region has experienced summer drought frequently, and irrigation is practiced on most sites every year.

A reliable supply of water is so crucial to success that many would be unwilling to plant a vineyard in southern Australia without providing some form of irrigation. The water may come from rivers and streams, bores, wells or springs, dams or public supply. Irrigation water is now licenced by State Governments, and licences must be purchased to access local supplies. Furthermore, there can be restrictions of dam capacity and run-off capture. It is necessary to determine

Figure 10.3 Excessive vegetative growth on a deep, fertile soil (Mornington Peninsula, Vic.).

Figure 10.4 Sod culture (mown sward) is generally used in vineyards in the Adelaide Hills, SA to decrease erosion. The row spacing in this case is 2.0 m.

irrigation requirements and water availability prior to land purchase and certainly planting. Increasingly irrigation water is being made available through community irrigation schemes, e.g. Hunter (NSW), Barossa Valley, McLaren Vale (SA).

The amount of water (irrigation or rainfall) required for assured vine growth in most seasons varies from 150 mm per season in cool humid districts to 700 mm in hot and dry districts. If rainfall and evaporation records are available the irrigation requirements can be roughly estimated by the difference between half of Class A Pan evaporation (an estimate of vineyard evapotranspiration) and rainfall during the growing season. A more precise water budget can be calculated by taking soil water storage capacity and run-off factors into consideration (see Volume II, Chapter 6).

10.4.2 CLIMATE

The climate requirements for grapegrowing are described in detail in Chapter 4. It is worthwhile noting that of the climate components that affect viticulture (temperature, rainfall, sunshine, wind and evaporation), there are limited opportunities to modify them commercially. Those that can be modified are low temperatures using frost avoidance fans or sprinkler irrigation, rainfall deficit using irrigation, and wind speed using windbreaks. For the remaining components, site selection is the primary means of selecting climate values within a desired range. Once the desired macroclimate has been selected (perhaps using the 'homoclime' approach — see 10.5), the climatic factors important in site selection may be further modified by topography, aspect and elevation (10.1.3). If a site has misty, foggy mornings, a westerly aspect may be chosen to increase sunlight interception; on the other hand, in regions where afternoon cloud is common, an easterly aspect may be best.

The flow of cold air during sunlight frost conditions is influenced by topography and there is a close correlation between frost hazard and contour height. Any

obstruction of air flow by windbreaks etc. will raise the frost hazard above them. It is often possible to avoid or remove obstructions on slopes, but hollows and closed valleys present a permanent hazard demanding special management practices or frost-prevention measures. In narrow valleys, vineyards must be kept at higher elevations above the valley floor than in broad valleys. Frost is particularly hazardous for a young vineyard because the developing shoots are closer to the ground where temperatures may be two or three degrees Celsius lower than at trellis height. Frost risk may be calculated for a region by use of probability curves and minimum temperature records.

Lower night temperatures in valleys also lead to higher relative humidity. Since vineyards on valley floors are often vigorous and poorly ventilated, the risk of fungal diseases is greater. Wind not only affects grapevine physiology directly (see Chapter 4) but also affects the heat budget of a site. For example, in northern Tasmania, a northerly aspect has the highest potential energy gain; however, strong cold winds from the north-west are

Figure 10. 5 Retention of native forest around vineyards at Margaret River, WA may provide protection from wind and an alternative food source for bird pests.

frequent during sunny weather and consequently the more protected north-east to east-facing slopes may be preferred for grapegrowing. Wind can limit the yield on coastal sites, e.g. Margaret River (WA), Southern Fleurieu (SA), southern Victoria (Henty, Geelong, Mornington Peninsula, Gippsland) and Tasmania, and those inland at higher elevations, e.g. Eden Valley, Adelaide Hills (SA), Macedon Ranges (Vic.). In the latter region, the frequency of moderate to strong winds during the growing season is high; it is estimated that the stomates are at least partially closed (and thus photosynthesis is impaired) for an average of two to five days per week during the whole of the growing season (Dry and Smart 1986). It is ironic that both Kelly (1861) and Ward (1864) emphasized the importance of choosing vineyard sites in southern Victoria with protection from cold southerly winds, and that this advice is being heeded 140 years later. Wind data is infrequently available in many regions, but the presence of strong wind can be assessed by the shape and form of trees and shrubs.

10.4.3 SOIL
The potential of soils for grapegrowing, including site selection, and the criteria for good soils are described in detail in Chapter 3.

In hot, dry areas, the criteria for evaluating soils will be different to those in cool, wet areas. For example, in the former areas, good soil depth with a moderately high silt, loam or clay content may be important for water storage capacity. In cool, wet areas good drainage may be more important to avoid waterlogging and to increase soil temperature, particularly in early spring.

Problems with acid soils, on the one hand, and excessive vigour on the other, have been encountered in many new vineyards in high rainfall areas. Acid soils are often found in high rainfall areas, and can be difficult to ameliorate if the acidity occurs at depth. The latter problem of high vigour is often a consequence of vineyard establishment on deep, fertile, moist soils, e.g. the volcanic soils of Mornington Peninsula and Henty (Vic.) and north-east Tasmania. In a few cases, there has been a deliberate attempt to choose sites with less deep and fertile soils to decrease the vigour problem; an example is a Mornington Peninsula (Vic.) vineyard that has been established on a duplex soil with a sandy loam A horizon (Anon. 1987).

Corrective measures on problem soils can be initially expensive (e.g. addition of gypsum, lime and other ameliorants, installation of drains, deep-ripping through calcrete and removal of stones) so judicious site selection is an important economic decision.

10.4.4 DISEASE AND PESTS
Certain pests and diseases obviously can be avoided by planting grapevines in regions without those problems. For example, downy mildew (*Plasmopora viticola*) is of limited occurrence in Western Australia (McLean et al. 1984)

and phylloxera is absent from most regions in Australia (see Volume II, Chapters 10, 11). However, there is no guarantee that this latter situation will last indefinitely, as phylloxera is currently limited by quarantine.

Regions with high growing-season rainfall have been less preferred for grapegrowing in the past due to problems with fungal diseases, notably downy mildew. Some exceptions such as the Hunter (NSW) were established prior to the introduction of downy mildew to Australia; downy mildew was first recorded in the Hunter in 1896 (Halliday 1985). The advent of fungicides, modern spray application technology and improved, resistant varieties has diminished this problem, and new vineyards have been established in high summer rainfall areas such as Port Macquarie, Nowra (NSW) and in south-east Queensland. The likely incidence of downy mildew and botrytis bunch rot in new areas can be predicted from long-term climatic data (Dry 1979), and models for downy and powdery mildews and botrytis bunch rot are now being tested (see Volume II, Chapter 11).

A moderate to high incidence of downy mildew is expected where:
- Rainfall (October to March) exceeds 200 mm
- Rainfall (November) exceeds 40 mm
- Raindays (October to March) exceed 40
- Relative humidity (9 am, November) exceeds 60%

A moderate to high incidence of botrytis bunch rot is expected where, in the harvest month:
- Rainfall exceeds 60 mm
- Raindays exceed 8
- Relative humidity (9 am) exceeds 60%

TABLE 10.2 lists rainfall, raindays and relative humidity for a range of viticultural regions in Australia. Note the high potential disease risk in regions such as Macedon Ranges, Henty (Vic.), Launceston (Tas.) and Adelaide Hills (SA). Although the incidence of downy mildew in drier regions like the Barossa Valley (SA) is generally low, epidemics can occur in occasional wet seasons, e.g. 1973/74.

10.4.5 VEGETATION ANALYSIS
The local vegetation has been used as an indicator of site quality since the early days of Australian viticulture when particular Eucalyptus species were found to be associated with deep well-drained soils. Vegetation, whether native or introduced, reflects the integral effect of all of the physical, chemical and biotic factors of the environment.

Indicators of good sites for grapegrowing in eastern Australia include *Eucalyptus macrorhynca* (red stringy bark), *Eucalyptus obliqua* (messmate stringy bark), *Eucalyptus rubida* (candlebark) and *Eucalyptus viminalis* (manna gum); sites to be avoided have *Eucalyptus fasciculosa* (pink gum), *Eucalyptus leucoxylon*, *Eucalyptus ovata* (swamp gum) and *Eucalyptus sideroxylon* (red

Table 10.2 Rainfall, raindays and relative humidity data for some Australian regions[1]

Region	Station	Rainfall (mm)			Raindays		Relative Humidity (9 am,%)	
		Oct to Mar	Nov	Harvest month[2]	Oct to Mar	Harvest month	Nov	Harvest month
Granite Belt	41095	488	74	67 (Mar)	55	9	59	71
Hunter	61009	436	59	88 (Feb)	45	8	54	67
Yarra Valley	1	375	77	69 (Apr)	59	11	73	78
Adelaide Hills	23785	329	62	97 (Apr)	56	12	64	71
Macedon Ranges	88036	293	52	54 (Apr)	43	9	65	76
				75 (May)		12		84
Tasmania[3] (Launceston)	1	290	54	61 (Apr)	52	10	69	80
				75 (May)		12		87
Henty	90048	285	59	66 (Apr)	70	15	73	82
Barossa Valley	23321	163	29	22 (Mar)	38	5	56	58
Barossa Valley (1973/74)	23321	343	29	54 (Mar)	48	7	64	74
Margaret River	9574	193	42	28 (Mar)	42	6	70	68
				67 (Apr)		10		79

[1] Refer to Table 2.1 for sources of data
[2] Harvest month indicated only for rainfall; also applies to raindays and relative humidity
[3] Zone

ironbark) (Due 1979). The performance of improved pastures of perennial grasses and other woody perennials, e.g. *Pinus radiata* and apple, can also provide useful information. A word of caution should be introduced here. While vegetation analysis can be useful to identify problem soils, one should not assume that deep and fertile soils as indicated by vegetation are most suitable for grapegrowing. This is especially the case in cool, wet regions. Rushes are very good indicators of poor drainage, and it is most useful to note their presence in any intended vineyard site.

10.4.6 OTHER FACTORS
The choice of a particular site may be determined as much by the following factors as those mentioned so far.
Cost of land, which is typically cheap if in a 'new' vineyard region, and if used for grazing.
Proximity to skilled labour and services. In new regions there will often be a lack of skilled or available labour for vineyard establishment and operation, supplies (chemicals, spare parts, etc.) and technical expertise.
Proximity to markets, including good visibility from and access to major roads if a cellar door operation is countenanced.
A demonstrated performance of grapevines in the area. This may be limited to a few vines in a backyard, or commercial vineyards. Sometimes the reputation of the new area grows to such an extent that nearby 'old-fashioned' established areas may wish to take advantage of its newly acquired status. The recent expansion of the Adelaide Hills viticultural region is one example.
Community co-operation in such matters as irrigation, drainage, control of herbicide use on neighbouring land (particularly hormone herbicides), council permits etc.
Environmental controls e.g. dam construction, restrictions

on bird control devices, planting in catchment areas etc. *Birds* can devastate isolated vineyards. In larger areas of vineyard the problem is shared, particularly where there are 250 ha or more of contiguous vineyards. Control of a bird problem may be expensive.

10.5 The homoclime approach

A homoclime is a place of similar climate to another. There has been a long-term fascination of Australian vignerons to match climates in Australia with prestigious vineyard regions of Europe. Wines from European regions have been used as standards for the development of similar styles in Australia since the early 1800s, in particular Bordeaux, Burgundy, Champagne, Sherry and Port. In the absence of long-term climatic data, the early settlers instinctively attempted to match the varieties from these regions with similar environments in Australia; for example, Kelly (1861) recommended Pedro Ximenes and Palomino in recognition of the perceived similarity between areas near Adelaide (SA) and the south of Spain.

Several approaches have been tried, the early ones using climatic indices. Such methods relied on averaging sets of temperature data, and were easy to calculate with the facilities of the time (calculators). Such studies included the classic one by Prescott (1969) using mean temperature of the warmest month, and those of Pirie (1978), Smart and Dry (1979), and Dry and Ewart (1986). The reverse approach has also been used, i.e. the search for homoclimes of Australian regions in Europe as a guide to variety use, management practices and so on (Dry and Smart 1980, Helm and Cambourne 1987, Kirk 1987). There was also use of climate maps as were published for Australia by the Bureau of Meteorology.

Table 10.3 Climatic data for viticultural regions in Australia and Europe[1]

| Region | Station | Temperature °C | | Rainfall (mm) | | Raindays | Rel. Humidity | Bright sunshine |
		MJT[2]	CTL[3]	Annual	GS[4]	GS[4]	(9am, %)	(GS[4], h/day)
Australia								
Margaret River	1	20.4	7.6	1192	198	42	65	7.9
Padthaway	26091	20.3	10.5	509	159	47	68	8.5
Tumbarumba	72043	20.1	15.0	986	425	43	61	8.5
Mornington Peninsula	86079	19.0	9.6	740	323	53	67	7.0
Adelaide Hills	23785	18.7	10.7	1118	329	56	60	8.7
Macedon Ranges	88036	18.5	12.7	713	293	43	58	8.0
Tasmania[5] (Launceston)	1	17.7	10.6	730	290	52	69	8.1
France								
Bordeaux	Bordeaux	19.5	14.1	893	384	53	74	7.6
Burgundy	Dijon	19.1	17.7	737	398	68	67	7.8
Alsace	Strasbourg	19.1	18.5	610	390	79	71	6.6
Champagne	Reims	18.3	16.3	596	322	76	73	6.7

[1] See Table 2.1 for sources of data for Australian regions; data for France sourced from Table 10.4, Dry and Smart (1988).
[2] Mean January and mean July temperature in southern and northern hemisphere respectively
[3] Continentality - see text of Chapter 2 for explanation
[4] Growing season: October to March and April to September in southern and northern hemisphere respectively
[5] Zone

These could be used with transparent overlays to find homoclimes in Australia of classic European areas, and could be extended to more than one climate parameter. **TABLE 10.3** presents climatic data for some Australian viticultural regions that were selected in the latter half of the 20th century and for those regions in France that were used as standards in homoclime studies at the time.

The facilities available for homoclime searching have changed considerably over the last decade. Personal computers have become widely available along with software allowing for mapping and spatial analysis. Furthermore, climate records from Australian and world-wide recording stations are more readily available from many sources including the Internet, and are more up to date. Lastly, climate data in Australia and some other countries is no longer restricted to the network of climate stations, but has been extrapolated to finer resolution using correlations with elevation etc. This is so-called gridded data, and in Australia is available for most climate components down to about 2 km by 2 km cells. This is almost to the individual farm level.

Such facilities now allow homoclime searching on a very sophisticated scale. The results to follow are from the unpublished work of R. Smart and J. Gwalter. They have compiled computer databases of climate data and variety information, and use sorting and statistical testing to reveal 'goodness of fit' in homoclime matching. Composite maps can be created with several climate components and also assessments of frost and disease risk. They have found that use of indices which rely on averaging temperature data (such as Heat Degree Days HDD, Mean January Temperature MJT) may give spurious results in homoclime searching, especially in comparisons between regions. Rather, it is better to separately search for similarity to individual curves of monthly maximum and minimum temperatures, rather than using a curve which is the average of the two.

FIGURE 10.6. shows homoclimes in Australia of Avignon (France) produced by John Gwalter using this method. The grading represents 'goodness of fit' to 8 month (September to April) growing-season maximum and minimum temperature conditions of Avignon. In this instance good temperature homoclimes were found in southern Australia. However, in general, much of Europe is more continental (that is, a larger difference between summer and winter temperatures) than is much of Australia (see **TABLE 10.3**), and so it is not always possible to find places where maximum and minimum temperatures are both matched, especially for early spring and late autumn. Bordeaux is a good example, as is shown in **FIGURE 10.7.** Here the places corresponding to Bordeaux maximum temperature homoclimes are different to those with correspondence to the minimum. Yet, a homoclime search using HDD or MJT yielded good matches, as is shown in **FIGURE 10.8.** This indicates the potential flaws in searching for homoclimes using averaged data rather than the actual maximum and minimum data. Similar results have been found for other European sites, most of which are more continental than Bordeaux.

FIGURE 10.9 shows the opposite approach, that of finding homoclimes in Australia of nominated overseas regions, in this instance Spain. For each of the major vineyard regions of Spain, the closest growing season temperature homoclimes in Australia are shown. It has been found that south-east Australia has close growing season temperature homoclimes with vineyard regions of New Zealand, South Africa, Chile, Argentina, parts of Europe, and some states of USA including California, Texas and Oregon. This is illustrated in **FIGURE 10.10**, which shows as an example for parts of south-east

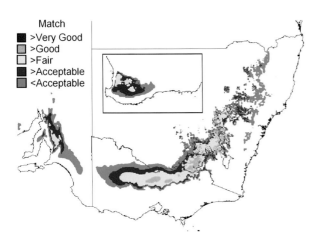

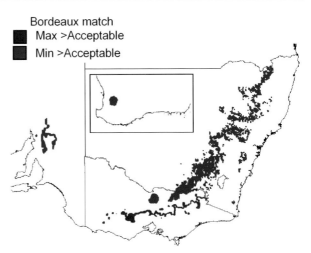

Figure 10.6 Homoclimes of the French vineyard region of Avignon in Australia, determined by comparing separately maximum and minimum temperature curves for the growing season (equivalent to September to April in the southern hemisphere).

Figure 10.7 Location of Australian places which match closely the maximum and minimum (separately) temperature curves for Bordeaux, France, growing season as September to April equivalent southern hemisphere months.

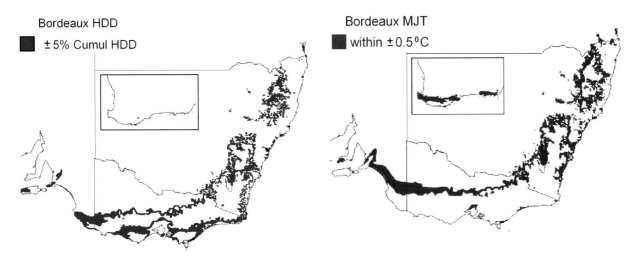

Figure 10.8 Location of homoclimes of Bordeaux, France in Australia indicated by matching using a) Heat Degree Days and b) Mean January temperature. Note that these places do not coincide with locations having similar maximum nor minimum temperature conditions, as shown in Figure 10.7 above.

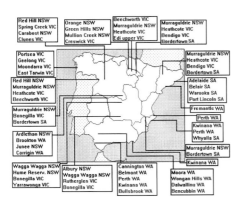

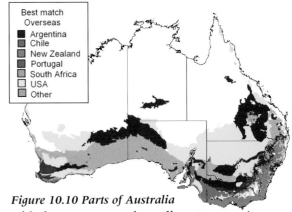

Figure 10.9 The closest 8-month temperature homoclimes in Australia shown for famous Spanish wine producing regions.

Figure 10.10 Parts of Australia with close temperature homoclimes to vineyard regions in other countries.

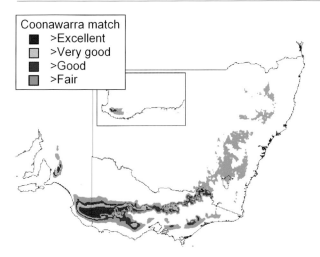

Figure 10.11 Growing season maximum temperature for Coonawarra, SA, Australia and minimum temperature homoclimes.

Australia, the country with a vineyard region which is the closest growing season temperature homoclime. Those zones with closest temperature homoclimes to Europe are limited to parts of southern NSW and northern Victoria.

Another use of homoclime searching is to find new regions with cheaper land in Australia with climates similar to established and distinguished Australian regions. An example is shown in **FIGURE 10.11** which indicates 8-month temperature homoclimes of Coonawarra in South East Australia.

10.6 Choice of grape variety

The choice of grape variety can be dictated by climatic considerations as well as by market forces. The latter are not discussed further here except to state that these pressures are dynamic and change with time, albeit often slowly. Varieties vary in their tolerance to climate conditions in terms of wine quality. The Burgundian varieties Pinot Noir and Chardonnay represent the opposite extremes of tolerance. Pinot Noir is known to be extremely fastidious, producing acceptable wine quality in only a few regions, and cool ones at that. Chardonnay on the other hand is well suited to cool climates, but also produces wines of good commercial quality in both warm and hot regions. Other varieties are positioned between these two extremes. The variety Shiraz produces distinctly different wine styles in different regions; when it is grown in cooler regions the wines are less alcoholic and more 'peppery' in aroma. It should also be stated that the climatic tolerance of varieties is not always known. For example, the white aromatic variety Alvariñho is grown in north west Spain and northern Portugal, but little elsewhere. While this region has temperature homoclimes in southern Victoria (see **FIGURE 10.9**), it is not to say that there might not

be other regions that could grow premium quality wines from this variety.

For the hot inland regions the choices of varieties for table grapes, and raisins are relatively straightforward (see Chapter 6). In the past there has been a temptation to plant in-demand varieties of wine grapes in these regions, but many of them have been found unsuited to high temperatures, for example Sauvignon Blanc, Traminer, Riesling and Pinot Noir. For cooler regions, the matching of varieties to sites, particularly for the production of quality winegrapes, is more difficult. The past success of a particular variety in a macroclimatic zone is not necessarily a guide if the variety is planted away from its traditional sites and/or cultural practices are changed. For example, Shiraz has been successful in the southern Hunter for red table wine when grown on the traditional 'low vigour' sites, i.e. non-irrigated, low fertility soils of moderate depth; however, when grown on the 'high vigour' sites, i.e. irrigated, deep, fertile soils, then inadequate ripening, poor wine colour and bunch rot are common in the absence of good canopy management.

The earliest recommendations based on actual performance of varieties on sites in Australia were published in the 1890s (de Castella 1891, Sutherland 1892). For example, Riesling was recommended for '...cool high slopes of fairly deep soil and subsoil of schist or decomposed granite' in South Australia (Sutherland 1892). Since that time, recommendations for the established areas have been published at regular intervals; in these cases the recommendations have been based as much on market demand as on varietal performance. For example, Grenache ripens well on hot, dryland sites and it was widely planted in the 1930s when the wine export bounty put a premium on sugar concentration (Hankel and Hall 1979). Interestingly the late 1990s saw a resurgence in demand for this variety especially from old vines on dryland vineyards, for use in blends with Shiraz and Mataro.

Choice of variety for new vineyard sites is a more difficult task. The ideal approach is to assess a range of varieties over several seasons; this has been done in several Australian locations, e.g. Padthaway, Drumborg; in Washington State, USA (Nagel et al. 1972); and in British Columbia, Canada (Vielvoye 1988b). A more rapid approach is to plant varieties based on their performance in homoclimes in Australia and overseas (Gladstones 1977, Dry and Smart 1980, Smart 2003).

Other factors which should be considered in variety choice include:

(a) Recovery after frost. Some varieties recover better after spring frost than others because they have more fruitful secondary buds, e.g. Gamay.

(b) Disease and pest resistance. Varieties with resistance to diseases and pests will be necessary in some locations. For example, Chambourcin has been successful at Port Macquarie (NSW) because it is resistant to downy mildew.

(c) Poor set. Pinot Noir, Riesling, Traminer and Chardonnay set poorly at Margaret River whereas the Bordeaux varieties, e.g. Cabernet Sauvignon and Sauvignon Blanc, have fewer problems (Gladstones 1987). A similar situation exists for other exposed, coastal sites in Australia.

(d) Ability to ripen. In cool regions, such as southern Victoria and Tasmania, the ability of a variety to reach an adequate sugar level is usually the most important criterion. There have been many attempts to correlate this ability with climatic indices, e.g. Prescott (1969), Gladstones (1977), Dry and Smart (1980), Jackson and Cherry (1988). In hot regions, the optimal composition for harvest might exist in the crop for only a few days (Coombe 1987) — the increase in sugar and decrease in malate are more rapid than in cool regions. Also, once harvested, the fruit is more subject to oxidation. Therefore, the criteria for variety selection in hot regions may be very different from those in cool regions (see Chapter 6 for further discussion).

Overall, it is the market forces of supply and demand that are most likely to determine variety choice (Dry 1988); it has always been this way in Australia and perhaps always will be. Despite this there is increasing interest in new varieties in the early 2000s, although proponents recognise that it may take generations for new varieties to become widely known and accepted.

10.7 Concluding remarks

Early viticultural pioneers in Australia had little opportunity for site selection as it is now understood. The country was largely unexplored, climatic records were not available, vegetation and soils were unfamiliar, only a limited range of varieties was available and there were no fungicides, pesticides, herbicides, or irrigation. Over the two centuries of European settlement in Australia, all of these factors have changed for the better. Even the pattern of wine consumption has stabilised since the 1960s to a preference for table wines instead of fortified wines. Now the modern site selector has available well-mapped resources of climate, soils and vegetation. Site selection in Australia increasingly has a focus of maximising wine quality, and also minimising climate risks of grapegrowing.

One problem is now emerging which did not exist 200 years ago and that is the prospect of climatic change due to the so-called 'greenhouse effect', caused by an increasing concentration of certain gases (principally carbon dioxide) in the atmosphere (Boag et al. 1988, Schultz 2000). Temperature rises of 1-2°C over the next 50 years are suggested. In addition, in southern Australia, summers may be up to 50% wetter and winters 20% drier. This may mean that present sites selected may, in time, become too warm for the original varieties planted there, and that site selection may be an on-going process with grape production possibly moving south to future cooler regions.

REFERENCES

Aney, W.W. (1974) Oregon climates exhibiting adaptive potential for vinifera Amer. J. Enol. Vitic. **25**, 212-218.

Anon. (1984) Atlas of suitable grape growing locations in the Okanagan and Similkameen Valleys of British Columbia (Agriculture Canada and Assoc. British Columbia Grapegrowers: Kelowna).

Anon. (1987) Mornington Peninsula Regional Report, Aust. NZ Wine Industry J. **1**, 11-23.

Becker, H. (1988) Mapping of soils and climate in the Rheingau. In: Proc. 2nd lnt. Symp. Cool Climate Vitic. Oenol., Auckland NZ 1988. Eds R.E. Smart, R.J. Thornton et al. (NZ Soc. Vitic. Oenol.), pp. 21-22.

Becker, N.J. (1977) Selection of vineyard sites in cool climates. In: Proc. 3rd Aust. Wine Industry Tech. Conf., Albury 1977 (Aust Wine Res. Inst.), pp. 25-30.

Becker, N.J. (1985) Site selection for viticulture in cooler climates using local climatic information. In: Proc. lnt. Symp. Cool Climate Vitic. Oenol., Eugene OR 1984, pp. 20-34.

Belperroud, J. (1859) The vine; with instructions for its cultivation, for a period of six years; the treatment of the soil, and how to make wine from Victorian grapes. Geelong, 1859 (Reprinted by Casuarina Press 1979).

Boag, S., Tassie, L. et al. (1988) The greenhouse effect: implications for the Australian grape and wine industry. Aust. NZ Wine Industry J. **3**, 30-36.

Boehm, E.W. (1970) Vine development and temperature in the Barossa. Experimental Record, South Aust. Dept. Agric. **5**, 16-24.

Busby, J.A. (1825) A treatise on the culture of the vine and the art of making wine. Sydney, 1825. (Reprinted by The David Ell Press, 1979).

Coombe, B.G. (1987) Influence of temperature on composition and quality of grapes. Acta Horticulturae **206**, 23-35.

de Castella, F. (1891) Handbook on Viticulture for Victoria. Melbourne, 1891.

Dry, P.R, (1979) Prediction of disease, pest and frost incidence. In: Vineyard Site Selection. Eds R.E. Smart and P.R. Dry (Roseworthy Agric. College), pp. 123-130.

Dry, P.R. (1984) Recent advances in Australian viticulture. In: Proc. 5th Aust. Wine Industry Tech. Conf., Perth 1983. Eds T.H. Lee and T.C. Somers (Aust Wine Res. Inst.), pp. 9-21.

Dry, P.R (1988) Wanted: one crystal ball. In: Proc. 2nd lnt. Symp. Cool Climate Vitic. Oenol., Auckland NZ 1988. Eds R.E. Smart, R.J. Thornton et al. (NZ Soc. Vitic. Oenol.), p. 59.

Dry, P.R. and Smart, R.E. (1980) The need to rationalise winegrape variety use in Australia. Aust. Grapegrower & Winemaker No. 196, 55-60.

Dry, P.R. and Ewart, AJ.W. (1986) Sites and variety - selection for premium grapes for Australian sparkling wine. Production of sparkling wine by the 'methode champenoise' (Aust. Soc. Vitic. Oenol.: Adelaide), pp. 25-40.

Dry, P.R, and Smart, R.E. (1986) Wind may be limiting grapevine yield. Aust. Grapegrower & Winemaker No. 269, 17.

Dry, P.R, and Smart, R.E. (1988) Vineyard Site Selection. In: Viticulture Vol. I, Edition 1. Eds B.G.Coombe and P.R.Dry (Australian Industrial Publishers: Adelaide), pp. 190-204.

Dry, P.R. and Botting, D.G. (1993) The effect of wind on the performance of Cabernet Franc grapevines. 1. Shoot growth and fruit yield components. Aust. NZ Wine Industry J. **8**, 347-352.

Due, G. (1979) The use of vegetation as a guide to site selection. In: Vineyard Site Selection. Eds R.E. Smart and P.R. Dry (Roseworthy Agric. College) pp. 79-89.

Dundon, C.G., Smart, R.E. et al. (1984) The effect of potassium fertilization on must and wine potassium levels of Shiraz grapevines. Amer. J. Enol. Vitic. **35**, 200-205.

Ewart, A.J.W., Iland, P.C. et al. (1987) The use of shelter in vineyards. Aust. Grapegrower & Winemaker No. 280, 19-22.

Gladstones, J.S. (1965) The climate and soils of south-western Australia in relation to vine growing. J. Aust. Inst. Agric. Sc. **31**, 275-288.

Gladstones, J.S. (1966) Soils and climate of the Margaret River-Busselton area: their suitability for wine grape production. Dept. of Agron., Univ. of WA, mimeo, 11 pp.

Gladstones, J. (1977) Temperature and wine grape quality in European vineyards. In: Proc. 3rd Aust. Wine Industry Tech. Conf., Albury 1977 (Aust Wine Res. Inst.), pp. 7-11.

Gladstones, J.S. (1987) Why Manjimup? In: Winegrapes at Manjimup. Papers from a field day at Manjimup Res. Station, 27 Feb. 1987; WA Dept. Agric.

Hankel, V. and Hall, D. (1979) The eager oenographers. In: The Australian Wine Browser. Ed A. Ousback (The David Ell Press: Sydney), pp. 59-71.

Hamilton, R.P. (1988) Wind effects on grapevines. In: Proc. 2nd lnt. Symp. Cool Climate Vitic. Oenol., Auckland NZ 1988. Eds R.E. Smart, R.J. Thornton et al. (NZ Soc. Vitic. Oenol.), pp. 65-68.

Heinze, R.A. (1977) Regional effects on vine development and composition. In: Proc. 3rd Aust. Wine Industry Tech. Conf., Albury 1977 (Aust Wine Res. Inst.), pp. 18-25.

Helm, K.F. and Cambourne, B. (1987) The Canberra district: a multi-climatic wine region. Aust. Grapegrower & Winemaker No. 280, 109.

Jackson, D.I. and Cherry. N.J. (1988) predictions of a district's grape-ripening capacity using a latitude- temperature index. Amer. J. Enol. Vitic. **39**, 19-28.

Jackson, D.I. and Schuster. D. (1987) The production of grapes and wine in cool climates (Nelson Publishers: Melbourne).

Kelly, A.C. (1861) The Vine in Australia. Melbourne. 1861 (Reprinted by The David Ell Press, 1980.)

Kirk, J.T.O. (1987) Canberra District, Bordeaux and The Upper Rhine Valley: a climatic comparison. Aust. NZ Wine Industry J. **2**, 21-24.

McCandless, L. (1999) New York State: mapping vineyards online and in time. Wines and Vines, July, 58-59.

McLean, G.D., Magarey, P.A. et al. (1984) A climatic evaluation of the question: could grapevine downy mildew develop in Western Australia. In: Proc. 5th Aust. Wine Industry Tech. Conf., Perth 1983. Eds T.H. Lee and T.C. Somers (Aust Wine Res. Inst.), pp. 249-260.

Olmo, H.P. (1956) A Survey of the Grape Industry of Western Australia. Vine Trust Research Trust, Perth.

Pirie, A.J.G. (1978) Comparison of climates of selected Australian, French and Californian wine-producing areas. Aust. Grapegrower & Winemaker No. 172, 74-79.

Prescott, J. (1969) The climatology of the vine (Vitis vinifera) 3. A comparison of France and Australia on the basis of the temperature of the warmest month. Trans. Roy. Soc. South Aust. **93**, 7-16.

Schultz, H. R. (2000) Climate change and viticulture: A European perspective on climatology, carbon dioxide and UV-B effects. Aust. J. Grape and Wine Res. **6**, 2-12.

Smart, R.E. (1977) Climate and grapegrowing in Australia. In: Proc. 3rd Aust. Wine Industry Tech. Conf., Albury 1977 (Aust Wine Res. Inst.), pp. 12-18.

Smart, R.E. and Dry, P.R. (1979) Vineyard Site Selection (Roseworthy Agric. College).

Smart, R.E. (1984) Canopy microclimates and effects on wine quality. In: Proc. 5th Aust. Wine Industry Tech. Conf., Perth 1983. Eds T.H. Lee and T.C. Somers (Aust Wine Res. Inst.), pp. 113-132.

Smart, R.E. (2003) Portuguese homoclimes in Australia. Aust. NZ Wine Industry J. **18** (1), 48-50.

Spurling, M.B. and Jennings, J.P. (1956) Frost: occurrence, prediction, control. J. South Aust. Dept. Agric., August, 18-25, 53-54.

Sutherland, C. (1892) The South Australian Vinegrower's Manual; a practical guide to the art of viticulture in South Australia (Government Printer: Adelaide).

Vielvoye, J. (1988a) Development of a climate and soil atlas for vineyard site selection. In: Proc. 2nd lnt. Symp. Cool Climate Vitic. Oenol., Auckland NZ 1988. Eds R.E. Smart, R.J. Thornton et al. (NZ Soc. Vitic. Oenol.), pp. 9-12.

Vielvoye, J. (1988b) Rapid screening of winegrape cultivars. In: Proc. 2nd lnt. Symp. Cool Climate Vitic. Oenol., Auckland NZ 1988. Eds R.E. Smart, R.J. Thornton et al. (NZ Soc. Vitic. Oenol.), pp. 39-42.

Ward, E. (1862) The vineyards and orchards of South Australia - a descriptive tour of Ebenezer Ward in 1862 (Reprinted by Sullivans Cove 1979).

Ward, E. (1864) The vineyards of Victoria as visited by Ebenezer Ward in 1864 (Reprinted by Sullivans Cove 1980).

Wolf, T.K. and Boyer, J.D. (2001) Site selection and other vine management principles and practices to minimize the threat of cold injury. Proc. Amer. Soc. Enol. Vitic. 50th Annual Meeting, Seattle WA 2000, pp. 49-59.

Wolf, T.K. and Boyer, J.D. (2003) Vineyard site selection. Virginia Cooperative Extension Publication 463-020.

Zakosek, H., Becker, H. et al. (1972-1985) Weinbaustandortkarte Rheingau, 1:5000. Hess Landesamt fur Bodenforschung.

Zakosek, H. Becker, H. et al. (1979) Einfuhrung in die Weinhaustandortkarte Rheingau i. M. 1:5000; Geol. Jb. Hessen, 261-281.

CHAPTER ELEVEN

Grape Berry Development and Winegrape Quality

B.G. COOMBE and P.G. ILAND

INTRODUCTION

Two international symposia have been held dealing with the topic 'Winegrape Quality'. The first was in South Africa in 1977 under the aegis of the International Vine and Wine Office (OIV) and the second in Italy in 1995 sponsored by the International Society for Horticultural Science (Poni et al. 1996). These events attest the wide recognition of the crucial importance of the *prima materia* for the quality of wine. The first symposium was notable in bringing together views from both the Old and the New World in ways that emphasised differences in approach to methods for improving wine quality, but, at the same time, unanimity in the desire for better methods. The symposium proceedings indicate the need for new concepts and better understanding of the interaction

between, on the one hand, the development of the chemical components of grape berries and their balance at harvest and, on the other, the subjective judgement of wine.

This chapter spans the conjunction of viticultural science and oenology. The poor understanding of this zone of knowledge and the newness of relevant research, much of which involving new scientific methods, has necessitated a review-like presentation of the arguments and ideas. It begins with an account of the fundamental determinants of quality potential, namely, the development of the grape berry itself and factors affecting fruit composition. The negative effects of faulty and variable development are discussed. Then follows a review of methods used for assessing winegrape quality potential, with suggestions for research directions that might improve assessments at the winery crusher. Finally a critical assessment is made of vineyard factors that affect grape quality. The related and important research on the effects of region, climate, seasons and vineyard establishment methods on grape and wine quality are considered elsewhere in this textbook.

Definitions

Some of the major components of wine that influence its sensory perception are acids, sugars, phenolics and varietal aroma/flavour compounds. These components originate largely in the berry. The *objective measurement* of the chemical composition of the harvested grapes, and preliminary sensory assessments, influence the winemaker's decisions about the **wine style** and hence the vinification methods that are appropriate. Within any style category, grades of **wine quality** are recognised by *subjective assessment*. For this, the concentrations, balance and interactions of the components in each wine are evaluated sensorily by humans against set criteria.

Throughout this chapter we focus on the understanding of the composition of the grape and of the studies that link grape composition to sensory assessments of resultant wine. Thus winegrape quality, as distinct from wine quality, *represents the **suitability** of a batch of grapes to produce a wine of the highest quality* in a targeted style. The term we have adopted to convey this meaning is **grape quality**.

11.1 Grape berry development

The key determinant of wine quality is the composition of grape berries at the time of harvest. Berry composition at harvest, in turn, depends on how and under what conditions each berry develops. To provide an understanding of the former aspect, this section gives a description of present knowledge about the development of berry structure and of the accumulation of chemical components, beginning with ovaries before and at flowering through to ripeness i.e. best for consumption or a targeted wine style. A recent review by Ollat et al. (2002) covers similar material more extensively, especially metabolic aspects.

The berry sections in **FIGURE 11.1** illustrate the development of grape parts from flowering until maturity. The grape berry has a double-sigmoid growth curve with two growth phases, very different in character (**FIGURE 11.3**). We term the first phase 'berry formation' during which berry structure and tissues are initiated. The second phase embraces 'berry ripening'. Commonly, descriptions of double-sigmoid fruit growth curves use three divisions called stages I, II and III,

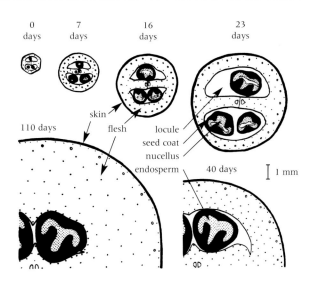

Figure 11.1 Outline transversal sections of berries of Muscat Gordo Blanco from day 0 (ovary at flowering) to day 110 (at ripeness) (from Coombe 1960).

number II being the lag-phase; but the boundary between I and II is often unclear. In fact this division is artificial physiologically—the two stages belong together since the lag-phase is the slowing part of the first sigmoid curve, ending when ripening begins. The lag is brief if the onset of ripening is early, prolonged if it is late.

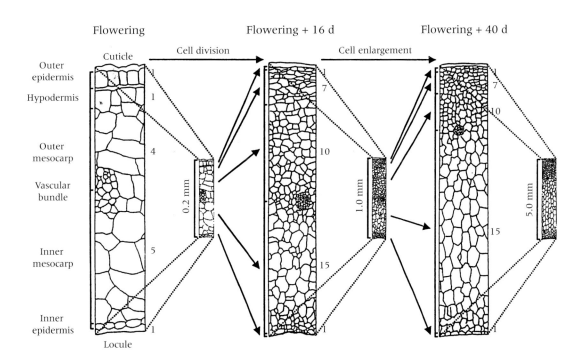

Figure 11.2 Median cross sections of the pericarp (skin and flesh) of Muscat Gordo Blanco berries at flowering and 14 and 40 days later showing changes in cell size and number; the number of cell layers in each of the five tissues is indicated (from data in Considine and Knox, 1979a, 1979b, 1981, and Coombe unpublished; drawing by B.G. Coombe and J.G. Gray).

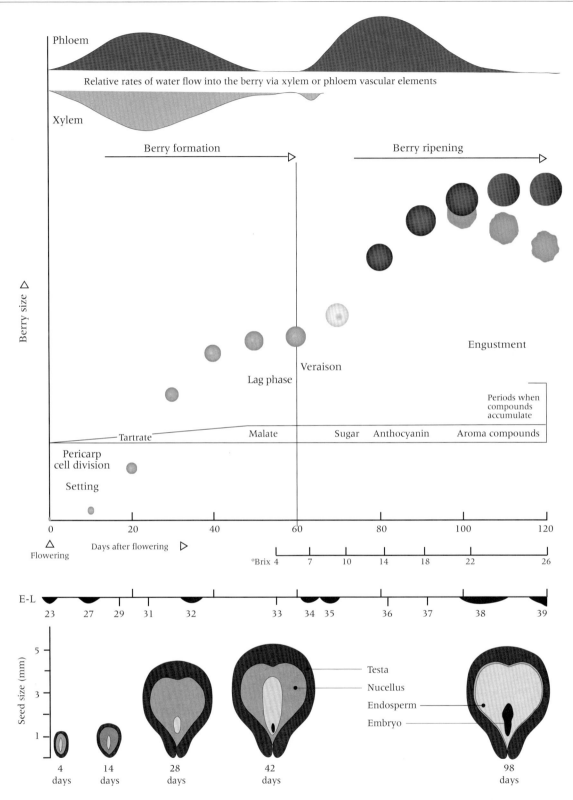

Figure 11.3 Central diagram: Appearance of berries at 10-day intervals revealing the two successive sigmoidal growth curves of a grape berry, designated 'berry formation' and 'berry ripening'. Three generalised x-axes are shown—days after flowering, approximate juice °Brix values during ripening, and developmental growth stages using the modified E-L system. The key growth stages and the approximate timing of the accumulation of major solutes are shown. At top: Sketch indicating present ideas on the relative activity of phloem and xylem transport into the berry. At bottom: Scale drawings of anatomical features in the longitudinal sections of developing grape seeds at days 4, 14, 28, 42 and 98 days after flowering (from data in Coombe and McCarthy 2000, Coombe 2001 and Ebadi et al. 1996b).

11.1.1 First phase – berry formation

The life of a seeded winegrape berry is potentiated at flowering when a sperm cell from a pollen tube fertilises an egg in at least one of its four ovules. Its potential is evidenced when the berry has set i.e. when the ovary persists and grows to become a fruit. The percentage of flowers that set in any one bunch can vary from nil to 95, but in most winegrape varieties the range is from 20 to 50%. Poor setting is a major contributor to low yields of some varieties in some seasons e.g. Chardonnay in cool regions. May (1992) showed that poor set resulted when pollen and ovules developed abnormaly following low temperatures before and during flowering. Nearly all winegrape varieties are seeded and, although four seeds are possible within each berry, usually only one to three develop; some set berries have imperfect seeds and are classified as seedless[1].

The berry's final shape, size and texture is strongly influenced by the number, shape and size of cells in the flesh and skin and their cell wall properties. Size increase of berry flesh is determined initially by cell division in the pericarp. FIGURE 11.2 summarises data showing that pericarp expansion during the first two weeks after flowering is associated with a three-fold increase in radial cell number of the inner and outer mesocarp (forming the flesh) and a seven-fold increase in the hypodermis (forming most of the skin). Expansion of pericarp (i.e. skin plus flesh) in the subsequent four weeks is predominated by cell enlargement in the inner mesocarp, positioning vascular bundles towards the skin. The number and size of pericarp cells have been quantified by analysis of the DNA content of Shiraz berries by Ojeda et al. (1999). This confirmed that cell division in flesh cells is most active during the first 14 days after anthesis, especially during the first week.

Meanwhile, cells are enlarging, there being two main cell enlargement episodes—from one to five weeks after anthesis, then during Stage III (ripening). It has been assumed that berry size is determined by the number of cells in the pericarp since in the smallest berries (parthenocarpic) there is no cell division after flowering and in large-seeded berries there is much. The relative contributions of variations in cell division and cell enlargement to the final size of grape berries under different development circumstances requires more study. For instance Ojeda et al. (2001) have suggested that the reduced berry size following post-anthesis water deficit is due more to inhibited cell wall extensibility than lessened cell division. Further, Colin et al. (2002) observed that the cell walls of 'chick' berries have high amounts of wall-bound diaminopropane; they suggest that the presence of this polyamine may inhibit cell wall

development leading to the small size of these berries.

Seeds complete much of their development during the formation period as can be seen in FIGURES 11.1 and 11.3. The amount of seed development has a profound effect on the development of the fleshy bulk of the berry, an effect probably mediated by hormones, especially gibberellins. The strength of this influence is shown by the relationship found in ripe berries between *total weight of all seed structures (large and small) within each berry and that berry's total fresh weight* (FIGURE 11.16). Even partial seed growth provides some stimulus for the ovary to develop although such berries are small e.g. the chickens of 'hens and chickens' which have incompletely developed, soft seeds (stenospermocarpic). Similarly, hollow seeds with normal, hard seed coats but without endosperm (floaters) contribute to the stimulus.

The relative size and structure of seeds in relation to the whole fruit is shown in cross sections in FIGURE 11.1 and in the longitudinal sections along the bottom of FIGURE 11.3. Seed and flesh development continue in parallel to the end of the formation stage whereupon lengthening of seed stops (their seed coats are now woody) but the growth of flesh resumes. Note that, at this stage, endosperm and embryo are incompletely developed.

11.1.2 Second phase – berry ripening

Origins of the ripening syndrome

Véraison in French means the commencement of berry colour change. In English, the word has become used generically to include all events that together mark the ending of the quiescent lag phase and the onset of the second phase i.e. berry ripening (FIGURE 11.3). Chief among the changes are:

- berry softening,
- sugar increase in the berry,
- malate decrease in the berry (and associated acidity changes),
- accelerated growth of the berry, and
- colour change in the skin   (Coombe 1984)

The above events are listed in the approximate order of their inception, covering about a week. Many others can be included e.g. the change in seed colour from yellow to brown (Ristic 2004) and the temporary swelling of hypodermal cell walls (which may be associated with glycosylation, Considine and Knox 1979b).

Berry softening and berry sugaring appear to be the earliest events and occur together: for the first few weeks of ripening, berry deformability measurements correlate directly with juice °Brix. This has provided a valuable research tool because sequential, non-destructive, daily measurements of the diameter and deformability of single berries *in situ* avoids berry-to-berry variation and reveals the relative progress of softening, juice °Brix and berry growth (Coombe and Phillips 1982, Coombe et al.

---

1. May (2004) has provided an important source of information on grape flowering and setting. The reference is listed at the end of this chapter, but due to the timing of its publication, only a few comments have been included in this text. (See also chapter 7, 7.4.1)

1987). Using this method, it was found that softening and sugaring begin together during a single day while, on average, berry expansion and skin colouring start later. The berries on each bunch do not undergo these changes synchronously; the time between first and last onset was found to be 10 days on one Muscat Gordo bunch and 23 days on another. Also, there was no evidence of patterns of onset due to proximity between berries i.e. each berry remained independent. May (2000) has suggested that differences in the timing of development of berries, set in train before flowering (**FIGURE 11.15**), continue through to veraison, thence to harvest (see 11.2.3).

Berry enlargement (expansion of pericarp cells) begins a few days after the increase in sugar concentration (and osmotic pressure); this might be due to delayed yielding of the confining skin 'jacket' involving plastic extensibility changes in skin cell walls (Matthews et al. 1987). Investigation by Considine (1982) of the histochemistry of the grape berry's dermal system during development led to the conclusion that the cuticle, being less extensible but more elastic than the underlying epi- and hypodermal cell layers, is the agent of the skin's constraining effect.

Another delayed event, apparently coincident with the expansion of flesh cells, is the stretching and breakage of xylem tracheid wall membranes in peripheral bundles at their entry through the brush (Findlay et al. 1987). The effect is that the water flow into the berry via xylem elements becomes impeded and supply is then dependent on phloem transport. This has a profound effect on the berry's physiology in that sugary phloem-sap flow becomes the major source of berry water throughout the rest of berry ripening and other processes are subject to this influence. The interpretation accords with the fact that sugar increments into the berry during ripening are tied with water increments in such a way that, *as berries grow, sugar concentration shows a steady and inexorable rise*. Time curves of °Brix in berries on the same vine, but of different sizes and on early and late bunches, follow similar upward paths after inception (Coombe 1992). Calculations of sap flow rates based on rates of sugar input per berry, and the per cent sucrose estimated to be in such sap, show that the idea is sustainable provided allowance is made for the daily loss of water transpired through the skin of berries (McCarthy and Coombe 1999).

There are a large number of other compositional changes that begin at veraison indicating a profound change in metabolism in these tissues compared with their relatively inactive state during the lag-phase. Such events must have important consequences for ripe berry composition (11.1.4). The search for hormonal changes that might trigger the events has been inconclusive: unlike climacteric fruits, ethylene does not seem to be a candidate in the grape berry, but abscisic acid (ABA) may

be because of its association with senescence events and since its concentration increases as softening begins (Coombe 1992). Changes in the expression of specific genes and synthesis or activation of relevant enzymes will undoubtedly help in the untangling of this phenomenon (Robinson and Davies 2000).

Phloem sap transport into the berry

The mechanism by which sugar is transported long distances from its source (sites of synthesis and storage) into sinks (such as other storage zones or growing points such as fruits or roots) has long been debated. It is widely agreed that translocation involves the flow of a sugary sap through the phloem sieve tubes driven by an axial turgor-pressure gradient. That there is a close association between the movements of both water and sugar is well appreciated because, in many fruits including grapes, water is accumulated along with sugar. This link is evidenced in grape varieties that differ in their timing of veraison and ripeness (Coombe 1960). According to the popular Münch translocation hypothesis the axial turgor-pressure gradient sap flow is generated osmotically because of an elevated sucrose concentration in the source sieve tubes and a depressed one in the sink sieve tubes.

The present discussion invokes a novel alternate mechanism for the sudden acceleration in translocation of phloem sap into grape berries that begins at veraison. The idea arose with the discovery of a functional breakdown in the membranes of flesh cells (Lang and Düring 1991 which paper cites an earlier 1986 reference and was extended in Coombe 1992, Dreier et al. 1998 and Hunter and Ruffner 2001). The plasma membranes previously formed compartmental barriers between symplasm (cytoplasts and vacuoles) and apoplasm (the surrounding wall space). With compartmentation breakdown, molecules are enabled to move from the vacuoles into the apoplast including invertase enzymes which have long been known to occur in the acidic vacuolar sap (Davies and Robinson 1996). Invertase causes rapid hydrolysis of sucrose in the wall solution into glucose and fructose with a resultant doubling of the osmotic activity of sugars. The consequence of both the symplastic leakage and the sucrose hydrolysis is a dramatic lowering of the water potential (much more negative) of the apoplast solution of the berry. Because this apoplast solution also bathes the sieve tubes of the phloem, their turgor pressures also fall thus steepening the source-sink turgor pressure gradient that drives sap phloem. In this way, the rate of translocation flow to the berry increases sharply. The cause of asynchronous ripening development between berries on a bunch appears due to asynchrony in the onset of plasma membrane leakiness. This sequence of events provides a simple mechanistic explanation for the close coupling of the onset of sugaring at veraison and berry softening.

(We acknowledge the help of Dr A. Lang in this description of the leakiness idea).

An additional factor contributing to the forces interacting within the berry is that of the skin tissue in influencing osmotic forces inside the berry and those that bring about unloading of phloem sap into the berry. Recent research suggests that sugar transport into berries can be influenced by factors affecting the rate of evaporation of water from the berries (Chapter 4, section 4.4.5). It is interesting to note that the berry flesh is bounded by dermal cells having distinctive morphology and metabolism and that are particularly rich in phenolics (Considine and Knox 1979b, Moskowitz and Hrazdina 1981). An additional contiguous tissue, also highly phenolic, is the aerenchymatous brush at the 'entrance' to the berry (Nii and Coombe 1983).

The leakiness proposal, if sustained, raises the question —what causes the membranes to become leaky? This, in turn, must permit an explanation of the variability of onset between neighbouring berries on each bunch given that the phloem sap available within each bunchstem is presumably of a common composition. It suggests that the cause is associated with some aspect of the development of each individual berry resulting in asynchronous onset of membrane leakiness.

Whatever the mechanisms, it is clear that the ripening grape berry is a very strong sink for dry matter transported into it from current photosynthesis in green tissues and from reserves in wood (Howell 2001). An illustration of this fact is provided by the results of Conradie in South Africa (Coombe 1989) which indicated that berry dry mass of container-grown vines increased 400% between veraison and harvest while dry mass in the rest of the vine increased by only 5% (all of which was in roots). Another illustration of sink strength is the ability of vines to partially ripen a crop after being stripped of most leaves (Coombe et al. 1987). The total dry matter in grape crops is largely determined by the size of the sinks since, once triggered, sugar transportation continues into the berries together with its solvent, water. Thus, ultimately, *the major representation of grape yield per hectare becomes a function of the total berry water in the crop (which, in essence, is approximated by the number of berries per hectare moderated to an extent by average berry size)*.

Flavour ripening – Engustment

The major weight changes in non-water components of berry flesh during ripening are the increase in hexose sugars and potassium (via phloem sap inflow) and the loss of malate (by berry respiration). Sugar and acid levels are paramount factors of berry ripeness (see discussion in 11.3.4). However, this observation disregards the *raison d'etre* for growing winegrapes, namely, their aroma and flavour[1].

As berries ripen, their composition becomes more complex and their flavour more acceptable and interesting. The entire compositional changes that contribute to the development of attractive berry flavour e.g. sugar/acid balance, aroma volatiles, phenolics, is called **flavour ripening**. The part of this contribution that is detected as aroma in berries when tasted or crushed is called **engustment** (the syllable 'gust' means 'tasting with pleasure' thus acknowledging the crucial contribution made by aroma compounds to berry taste; Coombe and McCarthy 1997). While the term engustment could apply to other parts of flavour ripening it is directed at aroma because of its more precise focus and is arguably one of the most distinctive events of grape berry ripening. In most grape varieties engustment develops mainly during the later phases of ripening and can only be examined by tasting berries, or measuring aroma and related compounds chemically; no visible indicators are manifest.

Growers and winemakers who taste berries as they ripen often remark upon the suddenness of the arrival of aroma and flavour sensations in berries of each vineyard. Quantification of the aroma scores of successive samples of Riesling juice in **FIGURE 11.24** provides an illustration of the phenomenon. A chemical example is given by the curve in **FIGURE 11.19** of non-anthocyanin glucosides (red-free G-G) in ripening Shiraz berries, a measure which should include aroma compounds. In both cases the increase began late during ripening. In another case, terpene levels increased in Muscat Gordo Blanco berries during initial sugaring but continued to higher levels during the second month of ripening (Wilson et al. 1983). In general, the results thus far confirm that sugar and acid levels are, alone, inadequate indicators of flavour ripeness.

An unusual aspect concerning the flow of phloem sap into berries was revealed by the results of McCarthy's irrigation experiment on Shiraz (described in 11.4.3). Berries on these vines showed a systemic shrinkage beginning at about 90 days after flowering when juice was about 20°Brix. The best explanation for these happenings is that phloem tubes had become blocked. Inception of shrinkage coincided with cessation of inflow of solutes and water, whereas the continuation of the normal loss of transpiration water from the berry led to a decline in berry weight. On this interpretation, and given the lack of xylem inflow, it would seem that these berries then continued their engustment and flavour ripening development *with minimal vascular connection to the rest of the vine!* (Coombe and McCarthy 2000). Indeed it is probable that synthesis of aroma compounds may

1. Definitions of aroma and flavour used by the Australia Wine Research Institute. **Aroma:** nasal perception of air-borne volatiles i.e. smell; **Flavour:** the totality of perceptions in the mouth during tasting including the retronasal perception of volatiles (smell) plus sensations perceived on the tongue and other mouth surfaces (such as sweetness, acidity, saltiness, bitterness, astringency, pungency and interactions between them).

continue in berries that have been cut from the plant as occurs in other horticultural crops.

While the Shiraz berry shrinkage phenomenon has raised interesting possibilities, it must be noted that there was evidence from another experiment that solute flow into the berries of Muscat Gordo Blanco continued undiminished to ripe °Brix levels and the berries did not shrink. This means that engustment can proceed under both circumstances i.e. with either full or minimal phloem sap contribution. These results accord with the bunch-grafting experiments of Gholami (1996) which showed that accumulation of flavour compounds was determined by the genotype of the grafted bunches, not by that of the scion tissues.

We suggest that synthesis of aroma and flavour compounds occurs independently of sugar accumulation by processes within the berry itself, much of it towards the later phases of ripening. Metabolism in cells of the skin appears to be crucial (Pirie and Mullins 1977; also note discussion relating to **FIGURE 11.22** in 11.3.4 – anthocyanins).

Rate of ripening

Crops in any particular vineyard ripen at a rate distinctive for that site but varied by cropping level and seasonal conditions. There is a view (commonly expressed on wine labels) that best quality years are those with weather that leads to long, slow ripening (colloquially called 'hang-time') during which deficiencies in flavour are thought to be remedied. There are no research results to support this view; in fact, the reverse is the case. One such was alluded to by Coombe and Iland (1987, legend to Figure 2 of that paper) where it was pointed out that a premier wine quality year was associated with grapes that ripened early and rapidly. In a discussion of the benefits of equable temperatures during ripening, Gladstones (1992) expressed similar sentiments "... rapid and complete ripening favours the best compositional balance with desirable flavour characteristics of full ripeness and least loss of volatiles. Also it reduces the time available for loss of quality due to environmental insults...".

Research comparing ripening rates and harvest quality support the concept. The survey data from hot irrigated vineyards in the Riverland of South Australia by Botting et al. (1996) showed a significant inverse correlation between G-G concentration and 'days to reach 23°Brix'. For instance, of the vineyards with grapes at the highest level of G-G (>2.8), 90% belonged to the fastest ripening group while those that took two to four weeks longer to ripen had lower concentrations of G-G and anthocyanins (Dry et al. 1999). Additional experimental support is provided by the irrigation/thinning experiment on Riesling shown in **FIGURE 11.24** (McCarthy 1986)—the faster the ripening, the higher the PVT concentration and aroma score. Note that in the above examples the effects were tied to fastest ripening (the interval from

veraison until ripeness), not necessarily to earliest ripening.

The suggestion that faster ripening (sugaring) favours higher grape quality needs further investigation but, if it is supported, what might be an explanation? Such must await the outcome of research on the mechanisms of accumulation of flavour and phenolic compounds in grape berries. But a different possibility is provided in the discussion of section 11.2.1 'Variability between berries' which demonstrates that the rate of ripening of a grape crop can be strongly influenced by the degree of asynchrony in the rate of development of the individual berries in the crop. This is illustrated theoretically in **FIGURE 11.7** where it is suggested that the greater the variation between berries in their rate of ripening the slower will be the rate of ripening of the mix and the lower will be the maximum potential grape quality. Other sources of variation, e.g. seed number, berry mass, skin colour, etc., would exacerbate slowness of ripening and debilitation of quality.

11.1.3 STRUCTURE OF THE RIPE BERRY

Grape berries are borne on a bunch framework (peduncle) via the berry stem (pedicel) which together make up the bunchstem tissues (incorrectly called 'rachis' which strictly is the central axis of a panicle; also incorrectly called 'stalks'). These stem tissues contain vascular bundles that provide a connection from the vine into each berry. The internal structure of the ripe berry is illustrated in **FIGURE 11.4** which provides a different perspective to the cross-section images of berry development in **FIGURE 11.1**. All of the non-seed parts of the ripe berry are fleshy and sugary, nourished by the phloem sap from the bundles penetrating up the centre and around the periphery in a chickenwire-like network joined at the top and bottom of the central bundle. The seeds are also connected to the vascular system by branches from the base of the central bundle. The seed bundle does not connect with the internal seed parts (nucellus, endosperm and embryo) which are therefore placental.

Berry skin has three layers: the outer cuticle, the outer epidermal layer, and then the hypodermal layers which are about six cells deep. Hypodermal cells are paving-stone shaped with thick walls and well-developed cytoplasmic organelles. The outer hypodermal layers have cells especially rich in tannins and are called 'tannin cells' by Riberau-Gayon et al. (2000). The enveloping cuticle is tough and has low water permeability, all water movement being through cutin and wax platelets, not through stomates or lenticels which become plugged. Transpiration proceeds at slow rates, governed by skin permeability and water potential differences between inside and out.

The flesh cells in the non-skin parts of the pericarp vary in size, shape and texture according to variety and growing conditions. Their size characteristics vary

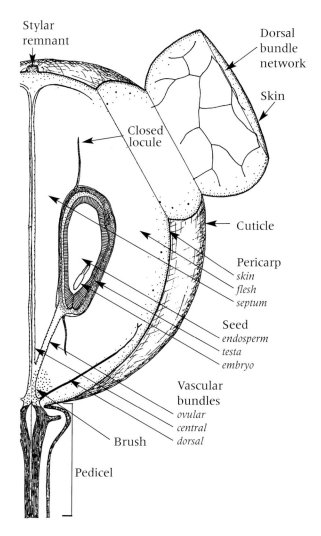

Stylar
remnant

Dorsal
bundle
network

Skin

Closed
locule

Cuticle

Pericarp
skin
flesh
septum

Seed
endosperm
testa
embryo

Vascular
bundles
ovular
central
dorsal

Brush

Pedicel

Figure 11.4 Diagram of a longitudinal section of one side of a grape berry showing its constituent tissues (modified from Coombe 1987).

to decline (due to some water loss). During the last few weeks of ripening, the chalaza develops its sculpted appearance. The internal changes in the seed during berry ripening are shown in **FIGURES 11.1** and **11.3**: the endosperm fills the space inside the testas and consumes the nucellus tissue as it develops; also the embryo develops to its full, though small, size.

11.1.4 CHEMICAL COMPOSITION OF THE DEVELOPING BERRY

Most of the chemicals in grapes that contribute to wine are in water solution, and water is the berry's principle compound. Of the non-water components the largest proportion is made up of the solutes glucose and fructose (**FIGURES 11.5 A** and **B**). It is the small proportion of non-sugar solutes, consisting of hundreds of other compounds, that make the grape distinctive and fascinating. The concentrations of some of the principle solutes found in free-run juice at harvest are listed in **TABLE 11.1**, but be aware that the concentrations that

Table 11.1 Concentration (g/L and mM) of some components of free-run juice from grapes at a later stage of ripeness.

Component	Range of g per L			mM
	Low	Mid	High	Mid
Water	700	750	800	–
Carbohydrates				
Glucose	80	105	130	580
Fructose	70	95	120	530
Sucrose	trace	1	5	3
Pectin	0.1	0.5	1	–
Inositol	0.2	0.5	0.8	3
Acids				
TA as tartaric	3	7	12	–
Tartrate	2	6	10	40
Malate	1	5	9	40
Citrate	trace	0.3	0.5	2
Nitrogen (N)				
Total–N	0.2	0.8	2	–
Amino acid–N	0.1	0.4	1	3
Ammonia–N	0.01	0.06	0.12	3.3
Phenolics total	0.1	0.5	1	–
Lipids	–	0.5	–	–
Minerals–Ash	2.5	3	6	–
Potassium	1	2	3	50
Phosphate	0.2	0.35	0.5	4
Sulfate	0.03	0.2	0.35	2
Magnesium	0.1	0.2	0.25	8
Calcium	0.04	0.14	0.25	4
Boron	trace	0.03	0.07	3
Manganese	trace	0.03	0.05	0.5
Iron	trace	0.02	0.03	0.4
Copper	trace	0.002	0.003	0.03
Zinc	trace	0.002	0.005	0.03
Terpenoids	0.05	0.2	0.5	–

according to position in the berry—bigger towards the centre with long axes positioned radially, grading to those at the outside which lie tangentially (**FIGURE 11.2**). The sugary flesh cells pack inside the enveloping skin filling the whole space. A study of the composition of flesh cell walls of ripe berries of Muscat Gordo versus that of the table grape Ohanez indicated that the firm texture of the latter is associated with their greater percentage of cellulose and xyloglucans in cell walls and a higher content of hydroxyproline in their cell-wall proteins (Nunan et al. 1997).

The seeds maintain the same general proportions to the whole berry throughout berry formation and are full-sized by the end of the lag phase, their colour changing from greenish then to yellow at the end of the lag-phase (Ristic 2004). At veraison, seed lengthening stops, the testas develop a brownish colour (due to oxidation of procyanidins) and seed fresh weight starts

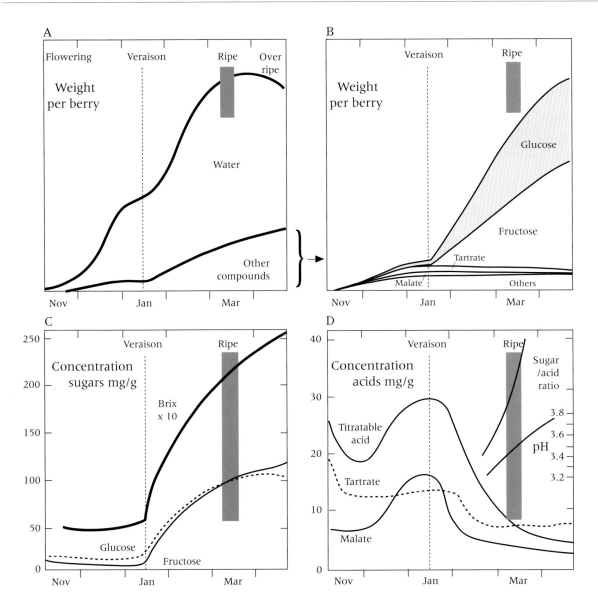

Figure 11.5 Generalised graphs of the development of chemical components of grape berries from flowering to the over-ripe stage. A. Changes in berry weight apportioned to water and the total of other compounds. B. Changes in the weight per berry of sugars (glucose and fructose), acids (tartrate and malate) and other compounds. C. Concentrations of glucose and fructose, and changes in °Brix of the juice. D. Concentrations of tartrate and malate, titratable acidity and pH, and changes in the sugar/acid ratio of the juice.

are measured in macerated whole berries, or in must after crushing of whole bunches, will vary from this list because of differences in concentrations between flesh and skin (**FIGURE 11.6**), and also seeds and stems. Variation in the accumulation of water into the berry (indicated by berry size) contributes a further variation to concentration when compared with changes in amount per berry, i.e. content versus concentration.

There are significant *differences between skin and flesh* in the concentrations of different solutes during ripening. **FIGURE 11.6** shows that levels in the flesh exceed those in the skin of solutes that accumulate

massively—malate before veraison and the hexoses after. With other solutes, concentrations are higher in the skin, e.g. potassium, inorganic anions, phenolics, tartrate, abscisate, lipids. These differences, and the microscopic structure of the tissue cells, suggest that flesh and skin have distinct functions—those of the flesh indicate a storage role while the structure of the dermal cells of skin suggest both a protective and an active metabolic role. In *vinifera* grapes, the skin is the site of pigment changes that begin during veraison; pigment concentrations have attracted considerable attention because of their possible connection with wine quality

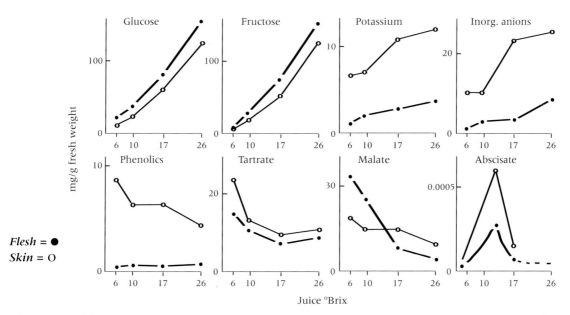

Figure 11.6 Differences between skin and flesh in the development of concentrations (mg/g fr wt.) of eight components in flesh (●) and skin (O) of the white grape Muscat Gordo Blanco berries at four ripeness stages – from veraison to over-ripe as indicated by the °Brix x-axis. Note the different y-axis scales (Coombe 1992).

(see 11.3.4). Of other compounds, the differences between concentrations in the skin versus the flesh are especially evident with potassium which accumulates strongly in skin tissue throughout ripening: at ripeness, a half of each berry's potassium may be in skin tissues which only constitute about one tenth of the whole berry weight. Inorganic anions (including sulfate, chloride and phosphate) also accumulate in skin. Phenolics are another group that are at high levels in skin but their deposition occurs before veraison: during ripening, their levels decline while that of the anthocyanin sub-group increase in black berries. There are also high concentrations of phenolics in the brush.

Sugar accumulation. The dramatic solute accumulatory process begins with that of the two hexoses, glucose and fructose. It starts at veraison, glucose concentration at that stage being several times greater than that of fructose; the levels soon equalise and continue together to ripeness, but, in over-ripe grapes, fructose (which is sweeter) often exceeds glucose (**FIGURE 11.5 B** and **C**). Of other saccharides, small amounts of sucrose are found in berry skin and the central bundles, and also in the pedicel of over-ripe berries (Coombe 1987). For further information on sugar accumulation see section 11.1.2.

Acidity in grapes is determined largely by the amounts of tartaric and malic acids and the proportion of the salt forms of tartrate (Iland and Coombe 1988). These acids have quite different properties and developmental patterns. Both acids are important for wine making; tartaric as the stronger and more stable acid while malic acid plays a significant role in the malolactic

fermentation. As shown in **FIGURE 11.5 D**, tartrate concentrations begin increasing during the first few weeks of berry growth. During the middle of the formation phase the berry accumulates little other than water and at this stage the per cent dry weight declines to its lowest level. Thereafter, throughout the latter half of berry formation, including the lag-phase, accumulation of the two acids accelerates, especially that of malate. Significant levels of juice acidity are attained reaching its highest point by veraison—about 3% w/v (half that of lemon juice). After veraison, the amounts of tartrate per berry remain relatively constant from then until harvest so that the main cause of decline in concentration is dilution by 'growth' water. On the other hand malate concentration declines throughout the ripening phase. Malate is an energy-rich compound and its high rate of loss parallels respiration rate, being faster at higher temperature (and, perhaps, in berries that accumulate sugar rapidly). There are indications that malate loss is most rapid near to vascular tissue when sugars are accumulating (Coombe 1987)—is there a causal connection?

Nitrogenous compounds occur in the reduced state and figure in the metabolism of many classes of compounds, some yielding forms that have sensory significance. In free-run juice, total N ranges from 0.2 to 2 mg/L (higher in whole berries). Amino acids make up more than half of total N and are important for yeast growth during fermentation except for proline which is not assimilated by yeast. Proline and arginine are the most abundant (each about 1 mg/g); arginine increases from before veraison and throughout ripening, but proline increase occurs late in ripening. Of the other 19 amino acids, eight are next in abundance with an average concentration of about 0.1 mg/g, namely, glutamine, gamma-aminobutyric acid, alanine, threonine, lysine, glutamate, serine and histidine (Stines et al. 2000). Polyamines are another class in this group which are emerging as physiologically important because of their growth regulating and toxicity properties. *Vitamin levels* do not influence grape harvest decisions but nevertheless affect yeast metabolism during fermentation. The concentrations of most vitamins increase with ripening. Their amounts in grapes are not large—about 1 ppm or more for vitamin A, niacin, pyridoxine and pantothenic acid, 0.1 ppm for vitamin C, thiamine and riboflavin, and 0.001–0.01 ppm for biotin and folate. Alleged vitamin P, a flavone form, is abundant in grape juice but its credentials as a vitamin are contentious; nevertheless grape phenolics, especially flavonols and flavanols, are significant health-promoting compounds because of their evident cardioprotective properties.

Aroma and flavour compounds are detailed in section 11.3.4 of this chapter because of their obvious importance in grape composition at harvest and in the assessment of grape berry quality. The remarks here are general. The compounds include many types of secondary metabolites including monoterpenoids, C13-norisoprenoids and methoxypyrazines. They occur in the berry in minute amounts as free compounds, many of which are categorised as volatiles hence it is not surprising that (with the exception of methoxypyrazine) synthesis is accompanied by the formation of conjugated forms. Maybe this conversion contributes to their accumulation? Chief among the binding agents is ß-D-glucose. Glucosylation transforms the aglycones to a non-volatile, water-soluble form suited for storage and available for later reversion to the parent aglycone. Conjugated forms usually predominate and are termed 'flavour-precursors' because their subsequent breakdown in wine leads to an increase in flavour concentration.

The glycosyl-glucose assay. Extraction of glycosides from the grape berry and then release and measurement of glucose gives a convenient method of quantifying the glycoside levels—the glycosyl-glucose assay (G-G, Williams et al. 1995) and the non-anthocyanin (red-free) G-G assay (Iland et al. 1996). These collective measures should be more likely to have general applicability as a flavour index than measurement of single compounds. Further fractionations of a glycoside extract and a method for measuring phenol-free G-G (PFGG) have been developed by Zoecklein et al. (2000) and Whiton and Zoecklein (2002) which together provide a more focused estimate of the pool of flavour and aroma precursors. The general approach looks promising (for more details see 11.3.4 and various test results through 11.4).

Tannins are large, complex polymers of procyanidins that form stable combinations with proteins and polysaccharides (Riberau-Gayon et al. 2000). These molecules confer important sensory qualities of astringency and bitterness in wine ranging from positive to negative depending on their content and composition. They derive from skins, seeds and bunchstem tissues but in different types and amounts varying with berry ripeness. The skins of immature grapes have simple tannins of high reactivity (and hence high astringency); as the berry ripens the skin tannins increase in complexity and become desirably 'softer'. The tannins of seeds and stems, which react strongly with proteins, confer high tannic astringency. Examination of Shiraz wines showed that a better quality wine had higher concentrations of skin anthocyanins and phenolics and lower concentrations of seed flavan-3-ols and proanthocyanidins (tannins) (Ristic et al. 2002).

Skins, seeds and stems undoubtedly contribute many other chemical compounds to grape must. Skins contain the all-important pigments—red anthocyanins and yellow flavonoids—in addition to the array mentioned above. Seeds contain, in addition to tannins, starch and oils. The composition of the tissues of the pedicels and bunchstems must have an effect on wine but understanding is meagre. The published composition of bunchstems shows resemblance to shoot stem tissues but perhaps with more sugars and acids. Another aspect that deserves exploration is the finding that water washings of the surface of bunchstems contained significant levels of glycosides which included, in their aglycone form, many flavour compounds (Gholami 1996).

Conclusions about composition

Concentration of any solute in a tissue at one time and place is influenced by any of six different events (i.e. three pairs): (a) its synthesis or alteration, (b) movement of the solute to or away, and (c) movement of the solvent water to or away from that place. The variations that may occur in the composition of grapes, and hence of wine, are readily apparent when one considers the variety of constituent tissues and the multitude of solutes, each following individual concentration fluxes during ripening, (see **FIGURE 11.6**). Research has provided some understanding of parts of this complex but much remains unexplained. Better understanding of the factors affecting concentration fluxes is needed to help unravel the mysteries of winegrape quality.

11.2 Variability; effects on berry composition

The berries in every grape crop are variable. Rarely is such variability measured or recorded and the fact of its existence has generally not been regarded with concern. We aim to show that high variability between berries in their development can be a serious negative factor for grape quality.

The potential of the quality of a harvested batch of grapes will be an average of all berries contributing to that batch. It is obvious that berries do not develop synchronously or homogeneously and that variation is the norm. As more attain peak quality synchronously and homogeneously, the better will be the quality potential of the harvest. Conversely, the larger the proportion that are under-ripe, over-ripe or defective, the lower will be the quality potential of the batch. Some winemakers hold that uneven maturity benefits wine quality. This relies upon chance. We suggest a better tactic is to grow a winegrape crop in which the composition of berries is as uniform as possible, to harvest that crop when the majority of berries are at a designated composition, then, after wine is made, use blending to achieve the quality mix that is sought.

The quality potential of each berry, as it develops, can be considered to follow a bell-shaped quality/time course of the general form shown in **FIGURE 11.17**, that is, a rise to a maximum, then a fall. If all berries have synchronous and uniform development, the curve for one is the same as for all and the collective peak is higher. In the illustration of this concept in **FIGURE 11.7**, in which the only measured variation is due to timing of development, the quality of the mix develops more slowly and reaches only 60% of full potential. This idea was mentioned in 11.1.2 (Rate of ripening). A graph showing the effects of mixing berries of diverse types of development, additional to asynchrony, would show additional negative effects.

Singleton et al. (1966) raised this problem when commenting upon unexplained quality differences between varietal wines prepared from musts having the same °Brix levels. They suggested different degrees of variation among berries as a cause; from a sequence of samples taken during ripening, berries were separated into °Brix groups (using flotation on graded sucrose solutions) and a two-fold range in °Brix levels of berries was found. In a later study (Long 1987), 400-berry samples were taken from two Cabernet Sauvignon vineyards in California with equal average °Brix but which differed in evenness of berry ripening. The spread of TSS concentration in individual berries at harvest was large in both samples but more so in that reputed to have greater unevenness. The wines made in the subsequent vintage confirmed the poorer quality from the vineyard with more uneven ripening.

11.2.1 RESEARCH TACTICS

Assessment of variation involves statistical calculations of variance e.g. standard deviation (SD), or coefficient of variation (CV) which is SD as a percentage of the mean; the lower the CV, the more uniform is the population. The populations from which the means derive have to relate to the question being asked. To compare populations it is necessary to measure all individuals; for

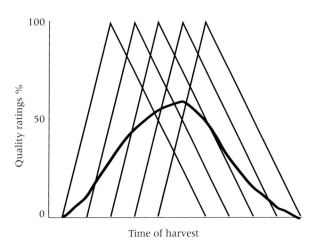

Figure 11.7 Theoretical illustration of the negative effect on wine quality potential of asynchronous berry development within a grape crop. The crop shown contains five types of berries each with the same rise and fall in quality potential (from nil to 100% maximum, then back to nil) but with a succession of timing of development. The thick line, which is the average of the ratings at each vertical group, shows how the average quality potential of the crop would vary according to harvest date.

instance, to measure berry variation within a bunch entails measuring selected parameters on every berry on that bunch. This is rarely done; instead a proportion is chosen with the hope that the sample represents the whole. But, if the sample is not representative, information is lost about an important component of the determination of grape quality.

The problem is compounded by the choices of measurement to be made, for example, berry dimensions, juice °Brix (TSS), pH and acidity, berry deformability and skin colour. Some of these can be measured on attached berries permitting a succession of data on the same fruit during early ripening development. This has been done for dimensions and deformability (from which °Brix can be estimated once correlations have been established). If this tactic could be adopted for the important quality indicators of berry colour and flavour, research in this area would be greatly advanced. The use of Near-Infra-Red spectroscopy offers promise as a possibility for this purpose. Removal of berries (i.e. sampling) ends the record of development of that fruit and thereby necessitates substitution and replication of berries and bunches and hence a different statistical approach.

The subject is sparsely researched because of its difficulty. To help appreciate the problem, consider the variation between berries of a 20 tonne load of grapes. Before crushing there might be, say, 20 million individual berries although, after crushing, this becomes one aqueous mixture. Understanding of the

CV of any parameter in the berries of this formidable berry number is helped by the fact that, before harvest, the berries can be considered at three distinct levels:

(a) *between vines* within the vineyard.

(b) *between bunches* within the vine and

(c) *between berries* within the bunch.

[The text in 11.2.2 to 11.2.4 is arranged in this order]. We have emphasised results where statistical analysis is reported, but in one study of variation between berries we propose the use of subjective judgment of distribution patterns.

Variation between years in performance of a vineyard is not part of this chapter but is important to vineyard profitability; useful aspects are considered by Dunn et al. 2002 (see also 11.4.2).

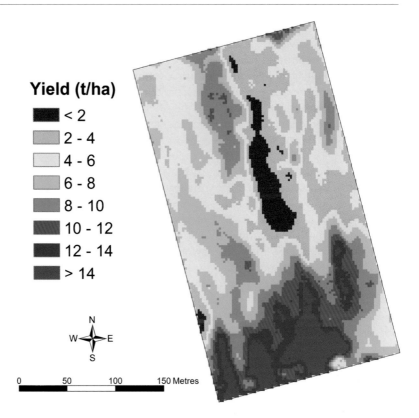

Yield (t/ha)

■ < 2
▨ 2 - 4
□ 4 - 6
▨ 6 - 8
▨ 8 - 10
▨ 10 - 12
■ 12 - 14
▨ > 14

N
W — E
S

0   50   100   150 Metres

Figure 11.8 Yield variation over a 5.4 ha Clare Valley vineyard obtained by a GPS-equipped yield monitor fitted to a mechanical harvester (R.G.V. Bramley, CSIRO Land and Water, Adelaide - pers. comm.).

11.2.2 QUANTIFICATION OF VARIATION

Variation between vines within a vineyard

Examining the question of variability between vines involves consideration of the functioning of each vine as a whole—roots, wood, canopy, and their interactions with fruit. In particular, it introduces the over-arching effect of soil. Study of the effects of soil on a deep-rooted, perennial, woody plant like the grapevine is complicated. Recording the degree of variation in vine-by-vine fruiting levels by hand is a useful beginning but even this is not simple and such studies are not widely reported.

The whole approach is moving in an encouraging direction due to the use of a suite of tools and termed 'Precision Viticulture' (Lamb and Bramley 2002). Remote sensing of vine canopy size and condition, coupled with the use of Global Positioning Systems (GPS) and other sensing technologies, followed by analysis using Global Information Systems (GIS), has provided a basis for understanding vineyard variability. Grape yield monitors and GPS-fitted mechanical harvesters have enabled within-vineyard and variation to be mapped; **FIGURE 11:8** is an example. This vineyards average yield was 7 t/ha but actual yield within it ranged from less than 1 t/ha to more than 19 t/ha. Such studies have shown that large yield variation between vines and across blocks is common—8 to 10-fold ranges being typical. Such variations would be expected to lower average grape

quality (unless harvesting was targeted, Bramley and Hamilton 2004). An extension of these approaches has permitted the prediction of berry colour of Cabernet Sauvignon grapes at harvest (Lamb et al. 2004).

Variation between bunches within a vine

A unique set of comparisons of the relative proportion of total variance that is attributable to each of four groups of data has been documented by Nayler (2001) in New Zealand using the variety Sauvignon Blanc (see data in columns of **TABLE 11.2**). In all sets, which deal with flowering, veraison and fruit composition, variance between bunches was high, especially with °Brix at harvest. He found that a major contribution to the variation between bunches was the difference caused by position on the shoot: proximal (basal) bunches flowered earlier and this difference in development persisted through all stages to harvest. Similar differences were attributable to shoot position. All of these differences contributed to overall variability between bunches.

From the same experiment, Nayler calculated mean and variance of the °Brix of contributing populations on three occasions during ripening (**FIGURE 11.9**). The average °Brix at each of the three stages was 12, 18 and 21.6 with ranges of 22°Brix for the first two but

Table 11.2 Proportion of total variance, obtained in one season from a factorial experiment on Sauvignon Blanc vines, attributable to each of four groups of data. Compiled from data in Nayler (2001).

Data Group	Proportion of total variance				
	Vineyard blocks	Trellis types	Shoots	Bunches	Total
Flowering scores					
5/12/98	34	7	32	27	100
9/12/98	5	10	53	32	100
16/12/98	0	4	28	68	100
Veraison scores					
7/2/99	20	31	19	30	100
13/2/99	12	25	26	37	100
Composition at harvest					
°Brix	14	28	11	47	100
T.A.	28	23	17	37	100
pH	1	40	26	33	100

only 13° for the last (near harvest); respective CVs were found to be 26, 17 and 10%. This lessening of the °Brix variance as fruit ripens (resynchronisation) results from a greater percentage of berries attaining the ripeness plateau. Variation in °Brix between berries has serious implications for those factors in ripening that change rapidly e.g. flavour and aroma; (these may not resynchronise in the same way e.g. FIGURE 11.14). Note that the three companion graphs of TSS-content per berry (obtained from the same data by multiplying °Brix by berry weight) show a range that increased as berries ripened. This increase reveals the additive effect of combining two variables, °Brix and berry weight, each with high variability between berries.

Variation between berries within a bunch

(Not all of the following deals strictly with variation within single bunches as some relate to localised populations of berries). Differences in the degree of fruit set affects the within-bunch variation in many ways e.g. berry size, rate of ripening, colour and composition as is indicated by FIGURE 11.10; these are additional to the effects on number of berries per bunch which can result in fluctuating yield levels.

An illustration of the variation of both berry weight and °Brix in one population of berries is shown in FIGURE 11.11 being measurements of 930 Chardonnay berries collected on one day in the middle of berry ripening (when variation is large). Despite the huge scatter, there is evidence of two groupings: the large group occupying the middle of the figure undoubtedly represents seeded berries with weights from 0.6 to 1.6 g, and °Brix from 7 to 14; the second group in the top left corner of this graph with weights

from 0.07 to 0.6 g would be the 'chickens' part of the 'hen-and-chickens' phenomenon ('millerandage'); these showed higher TSS values (8-18°Brix).

Small berries, compared with large, have a greater skin/flesh ratio which is often said to benefit wine quality, especially red wine, although their smaller size reduces their contribution to must components (May 2004). The evidence for this is largely circumstantial but has been strengthened by the results shown in FIGURE 11.22 in which berries of two black varieties were divided into skins and juice and measurements made of the concentrations of red-free G-G. From each of these samples, a glycoside precursor fraction was isolated and the glycosides were hydrolysed to release volatile compounds. Their aroma was assessed by a sensory panel and was found to correlate with red-free G-G. The juices were relatively low in both red-free G-G values and aroma scores, while for the skin extracts the values ranged from low to high and were correlated with each other (see also 11.3.4). The results suggest that skin contains compounds that contribute desirable aroma volatiles and therefore, other things being equal, that musts would benefit by having higher proportions of skins.

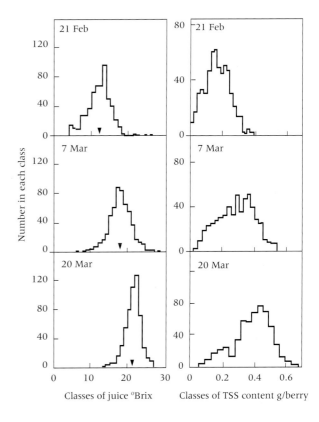

Figure 11.9 Frequency distributions of TSS readings of 900 individual berries of Sauvignon Blanc at three ripening stages. Histograms at left are of juice TSS concentration (°Brix); those at right are TSS content (g per berry). Arrows indicate °Brix means. Redrawn from data in Nayler (2001).

Figure 11.10 A poorly set grape bunch with few developed berries and some 'chicken' and 'shot' berries.

Variations in berry size and TSS shown above pose questions about the consequences for other parameters associated with grape quality. The evidence is meagre because such measurements at a per berry level are difficult. Clearly, a mix of ripening stages should cause a dilution and lowering of the levels of flavour and aroma compounds if these characteristics rise and fall as suggested in **FIGURE 11.17**. The picture presented by the array of skin colours in bunches of black varieties at the beginning of colouring (of which **FIGURE 11.12a** is an extreme example) lends credence to this overall story on flavour and aroma.

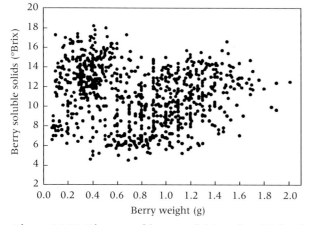

Figure 11.11 Diagram of berry weight against °Brix of 930 individual Chardonnay berries taken from two bunches from each of 15 shoots six weeks before harvest when fruit averaged about 11°Brix and berry weight averaged 0.8 g (Trought 1996).

The occurrence of 'chickens' is a feature of some varieties growing in cool regions, e.g. Pinot Noir and Chardonnay in Burgundy where the boost to sugar levels has been associated with better grape quality at harvest (Bessis et al. 2000). However, for quality in red wine, uniformly small size of berries-with-seeds compared with 'chickens' might be better because 'chickens' lack the seed influence on berry composition. The aspect of the contribution to quality of tannin extraction of polyphenols from seed coats raises the question of the effect of varying proportions of seeds in the crush; excessive extraction of phenolic compounds from seeds may lead to overly tannic wines. Another question is whether an empty seed (floater) contributes the same amount and type of phenolics as a full seed (sinker). Uniformity in seed number per berry seems desirable.

A ripening disorder, 'sweet and sour', that led to extreme variation in berry sugar levels is illustrated in **FIGURE 11.12a**. In the vineyard under study, seed and berry development proceeded normally up to the stage when veraison had just started under max./min. temperatures averaging 24/13°C. Then followed an 8-day spell of hot days and nights with max./min. temps averaging 37/25°C. It became apparent afterwards that only the early berries (7%) were expanding and colouring normally, unaffected by the heat; the rest remained green. During the ensuing week or two when temperatures reverted to 24/13°C, the green berries commenced ripening, but asynchronously as is illustrated by measurements made when the 7% of unaffected berries were becoming ripe (21 to 25°Brix)— the measures showed that 60% of berries had °Brix levels of 13° to 20° and were coloured purple, 18% were 9° to 13° and coloured pink, and 15% were 4° to 9° and still green. Nearly all berries were seeded and hence this disorder differs from 'hen and chickens' (Coombe 2000). Note the contrast between the bunch in **FIGURE 11.12a** and the 'ideal bunch' in **FIGURE 11.12b**.

Other disorders of berries such as sunburn and bunchstem necrosis (early and late forms) will affect quality if the berries on the affected portions have not raisined and contribute juice to the harvested crop. Shrinkage of Shiraz berries at about 20°Brix (see engustment section of 11.1.2 and RDI section of 11.4.3) appears to decrease berry variation because of its systemic nature (**FIGURE 11.13**). But variable levels of skin cracking after rain would be likely to reduce quality potential.

In summary, natural variation in berry size, rate of ripening and various non-parasitic disorders affecting between–berry development are likely detriments to grape quality but there is little data available other than °Brix and berry size to test the degree of their effects. The absence of measures of variation in flavour compounds is a serious omission, although the measurements of terpenoids in successive samples during development of

Figure 11.12a Cabernet Franc bunch with an extreme range of TSS levels in its berries which are not 'hen and chickens'. The phenomenon is thought to be the consequence of an 8–day spell of hot days and nights during veraison (see text).

Figure 11.12b An ideal bunch? The bunch is small, and has a well-ventilated and loose form, reasonably uniform berry size and development, and is moderately exposed to sunlight. Perhaps berries should be smaller although this depends on each variety's optimum berry size for the intended wine styles.

Muscat Gordo Blanco berries suggest that the variation was puzzlingly high (Wilson et al.1983). The problem of variability in fruit composition looms large in fruit sampling for prediction of harvest date and choice of methods that match measurements made from fruit delivered to the winery. This is considered by Krstic et al. (2002) and in Volume II, Chapter 13.

11.2.3 CAUSES OF VARIATION

Between vines

Much of the variations between vines in a vineyard are traceable to errors in factors associated with selection of the land for planting and layout of the planting (especially the allocation of uniform soil patches for harvesting units). Equally important is the use of good, virus-free planting material (see Volume II, Ch.1). In fact, many modern methods of vineyard establishment (see Volume II, Ch.2) encourage uniform budburst and subsequent shoot development thus minimising variation within and between vines. It is appropriate in this context to read the Section headings and Conclusions of Volume II, Chapter 2 'Vineyard Establishment' and to scan the text. A well organised and managed vineyard is readily recognisable and the harvested fruit shows the rewards.

Between bunches

Many studies have shown treatments that affect bunches and lead to effects on grape quality. These are considered in section 11.4 and are reviewed by Jackson and Lombard (1993), Reynolds and Wardle (1997) and many others. They deal with treatments such as shoot and bunch thinning, exposure or shading of bunches, bunch placement, leaf removal near bunches, etc. But the results are usually presented as means of treatments accompanied by the variance of the treatment means, rarely with the variance within the whole of each population which, as has been shown, can further influence the differences. Nevertheless they give leads for research on between–bunch variation.

The development of a bunch, being a grouping of berries, has been shown to be influenced by many factors transcending those that influence its units, i.e. berries. The fact of each bunch being organised morphologically on a bunchstem is a distinctive feature evident when stem disorders, diseases, pests and the like affect the development and functioning of the bunch as a whole. Another feature is that bunches are appendages on shoots which constrains their positioning in space and ties the growth rates of their bunches, tendrils and leaves closely to the vigour of the shoots. Vigorous shoots can bring crowded and shady conditions with negative consequences for berry development.

Yet another anatomical feature of grape shoots is the number of bunches per shoot. The results of Nayler in **TABLE 11.2** emphasise the large contribution to variability caused by differences between basal bunches and those above; this reveals an undesirable source of variability if shoots have two or more bunches. Initiation of anlagen in the previous spring, and their transformation into inflorescences, involves a long, slow sequence of developments over the next 12 months when, at budburst, cell division is activated and flower primordia formed. May (2000) has described these processes and has commented on the factors that influence flower formation and their development into berries. Variability can develop at many points during these events but only within the controls exercised by the genotype of each vine. The aim of producing shoot and bunch forms that experience suggests are desirable e.g. **FIGURE 11.12b**, will involve genetic methods.

Between berries

The development of the grape berry is prolonged and subject to many hazards which may promote variability. It should be possible to gauge at what stage variability increases or decreases by comparing the trends in CV during development. Gray (2002) did this for berry weight of Shiraz at seven growth stages, from setting to post-harvest, in a commercial vineyard at Willunga (MJT = 21°C). He sampled four bunches at each of the seven stages and assessed several non-destructive physical parameters of every berry (3,210 in total). The berries were then parceled separately and frozen for measurements of seed weights and chemical analysis.

The graph of berry weight at these seven stages in **FIGURE 11.13** shows a growth curve distinctive for

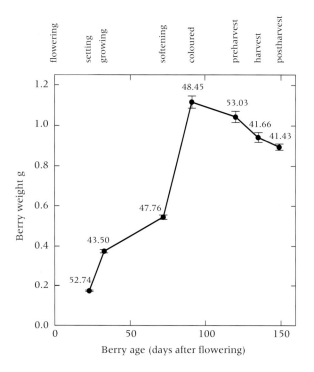

Figure 11.13 *Changes and variation in berry weight of Shiraz during development. Four bunches were harvested at seven stages indicated across the top, and their age along the bottom. (Gray 2002). Each point represents the mean ± S.E and the value above is the CV% of each population. Note berry shrinkage after day 91 (Gray 2002). (See also Table 11.3 results).*

many Shiraz berries in Australia with its episode of shrinkage after about 90 days post-flowering (McCarthy and Coombe 1999). The CVs of berry weight were high but fairly uniform throughout development (**FIGURE 11.13**). The largest CV was at setting (possibly because the period of berry set spanned several days) and again at two weeks before harvest; the smallest occurred at harvest (because of shrinkage?). However the results show clearly that, on these vines, the high variability in berry size was already established by the time of the first sampling (setting).

The mean values for deformability started to rise at the inception of softening, thereafter declining, while CVs were highest at the inception stage (**Table 11.3**).

From the frozen samples Gray selected two bunches at each of three stages (E–L 31, 34 and 37) and estimated spectrophotometrically the content and concentration of three flavonoid groups—anthocyanins, flavonols and total phenolics—in flesh plus skin of the 693 berries on these six bunches. The calculations of content and concentration were based on absorbance at appropriate wavelengths of reference compounds—malvidin-3-glucoside for anthocyanins (absorbance 528), quercetin-3-glucoside for flavonols (absorbance 364). and catechin for other-phenolics (absorbance 275 after subtraction of the contribution of anthcyanins and flavonols) including cinnamic acids and procyanidins (tannins) (Somers 1998). Additional chromatographic techniques would have provided greater detail and accuracy, indeed, the data of Downey et al. (2003) of berry skins from the same vines have lower values for catechins (other-phenolics). These differences may be due to the type of berry tissue measured but in any case the variation data presented here should remain valid.

The results of content per berry are shown in **TABLE 11.3**. The CVs for the estimates of anthocyanins, flavonols and other-phenolics per berry were similar at all three stages of development and were of the same order as the CVs of berry weight and deformability. The concentrations of flavonoids in individual berries shown in **FIGURE 11.14** are strikingly different and provide a unique picture of the array of these components contributing to fruit composition. Because of the complexity of the results we describe the differences by subjective assessment of patterns rather than by statistics.

The scatter-diagrams at **4°Brix** (pea-size) of concentrations mg/g equivalents of each reference compound show wide differences between compounds—about 0.01 for anthocyanins, 0.1 for flavonols and 2 to 3 for other-phenolics—but all show a large effect of berry weight viz. at least a 10-fold difference between small and large berries. At **7°Brix** (softening) the general forms of the distributions remain similar to those at 4°Brix but there is a striking reduction in variation between berries, especially with flavonol concentrations. This is a resynchronisation phenomenon.

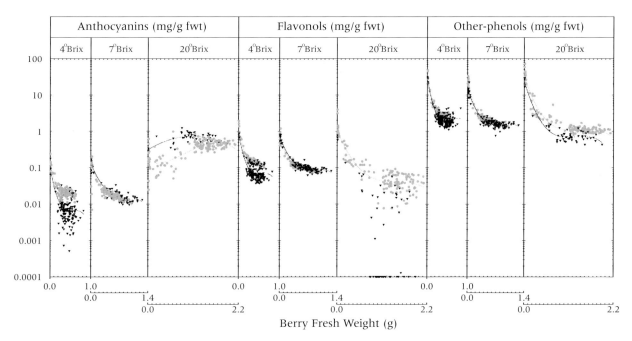

Figure 11.14 Concentration of flavonoids (log-scale) in individual berries from pairs of Shiraz bunches sampled at three growth stages—pea-size (4°Br), softened (7°Br) and preharvest (20°Br). Seeds were removed and flesh and skin of each berry extracted and prepared for spectrophotometer scanning to give absorbances at selected wavelengths for the three flavonoid groups—anthocyanins, flavonols and other-phenolics (see Table 11.3). Concentrations are given in flavonoid equivalents. (Drawn from data in Gray 2002).

At **20°Brix** (preharvest), concentrations display a wide scatter i.e. ripening has brought a general decline in synchrony, especially with flavonols (perhaps reflecting differences in degree of berry shading, Downey et al. 2004). The distribution of anthocyanin concentrations is distinguished by the decline in scatter no doubt associated with the general effect of accumulation that accompanies berry ripening. Berries weighing more than 1 gram appear to have a more uniform level of anthocyanins. These findings suggest new approaches in exploring the relationships between berry composition and quality of wine during the progress of ripening in Shiraz berries.

Gray then examined Chardonnay growing in the cooler climate of the Adelaide Hills (MJT = 19°C) and found results quite different from those with Shiraz. At the beginning of capfall a half of selected vines were trunk-girdled, the rest not; capfall date was recorded at every flower on selected bunches. At 15 days after first capfall, and again at 43 days, bunches were picked, all berries weighed and CVs calculated. The results in **TABLE 11.4** show that, at 15 days, CVs of berry weight were similar to those of Shiraz at setting discussed above. But, by 43 days, the response of these cool-grown Chardonnay was very different to that of Shiraz at

Table 11.3 Coefficients of variation (%) of some berry variables and content and concentration of some flavonoid groups selected from the same Shiraz experiment reported in Figures 11.13 and 11.14 (Gray 2002).

	Growth Stages				
E–L stage	27	31	34*	36**	37
Description	Setting	Pea-size	Softening	Coloured	Preharvest
Est. juice °Brix	–	4	7	15	20
	Coefficients of variation				
Berry variables					
Berry weight †	53	44	48	49	53
Deformability	23 _0.5_	27 _0.3_	48 _0.6_	34 _1.9_	32 _2.4_
Amount per berry					
Anthocyanins (malv-3-gluc. equivalents)	–	Δ	Δ	–	64 _0.55_
Flavonols (quercetin-3-gluc. equivalents)	–	43 _0.04_	37 _0.05_	–	76 _0.05_
Other-phenolics (catechin equivalents)	–	37 _0.91_	35 _0.97_	–	43 _1.32_

* Inception of ripening determined by deformability measurements.
** Stage 36 is maximum berry weight; thereafter berries are shrinking.
† CVs for berry volume and berry surface area were similar to those for berry weight.
Small subscript values are the actual means of deformability (mm) and content (mg/berry) and are not CVs. (Δ Values are low and hence not reported.)

Willunga. All berries had grown considerably but especially those on girdled vines (which were 250% bigger). The difference between the CVs of these two populations was large—ungirdled CV = 137% versus girdled = 61%. The high variation in berry weight of ungirdled at 43 days may result from Chardonnay's susceptibility to cool conditions which often causes poor set (coulure) and 'hen and chickens' (millerandage). The growth stimulus provided by girdling resulted in bigger and more uniform berries. Interestingly, the relationship between berry weight and seed weight was unaffected by girdling which suggests the girdling stimulus may have operated via enhanced seed growth (see three paragraphs below).

Table 11.4 Average berry weight and CV% of the berry weights on single bunches of Chardonnay, Adelaide Hills taken from bunches on ungirdled and girdled vines at 15 and 43 days after capfall. Each value is the mean from two bunches from each of three clones. (Capfall date was recorded for each flower) (Gray 2002).

Days after capfall	Berry wt. (mg)		CV %	
	Ungirdled	Girdled	Ungirdled	Girdled
15	3.3	4.0	39	42
43	38.9	104.2	137	61

There is a need to interpret differences in berry size due to growth or to various treatments in terms of average cell size and also of variation in fruit size in terms of variation in cell size. The development of confocal microscope techniques (Gray et al. 1999) permitted the measurement of the volume and number of cells in the flesh of selected berries and the relation of these and their CVs to the differences in berry weights (Gray 2002). For instance, the CVs of flesh cell volumes of both 'chicken' and 'hen' berries were similar at 15 and 43 days after capfall yet actual volumes of 'hen' cells were 1.6x (15d) and 4.6x (43d) those of 'chicken' cells. Girdling, compared with ungirdled, had little effect on the CVs of cell volume of 'chicks' despite its large effect in enlarging their cell volume.

The cause of high size variability between berries at setting is indicated by measurements made on developing ovaries throughout their pre-flowering development (May 1987, 1992, 2000). As early as four weeks after budburst (six weeks before flowering) microscope images show large differences between flowers in size and development stage. The extent of variation is illustrated in **FIGURE 11.15** of immature flowers on an inflorescence one month before flowering (E–L stage 17, single flowers separated). The flowers varied in size and state of development according to their position on the inflorescence, and in particular their position on each dichasium and of the branchlet on the branch (May 2004); diameters ranged from 0.25 to 0.7 mm. From such measurements, made at four stages, May showed that this spread of diameters was maintained through to flowering and might reflect large differences in cell numbers per pericarp. May showed further that patterns of flower distribution and size variation were similar over bunch laterals and between bunches and were the same in vines with different pruning systems and varying crop levels. He suggested that size variation, apparent at flowering, persisted through veraison up to harvest and that it was probable that berry composition patterns were influenced similarly.

Variation in berry size that is associated with variation in the development of reproductive parts is emphasised by the results of May (2000) and further detailed by Ebadi et al. (1996a, **FIGURE 11.16**). The harvest weights of Chardonnay berries were related to the collective weight of seeds, being a summation of the number and type of seed. 'Sinker' seeds (heavier in weight because of fully developed endosperms) were associated with heavier pericarps. Berries with 'floater' seeds (normal seed coats but empty inside) weighed less as did the associated pericarps. The five categories of seed fresh weight—one versus two seeds, floaters versus sinkers—had significantly different pericarp weights proportional to their total weight of seed structures. Parthenocarpic berries without any seed growth, such as Zante Currant, commonly weigh about 200 mg, but even the presence of small, abortive seed traces, as in 'chickens', causes some stimulus to berry growth (stenospermocarpic). It is hypothesised that the berry size differences reflect the amount of the seed stimulus; this effect could be on cell division differences in the pericarps during weeks 1 and 2 after anthesis (but see the suggestion of Ojeda et al. (2001) that water deficit may cause reduced cell wall extensibility).

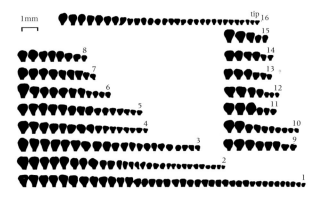

Figure 11.15 Shadowgrams of all of the immature flowers on one Pinot Noir inflorescence from a Burgundy vineyard about one month before flowering; the flowers are arranged in ascending order of the branches (No.1 to the bunch tip, No.16) and each row indicates the variability in flower size on each branch (as displayed by size decreasing from left to right). (May 2000).

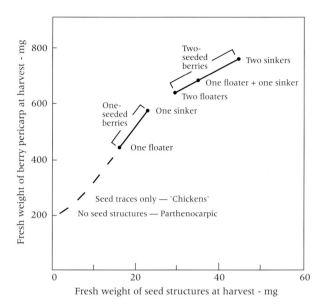

Figure 11.16 Weights of Chardonnay pericarps at harvest against total fresh weight of the combined seed structures in five categories according to the number and state of the seeds. Redrawn from data in Ebadi et al. (1996a).

Variation in seed development is associated with various types of defects in parts of the ovule as compared with the structure of normal developing seeds shown in **FIGURE 11.3**. Ebadi et al. (1996b) describe three groups of defects: a) ovule abortion (due to defects in development of embryo sacs, nucellus and integument) with the result that ovules cease growth and ovaries do not develop; (b) defective pollination or fertilisation of ovules so that no zygote forms and testa development is incomplete; these are the seed traces found in 'chickens' which provide enough growth stimulus for setting and limited pericarp development; (c) ovules which follow a normal path of development forming a full-sized seed coat, but pro-embryos abort and both the nucellus and endosperm degenerate—such seeds are 'floaters' and provide enough stimulus for ovaries to set but berry growth is less than those with 'sinkers' (complete seeds).

The usual cause of defective seed growth is the sensitivity of grape ovules to low temperatures as was shown by Ebadi et al. (1996a) using pot-grown Chardonnay vines exposed to three temperature regimes. Daily temperatures of 12°/9°C for one week before flowering at E–L 15 ('flowers single but compact') and at E–L 17 ('flowers separated') caused fewer berries to set and, in those that did, many seeds were floaters. Shiraz vines were less affected. Coincident shading of experimental vines by up to 72% shadecloth had only minor effects. The degree and timing of cold that impairs seed growth is not clear but, certainly, cold weather before and during flowering is a danger. Other negative factors are those that inhibit pollination, or pollen tube

growth down the style, or double fertilisation of the egg. As well as low temperatures, these growth events are sensitive to other extremes of weather such as heavy rain or drying winds. These conditions are known to affect berry set adversely. Setting probably reduces the extent of berry size variation implied by the image in **FIGURE 11.15** in that the 20 to 50% that do set are likely to be the 'fittest' and to out-compete the rest.

The physiological cause of the disorder 'sweet and sour' (**FIGURE 11.12a**) is unknown. One possibility is that the sudden change to hot weather prevented the inception of phloem transport of sugar and other ripening processes except in the early berries in which ripening had already been triggered; during the subsequent month with a return to cooler conditions, repair of the ripening mechanisms may have permitted resumption of development, but repair was slow and not synchronous. It appears that hot days and nights severely delayed the inception of ripening which was subsequently activated during lower temperatures—possibly, by repair of phloem transport mechanisms?

11.2.4 ALLEVIATION AND AVOIDANCE OF VARIATION

The variations between vines found in established vineyards by GPS methods (see **FIGURE 11.8**) provide valuable information to help unify the vines by traditional management methods e.g. training and pruning, soil amendments and fertilisers, drainage and targeted irrigation. Importantly, the information permits unifying the harvest by dividing vineyards into 'management zones'. Attempts are being made to supplement such information with data on fruit composition e.g. total soluble solids, acidity, colour and phenolics by measurements of samples from a grid of positions in each vineyard. Also methods are being sought to build upon these approaches by various physico-chemical techniques such as Near-Infra-Red spectroscopy (NIR) (Gishen et al. 2002). The Australian Cooperative Research Centre for Viticulture (CRCV) is coordinating relevant research under two topic headings: 'Winegrape Quality' and 'Variability within Vineyards' (Lamb et al. 2004). The understanding of these and related problems will undoubtedly be improved.

In summarising his research on variation between bunches, Nayler (2001) recommended that variation might be reduced by improving the uniformity of fruit exposure and reducing growth stage variability, both of which should benefit berry flavour development. Viticultural practices that foster uniformity during budburst, initial shoot growth, inflorescence development, flowering, bunch exposure and berry development should all help improve grape quality. Nayler also showed that variation between bunches on each shoot contributed to variation. One solution to this would be to seek genotypes that only initiate one bunch per shoot. Or, hand-thin the crop midway between budburst and flowering (eg E-L 12), when bunches are most accessible, by cutting off all except the basal (most developed) bunch; obviously this is an expensive operation but it might bring surprising rewards.

An aspect of fruit development in the grapevine that deserves research is that of the functioning of vascular elements into each berry. Three events have come to attention: (a) Impedance of xylem sap flow into berries when size expansion resumes after the lag phase with the consequence that phloem sap becomes the major source of berry water during the ripening phase. (b) The apparent shut-down of development of individual berries at veraison due to hot weather with recovery of function when cooler conditions prevail; this suggests a blockage of phloem elements, then a reopening (maybe due to dissolution of callose plugs). (c) Shrinkage of Shiraz berries 13 weeks after flowering affecting all berries on each vine suggesting a systemic shut-down of phloem sap flow into all berries which therefore become devoid of vascular connection with the rest of the vine yet continue with the engustment part of ripening. Event (b) greatly increases variation between berries while (a) and (c) appear not to.

The vine's genotype largely determines the geometry of the bunchstem which, depending on the level of berry set, influences bunch tightness at harvest; this, in turn, has significant consequences for disease and berry composition. May (2000) pointed to the merits of bunches that are small (less variation) and loose (well ventilated) (FIGURE 11.12b). Least size variation coupled with balanced and stable proportions of flesh, skin and seed would benefit must composition. Such would be helped if all berries had only a single well-developed seed. The cause of asynchronous ripening between berries on a bunch reflects asynchrony between berries in the onset of their plasma membrane leakiness.

Conclusions

The foregoing has excluded significant contributions to quality debilitation caused by damage to fruit due to berry splitting and mould following rain and contamination by MOG (matter-other-than-grapes). These are discussed in Volume II, Chapter 13, Harvesting of Winegrapes.

Variability in the composition of berries arises from differences in their morphological and physiological development which vary between berries for many reasons additional to a background of a natural developmental spread. As has been illustrated, the spread can by exaggerated by the seasonal weather e.g. cold before flowering, or heat at veraison; these are 'acts of nature' and are regarded as unavoidable and untreatable. But better understanding of how their effects arise could lead to the development of avoidance or corrective measures. The research thus far has emphasised physical rather than chemical

(compositional) variation; hopefully this deficiency will be corrected as methods become available.

A model for future research on grape berry variability is provided by the PhD thesis of J.D. Gray (2002). While this model has yet to be assessed by his peers, its significance is indicated by the basic questions being addressed and the innovative and appropriate methods used. The following conclusions selected from the research indicate its promise: (a) Comparisons of trends in variability during berry development (e.g. FIGURE 11.13) indicate that much arises during flower formation; (b) A large contribution to variability arises from differences between bunches on each shoot; (c) The waves of synchrony and asynchrony occurring in content and concentration of compounds in berries indicate unsuspected periods of change in berry metabolism (e.g. FIGURE 11.14); (d) The factors controlling berry growth may be an interplay of hormonal stimulus from developing seeds and organic nutrition of the pericarp cells; (e) The development and application of Confocal Laser-scanning Microscopy to measure size and shape of individual cells in blocks of flesh showed that variation in cell volume remained relatively constant during early postflowering development, while variation in berry weight increased. Some of these are new findings.

11.3 Methods for assessing grape quality

This section reviews methods that have been used for assessing winegrape quality potential (which we term 'grape quality') and to provide suggestions for research directions that might improve assessments. The focus is the vineyard and the grape harvest but with recognition of the fact that 'grape quality' impinges on the quality of wine made; wine quality is more readily assessed and investigated and must therefore, at some point, be a part of grape quality research.

11.3.1 WINE SHOWS, REPUTATION AND CONSUMER CONSENSUS

The global guide to public preferences between Australian wines has been provided by Wine Shows, the history of which is described by Dunphy and Lockshin (1998). The Shows started over 150 years ago to provide guidance to producers of grapes newly planted in untested, scattered regions. They have provided a forum for comparison and rating of qualities and styles of wines submitted. Essentially, wine shows are a self-help and promotional exercise but unfortunately they do not provide data for scientific analysis. The number of entries has grown to such an extent that the necessity of changing the judging methods is being considered (Walsh 2002). Questions have been raised about the relevance of judgements thus made to the assessments of wines made by consumers at the meal-table. The advent of judges to represent consumers could be useful, but the introduction of disciplined consumer preference testing as advocated by Noble (2001) seems desirable. Nevertheless, in the Australian context, show results have provided a benchmark of relative wine qualities and, thus, indirectly, of grape qualities.

Wine auctions provide another forum for comparing qualities of wines and have the merit that they are part of the realities of marketing. However, the progress of wine sales provides the ultimate arbitration and acceptance of wine value. Reputation gained by individual lots of wine has a predominating effect on the public's opinion of the quality of a region's wine. Promotion and advertising aid this process, augmented by the large amount of media attention given to wine. Ultimately, however, there is dependence on the judgments made by consumers. These in turn mean that such judgements are related to the condition and composition of the grapes at the moment of crushing.

Through most of Europe there are detailed classification systems, in particular, the Controlled Appellation laws developed in France. These were conceived in the 1930s to counter a number of serious production problems, negative to wine quality. Systems were devised for legally-binding wine labellings that were based on geographical zones within each of which viticultural methods were assured. The methods varied across zones but included such prescriptions as vine varieties, planting density, pruning and training methods, yield limits and minimum alcohol levels in the wine. The system has survived (with modifications) for over 70 years and indeed is expanding through other European countries: an Appendix in the Oxford Companion to Wine, 2nd edition (Robinson 1999), shows a list of over 500 appellation zones enacted in 12 countries; the list uniquely details the varieties officially permitted for each appellation wine.

There are negative aspects of the Controlled Appellation concept. Such laws do not encourage the testing and adoption of different varieties and of the use of new viticultural methods. The development of many production methods as described in this textbook—practices which have lowered costs of production and yet seem not to have affected wine quality adversely—would undoubtedly have been delayed under such a system.

11.3.2 VINEYARD CANOPIES, SCORECARDS AND GRAPE TASTING

Assessing grapevine canopies

Scientific investigation of grapevine canopy management is relatively recent. The new ideas about vineyard canopies arose from the work of Shaulis et al. (1966) with the *labruscana* variety Concord and, later, with Sultana by Shaulis and May (1971). The concepts were developed further on the black winegrapes

Cabernet Sauvignon in Bordeaux and Shiraz at Roseworthy (Smart et al. 1990) and have now been tested widely in many regions and countries. A treatise on winegrape canopy management by Smart and Robinson (1991) is the basis of Volume II, Ch. 5. The basic principles stemmed from the realisation that excessive shading of leaves and bunches lowered fruit quality, and that such conditions were associated with excessive shoot vigour and crowded canopies. Smart later proposed that an ideal canopy could be conceived. He described components of a canopy on a scale, from good to bad, and the total figure of the scorecard indicated the potential winegrape quality (see Volume II, Ch. 5). There is little doubt that the exercise alerted growers to an assessment of their vineyards in these terms and provided direction for the correction of faults.

A large Australian wine company took up the scorecard principle with the aim of improving the assessment of potential grape quality from individual grape suppliers. The assessed factors were compared statistically with an index of value of the wine from each grape lot using the allocations to 'end-use' made at the first classification tasting of the young wines. The first attempt, involving over 1,000 vineyards in six South Australian regions with three years of assessments of four varieties, was overly ambitious and largely unsuccessful (Gray et al. 1994). While an indication of some significant differences in Value Index (VI) between regions was shown, and some slight trends for correlations, the main outcome was that huge variability and inadequate data precluded predictions of the potential for wine quality of any vineyard lots.

A follow-up project was pursued using 148 Shiraz vineyards and an improved scoresheet involving quantitative measures, and with attempts to reduce the incidence of missing values. The results (Gray et al. 1997) were better: linear regression analysis showed small trends for lower VI from vineyards with leafy, dense canopies, poor fruit exposure, lower anthocyanin levels, larger berries and higher yields. But the high variability of the data would prejudice reliance on these vineyard assessment methods. Disappointingly, the assessments made at veraison were much less successful than those made at harvest and indicate that other measurement stages may need to be considered, e.g. at specified intermediate concentrations of total soluble solids (comments on such stages are made in Chapter 7, section 7.2). The above results do not invalidate the concept, but better methods are needed. Particularly, there is a pressing need for more research on the problem of within-vineyard variability (see 11.2.2).

Juice and grape tasting

Winegrape growers and winemakers with a concern for timing the harvest to target a particular wine style specified by the winemaker have adopted various methods of organoleptic assessment of grapes before harvest. These exercises are useful; some would say, essential. The simplest is to taste berries through the vineyard. Many have remarked how sudden and distinctive the revelation of flavour can be, especially in berries of aromatic varieties such as Riesling and the Muscat group. The same sensation follows the sniffing of juice preparations as proposed by Jordan and Croser (1984); McCarthy (1986) used such an approach in comparing the effects of viticultural treatments on the quality of Riesling using a panel of judges (**FIGURE 11.24**). A similar approach could be extended to juice of other varieties, quantifying aroma and flavour sensations appropriate to the varieties. Note, however, that in certain varieties, especially black grapes, flavour and mouthfeel qualities remain hidden until vinification.

11.3.3 SMALL-LOT WINEMAKING, SENSORY STUDIES

The most realistic method of assessing the quality of a batch of grapes is to make wine and assess it by sensory methods. The difficult task of quantifying quality is tackled by using comparative tests coupled with statistical analysis. Numerous research centres around the world have set up assessment systems giving results that are respected.

Making wine in small lots is essentially miniaturisation of normal winemaking methods. Descriptions of the methods used at CSIRO, Merbein by Antcliff and Kerridge (1975) and at Roseworthy Agricultural College by Ewart and Sitters (1991) are typical of other descriptions. The size of fermentation lots for experimental wines varies. Large lots (100 to 1,000 kg) are theoretically less likely to permit faults, but modern wine-making methods with precise control of conditions and careful monitoring have allowed the adoption of small units (1 to 20 kg) such as are needed for the evaluation of viticultural trials. A sensory comparison of wines made from 2, 20 and 20,000 L of juice or must of Riesling and Shiraz grapes was carried out by Ewart and Sitters (1991). No significant quality differences were found by both difference tests and wine scoring; however, 2 L lots were too small for adequate sensory evaluations. They recommended at least three replicate fermentations of 20 L lots. Such a prescription greatly constrains the type of viticultural experiment that is possible.

An aspect of sensory evaluation receiving much attention is that of statistical methods. Formerly, panellists allotted overall scores that were analysed by analysis of variance, with tasters results incorrectly used as replicates. Later development was the on-going assessment of panellists' performances in their reliability, agreement, variability, discrimination, and stability (Brien et al. 1987, Ewart and Sitters 1991). Also sensory assessments are increasingly being based on individual attributes, analysed separately. These are likely to be more homogeneous. Another trend is for assessments to be compiled by a disciplined series of difference tests (Noble 1988). Matthews et al. (1990) have described a novel protocol for paired comparisons in the sensory analysis of wines from an irrigation experiment.

The large outlay in personnel, buildings and equipment restricts the number of experimental wine laboratories. Hence the effort that is being made to seek methods of measurement of grapes from experimental plots that correlate with sensory assessments of wine style and quality. Good, reliable correlations are needed to facilitate the interpretation of viticultural field experiments.

11.3.4 GRAPE COMPOSITION AT HARVEST

Grape quality (i.e. wine quality potential) depends on the composition of the grapes when harvested. Theoretically, it should be possible to predict the potential for wine quality from chemical analysis of the harvested grapes. The aim in this approach is: (a) to select candidate compounds for this purpose (from among the many hundreds of chemicals in the mix), (b) to select measurement methods to quantify them, then (c) to compare the measures with assessments of the sensory properties of wine made. What is being sought is a measure that gives the best and most reliable correlation (positive or negative) with wine quality and thus provide a guide for harvesting (see Volume II, 13.2) and for assessing the subsequent vinification fate. The measures might be physical or chemical and relate to a single unit, a compound class, or a 'bundle of attributes'.

The following sections on method and time of sampling grapes in the vineyard should be read in conjunction with section 13.2 of Volume II.

Grape sampling methods

Any measure of winegrape composition, and hence of potential wine quality, must involve grape sampling and measurement. Commercial sampling has to allow for fruit variation between and within vines to arrive at a sample that represents the whole crop. A selection of whole bunches has the merit of coping with variable berry development within bunches and present commercial methods are described in Krstic et al. (2002). A small bucketful of bunches (~10 L per hectare) gives measures close to that from the whole crop. Where this is too large a proportion of the crop, picking single bunch laterals copes with berry variability yet gives comparable results. The results of May (2000) suggest that laterals in the proximal third of each bunch are representative or, even branches three and four. Single berry sampling has been a common method and has the merit of removing less crop; however the sample is often biased towards larger berries, especially in varieties with tight bunches.

Fractions taken from fruit samples for assessment include cleared juice, macerated berries or grape must. By and large, grape juice is a satisfactory fraction for many purposes except when information is needed on the contribution of skins and seeds such as for pH, colour and tannins (see 11.1.4). Must samples, taken after crushing, include juice, broken pulp and solids from flesh, skin and seeds of berries and crushed bits of tissue from pedicels and bunchstems, plus anything else that is collected in the harvest bins (MOG); such samples are more representative of commercial practice.

In all sampling cases, parallel information on berry size is valuable for interpretation of berry size effects on concentration measures.

When to sample

As berries ripen, the relative concentrations of most compounds in the fruit are changing, day by day. Long experience and numerous experiments have shown that wine made from grapes picked before they are ripe is of poor quality and, similarly, that wine quality declines when grapes are picked over-ripe. This image is expressed in the bell-shaped curves of wine quality graphed against harvest date or some component of grape composition (**FIGURE 11.17**). *Winegrapes are deemed ripe when their chemical composition is best suited for a wine of a targeted style and quality.* Different standards operate for different varieties and regions; note in **FIGURE 11.18** the lower Brix/acid indices for peak quality in the two white varieties compared with the two black varieties. The duration of peak ripeness is often briefer in hot climates than in cool.

To pin-point the peak, a regular sequence of samples is needed beginning some time before the anticipated harvest date. Measurement of sample components must be done quickly enough to follow the progress of ripening towards the composition desired. Records from a sequence of measures are essential for subsequent post-mortems of the seasonal effects or experimental results.

Interpreting measurements of grape quality becomes complicated when dealing with plots of field experiments in which treatments have caused differences in grape ripening rate. All plots should be harvested on the day a specified index is reached. Harvesting of such plots on a single day will, by definition, give samples with differing ripeness and hence differences in subsequent measurements; but it will be unclear whether the differences are due to treatment or stage of ripeness, or both. This fault has unfortunately been common and has prejudiced the acceptance of claims made in some viticultural papers (see the second paragraph of section 11.4 below).

What to measure?

We now consider candidates for quality prediction. Primary metabolites are dealt with first; these are compounds that are essential for life processes and occur in ripe grapes at concentrations usually greater than 1 millimolar; **TABLE 11.1** lists some examples. Then,

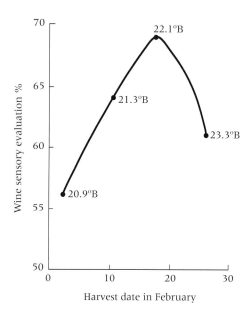

Figure 11.17 Variation in the sensory evaluation of wine quality of Chenin Blanc grapes harvested at different dates (and hence °Brix) from the same vineyard and year (Du Plessis 1977).

secondary metabolites are considered; these occur at concentrations as low as micromolar, or even nanomolar, but may contribute significantly to flavour by virtue of their high potency (low perception threshold).

Sugars, total soluble solids (TSS)

The most-used entity of grape components as a predictor of ripeness and quality is that of TSS concentration of which hexose sugars predominate. This is universally used because it is the principle solute group, is simple to measure, increases regularly as grapes ripen, and has proved to be a useful indirect guide to quality. Any of a number of methods serve for measuring TSS provided they are done consistently and accurately; these include total soluble solids by refraction or hydrometry, or total or reducing sugars by chemical methods. Knowledge of TSS concentration is an essential indicator for wine style but, by itself, fails as a guide to quality differences between lots and regions; this is illustrated by the fact that the same percent alcohol (which generally reflects sugar concentration in the must) is seen on the labels of both high and low quality wines within each style. Note that a deficiency of sugar in the harvested grapes can be corrected by addition, after crushing, of sugar or grape juice concentrate depending on regulations in the country of production.

Acidity and pH

A specified range of *acidity* and *pH range* are absolute requirements for good wine. Extensive research on the use of acidity and/or pH as guides to grape quality has

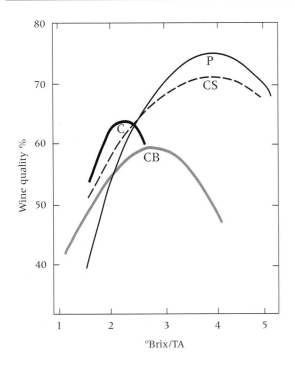

Figure 11.18 Fitted curves relating wine quality to the grape ripeness index, °Brix / T.A., of free-run juice of Colombard (C) and Chenin Blanc (CB) (average of six years) and of Pinotage (P) and Cabernet Sauvignon (CS) (average of five years). (Redrawn from graphs in Du Plessis and Van Rooyen 1982).

been carried out. Du Plessis and Van Rooyen (1982) and Du Plessis (1984) collated this information and concluded that guides using both sugar and acid were an improvement over sugar alone e.g. sugar/acid indices (°B/TA), sugar x pH or sugar x pH^2. The bell-shaped curves of wine quality against °B/TA for two white and two black varieties in **FIGURE 11.18** show peaks at distinct ratios of °B/TA—2.2 for Colombard, 2.8 for Chenin Blanc and 3.8 for Pinotage and Cabernet Sauvignon. Note, however, that in one of the three years with Chenin Blanc no such peak was found (data not shown). Further tests with Pinotage and Cabernet Sauvignon of the above three indices showed that optimum quality was defined more precisely by °Brix × pH (Van Rooyen et al. 1984). This index, and its relative, °Brix × pH^2, would seem appropriate for black grapes with higher potassium concentrations and lower malate levels, hence higher juice pH levels. As with sugar, deficiencies can be corrected by addition of acid (e.g. tartaric) after crushing (depending on regulations in the country of production).

Du Plessis (1984) supported the recommendations of Cootes et al. (1981) of the adoption of specified ranges of sugar, acidity and pH as initial guides for each vineyard, followed by those of Jordan and Croser (1984) of aroma and taste tests of the juice from the series of fruit samples used for chemical tests.

From time to time, other primary compounds that either increase or decrease in concentration during berry ripening have been considered as candidates for harvest indices. The amino acids proline and valine increase in concentration as ripening progresses, and there is also a steady decline in the concentration of ammonium ions, but these changes do not appear to provide successful indices.

Anthocyanins and other glucosides

For black grapes used for making red wine, P. G. Iland demonstrated in 1987 the potential of using a *grape colour measure* to predict wine sensory properties. This idea derived from preliminary recordings using grapes from three different Shiraz vineyards which produced wines with different sensory properties; these properties were compared with measurements of grape anthocyanins from each vineyard with the following result:

Grape anthocyanins mg/g berry wt.	Sensory properties of the wines
2.3	deep colour, ripe, very intense flavours and powerful tannins
2.0	deep colour, intense flavour and tannins
1.2	light colour, lacking intensity of flavours and tannins.

In previous work on red wines, Somers and Evans (1977) had shown that the colour density of young red wines was correlated with subjective assessments of their quality. These important findings have been widely acknowledged and used by the wine industry. Note however that, in contrast to previous claims, purified anthocyanins have recently been described as tasteless and non-astringent molecules (Vidal et al. 2004). Yet their levels in grapes appear often to correlate with quality of resultant red wine over a wide array of growing conditions (Francis et al. 1998a, 1999); this is especially so with Shiraz, but also with Pinot Noir (P.G. Iland, unpublished). The assay of red colour is becoming an important predictive measure for ripeness and quality in black grapes, additional to sugar and acid. The reasons for the good correlations between grape anthocyanins and red wine quality have yet to be sorted out (Iland 2001) but would appear to stem from a correlation with aroma and flavour compounds. Future studies may show similar associations with mouthfeel properties of red wines.

The development of an assay method to measure the concentration of glycosides (*the glycosyl-glucose or G-G assay*) has provided a useful additional tool. This idea developed from the recognition that a significant proportion of grape flavour compounds occur in the glycoside form and that hydrolytic release and measurement of the conjugating glucose of a glycoside extract would quantify the concentration of total

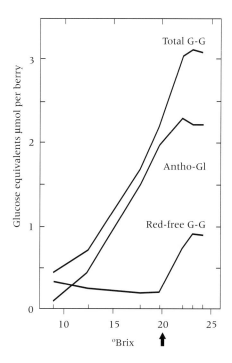

Figure 11.19 Content of glycosides per berry (as glucose equivalents, G-G) during ripening of Shiraz berries. Total G-G is partitioned into two components—anthocyanin glucose and non-anthocyanin glucose (red-free G-G). The points are means of five values in each of seven groups of ascending °Brix levels. The arrow head shows when berry shrinkage began. Compiled from data in McCarthy 1997b.

glucosides. Further, it was found that spiking of a base wine with hydrolysed glycoside extracts from Shiraz grapes of differing quality yielded sensory assessments that paralleled those of the relative red wines (Abbott et al. 1991). Subsequently an assay protocol was developed

by Williams et al. (1995). In **FIGURE 11.19**, G-G values are compared with anthocyanin measures during ripening of the black winegrape variety, Shiraz. This has led to experiments testing whether measures of total glycosyl-glucose (G-G) in grapes correlate with assessments of flavour in wine. Several encouraging correlations with wine flavour intensity scores from sample sets have been found. Tests with samples from commercial Shiraz vineyards showed positive correlations between grape G-G concentrations at harvest and flavour intensity scores of relevant wines (Francis et al. 1999, **FIGURE 11.20**). A second graph in the same reference from five other vineyards in which fruit °Brix was more uniform (22.6 to 23.4) quoted a high regression coefficient value (0.97). Both figures also displayed parallel results of grape colour measurements which showed correlations similar to those with flavour intensity. This is not surprising since the glucose from anthocyanin is a high proportion of the total glycoside (as is apparent in **FIGURE 11.19**). Because of its simplicity the measurement of colour is preferred but, unlike G-G, colour measurements cannot be tracked during vinification. In the case of white grapes (lacking anthocyanins), G-G values are low. Nevertheless, as shown in **FIGURE 11.21**, a correlation was evident between grape G-G and wine flavour intensity score for the varieties Chardonnay and Semillon; in each variety, the two highest G-G samples both had the highest intensity scores.

If anthocyanins are not significant flavour compounds, yet a total glycoside fraction contains flavour glycosides, the difference in concentration between total glucoside (G-G) and anthocyanins, both determined as glucose equivalents, should provide a better correlation with flavour of black grapes. [With white grapes, in which the complication caused by anthocyanins is absent, the two

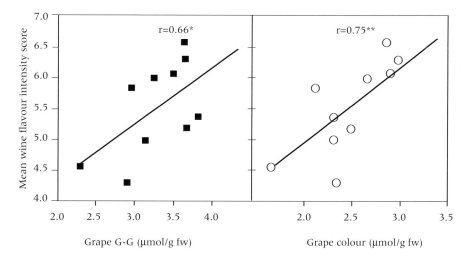

Figure 11.20 Relationship of wine flavour intensity scores and grape G-G and grape colour of Shiraz samples harvested from commercial vineyards in three regions. TSS values ranged from 22.4 and 24.9°Brix; small-lot wines were made under identical conditions (Francis et al. 1999).

measures, total G-G and red-free G-G, are of course the same value]. Protocols for the measurement of what has been called the *red-free G-G assay* were developed by Iland et al. (1996); some values are shown in **FIGURE 11.19**. Unfortunately, early results indicated that red-free G-G values in ripe black grapes gave inconsistent correlations with sensory assessments of wine (Francis et al. 1999, Iland 2001). The development of a promising alternative to the red-free G-G method—the phenol-free G-G (PFGG)— appears to have overcome many difficulties: Using different glycoside extractants, good recoveries of alkyl and benzenoid glucosides were found, suitable for the assay of aroma and flavour compounds of low-terpene varieties such as black grapes (Whiton and Zoecklein 2002).

Another encouraging finding is the measurement of the red-free G-G concentrations in skin and flesh hydrolysates of grapes from two black varieties and compared with wine aroma assessments from the same samples (Francis et al. 1998b). The results in **FIGURE 11.22** show an overall correlation between red-free G-G and a rating of aroma attributes found in their hydrolysed glycosides; importantly, *most of this correlation arose from red-free G-G measurements on berry skin and not juice* (see also 11.2.2). This difference between skin and juice suggests that more attention should be given to the red-free G-G or PFGG content of separated skins of black grapes (and maybe also of white grapes).

Recent work on extractability of colour from black grapes has led to a method that might improve the utility of colour measurements. The method, termed *'phenol maturity'*, was developed by Glories in Bordeaux and is described in Ribéreau-Gayon et al. (2000). It relates to the capacity of berry skin cells to break down during vinification and thus influence the degree of release of anthocyanins. In essence, the protocol quantifies the field practice of squashing berry skin between two fingers and assessing the colour. The data in **TABLE 11.5** compares measures from three harvest dates: the middle date showed the highest anthocyanin value in skins, but the sample picked eight days later had the highest wine anthocyanin level and wine colour intensity matching the high coefficient of extractability from crushed,

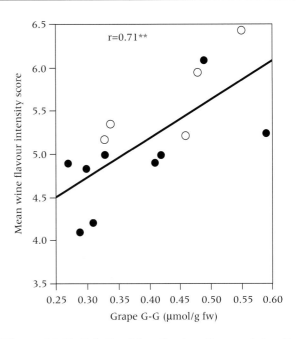

Figure 11.21 Relationship of wine flavour intensity scores to grape G-G of Chardonnay (○) and Semillon (●) grape samples harvested with TSS between 20.3 and 22.5°Brix (Francis et al. 1999).

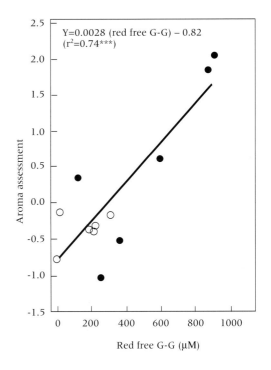

Figure 11.22 Concentrations of non-anthocyanin (red-free) G-G extracted from skin (●) and juice (○) of six samples of black grapes—Cabernet Sauvignon and Merlot each sourced from South Australia, Napa and Davis—and aroma assessment scores of the same isolates after addition to base wine. The aroma assessment (rotated component 1) encompassed largely 'dried fig' and 'tobacco' attributes (Francis et al. 1998 b).

Table 11.5 Effect of harvest date on anthocyanin levels in Cabernet Sauvignon skins and wine, related to the measurement of extractability during vinification (data from Ribereau-Gayon et al. 2000).

| Harvest date in September | Skins | | Wine | |
	Anthocyanin concenctration mg/L	Extraction coefficient %	Anthocyanin concenctration mg/L	Colour intensity
13	1550	61	930	0.686
20	1743	59	1046	0.812
28	1610	75	1207	0.915

fermenting berries. The table shows that, in these circumstances, the higher extractability at the later harvest more than compensated for the, by then, lower level of grape anthocyanin concentration (°Brix is not reported). The significance of this factor may vary between varieties, vineyards and season, and also will relate to the vinification methods in each winery, but should be worth investigation. The laboratory method for measuring extractability percentage is detailed in this reference.

Phenolics

Phenolics in grapes, (other than anthocyanins, considered above), include phenolic acids (e.g. cinnamic acid), flavonoids (yellow pigment flavonols, dihydroquercetin) and tannins (bulky molecules condensed in varying sizes from procyanidins—polymers of flavan-3-ols or catechins). Tannins are found in skins, seeds and stems. According to Ribéreau-Gayon et al. (2000) "... a ripe grape is characterised by skins rich in anthocyanins and tannins which are complex and relatively inactive, while seeds have a low content of extractable polymerised tannins that react strongly with proteins...". The value of anthocyanin measures for quality prediction of black grapes was discussed above but phenolic compounds other than anthocyanins are also regarded as important elements of quality in all winegrapes. However their diverse and difficult chemistry has precluded the use of their measurement for prediction of quality potential.

Aroma and flavour compounds

Given the diversity of styles and qualities of wine it would seem improbable that measures of single entities of grape composition could become successful as broadly applicable wine quality indicators across varieties. At present, no single grape volatile compound has been suggested as an indicator of best harvest time or of best potential wine quality (I.L. Francis, personal. comm.). However there are developments that offer promise for specific groups of related varieties. Impressive progress is being made in the study of flavour-active and precursor molecules in particular varietal wines. Others may develop from the work described in the book 'Chemistry of Wine Flavour' edited by Waterhouse and Ebeler (1998). The emphasis is on compounds and compound groups that contribute aroma and flavour to wine, and which can be measured by innovative chemical methods coupled with well-managed sensory evaluations of wines. In addition, the phenol-free G-G assay (mentioned four paragraphs above) could become a valuable collective measure of aroma and flavour compounds.

Monoterpenoids—These are volatile monoterpenes that are largely responsible for the distinctive aroma and flavour of a number of winegrapes, especially white winegrapes such as Riesling, Traminer and the Muscat family. Research on these grape volatiles has been intensive during the last quarter-century especially following the realisation of the important role of bound forms such as glycosides and polyols (termed flavour precursors or potential volatile terpenes—PVT). Free volatile terpenes (FVT) occur in smaller amounts and are released *in vitro* from PVT by acid or enzyme hydrolysis (Wilson et al. 1983). Viticultural studies were accelerated by the development of a simple distillation and colorimetric method by Dimitriadis and Williams (1984) for quantifying the concentrations of free (FVT) and bound (PVT) volatile monoterpenes.

Encouraging results using this method were obtained in comparisons of aroma scores of Riesling juice and PVT concentration by McCarthy (1986, **FIGURE 11.24**) and with total volatile terpene concentrations by Ewart (1987). There followed a large number of experiments in other countries the most intensive being those at Summerland, Canada, much of which has been summarised in a review by Reynolds and Wardle (1997). Their results showed that many viticultural treatments increased FVT and PVT levels in several varieties of white winegrapes, e.g. low crop load, fruit exposure to sunlight, vine hedging, basal leaf removal, wide vine spacing, selected training methods, and cooler vineyard sites. Of the two terpene types, PVT was the most responsive to these practices. Increases in grape monoterpene concentration were in many cases correlated with organoleptic assessment of wines made, but rarely with juice TSS, TA or pH. Note, however, that these promising results are confined to studies on those varieties in which terpenoids contribute significantly to overall aroma and flavour.

Norisoprenoids—This group of 13-carbon terpenoids contains many that are odoriferous and contribute to the aroma properties of a wide array of grape varieties, both whites and blacks. ß-damascenone is a significant part of the odour of Cabernet Sauvignon, Cabernet Franc and Merlot while ß-ionone is important for Pinot Noir. The megastigmane sub-group includes two compounds that develop during the ageing of wines, especially in Riesling: trimethyldihydronaphthalene (TDN) with a kerosene-like odour, and vitispirane with an odour resembling camphor. It is possible that the abundance of these and related compounds may correlate either negatively or positively with grape quality but faster assay methods and more detailed testing are needed.

Methoxypyrazines—These potent compounds differ from those above in that their aroma is not so much a fragrance but rather is herbaceous and vegetative. They are found in the free state in grapes of important varieties including Cabernet Sauvignon, Sauvignon Blanc, and Semillon. They occur at very low concentrations in grapes and wine, mostly in the isobutyl-substituted form. Their levels are highest in immature and shaded grapes and in those grown in cool climates. Moderate levels are important for the varietal character of these varieties, but high levels are negative for quality. The compounds are difficult to measure and results would apply only to a select group of varieties.

New laboratory techniques

The preparation by hand of samples for measuring colour and G-G of black grapes involves the homogenisation of whole berries which is tedious and inhibits the application of these methods. The Australian Wine Research Institute has been involved in the development of a machine that reduces this problem: it is fully automated and successfully carries out sample homogenisation, subsampling, weighing, addition of extraction solvent, mixing during extraction, and finally centrifugation (Francis et al. 2004).

Several new methods being used to study wines may prove to be useful for grapes. Gas chromatography-olfactometry has provided much information about the identity and odour activity of the array of individual odorants in wine and food. Variants in the methods include 'Charm-analysis', 'Osme value', 'aroma extract dilution analysis', 'static headspace analysis-olfactometry', 'the electronic nose' and probably others. These are specialised methods which hopefully may lead to more effective analytical tools for predicting composite levels of grape flavour. There is current enthusiasm for the potential of measuring a wide array of components in grape juice and crushed grapes by Near-Infra-Red spectroscopy (NIRS) since it offers speed and adaptability and should help field studies (Dambergs et al. 2000, Gishen et al. 2002).

Conclusions about grape composition

Analysis of chemical components of grapes is likely to be the most successful tool in the search for methods of predicting the best harvest date and/or potential grape quality level. It seems improbable that analysis of a single component would serve these purposes in all cases. Analyses of compound groups, such as glycosides or terpenoids, would seem a more logical target. No matter what is the factor, its selection will be the result of testing correlations with a range of sensory assessments of grapes and wine. This should be coupled with careful fruit sampling in the vineyard and analyses of a sequence of samples taken before, at, and (if possible) after, peak 'ripeness'.

11.4 Vineyard factors affecting grape quality

Long experience and copious discussion have been collated in the wine literature about the differences in wine quality from different grape-growing regions, climates, soils and factors concerned with site selection and planting material. These are significant determinants of grape quality and are considered in Volume 1,

Chapters 3, 4, 8, 9 and 10. However, since grape quality is an important vineyard resource, this present chapter considers the effects on harvest quality of the variables that are in the hands of growers. To clarify the discussion, we continue the approach of regarding growers (sellers, whose income derives from grape sales) and winemakers (buyers, whose income derives from wine sales) as different parties, with a negotiation leading to a valuation of the grapes at harvest.

The rapid changes in grape composition that take place as grapes proceed through their ripening development, and the overwhelming influence of composition on wine quality, are described in sections 11.1.2, 11.1.4 and 11.3.4. Comparisons of viticultural practices that are claimed to show differences in wine quality must therefore allow for, or remove, differences that may be due to the degree of ripeness of the grapes at harvest. If experimental plots are harvested on the same day, as has been common, and plots show different composition and/or quality, the differences may not be able to be ascribed to the effect of the treatments alone—they may be due to differences in ripeness. To avoid this, each plot should be harvested at a specified harvest index e.g. a narrow range of juice °Brix or Brix/acid ratio. Alternatively, a sequence of harvests from each treatment might be used, straddling the specified criteria and thus permitting interpolation of results to the specified stage. These constraints complicate experimental work aimed at determining effects of viticultural practices on grape composition and quality but are necessary to avoid the work being discounted. The approach in this chapter is to downplay experimental work in which the differences in the degree of ripeness at the point of comparison are considered too large for valid interpretation of treatment effects.

11.4.1 CANOPY MANAGEMENT AND GRAPE QUALITY

Fruit composition and wine quality are improved by moderating shoot vigour and ensuring adequate but not excessive fruit exposure i.e. by achieving open canopies (Smart and Smith 1988). Coupled with these characteristics are good sunlight penetration into, and air ventilation through the canopy and lowered susceptibility to pests and diseases (Smart and Robinson 1991). The central importance of vine balance—ratio of vine growth to fruit production—for long-term sustainable production is emphasised by Howell (2001). The evidence for these concepts and their application in different climatic regions is outlined in Volume II, Ch.5 'Canopy Management'. Here, the basis of the connection between canopy faults and winegrape quality is considered.

Canopy effect on bunch shading

Shading of bunches has been found to have significant effects on grape quality. A review of this subject with an emphasis on cool climate viticulture is provided by Jackson and Lombard (1993). In particular, they have summarised the confusing literature on the effects of the type and timing of shading treatments on grape quality; exposure of bunches to light in cool climates has been shown to increase levels of terpenoids, phenolics and anthocyanins with benefits to wine quality. Carbonneau (1996) emphasises the negative effects of bunch exposure that is too great (overly exposed) but, equally, that which is too little (overly shaded). Shading may increase herbaceous characters due to higher levels of methoxypyrazines.

In hot climates excessive berry exposure and resultant reduced anthocyanin levels are generally detrimental to grape quality. Where daytime temperatures regularly exceed 35°C moderate fruit exposure appears to be superior to full exposure (Haselgrove et al. 2000). This conclusion was supported by a Barossa Valley Shiraz experiment comparing different training systems (Wolf et al. 2003): consequent differences in canopy characteristics created large differences between treatments in berry exposure which demonstrated the interaction of light and heat on berry ripening. An explanation of the results was that, initially, exposed berries developed more berry colour and phenolics but, by harvest, these differences were lost due to excessive radiant heating of exposed berries. A more direct testing of the separate and interactive effects of sunlight and temperature on berry composition by Spayd et al. (2002) shows promise of untangling this complex matter.

Note added in proof: Downey et al. (2004) shaded Shiraz bunches in a way that avoided effects on berry temperature and humidity. Compared with exposed bunches there was little effect of shading on berry development and ripening, including accumulation of anthocyanins, but flavonol levels in grape skins were significantly reduced.

Shoot vigour

Excessive vigour in shoots is a common phenomenon in present vineyards because of the combined effects of modern viticultural methods and the grapevine's rapid response to such methods (Dry and Loveys 1998). This problem is difficult to overcome but, unless it is, grape quality suffers because of excessive shading of bunches and greater likelihood of pest and disease damage. It is less common in hot dry regions, perhaps because of the inhibitory effects of dry atmosphere on shoot elongation.

Increasing the number of buds left at pruning, i.e. more shoots per vine, leads to devigoration but this must be accompanied with adequate shoot spacing and/or orientation; in other words, improving the balance between shoots and roots but maintaining an open canopy. To handle this extra 'charge', the vine framework usually needs expansion, often entailing

added trellis wires. Vigour problems are less with hedge-pruned vines unless the hedging is severe. Minimally pruned vines generally have short shoots and open canopies but, in cool regions, may develop zones of dense foliage inside the canopy.

Vigorous shoots may indicate that rootstocks are too invigorating, pruning is too heavy, or nitrogen status of the vineyard is too high (a problem that is easily diagnosed and corrected). However, the most common cause of high shoot vigour is high soil water status. Depending on the incidence of rainfall, lessening or eliminating irrigation leads to reduction of shoot vigour. There is usually an accompanying reduction in fruit yield although the examples given in section 11.4.3 provide exceptions, in particular the technique of Partial Rootzone Drying which has been spectacularly successful in providing the yield benefits of irrigation without encouraging excessive shoot growth (see 11.4.3, Dry and Loveys 1998).

Shoot manipulation

There are a variety of shoot manipulations that can be used as shoots develop. These are reviewed by Jackson and Lombard (1993). All of them are labour-intensive and therefore costly unless they are amenable to mechanisation. They resemble fruit and leaf thinning in that they can be viewed as correctives inherited from faulty trellising, training and pruning and subsequent vine management methods that result in unbalanced vines.

Shoot thinning, especially the removal of barren and 'twiggy' shoots, can reduce errors in bud positioning at pruning and improve spacing of shoots and the maintenance of better leaf and bunch exposure, all of which should be beneficial to quality. A degree of berry thinning can also be achieved. Shoot positioning, by hand or as part of Vertical-Shoot-Positioned trellis systems, can serve the same purposes unless shoots are inadvisedly clumped together.

Topping and hedging of vines is commonly done to maintain access along row alleys in vigorous vineyards. Benefits to grape composition and quality have been reported in some cases but not in others. The consequences of topping on vine growth are complex because of interacting effects on lateral shoot growth, carbon assimilation effects and bunch exposure to light.

Basal leaf removal (fruit-zone leaf thinning) reduces leaf shading of bunches with benefits through reduced disease and pest damage and also increased bunch exposure. It has been shown to improve fruit quality, especially in cool regions. Several authors have reported consequential increases in the concentrations in berries of phenolics, anthocyanins, monoterpenes (both FVT and PVT) and glycosyl glucose.

These practices are detailed in the canopy management chapter (Volume II, Ch. 5).

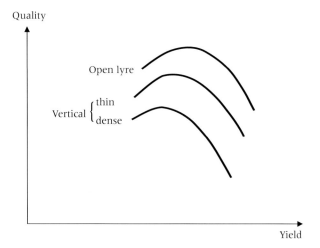

Quality

Open lyre

Vertical {thin / dense

Yield

Figure 11.23 Generalised relation between grape yield and wine quality from three training methods (Carbonneau 1996).

11.4.2 GRAPE YIELD AND GRAPE QUALITY

Champagnol (1977) has stated that "great wines have never been obtained except from weak vines". It is widely believed that the lower the yield the higher the quality of the wine (i.e. an inverse relationship) and that highly flavoured wines derive only from low-yielding vines. There are many examples supporting these generalisations but, equally, there are many that do not. An example of the complexity of the matter is provided by an analysis by Jones and Davis (2000) of 46 years of records of red wine production from selected chateaux in Bordeaux. They showed that the correlation between vintage quality and Bordeaux AOC red wine production (adjusted using a predictive time series) was significantly positive, not negative. For example, in the 10 years in which quality was rated 'exceptional', production from the total selected area was high (~4 mill. hL) in six years and low (~1 mill. hL) in only four years. These differences were mainly attributable to weather factors (temperature and rain), and not vineyard management, but sound a warning about the yield/quality concept.

The interaction of yield/quality/price is of crucial importance for determining a vineyard's profitability. Graphs of vineyard yield against wine quality are often shown to have a bell-like shape (**FIGURE 11.23**) rather than a line of negative slope. This is because both low yields and high yields may give poorer quality wines due to an array of faults in grape composition. Arguments abound about the details of these graphs but not about the truth of their general form. The shape of the middle sections indicate that there is a maximum in wine quality at some intermediate level of yield. Determining this point for each vineyard is the challenge. Graphs of *vineyard profit* against yield, set alongside those of grape quality versus yield (not shown), would reveal that the maximum profit was usually at a higher yield. The shape

difference between the value and profit graphs depends on quality as assessed by winegrape buyers and on price received. Growers will be influenced by an awareness of these two maxima in making decisions about yield levels. An understandable aim of most growers is to maximise vineyard profit by increasing yield without lowering net returns. An aim of winemakers is to maximise profit per tonne of grapes. The current efforts to improve the assessment of winegrape quality should provide clearer guidelines.

Vineyard yield levels

Inherently, grapevines are highly productive plants which, under certain conditions, produce exceptionally high yields, e.g. up to 100 t/ha. Grape producers run the risk of using practices that result in overcropping with a consequent lowering of quality. Overcropping occurs when the yield is such that the grape crop cannot be ripened to an appropriate composition for a targeted wine style. The trend for overcropping decreases when better grape quality is rewarded adequately by higher prices. After the cessation of prohibition in the USA, overcropping was rife in California (Winkler 1954) and, in the absence of official controls, was gradually reduced by carefully directed research work and associated publicity. Similar problems early in the 1900s which bedevilled wine production in the Republic of South Africa were solved by the formation of a cooperative (KWV) which adopted a sequence of laws influencing wine marketing, then grape prices, and finally grape yield quotas for each wine farm (Orffer 1968).

When minimum grape price schemes were legislated in Australia there was a tendency for viticultural methods that permitted overcropping which had the undesirable outcome of fostering low grape prices. This was coupled with a winemaking ethic of 'buy-vinify-classify'. In the mid-1980s there developed a trend for the operation of market forces in which buyers to an extent rewarded quality. As a result, grape prices rose dramatically. A desirable middle ground for the industry is for winegrape buyers to work in concert with growers, both aiming towards a balance between quality, yield and price. If growers feel they are not rewarded for quality, the tendency will be towards higher yields and hence average quality may decline.

Currently in Australia, growers and buyers may arrange term contracts with pricing criteria involving base prices per tonne plus bonuses depending on quality criteria such as yield, TSS, colour, etc. Buyers are stressing the importance of lower yield. This development will be helped by better information on which to base criteria such as that provided by recent survey projects of commercial vineyard blocks. The first, of 25 irrigated Shiraz vineyards in the hot Riverland region of South Australia, provided results of the type shown in **TABLE 11.6**. The vineyards represented by the column labelled 'lowest wine score' had grapes with G-G < 2.8 and colour < 1.0, and the vines had longer shoots (> 90), bigger berries (> 1.0) and poorer bunch exposure (< 225) [see table for units]. The yields from the group of vineyards that produced poor wine tended to be higher than the rest although the yield/quality correlation was not significant indicating that vineyard factors other than yield were also important in the search for good quality potential. Another Shiraz survey, this time in the NSW Riverina (Holzapfel et al. 1999), showed that vineyards with high yields (e.g. > 32 t/ha) had low berry colour (~ 0.5 mg/g); at lower yields, e.g. 16 t/ha, colour averaged about 0.8 mg/g (still a low value, see **TABLE 11.6**).

It is widely believed that small berries, compared with large, give musts with higher phenolics, and, in black grapes, higher colour and hence better quality (Johnstone 1996). This relationship needs further examination because of the link between berry size and crop yield.

Trellising and vine training

Trellis needs are generally dictated by vine size which in turn is broadly set by vine genotype and soil water and fertility. Nevertheless, at any one site, a huge array of training methods are possible bringing differences in vine yield and grape composition (see Volume II, Chs 3 and 5). In 1977, Safran proposed that, depending on the trellising methods compared, yield increase need not bring about a lowering of wine quality. Examples are provided by many South African trellising experiments, a selection of which is shown in **TABLE 11.7**. Note that, within each pair in this table, the trellised plots increased *both* yield and wine quality score compared with bush training.

A further illustration of both responses is given by the

Table 11.6 Measurements of selected vine and wine variables from two Riverland Shiraz vineyards. From a detailed survey in 1995 of 25 vineyards, five with a range of vine types were harvested at 23 ± 0.4 °Brix and wines made under comparable conditions; the two lots shown are those with the lowest and highest wine quality score of these five.

Measurement	Wine Scores	
	Lowest	Highest
*Shoot length (cm)	125	67
*Bunch exposure (µmol/m²/s)	169	293
*Berry weight (g)	1.2	0.7
*Yield (t/ha)	30	24
†Juice °Brix	23.3	23.0
†Grape colour (mg/g fr wt.)	0.83	1.28
†Grape G-G (µmol/g fr.wt.)	2.0	3.7
†Wine score (out of 20)	12.4	15.6

* From Botting et al. (1996)   †From Francis et al. (1999)

Table 11.7 Effects of training on yield and wine quality rating from experiments on three varieties showing treatment pairs selected with similar vine spacing (rows 3 or 3.7 m) and similar °Brix and TA in the harvest lots. The vineyard had good soil and the vines were not irrigated. Values are the average of eight years of results (Zeeman 1977).

Variety and treatment	°Brix	TA g/L	Yield t/ha	Quality score (%)
Riesling				
Bush vine	21.5	7.1	7.2	55.5
Trellis 1.5m slant	21.2	7.6	15.5	71.1
Chenin Blanc				
Bush vine	20.6	8.0	8.3	55.5
Trellis 3m slant	20.6	8.8	20.3	76.0
Cabernet Sauvignon				
Bush vine	22.2	7.4	8.3	83.3
Trellis 4-wire Perold	22.1	7.2	11.2	84.5

three curves in **FIGURE 11.23** comparing training methods from experiments in Bordeaux: the more open Lyre system gave both higher yield and wine quality than two vertical trellis systems.

Two papers describing experiments in hot irrigated regions in Australia provide supporting evidence: (a) From a trellis/pruning level experiment on Crouchen at Mildura, Victoria, May et al. (1976) showed a yield increase of 25–30% due to widening the trellis from 0.3 m to 1.4 m but with no measurable difference in wine quality; (b) Dry et al. (1999) describe results with five modern trellising methods which were compared on Shiraz at Waikerie, South Australia; despite significant differences in bunch number per vine and yield, grapes were similar in composition and colour.

A Shiraz training experiment in the Barossa Valley, South Australia has provided some new perspectives (Wolf et al. 2003). The training system widely favoured locally is a simple trellis with a single wire at about 1 m which is regarded as sufficient given the aridity of the region and the restrictions on irrigation with consequent low vine capacity. Five training systems were compared during four years seeking improvements over the presently-used system. Minimal pruning treatment produced more fruit on average but quality was poorer in high-yield years. The advantages shown by two more elaborate training methods were countered by significant disadvantages—poorer fruit exposure with Vertical Shoot Positioning, and variable fruit composition with a Scott-Henry system using up-down cordons from alternate vines. Consequently their higher canopy management costs could not be justified. The widely used single-wire system with its open canopy of splayed shoots ('spiky') was commended for moderate and consistent yields of high quality fruit involving minimal labour costs.

Finally, in a recently published paper on this topic (Reynolds et al. 2004) compared the response of Riesling in Summerland, British Columbia, to five training systems over four harvests. They concluded that *'high wine quality may be obtained from divided canopies despite large crop size and high crop loads'* (Y/P).

In his thoughtful review of vine balance and the concept of growth-yield relationship, Howell (2001), amongst many other matters, discussed the concept of the effect of the amount of wood in the perennial part of each vine and quoted examples where higher amounts favoured both yield and fruit composition.

Bunch thinning experiments

The testing of the effects of bunch thinning on grape quality has been popular because it is simple to do and constitutes a direct test of the central hypothesis that high yield reduces wine quality without confounding effects as occur for example with irrigation.

The developmental stage when bunch thinning has been tested has varied widely. When done near to flowering, the consequent possibility of better fruit-set and larger berries complicates interpretation of results. This can be avoided by delaying thinning until after both setting and pericarp cell division have been determined (when berry diameters are from 4 to 7 mm). Similarly, thinning late when berry ripening processes have been set in train may not show any benefits. Commonly, bunch thinning has been tried during the lag-phase before veraison (E–L 31 to 33) when berry and shoot growth are relatively unaffected and the measured effects of yield on grape quality are not confounded by change in berry size. Hand thinning during veraison provides an opportunity to improve fruit uniformity and quality by selectively removing green-berried bunches while retaining the colouring and faster-ripening bunches.

During the 1980s and 1990s there were about a hundred papers in the literature on thinning and grape quality. The majority showed that thinning did cause changes in grape composition held to indicate an improved wine quality. In a small proportion of papers, there was an improvement in sensory scores of wine made, especially of varietal flavour. Unfortunately, much of this research had the serious defect that the experimental plots were harvested with differing maturities, or that quality differences were not adjudged by making and assessing wine; they are therefore disregarded here.

The most comprehensive series of papers that meet the prescriptions for acceptability of results—equal sugars of the harvest and sensory assessment of small-lot wines or a chemical correlate thereof—are those by Bravdo's group in Israel who tested the effects of bunch thinning on several varieties. Results of factorial treatments of thinning x irrigation of Cabernet

Table 11.8 Factorial of twelve treatments (three bunch number levels x four irrigation schedules) on Cabernet Sauvignon vines in Israel. Plots were harvested when grapes were 23.1 ± 0.4 °Brix. Values are means of five years of results and have been rounded and statistical difference symbols omitted. Transposed from histograms in Figures 5 and 6 of Bravdo et al.(1985).

Thinning bunch no. per vine*	Irrigation schedule mm applied#	Prunings t/ha	Yield t/ha	Yield/ prunings ratio	Wine quality score
20	220	5.1	15	2.9	12.9
	260	4.5	13	2.9	12.6
	320	5.2	15	2.9	13.2
	400	*5.8 (+)*	*13*	*2.2 (−)*	*9.5 (−)*
(Mean)		(5.2)	(14)	(2.7)	(12.0)
40	220	4.3	20	4.7	13.0
	260	3.8	19	5.0	12.3
	320	4.4	18	4.1	12.4
	400	5.3	19	3.6	10.7
(Mean)		(4.6)	(19)	(4.4)	(12.1)
65	220	4.0	24	6.0	12.7
	260	*3.5 (−)*	*23*	*6.6 (−)*	*13.7 (+)*
	320	4.2	24	5.9	12.6
	400	4.7	25	5.3	10.4
(Mean)		(4.1)	(24)	(6.0)	(12.3)

* *Unthinned (65/vine); bunch thinned:-moderately (40/vine) and severely (20/vine).*

\# *Drip irrigated from shortly after flowering to harvest at two rates - weekly (3.3mm/day, 400mm/season) or fortnightly (2.0mm/day, 260mm/season) and repeated for the other two treatments but with a 50% cut-back from about 12°Brix until harvest (1.7mm/day, 320/season and 1.0 mm/day, 220 mm/season). The symbols beside selected values in the two italicised rows denote the highest (+) and the lowest (−) values in those three columns.*

Sauvignon vines are shown in **TABLE 11.8** (Bravdo et al. 1985). [The effects of irrigation are discussed in 11.4.3].

Compared with unthinned, two levels of bunch thinning, moderate and severe, increased pruning weight and *lowered yield but had no effect on wine quality* score. In parallel work on high-yielding Carignane, thinning also increased pruning weight and *lowered yield but significantly increased wine quality* scores. In a later experiment with Sauvignon Blanc (Gal et al. 1996), a wider range of bunch numbers was achieved by combining shoot number (14 and 44 shoots per vine) with two bunch numbers per shoot (1 and 2); a large spread of yields was obtained and, *as yields decreased* from 32 down to 9 t/ha, *quality scores increased* linearly from 9.3 to 13.3.

In summary, the Israeli results obtained by bunch thinning of Carignane and Sauvignon Blanc vines support the hypothesis that lower grape yields lead to higher wine quality, but bunch thinning of Cabernet

Sauvignon vines did not.

Two Australian experiments support the hypothesis that lowering of yield improves quality potential. Bunch thinning of irrigated Riesling (to a degree that halved the crop) hastened ripening, increased juice terpenoid concentration, and increased juice aroma score (**FIGURE 11.24**, McCarthy 1986). Thinning of minimally-pruned vines presents a problem because of their large number of dispersed, small bunches. This has been tackled by the use of shaker-harvesters, with promising results (Clingeleffer et al. 2002): Shiraz vines at two sites—Coonawarra (cool) and Sunraysia (warm)—were thinned at the pea-sized berry stage producing a 30–35% reduction in yield coupled with a large effect on fruit composition at harvest—higher colour density, total phenolics, total anthocyanins and ionised anthocyanins plus an increased sensory score. Although the thinned Sunraysia fruit did not compare with Coonawarra berries (either unthinned or thinned), the degree of improvement in their quality would help counter the yield reduction.

A decision to try bunch thinning for the prospect of better quality would need to balance the question: will the harvest be rewarded by higher prices sufficient to cover the smaller yield and the cost of thinning? For many vineyards, interpretation of the effects of thinning may be better viewed as a need for corrective measures and, in the longer term, as a need to review vine balance variables. However Howell (2001) has pointed out that bunch thinning can be a valuable tool in years when low temperatures threaten to jeopardise the ripening of a crop; he suggests that this need could be quantified by assessing the accumulated growing-degree-days at a specified stage halfway between flowering and veraison, e.g. pea-sized berries.

From the results presented in this section (11.4.2) we have questioned the commonly held view that low yields are essential for better quality wine. Instead, emphasis is given to the desirability of vineyards having moderate vigour and with spaced shoots so that fruit is not overly shaded or exposed and ripens evenly and quickly. This requires balanced vines with appropriate yield/pruning weight ratios. Further discussion of yield is found in the following section.

11.4.3 SOIL WATER AND GRAPE QUALITY

A basic tenet of plant physiology is that plant biomass production is proportional to crop water use which, in turn, is influenced largely by water supply to the plants and stomatal opening. The simple logic behind this is that open stomata permit, simultaneously, the egress of H_2O (water loss) and ingress of CO_2 (carbon assimilation). Thus an important way to alter grape production is to increase or decrease soil water status and to control stomatal opening. Unlike thinning, which reduces yield, irrigation is done to increase production. This increase is

often considered to reduce quality, a belief that is embedded in European appellation laws in which the irrigation of vineyards is forbidden or prescribed. Admittedly, highest priced wines often originate from moderate-to-low yielding vines, commonly unirrigated, which represent an important but small segment of production. However, there is great interest in the question, 'how high can yields be taken without any negative effect on quality becoming counterproductive?'.

Experimental evidence on the relationship between soil water status and wine quality has been difficult to obtain but the advent of better methods of water application and monitoring, coupled with improved measurements of vine performance, has led to some significant experiments. Six are described here. They were all continued for several years (2–5) with irrigation being by drip or microjet. Similar juice °Brix or Brix/acid ratios were ensured at harvest, and small-lot wines were assessed. In some cases, records of indicative flavour or glycoside compositions were provided. They are grouped under four headings.

All season irrigation

McCarthy (1986) compared thinning and irrigation treatments on Riesling vines at Nuriootpa, South Australia; irrigation involved weekly replacement of 40% of evaporation. The graphs in **FIGURE 11.24** derive from samples taken at regular intervals in the fourth year of the experiment. Compared with irrigated, 'no irrigation' caused a hastening in the juice °Brix curve (as is usual with lower yields) and also higher levels of PVT ('potential volatile terpenes') and of aroma scores of juice samples. Fruit from vines that had been irrigated but bunch-thinned (so that the yields were reduced to the same level as 'no irrigation') showed a °Brix increase that was faster than in the other two treatments, as was that of juice PVT and aroma. The methods permitted interpolation of an equivalent Brix/acid ratio (see figure) which indicated that, at this selected harvest stage, *yields were halved by not irrigating and juice PVT and aroma were increased*. However thinning of irrigated plots, which removed the yield differential due to irrigation, produced fruit with the fastest ripening, restored PVT levels and gave an improved aroma score compared with fruit from the irrigated, unthinned treatment.

The above-mentioned Israeli experiment on Cabernet Sauvignon by Bravdo et al. (1985, **TABLE 11.8**) did not have an unirrigated treatment but the four full-season irrigation schedules covered a wide range of water applied (from 220 to 400 mm). These treatments had little effect on yield within each of the thinning groups, and the only effect on wine quality score was that the treatments that received most irrigation had significantly poorer quality i.e. better wine quality resulted from vines receiving less irrigation but having the same yield. The authors pointed to the higher weight of prunings in

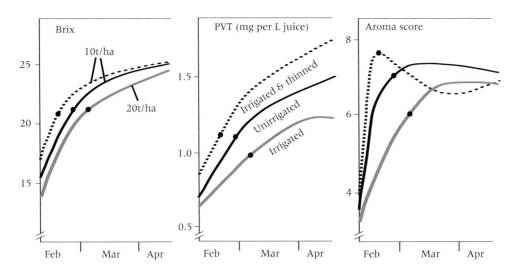

Figure 11.24 Developmental changes in °Brix, PVT and aroma score of juice from Riesling grapes subjected to three treatments: no irrigation; irrigated (by dripper weekly to 0.4 of evaporation); irrigated and bunch-thinned (half of the bunches removed before veraison) ● *= °Brix/acid ratio of 25 (a potential harvest date). Reproduced from Coombe (1992), from data in McCarthy (1986).*

the wet plots and concluded that *the weight ratio of yield to prunings (Y/P)[1] provided a better indication of performance than did yield alone*. A graph of Y/P against quality (not shown) reveals that, within each thinning group, an increase in Y/P was associated with better quality. For example, as denoted in **TABLE 11.8**, the treatment with the lowest quality score (20 bunches/400 mm) had the biggest berries, highest pruning weight and lowest Y/P ratio (2.2) (indicating diversion of growth from fruit to shoots). The treatment with the highest quality score (65 bunches/260 mm) was the opposite—smaller berries, high berry colour, lowest pruning weight and highest Y/P ratio (6.6). In general, while the effects of irrigation on yield were overshadowed by the effects of thinning, yields within each thinning group were relatively unaffected by irrigation (with the exception that the heaviest irrigation gave poorest quality). Thus, effects of irrigation on the interaction between shoot development and berry development and composition appear to be predominating influences.

Irrigation at prescribed growth stages

Van Zyl and Weber (1977) compared nine irrigation schedules on Chenin Blanc vines in South Africa over three years. The schedules consisted of waterings of about 140 mm at prescribed stages (setting, green berry or veraison) in various combinations. There were consistent effects, one of which is relevant here: plots irrigated at flowering and again at veraison yielded 25

t/ha while untreated yielded only 18 t/ha but, *despite this large yield difference, small-lot wines from both treatments had equivalent quality scores.*

Regulated deficit irrigation (RDI)

The RDI system means that deficits are imposed during designated phenological intervals. Such an experimental approach was used by Matthews group who compared the effects of drip irrigation deficits over specified intervals on Cabernet Franc in St. Helena, California during two seasons. Two papers describe the effects on fruit ripening and reproductive development, and a third (Matthews et al. 1990 in which all papers are cited) described sensory evaluation of wines made. Compared with continual irrigation, all deficits, especially pre-veraison deficits, had fewer berries per bunch and reduced berry volume and yield. Those which had experienced *a water deficit just before or after veraison* had higher concentrations of anthocyanin and phenolics that were matched by similar differences in wines; *wine flavour, aroma and taste were improved.* These composition differences were unrelated to berry size and yield differences. They concluded that, "where vine water status can be altered, irrigation offers a means to manipulate wine sensory characteristics in the vineyard". Their later experiments have confirmed that the *beneficial effects on tannin and anthocyanin concentrations following water deficits are due more to direct compositional effects than to berry size effects.*

Another detailed experiment was carried out on a mature Shiraz vineyard in the hot, arid Riverland region of South Australia which ran for four years (McCarthy 1997a). There were eight treatments comparing 'full' and 'nil' with combinations of four deficit intervals, each of

---

1. The ratio yield/pruning weight (Y/P) is termed 'crop load' by these authors. This terminology is avoided in this book since the term 'crop load' has been, and is being, widely used synonymously with 'crop level' or 'crop yield'. Note that the Y/P ratio has also been termed the Ravaz Index.

about one month—'post-flowering', 'pre-veraison', 'post-veraison' and 'pre-harvest'. Deficits, especially post-flowering (after setting), led to reduced berry size, yield and rate of juice °Brix increase. Increase in solutes-per-berry was slowed by post-veraison deficits. Examination of wines made from fruit of three treatments in years 3 and 4 of the experiment showed that the concentrations of total G-G and anthocyanin-glucose were generally higher in fruit from *unirrigated and post-veraison deficit treatments* compared with fruit from irrigated; these in turn *were associated with higher wine flavour intensity values.* No such relationship between treatments and red-free G-G was found (Iland, 2001). However, note the result reported in **FIGURE 11.22** which indicates that further investigation of red- or phenol-free G-G levels in skins of black grapes is warranted.

A remarkably consistent event was found to occur at 90 ± 2 days after flowering (when juice °Brix was about 20) in that berries started to shrink (McCarthy and Coombe 1999). This has been attributed to the blockage of phloem sap transport into the berries—phloem-transported solutes stopped accumulating and loss of water by transpiration from the berry caused berry shrinkage coupled with juice °Brix increase. Anthocyanin increase also slowed and stopped. Significantly, the rapid accumulation of non-anthocyanin glycosides ('red free G-G') began at this time (**FIGURE 11.19**); this group of chemicals would include glycosides of many aroma and flavour compounds. The increase in red-free G-G was not influenced by soil water deficit in the same way as was solutes-per-berry but did show a large difference in their levels between years 3 and 4 of the trial. This supports the notion that accumulation of primary compounds (sugar etc.) and secondary metabolites (flavour etc.) may be independent of each other (at least in var. Shiraz).

Partial rootzone drying (PRD)

The method of PRD (partial rootzone drying) was created during the 1990s. An account of its history and the current state of the concept in relation to grapevines is reported in Dry and Loveys (1998), Dry et al. (2000) and Stoll (2000). The principle relies on drip irrigating one half of each vine's roots while at the same time leaving the other half to dry out. The roots of the wet half maintain an adequate supply of water to the whole vine top while the roots in the dry half react to their droughted state by synthesising various chemical signals, including the hormone abscisic acid (ABA). These chemicals are transported to the whole of the top conveying the message—'slow vegetative growth'—the outcome being shorter shoots, fewer lateral shoots and less total leaf area on both sides; fruit development is not slowed. In the meantime, enough water is moved to the dry-zone roots to maintain their function. It was found that the effect was temporary: the production of the chemical signals by

the drying roots decreased after 10 to 15 days. This problem was solved by using a two-part drip irrigation system that alternately watered one or the other half of each vine, the non-irrigated half being left to dehydrate. The net result of this cycling from one side to the other (on say a 2-week cycle) is that the whole vine is not water-stressed but vegetative growth is lessened; further, *yield of PRD vines is maintained at the level of comparable fully irrigated vines but only half the amount of irrigation water is used.* The main capital cost involved is the doubling of the dripper lines and the provision of switching controls. The water status of both halves needs monitoring as it is crucial that the wet side does not dry out.

With PRD, *berry and crop weights are the same as with continual watering, and fruit quality is in many cases improved.* The fruit benefits from the better exposure to light and ventilation. In some experiments, juice pH has been lowered and the concentration of phenols and anthocyanins increased. Stoll (2000) showed that benefits of PRD to wine quality were due to related effects on light penetration into the canopy and effects on anthocyanin and phenolics rather than to PRD *per se.* PRD is a significant development and is attracting world-wide interest. The significant reduction in water usage is important in environments such as occur in Australia.

Regions that experience rains that preclude drying of the 'dry zone' may be unable to use the method; in these circumstances, selected covercrops grown in spring may help to control shoot vigour (Proffitt 2000). Also if reduced berry weight is desired then judicious supplemental RDI can be imposed (McCarthy 1998).

The summary in **TABLE 11.9** of the yield/quality relationships from these six groups of irrigation experiments shows that half of them support the idea that deficits in the irrigation of grapes, and the associated yield decrease, resulted in improved wine quality. But the other three were different: in one case a yield decrease was not accompanied by any change in quality, but with the other two there was no change in yield but quality was improved. There are strong indications that

Table 11.9 Contrasting effects of water deficits on yield and grape quality in viticultural experiments in which the complications of harvest ripeness differences were controlled.

Author*	Variety	Treatment methods	Comparison with full irrigation:	
			−on yield	−on quality
McCarthy	Riesling	± irrigation	Decreased	Improved
McCarthy	Shiraz	Deficit periods	Decreased	Improved
Matthews	Cabernet Fr.	Deficit periods	Decreased	Improved
van Zyl	Chenin Blanc	Watering periods	Decreased	No change
Bravdo	Cabernet Sauv.	Variable	No change	Improved
Dry, Stoll	Several	PRD	No change	Improved

* see text for reference citations.

good, even excellent, wine quality can be obtained from vines with respectable yields.

The main lesson is to avoid the ill-effects of excessive vegetative growth. Deficits early after setting result in smaller berries and improved quality (unless seed tannins become excessive) but the reduced yield may counter the benefit. Deficits before and after veraison have little effect on berry size and yield but, in some cases, give an improved quality. PRD may halve the amount of irrigation water applied yet maintains the same yield and gives indications of quality benefits.

The foregoing discussion of Soil Water and Grape Quality (11.4.3) emphasises effects on fruit yield and consequences for wine quality. The remarks add to the former section on the relation between Grape Yield and Grape Quality (11.4.2) which examines related aspects.

11.5 Concluding Remarks

The need for manipulations to improve winegrape quality are best decided upon by experimentation in each vineyard because of large over-riding influences of climate, soil variety, etc. The experiments can be focussed from general principles that relate to the effects on grape potential of such factors as vine balance, shoot vigour, canopy openness, yield and soil water. The negative effects on grape quality of variation between berries has been emphasised in this chapter. Remedies for these defects are more difficult to devise but begin at vineyard establishment and continue through annual vineyard maintenance operations. Some are discussed.

It can be seen from the above that much can be done to improve grape quality, even with higher cropping levels, but it is also apparent that there is a lot we do not understand. While it is indisputable that faulty canopies depress winegrape quality, as does departure from a desirable balance between crop levels and vegetative growth (expressed conveniently by Y/P), the research thus far has provided indications that we are missing many things about the determination of quality. What triggers the onset of ripening? What controls the rate of ripening and what are the consequences for quality? What is the basis of the water deficit effect on berry composition? What is the real effect of light on metabolism in skin compared with flesh? What is the connection between accumulation and metabolism in berries of primary metabolites versus secondary metabolites? What are the mechanisms controlling synthesis of flavour compounds and their glycosides within berries and, especially, the skin versus the flesh? Do flavour volatiles evaporate from the berry? And so on.

Compounding this ignorance are the difficulties encountered in the quantification of winegrape quality. While progress has been made with organoleptic assessment methods, a key limitation in research on the living fruit of the grapevine is that of what to measure

that correlates with quality. It must be some measure of chemical composition, but what? The large number of compounds involved and the difficulty of their measurement suggests a challenge to instrumentation and the coupling of measurements to grape and wine samples. The recent ideas of measuring grape glycosides and of monoterpenes in juice of floral white grapes are encouraging steps in this direction.

This chapter has raised more questions than answers, but the prospect for focussed research looks good. Related problems concerning yield and harvest such as yield forecasting and year-to-year yield variation are referred to in Volume II, Chapter 13 together with more on bunch sampling.

REFERENCES

Suggestions for further reading are marked (•).

Abbott, N.A., Coombe, B.G. et al. (1991) The contribution of hydrolyzed flavor precursors to quality differences in Shiraz juice and wines: an investigation by sensory descriptive analysis. Amer. J. Enol. Vitic. **42**, 167-174.

Antcliff, A.J. and Kerridge, G.H. (1976) Developments in small scale winemaking. Food Technol. in Aust. **27**, 523-525, 536.

Bessis, R., Charpentier, N. et al. (2000) Grapevine fruit set: physiology of the abscission zone. Aust. J. Grape and Wine Res. **6**, 116-124.

Botting, D., Dry, P.R. et al. (1996) Canopy architecture - implications for Shiraz grown in a hot, arid climate. Aust. Grapegrower & Winemaker No. 414a, 53-57.

Bramley, R.G.V. and Hamilton, R.P. (2004) Understanding variability in winegrape production systems. 1. Within vineyard variation in yield over several vintages. Aust. J. Grape & Wine Res. **10**, 32-45.

Bravdo, B., Hepner, Y. et al. (1985) Effect of irrigation and crop level on growth, yield and wine quality of Cabernet Sauvignon. Amer. J. Enol. Vitic. **36**, 132-139.

Brien, C.J., May, P. et al. (1987) Analysis of judge performance in wine-quality evaluations. J. Food Sci. **52**, 1273-1279.

Carbonneau, A. (1996) General relationship within the whole-plant: examples of the influence of vigour status, crop load and canopy exposure on the sink Òberry maturationÓ for the grapevine. Acta Hort. No. 427, 99-118.

Champagnol, F. (1977) Physiological state of the vine and quality of the harvest. O.I.V. Int. Symp. on the Quality of the Vintage (Oenol. Vitic. Res. Inst., Stellenbosch, South Africa), pp. 107-116.

Clingeleffer, P., Krstic, M. et al. (2001) Production efficiency and relationships among crop load, fruit composition, and wine quality. Proc. Amer. Soc. Enol. Vitic. 50th Anniv. Meeting, Seattle 2000, pp. 318-322.

Clingeleffer, P.R., Krstic, M. et al. (2002) Effect of post-set crop control on yield and wine quality of Shiraz. In: Proc. 11th Aust. Wine Industry Tech. Conf., Adelaide 2001. Eds R.J. Blair, P.J. Williams et al. (Aust. Wine Industry Tech. Conf.), pp. 84-86.

Colin, L., Cholet, C. et al. (2002) Relationship between endogenous polyamines, cellular structure and arrested growth of grape berries. Aust. J. Grape and Wine Res. **8**, 101-108.

Considine, J.A. (1982) Cuticular fracture and fracture patterns in relation to fruit structure in Vitis vinifera. J. Hort Sci. **57**, 79-91.

Considine, J.A. and Knox, R.B. (1979a) Development and histochemistry of the pistil of the grape, Vitis vinifera. Ann. Bot. **43**, 11-22.

Considine, J.A. and Knox, R.B. (1979b) Development and histochemistry of the cells, cell walls and cuticle of the dermal system of the fruit of the grape, Vitis vinifera. Protoplasma **99**, 347-365.

Considine, J.A. and Knox, R.B. (1981) Tissue origins, cell lineages and patterns of division in the developing dermal system of the fruit of Vitis vinifera. Planta **151**, 403-412.

Coombe, B.G. (1960) Relationship of growth and development to changes in sugars, auxins and gibberellins in fruit of seeded and seedless varieties of Vitis vinifera. Plant Physiol. **35**, 241-250.

Coombe, B.G. (1975) Development and maturation of the grape berry. Aust. Grapegrower & Winemaker No. 136, 60, 66.

Coombe, B.G. (1984) The inception of ripening in the grape berry. Quad. Vitic. Enol. Univ. Torino **8**, 87-99.

Coombe, B.G. (1987) Distribution of solutes within the developing grape berry in relation to its morphology. Amer. J. Enol. Vitic. **38**, 120-127.

Coombe, B.G. (1989) The grape berry as a sink. Acta Hortic. **239**, 149-158.

- Coombe, B.G. (1992) Research on development and ripening of the grape berry. Amer. J. Enol. Vitic. **42**, 101-110.

Coombe, B.G. (2000) Hen and chickens v. Sweet and sour. Aust. NZ Wine Industry J. **15** (2), 13.

Coombe, B.G. (2001) Ripening berries - a critical issue. Aust. Vitic. **5**, 28-34.

Coombe, B.G., Bovio, M. and Schneider, A. (1987) Solute accumulation by grape pericarp cells. V. Relationship to berry size and the effects of defoliation. J. Exp. Bot. **38**, 1789-1798.

Coombe, B.G. and Iland, P.G. (1987) Grape berry development. In: Proc. 6th Aust. Wine Industry Tech. Conf., Adelaide 1986. Ed T.H. Lee (Aust. Industrial Publ.: Adelaide), pp. 50-54.

Coombe, B.G. and McCarthy M.G. (1997) Identification and naming of aroma development in ripening grape berries. Aust. J. Grape and Wine Res. **3**, 118-120.

Coombe, B.G. and McCarthy M.G. (2000) Dynamics of grape berry growth and physiology of ripening. Aust. J. Grape and Wine Res. **6**, 131-135.

Coombe, B.G. and Phillips, P.E. (1982) Development of the grape berry. III Compositional changes during veraison measured by sequential hypodermic sampling. Proc. Int. Symp. Grapes and Wine, Davis, Calif. 1980, pp. 132-136.

Cootes, R.L., Wall, P.J. et al. (1981) Grape quality assessment. Seminar on Grape Quality: assessment from vineyard to juice preparation (Aust. Wine Res. Inst.: Adelaide), pp. 132-136.

Dambergs, R.G., Kambouris, B. et al. (2000) Measuring fruit quality. In: Modern Viticulture - meeting market specifications. Eds C. Davies, C. Dundon et al. (Aust. Soc. Vitic. Oenol.: Adelaide), pp. 45-47.

Davies, C. and Robinson, S.P. (1996) Sugar accumulation in grape berries. Plant Physiol. **111**, 275-283.

Dimitriadis, E. and Williams, P.J. (1984) The development and use of a rapid analytical technique for the estimation of free and potentially volatile monoterpene flavorants of grapes. Amer. J. Enol.Vitic. **35**, 237-250.

Downey, M.O., Harvey, J.S. and Robinson S.P. (2003) Analysis of tannins in seeds and skins of Shiraz grapes throughout berry development. Aust. J. Grape and Wine Res. **9**, 15-27.

Downey, M.O., Harvey, J.S. and Robinson S.P. (2004) The effect of bunch shading on berry development and flavonol accumulation in Shiraz grapes. Aust. J. Grape and Wine Res. **10**, 55-73.

Dreier, L.P., Hunter, R.R. et al. (1998) Invertase activity, grape berry development and cell compartmentation. Plant Physiol. **36**, 865-872.

Dry, P.R. and Loveys, B.R. (1998) Factors influencing grapevine vigour and the potential for control with partial rootzone drying. Aust. J. Grape and Wine Res. **4**, 140-148.

Dry, P.R., Loveys, B.R. et al. (1999) Vine manipulation to meet fruit specifications. In: Proc. 10th Aust. Wine Industry Tech. Conf., Sydney 1998. Eds R.J. Blair, A.N. Sas et al. (Aust. Wine Industry Tech. Conf.), pp. 208-214.

- Dry, P.R., Loveys, B.R. et al. (2000) Partial rootzone drying - an update. Aust. Grapegrower & Winemaker No. 438a, 35-39.

Dunphy, R. and Lockshin, L. (1998) The evolution of the Australian wine show system. Aust. NZ Wine Industry J. **13**, 395-402.

Dunn, G.M., Martin, S.R. et al. (2002) Yield targets: how do we hit them and how important are they? In: Proc. 11th Aust. Wine Industry Tech. Conf., Adelaide 2001. Eds R.J. Blair, P.J. Williams et al. (Aust. Wine Industry Tech. Conf.), pp. 61-67.

Du Plessis, C.S. (1977) Grape components in relation to white wine quality. In: OIV Int. Symp. on Quality of the Vintage (Oenol. Vitic Res. Inst.: Stellenbosch, South Africa), pp. 117-128.

Du Plessis, C.S. (1984) Optimum maturity and quality parameters in grapes: a review. S. Afr. J. Enol. Vitic. **5**, 35-42.

Du Plessis, C.S. and Van Rooyen P.C. (1982) Grape maturity and wine quality. S. Afr. J. Enol. Vitic. **3**, 41-45.

Ebadi, A., May, P. et al. (1996a).Effect of short-term temperature and shading on fruit-set, seed and berry development in model vines of V. vinifera, cvs Chardonnay and Shiraz. Aust. J. Grape and Wine Res. **2**, 2-9.

Ebadi, A., Sedgley, M. et al. (1996b) Seed development and abortion in Vitis vinifera, cv. Chardonnay. Int. J. Plant Sci. **157**, 703-712.

Ewart, A.J.W. (1987) Influence of vineyard site and grape maturity on juice and wine quality of Vitis vinifera cv. Riesling. In: Proc. 6th Aust. Wine Industry Tech. Conf., Adelaide 1986. Ed T.H. Lee (Aust. Industrial Publ.: Adelaide), pp. 71-74.

Ewart, A.J.W. and Sitters, J.H. (1991) Small scale winemaking as a research tool: the influence of fermenter size and juice clarification on resultant wine quality. Aust. NZ Wine Industry J. **6**, 128-132.

Findlay, N., Oliver, K.J. et al. (1987) Solute accumulation by grape pericarp cells. IV. Perfusion of pericarp apoplast via the pedicel and evidence for xylem malfunction in ripening berries. J. Exp. Bot. **38**, 668-679.

Francis, I.L., Cynkar, W. et al. (2004) The Bioprep 5 robotics system Aust. NZ Wine Industry J. **19**, 12-16.

Francis, I.L., Armstrong, H. et al. (1998a) The 1997 CRCV National Vineyard Fruit Composition Survey - Shiraz data. Aust. NZ Wine Industry J. **13**, 377-379.

Francis, I.L., Kassara, S. et al. (1998b) The contribution of glycoside precursors to Cabernet Sauvignon and Merlot aroma. Sensory and compositional studies. In: Chemistry of Wine Flavour. ACS Symposium series 714. Eds A.L. Waterhouse and S.E. Ebeler (Amer. Chem. Soc., Washington), pp. 13-30.

- Francis, I. L., Iland, P.G. et al. (1999). Assessing wine quality with the G-G assay. In: Proc. 10th Aust. Wine Industry Tech. Conf., Sydney 1998. Eds R.J. Blair, A.N. Sas et al. (Aust. Wine Industry Tech. Conf.), pp. 104-108.

Gal, Y., Naor, A. et al. (1996) Effect of shoot density, crop level and crop load on fruit and wine quality of Sauvignon blanc grapes. Acta Hort. **427**, 151-159.

Gholami, M. (1996) Biosynthesis and translocation of secondary metabolite glycosides in the grapevine Vitis vinifera L. PhD thesis, University of Adelaide.

Gishen, M. et al. (2002) Objective measures of grape and wine quality. In: Proc. 11th Aust. Wine Industry Tech. Conf., Adelaide 2001. Eds R.J. Blair, P.J. Williams et al. (Aust. Wine Industry Tech. Conf.), pp. 188-194.

Gladstones, J. (1992) Viticulture and Environment (Winetitles: Adelaide).

Gray, J.G. (2002) The basis of variation in the size and composition of grape berries. PhD thesis, University of Adelaide.

Gray, J.D., Gibson, R.J. et al. (1994) Assessment of wine grape value in the vineyard - a preliminary, commercial survey. Aust. NZ Wine Industry J. **9**, 253-261.

Gray, J.D., Gibson, R.J. et al. (1997) Assessment of winegrape value in the vineyard - survey of cv. Shiraz from South Australian vineyards in 1992. Aust. J. Grape and Wine Res. **3**, 109-116.

Gray, J.D., Kolesik, P. et al. (1999) Confocal measurement of the three-dimensional size and shape of plant parenchyma cells in a developing fruit tissue. The Plant J. **19**, 229-236.

Haselgrove, L., Botting, D. et al. (2000) Canopy microclimate and berry composition: the effect of bunch exposure on the phenolic composition of Vitis vinifera cv. Shiraz grape berries. Aust. J. Grape and Wine Res. **6**, 141-149.

Holzapfel, B., Rogiers, S. et al. (1999) Ripening grapes to specification: effect of yield on colour development of Shiraz grapes in the Riverina. Aust. Grapegrower & Winemaker No. 428, 24-28.

Howell G.S. (2001) Sustainable grape productivity and the growth-yield relationship. A review. Amer. J. Enol. Vitic. **52**, 165-174.

Hunter, J.J. and Ruffner, H.P. (2001) Assimilate transport in grapevines - effect of phloem disruption. Aust J. Grape and Wine Research. **7**, 118-126.

Iland, P.G. (2001) A study of glycosides in grapes and wines of Vitis vinifera cv. Shiraz. PhD thesis, Adelaide University.

Iland, P.G. and Coombe, B.G. (1988) Malate, tartrate, potassium and sodium in flesh and skin of Shiraz grapes during ripening: concentration and compartmentation. Amer. J. Enol. Vitic. **39**, 71-76.

Iland, P.G., Cynkar, W. et al. (1996) Optimisation of methods for the determination of total and red-free glycosyl glucose in black grape berries of Vitis vinifera. Aust. J. Grape and Wine Res. **2**, 171-178.

- Jackson, D.I. and Lombard, P.B. (1993) Environment and management practices affecting grape composition and wine quality. Amer. J. Enol. Vitic. **44**, 409-430.

Johnstone, R. (1996) Specifying grape flavour. ASVO Seminar on Quality Management in Viticulture (Aust. Soc. Vitic. Oenol.: Adelaide), pp. 7-9.

Jones, G.V. and Davis, R.E. (2000) Climate influences on grapevine phenology, grape composition, and wine production and quality for Bordeaux, France. Amer. J. Enol. Vitic. **51**, 249-261.

Jordan, A.D. and Croser, B.J. (1984) Determination of grape maturity by aroma/flavour assessment. In: Proc. 5th Aust. Wine Industry Tech. Conf., Perth 1983. Eds T.H. Lee and T.C. Somers (Aust Wine Res. Inst.), pp. 261-274.

Krstic, M.P , Leamon, K. et al. (2002) Sampling for wine grape quality parameters in the vineyard: variability and post-harvest issues. In: Proc. 11th Aust. Wine Industry Tech. Conf., Adelaide 2001. Eds R.J. Blair, P.J. Williams et al. (Aust. Wine Industry Tech. Conf.), pp. 87-90.

- Krstic, M. Moulds, G. et al. (2003) Growing quality grapes to winery specification (Winetitles: Adelaide).

Lamb, D.W. et al. (2004) Using remote sensing to predict grape phenolics and colour at harvest in a Cabernet Sauvignon vineyard: Timing observations against vine phenology and optimising image resolution. Aust. J Grape & Wine Res. **10**, 46-54.

Lamb, D.W. and Bramley, R.G.V. (2002) Precision viticulture - tools, techniques and benefits. In: Proc. 11th Aust. Wine Industry Tech. Conf., Adelaide 2001. Eds R.J. Blair, P.J. Williams et al. (Aust. Wine Industry Tech. Conf.), pp. 91-97.

Lang, A. and Düring, H. (1991) Partitioning control by water potential gradient: evidence for compartmentation breakdown in grape berries. J. Exp. Bot. **42**, 1117-1122.

Long, Z.R. (1987) Manipulation of grape flavour in the vineyard: California, North Coast region. In: Proc. 6th Aust. Wine Industry Tech. Conf., Adelaide 1986. Ed T.H. Lee (Aust. Industrial Publ.: Adelaide), pp 82-88.

Matthews, M.A., Cheng, G. et al. (1987) Changes in water potential and dermal extensibility during grape berry development. J. Amer. Soc. Hort. Sci. **112**, 314-319.

Matthews, M.A., Ishii, R. et al. (1990) Dependence of wine sensory attributes on vine water status. J. Sci. Food Agric. **51**, 321-335.

May, P. (1987) The grapevine as a perennial, plastic and productive plant. In: Proc. 6th Aust. Wine Industry Tech. Conf., Adelaide 1986. Ed T.H. Lee (Aust. Industrial Publ.: Adelaide), pp. 40-49.

May, P. (1992) Studies on fruit set in winegrapes: comparison of Chardonnay vines in the Adelaide Hills and Southern Vales. Aust. NZ Wine Industry J. **7**, 187-188.

• May, P. (2000) From bud to berry, with special reference to inflorescence and bunch morphology in Vitis vinifera L. Aust. J. Grape and Wine Res. **6**, 82-98.

May, P. (2004) Flowering and Fruitset in Grapevines (Phylloxera and Grape Industry Board of South Australia and Lythrum Press).

May, P., Clingeleffer, P.R. et al. (1976) The response of the grape cultivar Crouchen to various trellis and pruning treatments. Aust. J. Agric. Res. **27**, 845-856.

McCarthy, M.G. (1986) Influence of irrigation, crop thinning and canopy manipulation on composition and aroma of Riesling grapes. M.Ag.Sc. thesis, University of Adelaide.

McCarthy, M.G. (1997a) The effect of transient water deficit on berry development of cv. Shiraz (Vitis vinifera L.) Aust. J. Grape and Wine Res. **3**, 102-108.

McCarthy, M.G. (1997b) Timing of water deficit on fruit development and composition of Vitis vinifera, cv.Shiraz. PhD thesis, University of Adelaide.

McCarthy, M.G. (1998) Irrigation management to improve winegrape quality - nearly 10 years on. Aust. Grapegrower & Winemaker No. 414, 65-71.

McCarthy, M.G. and Coombe, B.G. (1985) Water status and winegrape quality. Acta Hortic. **171**, 417-419.

McCarthy, M.G. and Coombe, B.G. (1999) Is weight loss in ripening grape berries cv. Shiraz caused by impeded phloem transport? Aust. J. Grape and Wine Res. **5**, 17-21.

Moskowitz, A.H. and Hrazdina G (1981) Vacuolar contents of fruit subepidermal cells from Vitis species. Plant Physiol. **68**, 686-692.

Nayler, A.P. (2001) The effects of row orientation, trellis type, shoot and bunch position on the variability of Sauvignon Blanc (Vitis vinifera L.) juice composition. M. Appl. Sci. thesis, Lincoln University, NZ.

Nii, N. and Coombe. B.G. (1983) Structure and development of the berry and pedicel of the grape Vitis vinifera L. Acta Hort. **139**, 129-140.

Noble, A.C. (1988) Analysis of wine sensory properties. In: Wine Analysis (new series Volume 6). Eds H.F. Linskens and J.F. Jackson (Springer-Verlag: Berlin, Heidelberg), pp. 9-28.

Noble, A.C. (2001) Consumer preference testing. An under-utilised resource. In: Proc. Ann. Mtg. Amer. Soc. Enol. Vitic., Seattle 2000.

Nunan, K.J, Sims, I.A. et al. (1997) Isolation and characterization of cell walls from the mesocarp of mature grape berries (Vitis vinifera). Planta **203**, 93-100.

O.I.V. (1977) International symposium on the quality of the vineyard (Oenol. and Vitic. Res. Inst.: Cape Town, South Africa).

Ojeda, H., Deloire, A. et al. (1999) Berry development of grapevines: Relations between the growth of berries and their DNA content indicate cell multiplication and enlargement. Vitis **38**, 145-150.

Ojeda, H., Deloire, A. et al. (2001) Influence of water deficits on grape berry growth. Vitis **40**, 141-145.

Ollat, N., Diakou-Verdin, P. et al. (2002) Grape berry development: a review. J. Int. Sci. Vigne Vin **36**, 109-131.

Orffer, C.J. (1968) To the southern point of Africa. In: Spirit of the Vine. Ed D.J. Opperman (Human and Rousseau: Cape Town), pp. 152-181.

Pirie, A. and Mullins, M.G. (1977) Interrelationships of sugars, anthocyanins, total phenols and dry weight in the skin of grape berries during ripening. Amer. J. Enol. Vitic. **28**, 204-209.

Poni, S., Peterlunger, E. et al. (1996) Proceedings of the First ISHS workshop on Strategies to Optimize Wine Grape Quality. Acta Hort. No. 427.

Profitt, T. (2000) Using cover crops and root pruning to affect water uptake. Aust. Vitic. **4**, 45-51.

Ravaz, L. (1904) La brunissure (Coulet, editeur: Montpellier).

• Reynolds, A.G. and Wardle, D.A. (1997) Flavour development in the vineyard: impact of viticultural practices on grape monoterpenes and their relationship to wine sensory response. S.Afr. J. Enol. Vitic. **18**, 3-18.

Ribereau-Gayon, P., Glories, Y. et al. (2000) Handbook of Enology. Volume 2: The Chemistry of Wine (John Wiley: London).

Ristic, R. et al. (2002) Relationship between seed composition and grape and wine quality. In: Proc. 11th Aust. Wine Industry Tech. Conf., Adelaide 2001. Eds R.J. Blair, P.J. Williams et al. (Aust. Wine Industry Tech. Conf.), pp. 145-149.

Ristic, R. (2004) A study of seed development and phenolic compounds in seeds, skins and wines of Vitis vinifera L. cv Shiraz. PhD thesis, University of Adelaide.

Robinson, J. Ed (1999) The Oxford Companion to Wine, 2nd edition (Oxford Univ. Press: Oxford).

Robinson, S.P., and Davies, C. (2000) Molecular biology of ripening. Aust. J. Grape and Wine Res. **6**, 175-188.

Safran, B. (1977) Effects of cultivation practices on the quality of the vintage in hot regions. OIV Int. Symp. on the Quality of the Vintage (Oenol. Vitic. Res. Inst.: Stellenbosch, South Africa), pp 243-262.

Shaulis, N.J., Amberg, H. et al. (1966) Response of Concord grapes to light, exposure and Geneva Double Curtain training. Proc. Amer. Soc. Hort. Sci. **89**, 268-280.

Shaulis, N.J. and May, P. (1981) Response of Sultana vines to training on a divided canopy and to shoot crowding. Amer. J. Enol. Vitic. **22**, 215-221.

Singleton, V.L., Ough, C.S. et al. (1966) Density separations of wine grape berries and ripeness distribution. Amer. J. Enol. Vitic. **17**, 95-105.

Smart, R.E., Dick, J.K. et al. (1990) Canopy management to improve grape yield and wine quality - principles and practices. S. Afr. J. Enol. Vitic. **11**, 3-17.

Smart, R.E. and Robinson, M.D. (1991) Sunlight into Wine: a handbook for winegrape canopy management (Winetitles: Adelaide).

Smart, R. and Smith, S. (1988) Canopy management: identifying problems and practical solutions Amer J. Enol. Vitic. **37**, 325-333.

Somers, T.C. (1998) The Wine Spectrum (Winetitles: Adelaide).

Somers, T.C. and Evans, M.E. (1977) Spectral evaluation of young red wines: anthocyanin equilibria, total phenolics, free and molecular SO2, 'chemical age'. J. Sci. Food and Agric. **28**, 279-287.

Spayd, S.E., Tarara, J.M. et al. (2002) Separation of sunlight and temperature effects on the composition of Vitis vinifera cv. Merlot berries. Amer. J. Enol. Vitic. **53**, 171-182.

Stines, A.P., Grubb, J. et al. (2000) Proline and arginine accumulation in developing berries of Vitis vinifera L. cv. Shiraz in Australian Vineyards: Influence of vine cultivar, berry maturity and tissue type. Aust. J. Grape and Wine Res. **6**, 150-158.

Stoll, M. (2000) Effects of partial rootzone drying on grapevine physiology and fruit maturity. PhD thesis, University of Adelaide.

Trought, M.C.T. (1996) The New Zealand terroir: Sources of variation in fruit composition in New Zealand vineyards. In: Proc. 4th Int. Symp. on Cool Climate Vitic. and Enol., Rochester, pp. 23-27.

Van Rooyen, P.C., Ellis, L.P. and Du Plessis, C.S. (1984) Interactions between grape maturity indices and quality for Pinotage and Cabernet Sauvignon wines from four localities. S. Afr. J. Enol. Vitic. **5**, 29-34.

Van Zyl, J.L. and Weber, H.W. (1977) Irrigation of Chenin Blanc in the Stellenbosch area within the framework of the climate-soil-plant continuum. OIV Int. Symp. on the Quality of the Vintage (Oenol. Vitic. Res. Inst.: Stellenbosch, South Africa), pp 331-350.

Vidal, S., Francis, L., et al. (2004) Tast and mouth-feel properties of different types of tannin-like polyphenolic compounds and anthocyanins in wine. Anal. Chim. Acta 513(1), 57-65.

Walsh, B. (2002) Roles and relevance of the Australian Wine Show System. In: Proc. 11th Aust. Wine Industry Tech. Conf., Adelaide 2001. Eds R.J. Blair, P.J. Williams et al. (Aust. Wine Industry Tech. Conf.), pp. 140-144.

Waterhouse, A.L. and Ebeler, S.E. Eds (1998) Chemistry of Wine Flavor. ACS Symposium Series 714 (American Chem. Soc.: Washington).

Whiton, R.S. and Zoecklein, B.W. (2002) Evaluation of glycosyl-glucose analytical methods for various glycosides. Amer. J. Enol. Vitic **53**, 315-317.

Williams, J.P., Cynkar, W. et al. (1995) Quantification of glycosides in grapes, juices and wines through a determination of glycosyl glucose. J. Agric. Food Chem. **43**, 121-128 .

Wilson, B., Strauss, C.R. et al. (1983) The development of free monoterpene flavourants and precursor compounds in ripening Muscat Gordo Blanco berrries. In: Proc. 5th Aust. Wine Industry Tech. Conf., Perth 1983. Eds T.H. Lee and T.C. Somers (Aust Wine Res. Inst.), pp 331-338.

Winkler, A.J. (1954) Effects of overcropping. Amer. J. Enol. Vitic. **5**, 4-12.

Wolf, T.K., Dry, P.R. et al. (2003) Response of Shiraz grapevines to five different training systems in the Barossa Valley, Australia. Aust. J. Grape and Wine Res. **9**, 82-95.

Zeeman, A.S. (1977) Some practical results on more efficient moisture utilization obtained by means of cultural practices. OIV Int. Symp. on the Quality of the Vintage (Oenol. Vitic. Res. Inst.: Stellenbosch, South Africa), pp. 233-240.

INDEX

ACKNOWLEDGEMENT OF ILLUSTRATIONS

The publisher wishes to thank the following individuals and organisations who have kindly given permission to reproduce illustrations in the Figures indicated. Unless otherwise indicated, all diagrams are original works of the author(s) of each chapter.

DIAGRAMS

1.1   Redrawn by C. Potter (Winetitles) from original Geographical Indications maps by Aust. Wine and Brandy Corporation

1.3   B. Coombe

1.12   Redrawn from Clingleffer et al. (1997)

2.2   Redrawn by C. Potter from original GI maps by Aust. Wine and Brandy Corporation

2.8   Phylloxera and Grape Industry Board of SA

3.1   D. Maschmedt (Department of Water, Land and Biodiversity Conservation South Australia) and R. Schuster (CSIRO)

3.18   CSIRO

4.3   Originally published in Coombe and Dry (1988)

5.1   Originally published in Coombe and Dry (1988): redrawn by G. Lavis from an original figure from Galet (1979)

7.6-7.7   M.G. McCarthy (SARDI)

7.8   Redrawn by B. Coombe from an original figure of Jones and Davis (2000)

7.9   D.G. Botting (formerly CRC for Viticulture)

10.1   Reproduced from Jackson and Schuster (1987)

11.2   B. Coombe and J. Gray

11.8   R. Bramley (CSIRO Land and Water) and A. Proffitt (formerly Southcorp)

11.9   Redrawn by B. Coombe from data of Nayler (2001)

11.13 Redrawn by B. Coombe from data of Gray (2002)

11.14 Redrawn by B. Coombe from data of Gray (2002)

11.15 P. May

11.16 Redrawn by B. Coombe from data of Ebadi et al. (1996a)

11.17 Redrawn by B. Coombe from an original figure of Du Plessis (1977)

11.18 Redrawn by B. Coombe from an original figure of Du Plessis and Van Rooyen (1982)

11.19 Redrawn by B. Coombe from an original figure of McCarthy (1997b)

11.20-11.22 L. Francis (Aust. Wine Research Institute), Aust. Wine Industry Technical Conference Inc.

11.23 Redrawn by B. Coombe from an original figure of Carbonneau (1996)

PHOTOGRAPHS

Frontispiece P. Dry (Univ. of Adelaide)

1.4, 1.5   G. Gregory (originally published in Gregory, G. (1988) Development and Status of Australian Viticulture. In: Viticulture Vol. 1 Resources, 1st edn. Eds B.G. Coombe and P.R. Dry (Winetitles: Adelaide), pp. 1-36)

1.6   Winetitles

1.7   Angoves Pty. Ltd.

1.8-1.10 Winetitles: Australian Viticulture

1.11   P. Dry (Univ. of Adelaide)

1.13a La Trobe Picture Collection, State Library of Victoria

1.13b Yering Station Vineyard

2.3, 2.7, 2.9, 21.3, 2.14 Winetitles: Australian Viticulture

2.4, 2.5, 2.6, 2.10, 2.11, 2.12, 2.15-2.20 P. Dry (Univ. of Adelaide)

3.2-3.10, 3.13-3.16, 3.19, 3.22-3.24, 3.28, 3.32, 3.35, 3.37, 3.39 3.45, 3.47-3.49, 3.51-3.53, 3.58, 3.59 D. Maschmedt (Department of Water, Land and Biodiversity Conservation South Australia [DWLBC])

3.11, 3.12, 3.21, 3.25, 3.26, 3.36, 3.46, 3.50 A. McCord (DWLBC)

3.17   G. Gale (DWLBC)

3.20   R. Stevens (South Australian Research and Development Institute [SARDI])

3.27   J. Coppi (CSIRO)

3.29   K. Wetherby (formerly South Australian Dept. of Agric.)

3.30, 3.31 B. Billing (DWLBC)

3.33   R. Doyle (Univ. of Tasmania)

3.34   M. Inhof (Dept. of Primary Industries Victoria)

3.38   A. Brown (DPI Vic.)

3.54   D. Woodard (Primary Industries and Resources South Australia [PIRSA])

3.55   P. Tille (Dept. of Agriculture Western Australia)

3.56   M. Cann (formerly PIRSA)

3.57   D. Farquhar (Department of Primary Industries, Water and Environment Tasmania)

5.2-5.4 CSIRO Plant Industry, Merbein, Vic.

8.1-8.3 J. Whiting (DPI Vic.)

9.1   N. Habili (Waite Diagnostics)

10.2-10.5 P. Dry (Univ. of Adelaide)

11.10, 11.12 Winetitles